INTERNATIONAL ECONOMICS

THEORY, APPLICATION, AND POLICY

CHARLES VAN MARREWIJK

ERASMUS UNIVERSITY ROTTERDAM

in cooperation with

DANIËL OTTENS

STEPHAN SCHUELLER

OXFORD
UNIVERSITY PRESS

OXFORD
UNIVERSITY PRESS

Great Clarendon Street, Oxford OX2 6DP

Oxford University Press is a department of the University of Oxford.
It furthers the University's objective of excellence in research, scholarship,
and education by publishing worldwide in

Oxford New York

Auckland Cape Town Dar es Salaam Hong Kong Karachi
Kuala Lumpur Madrid Melbourne Mexico City Nairobi
New Delhi Shanghai Taipei Toronto

With offices in

Argentina Austria Brazil Chile Czech Republic France Greece
Guatemala Hungary Italy Japan Poland Portugal Singapore
South Korea Switzerland Thailand Turkey Ukraine Vietnam

Oxford is a registered trade mark of Oxford University Press
in the UK and in certain other countries

Published in the United States
by Oxford University Press Inc., New York

British Library Cataloguing in Publication Data

Data available

Library of Congress Cataloging in Publication Data

Marrewijk, Charles van.
International economics : theory, application, and policy / Charles Van
Marrewijk in cooperation with Daniël Ottens, Stephan Schueller.
    p. cm.
  ISBN 978-0-19-928098-8
  1. International economic relations. I. Ottens, Daniel. II. Schueller,
Stephan. III. Title.
  HF1359.M369 2007
  337—dc22   2006034949

Typeset by Newgen Imaging Systems (P) Ltd., Chennai, India
Printed in Great Britain
on acid-free paper by
Ashford Colour Press Ltd, Gosport, Hampshire

ISBN 978-0-19-928098-8

10 9 8 7 6 5 4 3

CONTENTS

DETAILED CONTENTS

LIST OF FIGURES

LIST OF TABLES

LIST OF BOXES

LIST OF TECHNICAL NOTES

The objective of this book is to give a succinct, yet fairly complete, up-to-date, and thorough introduction to the most important aspects of international economics, including, for example: trade and investment flows, international money, exchange rates, perfect and imperfect competition, international institutions, policy (fiscal, monetary, and trade), multinationals, economic (monetary) integration, and financial crises. The book's target audience includes first- and second-year university and college students in economics, management, and business with a working knowledge of microeconomics and macroeconomics. Elementary comprehension of mathematics for economists (simple functions and differentiation) is recommended. The approach is based on the student's active participation using the selected questions at the end of each chapter and those in the remainder of the *Study Guide* expertly compiled by Daniël Ottens and Stephan Schueller, available on the online resource centre at www.oxfordtextbooks. co.uk/orc/vanmarrewijk/. This site provides, for example, empirical questions to test theories and simulation questions to get a better feel for the structure of economic models by performing small, user-friendly computer simulations and interpreting the results. I briefly discuss the main features of the book below.

Three for the price of one

After the successful introduction of my book *International Trade and the World Economy* (Oxford: Oxford University Press, 2002), which focused on the real aspects of international economics, I was asked by OUP's Tim Page to (i) prepare a second edition and (ii) provide a *complete* introduction to international economics by writing an international money counterpart to complement the international trade book. In view of the excellent cooperation with OUP, I was happy to oblige. Initially, we thought it would be best to produce two separate volumes (*International Trade* and *International Money*). It soon became apparent, however, that the economies of scale at the printing stage would make it more cost-efficient to combine the two volumes in one book. In addition, the authors of the *Study Guide to International Trade and the World Economy*, Daniël Ottens and Stephan Schueller, agreed that it was sub-optimal to sell the *Study Guide* separately. We therefore decided to include a selection of the exercises of the *Study Guide* in this book and make the remaining questions, simulations, and study material available on the online resource centre. The combination of *International Trade*, *International Money*, and the *Study Guide* in one package enabled us to offer the student 'three for the price of one'.

Organization of the book

As illustrated in Figure I, the book's primary organizational structure is in four simple parts. We start with a two-chapter introduction to the book which provides background information on the world economy and the basics of the balance of

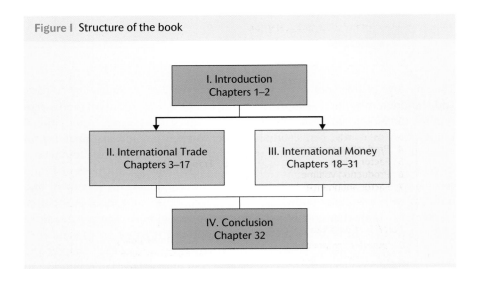

Figure I Structure of the book

payments and capital flows. The reader can then either move on to Part II on international trade (consisting of Chapters 3–17) or to Part III on international money (consisting of Chapters 18–31). Part II can be studied independently of Part III. Similarly, Part III can be studied independently of Part II, with the exception of the last chapter, Chapter 31, which assumes prior knowledge of Chapters 10 and 14. We conclude in Part IV.

Organization of international trade

As illustrated in Figure II, the international trade section of the book is sub-divided into three parts. Part II.A (comparative advantage) analyses international trade flows in perfectly competitive markets based on differences in technology (classical trade) or factor abundance (neoclassical trade). It concludes with a discussion of the (distributional) welfare implications of trade policy, such as tariffs, quotas, and voluntary export restraints in this framework. Part II.B (competitive advantage) investigates the impact of imperfect competition, economies of scale, and product differentiation (new trade) on the structure of the international economy and the size and type of its trade flows. This part also analyses the impact of new trade theory on (strategic) trade policy, discusses the main international organizations, and applies the economic insights gathered so far to an investigation of the process of (European) economic integration. Part II.C (trade interactions) brings the reader up to date with recent developments based on interactions between international economics and other fields of economics; with economic geography leading to a better explanation of location, with international business leading to a better explanation of multinational firms, and with economic growth theory leading to a better understanding of international differences in growth and development. This part concludes with a discussion of the implications of these developments for applied trade policy modelling. As

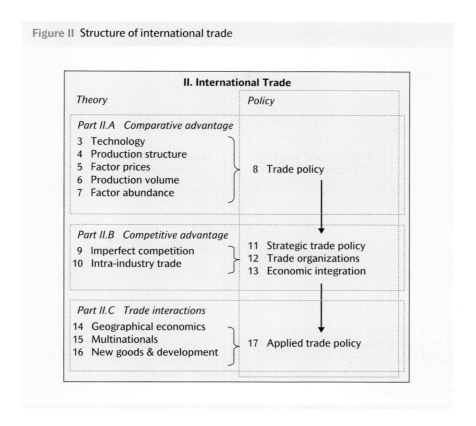

Figure II Structure of international trade

indicated in Figure II, we discuss both theoretical models and the policy implications derived from these models. In all chapters, the newly acquired insights are applied and illustrated using empirical data and discussing case studies.

Organization of international money

As illustrated in Figure III, the international money section of the book is also subdivided into three parts. Part III.A (money basics) provides a brief review of the money market and then discusses the size and structure of foreign exchange markets, purchasing power parity, and interest rate parity. This part concludes with an overview of the main international money organizations and institutions. Part III.B (exchange rates) provides an overview of basic exchange rate theories and discusses the elasticity and absorption approach, the (long-run) monetary approach, the (short-run) effects of monetary and fiscal policy, and the transition from short-run to long-run in a sticky-price model with rational expectations. Part III.C (policy and credibility) provides a policy framework (objectives, targets, and instruments) and applies it to fixed exchange rates (target zones), financial crises, and European monetary unification. This part concludes with a brief discussion of recent developments in new open economy macroeconomics, which provides a bridge between international trade and international money

Figure III Structure of international money

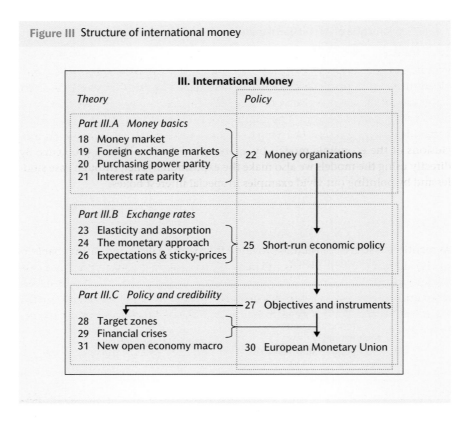

(as discussed in Part IV). As indicated in Figure III, the international money framework is quite similar to the international trade framework: we discuss both theoretical models and the policy implications derived from these models. Again, in all chapters the newly acquired insights are applied and illustrated using empirical data and discussing case studies. We now continue with a discussion of the general characteristics of the book.

Two-tier analysis

The body of the text represents the first tier of analysis, by providing extensive verbal, graphical, and intuitive explanations of the structure of the international economic system. The reader's understanding of the first tier is supported by limited structural analysis, empirical data, special interest boxes, and applications. The second tier of analysis is provided by the Technical Notes at the end of most chapters, which explicitly derive most results used and discussed in the body of the text. As such, the second tier represents background information for a better understanding of the body of the text. A proper understanding of the first tier, however, does not require knowledge and comprehension of the Technical Notes, as long as the reader is willing to take the results derived in those notes for granted.

Empirics: applications, boxes, and examples

The ultimate objective of economic model building is to provide a better understanding of the (forces of the) world economy. The empirical information provided throughout the book therefore serves a dual purpose: first, to give a better insight in the structure of the world economy, e.g. on the size of trade and capital flows or the rising importance of multinational firms, such that the reader has a better idea what we should be trying to explain, and second, to test the main conclusions of the economic models by applying them to real-world problems. By directly using the models we also make the exposition livelier, through case studies and by pointing out vivid examples in special interest boxes.

Thorough, but simple

As mentioned above, we want to provide a thorough analysis, indicating that (virtually) all the results we discuss will be based on explicit economic models. None the less, we want to keep the analysis as simple and tractable as possible. Without reservation, therefore, all the discussions in the text and derivations in the Technical Notes at the end of each chapter will be based on the most simple functional forms.

Study Guide

There is a clear and consistent interaction between the book and the *Study Guide*, which is partially included in this book (selected questions at the end of each chapter), the remainder of which is provided on the online resource centre. For example, since the exposition in the text and many illustrations are based on actual calculations using specific functional forms (see the feature above), we can use this to our advantage in the 'simulation' questions of the *Study Guide*. These questions are based on the figures in the book and are available on the online resource centre. The student not only immediately recognizes the material in the questions of the *Study Guide*, but also becomes acquainted with practical computer tools, thus learning first hand what happens with production and consumption if the capital stock increases or the preference structure changes.

C.v.M.

www.charlesvanmarrewijk.nl

ACKNOWLEDGEMENTS

In the course of writing this book I have accumulated a substantial intellectual debt to the co-authors of work forming the basis for some chapters or sections, in particular Steven Brakman, Harry Garretsen, Jeroen Hinloopen, and Arjen van Witteloostuijn, and to persons providing comments and suggestions for improvements on earlier versions of (parts of) this book, in particular Brian Bentick, Koen Berden, Steven Brakman, Wilfrid Csaplar, Joe Francois, Franz Xaver Hof, Ger Lanjouw, Doug Nelson, Okè Onemu, Teun Schmidt, Albert de Vaal, Jean-Marie Viaene, Alex Wubben, Maurizio Zanardi, and an anonymous student. Of these persons Koen Berden and Teun Schmidt were my excellent and inspirational colleagues for the course *International Economics* at Erasmus University, where Koen reaches levels of student praise in the evaluations which I unfortunately will never achieve, and Teun has been my valuable mentor in the history of (international) economic thought for two decades. My special thanks go to Stephan Schueller and Daniël Ottens, the authors of the *Study Guide*, who not only worked very hard, provided and processed a substantial part of the data material, gave detailed comments, did a wonderful job on writing the *Study Guide*, refining the simulations, and providing empirical exercises, but through their presence also made it a pleasure to go to work and continue our collaboration after they graduated.

Rotterdam
20 January 2006

PART I
INTRODUCTION

Part I (Introduction) gives an overview of the main economic forces in the world economy today and of the basics of the balance of payments, providing useful information for both international trade and international capital flows.

THE WORLD ECONOMY

$\boxed{1}$

Objectives/key terms

- International real/monetary analysis
- Land area
- Gross domestic product (GDP)
- Purchasing power
- International comparison project (ICP)
- Exports/imports

- General equilibrium approach
- Population
- Gross national product (GNP)
- Tradable/non-tradable
- Income per capita
- Globalization

We present basic information on (the development of) the structure of the world economy in terms of land area, population, income, and (the connection between) trade flows and capital flows. This serves as background information for observations to be explained by international economics models discussed in the remainder of this book.

1.1 Introduction[1]

What is international economics? To paraphrase a well-known definition of economics, it is 'what international economists do'. Although this does not seem very helpful at first sight, the underlying message is clear: you will only know what international economics is about once you have studied it yourself. In fact, this probably holds for many fields of study outside economics. This does not mean that you have to devote four years of your life to studying international economics before you get an idea of why we like this field so much, although I can highly recommend it. Instead, you can get a good overview by studying this book. The field of international economics is divided into two parts, namely international *real* analysis and international *monetary* analysis. International real analysis is covered in Part II (International Trade; Chapters 3–17) and investigates trade and investment flows, imperfect competition, trade policy, multinationals, economic integration, etc. International monetary analysis is provided in Part III (International Money; Chapters 18–31) and investigates the demand for and supply of (international) money and the interactions between nations through the exchange rate and other means.

The remainder of this chapter gives a brief empirical overview of the world economy, based on data from the World Bank Development Indicators CD-ROM 2005, covering the forty-odd years from 1960 to 2003.[2] This serves as background information for observations to be explained by international economics models discussed in the rest of this book. More detailed empirical information on specific topics, raising new questions to be answered, will be presented as we go along. A final remark before we get started. I was asked by students what sets international economics apart from other fields of study. After contemplating the question for a while, I think an important distinguishing characteristic is the *general equilibrium* nature of the approach. It is true that many discussions in the chapters to follow are of a *partial equilibrium* nature, for example determining the optimal production level for

Famous economists	Angus Maddison
 **Fig. 1.1** Angus Maddison (1926–)*	Born in Newcastle upon Tyne (England) and educated at Cambridge, McGill, and Johns Hopkins, Angus Maddison spent most of his professional career in various functions at the Organization for Economic Cooperation and Development (OECD; see Chapter 12) in France and as a professor of economics at the University of Groningen in the Netherlands. As one of the most important economic historians and a self-confessed chiffrephile, he has published a wide range of articles and books on historical statistical data. He estimated, for example, the levels of population, income, trade, and urbanization throughout the world for the past 2000 years. Of his many accomplishments, also used as a source of data throughout this book, we should at least mention *Monitoring the World Economy, 1820–1992* and *The World Economy: A Millennial Perspective*, published in 1995 and 2001, respectively. * The portrait was painted by Carla Rodenburg in 2001. I am grateful to Angus Maddison for his permission to reproduce this painting.

a producer *given* the demand for its good, or determining the optimal consumption level for a labourer *given* the wage rate she earns and the prices charged for the goods on the market. However, international economists are not truly satisfied with an explanation of empirical observations until the partial equilibrium explanations are put together like a jigsaw puzzle in a consistent general equilibrium framework, providing a miniature world in which the producer's demand for its goods is explained by the consumer's optimization problem and in which the wage rate and the prices are also determined within the model. The main advantage of insisting on a general equilibrium framework is, of course, that it forces us to be precise and complete in our explanations. Essentially, it prevents us from cheating. It is important to keep this in mind as we continue.

1.2 Land area and population

There are many countries in the world. On its CD-ROM the World Bank distinguishes 208 different countries, a fair number of which are so small in terms of land area, population, and economic clout that you may never have heard of them. As a result of political pressure from China, which considers it one of its provinces, Taiwan is the only significant country missing on the World Bank CD-ROM. In the discussions in this chapter, we focus attention on the most important countries. But important in what sense? Clearly, if you are one of the few inhabitants of Vanuatu, this is an important country to you and your family. However, for the world as a whole we will assume that 'large' countries are important. Again, the question is raised: large in what sense? There are, of course, several options available, their suitability depending on the object of study. In general terms, we can look at land area or population. Since this is a book on economics, we can look at various income measures. More specifically, since this is a book on *international* economics, we can look at exports or international capital flows. In the rest of this chapter and the next we will look briefly at all these aspects, indicating some of the relationships between them if appropriate.

Land area

As the central piece left over after the break-up of the Soviet Union, the Russian Federation, henceforth Russia for short, is still by far the largest country in the world in terms of land area. With almost 17 million km^2, as indicated in Table 1.1, some 13 per cent of the world total, Russia is more than 80 per cent larger than China, the world's second-largest country. Other non-surprising large countries are Canada, the USA, and Brazil. Perhaps more remarkable countries in the top fifteen list are the ninth place for Kazakhstan, formerly a part of the Soviet Union, and the African countries: Algeria (tenth), Sudan (eleventh), and Congo (Zaire[3], twelfth). As a result of the most frequently used methods for projecting the world globe on a flat piece of paper, most people tend to underestimate the size of the African land area. Finally, note that, taking into consideration that by far the biggest part of Russia is on the Asian continent, there are no European countries in the top fifteen of Table 1.1, which taken together account for about 63 per cent of the total land area in the world.

Population

As an indicator of economic importance, a country's land area is of limited use. Many of the countries listed in Table 1.1 incorporate vast stretches of desert, rocks, swamps, or areas frozen

Table 1.1 Top fifteen land area (1,000 km²), 2003

Country	Size	% of world	Sum %
1 Russia	16,889	13.0	13
2 China	9,327	7.2	20
3 Canada	9,221	7.1	27
4 USA	9,159	7.0	34
5 Brazil	8,457	6.5	41
6 Australia	7,682	5.9	47
7 India	2,973	2.3	49
8 Argentina	2,737	2.1	51
9 Kazakhstan	2,671	2.1	53
10 Algeria	2,382	1.8	55
11 Sudan	2,376	1.8	57
12 Zaire	2,267	1.7	58
13 Saudi Arabia	2,150	1.6	60
14 Mexico	1,909	1.5	62
15 Indonesia	1,812	1.4	63
World	130,330		

solid year round. Such uninhabitable land cannot be used to sustain and feed a population engaged in commerce, production, and trade. In this respect, the total population of a country is a better indicator of its fertility and potential economic viability. Table 1.2 lists the top fifteen countries in terms of population, only seven of which also make it to the top fifteen in terms of land area.

Two Asian countries, China and India, clearly stand out in terms of total population. Together they have 2.35 billion inhabitants, or almost 38 per cent of the world total of 6.3 billion people. The USA, ranked third with 291 million inhabitants, has less than 28 per cent of the Indian population, which is ranked second. Asian countries dominate the population list. Apart from China and India, this includes Indonesia (fourth), Pakistan (sixth), Bangladesh (eighth), Japan (tenth), the Philippines (thirteenth), Vietnam (fourteenth), and Turkey (fifteenth). Note that we do not include Russia in this list of Asian countries, despite the fact that its largest land mass is in the Asian continent, because the largest share of its population is on the European continent. Thus, together with Germany (twelfth), there are two European countries in the top fifteen. With 136 million people, Nigeria is the only African country. The top fifteen countries together account for about 66 per cent of the world population.

Table 1.2 Top fifteen population (millions), 2003

Country	Size	% of world	Sum %
1 China	1,288	21.0	21
2 India	1,064	16.7	38
3 USA	291	4.7	42
4 Indonesia	215	3.5	46
5 Brazil	177	2.8	48
6 Pakistan	148	2.4	51
7 Russia	143	2.3	53
8 Bangladesh	138	2.1	55
9 Nigeria	136	2.1	57
10 Japan	128	2.1	59
11 Mexico	102	1.6	61
12 Germany	83	1.4	62
13 Philippines	82	1.3	64
14 Vietnam	81	1.2	65
15 Turkey	71	1.1	66
World	6,273		

 Box 1.1   **Are nations rational?**

Sometimes it is hard for outsiders to understand the disagreements between nations. In July 2001 the government of South Korea became so upset about the 'missing' parts in a Japanese history book for 13–15-year-old students that it decided to break off the (limited) military cooperation with Japan and not to open up its market for Japanese cultural goods, such as computer games. The South Korean government objected to the portrayal of history in the Japanese book on about thirty-five points. Partially, this reflects irritation at the fact that the book does not acknowledge that many cultural innovations, such as Chinese writing, Buddhism, and baking porcelain, reached the Japanese islands through the Korean peninsula. Most irritation, however, is related to the occupation of Korea by Japan in the twentieth century, in particular the fact that the book does not mention the 'comfort girls', a gentle term for (Korean) women forced into prostitution by the Japanese military in the Second World War. The description of the Korean–Japanese history in the book is biased. Whether this is important enough to warrant the Korean excitement and (trade) restrictions is another matter. The costs of trade restrictions are discussed in the sequel.

Information source: NRC (2001d).

1.3 Income

The best indicator of the economic power of a nation is, of course, obtained by estimating the total value of the goods and services produced in a certain time period. Actually doing this and comparing the results across nations is a formidable task, which conceptually requires taking three steps. First, a well-functioning statistics office in each nation must gather accurate information on the value of millions of goods and services produced and provided by the firms in the economy. This will be done, of course, in the country's local currency, that is dollars in the USA, pounds in the UK, yen in Japan, etc. Second, we have to decide what to compare between nations: gross domestic product or gross national product? Third, we have to decide *how* to compare the outcome for the different nations. We will elaborate on the second and third steps below.

Domestic or national product?

As mentioned above, we can compare either gross domestic product (GDP) or gross national product (GNP) between nations. GDP is defined as the market value of the goods and services produced by labour and property *located* in a country. GNP is defined as the market value of the goods and services produced by labour and property of *nationals* of a country. If, for example, a Mexican worker is providing labour services in the USA, these services are part of American GDP and Mexican GNP. The term 'located in' sometimes has to be interpreted broadly, for example if a Filipino sailor is providing labour services for a Norwegian shipping company, this is part of Norwegian GDP despite the fact that the ship is not actually located in Norway most of the time. The difference between GNP and GDP not only holds for labour services, but also for other factors of production, such as capital, that is:

(1.1)   GDP + net receipts of factor income = GNP

So does it really matter whether we compare countries on the basis of GDP or GNP? No. This is illustrated in Figure 1.2 for the GDP and GNP values measured in current US$, using a logarithmic scale with the size of circles proportional to the size of GDP. Since almost all observations are very close to a straight 45-degree line through the origin, the values of GDP and GNP are usually very close to one another. For example, French GDP was $1,758 bn, about 0.1 per cent above its GNP of $1,755 bn. The relative difference is about 0.5 per cent for the USA and Germany. The difference between GDP and GNP is not always small, at least not in relative terms. For example, capital income from abroad for some of the small oil-producing nations, such as Kuwait, ensures that the GNP level is some 7 per cent higher than the GDP level. Similarly, labour income from its many sailors and other workers abroad makes GNP for the Philippines about 7 per cent higher than its GDP.

Comparison

Table 1.3 reports the top fifteen countries in terms of GNP level when the outcome for each nation in local currency is simply converted to the same international standard currency, usually the US$, on the basis of the average exchange rate in the period of observation.[4] These are called current $. The total value of all goods and services produced in the world in 2003 was estimated to be $36,362 bn. Taken together, the top fifteen countries account for about 80 per cent of the world production value.

Figure 1.2 Gross domestic and gross national product, 2003 ($ billion)

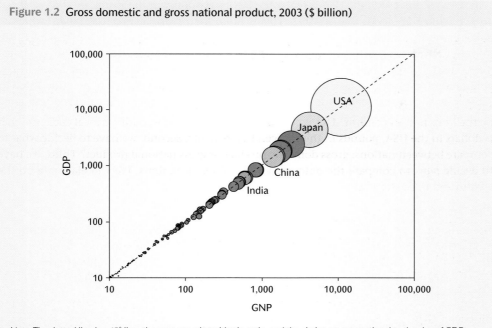

Note: The dotted line is a 45° line, the axes use a logarithmic scale, and the circles are proportional to the size of GDP.

Table 1.3 Top fifteen gross national product (current $bn), 2003

Country	Size	% of world	Sum %
1 USA	11,004	30.3	30
2 Japan	4,374	12.0	42
3 Germany	2,391	6.6	49
4 UK	1,831	5.0	54
5 France	1,755	4.8	59
6 Italy	1,452	4.0	63
7 China	1,409	3.9	67
8 Canada	839	2.3	69
9 Spain	830	2.3	71
10 Mexico	613	1.7	73
11 South Korea	606	1.7	75
12 India	598	1.6	76
13 Australia	507	1.4	78
14 The Netherlands	497	1.4	79
15 Brazil	474	1.3	80
World	36,362		

In terms of current $, the USA is by far the largest economy in the world, producing about 30 per cent of all goods and services. This is more than twice as much as Japan, which is ranked second, which in turn is about twice as large as Germany, which is ranked third. All other European countries in the production top fifteen, that is, the UK (fourth), France (fifth), Italy (sixth), Spain (ninth), and the Netherlands (fourteenth), are not listed in the population top fifteen. In fact, of the fifteen largest countries in terms of population listed in Table 1.2, only seven make it to the top fifteen in terms of income level. Having a large population is therefore not at all synonymous with having a large production value. A striking example is provided by the Netherlands, which has a small population of 16.2 million people (ranked fifty-sixth), but a production value of $497 bn, only 17 per cent below the value produced by the more than 1 billion inhabitants of India. Australia is another relatively small country in terms of population, but large in terms of production value.

Purchasing power

The ranking of production value in Table 1.3 is deceptive because it tends to overestimate production in the high-income countries relative to the low-income countries. To understand this we have to distinguish between *tradable* and *non-tradable* goods and services. As the name suggests, tradable goods and services can be transported or provided in another country, perhaps with some difficulty and at some costs. In principle, therefore, the providers of tradable goods in different countries compete with one another fairly directly, implying that the prices of such goods are related and can be compared effectively on the basis of observed (average) exchange rates. In contrast, non-tradable goods and services have to be provided locally and do not compete with international providers. Think, for example, of housing services, getting a haircut, or going to the cinema.

Since (i) different sectors in the same country compete for the same labourers, such that (ii) the wage rate in an economy reflects the average productivity of a nation (see also Chapter 3), and (iii) productivity differences between nations in the non-tradable sectors tend to be smaller than in the tradable sectors, converting the value of output in the non-tradable sectors on the basis of observed exchange rates tends to underestimate the value of production in these sectors for the low-income countries. For example, on the basis of observed exchange rates, getting a haircut in the USA may cost you $10 rather than the $1 you pay in Tanzania, while going to the cinema in Sweden may cost you $8 rather than the $2 you pay in Jakarta, Indonesia. In these examples the value of production in the high-income countries relative to the low-income countries is overestimated by a factor of 10 and 4, respectively.

To correct for these differences, the United Nations International Comparison Project (ICP) collects data on the prices of goods and services for virtually all countries in the world and calculates 'purchasing power parity' (PPP) exchange rates, which better reflect the value of goods and services that can be purchased in a country for a given amount of dollars. Reporting PPP GNP levels therefore gives a better estimate of the actual value of production in a country.

Figure 1.3 illustrates the impact on the estimated value of production after correction for purchasing power. Two top-income countries from Table 1.3 do not make it to the PPP top fifteen of Figure 1.3, namely the Netherlands (which drops to twentieth place) and Australia (which drops to sixteenth place). They are replaced by Russia and Indonesia. The USA is still the largest economy, but now 'only' produces 21.4 per cent of world output, rather than 30 per cent. The estimated value of production for the low-income countries is much higher than before. The relative production of China (ranked second) is more than three times as

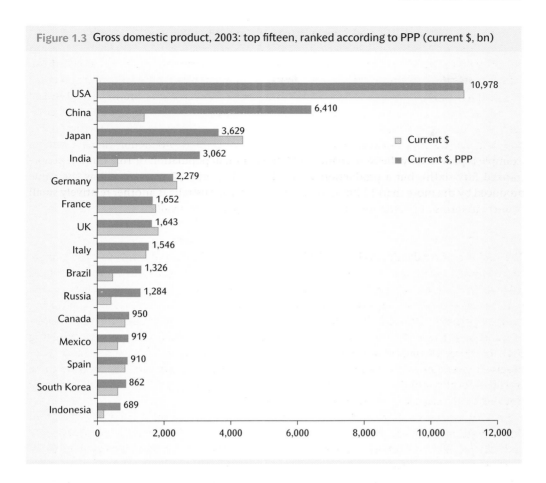

Figure 1.3 Gross domestic product, 2003: top fifteen, ranked according to PPP (current $, bn)

high as before (rising from 3.9 per cent to 12.5 per cent), similarly for India (rising from 1.6 per cent to 6.0 per cent), Russia (rising from 1.2 per cent to 2.5 per cent), and Indonesia (rising from 0.5 per cent to 1.3 per cent).[5] The drop in the estimated value of output is particularly large for Japan (falling from 12.0 per cent to 7.1 per cent), reflecting the high costs of living in Japan. See Chapter 20 for further details.

1.4 Income per capita

For an individual inhabitant of a country the total production value of the country is hardly relevant. More important is the production value per person, that is per capita. It should be noted that income per capita gives an idea of the well-being for the 'average' person in the country, but gives no information on the distribution of the income level within the country. If Jack and Jill together earn $100, the average income level is $50, which holds if they both earn $50 *and* if Jack earns $1 while Jill earns $99. The average income level is therefore a poor indicator of the 'representative' situation in a country if the distribution of income is more uneven. In general, the income level is more evenly distributed in Europe and Japan than in the USA, where it is in turn more evenly distributed than in many low-income countries.

Table 1.4 Top fifteen gross national income per capita (PPP $), 2003

Country	Size	% of world average
1 Luxembourg	55,500	678
2 Norway	37,910	463
3 USA	37,750	461
4 Switzerland	32,220	393
5 Denmark	31,050	379
6 Ireland	30,910	377
7 Iceland	30,570	373
8 Canada	30,040	367
9 Austria	29,740	363
10 Belgium	28,920	353
11 Australia	28,780	351
12 Hong Kong, China	28,680	350
13 Netherlands	28,560	349
14 Japan	28,450	347
15 UK	27,690	338
World	8,190	100

Table 1.4 gives the top fifteen countries in terms of income per capita, corrected for purchasing power. The average income level in the world was $8,190 per person. The highest income level, almost seven times the world average, was generated in the tiny country of Luxembourg. The lowest income level ($530 per capita) was measured in Sierra Leone, a small African nation. High income levels per capita are generated in North America (USA and Canada), Japan, and Australia. All other high income per capita countries in Table 1.4 are located in Europe.

1.5 International trade

As the title of this book suggests, the interactions between nations, their underlying forces, and the implications of economic policy are our primary focus of attention. Before we continue it should be noted that the comparison problems between countries discussed in Sections 1.3 and 1.4 arising from the distinction between tradable and non-tradable goods do not occur when investigating and comparing trade flows, which can readily be compared using the exchange rates. So what are the large trading nations? We will distinguish between merchandise trade (Table 1.5) and trade in commercial services (Table 1.6). The left-hand side of Table 1.5 lists the top fifteen countries in terms of merchandise trade export value, while the right-hand side lists the top fifteen countries in terms of import value. With the exception of Russia (which is replaced by Spain), the same countries appear on both sides, only in

Table 1.5 Top fifteen merchandise trade ($ bn), 2004

Country	Exports	% of world	Country	Imports	% of world
1 Germany	915	10.0	USA	1,526	16.1
2 USA	819	9.0	Germany	718	7.6
3 China	593	6.5	China	561	5.9
4 Japan	566	6.2	France	464	4.9
5 France	451	4.9	UK	462	4.9
6 Netherlands	359	3.9	Japan	455	4.8
7 Italy	346	3.8	Italy	349	3.7
8 UK	346	3.8	Netherlands	320	3.4
9 Canada	322	3.5	Belgium	287	3.0
10 Belgium	309	3.4	Canada	276	2.9
11 Hong Kong	266	2.9	Hong Kong	273	2.9
12 South Korea	254	2.8	Spain	250	2.6
13 Mexico	189	2.1	South Korea	224	2.4
14 Russia	183	2.0	Mexico	206	2.2
15 Taipei, Chinese	181	2.0	Taipei, Chinese	168	1.8
World	9,124	100	World	9,458	100

Source: WTO press release, 14 April 2005.

a slightly different order. The total value of world merchandise exports is $9,124 bn (note the small statistical discrepancy between the export and import value).

Germany was the world's largest merchandise trade exporter in 2004, followed by the the USA and China. Taking into consideration that the USA's share of world production is 30 per cent (see Table 1.3), the USA's share of world exports (9.0 per cent, see Table 1.5) is rather modest. Most countries in Table 1.5 have a larger share in world exports than in world production. To some extent this can be explained by the artificiality of drawing borders between nations on the globe. For example, if an American firm in Boston sells goods 5,000 km away in Los Angeles, this is not counted as exports because both cities are located in the USA. Compare this to a Dutch firm in Rotterdam, Europe's largest harbour, selling goods to a Belgian consumer in Antwerp less than 100 km away, which of course is part of Dutch exports. Consequently, many countries in Table 1.5 are relatively small, high-income open economies: such as the Netherlands (sixth), Canada (ninth), Belgium (tenth), Hong Kong (eleventh), and Taiwan (fifteenth).

Table 1.6 lists the top fifteen commercial services exporters and importers, the total value of which is almost one quarter the size of merchandise trade. Relative to Table 1.5 there are only three new countries on the export list, namely Spain, Austria, and Ireland, which replace Mexico, Russia, and Taiwan. Although we can therefore conclude that large merchandise trade exporters are generally also large commercial services exporters, the order on the list differs quite remarkably. The USA, for example, moves up to first place (from second) and the

Table 1.6 Top fifteen commercial services trade ($ bn), 2004

Country	Exports	% of world	Country	Imports	% of world
1 USA	319	15.2	USA	259	12.4
2 UK	169	8.1	Germany	191	9.2
3 Germany	126	6.0	UK	135	6.5
4 France	108	5.2	Japan	134	6.4
5 Japan	94	4.5	France	95	4.5
6 Italy	85	4.0	Italy	80	3.8
7 Spain	84	4.0	Netherlands	72	3.5
8 Netherlands	72	3.4	China	70	3.3
9 China	59	2.8	Ireland	58	2.8
10 Hong Kong	54	2.6	Canada	56	2.7
11 Belgium	50	2.4	Spain	53	2.6
12 Austria	47	2.2	South Korea	50	2.4
13 Canada	47	2.2	Belgium	48	2.3
14 Ireland	46	2.2	Austria	48	2.3
15 South Korea	40	1.9	India	38	1.8
World	2,100	100	World	2,080	100

Source: WTO press release, 14 April 2005.

UK moves up to second place (from eighth). Germany, on the other hand, drops from first to third place, while Canada drops from ninth to thirteenth. Evidently, the USA and the UK specialize to some extent in exporting commercial services while Canada and Germany specialize in exporting merchandise trade.

Exports relative to imports

Figure 1.4 illustrates the export value of goods and services relative to the import value for 155 countries using a logarithmic scale.[6] It also depicts a 45-degree line where exports are equal to imports and the trade balance is zero (see also the next section). Although a country's export value is generally roughly in line with its import value, the deviations between the two are clearly more substantial than the deviations between GDP and GNP illustrated in Figure 1.2. Germany had the largest trade balance surplus ($101 bn), followed by Japan ($72 bn) and Russia ($49 bn). The USA had by far the largest trade balance deficit ($497 bn, see Box 31.1), followed by the UK ($50 bn) and Australia ($16 bn). In relative terms, Venezuela is a large net exporter while Haiti, and Bosnia and Herzegovina are large net importers; see Figure 1.4.

Exports relative to production

The reader may wonder how it is possible that a small country like Hong Kong, which has only 7 million inhabitants, is able to reach the world's top fifteen in export and import value. The reason is that countries may re-export goods and services they import to other countries,

Figure 1.4 Exports and imports of goods and services, 2003 ($ bn)

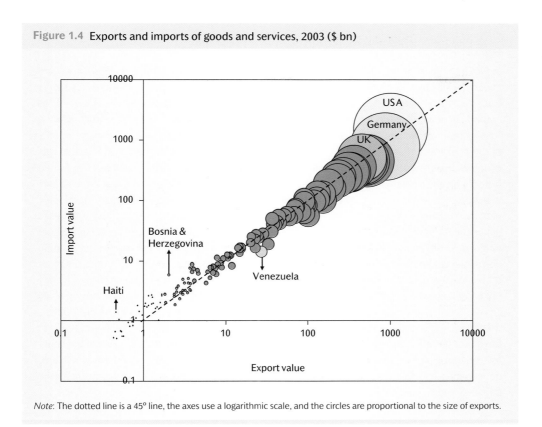

Note: The dotted line is a 45° line, the axes use a logarithmic scale, and the circles are proportional to the size of exports.

Figure 1.5 Relative exports of goods and services, 2003 (% of GDP)

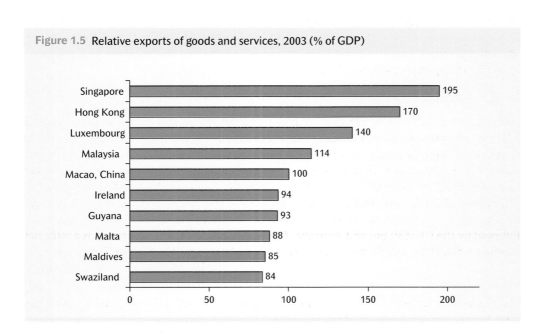

Box 1.2   **Tariffs as a source of government revenue**

In Part II of this book we will analyse the forces underlying international trade flows, their welfare impact for different agents in the economy, and the consequences of policy measures restricting trade flows. In general we will argue not only that international trade flows lead to efficiency gains and welfare improvements for a country as a whole, but also that policy measures restricting trade flows deteriorate welfare and reduce efficiency, sometimes in unexpected and covert ways. In view of these conclusions, supported by almost all international economists, the question arises *why* countries impose (welfare-deteriorating) trade restrictions. We will discuss the more complicated distribution effects of trade restrictions, which may help to explain these phenomena, in the sequel. In this box, however, we want to point to the problems facing the governments of many developing nations which do not have an efficient tax-collecting system available. After all, this requires detailed information on the inhabitants of the country, their income level, specific circumstances that may be relevant for an individual, and many public servants to gather and process the information. None the less, the government of any nation requires funds to perform its basic duties, such as protecting the country, providing law, order, and education, etc. In the absence of an efficient tax-collecting apparatus it is therefore tempting to collect government revenue by imposing tariffs on the (relatively easily controlled) international trade flows (imports duties, export duties, exchange profits, and the like). This is illustrated in Figure 1.6, which ranks countries in terms of taxes on international trade as a percentage of goverment revenue. It shows not only that the countries imposing high tariffs are generally developing nations, but also that some countries are highly dependent on taxing international trade flows for their tax revenue (for example 59 per cent for the Bahamas and 50 per cent for Swaziland).

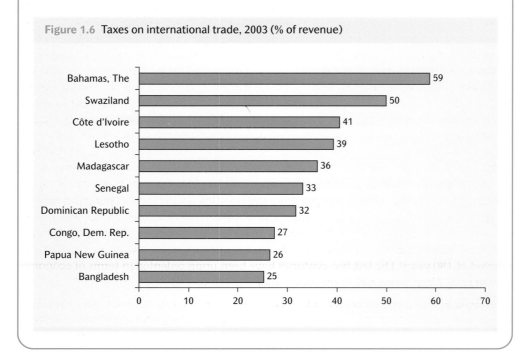

Figure 1.6 Taxes on international trade, 2003 (% of revenue)

with only modest value added in the country itself. This is illustrated in Figure 1.5, which shows the top ten value of exports of goods and services relative to GDP. Note that Singapore, the highest-ranked economy, exports a value of goods and services which is 95 per cent higher than the total value of production, which can be explained by re-exports. Four other countries in Figure 1.5, which are all small economies, also export more than the total production value.

1.6 Globalization

The term 'globalization' means different things to different people. Brakman et al. (2006) distinguish, for example, between cultural, geographical, institutional, political, and economic globalization. We will concentrate on economic globalization as defined by Neary (2002): the increased interdependence of national economies, and the trend towards greater integration of goods, labour and capital markets. Extensive research over the past decade has shown that economic globalization is not as new a phenomenon in history as previously thought; see O'Rourke and Williamson (1999), Maddison (2001), and Bordo, Taylor, and Williamson (2003).

Globalization and income[7]

In his impressive work full of historical detail entitled *The World Economy: A Millennial Perspective* (published in 2001), Angus Maddison collects detailed statistics on a wide range of economic variables, such as income, population, international trade, and capital flows, for all major regions and countries in the world over the past two thousand years. To describe the evolution of income over time Maddison uses so-called '1990 international dollars', which correct for purchasing power parity, and takes great care to ensure transitivity, base country invariance, and additivity. The development of world per capita income is illustrated in Figure 1.7 using a logarithmic scale. The main advantage of using a logarithmic scale is the simultaneous depiction of the *level* of a variable (measured by its vertical height) and the *growth rate* of that variable (measured by the slope of the graph) in one figure. Average world per capita income in the year zero was estimated to be $444. The subsistence income level is $400. Where the governing elite could maintain some degree of luxury and sustain a relatively elaborate system of governance, Maddison estimates the income level in the year zero to be $450, as was the case for the Roman Empire, China, India, other Asian countries, and the northern part of Africa. As indicated in Figure 1.7, there was no advance in per capita income on a global scale in the first millennium (the small advance in Japan was compensated by the decline in Western Europe). From the year 1000 to 1820 global per capita income started to increase in what we now consider a slow crawl – the world average rose by about 50 per cent in 820 years, to $667. A clear increase in the global economic growth rate started in 1820 with the industrial revolution. Since then per capita income rose more than eightfold in a period of 180 years! The last two centuries have been unprecedented in terms of economic growth rates. Note, moreover, as Maddison argues (2001, p. 17):

> Per capita income growth is not the only indicator of welfare. Over the long run, there has been a dramatic increase in life expectation. In the year 1000, the average infant could expect to live about 24 years. A third would die in the first year of life, hunger and epidemic disease would ravage the survivors. . . . Now the average infant can expect to survive 66 years.

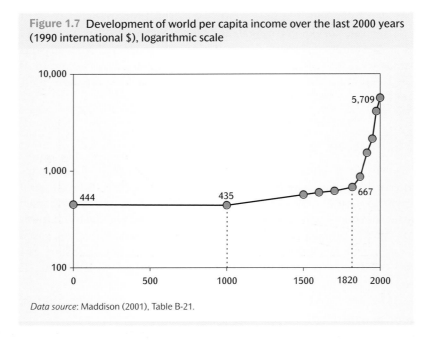

Figure 1.7 Development of world per capita income over the last 2000 years (1990 international $), logarithmic scale

Data source: Maddison (2001), Table B-21.

Globalization and trade

Britain became the leading economy in the eighteenth century, initially by improving its financial, banking, fiscal, and agricultural institutions along the lines pioneered by the Dutch, and subsequently by a surge in industrial productivity. The latter was not only based on the acceleration of technical progress and investments in physical capital, education, and skills, but also on commercial trade policy, which in 1846 reduced protective duties on agricultural imports and by 1860 unilaterally removed all trade and tariff restrictions. The British willingness to specialize in industrial production and import a large part of its food had positive effects on the world economy and diffused the impact of technical progress, but most of all it allowed Britain to achieve unprecedented rates of economic growth and establish a global economic and political power. This progress came to end as a result of two world wars (1914–1918 and 1939–1945) and the Great Depression in the 1930s, which drastically raised trade impediments and led to a collapse of trade, capital, and migration flows. As a consequence, the world economy grew much more slowly from 1913 to 1950 than from 1870 to 1913.[8]

The institutional arrangements with codes of behaviour and cooperation set up after the Second World War created a new liberal international order which contributed to remarkable growth rates of income per capita (3 per cent per year), total world income (5 per cent per year), and world trade flows (8 per cent per year). At the same time, the world economy became more closely connected than ever before. These 'two waves of globalization' are illustrated in Figure 1.8 in terms of trade flows relative to GDP. During the first wave of the nineteenth century there was an increase of trade in basic and homogeneous commodities. During the second wave after the Second World War, there was an increase of trade in basic and differentiated manufactured products. Decreases in transport costs, technological improvements, falling trade restrictions, international cooperation, and improved communication possibilities have all been important underlying forces in the two waves of

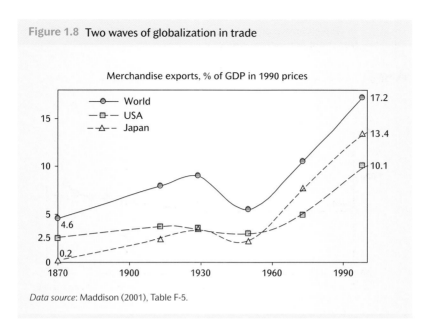

Figure 1.8 Two waves of globalization in trade

Merchandise exports, % of GDP in 1990 prices

Data source: Maddison (2001), Table F-5.

globalization; think of the railway, the steamship, the opening of the Suez canal and the Panama canal (which cut travel times and avoided the dangerous routes around the Cape of Good Hope and Cape Horn), and technological inventions, such as effective means of refrigeration which enabled the transportation of perishable goods (meat and fruit).

Globalization and capital

Two similar waves of globalization are also visible on the capital market. There was a reduction in the interest rate spread during the first wave of globalization and an increase in the interbellum. The two waves are illustrated in Figure 1.9, which measures foreign capital stocks relative to world GDP. There is a first peak towards the end of the nineteenth century, a sharp drop in the interbellum, and a second peak towards the end of the twentieth century after the capital market liberalizations starting in the 1960s.

Globalization and migration

Historians have identified two modern waves of migration. The first took place between 1820 and 1913. More than 50 million migrants departed (mostly) from Europe to the USA, Canada, South America, and Australia. Almost 60 per cent of the migrants went to the USA. Most were young, and relatively low skilled. After 1850 most migrants came from Ireland. The second wave started after the Second World War, and has not yet ended. In view of the rising population levels, it is smaller in relative terms; see Figure 1.10. Between 1913 and 1950 migration was only a fraction of what it had been during the nineteenth century. The USA remained the main destination country. Immigration grew from a low of 252,000 per year in the 1950s to 916,000 in the 1990s. The source countries changed dramatically. Before the 1950s most immigrants came from Europe, in the 1990s most came from Asia and from 1990 on, also from former Eastern Europe. During this second wave immigration restrictions became more binding than before. Many countries use quota, and only allow migrants for

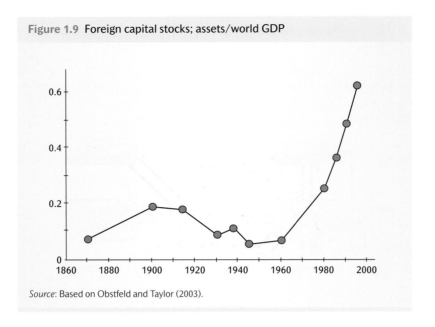

Figure 1.9 Foreign capital stocks; assets/world GDP

Source: Based on Obstfeld and Taylor (2003).

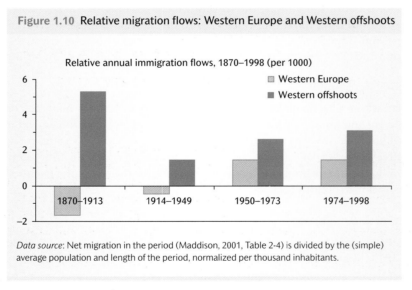

Figure 1.10 Relative migration flows: Western Europe and Western offshoots

Relative annual immigration flows, 1870–1998 (per 1000)

Data source: Net migration in the period (Maddison, 2001, Table 2-4) is divided by the (simple) average population and length of the period, normalized per thousand inhabitants.

reasons such as family reunion or specific labour demands. In Europe immigration from Africa and Eastern Europe is relatively small compared to intra-EU migration. It is clear, however, that labour markets are less globally integrated than goods and capital markets.

1.7 Trade connections in the world economy

To conclude the first chapter, we want to give an impression of the most important international trade connections in the world economy. The World Bank identifies seven global regions, namely (i) East Asia and the Pacific (EAP; including China and Indonesia),

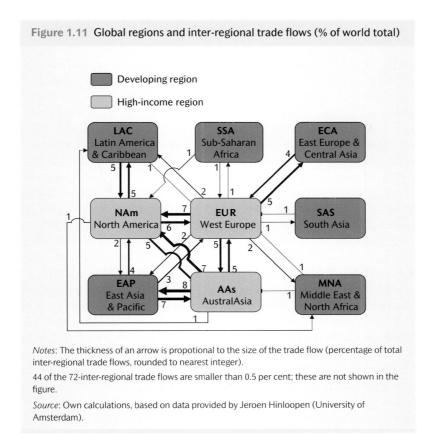

Figure 1.11 Global regions and inter-regional trade flows (% of world total)

Notes: The thickness of an arrow is propotional to the size of the trade flow (percentage of total inter-regional trade flows, rounded to nearest integer).

44 of the 72-inter-regional trade flows are smaller than 0.5 per cent; these are not shown in the figure.

Source: Own calculations, based on data provided by Jeroen Hinloopen (University of Amsterdam).

(ii) (East) Europe and Central Asia (ECA; including Russia and Turkey), (iii) Latin America and the Caribbean (LAC; including Brazil and Mexico), (iv) Middle East and North Africa (MNA; including Egypt), (v) South Asia (SAS; including India), (vi) Sub-Saharan Africa (SSA; including Nigeria and South Africa), and (vii) the high-income countries. For the purposes of this section we have subdivided the group of high-income countries into three subgroups, namely North America (NAm), Western Europe (EUR), and AustralAsia (AAs, including Japan and Australia), leading to a total of nine global regions.[9] Figure 1.11 illustrates the inter-regional trade flows as a percentage of total inter-regional trade flows (rounded to the nearest integer and thus depicting only inter-regional trade flows larger than 0.5 per cent).[10] The figure leads to several conclusions. First, South Asia and Sub-Saharan Africa scarcely participate in the global economy as they have only a few small connections to the rest of the world (mainly Western Europe). Second, Western Europe is a spider in the web of global international trade connections as it is the only region with sizeable trade flows to all other regions. Third, the largest inter-regional trade flows are from the high-income global regions to the other high-income regions. Fourth, and finally, there is a local character to trade flows with strong links between North and Latin America (NAm and LAC), between West and East Europe (EUR and ECA), and between AustralAsia and East Asia and the Pacific (AAs and EAP).

1.8 Conclusions

This chapter presents basic, but essential, information on the structure of the world economy. We give an impression of the importance of various countries using different measures. In terms of land area, Russia is the largest country, while some relatively unknown African nations are also important. In terms of population, China and India stand out, as do Asian nations in general. In terms of income, using either GDP or GNP, North America, Japan, and many European nations are important. This holds even when current dollars, which tend to overestimate the importance of high-income countries, are corrected for purchasing power. Japan and nations from North America and Europe also hold top positions with respect to income per capita. The differences in this respect are enormous. International trade flows are dominated by relatively small European and South-East Asian countries. In general, the different rankings change the composition of important countries considerably. Only five, namely Brazil, China, India, Mexico, and the USA, make it to the top fifteen lists in terms of land area, population, and total income (Tables 1.1–1.3). We showed that per capita income levels have been rising very rapidly only fairly recently (in the last two centuries). Historians have identified two big waves of economic globalization: at the end of the nineteenth century and since the end of the Second World War. These episodes coincide with drastic decreases in international price gaps for goods and services and drastic increases in relative international trade and capital flows (conclusions with respect to migration are less clear cut).

With this information in the back of our minds we are ready to embark on our journey into international economics, which values the consistency of a general equilibrium approach. Clearly, we will not be able to 'explain' all the empirical observations above, although international economists do work on all these issues. We will discuss how the insights we derive can be helpful for tackling important policy problems. Many other topics touched upon above will also be explored. Along the way we will present more detailed empirical information on specific topics to raise new questions and guide us in our search. Before we can analyse these issues, however, we have to get a firm grip of international accounting principles and practices to understand the interconnections between goods and services flows on the one hand and international capital flows on the other. This knowledge, provided in the next chapter, is crucial for a thorough understanding of both Part II (International Trade) and Part III (International Money) of this book.

QUESTIONS

Question 1.1

Imagine you work at the Statistical Bureau of Singapore and have to record the value changes in GDP, GNP, exports and imports. What value changes do you record when:

1.1A A shipload of 1,000 trousers arrives from India that has cost the Singapore importer 5 Singapore dollars per piece. This shipload is immediately re-exported to the USA for 6 Singapore dollars per piece.

1.1B A bundle of 1,000 trousers has been purchased from a Singapore producer for 5 Singapore dollars per piece. This bundle is exported to the USA for 6 Singapore dollars per piece.

1.1C The same transaction is executed as in 1.1A but this time the Indian producer of trousers has to pay 1 Singapore dollar per trouser to a Singapore investor who has helped to establish the Indian trouser factory.

1.1D An Indonesian nanny returns home after babysitting in Singapore for four months. She takes her total wage of 1,000 Singapore dollars with her.

1.1E An Indonesian woman, married to a Singapore man, returns home and gives her parents 1,000 Singapore dollars.

Question 1.2

The difference between GDP converted by the current and the PPP exchange rate can be illustrated with a simple example. Assume that Germany and Poland both produce every year a thousand machines (to remove oil remains) and five hundred pedicure treatments. Machines can be traded between both countries while pedicure treatments cannot be traded. Further assume that the current exchange rate is one euro for four Polish zloty, the hourly wage in Germany is 10 euro and the number of hours it takes to produce one machine or to give one pedicure treatment in both countries is given in the following table:

Number of hours to produce one unit		
	Germany	Poland
Machine	10	20
Pedicure treatment	2	2

1.2A If machine producers do not make any profit, what is the price of a machine in Germany (in euro) and in Poland (in zloty)?

1.2B What is the hourly wage rate in Poland?

1.2C If also pedicures do not make any profit, what is the price of a pedicure treatment in Germany (in euro) and in Poland (in zloty)?

1.2D What is the GDP figure in Germany (in euro) and in Poland (in zloty)?

1.2E What is the PPP exchange rate between the euro and the zloty?

1.2F Convert the Polish GDP figure to euro with the current exchange rate and the PPP exchange rate. Explain the difference between these two figures.

Question 1.3

Trade statistics are not always reliable. It is a well-known fact that there is a discrepancy between figures on the value and number of products leaving a country and the figures on the value and number of products entering another country as reported by the national statistical agencies. The table below gives a striking example.

Indonesian sawnwood exports to major trading partners in thousand m3 according to Indonesian statistics (EX) and statistics of importers (IM)

	1998			1999			2000		
	EX	IM	% diff	EX	IM	% diff	EX	IM	% diff
Japan	148	336	127	109	261	139	35	271	674
China	52	317	510	77	580	653	20	931	4555
Malaysia	4	335	8275	7	289	4029	7	450	6329

Source: Johnson (2002), 'Documenting the undocumented', *Tropical Forest Update*, vol. 12, no. 1.

1.3A Why do statistics on exports and imports differ between different national statistical agencies?

1.3B What do you think is the main source of discrepancy in the case of Indonesian sawnwood?

See the Online Resource Centre for a Study Guide containing more questions
www.oxfordtextbooks.co.uk/orc/vanmarrewijk/

NOTES

1 I am grateful to my co-authors Steven Brakman, Harry Garretsen, and Arjen van Witteloostuijn for allowing me to use some of our joint work (see Brakman et al., 2006) as the basis for parts of this chapter.

2 Unless stated otherwise, the source of all data in this chapter is the World Bank Development Indicators CD-ROM 2005. If data for 2003 are reported, the most recent observation in the period 2000–2003 was used, which in most cases is indeed the 2003 observation.

3 There are two 'Congo' countries in Africa, the largest of which in terms of both population and size, a former Belgian colony, is better known under the old name Zaire.

4 Henceforth the $ sign always refers to the US$.

5 These percentages are not listed in Figure 1.2. More details are provided on the book's website.

6 Note that the data in the figure are for 2003 while the data in Tables 1.5 and 1.6 are for 2004.

7 Unless indicated otherwise, all data in this section are from Maddison (2001).

8 Namely 0.91 per cent per annum rather than 1.30 per cent. Although this difference might seem to be small, world income would have been 15 per cent higher in 1950 if the slow-down had not occurred and the economy had maintained its 1.30 per cent growth rate.

9 The online resource centre specifies exactly to which global region a country belongs.

10 Note that the (large) trade flows within the same regions, such as between France and Germany or between China and Indonesia, are not depicted in Figure 1.11.

THE BALANCE OF PAYMENTS

2

Objectives/key terms

- Balance of payments
- Current account
- Capital inflows and outflows
- Louisiana purchase
- Feldstein–Horioka puzzle

- Trade balance
- Capital account
- Sales and value added
- Benefits of capital flows

The balance of payments records a country's transactions with the rest of the world. As such, it provides essential information on a nation's trade and capital flows in a consistent (accounting) framework. We discuss the link between the current account balance and net capital flows, of which we provide some empirical evidence.

2.1 Introduction[1]

Accounting may not be viewed as the most exciting field of economics, but the products provided by accountants, such as a country's balance of payments or a firm's annual report, are indispensible as building blocks for other research. As we will see, it helps us, for example, to establish the link between international trade and capital flows. By discussing some definitions and accounting principles regarding the balance of payments, this chapter provides the basis for a proper understanding of Part II on international trade flows as well as for Part III on international money (and capital) flows. In the process, we clarify some confusion regarding the power of multinationals relative to the nation-state and discuss the major advantage of international capital flows.

2.2 The balance of payments

This section is divided into two parts. First, we briefly review some accounting principles. Second, we discuss some accounting identities at the macroeconomic level.

Accounting principles

The balance of payments records a country's transactions with other countries on the basis of a set of agreed-upon accounting definitions and principles. The balance of payments thus involves macro-level accounting for nation-states and is based on the rules of double-entry bookkeeping, with matching credit and debit entries. By definition, the balance of payments is therefore equal to zero. We distinguish between two main parts of the balance of payments, namely the current account on the one hand and the capital and financial account on the other hand, each with subdivisions as summarized in Figure 2.2.

The transactions on the current account are income related, pertaining to produced goods, provided services (also known as invisibles), income (from investment), and unilateral transfers. Exports are recorded as credit items (+) and imports as debit items (−). After all, with exports money is earned, and with imports it is spent. The sum of the merchandise and services balance is called the trade balance, indicating the net money earned with trade (exports minus imports), which may of course be negative if more is imported than exported, in terms

Famous economists	Adam Smith

Scottish philosopher, considered by many to be the founder of modern economic science as we know it. Famous for the 'invisible hand', that is how people pursuing their own self-interest actually benefit society as a whole, and the advantages of increasing 'specialization' (the pin factory example). Major publications are *The Theory of Moral Sentiments* (1759) and *An Inquiry into the Nature and Causes of the Wealth of Nations* (1776).

Fig. 2.1
Adam Smith
(1723–1790)

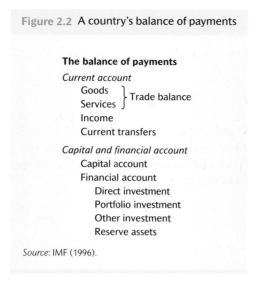

Figure 2.2 A country's balance of payments

The balance of payments

Current account
    Goods   ⎫
               ⎬ Trade balance
    Services ⎭
    Income
    Current transfers

Capital and financial account
    Capital account
    Financial account
        Direct investment
        Portfolio investment
        Other investment
        Reserve assets

Source: IMF (1996).

of money value. More important, however, is the current account balance, which also includes income and unilateral transfers because investment income, such as dividend payments, reflects the remuneration for the use of capital, a factor of production, by another country. It is therefore essentially the payment for trade in (capital) services. Unilateral transfers, such as foreign aid to a developing nation, remittances or military aid, are included as they represent income transfers to another country and not claims on another country. As a result, the current account balance measures the net change in claims on the outside world, which is recorded on the capital and financial account. This includes, in the capital account, capital transfers and transactions (purchases/sales) in an economy's non-produced, non-financial assets (such as patents and copyrights) and, in the financial account, transactions in an economy's external financial assets and liabilities.

Accounting identities

The transactions on the capital and financial account are asset related. An increase in claims on foreigners is a *capital outflow* and appears as a debit. An increase in claims by foreigners on our country is a *capital inflow* and appears as a credit. If the claim is longer than one year, it is called long-term capital – for example, foreign direct investment and long-term portfolio investment, such as securities and loans. Otherwise, it is called short-term capital. Sometimes, the classification is difficult. Purchasing foreign stocks is a short-term capital flow, unless you buy so much of the company that it becomes a foreign direct investment. Changes in reserve assets may refer to changes by the central banking system in gold stocks, IMF credits, Special Drawing Rights (SDRs), or foreign exchange reserves. As mentioned above, the balance of payments is zero by definition such that

(2.1)   *current account balance + capital and financial account balance* = 0

Suppose there is a surplus on the current account. This implies, roughly speaking, that the value of our exports (credit) is higher than the value of our imports (debit) – that is, the current account represents a net credit item. By the rules of double-entry accounting this must be matched by a net debit item on the capital account, and thus a net capital outflow, that is:

(2.2)   *surplus current account ⇔ net capital and financial outflow*

To see how the current account and capital account are related and how the 'books are balanced', consider the following example. Suppose a country exports goods for 1 billion euro (net proceeds) and imports no goods at all. The country has a current account *surplus*. If the exporting firms decide to spend their proceeds on buying financial assets abroad, like foreign shares or bonds, this constitutes a capital outflow and hence a debit because by buying these assets the country has *imported claims (on future production) on foreigners*. This means that the capital account will display a *deficit* because of the capital outflow of 1 billion euro. Of course, the net export proceeds do not have to be spent on foreign financial assets. The exporting firms may simply put their money on deposit with their bank. But in that case the reserve asset position of this country will increase by 1 billion and the result will be the same as with the acquisition of foreign shares or bonds. To see this, note that our exporting firms will have to be paid in local currency, which means that the foreigners who have bought the goods will first have to go to the bank to exchange their currency for that of the exporting firms, leading to an increase in the foreign exchange reserves of the exporting country (see item reserve assets in Figure 2.2). A similar line of reasoning helps to explain why a net capital inflow is booked as a credit.

The principle underlying the balance of payments is exactly the same as the one related to an individual's budget constraint.[2] If the income you earn this month (export of labour services, your only factor of production) is higher than the money you spend on consumption (import of goods and services), this will increase your claims on the outside world (for example, by an increase of the balance on your cheque account). If your income is less than your consumption spending this month, this will reduce your claims on the outside world. Table 2.1 provides a recent example for Germany and the USA.

2.3 Capital flows

As is clear from equation (2.2), analysing a country's current account balance over a somewhat longer period of time gives a good idea of the net change in claims on the rest of the world. This is illustrated in Figure 2.3 for a selection of countries, where the current account balance is measured relative to GDP. Note that the scale on the vertical axis is not the same for the various panels in Figure 2.3. The USA, which used to be a net creditor, has accumulated such large current account deficits over the past two decades that it is now the world's largest debtor (see also Box 31.1). Considering the enormous size of the US economy, the recent current account deficit of almost 5 per cent in 2003 is very large. In the aftermath of the Iraq War and the expansionist policies of the Bush administration (such as huge defence budgets and tax reductions, which produced large federal budget deficits), the account deficit deteriorated even further.

Japan has had a current account surplus fluctuating around 2 per cent of GDP, and thus has accumulated claims on the rest of the world, becoming a large creditor. Similar observations on a (relatively) somewhat larger scale hold for the Netherlands (which is consistently accumulating claims on the outside world) and Australia (which is borrowing from the rest of the world). Developments are more dramatic for the small South-East Asian nations involved in

Table 2.1 Balance of payments for Germany and the USA, 2002 ($ billion)

		Germany	USA
A	Current account	46.59	−480.86
	goods: exports fob	615.02	685.38
	goods: imports fob	−492.84	−1,164.76
	balance on goods	*122.18*	*−479.38*
	services: credit	106.00	288.72
	services: debit	−150.49	−227.38
	balance on goods and services	*77.69*	*−418.04*
	income: credit	103.26	255.54
	income: debit	−109.26	−259.51
	balance on goods, services, and income	*71.69*	*−422.01*
	current transfers: credit	15.83	11.50
	current transfers: debit	−40.94	−70.35
B	Capital account	−0.23	−1.29
	capital account: credit	2.09	1.11
	capital account: debit	−2.32	−2.39
	total: groups A plus B	*46.36*	*−482.14*
C	Financial account	−77.08	531.68
	direct investment abroad	−25.30	−137.84
	direct investment in Germany/USA	37.30	39.63
	portfolio investment assets	−63.32	15.80
	portfolio investment liabilities	98.70	421.44
	financial derivatives	−0.79	..
	other investment assets	−151.21	−53.27
	other investment liabilities	27.55	245.91
	total: groups A through C	*−30.72*	*49.54*
D	Net errors and omissions	28.74	−45.84
	total: groups A through D	*−1.98*	*3.69*
E	Reserves and related items	1.98	−3.69
	Overall balance	0.00	0.00

Source: IMF, *Balance of Payments Statistics Yearbook 2003*.

the Asian crisis of 1997, as illustrated for Malaysia and the Philippines in Figure 2.3. Both countries were borrowing on a large scale in the 1990s, in part to finance the rapid development processes and in part to finance consumption. There was an abrupt break in the capital inflow as a result of the Asian crisis, which forced both countries to repay part of their debt. This, in turn, forced them to generate large current account surpluses (see Chapter 29). In terms of relative magnitude, the oil-producing nations, such as Kuwait and Saudi Arabia, are in a class of their own, with years in which 60 per cent of GDP was recorded as a capital or financial outflow. In the case of Kuwait, the impact of the Gulf war in the early 1990s is immediately evident (the current account deficit was 240 per cent of GDP in 1991).

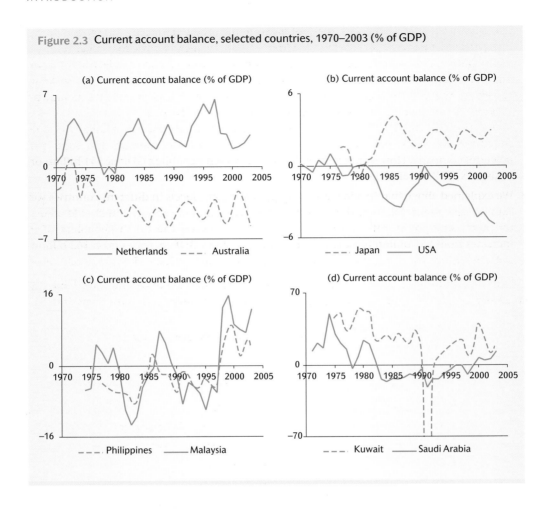

Figure 2.3 Current account balance, selected countries, 1970–2003 (% of GDP)

2.4 Nations and firms: a classic mistake

The usefulness of accounting is also, inadvertently, illustrated by Noreena Hertz (2001) and Naomi Klein (2001). They are very critical of many aspects of the globalization process and warn, for example, of the ever-increasing power of multinational firms, arguing that large companies such as Wal-Mart (with total sales of $165 billion in the fiscal year 2000) are even more powerful than entire nations, such as the Czech Republic (with a population of 10 million people generating a GDP of $51 billion in the year 2000) or Pakistan (with a population of 138 million people generating a GDP of $62 billion). In doing so, they make a classic mistake by directly comparing the sales revenue of a company and the gross domestic product of a nation for three reasons.

1 The Czech Republic and Pakistan are sovereign states with the ability to pass laws and regulations imposing restrictions and conditions on individuals and firms, to impose taxes, organize police, justice, and defence systems, etc. Wal-Mart, or any other company in the world, does not even remotely have the same powers.

2 The sales revenue of a company does not measure the production value of that company, in contrast to a nation's GDP. Before Wal-Mart can sell its merchandise for a total value of $165 billion, it has to buy this merchandise and other inputs (such as electricity) from many different sources. The production value added to the merchandise by Wal-Mart consists of the difference between the sales revenue and what it has to pay for its inputs. This difference is needed to pay Wal-Mart employees, the use of capital, to make a profit, etc. In the year 2000 Wal-Mart's gross margin was 21.42 per cent, such that the company's value added was about $35 billion. This is a substantial amount and Wal-Mart is a large and powerful company. However, it is smaller than the Czech Republic's GDP of $51 billion or Pakistan's GDP of $62 billion.

3 We explained above that in adequately comparing income levels in different countries we cannot use current dollars as the basis for comparison (as done above), but should adjust for purchasing power. After correcting for purchasing power the Czech Republic's GDP increases from $51 billion to $144 billion, while Pakistan's GDP increases from $62 billion to $266 billion. Both are substantially larger than Wal-Mart's value added of $35 billion.

Tables 2.2 and 2.3 indicate the importance of the correct method of comparison. Table 2.2 constructs a ranking using GDP as the size measure for countries and sales for firms. Indeed,

Table 2.2 Top 100 nations and firms based on a sales–GDP ranking, 2002

Rank	Firm or country	Rank	Firm or country
1	USA	20	Sweden
2	Japan	21	Austria
3	Germany	22	Exxon Mobil Corporation
4	UK	23	Norway
5	France	24	Poland
6	China	25	Saudi Arabia
7	Italy	26	General Motors
8	Canada	27	Turkey
9	Spain	28	British Petroleum Co. Plc
10	Mexico	29	Royal Dutch/Shell Group
11	India	30	Denmark
12	Korea, Rep.	31	Indonesia
13	Brazil	32	Ford Motor Company
14	Netherlands	33	Hong Kong, China
15	Australia	34	Daimler Chrysler Ag
16	Russian Federation	35	Greece
17	Switzerland	36	General Electric
18	Belgium	37	Finland
19	Wal-Mart Stores	38	Toyota Motor Corporation

Table 2.2 (*Cont.*)

Rank	Firm or country	Rank	Firm or country
39	Thailand	70	Royal Ahold NV
40	Portugal	71	Pakistan
41	Ireland	72	New Zealand
42	Mitsubishi Corporation	73	Nestle
43	Mitsui & Co Ltd	74	Conoco Phillips
44	Iran, Islamic Rep.	75	Hewlett-Packard
45	South Africa	76	Peru
46	Israel	77	Algeria
47	Argentina	78	Vivendi Universal
48	ChevronTexaco Corp.	79	Fiat Spa
49	Total Fina Elf	80	Merck & Co
50	Malaysia	81	Metro AG
51	Venezuela, RB	82	Samsung Electronics Co., Ltd
52	Egypt, Arab Rep.	83	Bangladesh
53	Singapore	84	Unilever
54	Volkswagen Group	85	Romania
55	IBM	86	Electricite France
56	Colombia	87	Eni Group
57	Philip Morris Companies Inc	88	RWE Group
58	Philippines	89	France Telecom
59	Siemens AG	90	Suez
60	United Arab Emirates	91	Nigeria
61	Czech Republic	92	Procter & Gamble
62	Verizon Communications	93	Vodafone Group Plc
63	Hitachi Ltd	94	Ukraine
64	Hungary	95	AOL Time Warner Inc
65	Honda Motor Co Ltd	96	BMW AG
66	Carrefour SA	97	Motorola Inc
67	Chile	98	DeutschePostWorldNet
68	Sony Corporation	99	British American Tobacco Group
69	Matsushita Electric Industrial Co.	100	Johnson & Johnson

Source: Calculations based on World Bank Development Indicators CD-ROM (2004) and UNCTAD World Investment Report (2004).

Table 2.3 Top 100 nations and firms based on a value added–GDP ranking, 2000

Rank	Firm or country	Rank	Firm or country
1	USA	37	Egypt
2	Japan	38	Ireland
3	Germany	39	Singapore
4	UK	40	Malaysia
5	France	41	Colombia
6	China	42	Philippines
7	Italy	43	Chile
8	Canada	44	Wal-Mart
9	Brazil	45	Pakistan
10	Mexico	46	Peru
11	Spain	47	Algeria
12	India	48	Exxon
13	South Korea	49	Czech Republic
14	Australia	50	New Zealand
15	The Netherlands	51	Bangladesh
16	Argentina	52	UA Emirates
17	Russia	53	General Motors
18	Switzerland	54	Hungary
19	Belgium	55	Ford Motors
20	Sweden	56	Mitsubishi
21	Turkey	57	Mitsui
22	Austria	58	Nigeria
23	Hong Kong	59	Citigroup
24	Poland	60	Itochu
25	Denmark	61	DaimlerChrysler
26	Indonesia	62	Royal Dutch Shell
27	Norway	63	British Petroleum
28	Saudi Arabia	64	Romania
29	South Africa	65	Nippon T&T
30	Thailand	66	Ukraine
31	Venezuela	67	Morocco
32	Finland	68	AXA
33	Greece	69	General Electric
34	Israel	70	Sumitomo
35	Portugal	71	Vietnam
36	Iran	72	Toyota Motors

Table 2.3 (*Cont.*)

Rank	Firm or country	Rank	Firm or country
73	Belarus	87	IBM
74	Marubeni	88	CGNU
75	Kuwait	89	JP Morgan Chase
76	Total Fina Elf	90	Carrefour
77	Enron	91	Crédit Suisse
78	ING Group	92	Nissho Iwai
79	Allianz Holding	93	Bank of America
80	E.ON	94	BNP Paribas
81	Nippon LI	95	Volkswagen
82	Deutsche Bank	96	Dominicans
83	AT&T	97	Uruguay
84	Verizon	98	Tunisia
85	US Postal Service	99	Slovakia
86	Croatia	100	Hitachi

Source: De Grauwe and Camerman (2002).

in *sales* terms, multinationals are massive economic entities, frequently larger than economies populated with millions and millions of people (see the shaded entries in Table 2.2). There are 13 multinationals in the top 50 and 46 in the top 100, with the highest-ranking firm (Wal-Mart) at number 19, above such countries as Sweden, Poland, Turkey, and Indonesia. Indeed, in sales terms no less than 16 firms rank higher than the Philippines, an economy with about 80 million inhabitants. Table 2.3 gives a more appropriate ranking of firms and countries, using value added as the source for comparison; see De Grauwe and Camerman (2002) for details. In this case only two multinationals – Wal-Mart and Exxon – make it into the top 50. Using sales as a size measure inflates firm size by cumulating double counts. After all, many expenses of a multinational relate to intermediate transactions. For instance, DaimlerChrysler must pay billions of dollars or euros to suppliers of raw materials (such as steel) and intermediate products (such as tyres). Therefore, a multinational's sales cannot be compared with a country's GDP, which is a value added measure. For a true comparison, only value added matters: that is, the value that is really produced by the multinational itself, and not by its large set of suppliers. Note, however, that Table 2.3 does not correct for differences in purchasing power, as is needed for a true comparison of production value.

2.5 The benefits of international capital flows

Before continuing with an analysis of international trade flows in Part II of the book, we briefly explain one of the main benefits of international capital flows. Other advantages and disadvantages are taken up in Part III of the book. The capital market is a (virtual) place where

Box 2.1   **International financing of the Louisiana Purchase**

Some 200 years ago, on 20 December 1803, and only 27 years after the Declaration of Independence, the USA was involved in the best real-estate deal in history: the Louisiana Purchase.[3] The French general Napoleon Bonaparte acquired the huge territory west of the Mississipi river, an area of 828,000 square miles (more than two million square kilometres) from Spain only three years earlier. The USA was primarily interested in the harbour city of New Orleans, providing access from the mighty Mississipi to the Gulf of Mexico for its trade flows. France, however, urgently needed funds to finance its war efforts in Europe and was willing to sell the entire Louisiana Territory, raising the price from the initially offered 10 million dollars to 15 million dollars. The deal between American president Thomas Jefferson and Napoleon Bonaparte doubled the size of the USA, provided the desired harbour access, and enabled westward expansion; see Figure 2.4. In 1804, the famous Lewis and Clarke expedition embarked on charting the newly acquired territory.

The Louisiana Purchase was financed by the banks Hope & Co. in Amsterdam and Baring & Co. in London by issuing bonds on behalf of the American Treasury with an interest rate of 6 per cent. Business bankers, such as the Scotsman Henry Hope who lived in Amsterdam, were indispensible links in the global network of international financing. It was a lucrative deal for the bank, which made a return on investment of 6.5 per cent in the decades before the Louisiana Purchase and of 10 per cent for a substantial period afterwards. Hope was particularly well connected with Russia, which bought most of the bonds. Ironically, therefore, Napoleon financed his European expansion with a transaction of American land via Amsterdam and hostile London with funds provided in substantial part by Russia, his later target. Hope & Co. later evolved to the present Dutch bank MeesPierson, a subsidiary of the Dutch Fortis group. The London-based Baring & Co. went bankrupt in 1995 after massive speculation by one of its employees in Singapore. It was bought by another Dutch financial conglomerate: ING.

Information source: NRC Handelsblad (2003).

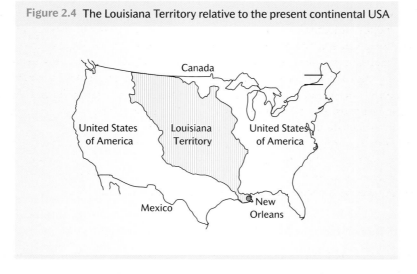

Figure 2.4 The Louisiana Territory relative to the present continental USA

savings are confronted with investments to be traded at a price called the interest rate. Savings are channelled directly through capital markets or indirectly through financial intermediaries (e.g. banks) towards investment opportunities in the expectation that the investments will yield a positive return or future income stream. To induce agents to save more and reduce current consumption, the interest rate, r, has to increase. Also, when the risk of financial transactions increases, the interest rate has to increase to compensate savers for the higher risk involved. These considerations suggest the following set-up for the savings function, S, for the home country (sub-index H) and the foreign country (sub-index F):

$$(2.3) \qquad\qquad S_H = S_H(r_H); \qquad S_F = S_F(r_F)$$

Turning to investment I, here too the interest rate is important. Each investment project increases the existing capital stock. This raises the productivity of capital, but each new addition to the capital stock makes a smaller contribution to the productivity of capital due to the law of diminishing marginal returns (see also Chapter 4). What is the optimal or equilibrium level of investment in this case? Investment takes place until the contribution of the latest, or marginal, investment project to productivity equals the cost of capital. The cost of capital, or the cost of financing an investment project, is equal to the interest rate r. Hence investment will take place until the marginal productivity of capital (MPC) equals the cost of capital r. These considerations suggest the following investment function, I, for the home country and the foreign country:

$$(2.4) \qquad\qquad I_H = I_H(r_H); \qquad I_F = I_F(r_F)$$

Figure 2.5 illustrates a major potential advantage of international capital mobility. For Home and Foreign, the respective national savings and investment schedules are drawn. The savings curves are upward sloping, and the investment curves are downward sloping. In the absence of international capital mobility the equilibrium interest rates at which national savings equals national investment are r_{H0} (at point 1 in the figure) and r_{F0} (at point 2 in the figure) for Home and Foreign, respectively. Note that, without international capital mobility, the Home interest rate is higher than the Foreign interest rate. Because at these equilibrium interest rates national savings equals national investment, we also have a current account balance. There is no net capital in- or outflow which is consistent with the assumption of no international capital mobility.

It is now straightforward to illustrate that the introduction of international capital mobility makes both countries better off. This follows from the fact that (in the absence of country-specific risks) international capital mobility implies that there will be one worldwide interest rate somewhere in between r_{H0} and r_{F0} for both countries. If this were not the case, profits could be made by redirecting savings towards (or away from) a country with the higher (lower) interest rate. Both countries gain *despite* the fact that the interest rate increases in one country and decreases in the other country. In Home, welfare improves because the increase in investor surplus (the area in between the Home investment schedule and the change in interest rates; see below for details) is larger than the decrease in savings surplus (the area in between the Home savings schedule and the change in interest rates). Similarly, in Foreign, welfare improves because the increase in savings surplus (the area in between the Foreign savings schedule and the change in interest rates) is larger than the decrease in investor surplus (the area in between the foreign investment schedule and the change in interest rates).

Figure 2.5 Capital mobility is welfare enhancing

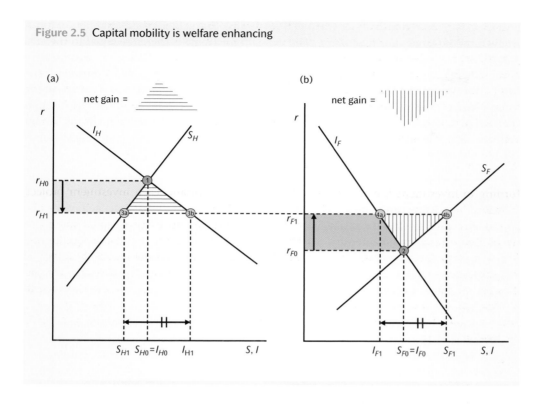

See also Chapter 8 for a similar analysis of the benefits of international trade flows and Box 2.1 for a vivid example of international capital flows and financing.

In autarky, Home finds itself in point 1 and Foreign in point 2 in Figure 2.5. Once capital mobility is permitted, capital will reallocate and start to flow from Foreign to Home because Home has higher interest rates than Foreign. Consequently, the interest rate in Home will fall because of the additional (foreign) savings that now become available. The drop in the Home interest rate will increase national investment and discourage national savings (compared to the case without international capital mobility). In Foreign the opposite will happen, such that foreign savings will increase and foreign investments will decrease. The incentive for further reallocation of international capital flows (from Foreign to Home) will stop if the two interest rates are equal ($r_{H1} = r_{F1}$). This situation is represented by the points labelled 3 and 4 in Figure 2.5: Foreign has a net capital outflow that corresponds with a savings surplus of $S_{F1} - I_{F1}$, whereas Home has an equally sized net capital inflow that corresponds with an investment surplus of $I_{H1} - S_{F1}$. Thanks to international capital mobility, Home is able to increase its level of investment (at a lower interest rate than in the case of capital market segmentation), and Foreign enjoys a higher rate of return on its savings compared to autarky. The net gain for both countries is indicated by the two triangles in Figure 2.5. The net gain for Home is positive because the gain for the demanders of funds (as represented by the investment schedule) outweighs the loss for the suppliers of funds (as represented by the savings schedule). The introduction of international capital mobility leads to a lower interest rate in Figure 2.5a. This amounts to a loss for the suppliers of funds equal to the area $r_{H0},1,3a,r_{H1}$ in Figure 2.5a (see Chapter 8 for details). The gain for the demanders of funds is given by the larger area $r_{H0},1,3b,r_{H1}$. The net gain for Home is therefore equal to the area 1,3a,3b, as indicated above the Figure. Similarly, the net gain for Foreign is also positive because here the gain for the suppliers of funds, equal to the area $r_{F0},2,4b,r_{F1}$ outweighs the loss for the demanders of funds, equal to the area $r_{F0},2,4a,r_{F1}$, which results from the rise in the interest rate in Foreign after the introduction of international capital mobility. The net gain for Foreign is therefore equal to the area 2,4a,4b, as indicated above the Figure. The net benefit arises because international capital mobility ensures that funds (savings) are directed towards the highest return internationally, rather than nationally.

 Box 2.2   The Feldstein–Horioka puzzle

From the analysis in section 2.2 we know that the current account balance (CA, say) is equal to the difference between national savings S and investments, that is $CA \equiv S-I$. The term 'national' indicates that both the private and government sector are included. From this accounting identity it becomes clear that a national savings surplus, $S-I > 0$, has to be invested abroad (as reflected in a corresponding capital outflow), and *vice versa* for a deficit. A major implication of international capital mobility and integrated financial markets (illustrated in Figure 2.5) is that national savings are not necessarily equal to national investment; that is, $S-I \neq 0$ is possible. National savings and investment no longer move in unison and there is no longer a perfect correlation between these two. Particularly for a small country, national investment will not be constrained by a lack of national savings: it is world savings that matter. Based on these observations, the seminal study by Feldstein and Horioka (1980) found, surprisingly, that the correlation between the national savings and invest-ment ratios was typically very high. For their sample of OECD countries they found this correlation to be almost equal to one. They concluded that the degree of international capital market integra-tion and hence of international capital mobility was still rather limited. This finding is puzzling because it is in contrast to the popular conviction that the world is highly globalized and that capital markets are highly integrated. Their result became known as the Feldstein–Horioka puzzle.

Table 2.4 The Feldstein–Horioka test (see equation 2.5)

Period	α_0	α_1	Explained variance (R^2)
1960–64	7.02 (1.50)	0.70 (3.75)	0.50
1965–69	8.78 (2.07)	0.65 (3.90)	0.50
1970–74	5.93 (1.96)	0.74 (6.62)	0.74
1975–79	6.47 (1.45)	0.78 (4.17)	0.54
1980–84	12.17 (4.36)	0.48 (3.81)	0.49
1985–89	10.41 (3.91)	0.54 (4.57)	0.58
1990–94	10.26 (5.88)	0.53 (6.46)	0.74
1995–97	7.83 (2.93)	0.56 (4.74)	0.58

Source: Ostrup (2002) based on OECD National Accounts; t-statistics in parenthesis.

> In response to the Feldstein–Horioka puzzle, Table 2.4 presents some evidence of increasing capital market integration based on a pooled estimate for a large set of countries of the equation:

(2.5)
$$\frac{I}{Y} = \alpha_0 + \alpha_1 \frac{S}{Y}$$

for various sub-periods of 1960–1997 (see Box 20.1 on basic econometrics). The core information is captured by the estimated coefficient α_1. The lower this coefficient, the lower the correlation between domestic savings and investment, and thus the higher the degree of international capital mobility. As discussed in Chapter 22, the year 1980 is often considered an important watershed year: on average international capital mobility gradually increased since then compared to the period 1945–1979. Table 2.4 illustrates this. The α_1-coefficient in the period after 1980 is lower than in the period 1960–1980, which suggests that international capital mobility and international capital market integration increased.

2.6 Services

We want to make some final observations regarding services and the production structure of various economies before continuing with the rest of the book. In the remainder we will use the term 'goods' to refer also to the production and trade of services, because our theories apply to both goods and services. This does not mean that the distinction between goods and services is unimportant, or that there are no special issues associated with dealing with services instead of goods, as will be discussed in Chapters 10, 12, and 16. In fact, as illustrated in Figure 2.6, the services sectors tend to become increasingly important as economies become wealthier and more sophisticated. In 2003, for example, average employment in the services sectors was 57.6 per cent of total employment, ranging from a minimum of 12.9 per cent for China (with a per capita GDP of $1,067) to a maximum of 80.3 per cent for Hong Kong (with a per capita GDP of $25,633). Typical examples in this respect are also provided by Bangladesh, with a GDP per capita of $395 and 23.5 per cent of employment in the services sector, and the USA, with a GDP per capita of $35,566 and 75.2 per cent employment in the services sector.[4] A popular method for distinguishing between goods and services is to argue that services, such as getting a haircut, are produced and consumed simultaneously, although not necessarily at the same place. A less sophisticated, but effective, method is to argue that if you can drop it on your foot it must be a good.

If the share of services employment increases, it must be at the expense of the share of some other type of employment. As illustrated in Figure 2.7, the agricultural sectors tend to become less important as economies become wealthier. In 2003, for example, average employment in the agricultural sectors was 17.1 per cent of total employment, ranging from a minimum of 0.1 per cent for Macao (with a per capita GDP of $15,892) to a maximum of 62.1 per cent for Bangladesh. Agricultural employment in the USA was 2.4 per cent of total employment. We return to these issues from a country perspective in Box 16.3.

Figure 2.6 GDP per capita and services employment: 82 countries, 2003*

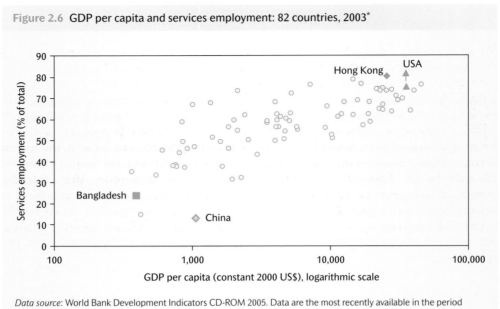

Data source: World Bank Development Indicators CD-ROM 2005. Data are the most recently available in the period 2001–2003.

Figure 2.7 GDP per capita and agricultural employment: 82 countries, 2003

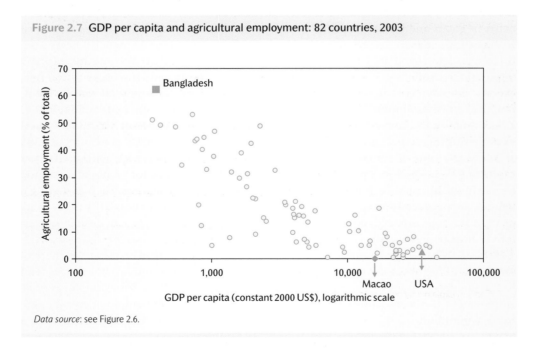

Data source: see Figure 2.6.

2.7 Conclusions

We provided some elementary information on the balance of payments, which records a country's transactions with the rest of the world. Our main distinction is between the current account on the one hand (which records flows from trade in goods, services, income from investment, and unilateral transfers) and the capital and financial account on the other hand (which records changes in claims on the rest of the world). Since the balance of payments is based on the rules of double-entry bookkeeping, the current account balance is always offset by an equal and opposite balance on the financial and capital account. As such, the current account balance measures the change in claims on the outside world. We use this identity to illustrate the size of international capital flows for a selection of countries. After a brief discussion on comparing the economic power of nations and firms, we discuss the benefits of international capital flows for both net capital exporters and importers. Based on the Feldstein–Horioka approach, we conclude by providing some evidence of increased international capital market integration and some evidence on the relation between income and services employment.

QUESTIONS

Question 2.1

'If there is more money flowing into a country than there is flowing out, that country has a positive balance of payments; if, on the other hand, more money flows out than in, the balance of payments is negative.'
Source: Wikipedia encyclopaedia, January 2006 (http://en.wikipedia.org/wiki/Balance_of_payments).

2.1A Is the definition above correct? Explain.

In this book, we follow the accounting principle that this balance equals zero. In practice, different definitions for the balance of payments exist. They sometimes exclude reserve assets or short-term capital account transactions from the balance, such that imbalances are possible. Consider the following quote: 'The USA is able to attract funds from the rest of the world to finance its balance of payments deficit'.

2.1B Explain the quote with the help of equation (2.1). What happens when the USA is unable to attract funds from the rest of the world?

Suppose that the Chinese central bank publishes a report that blames expected balance of payments surplus reductions on lower trade tariffs (taxes on imports) and higher oil prices.

2.1C Which balance of payments definition does the Chinese central bank probably use? Explain how tariff reductions and higher oil prices can contribute to a lower surplus.

When a country has a deficit in its balance of payments, politicians and the press often portray this as a cause of major concern. This concern is groundless for two reasons: (1) there never is a deficit, and (2) it wouldn't necessarily hurt if there were a deficit.

2.1D Explain for both reasons whether you agree or disagree.

2.1E Can you explain why politicians and the press are often concerned?

Question 2.2

The developments of the Chinese and US current account balance since 1990 are shown in the graph below. The current account is a flow variable. It represents the build-up of net foreign claims by an economy. Below you can also see a graph of the related stock variable, the international investment position for the USA. Many US politicians blame China for their country's growing current account deficit and negative international investment position.

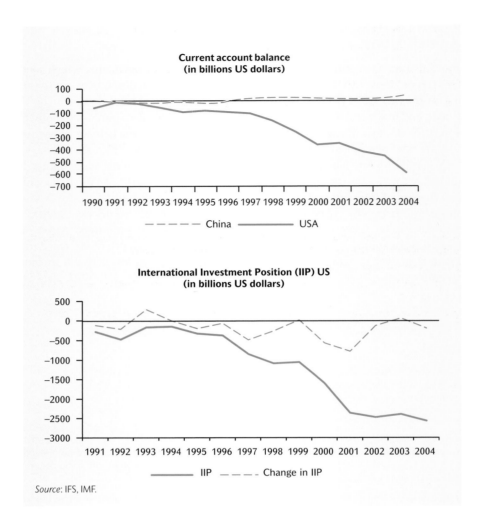

Source: IFS, IMF.

2.2A Why do US politicians blame China for their deficit, while the Chinese current account surplus is fairly small compared to the US deficit?

2.2B The current account balance is not exactly equal to changes in the international investment position. Can you explain why this is so?

2.2C The Chinese and US economies both attract a great deal of foreign direct investment (FDI). Does this represent a capital inflow or outflow?

2.2D If the current account remains unchanged, which offsetting capital account transactions can occur to maintain a balance of payments (use Table 2.1)?

2.2E Suppose the US government wants to improve relations with China and does so by giving emergency assistance after a flooding of the Yangtze River. How does this affect the Chinese balance of payments?

Question 2.3

Suppose that you live in the hermetically closed nation of North Korea. The economy has no outside economic links with the rest of the world. You save money in the bank and know that North Korean banks have the highest interest rates in the world.

2.3A What do you know about the saving and investment relationship in North Korea?

2.3B As a saver, do you favour capital mobility? Explain.

2.3C Do you expect the relationship between saving and investment to change after capital market integration? What will happen to the North Korean current account? Explain.

2.3D What impact does the Feldstein–Horioka puzzle have on your answer to 2.3C?

 See the Online Resource Centre for a Study Guide containing more questions
www.oxfordtextbooks.co.uk/orc/vanmarrewijk/

NOTES

1 I am grateful to my co-authors Steven Brakman, Harry Garretsen, and Arjen van Witteloostuijn for allowing me to use some of our joint work (see Brakman et al., 2006) as the basis for parts of this chapter.

2 In fact, budget constraints are additive, so we can do this for individuals in a country.

3 Arguably, the second-best deal is president Andrew Johnson's 1867 purchase of Alaska on behalf of the USA from Russia for $7.2 million.

4 The share of industrial employment tends to first increase and then decrease with income; see Chapter 16.

PART II
INTERNATIONAL TRADE

II.A

COMPARATIVE ADVANTAGE

Part II.A analyses comparative advantage in perfectly competitive economies, either based on differences in technology (classical trade; Chapter 3) or on differences in factor abundance (neoclassical trade; Chapters 4–7). It also discusses the (distributional) welfare implications of various trade policies, such as tariffs, quotas, and voluntary export restraints, in the classical and neoclassical settings (Chapter 8).

CLASSICAL TRADE: TECHNOLOGY

Objectives/key terms

- Productivity table
- Opportunity costs
- Comparative advantage
- Autarky
- Gains from trade
- Balassa index

- Constant returns to scale
- Absolute costs
- Production possibility frontier (PPF)
- Terms of trade
- World PPF
- Revealed (comparative) advantage

The classical driving forces behind international trade flows are technological differences between nations. If another country can produce a good (relatively) more cheaply than we ourselves can make it, it is better to import this good from abroad as it will increase our welfare. The per capita welfare level, however, depends on absolute cost differences, which also explains the large international differences in wage levels.

3.1 Historical introduction

Adam Smith (1723–90; see Chapter 2) will provide us with the starting point of our analysis. On the peculiar notions of the costs and benefits of international trade before Adam Smith, for example considering the role of merchants, the reader is encouraged to consult Douglas Irwin's (1996) *Against the Tide: An Intellectual History of Free Trade*. It suffices for our present purposes to note that various authors had already advocated a policy of free trade before the publication of Smith's (1776) influential masterpiece, *An Inquiry into the Nature and Causes of the Wealth of Nations*. The emergence of a doctrine of free trade at the time was largely a reaction to the Mercantilist literature of the seventeenth century, which advocated state regulation of trade to promote wealth and growth, maximize employment, achieve a favourable balance of trade, and protect the home industry.

If a free trade doctrine was already advocated by others before the *Wealth of Nations*, why do we pay so much attention to Adam Smith's analysis? First, because that's what it is, an *analysis* of economic reasons for advocating a policy of free trade. Second, because many people still needed to be convinced of the benefits of international trade, as illustrated by the work of James Steuart's (1767) *An Inquiry into the Principles of Political Economy*. Third, because Smith was able to put many different arguments and elements together in a coherent and systematic framework, organized using a few general principles, and thus providing a new way of thinking about political economy. After a few years, this had a large impact on the profession. As Irwin (1996: 75) put it:

> While drawing upon the work of others, Smith created such a compelling and complete case for free trade that commercial policy could no longer be seriously discussed without contending with his views, and herein lies one of Smith's foremost contributions to economics.

An issue associated with the theory of absolute cost advantages as set forth by Smith continues to puzzle thinkers up to this day, as illustrated by the well-known historian Paul Kennedy (1995), criticizing the case for free trade more than 200 years after Adam Smith argued his case (italics mine): 'What if there is *nothing* you can produce more cheaply or efficiently than anywhere else, except by constantly cutting labour costs?' The suggestion is that less developed nations cannot compete on the international scene, and that they do not benefit from the international exchange of commodities. How can you participate on the global market and gain from trading different goods and services if there is nothing you can produce more efficiently than anyone else? As we will see in Section 3.7, this is not merely a theoretical possibility; for all sixteen sectors of production for which we have data available, the EU is more productive than Kenya. So how can Kenya possibly trade with the EU? These problems were analysed in the first half of the nineteenth century in England by Robert Torrens, James Mill, and, most importantly, David Ricardo. All were in favour of free trade, and in the popular debate were particularly hostile towards the (in)famous Corn Laws, restricting grain imports into Britain. The most important contribution of this era was the *classical model*, or the *Ricardian model*. American Nobel laureate Paul Samuelson once even remarked that the theory of comparative advantage is 'one of the few ideas in economics that is true without being obvious'.

Famous economists	David Ricardo
 **Fig. 3.1** David Ricardo (1772–1823)	Born in London, the third son of a Jewish family emigrated from Holland, he married the daughter of a Quaker and was disinherited by his parents. Ricardo none the less accumulated a fortune as a stock-jobber and loan contractor. As Blaug (1986: 201) puts it: 'Ricardo may or may not be the greatest economist that ever lived, but he was certainly the richest.' His fame today rests mainly, of course, on his contributions to the theory of comparative advantage.

3.2 Smith's argument for free trade

Summarizing Smith's argument for free trade, it runs roughly as follows. First, he emphasizes the *opportunity costs* in regulations in general (IV. ii. 3):[1]

> No regulation of commerce can increase the quantity of industry in any society beyond what its capital can maintain. It can only divert a part of it into a direction into which it might not otherwise have gone; and it is by no means certain that this artificial direction is likely to be more advantageous to the society than that into which it would have gone of its own accord.

This aspect of the analysis, that regulations, for example promoting the interests of the shoemakers, imply that resources, such as capital and labour, are drawn away from other sectors of the economy, is probably Smith's most important contribution in this respect. Until then, the 'successfulness' of such regulations was measured for example by the increasing production of shoes, or by the increase in profits for the shoemakers. Smith pointed out that there were costs to this increase, now known as opportunity costs, because the extra capital and labour used for shoe production might have been more advantageously employed in some other sector.

Second, he applies the opportunity cost principle to individuals in a society (IV. ii. 11):

> It is the maxim of every prudent master of a family, never to attempt to make at home what it will cost him more to make than to buy. The taylor does not attempt to make his own shoes, but buys them of the shoemaker. The shoemaker does not attempt to make his own cloaths, but employs a taylor. The farmer attempts to make neither the one nor the other, but employs those different artificers. All of them find it for their interest to employ their whole industry in a way in which they have some advantage over their neighbours, and to purchase with a part of its produce, or what is the same thing, with the price of a part of it, whatever else they have occasion for.

His general conclusion is therefore that each individual is specializing in the production of those goods and services in which s/he has some advantage.

Third, he applies the same opportunity cost principle to international commercial policy (IV. ii. 12):

> What is prudence in the conduct of every private family, can scarce be folly in that of a great kingdom. If a foreign country can supply us with a commodity cheaper than we ourselves can

make it, better buy it of them with some part of the produce of our own industry, employed in a way in which we have some advantage. The general industry of the country, being always in proportion to the capital which employs it, will not thereby be diminished, no more than that of the above-mentioned artificers; but only left to find out the way in which it can be employed with the greatest advantage.

This leads to the conclusion that international trade flows reflect the fact that goods and services can sometimes be imported at lower cost from abroad than they can be produced at home. This increases the consumption opportunities for a nation, and is therefore beneficial for the nation as a whole, just as the specialization of the artificers, the shoemaker and the tailor, is advantageous at the individual level.[2]

3.3 Ricardo's contribution

As indicated in section 3.1, at the beginning of the nineteenth century various people were working on the same problem at the same time, namely how a country that is less efficient than another country in all sectors of production can still trade with other countries. They were all close to reaching the same conclusion. As Irwin (1996: 89) put it: 'Mill and Torrens were on the verge of an even more important insight', by which he means the theory of comparative advantage. After a quote from Torrens involving Poland, Irwin (1996: 90) concludes: 'this formulation lacks only the comparison of the cost ratios in both countries . . . whereby the theory is stated in its entirety. David Ricardo . . . provided this finishing touch in his *On the Principles of Political Economy and Taxation* in 1817.' In that work David Ricardo discusses a famous example of England and Portugal exchanging wine and cloth to complete the theory of comparative advantage, for which he therefore receives almost full credit (Ricardo, 1817, ch. VII):[3]

> England may be so circumstanced that to produce the cloth may require the labour of 100 men for one year; and if she attempted to make the wine, it might require the labour of 120 men for the same time. England would therefore find it her interest to import wine, and to purchase it by the exportation of cloth.
>
>   To produce the wine in Portugal might require only the labour of 80 men for one year, and to produce the cloth in the same country might require the labour of 90 men for the same time. It would therefore be advantageous for her to export wine in exchange for cloth. This exchange might even take place notwithstanding that the commodity imported by Portugal could be produced there with less labour than in England. Though she could make the cloth with the labour of 90 men, she would import it from a country where it required the labour of 100 men to produce it, because it would be advantageous to her rather to employ her capital in the production of wine, for which she would obtain more cloth from England, than she could produce by diverting a portion of her capital from the cultivation of vines to the manufacture of cloth.
>
>   Thus England would give the produce of the labour of 100 men for the produce of the labour of 80. Such an exchange could not take place between the individuals of the same country. The labour of 100 Englishmen cannot be given for that of 80 Englishmen, but the produce of the labour of 100 Englishmen may be given for the produce of the labour of 80 Portuguese, 60 Russians, or 120 East Indians.

Ricardo therefore argues that it is beneficial for Portugal to specialize in the production of wine and exchange the wine for cloth from England, even though it would require less

Portuguese labour to produce this cloth than English labour. The details of this reasoning will be further explained in the next section. The essence of the argument was summarized by James Mill in 1821 as follows:[4]

> When a country can either import a commodity or produce it at home, it compares the cost of producing at home with the cost of procuring from abroad; if the latter cost is less than the first, it imports. The cost at which a country can import from abroad depends, not upon the cost at which the foreign country produces the commodity, but upon what the commodity costs which it sends in exchange, compared with the cost which it must be at to produce the commodity in question, if it did not import it.

3.4 Technology as a basis for comparative advantage

In general, to convince modern economists of the validity of an argument, one must be precise. This implies that one must specify the exact circumstances in a small (general equilibrium) economic model under which the conclusion is valid. Although some econom- ists, and presumably many non-economists, lament the modern approach, for example because it implies that much of the richness of Smith's analysis (the eloquence of his writing, the examples he uses) is lost in the process, the advantages are substantial. First, and most importantly, because cheating is not allowed. You are forced to think your analysis through in detail and get your story right. The importance of this aspect cannot be stressed too much, because it is easy (and tempting) to sweep some of the loose ends and the details of the analysis (intentionally or unintentionally) under the mat in a purely verbal approach. Second, knowing the exact circumstances under which a conclusion is valid frequently points the way to a more general approach under which the conclusion is still valid, or to circumstances under which we may arrive at different conclusions.

To specifically point out the tools used in international economic analysis we usually draw attention to them in text boxes (see Box 3.1).

To show a specific set of circumstances such that under free trade all goods will be produced where their relative or comparative costs in terms of labour are lowest, assume that there are

---

 Box 3.1   **Tool: productivity table**

A rather simple tool used in this chapter is the productivity table, summarizing the state of technology in both countries, see Table 3.1. Since the production functions use only one input (labour) and exhibit constant returns to scale, they can be summarized using a table specifying how much labour is required to produce one unit of either good in either country. The left-hand side of Table 3.1 gives these labour requirements in general terms, where a_F^{EU} is the number of units of labour required in the EU to produce one unit of food, a_C^K is the number of units of labour required in Kenya to produce one chemical, etc. These are measured in flows of labour services over a certain time period, for example the number of men required to work 40 hours per week during 8 weeks to produce one unit of output. The right-hand side of Table 3.1 gives an example using specific numbers for the unit labour requirements.

two countries, the European Union (EU) and Kenya, producing two goods, food and chemicals, using one factor of production, labour (international economists refer to this setting as a $2 \times 2 \times 1$ model). The production function in both countries and for both goods exhibits constant returns to scale, indicating that if we double the amount of inputs in an industry (that is, labour), the output level (that is, production) will also double. We assume that there are many firms in both countries, each behaving perfectly competitively; that is, each firm wants to maximize profits, taking the price levels in the output and input markets as given. Taken together, the assumptions of constant returns to scale and perfect competition imply that if a good is produced in equilibrium, the price level in the output market must be equal to the unit cost of production; see Box 3.2.

Table 3.1 gives the productivity table, summarizing the state of technology in both countries. The left-hand side of Table 3.1 gives the labour requirements in general terms, where a_F^{EU} is the number of units of labour required in the EU to produce one unit of food, a_C^K is the number of units of labour required in Kenya to produce one unit of chemicals, etc. The right-hand side of Table 3.1 gives an example using specific numbers for the unit labour requirements.

As is clear from the table, the EU is more efficient in the production of both goods; it requires two rather than four units of labour to produce one unit of food and eight rather than 24 units of labour to produce one unit of chemicals. Based on a theory of absolute cost advantages, Kenya would not be able to trade with the EU. However, the theory of comparative cost advantages argues that only relative, or comparative, costs are important for determining a nation's production advantages. In the example we see that Kenya is twice as inefficient as the EU in producing food (requiring four units of labour, rather than two) but three times as inefficient as the EU in producing chemicals (requiring 24 units of labour, rather than eight). It should therefore specialize in the production of food, and export this to the EU in exchange for chemicals.

Let's see how this works exactly. Suppose Kenya produces one unit of chemicals less. This frees up 24 (i.e. a_C^K) units of labour. These 24 units of labour can be used in Kenya to produce $24/4 = 6$ (i.e. a_C^K/a_F^K) units of food. The opportunity costs of producing chemicals in Kenya are six units of food. Kenya has now produced one unit of chemicals less and six units of food more. Suppose, however, that it wants to consume the same quantity of chemicals as before. It must then import one unit of chemicals from the EU. To produce one extra unit of chemicals, the EU needs eight (i.e. a_C^{EU}) units of labour. These labourers must come from the food sector, where production therefore drops by $8/2 = 4$ (i.e. a_C^{EU}/a_F^{EU}) units of food, reflecting the opportunity costs of producing chemicals in the EU. Now note that this hypothetical reallocation of labour between sectors in both countries results in Kenya producing one unit of chemicals less, but six units of food more, while the EU produces four units of food less, but one unit of chemicals more. The total world production of chemicals therefore remains unchanged, while food production rises by two units. These two extra units of food reflect the potential gains from specialization if both countries concentrate in the production of the good for which they have a comparative advantage, that is the good they produce *relatively* most efficiently, namely chemicals for the EU and food for Kenya. In principle, therefore, there is room for both countries to gain from trading with each other. It is time to see what determines the terms of trade and the division of gains from trade in the classical setting.

Box 3.2   Constant returns to scale and perfect competition

In classical and neoclassical economics we frequently combine the technological assumption of constant returns to scale with the behavioural assumption of perfect competition. This implies a simple, but important, relationship between the costs of production and the equilibrium price of a good on the market.

Under constant returns to scale, knowing the (minimum) costs of producing one unit of a good, say c, gives us enough information to determine the (minimum) costs of producing an arbitrary number of goods, even if there are many different inputs into the production process. More specifically, if the firm wants to produce x units of a good, its costs are cx.

Under perfect competition, the firm takes the unit costs of production c as a parameter; that is, it assumes that it has no control over the unit cost level, which will depend in particular on the level of technology (the production function) and the cost of the inputs (for example the wage rate). Similarly, the firm will treat the price it can fetch for a unit of output, say p, as a parameter beyond its control determined on the marketplace. If a firm sells x units of a product, its total revenue will be px. The firm's profits π, total revenue minus total costs, can therefore be written as:

(3.1) $$\pi = px - cx = (p - c)x$$

Since the firm's objective function is to maximize profits and, as argued above, it treats the price p and the unit cost of production c as parameters, we can logically distinguish between three different possibilities:

- $p < c$. If the price p of the good on the marketplace is smaller than the unit cost of production c, profits are obviously maximized by not producing any units of the good: $x = 0$.

- $p = c$. If the price p of the good on the marketplace is equal to the unit cost of production c, profits are zero independently of the level of production; the production level x is undetermined at the firm level since the firm always maximizes profits independently of the scale of production (which in equilibrium can then be determined by other economic forces, such as the equality of total supply and demand for the good).

- $p > c$. If the price p of the good on the marketplace is larger than the unit cost of production c, profits are maximized at the firm level by producing an infinite number of goods ($x = \infty$), which also leads to infinite profits. Although this possibility may appeal to the entrepreneurs among the readers, an infinite production level cannot be reached in any economy with a finite number of inputs, implying that this logical possibility cannot be an economic equilibrium and therefore has to be discarded.

Summarizing the above arguments, we can conclude that under perfect competition and constant returns to scale: $p \leq c$, where $x > 0 \Rightarrow p = c$ and $p < c \Rightarrow x = 0$.

Table 3.1 Productivity table; labour required to produce one unit of output

	General specification		Example	
	Food	Chemicals	Food	Chemicals
EU	a_F^{EU}	a_C^{EU}	2	8
Kenya	a_F^K	a_C^K	4	24

3.5 Production possibility frontier and autarky

If we want to determine the terms of trade if two Ricardian-type countries are trading goods with each other, we have to determine the equilibrium relationships in the economy. Although this is not too complicated in the Ricardian model, it is instructive to start the analysis from a situation of *autarky*, that is if the two countries are *not* trading any goods. This is done most easily using the production possibility frontier (see Box 3.3).

To determine the production possibility frontiers for the EU and Kenya for the example of Table 3.1, we have to specify the available factors of production in each country. It suffices to specify the number of workers available since labour is the only factor of production, say 200 labourers for the EU and 120 labourers for Kenya. This implies that the EU can produce a maximum of 200/2 = 100 units of food if it produces no chemicals at all, or 200/8 = 25 units of chemicals if it produces no food at all. Similarly, Kenya can produce a maximum of 120/4 = 30 units of food, or a maximum of 120/24 = 5 units of chemicals. This is summarized in Table 3.2.

This is actually all the information we need to calculate in full the production possibility frontiers for Kenya and the EU in a Ricardian model, since there are constant returns to scale and there is only one factor of production. If the EU currently produces 100 food and 0 chemicals (which is a point on the production possibility frontier) and wants to produce one unit of chemicals, it has to transfer eight labourers from the food sector to the chemicals sector. These eight labourers could have produced 8/2 = 4 units of food, so food production drops to 100−4 = 96, which gives us another point on the production possibility frontier. Similarly, if the EU wants to produce another unit of chemicals (two rather than one), food production drops again by four units (to 92). These changes are therefore *equiproportional*, such that the Ricardian production possibility frontiers are *straight lines*. All we really have to do, therefore, is calculate the maximum production points and connect these with a straight line. This is illustrated using the information of Table 3.2 in Figure 3.2.

We can now determine the equilibrium price of chemicals in terms of food (which we take as our measurement unit, known as the numéraire) for both countries, provided we are willing to make one simple and very weak assumption: *both countries want to consume at least some units of both goods*. Why does this assumption suffice to determine the price of chemicals in terms of food? Well, recall Box 3.2 and take the EU as an example:

- If the price of chemicals is more than four food, entrepreneurs want to produce only chemicals and no food. Since the economy wants to consume at least some food, this cannot be an equilibrium price.

Box 3.3   Tool: production possibility frontier (PPF)

Another tool introduced in this chapter is that of the production possibility frontier (or curve). It is defined as *all possible combinations of efficient production points given the available factors of production and the state of technology*. The production possibility frontier therefore gives all production combinations for which it is not possible to produce more of some good without reducing the production of some other good. In our two-good setting of food and chemicals it either depicts the maximum amount of food one can produce for a given amount of chemical output or, equivalently, the maximum amount of chemicals the economy can produce for a given level of food production. An example for the Ricardian model is depicted in Figure 3.2, where point C is a production point beyond the scope of the production possibility frontier for the Kenyan economy (for lack of labourers or technology), while it is below, and therefore not part of, the production possibility frontier for the EU economy. Note, in particular, that the EU economy could produce more food without producing less chemicals at point D, or more chemicals without producing less food at point E. More examples will follow in the next chapters. Note that:

- the production possibility frontier is a technical specification: it does not depend on any type of market competition;

- the production possibility frontier depends on the available factors of production: if more labourers are available, more goods can be produced;

- the production possibility frontier depends on the state of technology; if new production techniques become available, more goods may be produced using the same amount of factors of production.

Table 3.2 Total labour available and maximum production levels

	Total labour available	Maximum production	
		Food	Chemicals
EU	200	100	25
Kenya	120	30	5

- If the price of chemicals is less than four food, the entrepreneurs want to produce only food and no chemicals. Since the economy wants to consume at least some chemicals this also cannot be an equilibrium price.

- The price of chemicals is therefore four units of food in autarky in the EU.

Similar reasoning for Kenya leads to the conclusion that the price of chemicals is six units of food in autarky. This implies that the production possibility frontier coincides with the economy's budget line generated by the production levels in autarky for both countries.

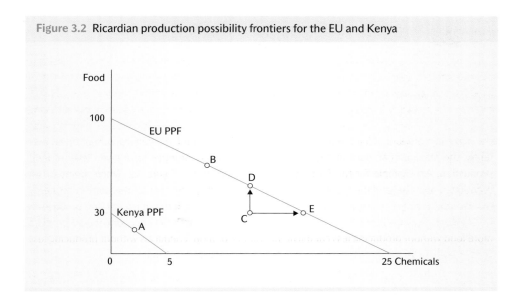

Figure 3.2 Ricardian production possibility frontiers for the EU and Kenya

The consumers in both countries therefore choose the optimal consumption point along the production possibility frontier in autarky, while the entrepreneurs adjust their production levels along the PPF to accommodate the wishes of the consumers, say point A for Kenya and point B for the EU in Figure 3.2.

Thus the autarky price ratio in a Ricardian model is exclusively determined by the technical coefficients of the productivity table; the price of chemicals in terms of food equals $a_C^{EU}/a_F^{EU} = 8/2 = 4$ in the EU and $a_C^K/a_F^K = 24/4 = 6$ in Kenya. Opportunities for trade between nations arise whenever the relative, or comparative, productivity ratios differ. They do not depend on absolute productivity levels.

3.6 Terms of trade and gains from trade

Determining the price of chemicals in terms of food in autarky in both countries does not allow us to determine exactly the terms of trade if the two countries decide to open up opportunities to trade with each other, as this requires more detailed information on the demand structure of the economies than the simple assumption made in Section 3.5. We can, however, determine the range within which the terms of trade can vary, and we can demonstrate that both countries may gain from trade. To start with the former, the autarky price of chemicals in terms of food is 4 in the EU and 6 in Kenya. The terms of trade can only vary within this range, endpoints included. If the price falls below 4, both countries want to produce only food, which cannot be an equilibrium, and if the price rises above 6, both countries want to produce only chemicals, which also cannot be an equilibrium.

As for the gains from trade, we can distinguish three separate cases: (i) if the terms of trade is strictly in between 4 and 6, both countries will gain; (ii) if the terms of trade is 4, only Kenya

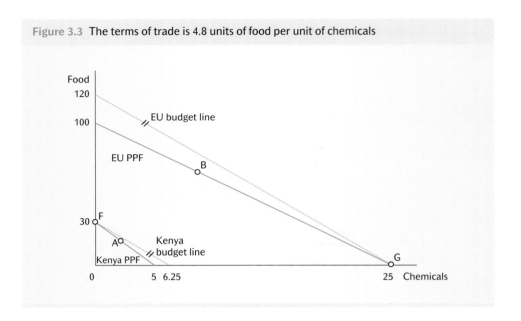

Figure 3.3 The terms of trade is 4.8 units of food per unit of chemicals

will gain while welfare in the EU will not change; and (iii) if the terms of trade is 6, only the EU will gain while welfare in Kenya will not change. Possibility (i) is illustrated in Figure 3.3, where we assume that the terms of trade is 4.8 units of food per unit of chemicals in the trading equilibrium. At that price Kenya will produce only food (30 units at point F) and will purchase abroad the required amount of chemicals at a price of 4.8 (to a maximum of 30/4.8 = 6.25 units). Similarly, at that price the EU will produce only chemicals (25 units at point G) and will purchase the amount of food it wants (to a maximum of 25 × 4.8 = 120 units).

How can we decide that if the terms of trade is 4.8 units of food per unit of chemicals, both countries will gain from trade? Quite simply because at those terms of trade the production decisions of the entrepreneurs allow the consumers to choose a consumption point *beyond* the old autarky optimum (point A for Kenya and point B for the EU) because the budget line has pivoted outwards (around point F for Kenya and around point G for the EU). By revealed preference the consumption point chosen on the new budget line must be preferred to the old consumption point at autarky. So *if* a price of 4.8 is a trading equilibrium, both countries will gain from trade (and similar reasoning holds for any other price strictly in between 4 and 6). The '*if*' above reflects the fact that a price of 4.8 can only be an equilibrium price if the consumers of the EU and Kenya combined at that price want to consume the total world production of both goods (30 units of food and 25 units of chemicals) given their income levels.[5]

Possibility (ii), that is, Kenya will gain and EU welfare will remain unchanged if the terms of trade is 4, is illustrated in Figure 3.4. The way the autarky production points are chosen in Figure 3.2 makes it unlikely that a terms of trade higher than 4 is an equilibrium trading price, simply because it implies that the EU will specialize completely in the production of chemicals and food production will drop drastically. A plausible outcome in this set-up in which the production levels of the EU are much larger than in Kenya is therefore that the

Figure 3.4 The terms of trade is 4 units of food per unit of chemicals

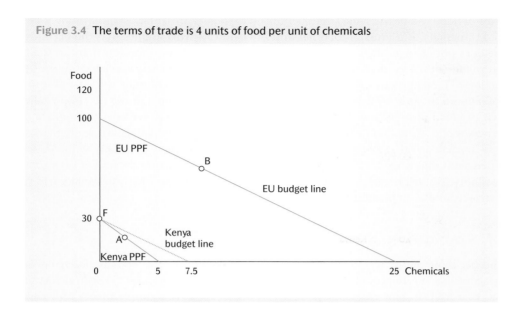

Box 3.4 **Comparative costs, absolute costs, and international wages**

This chapter argues that differences in comparative costs are crucial for determining international trade flows and gains from trade. Absolute cost advantages, however, are crucial for determining a country's per capita welfare level, and thereby explain differences in international wages. To be concrete, take the framework of section 3.4, more specifically the example in Table 3.1, as the point of departure. Assume that the EU specializes in the production of chemicals, that Kenya specializes in the production of food, that the exchange rate is 1, and take the wage rate in Kenya as the numéraire. In a perfectly competitive economy with constant returns to scale the price of a product is equal to the cost of production, see Box 3.2. Since food is produced in Kenya, the Kenyan wage is 1, and it takes four units of Kenyan labour to produce one unit of food, the price of food must be 4 ($= 4 \times 1$). Let w_{EU} be the EU wage. Since the EU produces chemicals and it requires eight units of EU labour to produce one unit of chemicals, the price of chemicals must be $8 \times w_{EU}$.

Now note that the EU can, in principle, also produce food. If it were to do this, and in view of the fact that it requires two units of EU labour to produce one unit of food, the price would be $2 \times w_{EU}$. Since we have assumed that only Kenya produces food, this price must be higher than the actual food price ($= 4$, see above). We conclude therefore that $2 \times w_{EU} > 4$, or $w_{EU} > 2$. Similarly, Kenya can, in principle, also produce chemicals. If it did, the price would be 24 ($= 24 \times 1$), since it requires 24 units of Kenyan labour to produce one unit of chemicals and the Kenyan wage is 1. Since Kenya does not actually produce chemicals, this price must be higher than the price currently prevailing ($= 8 \times w_{EU}$; see above). We conclude therefore that $8 \times w_{EU} < 24$, or $w_{EU} < 3$. Combining this information, we can conclude that the EU wage rate is at least twice as high as the Kenyan wage rate, and at most three times as high. (As with the terms of trade, to calculate the wage rate exactly requires information, on the demand structure to determine the trading equilibrium.) Evidently, this difference in the international wage rates depends on the difference in absolute costs in the two countries, that is on the difference in productivity levels. The EU per capita welfare level, based on this wage difference, therefore also depends on the difference in absolute cost levels, and is primarily based on its own productivity.

terms of trade will be the same after opening up to trade as the autarky equilibrium price in the EU, namely four units of food per unit of chemicals. This implies that the EU budget line does not change, such that point B is still the optimal consumption point in the EU and welfare in the EU does not change. Kenya, however, completely specializes in the production of food and can trade this at the most beneficial terms of trade with the EU (up to a maximum of 30/4 = 7.5 units of chemicals). The entrepreneurs in the EU simply adjust their production decisions along the production possibility frontier to accommodate the Kenyan wishes (who choose some point on their new budget line) and clear world markets. Note in particular that *Kenyan welfare rises* as a result of trading with the EU, while EU welfare remains unchanged, even though *Kenya is less efficient* in the production of both goods. Possibility (iii), if the terms of trade is 6, EU welfare will rise and Kenyan welfare will not change, is similar to possibility (ii) discussed above.

3.7 Application: Kenya and the EU

A proper econometric test of the various theories put forth in this book is clearly beyond our scope, but it is important to realize that it is ultimately the friction between theory and facts that leads to new economic insights. Now that we have a simple theory underlying international trade flows, a common-sense check on the validity of this theory implies simply gathering some statistical information, more readily available now than in the days of Smith and Ricardo, and confront the theory with these data.

First, we stick as closely as we can to the example given in the text. This requires us to gather information about the labour productivity in the EU and Kenya, for both food and chemicals. To this end we use the International Standard Industrial Classification (ISIC) revision II data on production and employment, reported for various industries. As an indicator of labour productivity we use total value added in a sector, divided by total employment in that sector; see Table 3.3 for 16 sectors. For those 16 sectors, the EU has considerably higher productivity than Kenya. Based on the theory of absolute advantage, the EU should only be exporting to Kenya, and not import anything at all. However, as is evident from the table, the EU does import goods from Kenya, which could be based on trade in accordance with comparative advantage.

As can be calculated from Table 3.3 (see also the questions in the study guide) the EU indeed has a comparative advantage in the production of chemicals, as assumed in Table 3.1, which is the EU's second largest exporting sector. Similarly, Kenya has a comparative advantage in the production of food, which is by far its largest export sector. Net trade flows for these two products are in accordance with the theory of comparative advantage. As illustrated in Table 3.3 by the shaded sectors, the prediction of net trade flows is in accordance with comparative advantage for only five of the 16 sectors. The theory of comparative advantage does better in terms of explanatory power than the theory of absolute advantage. Of the total trade flows (imports + exports) in Table 3.3, absolute advantage explains about 47.8 per cent of those flows, and comparative advantage explains about 68.4 per cent. If the differences in relative productivity[6] are very large, the net trade flow is generally in accordance with comparative cost advantage. This is illustrated in Figure 3.5 by calculating exports and imports for different categories as a percentage of total exports and imports, using the difference as an indication of net trade flows. The most

Table 3.3 Kenya and EU; value added, imports and exports, various sectors

ISIC	Industry	Trade (1,000 US$)		Value added/person	
		Export to EU	Import from EU	Kenya	EU4
322/3	Wearing apparel and leather products	15,027	5,350	663	193,017
311/2	Food products	783,658	120,997	233	45,341
385	Professional and scientific equipment	1,361	42,577	5,306	33,092
321	Textiles	11,805	64,422	83	17,347
382/3	Machinery	8,977	310,198	981	116,668
313	Beverages	118	5,278	559	107,718
324	Footwear	273	2,363	262	19,477
355	Rubber products	378	8,368	717	46,370
356	Plastic products	30	29,027	229	30,673
341/2	Paper and printing products	34	29,301	343	47,402
361/2/9	Non-metallic mineral products	11,088	14,096	423	97,593
384	Transport equipment	4,067	94,096	124	55,413
381	Fabricated metal products	2,105	22,851	227	18,368
332	Furniture	268	3,336	49	15,344
351/2	Chemicals	11,024	173,129	452	154,537
331	Wood products	2,146	908	91	31,472
Average value added per person				231	52,534

Figure 3.5 Kenya–EU exports and productivity, various sectors

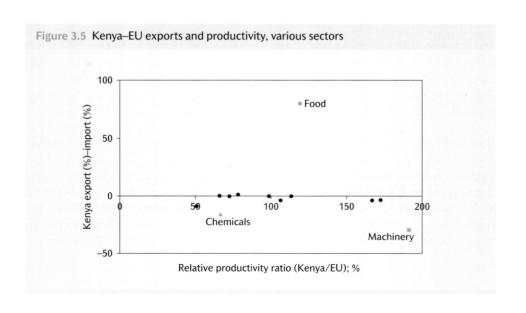

noteworthy exception is the 'machinery' sector. In Part II.B of this book we will argue that this is related to aggregation problems; the term 'machines' refers to many differentiated goods. There are several important reservations to be made with respect to the calculations underlying Table 3.3 to which we will return later in the book.

3.8 More countries and world PPF

The exposition in sections 3.5 and 3.6 uses two final goods and two countries. Both restrictions can be relaxed quite easily, as long as we continue to restrict ourselves to the analysis of only one production factor. Dornbusch, Fischer, and Samuelson (1977), for example, analyse a setting with many goods ranked from high to low in terms of comparative advantage, say for the EU. If we use the index i to identify a good and there are N goods, $i = 1, \ldots , N$, then the EU will have the highest comparative advantage for good 1, the second highest for good 2, etc. Dornbusch et al. show that there is a critical good, say n, such that the EU will produce the goods $1, \ldots , n$ and the other country produces the goods $n + 1, \ldots , N$.[7] Each country therefore produces the range of goods for which its comparative advantage is highest.

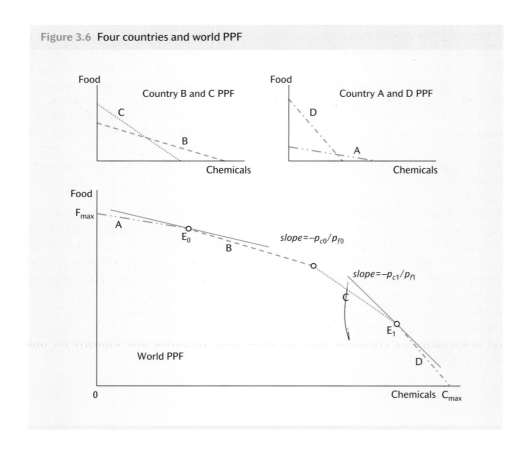

Figure 3.6 Four countries and world PPF

Box 3.5   Comparative advantage and the organization of firms

It should be noted that the principles underlying an efficient production process in the international economy also hold at the firm level. A company employing 2,000 people should steer its workers to those labour activities they perform relatively most efficiently. The wage rate paid to an individual worker depends on absolute costs; see Box 3.4. The vivid example sometimes used here is that of a hospital employing a brain surgeon who also happens to be the world's fastest typist. This brain surgeon should none the less leave the typing work to her secretary, as she has a comparative advantage performing surgery (assuming that the typist cannot perform this activity). To assist her in making this choice, the wage she can earn as a brain surgeon is higher than the wage she can earn as a typist.

Figure 3.6 illustrates the other case, in which there are two goods and more than two countries. This also allows us to discuss another concept, that of the world production possibility frontier. Suppose, to be concrete, that there are four countries, labelled A, B, C, and D, each able to produce two goods, food and chemicals. The top panel illustrates the production possibility frontiers of the four individual countries, where the slope of the PPF depends on the comparative advantage of the countries for producing food and chemicals. The bottom panel depicts the world production possibility frontier; that is, all combinations of efficient production points for the world as a whole (but without factor mobility). The maximum world production level of food, F_{max} say, obtains if all four countries only produce food. Since country A has the flattest slope of its production possibility frontier, indicating that its opportunity costs for producing food are highest, it will be the first country to stop producing food; that is, close to F_{max} the slope of the world PPF is equal to the slope of country A's PPF. Once point E_0 is reached, country A will have completely specialized in the production of chemicals. Since country B has the second flattest slope of its PPF, country B will be the second country to start producing chemicals. This process continues until all countries specialize in the production of chemicals at C_{max}. The various dashed lines connecting F_{max} and C_{max} depict the world PPF.

Once we have derived the world PPF it is easy to determine the world production point in a free trading equilibrium. Suppose, for example, that the relative price of chemicals is equal to p_{c0}/p_{f0}. Then the maximum value of world production is obtained at point E_0; that is, country A will produce chemicals and the other three countries will produce food. Country A will therefore export chemicals in exchange for food with the other three countries. Next, suppose that the relative price of chemicals is equal to p_{c1}/p_{f1}. Then the maximum value of world production is obtained at point E_1; that is, country D will produce food and the other three countries will produce chemicals. Country D will therefore export food in exchange for chemicals with the other three countries, and similarly for other relative prices.

3.9 Measuring trade advantages: the Balassa index[8]

We have seen that it is beneficial for a country to specialize in the production of those goods that it can produce relatively more efficiently than another country, and to export these goods in exchange of imports of goods it can produce less efficiently. As such it provides a small and simple explanation for international trade flows. Subsequently, section 3.7 provided some empirical information on the trade flows between the EU and Kenya. We can, however, also turn the question around, by first empirically investigating which countries are exporting which goods and then wondering which theory, or theories, may explain this export pattern. Since the idea is that investigating a country's actual exports 'reveals' the country's strong sectors, the first step in this procedure is known as establishing a country's 'revealed comparative advantage'.[9] The index most frequently used in this respect was pioneered by Liesner (1958), but refined and popularized by Bela Balassa (1965, 1989), and is therefore known as the *Balassa index*.

Many countries are, for example, producing and exporting cars. To establish whether a country, say Japan, holds a particularly strong position in the car industry, Balassa argued that one should compare the share of car exports in Japan's total exports with the share of car exports in a group of reference country's total exports. The Balassa index is therefore essentially a normalized export share. More specifically, if BI_j^A is country A's Balassa index for industry j, this is equal to:

$$(3.2) \qquad BI_j^A = \frac{\text{share of industry } j \text{ in country A exports}}{\text{share of industry } j \text{ in reference country exports}}$$

If $BI_j^A > 1$, country A is said to have a revealed comparative advantage in industry j, since this industry is more important for country A's exports than for the exports of the reference countries.

Before actually calculating the Balassa index, we have to decide which exports to which countries to include and which countries to use as 'reference' countries. In this section we restrict attention to the exports of 28 *manufacturing* sectors for the member countries of the Organization for Economic Cooperation and Development (OECD), which is also the group

Table 3.4 **Manufacturing sectors in the Ottens database**

Food	Wood products	Petrol and coal products	Non-ferrous metals
Beverages	Furniture	Rubber products	Metal products
Tobacco	Paper	Plastic products	Non-electrical machinery
Textiles	Printing and publishing	Pottery and china	El. machinery
Wearing apparel	Industrial chemicals	Glass and products	Transport equipment
Leather and products	Other chemicals	Non-metal products	Professional goods
Footwear	Petroleum refineries	Iron and steel	Other manufacturing

Table 3.5 Sectors with highest Balassa index, 1996

Australia		Germany		Norway	
Non-ferrous metals	5.60	Industrial chemicals	1.24	Non-ferrous metals	6.48
Food	3.91	Metal products	1.23	Petroleum refineries	6.14
Austria		*Greece*		*Portugal*	
Wood products	2.78	Wearing apparel	8.07	Footwear	13.32
Paper and products	1.94	Non-metal products	5.68	Pottery, china, etc.	7.83
Belgium		*Iceland*		*Spain*	
Other maunfacturing	4.56	Food	13.44	Footwear	3.60
Glass and products	2.04	Non-ferrous metals	5.25	Non-metal products	3.51
Canada		*Italy*		*Sweden*	
Wood products	6.46	Footwear	5.62	Paper and products	3.79
Paper and products	3.38	Leather and products	4.87	Wood products	3.49
Denmark		*Japan*		*United Kingdom*	
Furniture and fixtures	4.97	Electrical machinery	1.77	Beverages	2.01
Food	4.12	Professional goods	1.69	Printing and publishing	1.94
Finland		*The Netherlands*		*United States*	
Paper and products	7.83	Tobacco	4.31	Tobacco	2.73
Wood products	5.15	Petroleum refineries	3.66	Professional goods	1.40
France		*New Zealand*			
Beverages	3.42	Food	9.20		
Glass and products	1.68	Leather and products	4.20		

Source: Ottens (2000). The numbers indicate the Balassa index in 1996.

of reference countries; see Tables 3.4 and 3.5. This has the advantage that data are available for a fairly long time period (1970–96).

Figure 3.7 illustrates the evolution of the Balassa index in the period 1970–96 for the two sectors with the highest Balassa index for the USA, Japan, Finland, and Italy. In all cases the Balassa index is above 1, as it should be for the strong export sectors. Apparently, the USA has a revealed comparative trade advantage for tobacco and professional goods and Japan for electrical machinery and professional goods. Note the fairly small value of the highest Balassa index for both countries (about 2–3). This can be attributed to the fact that both countries have a large industrial base, exporting a wide variety of goods, which makes it more difficult to achieve high values for the Balassa index. This contrasts with the much larger highest values for countries with a smaller industrial base, such as Italy (about 6–8) and Finland (about 8–11). Italy's highest-ranking sectors are footwear (Italian shoes) and leather and products (e.g. handbags

Figure 3.7 Highest Balassa index, selected countries: (a) USA, (b) Japan, (c) Finland, (d) Italy

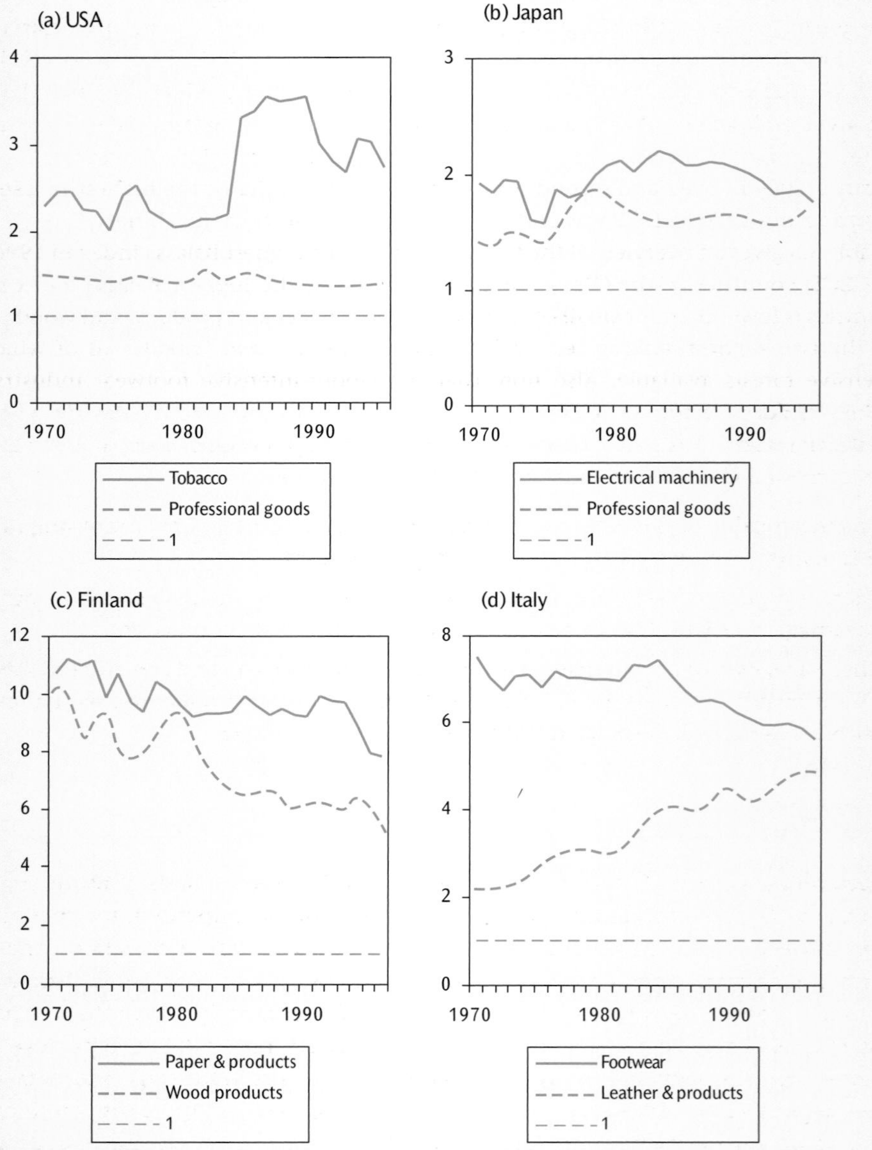
(a) USA
4
3
2
1
0
1970
1980
1990
Tobacco
Professional goods
1
(b) Japan
3
2
1
0
1970
1980
1990
Electrical machinery
Professional goods
1
(c) Finland
12
10
8
6
4
2
0
1970
1980
1990
Paper & products
Wood products
1
(d) Italy
8
6
4
2
0
1970
1980
1990
Footwear
Leather & products
1

for the Italian fashion industry). Finland's highest-ranking sectors are paper and products and wood products. This must have something to do with the easy availability of factor inputs, that is wood from the large Finnish forests, as will be discussed in Chapters 4–7.

In general, sectors with a high comparative advantage tend to sustain this advantage for a fairly long time. Tobacco, for example, is always the sector with the highest Balassa index in the USA. The same holds for footwear in Italy and paper and products in Finland. Changes over extended periods of time are, however, also possible. The Balassa index for leather and products in Italy has clearly increased in the period of investigation. This sector was ranked fourth in Italy in 1981 and second from 1984 onwards. Similarly, the highest-ranking sector in Japan from 1970 to 1979 was pottery and china, not electrical machinery.

Table 3.5 gives an overview of the two sectors with the highest Balassa index in 1996 for the 20 OECD countries in the Ottens database. In general, the highest Balassa index for large countries is lower than for small countries. Note that paper and products and wood products are the two highest-ranking sectors for Finland, Sweden, *and* Canada, all of which have extensive forests available. Also note that the labour-intensive footwear industry is the highest-ranking sector for Spain, Portugal, and Italy. Ottens investigates the changes in the distribution of the Balassa index and the relationships between comparative advantage, employment and labour productivity. His main conclusions are:

- The mean value of the Balassa index is slowly increasing over time. According to Ottens, this points to an increase in international specialization.
- There is a positive relationship between employment and industries with a comparative advantage. Specialization therefore tends to be in the 'correct' industries.
- There is no clear-cut relationship between labour productivity and comparative advantage. This probably indicates the importance of other factors of production, such as capital or natural resources, in also determining comparative advantage.

3.10 Conclusions

To determine a country's strong (export) sectors on the classical basis of technology differences, as well as its terms of trade, only comparative costs are important. International trade leads to welfare gains irrespective of absolute costs. Using empirical data on the EU and Kenya, we concluded that the theory of comparative costs is somewhat better than the theory of absolute costs in determining international trade flows. Note, however, that the per capita welfare level largely depends on absolute cost differences, rather than comparative cost differences. This may explain the large international differences in the wage rate, namely as the result of productivity differences. The analysis can be generalized quite easily to incorporate more goods and more countries. The incorporation of more than one factor of production, however, is more complicated. This issue is addressed in Chapters 4–7 of the book.

QUESTIONS

Question 3.1

The table below gives the units of labor needed to produce one ship, one bicycle and one airplane in Russia and the European Union.

Units of labour needed for the production of one unit			
	Ship	Bicycle	Airplane
Russia	200	50	500
EU	100	30	200

3.1A Which country has an absolute advantage in the production of ships, bicycles and airplanes?

3.1B What is the EU's comparative advantage if we look only at ships and bicycles?

3.1C What is the EU's comparative advantage if we look only at bicycles and airplanes?

3.1D Can you infer from your calculations in 3.1B and 3.1C which product the EU will export for sure and which product it will surely not export?

Question 3.2

Some politicians and trade activists argue that developing countries should not participate in the global economy as their industries cannot compete with their Western counterparts. According to these observers, trade does not benefit the developing countries and will only result in the exploitation of the labour force. Let's analyse this argument in a simple Ricardian framework. Suppose there are only two countries, Indonesia and the USA, producing only two goods, clothes and machines. Labour is the only factor of production. The table below shows how many man-hours are needed in Indonesia and the USA to make one unit of cloth or one machine. Assume that 2,000 man-hours are available in the USA and 36,000 in Indonesia.

3.2A Explain which country has a comparative advantage in which product.

3.2B What is the autarky price of machines in Indonesia and the USA?

3.2C Indicate exactly what range of prices for machines should be offered on international markets for both countries to profit from international trade. What will Indonesia and the USA import and export?

3.2D Explain in a consistent graph with production possibility frontiers why both countries gain from trade when prices on the international markets are within the range you indicated for 3.2C.

Number of man-hours needed to produce one unit		
	Indonesia	USA
Cloth	50	3
Machine	100	5

Some trade activists who think that developing countries are exploited on the international market may not be convinced by your arguments above. They will claim that even in the Ricardian framework trade is based on unequal wages between developed and developing countries.

3.2E Explain whether wages are unequal in the example of Indonesia and the USA. If both countries trade with each other, what is the maximum and minimum difference between the wage rate in Indonesia and the USA?

3.2F Discuss whether abolishing trade is an effective instrument to raise Indonesian wages. Use the observations you made in your analysis above.

Question 3.3

Bernhofen and Brown (2004)[10] use Japan's nineteenth-century period of trade liberalization as a 'natural historical experiment' to test the theory of comparative advantage. After two centuries of almost complete autarky, Japan was forced by Western powers in 1859 to move to a free trade regime. The figure below shows on the vertical axis how goods prices changed within Japan between 1851 and 1853 (state of autarky) and 1869 (free trade regime). On the horizontal axis it shows net exports in 1869. Explain whether the figure below supports the theory of comparative advantage.

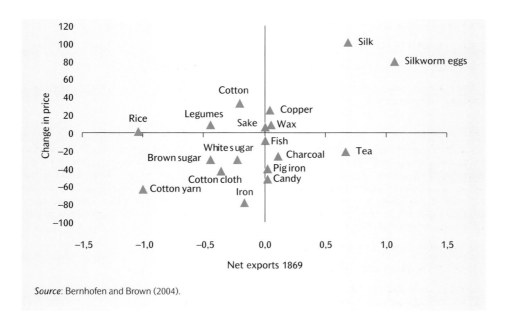

Source: Bernhofen and Brown (2004).

 See the Online Resource Centre for a Study Guide containing more questions
www.oxfordtextbooks.co.uk/orc/vanmarrewijk/

NOTES

1 The reference numbers for Adam Smith follow the Glasgow convention of book, section, paragraph.

2 An important forerunner of Adam Smith in terms of opportunity costs was Henry Martyn; see also Chapter 9, who in (1701) argued (Irwin 1996: 57): 'Things may be imported from India by fewer hands than as good would be made in England, so that to permit the consumption of Indian manufactures is to permit the loss of few men's labour . . . a law to restrain us to use only English manufactures, is to oblige us to make them first, is to oblige us to provide for our consumption by the labour of many when that of few might be sufficient'.

3 See Allen (1965: 63–4). Some economists question the contribution of Ricardo; see e.g. Chipman (1965: 480), or even suggest that James Mill rather than David Ricardo came up with the example (Thweatt, 1976). Since his contemporary James Mill gives full credit to David Ricardo on at least two occasions (Irwin, 1996: 91), I think it is fair to conclude that Ricardo does deserve most credit.

4 Irwin (1996: 91).

5 Equivalently, the 'trade triangles' have to coincide. This is discussed further in the sequel.

6 Let $VA^{k,i}$ be value added per worker in sector i in Kenya; similarly for the EU with superscript EU, and let a bar denote the country-wide average value added per worker, then the relative productivity ratio (Kenya / EU) used in Figure 3.5 is calculated as: $(VA_i^k/VA^k)/(\overline{VA_i^{EU}}/\overline{VA^{EU}})$.

7 In some cases, the other country may also produce good n.

8 This section is based on Ottens (2000) and Hinloopen and van Marrewijk (2001).

9 The 'comparative' part of this term also reflects the developments in the next few chapters.

10 D. M. Bernhofen and J. C. Brown, 'A direct test of the theory of comparative advantage: The case of Japan', *Journal of Political Economy,* vol. 112 no. 1, 2004.

PRODUCTION STRUCTURE

4

Objectives/key terms

- Production functions
- Cost minimization
- Constant returns to scale
- Isoquants
- Factor intensity
- Unit costs

The neoclassical driving forces behind international trade flows are differences in factor endowments between nations. The conclusions depend to a large extent on the production structure of the economy, based on identical technology, constant returns to scale, and perfect competition. This chapter briefly reviews the microeconomic foundations and main implications of this production structure.

4.1 Introduction

The classical theory of absolute and comparative cost advantages discussed in Chapter 3 focuses attention on technological differences between nations to explain international trade flows. At this point we may note at least three problems associated with the theory of comparative advantage.

First, the largest technological differences between nations presumably arise when these nations are very different in their state of economic development. Even if we acknowledge that only the relative differences are influential in determining comparative advantage, we would still expect substantial trade flows between nations with large differences in technology. However, as we saw in Chapter 1, there are only very small trade flows between developed and less developed nations.[1]

Second, the empirical discussion in Chapter 3 on the explanatory power of the theory of comparative advantage for the trade flows between the EU and Kenya was only moderately supportive of this theory. Some of the difficulties were discussed at the end of Chapter 3. The feeling does arise, however, that other economic forces may be useful for explaining some of the trade flows not explained by the theory of comparative advantage.

Third, the focus on only one factor of production in the theory of comparative advantage seems too restrictive and precludes the analysis of many interesting issues. In getting some intuitive feel for the empirical validity of the theory of comparative advantage, we had to mould the data in a straitjacket, in particular, because we attributed *all* value added in a final goods sector to only one factor of production: labour. Clearly, some sectors, such as oil refineries, are much more capital intensive than other sectors, such as hairdressers. A larger part of the value added in the oil refinery is used to remunerate the capital investments involved than for the hairdresser. Similarly, some sectors, such as electronics firms, use more highly educated labourers than other sectors, such as domestic services. Differences in remuneration therefore may reflect differences in years of education and skills. This is in line with the finding in Section 3.9 that there is no clear-cut relationship between revealed comparative advantage as measured by the Balassa index and labour productivity. To analyse these and other distributional economic aspects of production and trade flows requires the distinction of at least two different factors of production.

These observations bring us to the core of international trade theory: factor abundance theory, or the neoclassical theory of international trade, to be discussed in this and the next three chapters.

4.2 Neoclassical economics

A proper understanding of the forces behind international trade and capital flows cannot be obtained without thoroughly studying the foundations of neoclassical economics. For many practical applications and problems an understanding of the small general equilibrium model known as the neoclassical model provides valuable economic intuition for the most important forces playing a role in production and consumption decisions. The foundations for the neoclassical model were laid by Eli Hecksher and his pupil Bertil Ohlin, two Swedish economists. Undoubtedly the most influential publication in this respect is Bertil Ohlin's

Famous economists   **Paul Samuelson**

Born in Gary, Indiana, he has contributed from his MIT offices to virtually all parts of economic analysis. By applying and developing the neoclassical apparatus of optimization to the problems of consumers and producers, his influence on the mindset of today's economist cannot be overestimated. For international economics in particular he is important for the development of factor abundance theory.

Fig. 4.1
Paul Samuelson
(1915–)

(1933) *Interregional and International Trade*. After a brief discussion of some simplifications and the definition of a region, Ohlin (1933, ch. I) remarks:[2]

> We have evidently pushed the analysis one step further, to an inquiry under what circumstances relative commodity prices will actually be different in two isolated regions. The starting point for such an investigation is the fact that all prices, of goods as well as of industrial agents, are ultimately, in each region, at any given moment, determined by the demand for goods and the possibilities of producing them. Behind the former lie two circumstances to be considered as known data in the problem of pricing: (1) the wants and desires of consumers, and (2) the conditions of ownership of the factors of production, which affect individual incomes and thus demand. The supply of goods, on the other hand, depends ultimately on (3) the supply of productive factors, and (4) the physical conditions of production.

Ohlin is thus well aware that the circumstances under which relative commodity prices in two isolated regions differ depend on an interplay between demand and supply conditions, each in turn depending on various other factors. Before we can derive any definite conclusions, therefore, we have to specify these demand and supply conditions. We will elaborate on various details in the next three chapters. In this chapter, we provide some of the production structure preliminaries of neoclassical economics. First, however, we give an overview of the most important results of the neoclassical model.

Each serious student of international economics must be familiar with the four main results of neoclassical trade theory, namely:

- The *factor price equalization* proposition (Samuelson, 1948, 1949); see Chapter 5. This result argues that international free trade of final goods between two nations leads to an equalization of the rewards of the factors of production in the two nations.

- The *Stolper–Samuelson* proposition (Stolper and Samuelson, 1941); see Chapter 5. This result argues that an increase in the price of a final good increases the reward to the factor of production used intensively in the production of that good.

- The *Rybczynski* proposition (Rybczynski, 1955); see Chapter 6. This result argues that an increase in the supply in a factor of production results in an increase in the output of the final good that uses this factor of production relatively intensively.

- *The Heckscher–Ohlin* proposition (Ohlin, 1933); see Chapter 7. This result argues that a country will export the good which intensively uses the relatively abundant factor of production.

The precise formulation of these results and the conditions under which they can be derived will be the topic of Part II.A of this book. It is important to keep the final conclusion (the Heckscher–Ohlin proposition) to be derived in Chapter 7 clearly in mind: the neoclassical driving forces behind international trade flows are based on differences in factor endowments between nations; that is, a country will export those goods and services that use intensively its abundant factors of production. In a sense the other results, and the discussions in Chapters 4–6, only pave the way for the Heckscher–Ohlin proposition. Before we continue, we must point out that most technical details and the precise conditions under which the four main results of neoclassical trade theory can be derived were analysed and specified by Paul Samuelson. Instead of the term 'neoclassical trade theory' or 'factor abundance theory' the term 'HOS theory' (short for Heckscher–Ohlin–Samuelson) is also often used.

4.3 General structure of the neoclassical model

The general structure of the neoclassical model, to be used throughout Part II.A can be summarized as follows.

- There are two countries, Austria (index A) and Bolivia (index B), two final goods, manufactures (index M) and food (index F), and two factors of production, capital (index K) and labour (index L). This is, therefore, a $2 \times 2 \times 2$ model. When appropriate, we will point out if the results to be derived below can be generalized to a setting with more goods, more countries, and more production factors.
- Production in both sectors is characterized by constant returns to scale. The two final goods sectors have different production functions.
- The state of technology is the same in the two countries, such that the production functions for each sector are identical in the two countries. Any trade flows arising in the model therefore do not result from Ricardian-type differences in technology.
- The input factors capital and labour are mobile between the different sectors within a country, but are not mobile between countries.
- All markets are characterized by perfect competition. There are no transport costs for the trade of final goods between nations, nor any other impediments to trade.
- The demand structure in the two countries is the same (identical homothetic preferences). This assumption is only important for Chapter 7.
- Finally, the available amounts of factors of production, capital K and labour L, may differ between the two nations. These differences in factor abundance will give rise to international trade flows.

By imposing strong restrictions on the production structure (constant returns to scale) and the market structure (perfect competition) of the economy, the neoclassical model in general does not require strong restrictions on the functional form of the production functions to derive its four basic propositions. This is in contrast with the theories of absolute and comparative advantage discussed in Chapter 3, and with the new trade theories and geographical economic theories to be discussed in later chapters, all of which use simple specific functional forms to get the main points across as clearly as possible. As explained in the preface, for expository balance and clarity we will use only the simplest (Cobb–Douglas) production function to derive the main results of neoclassical economics. The remainder of this chapter will briefly review the main implications of the production structure of the neoclassical model.

4.4 Production functions

As indicated in Section 4.3, there are two final goods, manufactures and food, with Cobb–Douglas production functions, different for the two sectors but identical in the two countries for each sector. We let M denote the production level of manufactures, K_m the amount of capital used in the manufacturing sector, and L_m the amount of labour used in the manufacturing sector, and similarly for food. Production is given by:

(4.1)
$$M = \underbrace{K_m^{\alpha_m}}_{\substack{captial \\ input}} \underbrace{L_m^{1-\alpha_m}}_{\substack{labour \\ input}}; \quad F = \underbrace{K_f^{\alpha_f}}_{\substack{captial \\ input}} \underbrace{L_f^{1-\alpha_f}}_{\substack{labour \\ input}}; \quad 0 < \alpha_m, \alpha_f < 1$$

For reasons to be explained further below, the parameter α_m (α_f) is a measure of the capital intensity of the production process for manufactures (respectively food). Clearly, since we assumed these two parameters to be strictly in between 0 and 1, both capital and labour are indispensable inputs for both final goods sectors; at least some of both inputs is required to produce any output.

An important implication of the neoclassical production function specified in equation (4.1) is the ability to substitute one input for another, that is to produce the same level of output with different combinations of inputs. For example, if $\alpha_m = 0.5$, the entrepreneur is able to produce 1 unit of manufactures using 1 unit of capital and 1 unit of labour, or using 2 units of capital and 0.5 units of labour, or using 0.5 units of capital and 2 units of labour, etc. In principle, an infinite number of possible combinations is available to produce the same level of output. All possible efficient combinations of capital and labour able to produce a certain level of output is called an *isoquant* (see Box 4.1). This is illustrated for the isoquant $M = 1$ for three possible values of α_m in Figure 4.3.

 Box 4.1   **Tool: isoquants**

If there are two or more inputs needed and/or available to produce a final good, we call the set of all *efficient* input combinations an *isoquant;* see Figure 4.2.

The isoquant can be derived from the production function. Taking equation (4.1) as an example, the same level of output can be produced using many different combinations of capital and labour. Figure 4.2 illustrates this for the isoquant $M = 1$, where the shaded area shows all input combinations producing at least one unit of manufactures. The input combination at point A, therefore, enables the entrepreneur to produce one unit of manufactures. However, to produce one unit of manufactures the entrepreneur could use either less labour at point B than at point A, or less capital at point C than at point A, such that point A is not an efficient input combination to produce one unit of manufactures. As such, point A is not part of the $M = 1$ isoquant, in contrast to points B and C, which both are part of the $M = 1$ isoquant.   »

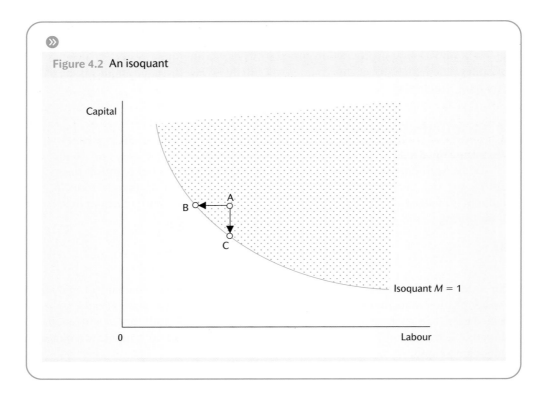

Figure 4.2 An isoquant

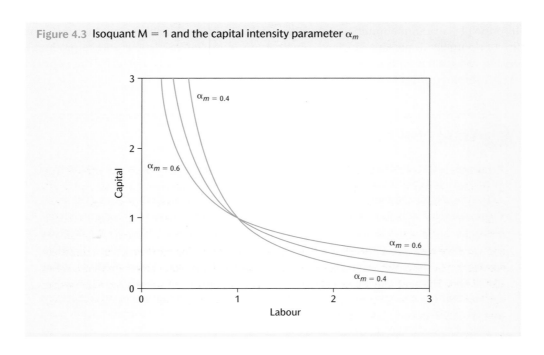

Figure 4.3 Isoquant M = 1 and the capital intensity parameter α_m

Note that, if very little of an input is used, it becomes harder to substitute this input for another input. This is illustrated in Table 4.1 for 10 combinations of capital and labour producing one unit of manufactures if $\alpha_m = 0.4$. Starting with 1 unit of capital and labour, the input of labour is gradually reduced by steps of 0.1 unit. To continue producing 1 unit of manufactures this implies that the required extra input of capital increases rapidly, from 0.171 to 20.442. The extent to which additional capital is needed to substitute for labour depends, of course, on the value of the parameter α_m. This is also illustrated in Figure 4.3, which shows that for higher levels of the capital intensity parameter α_m the isoquant is tilted towards the capital axis.

Table 4.1 Substitution possibilities ($\alpha_m = 0.4$)

L_m	K_m	Extra capital
1.0	1.000	—
0.9	1.171	0.171
0.8	1.398	0.226
0.7	1.707	0.310
0.6	2.152	0.444
0.5	2.828	0.677
0.4	3.953	1.124
0.3	6.086	2.133
0.2	11.180	5.095
0.1	31.623	20.442

 Box 4.2 Capital per worker

The neoclassical model discussed in this part of the book argues that countries will export the final goods making intensive use of the relatively abundant factor of production. Since we distinguish between two main types of factors of production, capital and labour, the empirical question arises as to what extent countries differ in their capital and labour endowments. This question is not so easy to answer because it requires us to aggregate many different varieties of capital and labour into one aggregate measure; see also Box 4.4 for a different approach. The construction of a consistent data set that can be compared for a large number of countries is therefore complicated and involves a lot of work. The most widely used data set was initiated by Lawrence Summers and Alan Heston; see their 1991 paper for a description and the National Bureau of Economic Research (NBER) website (http://www.nber.org) for updates.   »

As Table 4.2 shows, with a total value of $4,271 bn (1990, in 1985 constant $), the USA is estimated to have the largest capital stock. Japan has the second largest capital stock and West Germany the third largest. Since the West German workforce of 31 million people is considerably smaller than the American workforce of 123 million, the capital stock per worker is higher in West Germany ($50,116) than in the USA ($34,705), despite the higher total American capital stock. The distribution of the capital stock per worker is illustrated in Figure 4.4 for the 60 countries for which data are available. Swiss workers had the highest capital stock per worker available ($73,459). Workers from Sierra Leone had the lowest capital stock per worker ($223).

Table 4.2 Total capital stock ranking

	Capital stock ($ bn)	Workers (m)	Capital stock per worker ($)
1 USA	4,271	123	34,705
2 Japan	2,852	78	36,480
3 W. Germany	1,539	31	50,116
4 France	925	26	35,600
5 Italy	740	23	31,640
6 India	645	331	1,946
7 UK	601	28	21,179
8 Canada	566	13	42,745
9 Spain	386	14	27,300
10 Mexico	361	28	12,900
11 South Korea	321	18	17,995
12 Australia	298	8	37,854
13 Iran	258	17	15,548
14 Switzerland	248	3	73,459
15 Poland	232	20	11,890
16 Taiwan	229	9	25,722
17 The Netherlands	202	6	32,380
18 Turkey	185	24	7,589
19 Sweden	175	4	39,409
20 Belgium	152	4	36,646

Source: NBER website, data for 1990 in constant 1985 $.

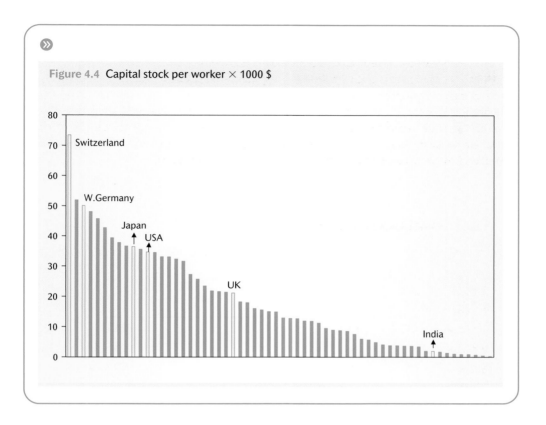

Figure 4.4 Capital stock per worker × 1000 $

4.5 Cost minimization

The objective function for the entrepreneurs inhabiting our economic models is quite simply profit maximization. Although some objections can be raised against this objective function, one of the strongest arguments in its favour is the fact that entrepreneurs not striving towards profit maximization will be driven out of business by those who do. This certainly holds in perfectly competitive economies characterized by constant returns to scale, as analysed here, where the best a firm can do is to ensure that it does not make a loss (a nicer term is 'excess profits are zero'). The entrepreneur can actually break down its production decision into two steps. First, for any arbitrary level of production determine how this output level is achieved at minimum cost. Second, taking the outcome of the first step into consideration, determine the optimum output level. This second step is discussed in Box 3.2. It is therefore time to analyse in somewhat more detail the first step, that of cost minimization. In this section we restrict attention to analysing the problem of producing one unit of output at minimum cost. Section 4.7 below will discuss this problem for arbitrary levels of output.

The problem facing an entrepreneur in the manufacturing sector trying to minimize the costs for producing one unit of output is illustrated in Figure 4.5. Recall that the production function is given in equation (4.1), which implies that the entrepreneur can choose between

Figure 4.5 Unit cost minimization

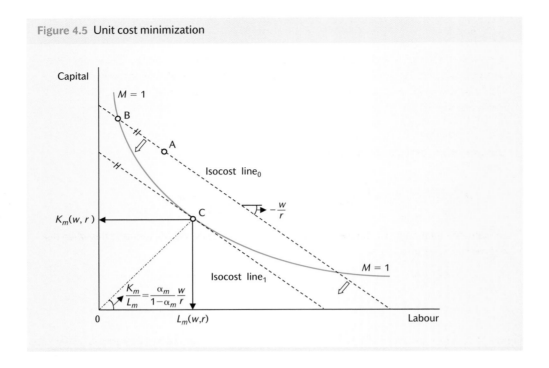

two different inputs: capital K_m and labour L_m. As discussed in section 4.4, many different combinations of capital and labour are available to produce one unit of manufactures. This is illustrated by the isoquant $M = 1$ in Figure 4.5. There are three points, A, B, and C, explicitly stated in Figure 4.5. All three points can produce one unit of output. Point A, however, is not part of the isoquant $M = 1$, since the same level of output can be produced using either less labour or less capital (or a little less of both inputs) than the amount used at point A, which is therefore not an efficient input combination to produce one unit of output.[3]

Since the entrepreneur can choose between two different inputs, we first have to determine the level of costs associated with a certain input combination before we can determine how to minimize the level of these costs. In this respect the assumption of perfect competition, which also applies to the input markets, is most convenient. The entrepreneur simply takes the price level of labour, the wage rate w determined on the labour market, and the price level of capital, the rental rate r determined on the capital market, as given. If the firm therefore hires L_m labour and K_m capital, total costs associated with this input combination are

$$(4.2) \qquad\qquad costs = \underset{\substack{labour \\ cost}}{wL_m} + \underset{\substack{capital \\ cost}}{rK_m}$$

Obviously, different input combinations of capital and labour can give rise to the same cost level. From equation (4.2) it is clear that such isocost combinations are straight lines in labour–capital space, with a slope equal to $-w/r$. This is illustrated for two isocost lines in

Box 4.3 **Capital-intensity parameter and the cost share of capital**

A simple and useful mnemonic for the capital intensity parameter α in the production function of equation (4.1) is the fact that it represents the share of total costs paid for the use of capital in the production process. This can be readily seen from equation (4.3), which can be rewritten as

$$\frac{(1 - \alpha_m)}{\alpha_m} rK_m = wL_m$$

Using this in the definition of total costs gives

$$rK_m + wL_m = rK_m + \left(\frac{1 - \alpha_m}{\alpha_m} rK_m\right) = \frac{rK_m}{\alpha_m} \Rightarrow \underbrace{\frac{\overbrace{rK_m}^{\text{cost of capital}}}{rK_m + wL_m}}_{\text{total cost}} = \alpha_m$$

Similarly, the total wage bill represents a share $1 - \alpha_m$ of total costs. We will return to this when discussing the demand side of the neoclassical model in Chapter 7.

Figure 4.5, with points A and B part of the same isocost line. Graphically, the cost minimization problem facing the entrepreneur is quite simple: move the dashed isocost line down to the south-west (in the direction of the arrows) as far as possible, with the restriction that at least one of the input combinations on the isocost line is able to produce one unit of manufactures (part of the $M = 1$ isoquant). The solution to this procedure applied to Figure 4.5 gives point C as the optimal input combination, using $K_m(w, r)$ units of capital and $L_m(w, r)$ units of labour. This notation makes explicit the fact that the optimal input combination depends on the wage rate w and the rental rate r; see also Section 4.6. Figure 4.5 also illustrates the optimal relative input combination K_m/L_m. This plays an important role in the sequel.

Technical Note 4.1 explicitly calculates the solutions $K_m(w, r)$ and $L_m(w, r)$ for the cost minimization problem, which gives the following optimal *relative* input combination (the capital–labour ratio) for manufactures and food:

(4.3)
$$\frac{K_m}{L_m} = \frac{\alpha_m}{1 - \alpha_m} \frac{w}{r} \; ; \quad \frac{K_f}{L_f} = \frac{\alpha_f}{1 - \alpha_f} \frac{w}{r}$$

It is important to note that the optimal capital–labour ratio depends on two factors:

- The capital–labour ratio is higher if the capital intensity parameter α rises.
- The capital–labour ratio is higher if the wage–rental ratio w/r rises (section 4.6).

For ease of exposition, and without loss of generality, we henceforth impose the following:

Assumption: the production of manufactures is relatively more capital intensive than the production of food for all w/r ratios, that is $\alpha_m > \alpha_f$.

4.6 Impact of wage rate and rental rate

As argued above, and derived in Technical Note 4.1, the optimal input of labour and capital depends on the wage–rental ratio. Three issues are important. First, the cost-minimizing input combination depends only on the wage–rental *ratio*, not on their absolute levels. This is intuitively obvious, as an equiproportional change in the wage rate and the rental rate does not change the *slope* of the isocost lines in Figure 4.5, and therefore does not affect the cost-minimizing input combination. An equiproportional change in input prices does, however, change the cost level, as derived in Technical Note 4.2. Second, an increase in the price of an input reduces the demand for that input; that is, an increase in the wage rate reduces the demand for labour, while an increase in the rental rate reduces the demand for capital. This is illustrated for $\alpha_m = 0.5$ in Figure 4.6: as the wage rate rises, the demand for labour falls. Third, and linked to the previous two observations, if the price of an input factor rises there is a substitution away from the more expensive input towards the other input. Thus, if the wage rate rises, the demand for capital rises, and if the rental rate rises, the demand for labour rises. This too is illustrated in Figure 4.6, where there is an increase in the demand for labour for any given level of the wage rate if the rental rate increases from $r = 1$ to $r = 2$.

These observations are explained in Figure 4.7, analysing the impact of a lower wage rate on the cost-minimizing input combination. Initially, the wage rate and rental rate are identical to those analysed in Figure 4.5, thus leading to the cost-minimizing input combination at point C. Suppose, then, that the wage rate falls from w_0 to w_1. As a result, the isocost line rotates counter-clockwise around point D. Consequently, production costs are no longer minimized at point C but, repeating the procedure described in section 4.5, at point E, using $K_m(w_1, r) < K_m(w_0, r)$ units of capital and $L_m(w_1, r) > L_m(w_0, r)$

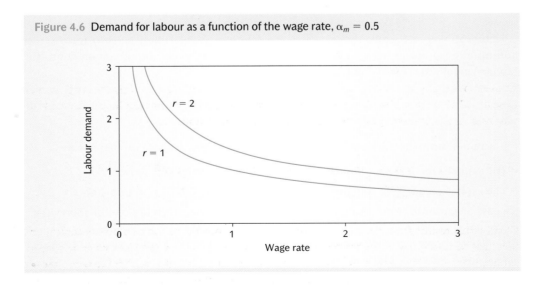

Figure 4.6 Demand for labour as a function of the wage rate, $\alpha_m = 0.5$

Figure 4.7 Impact of lower wage on cost-minimizing inputs

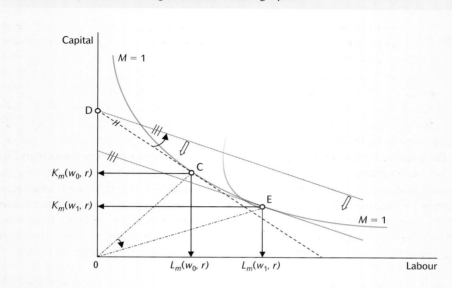

units of labour. Thus, there has been a substitution away from the now relatively more expensive capital towards the cheaper labour. This substitution effect is summarized in the lower capital–labour ratio at point E compared to point C. The actual cost level achieved for all possible combinations of wage rates and rental rates is derived in Technical Note 4.2.

4.7 Constant returns to scale

As mentioned in section 4.3, the production processes are characterized by constant returns to scale (CRS); that is, if we increase the use of both factors of production by the same multiplicative factor κ, the output produced also increases by that factor κ:

$$(4.4) \qquad \underbrace{\left(\kappa.K_m\right)}_{\substack{increase \\ capital}}^{\alpha_m}\underbrace{\left(\kappa.L_m\right)}_{\substack{increase \\ labour}}^{1-\alpha_m} = \kappa^{\alpha_m+1-\alpha_m}K_m^{\alpha_m}L_m^{1-\alpha_m} = \underbrace{\kappa}_{\substack{increase \\ production}}\left(K_m^{\alpha_m}L_m^{1-\alpha_m}\right)$$

Clearly, this results from the fact that we imposed the powers of the two inputs capital and labour to sum to unity in the production function ($\alpha_m + (1 - \alpha_m) = 1$).[4] The two main reasons for imposing constant returns to scale are ease of exposition (see Box 3.2 on the combination of perfect competition and constant returns to scale) and a replication argument; if the

Figure 4.8 Constant returns to scale and isoquants, $\alpha_m = 0.5$

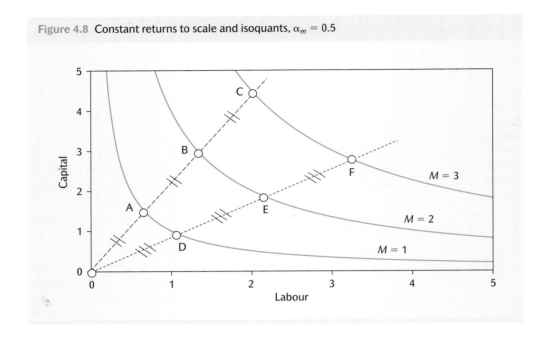

current mix of inputs produces four units of output, one should be able to double the output to eight units simply by replicating the current production process (thus doubling the use of all inputs). Imposing constant returns to scale in the production process gives us two important simplifications, namely (i) for the structure of the isoquants and (ii) for the cost minimization process.

Structure of the isoquants

For any constant returns to scale production process it suffices to derive only one isoquant. Quite literally, one can say 'if you have seen one isoquant you have seen them all'. This is illustrated in Figure 4.8 for $\alpha_m = 0.5$ and three isoquants. First, take an arbitrary point, such as point A, on the isoquant $M = 1$. By the constant returns to scale property of the production process we know that if we double the use of both inputs we double the output of the production process. Graphically, if we draw a straight line from the origin through point A, we can double the use of both inputs by measuring the distance from the origin to point A and adding this distance from point A along the line earlier drawn through the origin and point A. We thus arrive at point B. Since doubling the use of inputs doubles the output produced, point B must be part of the $M = 2$ isoquant. Similarly, by tripling the use of inputs from point A we arrive at point C, which must be part of the $M = 3$ isoquant. We can repeat this procedure for another point on the $M = 1$ isoquant, such as point D. Doubling the inputs leads to point E, which must be part of the $M = 2$ isoquant, and tripling the inputs leads to point F, which must be part of the $M = 3$ isoquant. Repeating this procedure for all other points on the $M = 1$ isoquant shows that all isoquants are radial blow-ups of the $M = 1$

isoquant. Thus, once we have drawn one isoquant, we have in principle drawn them all after rescaling the inputs.

Cost minimization

Imposing constant returns to scale in the production process considerably simplifies the cost minimization problem. In section 4.5 and Technical Note 4.1 we solved the cost minimization problem for producing one unit of manufactures. Due to constant returns to scale, this suffices to determine the cost minimization problem for all levels of output. As argued above, all isoquants are radial blow-ups of one another. This implies in particular that the slope of an isoquant is the same for any ray through the origin. This is illustrated in Figure 4.9 and shown in Technical Note 4.3. Clearly, point A in Figure 4.9 minimizes the cost of producing one unit of manufactures for the wage–rental ratio drawn in the figure (equal to 1 in the example). Since a doubling of inputs (from point A to point B) doubles the output to two units of manufactures and the slope of the isoquant at point B is equal to the slope of the isoquant at point A, point B minimizes the cost of producing two units of manufactures. Similarly, point C minimizes the cost of producing three units of manufactures, etc. At the wage–rental ratio drawn in Figure 4.9, the cost-minimizing input combination is a radial blow-up from the origin through point A. An increase or decrease of the scale of production therefore takes place along the expansion path drawn in the figure. Thus, once we have solved the cost minimization problem for producing one unit of manufactures, we have automatically solved this problem for all other output levels.

Figure 4.9 Constant returns to scale and cost minimization, $\alpha_m = 0.5$, $w = r = 1$

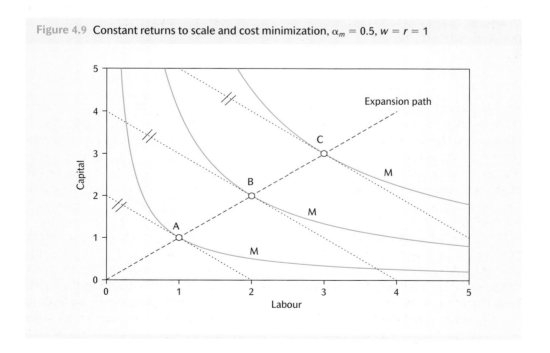

Box 4.4   **Primary products exporters**

Sections 4.4–4.7 have discussed the main properties of the neoclassical production functions by distinguishing between just two factor inputs and two final goods. In reality one can, of course, identify several thousand different factors of production and final goods. For example, many types of capital goods, such as printing presses, desks, and computers, or many types of labour, such as unskilled labour, engineers, and accountants. Empirical research usually tries to find some middle ground in between the two factors of production and two final goods used in the exposition of the book and the thousands one can identify in reality by distinguishing a limited number of each, say between five and ten factors of production and between five and 800 final goods.

The website of the International Trade Centre (ITC, see http://www.intracen.org), the joint UNCTAD/WTO organization, provides a good example of the empirical approach. To classify international trade flows, it distinguishes five factors of production and 257 final goods, based on the three-digit level of SITC classification Rev. 3. As we have argued in section 4.2 and will clarify in the next few chapters, the intensity with which different final goods use the production factors has important ramifications for international trade flows. The ITC therefore aggregates the 257 final goods into five broader categories based on the intensity of the five factors in the production process:

- primary products
- natural-resource-intensive products
- unskilled-labour-intensive products
- technology-intensive products, and
- human-capital-intensive products.

We briefly discuss the world's main exporters in relative and absolute terms for each of these five categories in special interest boxes in this chapter and the next four chapters.

The ITC classifies 91 goods as 'primary' products, incorporating meat, dairy, cereals, fruit, coffee, sand, minerals, oil, natural gas, iron ore, copper ore, etc. For the 151 countries for which the ITC provides data, total exports of primary products in 1998 were equal to $816 bn, some 17 per cent of all exports. The left-hand side of Table 4.3 lists the top ten exporters of primary products in absolute terms. With a value of $80 bn, the USA is the world's largest primary products exporter, shipping for example wheat, maize, soya beans, and cigarettes. With a value of $49 bn, Canada, shipping for example wheat, is the second largest primary products exporter, while France, shipping grapes, wheat, and bovine meat, is the third largest. With the exception of Saudi Arabia, the other large primary products exporters are all in Europe.

Since primary products represent 13 per cent of American exports, the USA is below the world average in relative terms. The right-hand side of Table 4.3 lists the top ten world exporters of primary products in relative terms, all of which are located in the Middle East and Africa. Note that the export of primary products is virtually the only source of foreign exchange for all these countries, as even Uganda, ranked tenth, depends for 97 per cent of its exports on primary products. Also note the very small absolute size of the trade flows for these countries. The top three are Burundi (mostly coffee), Iraq (oil), and Yemen (oil).

Figure 4.10 shows the relative dependence of countries on the exports of primary products. Its indicates clearly that Africa, the Middle East, and South America are the world's top primary products exporters in relative terms.   »

Table 4.3 Top ten primary products exporters, 1998

No.	Top 10 in absolute terms			Top 10 in relative terms		
	Country	Exports		Country	Exports	
		Value	%		%	Value
1	USA	80	13	Burundi	100	0.0
2	Canada	49	25	Iraq	100	0.0
3	France	46	16	Yemen	99	0.0
4	The Netherlands	40	25	Mauritania	99	0.0
5	Germany	36	7	Chad	98	0.0
6	Australia	30	60	Guinea-Bissau	98	0.0
7	Saudi Arabia	29	86	Equatorial Guinea	97	2.1
8	UK	29	11	Gabon	97	1.9
9	Russian Federation	24	49	Nigeria	97	1.7
10	Belgium	23	14	Uganda	97	1.4

Source: WTO/UNCTAD International Trade Centre website http://www.intracen.org; value in bn US$. The % shares are relative to the country's total exports.

Figure 4.10 Primary products exports, share 1998

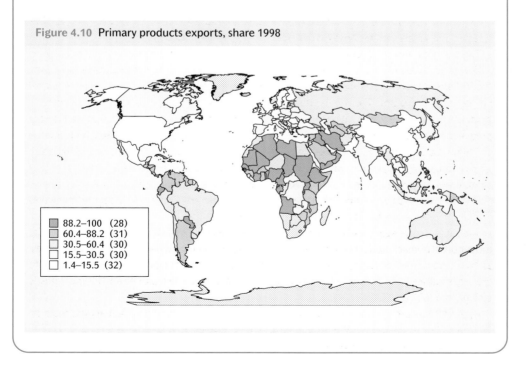

88.2–100 (28)
60.4–88.2 (31)
30.5–60.4 (30)
15.5–30.5 (30)
1.4–15.5 (32)

4.8 Conclusions

This chapter briefly reviews the microeconomic foundations and main implications of the neoclassical production structure. There are two factors of production, capital and labour, that can be partially substituted for one another in the production process. As a result of constant returns to scale, the isoquants (depicting efficient combinations of capital and labour for producing a given output level) are radial blow-ups of one another. As a result, the final goods producer equiproportionally adjusts the cost-minimizing inputs of capital and labour to change the output level for a given wage rate and rental rate. The cost-minimizing capital–labour input mix depends on (i) the wage–rental ratio, and (ii) a parameter measuring the capital intensity of the production process. The latter parameter can therefore be used to classify the final goods based on the intensity with which they use capital (relative to labour) in the production process; throughout the remainder of Part II.A we will assume that the production of manufactures is more capital intensive than the production of food.

TECHNICAL NOTES

Technical Note 4.1 Unit cost minimization

The problem for an entrepreneur who wants to minimize the cost of producing one unit of manufactures by choosing the input quantities of capital K_m and labour L_m, taking the rental rate of capital r and the wage rate of labour was given, is specified as:

$$(4.A1) \qquad \min_{K_m, L_m} w L_m + r K_m \ \ s.t. \ M = K_m^{\alpha_m} L_m^{1-\alpha_m} \geq 1$$

To solve this problem we define the Lagrangean Γ, using the Lagrange multiplier λ:

$$(4.A2) \qquad \Gamma = w L_m + r K_m + \lambda(1 - K_m^{\alpha_m} L_m^{1-\alpha_m})$$

Derive the two first-order conditions $\partial \Gamma / \partial K_m = \partial \Gamma / \partial L_m = 0$ for an optimum and note

$$(4.A3) \qquad w = (1 - \alpha_m)\lambda K_m^{\alpha_m} L_m^{-\alpha_m} \ \ \text{and} \ \ r = \alpha_m \lambda K_m^{-(1-\alpha_m)} L_m^{1-\alpha_m}$$

Taking the ratio of these two conditions and simplifying determines the optimal capital–labour ratio K_m/L_m for the production of manufactures, which depends in a simple way on the wage–rental ratio w/r and the capital-intensity parameter α_m

$$(4.A3) \qquad \frac{K_m}{L_m} = \frac{\alpha_m}{1 - \alpha_m} \frac{w}{r}$$

This relationship between the optimal use of capital and labour can be substituted in the production function to derive the actual amount of capital and number of labourers you need to produce one unit of manufactures at minimum cost.

$$(4.A4) \qquad M = K_m^{\alpha_m} L_m^{1-\alpha_m} = \left(\frac{\alpha_m}{1 - \alpha_m} \frac{w}{r} L_m \right)^{\alpha_m} L_m^{1-\alpha_m} = 1$$

Simplifying this, denoting the optimal choice of labourers $L_m(w, r)$ since it depends on the wage rate w and the rental rate r, and repeating the procedure for the optimal choice of capital $K_m(w, r)$ gives:

$$(4.A5) \qquad L_m(w,r) = \left(\frac{\alpha_m}{1 - \alpha_m} \frac{w}{r} \right)^{-\alpha_m} \quad and \quad K_m(w,r) = \left(\frac{\alpha_m}{1 - \alpha_m} \frac{w}{r} \right)^{1 - \alpha_m}$$

The interpretation of these results is discussed in the main text. Replacing the index m with the index f in the above two equations will give the demand for labour and capital in the food sector.

Technical Note 4.2 Duality

In Technical Note 4.1 we derived the optimal factor input mix of capital and labour to minimize the costs of producing one unit of manufactures; see equation (4.A5). For the entrepreneur it is, of course, important to know how high these minimum costs for producing one unit of manufactures really are. We will denote these[5] by $c_m(w, r)$, as they depend on the wage rate w and the rental rate r. They can be derived by substituting the *optimal* (i.e. cost-minimizing) factor inputs into the costs $wL_m + rK_m$:

$$(4.A6) \qquad c_m(w,r) = wL_m(w,r) + rK_m(w,r) = w \left(\frac{\alpha_m}{1 - \alpha_m} \frac{w}{r} \right)^{-\alpha_m} + r \left(\frac{\alpha_m}{1 - \alpha_m} \frac{w}{r} \right)^{1 - \alpha_m}$$

After some algebraic manipulations the unit cost function can be simplified to

$$(4.A7) \qquad c_m(w,r) = \gamma_m r^{\alpha_m} w^{1 - \alpha_m}, \text{ where } \gamma_m \equiv \alpha_m^{-\alpha_m} (1 - \alpha_m)^{-(1 - \alpha_m)}$$

(The symbol '$\equiv$' means 'is defined to be equal to'). Replacing the index m by the index f gives the unit cost function of food. Note that the structure of the unit cost function is similar to the structure of the production function. Both are Cobb–Douglas functions, with α as the power for capital in the production function and as the *price* of capital in the unit cost function, and $1 - \alpha$ as the power of labour in the production function and as the *price* of labour in the unit cost function. This is no coincidence, but a phenomenon known as duality. Before we discuss this, note that

$$(4.A8) \qquad \frac{\partial c_m(w,r)}{\partial w} = \left(\frac{\alpha_m}{1 - \alpha_m} \frac{w}{r} \right)^{-\alpha_m} = L_m(w,r) \text{ and}$$

$$\frac{\partial c_m(w,r)}{\partial r} = \left(\frac{\alpha_m}{1 - \alpha_m} \frac{w}{r} \right)^{-\alpha_m} = K_m(w,r)$$

That is, if we differentiate the unit cost function with respect to the price of labour, the outcome is identical to the unit-cost-minimizing number of labourers and if we differentiate the unit cost function with respect to the price of capital, the outcome is identical to the unit-cost-minimizing amount of capital. This result is known as *Shephard's lemma*. We can thus arrive at the cost-minimizing input combinations in two different ways. First, we can specify a production function and explicitly derive the cost-minimizing input combination as we did in Technical Note 4.1. Second, we can use the dual approach, that is specify a unit cost function as in (4.A7) above and simply differentiate with respect to the wage rate and the rental rate to derive the optimal combination of labour and capital. Taking some technical restrictions into consideration, these two approaches, specifying either a production function or a cost function, are *equivalent*. Depending on the problem to be analysed, one approach may be more convenient than another. In this book we will not use the dual approach; see however Dixit and Norman (1980), and Brakman and van Marrewijk (1998) for various applications of the dual approach to international economics.

Technical Note 4.3 Slope of isoquants

By definition, an isoquant depicts all possible efficient input combinations to produce a certain level of output, say $M = \bar{M}$. Totally differentiating the production function (4.1) for this level of output gives

$$(4.A9) \qquad \alpha_m K_m^{\alpha_m - 1} L_m^{1 - \alpha_m} dK_m + (1 - \alpha_m) K_m^{\alpha_m} L_m^{-\alpha_m} dL_m = d\bar{M} = 0$$

from which the slope on any point of the isoquant can be derived easily

(4.A10)
$$\frac{dK_m}{dL_m} = -\frac{1 - \alpha_m}{\alpha_m}\frac{K_m}{L_m}$$

Clearly, the slope of an isoquant depends only on the capital–labour *ratio*. Thus, if we change both inputs equiproportionally by the factor κ, where κ = 2 at point B relative to point A and κ = 3 at point C relative to point A in Figure 4.9, the slope of the isoquant remains the same. The implications are discussed in the main text.

QUESTIONS

Question 4.1

Dwell produces desktop computers using high-skilled labourers (H) and low-skilled labourers (L) with constant returns to scale. To maximize profits, it wants to minimize its cost of production. Computers are relatively intensive in low-skilled labour production and Dwell is a price taker on the labour market. The market for computers is perfectly competitive.

4.1A Draw a production isoquant for computers and an isocost line. Indicate in your graph the number of high-skilled and the number of low-skilled workers involved in the production process.

Dwell forecasts an increase in demand for its newest model and doubles its production.

4.1B Draw the new situation in your graph of A.

4.1C What happens to the isocost line and production isoquant? Why? How many new labourers does Dwell hire?

4.1D What impact does the production change have on Dwell's profitability?

Question 4.2

Dwell computers of question 4.1 has just doubled production. It wants to maintain its production level when it is confronted with a wage increase for high skilled-labour.

4.2A Draw the initial situation in a graph with a production isoquant and an isocost line. Indicate the change in the isocost line after the wage increase.

4.2B What implications does this have for Dwell's production process of computers? What happens to the demand for high-skilled labour from Dwell?

Dwell does some research and development and manages to improve its production process. As a consequence, producing computers after the innovation becomes more low-skilled labour intensive.

4.2C Show in your graph the effect of this technological innovation. Does this alter the input mix of high- and low-skilled labour?

4.2D What would be the consequences of this kind of technological development for wages of skilled and non-skilled workers?

Question 4.3

4.3A What are the two main determinants of the optimal capital–labour ratio for the producers of food and manufactures in the neoclassical model?

4.3B Suppose all countries in the world produce only food and manufactures, using the same technology in a neoclassical model without international trade. What do you think will be the pattern of wage–rental ratios in the food sector and manufacturing sector of the countries in Table 4.2?

See the Online Resource Centre for a Study Guide containing more questions
www.oxfordtextbooks.co.uk/orc/vanmarrewijk/

NOTES

1 Moreover, we will argue in this part of the book that a large proportion of the trade flows that do arise between developed and less developed nations result from a different underlying force for trade.

2 See Allen (1965: 173).

3 It is part of another isoquant, producing a higher output level of manufactures (not illustrated).

4 If their sum exceeds unity, there are increasing returns to scale; see Part IIB of the book. If their sum falls short of unity, there are decreasing returns to scale.

5 The reader may note that these unit costs $c_m(w, r)$ are labelled unit costs c in Box 2.1.

FACTOR PRICES

5

Objectives/key terms

- Factor price equalization
- Unit value isoquant/isocost line
- Magnification effect

- Stolper–Samuelson
- Lerner diagram
- Globalization debate

We discuss the connections between the prices of final goods and the rewards to factors of production, in particular how trade between countries can lead to factor price equalization. We apply these results to discuss and evaluate the 'globalization' debate of the 1990s.

5.1 Introduction

The first two main results of neoclassical economics, namely (i) factor price equalization and (ii) Stolper–Samuelson, are related to an economy's factor prices. The results will be more precisely stated below, and discussed and derived in more detail in this chapter. We start the discussion with result (i), as result (ii) derives almost immediately from it. The term 'factor price equalization' refers to the idea that trade in final goods between two nations leads to an equalization of the rewards for the factors used to produce these goods. As Bertil Ohlin (1933, ch. II) put it:[1]

> The most immediate effect of trade between a number of regions under the conditions which have been assumed to exist is that commodity prices are made to tally. . . . Trade has, however, a far-reaching influence also on the prices and the combination and use of the productive factors, in brief, on the whole price system. . . . In both regions . . . the factor which is relatively abundant becomes more in demand and fetches a higher price, whereas the factor that is scantily supplied becomes less in demand and gets a relatively lower reward than before.

Carefully reading the above quote makes it clear that Ohlin did not actually think that the rewards for the factors of production would be equalized between the two regions, just that there is a *tendency* for the rewards of the factors of production to become more equal between the regions (to understand this the reader must realize that the factor of production relatively abundant in one country is relatively scarce in the other country). The term factor price equalization derives from Paul Samuelson's (1948, 1949) work on the formalization of Ohlin's ideas on the tendency of factor prices between nations to converge as a result of international trade in final goods, which shows that these factor prices will in fact become equal. It is this version of the idea, discussed below, that became one of the cornerstones of the neoclassical economics framework. To be fair to Ohlin, however, in a more general setting, allowing for more final goods, more factors of production, and other complications, factor prices will not become equal as a result of trade in final goods, but there is a *tendency* for factor rewards to move closer together, just as Ohlin argued. This prompted Paul Samuelson (1971) to write an essay with the title 'Ohlin was right'.

Famous economists	Harry Johnson
 **Fig. 5.1** Harry Johnson (1923–1977)	Born in Toronto, Canada, Harry Johnson worked at the University of Cambridge (UK), the University of Chicago (USA), and the Graduate Institute of International Studies (Switzerland). He travelled all over the globe to lecture and give presentations. While travelling, and drinking large quantities of alcohol, he produced an enormous quantity of high-quality economic papers, books, pamphlets and journal articles, in particular in international economics and monetary economics. His work in international economics, using geometric rather than algebraic illustrations and proofs, focuses on policy-relevant issues, welfare economics, tariffs in the face of retaliation, and the theory of second-best.

5.2 Factor price equalization

Using the neoclassical production structure with two countries, two final goods, and two factors of production explained in more detail in Chapter 4, Samuelson's (1948, 1949) result can most usefully be stated as follows.

Factor price equalization proposition (FPE)

In a neoclassical framework with two final goods and two factors of production, there is a one-to-one correspondence between the prices of the final goods and the prices of the factors of production, provided both goods are produced. This implies

(i) *if the factor rewards (w, r) are known the prices of the final goods (p_m, p_f) can be derived, and*

(ii) *if the prices of the final goods (p_m, p_f) are known, the factor rewards (w, r) can be derived.*

Reading the statement of the proposition above, the reader may justifiably wonder why it is called the factor price equalization (FPE) proposition, since there is no mention of any equalization, nor even of countries involved in such an equalization process. The reason is that a simple application of the above proposition leads to the following:

Corollary

In a neoclassical framework with two countries, two final goods, and two factors of production, international trade of the final goods, which equalizes the prices of these goods in the two nations, also leads to an equalization of the rewards of the factors of production in the two nations, provided both final goods are produced in both nations and the state of technology in the two nations is the same.

The statement of the corollary makes two provisions, namely (i) both final goods must be produced in both nations, and (ii) the state of technology in the two nations must be the same. Provision (i) is also used in the FPE proposition. Clearly, if we want to apply that proposition, we also have to use the provision in the application. Why both goods must be produced in both countries will become clear in the discussion of the proposition in the sections below. Provision (ii), on the equality of the state of technology, is new because we now have the production functions in two countries to take into consideration. The reasoning in the corollary is quite simple. If international trade between Austria and Bolivia leads the prices of the final goods to be the same (recall that there are no transport costs or other impediments to trade), that is, $p_{mA} = p_{mB}$ and $p_{fA} = p_{fB}$, then applying the FPE proposition leads us to conclude that the factor rewards, the wage rate and the rental rate, must also be equalized for the two countries; that is, $w_A = w_B$ and $r_A = r_B$, if both countries produce both goods and the state of technology is the same (otherwise the same set of final goods prices could lead to a different set of factor prices, see also below).

5.3 The Lerner diagram

The FPE proposition makes two separate statements. It says that if the factor rewards (w, r) are known, the prices of the final goods (p_m, p_f) can be derived. It also says that if the prices of the final goods (p_m, p_f) are known, the factor rewards (w, r) can be derived. These two issues will

Box 5.1   **Tool: Lerner diagram**

The analysis below uses two intricately related tools of analysis, namely the unit value isocost line and the unit value isoquant, together forming the Lerner diagram. The *unit value isocost line* depicts all input combinations (L, K) giving rise to a cost level of one unit of measurement, taking the input prices (w, r) as given. This is illustrated in Figure 5.2. If you like big numbers, the unit of measurement could be $1 million or $1 billion, but this is simply a scale effect, so the same results are derived if the unit of measurement is $1. The *unit value isoquant* for a final good, say manufactures, is a regular isoquant; that is, it depicts all efficient input combinations (L_m, K_m) giving rise to a certain production level of manufactures, with the provision that the *value* of this production level is one unit of measurement, taking the final goods price p_m as given. This is illustrated in Figure 5.3, and discussed further below. Note that each final good gives rise to its own unit value isoquant, depending on the production function and its own price level. Combining these tools gives you Figure 5.4, which is known as the Lerner diagram, named after Abba Lerner (1952).

Figure 5.2 Unit value isocost line; effect of an increase in rental rate r

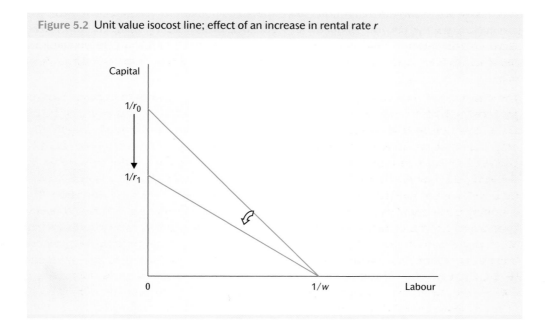

be addressed in Sections 5.4 and 5.5. The tool of analysis used in those sections is briefly discussed in this section.

Figure 5.2 depicts two unit value isocost lines, namely for the factor prices (w, r_0) and for the factor prices (w, r_1). Note that by definition the isocost line is given by

(5.1) $rK + wL = 1$

From equation (5.1) the intercepts of the unit value isocost line are easily calculated as $1/w$ for the labour axis and $1/r$ for the capital axis. Figure 5.2 depicts a situation in which the rental rate of capital rises from r_0 to r_1, causing a counter-clockwise rotation of the unit value isocost line around the point $(1/w, 0)$.

Figure 5.3 depicts one unit value isoquant for food if the price is p_f and two unit value isoquants for manufactures, namely if the price is p_{m0} and p_{m1}. Note that by definition the unit value isoquant for manufactures and food is determined by

(5.2) $p_m M = 1; \quad p_f F = 1$

Thus, if you know the price p_m of the final good it is easy to determine the number of goods (and thus the isoquant) you have to produce, namely $1/p_m$, to ensure that this production level represents one unit of value (since $p_m \cdot (1/p_m) = 1$). Clearly, if the price level of the final good rises, fewer goods are needed to produce one unit of value. Thus a price *rise* results in an *inward* shift of the unit value isoquant, as illustrated for manufactures in Figure 5.3.

A final remark on Figure 5.3, depicting three different isoquants, may be useful. As drawn, the isoquants intersect at two locations, point A and point B. The reader will recall from the microeconomics class that two isoquants cannot intersect, since the same input combination cannot give rise to two different output levels if both combinations make efficient use of the resources. None the less, the isoquants in Figure 5.3 do intersect. Is there an error in the figure? No, there is not. Note that at the two points of intersection A and B an isoquant for

Figure 5.3 Unit value isoquants: effect of an increase in the price of manufactures

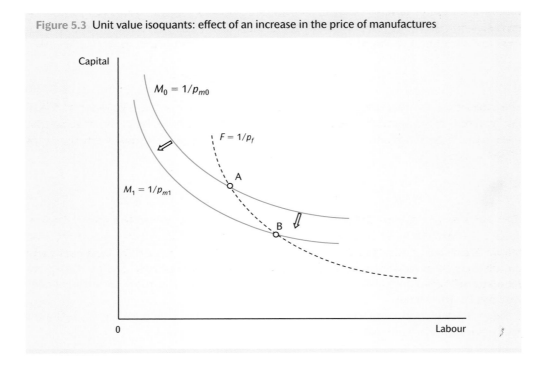

manufactures intersects with an isoquant for food. Since these are two different goods, there is no contradiction. The points A and B have no special interpretation, other than that apparently the same input combination produces the same value of output, namely 1, for both goods.

5.4 From factor prices to final goods prices

Now that we have briefly discussed the unit value isocost line and the unit value isoquants, we are in a position to derive the FPE proposition once we realize the connections between these tools in a perfectly competitive economy. As already discussed in Box 3.2, *if* a good is produced under perfect competition the price of the good is equal to the cost of production. In other words, there are no (excess) profits, such that if an entrepreneur can generate a revenue of one unit of measurement, this entrepreneur also incurs a cost of one unit of measurement. The FPE proposition makes only one provision, namely that both goods must be produced. Thus for both final goods one unit of revenue must be equal to one unit of costs.

The connections between costs and revenue are illustrated in Figure 5.4. If the price of manufactures is p_m and the wage–rental ratio is w/r, the entrepreneur minimizes production costs for the unit value isoquant of manufactures at point A. To be an equilibrium production point, the costs must be equal to the revenue, such that the unit value isocost line must be tangent at point A. Similar reasoning holds for the food sector at point B. Note also that, as assumed in Chapter 4, the relative capital intensity is higher in the manufactures sector than in the food sector; that is, $K_m/L_m > K_f/L_f$ because $\alpha_m > \alpha_f$.

With these preliminaries, it is relatively easy to show the first part of the FPE proposition; that is, if the factor rewards (w, r) are known, the prices of the final goods (p_m, p_f) can be derived. Once the factor prices are known, the unit value isocost line is known and we only have to determine which isoquant for either good is tangent to this unit value isocost line:

$$(w,r) \Rightarrow \text{isocost line} \Rightarrow \text{unit value isoquant} \Rightarrow (p_m, p_f)$$

The calculations have already been performed in Technical Note 4.2, see equation (4.A7): if the market is characterized by perfect competition and production by constant returns to scale, then *if* a good is produced in equilibrium the price of the good is equal to the unit costs of production:

(5.3)
$$p_m = \underset{constant}{\gamma_m}\, r^{\alpha_m} w^{1-\alpha_m}; \quad p_f = \underset{constant}{\gamma_f}\, r^{\alpha_f} w^{1-\alpha_f}$$

The constants γ_m and γ_f are defined in Technical Note 4.2; The relationship between the final goods prices and the input prices given in equation (5.3) is illustrated for changes in the wage rate in Figure 5.5. As an inspection of equation (5.3) shows, the price of food rises more quickly than the price of manufactures if the wage rate increases because $1-\alpha_f > 1-\alpha_m$. We return to this below.

Figure 5.4 The Lerner diagram

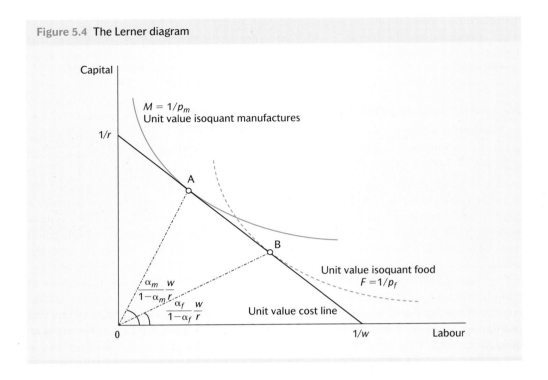

Figure 5.5 Final goods prices as a function of the wage rate, $r = 1$, $\alpha_m = 0.7$, $\alpha_f = 0.3$

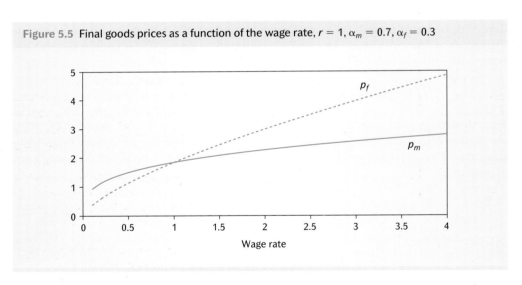

5.5 From final goods prices to factor prices

Showing the second part of the FPE proposition: that is, if the prices of the final goods (p_m, p_f) are known, the factor rewards (w,r) can be derived, is a little bit more complicated. Conceptually, we can reverse the logic of section 5.4. First, the two unit value isoquants for

Box 5.2 More countries, more goods, and more factors I

The two results discussed in this chapter, factor price equalization and Stolper–Samuelson, are derived in a framework with two countries, two goods, and two factors of production. This raises the question, of course, whether these results also hold in a more general setting. Ignoring the rather complex mathematical details of this more general setting, the answer is 'yes, sort of'. Factor price equalization, for example, does not hold in a strict sense (which would also be immediately refuted by empirical evidence). Instead, it is possible to distinguish so-called 'cones of diversification' for which FPE holds, leading to *groups* of countries with similar factor prices. The Stolper–Samuelson result holds in a weaker sense; that is, a higher price for some final good 'on average' increases the rewards of the factors used intensively in the production of that good. The magnification effect (see section 5.8) holds quite generally; that is, a higher price for some final good increases the relative reward to *some* factor of production ('friend') and reduces the relative reward of some other factor of production ('enemy').

manufactures and food can be determined from the identities $p_m M = 1$ and $p_f F = 1$. Second, the unit value cost line can then be determined by deriving the line tangent to both unit value isoquants:

$$(p_m, p_f) \Rightarrow \text{unit value isoquant} \Rightarrow \text{isocost line} \Rightarrow (w, r)$$

However, in this case it is easier to invert equations (5.3) above to get:

(5.4)
$$w = \underbrace{\gamma_w}_{constant} \left[p_f^{\alpha_m} p_m^{-\alpha_f} \right]^{\frac{1}{\alpha_m - \alpha_f}} ; \quad r = \underbrace{\gamma_r}_{constant} \left[p_m^{1-\alpha_f} p_f^{-(1-\alpha_m)} \right]^{\frac{1}{\alpha_m - \alpha_f}}$$

See Technical Note 5.1 for a derivation of these equations and the definition of the parameter constants γ_m and γ_r. The structure of the equations is similar to those of the production functions and the unit cost functions. Note, however, that this time the difference in the capital-intensity parameters $\alpha_m - \alpha_f$ plays a crucial role in determining the sign of the powers in the equation. In Chapter 4 we assumed that the production of manufactures is relatively more capital intensive than the production of food, such that $\alpha_m - \alpha_f > 0$. Equation (5.4) gives us a first indication that this assumption is important for the results to be derived and discussed below.

5.6 Stolper–Samuelson

Now that we have developed the economic tools to analyse factor price equalization, it is easy to derive the Stolper–Samuelson proposition, which relates the impact of a change in final goods prices to the rewards of the factors of production and the factor intensity of the production processes. In retrospect the basic reasoning is quite simple and widely applicable. However, when summarizing the impact of international trade for goods and factor prices, the production levels, and the international trade flows, Bertil Ohlin (1933, ch. II) argued:[2]

goods containing a large proportion of scantily supplied and scarce factors are imported, the latter hence becoming less scarce . . . . The price even of the factors which are made relatively less scarce may well rise in terms of commodities, for the total volume of goods increases, owing to the more efficient use of the productive facilities made possible through trade, and the *average* price of productive factors consequently rises in all regions.

As we will see below, the conclusion Ohlin draws here, that the average price of productive factors rises in all regions, is wrong. At least, it is wrong if this statement is interpreted as an indication that both the wage rate and the rental rate will rise against a 'suitable' combination of the prices of manufactures and food. The precise consequences were analytically derived for the first time by Wolfgang Stolper and Paul Samuelson (1941). Ohlin's remark above may be salvaged, as we will see in Chapter 7, if the statement is interpreted as an indication that the 'average' price of the wage rate and rental rate combined rises relative to the 'average' price of manufactures and food combined.[3] The formal link between the prices of final goods, the rewards to factors of production, and the relative intensity of the production process can be stated as follows.

Stolper–Samuelson proposition

In a neoclassical framework with two final goods and two factors of production, an increase in the price of a final good increases the reward to the factor of production used intensively in the production of that good and reduces the reward to the other factor, provided both goods are produced.

Using the assumption that the relative capital intensity for manufactures is higher than for food, the proposition thus leads to the following conclusions:

- If the price of manufactures rises, the rental rate will rise (because the production of manufactures is relatively capital intensive), and the wage rate will fall.
- If the price of food rises, the wage rate will rise (because the production of food is relatively labour intensive), and the rental rate will fall.

These conclusions, which are partly illustrated in Figure 5.6, show that the first interpretation of the Bertil Ohlin quote above must be wrong. Suppose, for the sake of argument, that the price of manufactures rises as a result of international trade. Then the wage rate will fall. If we realize that the price of food has not changed, it is clear that the wage rate has fallen relative to the price of *both* final goods. The reward to labour has therefore unambiguously fallen; that is, a labourer can now buy less of both goods than before the change in the price of manufactures. Similarly, from the conclusions we know that the rental rate of capital has risen, such that capital owners can now buy more units of food (the price of which has not changed). Moreover, as we will see in section 5.8, the rental rate of capital has also risen relative to manufactures, such that capital owners can also buy more units of manufactures. The reward to capital has therefore unambiguously risen relative to both final goods. These distribution aspects of the neoclassical production structure are interesting and receive considerable attention in applications. Whether or not the gains to the capital owners outweigh the losses to the labourers in our hypothetical example will be discussed in Chapter 7.

Figure 5.6 Impact of changing the price of manufactures, $p_f = 1$, $\alpha_m = 0.7$, $\alpha_f = 0.3$

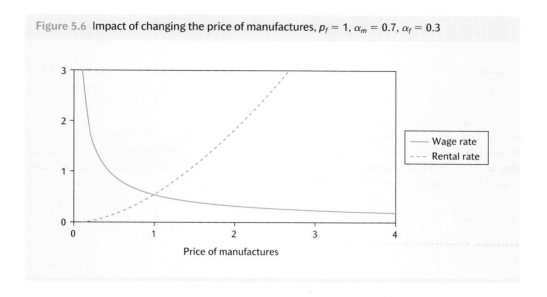

5.7 Graphical analysis

We analyse the impact of an increase in the price of manufactures for the factor rewards w and r using the Lerner diagram. We can do this because the Stolper–Samuelson proposition states that both final goods are produced, such that the price of both goods must be equal to the cost of production. Initially, the price of manufactures is equal to p_{m0}. As we know from the FPE proposition, the price p_{m0} for manufactures together with the price p_f for food, which does not change, determines the wage rate w_0 and the rental rate r_0 through the points of tangency at A and B in Figure 5.7.

If the price of manufactures rises from p_{m0} to p_{m1}, the unit value isoquant for manufactures shifts *in*ward, as indicated by the open straight arrows, because fewer goods are needed to generate one unit of value as a result of the price rise. Using the FPE proposition again, we can derive the new wage rate w_1 and rental rate r_1 through the points of tangency at A′ for the new unit value isoquant of manufactures and B′ for the old unit value isoquant of food. It is clear from Figure 5.7 that the rental rate of capital r has increased (because $1/r$ had decreased) and the wage rate has fallen (because $1/w$ has risen).

Figure 5.7 is drawn in accordance with the assumption that the production of manufactures is relatively capital intensive; the slope of the line OA, which is equal to the capital–labour ratio of manufactures, is steeper than the slope of the line OB, which is equal to the capital–labour ratio of food. Similarly, after the price change OA′ is steeper than OB′. Note that the capital–labour intensity falls for the production of both final goods, as indicated by the open curved arrows; there is a substitution away from the more expensive capital towards the cheaper labour in both sectors of production. We can conclude that, as a result of the increase in the price of the relatively capital-intensive manufactures, the rental rate of capital rises and the wage rate falls, in accordance with the Stolper–Samuelson proposition. We get similar conclusions in accordance with this proposition, as the reader may verify, for all other possible combinations (for example by changing the price of food).

Figure 5.7 Analysis of an increase in the price of manufactures

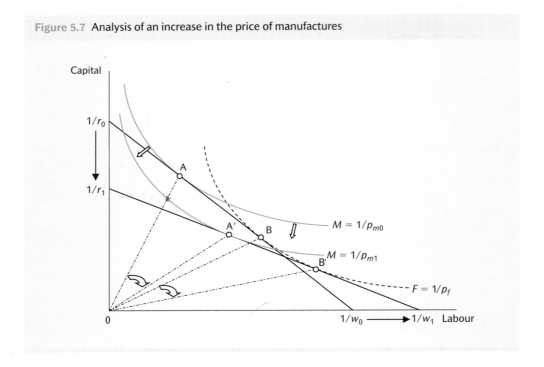

5.8 The magnification effect

The Stolper–Samuelson proposition says that if, for example, the price of manufactures rises, then the reward to the factor of production used relatively intensively in the production of manufactures, in our case capital, rises, and the reward to the other factor falls. Both the price of manufactures and the rental rate of capital rise, but there is no indication which rises faster. This issue is addressed by Ronald Jones (1965), who shows that the price of the factor of production rises *more* in relative terms than the price of the final good; that is, the rental rate rises faster than the price of manufactures. This can be seen in Figure 5.7 once we realize that the extent of the inward shift of the unit value isoquant is proportional to the price change of manufactures. The fact that the new unit value isoquant for manufactures cuts the line OA strictly above the line from $1/r_1$ to $1/w_0$ indicates that the relative change of the rental rate is larger than the relative change of the price of manufactures. Analytically, this can be verified by totally differentiating equation (5.4), see Technical Note 5.2.

Jones magnification effect

In a neoclassical framework with two final goods, M and F, and two factors of production, K and L, with factor rewards r and w, respectively, changes in the final goods prices are magnified in the factor rewards. If we denote relative changes by ~ and assume that the production of manufactures is relatively capital intensive, the following relationships hold:

Box 5.3 **An alternative (dual) approach**

The Stolper–Samuelson result can also be derived using the dual approach (see Technical Note 4.2), based on the fact that if food is produced in equilibrium the unit costs of production must be equal to its price, and similarly for manufactures. Recall:

(5.3) $$p_m = \gamma_m r^{\alpha_m} w^{1-\alpha_m}; \qquad p_f = \gamma_f r^{\alpha_f} w^{1-\alpha_f}$$

Based on equation (5.3), reproduced above, we can draw isocost *curves* in (r, w)-space, that is combinations of rental rate and wage rate giving rise to the same costs for the production of one good. This is done in Figure 5.8 for both food and manufactures. Initially, the price of both goods is 1, leading to equilibrium at point E_1, the only combination of rental rate and wage rate at which both goods can be produced.

Since the production of manufactures is relatively capital intensive ($\alpha_m > \alpha_f$), the isocost curve for the manufactures sector cuts that of the food sector from above in E_1.[4] Now suppose that the price of manufactures rises from 1 to 1.25. This shifts the combinations at which price is equal to unit costs *up* in Figure 5.8. The equilibrium moves to E_2, such that the rental rate rises and the wage rate falls, in accordance with the Stolper–Samuelson result.

Figure 5.8 Stolper–Samuelson in the dual approach, $\alpha_m = 0.6$, $\alpha_f = 0.3$

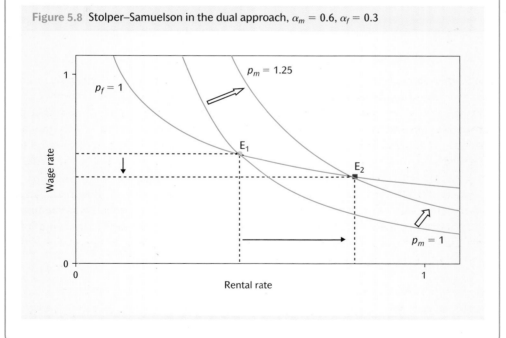

Box 5.4   Natural-resource-intensive manufacturing exporters

The ITC classifies 21 goods as 'natural-resource-intensive' products, incorporating leather, cork, wood, lime, precious stones, pig iron, copper, aluminum, lead, etc. For the 151 countries for which the ITC provides data, total exports of natural-resource-intensive manufactures in 1998 were equal to $248 bn, some 5 per cent of all exports. The left-hand side of Table 5.1 lists the top ten exporters of natural-resource-intensive manufactures in absolute terms. With a value of $19 bn (mostly gold), the USA is the world's largest natural-resource-intensive manufacturing exporter, closely followed by Germany and Belgium (mostly diamonds) with $17 bn each. With the exception of the Russian Federation, the other large exporters are all OECD countries.

Since natural-resource-intensive manufactures represent only 3 per cent of American and German exports, they do not make it to the right-hand side of Table 5.1, listing the top ten world exporters of natural-resource-intensive manufactures in relative terms. These are all located in Africa and Central Asia. The top three are the Democratic Republic of Congo (Zaire: diamonds and some cobalt), Gambia (diamonds), and the Central African Republic (diamonds). Note the small absolute size of these trade flows and the high dependence on the exports of natural-resource-intensive manufactures for all these countries, ranging from 77 per cent for Congo to 42 per cent for tenth-ranked Armenia. Figure 5.9 shows the relative dependence of countries on the exports of natural-resource-intensive manufactures. These are clearly distributed in a haphazard way around the globe, presumably largely depending on the availability of exportable natural resources.

Table 5.1 Top ten natural-resource-intensive manufacturing exporters, 1998

No.	Top 10 in absolute terms			Top 10 in absolute terms		
	Country	Exports		Country	Exports	
		Value	%		%	Value
1	USA	19	3	Congo, Dem. Rep.	77	0.2
2	Germany	17	3	Gambia	74	0.0
3	Belgium	17	10	Central African Rep.	71	0.1
4	Canada	15	8	Zambia	66	0.1
5	Russian Federation	13	26	Sierra Leone	65	0.0
6	Italy	12	6	Eritrea	60	0.0
7	UK	12	4	Bahrain	59	0.1
8	South Korea	11	9	Niger	58	0.1
9	France	9	3	Kyrgyzstan	49	0.2
10	Australia	9	18	Armenia	42	0.0

Source: WTO/UNCTAD International Trade Centre website http://www.intracen.org; value in bn US $. The % shares are relative to the country's total exports.

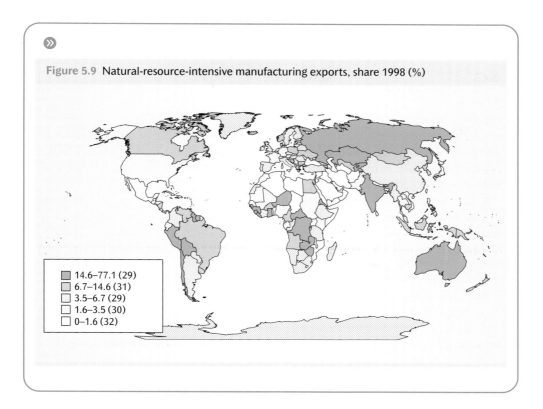

Figure 5.9 Natural-resource-intensive manufacturing exports, share 1998 (%)

14.6–77.1 (29)
6.7–14.6 (31)
3.5–6.7 (29)
1.6–3.5 (30)
0–1.6 (32)

(i)   if $\tilde{p}_m > \tilde{p}_f$, then $\tilde{r} > \tilde{p}_m > \tilde{p}_f > \tilde{w}$

(ii) if $\tilde{p}_m < \tilde{p}_f$, then $\tilde{r} < \tilde{p}_m < \tilde{p}_f < \tilde{w}$.

It is sometimes said that manufactures is a 'friend' of capital and an 'enemy' of labour, because a price increase for manufactures results in a higher factor price rise for capital and a relative factor price fall for labour. Similarly, food is a 'friend' of labour and an 'enemy' of capital.

5.9 Application: globalization, low wages, and unemployment

The neoclassical factor abundance model, and in particular the Stolper–Samuelson result, has been at the heart of a heated trade policy debate in the last decade of the twentieth century on the impact of 'globalization' for wages and unemployment in the high-income countries; see Lawrence and Slaughter (1993), Wood (1994), and Collins (1998). For a survey see Wood (1998). In Chapter 1 we pointed out that the term 'globalization' tends to be confusing, as it has different meanings for different people. In this particular debate it refers to increased imports and competition for the OECD countries from 'low-wage' countries in Asia, Latin America, and Africa.

Empirical observations

Two quite different empirical observations in Europe and America formed the basis for the debate, which distinguishes between two types of labour: high-skilled labour (so-called white-collar workers) and low-skilled labour (so-called blue-collar workers). The American problem is suggested in Figure 5.10. Initially, the wages for the white-collar and blue-collar workers are rising roughly equally fast. This changes in the 1980s (since 1984), when the wages of the white-collar workers start to rise relative to the blue-collar workers. In the same time period, as also illustrated in Figure 5.10, imports of goods and services from low-wage countries are rising, although the relationship with the development of the relative wages is not very clear. In the public debate the declining relative wage of blue-collar workers was widely attributed to imports and competition from low-wage countries.

The European problem is suggested for France in Figure 5.11. In the 1970s French unemployment starts to rise rapidly, from 600,000 in 1974 to more than 3 million in 1994. Simultaneously, imports from low-wage countries rise from about $600 million in 1974 to about $2 billion in 1997. As a result of this simultaneous occurrence, the high level of French unemployment, especially for low-skilled workers, was widely attributed in the public debate to imports and competition from low-wage countries.

Explaining the empirical observations

To see how the neoclassical model has been used to explain the above empirical observations, we have to interpret the model with some flexibility. First, rather than distinguishing the factor inputs capital and labour, as in Sections 5.2–5.8, we use the distinction

Figure 5.10 Smaller wage increases for blue-collar workers in the USA

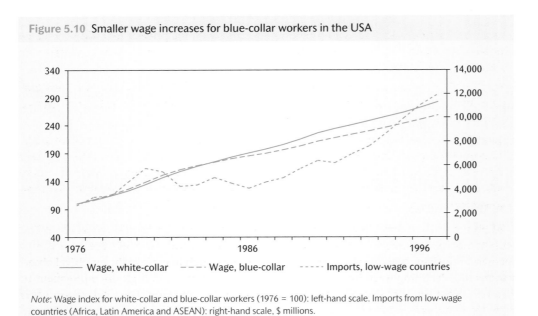

Note: Wage index for white-collar and blue-collar workers (1976 = 100): left-hand scale. Imports from low-wage countries (Africa, Latin America and ASEAN): right-hand scale, $ millions.

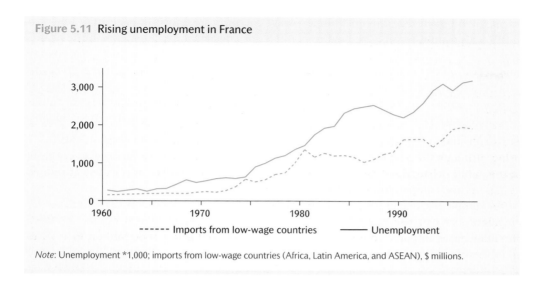

Figure 5.11 Rising unemployment in France

------ Imports from low-wage countries   —— Unemployment

Note: Unemployment *1,000; imports from low-wage countries (Africa, Latin America, and ASEAN), $ millions.

high-skilled (white-collar) workers and low-skilled (blue-collar) workers. Moreover, there are two types of goods, high-skill-intensive goods and low-skill-intensive goods. As a result of improved transportation possibilities and changes in trade policy for major countries (such as China; see also Chapter 17), imports from low-wage countries into the OECD countries increase. Clearly, low-wage countries are relatively abundant in low-skilled workers, while the OECD countries are relatively abundant in high-skilled workers. This leads to the following conclusions:

- as a result of increased trade with the low-wage countries, the price of high-skill-intensive goods rises relative to the price of low-skill-intensive goods in the OECD countries (see Chapter 7), such that;

- the OECD countries start to produce more high-skill-intensive goods and less low-skill-intensive goods. The fall in production of the low-skill-intensive sector is interpreted as a *de-industrialization* in the OECD countries;

- according to the Stolper–Samuelson result, the increase in the relative price of high-skill-intensive goods raises the wage rate for white-collar workers and reduces the wage rate for blue-collar workers. This is what we observe in the USA. In Europe, however, where labour markets are more rigid, the fall in demand for blue-collar workers does not lead to a lower wage rate for blue-collar workers, but to a higher unemployment level.

At present there is little doubt that the forces underlying the neoclassical model are in line with the observations and explanations elaborated upon above. Instead, the debate now focuses on the issue whether these forces are powerful enough to explain the empirical observations of a declining wage for low-skilled workers in America and high unemployment in Europe. To put these in a proper perspective, consider the following. The total import value from the low-wage countries of Figure 5.10 into the USA in 1999 was about $12 bn. Although this is a nice sum to have in your wallet, it is only 1 per cent of the USA's total imports of $1,116 bn in 1999. The latter, in turn, is only about 12 per cent of the USA's enormous GDP of $9,152 bn, such that imports from low-wage countries are only 0.13 per cent of American GDP.[5] This cannot possibly be held responsible for any actual developments in the relative wage rate of blue-collar workers in the USA. Instead, it is thought that technological changes and sector adjustments favouring white-collar workers relative to blue-collar workers are largely responsible for the empirical developments. Similarly, the rigid labour markets in Europe are largely responsible for the high unemployment levels in some European countries. The increased OECD trade levels with low-wage countries seem to have had limited influence in this respect.

5.10 Conclusions

There is a one-to-one connection between the prices of final goods and the rewards to the factors of production; that is, if we know the price of food and manufactures we can derive the wage rate and the rental rate, and vice versa. If trade between nations equalizes the prices of food and manufactures, it therefore also equalizes the wage rate and the rental rate (factor price equalization). If the production of food is labour intensive and the price of food rises, this raises the wage rate and reduces the rental rate. The opposite holds if the price of manufactures rises (Stolper–Samuelson). Moreover, the changes in the factor prices are larger in relative terms than the changes in the final goods prices (magnification effect). We apply these results and the neoclassical model to better understand the 'globalization' debate of the 1990s, where it was argued that increased international trade with low-wage countries led to higher unemployment in Europe and a deterioration in the relative wage rate of blue-collar workers in the USA. Countries with a high share of exports of natural-resource-intensive manufactures are distributed in a haphazard way around the globe, presumably largely depending on the availability of exportable natural resources.

TECHNICAL NOTES

Technical Note 5.1 Factor prices as a function of final goods prices

We start by recalling the relationships between costs and prices:

(5.A1) $$p_m = \gamma_m r^{\alpha_m} w^{1-\alpha_m} \ and \ p_f = \gamma_f r^{\alpha_f} w^{1-\alpha_f}$$

Now write the rental rate r as a function of the final goods price and the wage rate for both equations using the definition $\gamma_m \equiv \alpha_m^{-\alpha_m}(1 - \alpha_m)^{-(1-\alpha_m)}$ and similarly for γ_f

(5.A2) $$r = \alpha_m(1 - \alpha_m)^{\frac{1-\alpha_m}{\alpha_m}} p_m^{\frac{1}{\alpha_m}} w^{-\frac{(1-\alpha_m)}{\alpha_m}}$$ and $$r = \alpha_f(1 - \alpha_f)^{\frac{1-\alpha_f}{\alpha_f}} p_f^{\frac{1}{\alpha_f}} w^{-\frac{(1-\alpha_f)}{\alpha_f}}$$

Since we have two equations determining the rental rate r setting them equal to each other allows us to determine the wage rate w as a function of the final goods prices p_m and p_f, see below. A similar procedure gives the rental rate r as a function of the final goods prices p_m and p_f.

$$(5.A3) \qquad w = \gamma_w \, p_f^{\frac{\alpha_m}{\alpha_m - \alpha_f}} \, p_m^{\frac{-\alpha_f}{\alpha_m - \alpha_f}} \quad , \qquad \text{where} \qquad \gamma_w \equiv \left[\frac{\alpha_m (1 - \alpha_m)^{\frac{1 - \alpha_m}{\alpha_m}}}{\alpha_f (1 - \alpha_f)^{\frac{1 - \alpha_f}{\alpha_f}}} \right]^{\frac{-\alpha_m \alpha_f}{\alpha_m - \alpha_f}} , \text{and}$$

$$(5.A4) \qquad r = \gamma_r \, p_m^{\frac{1 - \alpha_f}{\alpha_m - \alpha_f}} \, p_f^{\frac{-(1 - \alpha_m)}{\alpha_m - \alpha_f}} \quad , \qquad \text{where} \qquad \gamma_r \equiv \left[\frac{(1 - \alpha_m)\alpha_m^{\frac{\alpha_m}{1 - \alpha_m}}}{(1 - \alpha_f)\alpha_f^{\frac{\alpha_f}{1 - \alpha_f}}} \right]^{\frac{(1 - \alpha_m)(1 - \alpha_f)}{\alpha_m - \alpha_f}}$$

Technical Note 5.2 Jones magnification

Quite frequently in economic analysis the relationships between different economic forces are rather complex when stated in levels, but surprisingly simple when stated in relative changes. This fact is, for example, fruitfully used in the Jones (1965) analysis of the neoclassical model in general. Suppose the relationship between the variables z and v is of the type $z = av^\eta$ for some constant a and parameter η. For any variable z, let $\tilde{z}$ denote the relative change of z, that is $\tilde{z} = \frac{dz}{z}$. Total differentiation of $z = av^\eta$ gives $dz = \eta a v^{\eta-1} dv$. Dividing the left-hand side by z and the right-hand side by av^η (which is the same as z) gives

$$(5.A5) \qquad dz = \eta \frac{av^{\eta-1} dv}{av^\eta}, \text{ or } \tilde{z} \equiv \frac{dz}{z} = \eta \frac{dv}{v} = \eta \tilde{v}$$

In relative changes, the relationship $z = av^\eta$ therefore reduces quite simply to $\tilde{z} = \eta \tilde{v}$ Applying this result to equation (5.4) gives

$$(5.A6) \qquad \tilde{w} = \frac{\alpha_m}{\alpha_m - \alpha_f} \tilde{p}_f - \frac{\alpha_f}{\alpha_m - \alpha_f} \tilde{p}_m; \quad \tilde{r} = \frac{1 - \alpha_f}{\alpha_m - \alpha_f} \tilde{p}_m - \frac{1 - \alpha_m}{\alpha_m - \alpha_j} \tilde{p}_f$$

Now apply these relationships for example if the price of manufactures rises ($\tilde{p}_m \geq 0$) and the price of food remains the same ($\tilde{p}_f = 0$):

$$(5.A7) \qquad \tilde{r} = \frac{1 - \alpha_f}{\alpha_m - \alpha_f} \tilde{p}_m > \tilde{p}_m > 0 = \tilde{p}_f > -\frac{\alpha_f}{\alpha_m - \alpha_f} \tilde{p}_m = \tilde{w}$$

Thus the rental rate of capital rises more than the price of manufactures, which uses capital intensively, which rises more than the price of food (= 0), which rises more than the wage rate (which actually falls relative to the price of both goods). This result, which holds more generally, is known as the *Jones magnification effect*.

Question 5.1

The Russians and the Germans both like vodka and beer. Suppose that these are the only two products they consume and produce. Moreover, suppose that as a result of regulations vodka and beer initially cannot be traded between Russia and Germany. Beer is produced with the help of machines largely controlled by computers. Beer breweries are therefore capital intensive. The production process of vodka, on the other hand, is more traditional and therefore quite labour intensive. Because of its large population and lack of capital goods, the wage–rental ratio (w/r) is initially lower in Russia than in Germany.

5.1A Explain whether the relative price ratio of vodka in terms of beer (p_{vodka}/p_{beer}) will be higher in Russia or in Germany in the initial situation (without trade).

Suppose that, after intensive international consultations, the regulations for vodka and beer are lifted, such that these goods can now be freely and costlessly exported and imported. In response, Russia starts to produce more vodka and less beer while Germany starts to produce more beer and less vodka. Russia exports vodka in exchange for beer.

5.1B Once the two countries can trade, will the price ratio of vodka in terms of beer (p_{vodka}/p_{beer}) be higher in Russia or in Germany?

5.1C What will happen to the wage–rental ratio in Russia and Germany? Why?

5.1D The trade liberalizations in Russia and Germany have not remained unchallenged. Explain which groups of people are likely to protest against the liberalizations.

5.1E What can the politicians in Russia and Germany do in response to these protests?

Question 5.2

We ask you to clarify the situation of question 5.1 graphically. Assume that the unit value isoquant for beer is equal for Russia and Germany (it is the numéraire).

5.2A Draw the unit value cost lines and unit value isoquants for both vodka and beer for both Russia and Germany in a situation of autarky.

5.2B What will happen to the price of beer and vodka in both Russia and Germany if both countries start to trade?

5.2C Draw the new unit value isoquants and unit value cost lines in the figure of question 5.2A in a situation in which Russia and Germany engage in international trade.

5.2D What happens to the wage rates and rental rates in both countries?

Question 5.3

The Stolper–Samuelson result shows that free trade may lead to a deterioration of labour conditions for low-skilled workers in developed countries. Based on this argument, opponents of free trade often call for trade protection in order to shield low-skilled workers from the forces of international competition. In their view, a lack of trade protection has already caused a relative deterioration of the wages of low-skilled workers in recent decades (see section 5.9). Proponents of free trade claim, however, that free trade is not the main cause of the relative deterioration of wages of low-skilled workers. They point to the fact that the share of low-skilled workers in total employment has decreased in recent years, as shown in the figure below for the case of the Netherlands. This, according to them, points to the fact that another factor is responsible for the relative deterioration of wages of low-skilled workers in developed countries.

5.3A Explain why a decrease in the share of low-skilled workers in total employment shows that free trade is not responsible for the relative decrease in wages of low-skilled workers in developed countries.

5.3B What other factor do you think is responsible for this decrease?

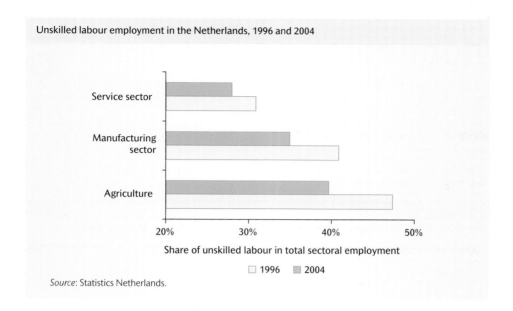

Unskilled labour employment in the Netherlands, 1996 and 2004

Share of unskilled labour in total sectoral employment

□ 1996   ■ 2004

Source: Statistics Netherlands.

 See the Online Resource Centre for a Study Guide containing more questions
www.oxfordtextbooks.co.uk/orc/vanmarrewijk/

NOTES

1 See Allen (1965: 185–6).

2 See Allen (1965: 201–2).

3 It seems clear to me that this is not what Ohlin meant.

4 Using Shephard's lemma, see Technical Note 4.2, it can also be shown that the slope of the isocost curve is equal to the capital-labour ratio.

5 Variations in the selection of 'low-wage' countries can increase this percentage somewhat, never to exceed 1 per cent of American GDP.

PRODUCTION VOLUME

6

Objectives/key terms

- Rybczynski result
- Contract curve
- Output magnification

- Edgeworth Box
- Sector-specific capital
- Labour migration in Israel

We analyse the connection between the production levels of final goods and the available factors of production (Rybczynski effect). We apply this result to discuss the effect of immigration from Russia into Israel in the 1990s.

6.1 Introduction

After the discussion of the relationship between the prices of final goods and the rewards to factors of production in Chapter 5, we now turn to the relationship between the level of production of final goods (food and manufactures) and the available production factors (labour and capital). The third main result in neoclassical trade theory, which investigates this relationship, is named after the Polish economist Rybczynski, who provided the first analysis in 1955 in a production equilibrium (such that all available inputs are employed). The Rybczynski result lies at the heart of the Heckscher–Ohlin proposition, relating the direction of international trade flows and factor abundance, as we will see in the next chapter.

The tool used to demonstrate the Rybczynski effect in this chapter is called the Edgeworth Box.[1] Named after Francis Edgeworth, it elegantly combines various aspects of an efficient production equilibrium in one graphical framework, and as such is a useful tool of analysis also in other areas of economics, such as microeconomics and game theory. The factor price equalization result, discussed in Chapter 5, will also prove to be useful in the sequel.

6.2 Rybczynski

The connection between the available factors of production, the output levels of final goods, and the relative intensity of the production processes for a given set of final goods prices with a neoclassical production structure can be stated as follows:

Rybczynski proposition

In a neoclassical framework with two final goods, two factors of production, and constant prices of the final goods, an increase in the supply of one of the factors of production results in an increase of the output of the final good that uses this factor of production relatively intensively and a reduction in the output of the other final good, provided both goods are produced in equilibrium.

Famous economists	Francis Edgeworth

Fig. 6.1
Francis Edgeworth
(1845–1926)

Born in Ireland, Edgeworth was educated in Dublin and Oxford, and worked initially in London and eventually at Oxford. After its foundation in 1891 he was editor of the *Economic Journal* for 35 years. He was the first to define the law of diminishing product in marginal, rather than average, terms. He was also the first to define a general utility function, depending on the quantity of all goods consumed and thus bringing substitutability and complementarity within reach. Moreover, he was the first to introduce indifference curves, the contract curve, and the core of an economy. Since all these concepts are still widely used in economics his influence is substantial.

Using the assumption made in Chapter 4 that the production of manufactures is relatively capital intensive, this leads to the following conclusions:

- If the available amount of labour rises, the output of food increases (because its production is labour intensive) and the output of manufactures falls.
- If the available amount of capital rises, the output of manufactures increases (because its production is capital intensive) and the output of food falls.

There are at least two points to note with respect to the Rybczynski proposition. First, the statement is made for *given* values of the final goods prices p_m and p_f. This is important to realize, since in a full general equilibrium framework we would expect an increase in the amount of a factor of production, which leads to output changes, also to affect the (relative) price level of final goods. The Rybczynski proposition can then be used as an indication for the direction of the price changes of final goods. We return to this issue below. Second, the reader of course realizes that, starting from some initial equilibrium with concomitant production levels, an increase in the available amount of a factor of production *in principle* allows the economy to produce more of *both* goods, by allocating some of the extra input to one sector and the rest to the other sector. The Rybczynski proposition states, however, that this is *not* what happens; the output of one final good rises and the output of the other final good *falls*. The remainder of this chapter will use the link between the two points above to show why this is true.

6.3 The Edgeworth Box

In Chapter 5 we introduced the Lerner diagram to analyse the links between the prices of final goods and the prices of factors of production in an economic equilibrium in which both goods are produced. This time we want to analyse the connections between the available factors of production and the quantity of output produced, for which a different tool is suitable: the Edgeworth Box.

The situation is illustrated in Figure 6.2. Panels (a) and (b) show different isoquants for manufactures and food. Obviously, an increase in the available amount of capital or labour leads to an increase in the output of the sector to which it is allocated. The question arises as to how to allocate the available capital and labour over the two final goods sectors, and how to show this problem clearly in one picture. Drawing the isoquants for the two goods from the same origin, as we did in Chapter 5 and as illustrated in panel 6.2(c), is not very useful as it does not help us to allocate the inputs efficiently.

The important step in constructing the Edgeworth Box is the realization that in an economic equilibrium all available inputs must be used either in one sector or in the other; that is both the capital market and the labour market must be in equilibrium.

(6.1) $$K_m + K_f = K; \; L_m + L_f = L$$

Once we know the total available amount of capital K, it suffices to know the capital input K_m to calculate the remaining use of capital $K_f = K-K_m$. Similarly, once we know how much labour L is available and the amount L_m used for manufactures, we also know how much is available for production of food, namely $L_f = L-L_m$. The Edgeworth Box uses this principle by transposing the origin for the isoquants of one of the final goods onto the total amount of capital K and labour L available for production, as explained in Box 6.1 and illustrated in Figure 6.4.

Figure 6.4 illustrates the Edgeworth Box for the Cobb–Douglas production functions of equation (4.1), assuming that $K = L = 5$. The origin for manufactures is in the south-west corner, as usual. The dashed lines in the figure give three different isoquants for manufactures, each having the well-known curvature. The origin for food is located exactly on top of the total available amount of capital and labour (in this case 5), and rotated 180 degrees. The

Figure 6.2 Isoquants for manufactures and food, $\alpha_m = 0.7$, $\alpha_f = 0.3$

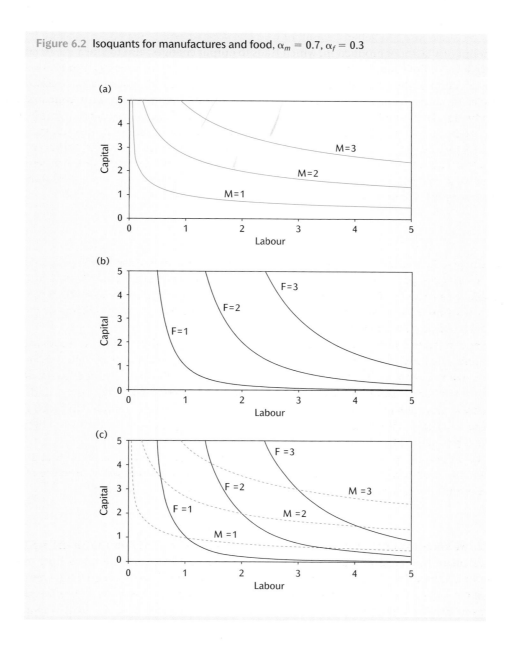

amount of labour used for food is thus measured from right to left, as indicated by the arrow in Figure 6.4, and the amount of capital used for food is measured from top to bottom, as indicated by the other arrow in Figure 6.4. There are also three isoquants for food drawn in the figure. At first sight, their curvature may seem strange and they may appear to be increasing in the wrong direction, but once it is realized that the axes for food are rotated (and the book is turned upside down), it is clear that these isoquants have the normal shape and production increases if more capital and labour is put into the production of food.

Box 6.1   Tool: Edgeworth Box

The Edgeworth Box is constructed using the field of isoquants for manufactures and food illustrated on the left-hand side of Figure 6.3 (using the isoquants $M = 2$ and $F = 1$ as an example). The origin and axes of one of the goods, in this case food, is turned around 180 degrees and placed exactly on the total amount of capital K and labour L available in the economy. The result is illustrated in Figure 6.4 and further discussed in the main text.

Figure 6.3 Construction of the Edgeworth Box

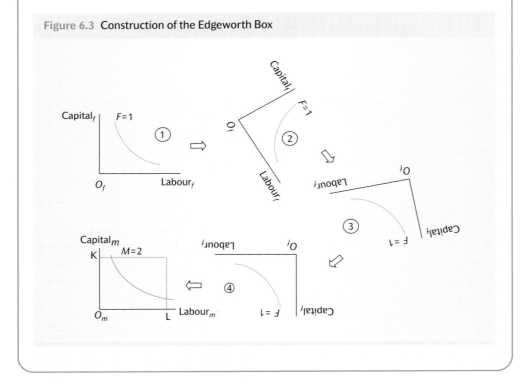

Figure 6.4 The Edgeworth Box, $K = L = 5$, $\alpha_m = 0.7$, $\alpha_f = 0.3$

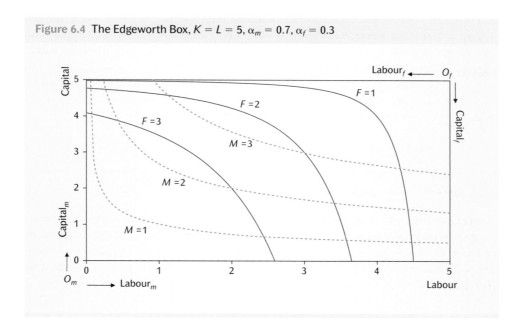

6.4 The contract curve

The Edgeworth Box constructed in section 6.3 depicts all possible distributions of capital and labour for the production of manufactures and food, and their concomitant output levels. We are interested, however, in finding *efficient* input combinations, that is, distributions of the allocation of capital and labour such that it is not possible to produce more of one good without reducing the production level of the other good. This concept is illustrated in Figure 6.5. Point A depicts an input combination of capital and labour that allows the economy to produce two units of manufactures. At the same time, this allocation of capital and labour allows the economy to produce three units of food.

Point A in Figure 6.5 is not an efficient input allocation. Keeping the output level of manufactures fixed, that is restricting ourselves to the isoquant $M = 2$, we could produce more units of food. This is illustrated in Figure 6.5 by point B, where the economy produces two units of manufactures and simultaneously produces 3.4 units of food. If, starting from point B, we want to produce more units of food, we have to reduce the production of manufactures. Similarly, if we want to increase the production of manufactures, we have to reduce the production of food. Point B is thus an efficient input allocation. Graphically, it is characterized by the tangency of the isoquants for the production of manufactures and food. Point C in Figure 6.5 is another efficient input allocation. The curve connecting all efficient input combinations in the Edgeworth Box is called the *contract curve*. It is analytically derived in Technical Note 6.1.

In Figure 6.5 the contract curve is drawn above the diagonal connecting the two origins O_m and O_f. This is because the production of manufactures is relatively capital intensive. The extent of the curvature of the contract curve depends on the difference in the degree of capital intensity. This is illustrated for four different cases in Figure 6.6. If the capital–labour intensity is the same for the two final goods, that is if $\alpha_m = \alpha_f$ (in which case the two production functions are identical), the contract curve coincides with the diagonal connecting the two origins. The larger the difference in capital intensity, the more pronounced the curvature of the contract curve and, as we will see in the next chapter, the more pronounced the curvature of the production possibility frontier.

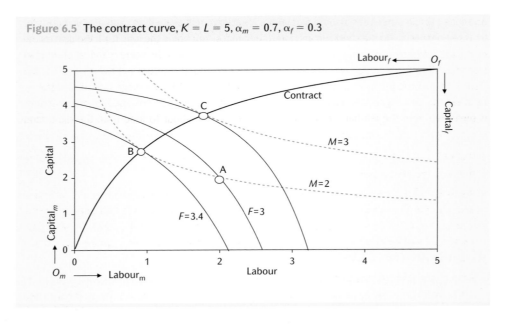

Figure 6.5 The contract curve, $K = L = 5$, $\alpha_m = 0.7$, $\alpha_f = 0.3$

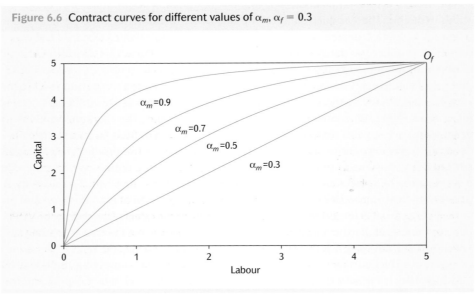

Figure 6.6 Contract curves for different values of α_m, $\alpha_f = 0.3$

Box 6.2   Sector-specific capital

A special case of the neoclassical model arises when we allow for sector-specific factors of production. Also adding a time dimension, a rapidly adjusting factor of production and a slowly adjusting factor of production, we can distinguish between the short term, the intermediate term, and the long term. Obviously, adjusting the allocation of factors of production after some exogenous change, say an increase in the price of manufactures, requires time to move capital and labour from one sector to the other. Let's assume that labour is easier to reallocate than capital, which we refer to as sector-specific (in the short run and intermediate run, but not in the long run). We discuss the reallocation of factors of production using Figure 6.7, which depicts the value marginal product of labour (VMPL) for manufactures (bottom left origin) and food (bottom right origin), *given* the distribution of capital. In equilibrium, a sector's VMPL is equal to the wage rate. The distance between the two origins is equal to the total labour force, the allocation of labour to manufactures is measured from the left-hand origin and the allocation of labour to food from the right-hand origin. In both sectors the marginal product of labour (and VMPL) declines as more labour is used.

- Point E_0 depicts the initial equilibrium, in which the wage rate for manufactures w_{m0} is equal to the wage rate in the food sector w_{f0}.

- Points E_0 and E_1 depict the short-term (Ethier) equilibrium, *given* the allocation of capital and labour to the two sectors, after an increase in the price of manufactures. Nothing changes for the food sector, such that the wage rate remains w_{f0}. The higher price of manufactures shifts the VMPL curve ($p_m \times MPL$) in that sector up, leading to a higher wage rate w_{m1} for manufactures than for food.

- Point E_2 depicts the medium-term (Neary, 1978) equilibrium. The higher short-term wage rate in the manufacturing sector leads to a reallocation of labour from food (where the wage rate starts to increase) to manufactures (where the wage rate starts to decline) until a new equilibrium (with equal wages) is reached. Obviously, this increases the production of manufactures and reduces the production of food.

- Point E_3 depicts the long-run (neoclassical) equilibrium. At the initial equilibrium point E_0 we implicitly assumed that the rental rate of capital was the same in the two sectors. However, after the price increase for manufactures (raising the value) and the reallocation of labour from food to manufactures (raising the marginal product of capital), the rental rate for manufactures is higher than for food. Over time, this will lead to a reallocation of capital from food to manufactures, leading to an upward shift of VMPL for manufactures and a downward shift of VMPL for food. These changes in turn require a reallocation of labour, which requires a reallocation of capital, etc. The process continues until both the wage rate and the rental rate are the same in the two sectors. Point E_3 depicts the ultimate long-run equilibrium. Note that in the intermediate term (point E_2) the wage rate is higher than at the initial equilibrium, while in the long run (point E_3) we have drawn the wage rate to be lower than at the initial equilibrium. When looking at Figure 6.7 this seems to be an arbitrary decision on our part, depending on the extent of the shifts in the VMPL curves as a result of the reallocation of capital. This is, however, not the case as the long-run equilibrium is determined by the neoclassical model and we know from the Stolper–Samuelson result that an increase in the price of manufactures (which is capital intensive) raises the reward to capital (rental rate) and reduces the reward to labour (wage rate). For the labourers, the impact of the price change is therefore beneficial in the short run and intermediate run, but detrimental in the long run.   »

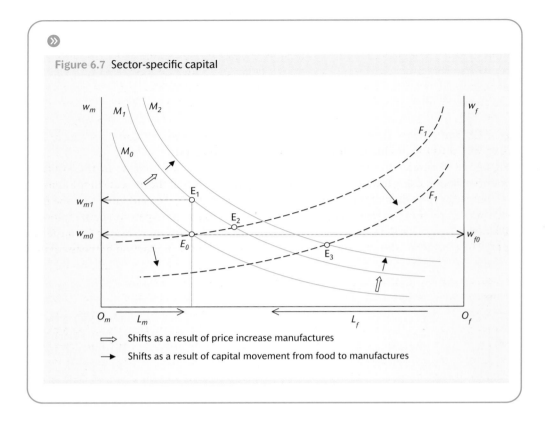

Figure 6.7 Sector-specific capital

⟹ Shifts as a result of price increase manufactures

→ Shifts as a result of capital movement from food to manufactures

6.5 The distribution of labour and capital

We are now in a position to derive the distribution of capital and labour in the economy and the concomitant production levels of manufactures and food. Moreover, we can illustrate this graphically in the Edgeworth Box and demonstrate the Rybczynski proposition stated in section 6.2. The basic reasoning involves three main steps.

- Given the prices of the final goods p_m and p_f, we can determine the wage rate w and the rental rate r using the factor price equalization proposition of Chapter 5, provided both goods are produced in equilibrium.

- If we know the wage rate w and the rental rate r, we can derive the optimal (cost-minimizing) capital–labour ratios for both goods K_m/L_m and K_f/L_f. It is important to realize that these capital–labour ratios do not change as long as the final goods prices p_m and p_f do not change.

- Using the full employment conditions, equation (6.1), and the capital–labour ratios K_m/L_m and K_f/L_f we can derive the equilibrium allocation of capital and labour in the two sectors, and thus the production levels in both sectors.

This is illustrated in Figure 6.8. Once the final goods prices, and thus the wage–rental ratio, are known we also know the capital–labour ratios K_m/L_m and K_f/L_f in the two sectors. Output of *manufactures* will expand or contract along the optimal capital–labour ratio line with slope K_m/L_m. The further away from the origin O_m, the larger the output of manufactures. Similarly, output of *food* will expand or contract along its optimal capital–labour ratio line with slope K_f/L_f. The further away from the origin O_f, the larger the output of food. Finally, given this information and the total available amount of capital K and initially available labour L_0 there is one, and only one, allocation in which all capital and labour is employed, namely at point E_0. This point is on the contract curve connecting the origin O_m with the origin O_f in Figure 6.8 (not drawn). Technical Note 6.2 analytically derives the allocation of capital and labour, and thus the production levels of manufactures and food.

Figure 6.8 illustrates the Rybczynski proposition if there is an increase in the available amount of labour, rising from L_0 to L_1. The first thing to note is that the increase in the amount of labour shifts the origin of the isoquants for food from O_f to O'_f. Second, note that the final goods prices, and thus the wage–rental ratio, have not changed, the expansion path for food is still along its optimal capital–labour ratio line with slope K_f/L_f, this time starting from the origin O'_f. Thus, as before, the allocation of capital and labour for the production of the two goods is determined by the intersection of the expansion paths, at point E_1. This point is on the contract curve connecting the origin O_m with the origin O'_f in Figure 6.8 (not drawn).

How can we conclude that the output level for food has increased and for manufactures has fallen, as required by the Rybczynski proposition? Quite simply, by measuring the distance of the allocation point from the origin. Since the line from O_m to E_0 is longer than from O_m to E_1, the output of manufactures has *decreased*. Similarly, since the line from O_f to E_0 is shorter than from O'_f to E_1, the output of food has *increased*. These conclusions are linked to the capital–labour intensity of the two sectors, as summarized in the Rybczynski proposition.

Figure 6.8 The Rybczynski proposition; expansion of labour

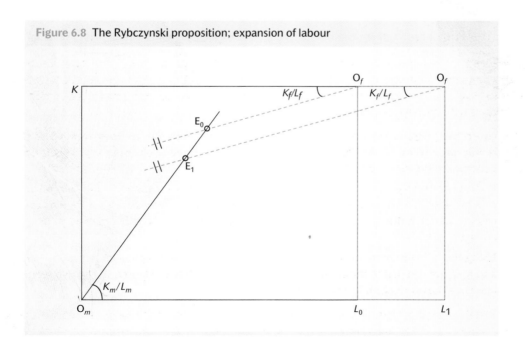

The proposition is also easy to understand if we let λ_m be the share of the labour force in manufactures, that is, $\lambda_m = L_m/L$, and take the ratio of equation (6.1) to get (see Technical Note 6.2):

$$(6.2) \qquad \underbrace{\frac{K}{L}}_{\substack{\text{economy}\\\text{cap. int}}} = \lambda_m \underbrace{\frac{K_m}{L_m}}_{\substack{\text{manuf}\\\text{cap. int}}} + (1 - \lambda_m) \underbrace{\frac{K_f}{L_f}}_{\substack{\text{Food}\\\text{cap. int}}}$$

Equation (6.2) shows clearly that the economy-wide capital–labour ratio K/L is equal to the weighted average of the sectoral capital–labour ratios K_m/L_m and K_f/L_f. Since the latter do not change for given final goods prices, a change in the available amount of one of the production factors, which changes the economy-wide capital–labour ratio K/L, can only be accommodated by changing the share of labour in manufactures λ_m. Obviously, an increase in the economy-wide capital–labour ratio must lead to an increase in the share of labour allocated to the capital-intensive sector, and vice versa for a decrease in the economy-wide capital–labour ratio. That, in a nutshell, is the Rybczynski proposition.

Finally, it is worthwhile to point out that Jones (1965) also shows that there is a magnification effect in output space, as was shown in Chapter 5 for the prices of factors of production. More specifically, given that the production of manufactures is capital intensive, the following relationships hold:

(i) if $\tilde{K} > \tilde{L}$, then $\tilde{M} > \tilde{K} > \tilde{L} > \tilde{F}$

(ii) if $\tilde{K} < \tilde{L}$, then $\tilde{M} < \tilde{K} < \tilde{L} < \tilde{F}$

 Box 6.3   Unskilled-labour-intensive manufacturing exporters

The ITC classifies 31 goods as 'unskilled-labour-intensive manufacturing' products, incorporating various textiles, clothing, glass, pottery, ships, furniture, footwear, and office supplies. For the 151 countries for which the ITC provides data, total exports of unskilled-labour-intensive manufactures in 1998 were equal to $610 bn, some 13 per cent of all exports. The left-hand side of Table 6.1 lists the top ten exporters of unskilled-labour-intensive manufactures in absolute terms. With a value of $78 bn, China is the world's largest unskilled-labour-intensive manufactures exporter, including ships, shoes, and wearing apparel, followed by Italy with a value of $48 bn (including furniture, footwear, and pullovers). The other large exporters are all OECD countries.

Despite the fact that unskilled-labour-intensive manufactures represent a sizeable 43 per cent of Chinese and 24 per cent of Italian exports, neither country makes it to the right-hand side of Table 6.1, listing the top ten world exporters of unskilled-labour-intensive manufactures in relative terms. The majority of these are located in Asia. The top three are Nepal (carpets), Bangladesh (clothing and textiles), and Pakistan (cotton and textiles). Note the small absolute size of these trade flows and the high dependence on the exports of unskilled-labour-intensive manufactures for all these countries, ranging from 89 per cent for Nepal to 62 per cent for tenth-ranked Albania. Figure 6.9 shows the relative dependence of countries on the exports of unskilled-labour-intensive manufactures. These are clearly concentrated in South-East Asia and Central Europe. ≫

Table 6.1 Top ten unskilled-labour-intensive manufacturing exporters, 1998

No.	Top 10 in absolute terms			Top 10 in relative terms		
	Country	Exports		Country	Exports	
		Value	%		%	Value
1	China	78	43	Nepal	89	0.3
2	Italy	48	24	Bangladesh	86	4.4
3	Germany	45	9	Pakistan	83	5.8
4	USA	45	7	Cambodia	82	0.6
5	France	30	10	Haiti	78	0.2
6	South Korea	28	22	Sri Lanka	69	2.8
7	Japan	25	7	Liberia	68	0.9
8	Taiwan	23	20	Laos	67	0.1
9	UK	22	8	Mauritius	64	1.1
10	Belgium	21	13	Albania	62	0.2

Source: WTO/UNCTAD International Trade Centre website http://www.intracen.org; value in bn US$. The % shares are relative to the country's total exports.

Figure 6.9 Unskilled-labour-intensive manufacturing exports, share 1998 (%)

24.1–88.6 (32)
10.1–24.1 (30)
4.9–10.1 (27)
1.3–4.9 (30)
0–1.3 (32)

6.6 Application: Russian immigrants in Israel

To see how the Rybczynski result can be useful for understanding empirical changes in production we discuss the study of Gandal, Hanson, and Slaughter (2000), who analyse the impact of Russian immigration into Israel in the 1990s. In late 1989 the Soviet Union relaxed emigration restrictions, which induced many Russian Jews to emigrate to Israel. From 1989 to 1996 some 670,000 Russian Jews arrived, increasing the Israeli population by 11 per cent and the labour force by 14 per cent. A notable aspect of this large influx of labour into Israel was the change in skills composition of the labour force. Gandal et al. distinguish between four different types of labour: LTH (less than high-school), HG (high-school graduate), SC (some college), and CG (college graduate). As illustrated in Figure 6.10, compared to the rest of the Israeli population the Russian immigrants had high education levels in the period 1989–96, with much higher shares in the SC and CG categories.

Despite the large influx of workers, particularly of workers with a high education level, there was no noticeable evidence of depressed wages, while the relative wage of high-skilled workers slightly increased (rather than decreased, as might be expected from the high-skill composition of arriving Russians). Gandal et al. point to two forces for explaining these observations. First, since Israel is a small open economy with limited influence on the world price of final goods, the Rybczynski result can be used to understand the constant wage rate, provided Israel increases the (relative) production in sectors requiring high education levels in the production process. Second, if changes in technology in general favour the demand for high education levels, this may explain the (small) increase in skill premium in the wage rate. The authors find empirical support for these two explanations in a framework with five factors of production (capital and the four types of labour) and nineteen sectors of production. Table 6.2 reports the estimated Rybczynski contribution to labour absorption in Israel, that is the extent to which a change in a factor's supply can be explained from a change in the composition of output, which ranges from about half for the LTH category to almost completely for the CG category.

Table 6.2 Rybczynski contribution to labour absorption in Israel

Labour type	Change in net factor supply	Rybczynski contribution
Less than high school	3.25	7.90
High-school graduate	3.71	5.32
Some college	1.78	3.62
College graduate	2.86	2.93

Note: Change in net factor supply is the change in the factor's share of Israeli employment, corrected for global technology changes.

Source: Gandal, Hanson, and Slaughter (2000).

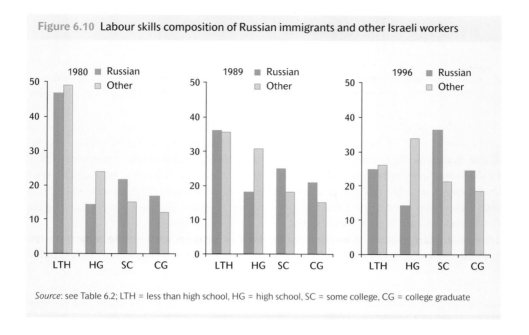

Figure 6.10 Labour skills composition of Russian immigrants and other Israeli workers

Source: see Table 6.2; LTH = less than high school, HG = high school, SC = some college, CG = college graduate

---

 Box 6.4   **More countries, more goods, and more factors II**

The Rybczynski result discussed in this chapter holds in a weaker sense in a more general setting allowing for more countries, more goods, and more factors of production. An increase in the available amount of a factor of production 'on average' increases the production of goods using this factor intensively in the production process. The magnification effect holds generally; that is, an increase in a production factor increases the production level of *some* good ('friend') and reduces the production level of some other good ('enemy').

6.7 Conclusions

We analyse the connection between the production levels of final goods and the available factors of production using the Edgeworth Box. The set of all efficient allocation combinations, leading to maximum output of one good given the output level of the other good, is called the contract curve. The curvature of the contract curve is determined by the difference in capital intensity in the production processes of final goods. For given prices of the final goods, an increase in the available amount of capital leads to an increase in the production of (capital-intensive) manufactures and a reduction in the production of food. The opposite holds for an increase in the available amount of labour (Rybczynski effect). We apply this result to discuss the effect of immigration from Russia into Israel in the 1990s. In accordance with the Rybczynski effect, the influx of relatively highly educated Russian workers led to a change in the output composition of final goods production in the direction of high-skill-intensive sectors. Countries with a high share of exports in unskilled-labour-intensive manufactures are concentrated in South-East Asia and Central Europe.

TECHNICAL NOTES

Technical Note 6.1 Determination of the contract curve

To determine the contract curve in the Edgeworth Box it is clear that the slopes of the isoquants must be the same. For the Cobb–Douglas production functions of equation (4.1) these are (see Technical Note 4.3)

$$(6.A1) \qquad \frac{dK_m}{dL_m} = -\frac{1 - \alpha_m}{\alpha_m}\frac{K_m}{L_m} \; ; \quad \frac{dK_f}{dL_f} = -\frac{1 - \alpha_f}{\alpha_f}\frac{K_f}{L_f}$$

Setting these two slopes equal to each other and realizing that $K_f = K - K_m$ and $L_f = L - L_m$ gives the following relationship between K_m and L_m

$$(6.A2) \qquad K_m = \frac{\alpha_m(1 - \alpha_f)KL_m}{\alpha_f(1 - \alpha_m)L + (\alpha_m - \alpha_f)L_m}$$

This is the contract curve. Note that if the capital intensity is the same in the two final goods sectors; that is, if $\alpha_m = \alpha_f$, the contract curve reduces to a straight line equal to the diagonal of the Edgeworth Box.

Technical Note 6.2 The distribution of capital and labour

Given the total available factors of production capital K and labour L, and the prices of the final goods, and therefore of the wage rate and the rental rate, we can determine the share of labourers working in each sector as follows. Take the ratio of equation (6.1), and let λ_m be the share of the labour force in manufactures, that is $\lambda_m = L_m/L$

$$(6.A3) \qquad \frac{K}{L} = \frac{K_m}{L} + \frac{K_f}{L} = \frac{L_m}{L}\frac{K_m}{L_m} + \frac{L_f}{L}\frac{K_f}{L_f} = \lambda_m\frac{K_m}{L_m} + (1 - \lambda_m)\frac{K_f}{L_f}$$

Now substituting the optimal capital–labour ratios in both sectors as a function of the wage–rental ratio gives

$$(6.A4) \qquad \frac{K}{L} = \lambda_m\frac{\alpha_m}{1 - \alpha_m}\frac{w}{r} + (1 - \lambda_m)\frac{\alpha_f}{1 - \alpha_f}\frac{w}{r}$$

We use this equation to determine the share of labourers in manufactures λ_m:

$$(6.A5) \qquad \lambda_m = \frac{(1 - \alpha_m)(1 - \alpha_f)}{\alpha_m - \alpha_f}\frac{(K/L)}{(w/r)} - \frac{\alpha_f(1 - \alpha_m)}{\alpha_m - \alpha_f}$$

This completely determines the distribution of capital and labour over the two final goods sectors. Finally, this distribution of capital and labour can be used to determine the production level for manufactures:

$$(6.A6) \qquad M = K_m^{\alpha_m}L_m^{1-\alpha_m} = \left(\frac{K_m}{L_m}\right)^{\alpha_m} L_m = \left(\frac{\alpha_m}{1 - \alpha_m}\frac{w}{r}\right)^{\alpha_m}\lambda_m L$$

And similarly for food.

QUESTIONS

Question 6.1

Armenia is a small country (changes in endowments do not result in price changes for factor inputs or final goods prices). Suppose that it produces two goods, manufactures and food. It produces these goods in a Heckscher–Ohlin world using high-skilled labour (*H*) and low-skilled labor (*L*). Manufactures make relatively intensive use of *H* and food is relatively *L* intensive. About 3 million Armenians are high skilled, while 1 million people are low skilled.

6.1A Draw the situation described above in an Edgeworth Box. Put the origin of food in the south-west corner and the origin of manufactures in the north-east corner. Measure high-skilled labour (*H*) on the horizontal axis and low-skilled labour (*L*) on the vertical axis. Draw the contract curve, one efficient point of production, and the isoquants of both goods through the chosen efficient production point.

6.1B What indicates in the Edgeworth Box the level of output of a good?

6.1C How can you determine the production levels of rice and clothes in full employment equilibrium?

After the fall of the Soviet Union and the declaration of Armenian independence, the socio-economic situation in Armenia deteriorates rapidly. As a consequence, people are voting with their feet. Estimates show that 2 million people have emigrated from Armenia since independence. It is the best (high-skilled) people who are going.

6.1D Show the effects of the Armenian emigration in the Edgeworth Box you have drawn in 6.1A.

Gross domestic product by sector (% of total at current prices)

	1990	1991	1992	1993	1994
Agriculture	16	24	29	49	44
Industry	30	35	30	22	29
Construction	18	1	6	4	7
Transport & communication	7	5	7	6	4
Services	47	37	34	24	23

Source: Economist Intelligence Unit.

6.1E What are the effects on the production of manufactures and food? What do we call this effect in theory?

The table above shows the contribution to Armenian GDP per sector.

6.1F Does the table provide support for the effect you have identified in question 6.1E? Explain your answer.

Question 6.2

Bangladesh is a developing country which ranks second in the top ten of unskilled-labour-intensive manufacturing exporters (see Table 6.1). These exports consist mainly of clothing goods. The Multi-Fibre Agreement, which imposed all kinds of restrictions on world trade in textiles, was officially ended at the start of 2005. We will analyse its impact with the help of the two graphs on the next page. The top graph shows the unit value isoquants for both goods. The bottom graph is an Edgeworth Box.

6.2A Draw the optimal production point in the Edgeworth Box.

6.2B What happens if the price of clothing increases as a result of the end of the Multi-Fibre Agreement in 2005? Draw the new situation in both graphs.

In isolation, the MFA agreement would affect Bangladesh as you have analysed in question 6.2B. Yet the labour force in Bangladesh has also expanded rapidly.

6.2C Expand the Edgeworth Box and analyse the combined effect of a labour force increase with a price increase for clothing. How does this affect the production level of rice?

Question 6.3

Section 6.6 of the book describes an empirical study of the effects of the influx of Russian immigrants into Israel, which changed the composition of the Israeli labour force. It offers an opportunity to investigate the Rybczynski proposition.

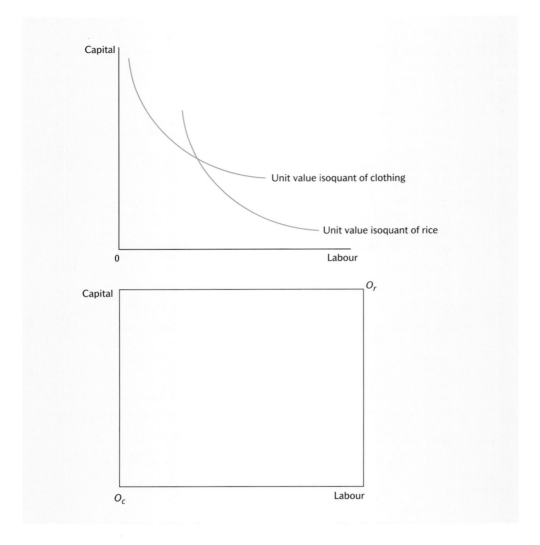

When confronting theory with empirical data, you have to be careful and correct for factors that are not explicitly modelled or assumed constant in theory.

6.3A   Which factors, not explicitly modelled or assumed constant in Chapter 6, played a role in this particular study?

6.3B   Do the assumptions of the model in Chapter 6 strengthen or weaken the theory?

 See the Online Resource Centre for a Study Guide containing more questions
www.oxfordtextbooks.co.uk/orc/vanmarrewijk/

NOTE

1 It is sometimes also called the Edgeworth–Bowley Box.

FACTOR ABUNDANCE

(7)

Objectives/key terms

- Heckscher–Ohlin result
- Rybczynski lines
- Marginal rate of transformation (MRT)
- Autarky
- General equilibrium

- Homothetic demand
- Marginal rate of substitution (MRS)
- Leontief paradox
- International trade
- Missing trade

We analyse the connection between the direction of international trade flows and the factor intensity of the production process. Countries tend to export goods making intensive use of the abundant factors of production (Heckscher–Ohlin result). We show the implications of the neoclassical model for a range of countries and discuss some empirical tests of the model.

7.1 Introduction

The fourth and last main result of the neoclassical trade model to be analysed in this book is the Heckscher–Ohlin proposition. Although the principle of the result is not difficult to comprehend, a complete understanding does require knowledge of all aspects of the neoclassical trade model, that is the production structure, the demand structure, and the equilibrium relationships between them. In short, it requires an understanding of the general equilibrium structure of the model. So far, we have not used any assumptions about the demand structure; the factor price equalization proposition, the Stolper–Samuelson proposition, and the Rybczynski proposition are all only dependent on the supply structure of the economy.

The Heckscher–Ohlin proposition relates the abundance of the factors of production in a region or country and the international trade flows of goods and services. As Ohlin (1933, ch. I) remarked in his *Interregional and International Trade*:[1]

> Australia has more agricultural land, but less labour, capital, and mines than Great Britain; consequently Australia is better adapted to the production of goods which require great quantities of agricultural land, whereas Great Britain has an advantage in the production of goods requiring considerable quantities of other factors. If both countries produced their own total consumption, agricultural products would be very cheap in Australia, but manufactured articles relatively dear, whereas the reverse would be the case in Great Britain, where owing to the scanty supply of land each acre would have to be intensely cultivated with much labour and capital to provide the necessary amount of food. The utmost economy would have to be exercised with land, and owing to the tendency to diminishing returns the yields of wheat, etc., from the last units of capital and labour would be very small. In Australia, on the other hand, the abundance of land would lead to an extensive method of cultivation, very little labour and capital being expended on each acre; hence the yield from each unit of capital and labour would be great.

Ohlin therefore argues that in autarky, that is if there are no international trade flows, the price of agricultural goods in Australia will be low compared to Great Britain because the

Famous economists	Bertil Ohlin

Fig. 7.1
Bertil Ohlin
(1899–1979)

Bertil Ohlin was a Swedish economist who studied at Lund and Stockholm, worked mostly at the Stockholm School of Economics, and was politically active as a member of parliament for 33 years and as the leader of the Swedish liberal party. He became well known after his dispute with John Maynard Keynes on the transfer problem, considering the German reparations payments after the First World War. (It was Ohlin, not Keynes, who was right on most issues; see Brakman and van Marrewijk, 1998.) His most important work, however, was on the theory of factor abundance, with the publication of *Interregional and International Trade* in 1933, inspired by the work of his old teacher Eli Heckscher. It won him the Nobel prize in economics in 1977.

production of agricultural goods is relatively land intensive (compared to the production of manufactured goods) and Australia has an abundant supply of agricultural land. This connection results from the fact that the abundant supply of agricultural land leads to a low price for the factor services of land, which are a substantial part of the costs of production of agricultural goods, thus leading to low prices for those goods. Moreover, since the price of agricultural goods is lower in Australia than in Great Britain in autarky, Australia will export those goods if international trade is allowed.

The final result, which can be summarized as 'Australia will export those goods which intensively use the relatively abundant factor of production', is simple to comprehend and intuitively appealing. As is clear from the detailed analysis in the preceding chapters, and the care to be taken in the sequel of this chapter, given the simplicity of the Heckscher–Ohlin proposition it is remarkable how much structure we have to impose on the economy before we can actually conclude that this connection between factor abundance, the capital–labour intensity in the production of final goods, and the direction of international trade flows exists.

7.2 Heckscher–Ohlin

We can state the main result of neoclassical trade theory, linking the available factors of production, the relative intensity of the production processes, and the direction of international trade flows as follows.

Heckscher–Ohlin proposition

In a neoclassical framework with two final goods, two factors of production, and two countries which have identical homothetic tastes, a country will export the good which intensively uses the relatively abundant factor of production.

Using the assumption made in Chapter 4 that the production of manufactures is capital intensive thus leads to the following conclusions.

- If a country is relatively capital abundant, it will export manufactures (because its production is capital intensive).
- If a country is relatively labour abundant, it will export food (because its production is labour intensive).

In the demonstration of the Heckscher–Ohlin result below we will use the previous results, in particular the factor price equalization proposition and the Rybczynski proposition. Evidently, the direction of international trade flows in the neoclassical trade model stems from the supply structure of the economy. Indeed, one can argue that the supply side of the economy over the centuries has received much more attention than the demand side of the economy, at least within international economics. None the less, as is evident from the Ohlin quote in Section 4.1, we must take the influence of the demand structure into consideration in a general equilibrium setting before we can draw any definite conclusions about the direction of international trade flows. Essentially, this problem is 'solved' by eliminating all demand bias, as explained in the next section.

7.3 Demand

Exports of goods and services from one country to another can be viewed as excess supply flows. After all, such exports can be defined as the difference between the quantity of goods produced and consumed within a nation.

(7.1)   exports = production − consumption

International trade flows therefore represent the outcome of the interplay between the supply structure and the demand structure of the economy. The supply structure determines the production level of goods and services in the economy. For the neoclassical trade model, this has been discussed at length in the previous three chapters. The demand structure of the economy determines the consumption level of goods and services in the economy. It will be discussed in this section.

As is immediately evident from equation (7.1), a relationship between the supply structure of an economy and international trade flows can only be derived if we somehow eliminate differences in demand structure between nations. The neoclassical trade model therefore makes the following:

Assumption: all consumers in all countries have identical homothetic preferences.

Rather than discussing what identical homothetic preferences are exactly, we will define a utility function for all consumers in accordance with the assumption above and briefly discuss the main implications of this function, see also Box 7.1. In economics we assume that consumers, that is you, I, and everyone else, try to maximize the utility derived from their income earned (through work or ownership of capital goods) by a suitable choice of consumption of goods and services, in accordance with our preferences. Since we have to pay for our consumption goods and we have a limited income level, this problem can be stated mathematically as a maximization problem. Let C_m be the consumption level of manufactures, let C_f be the consumption level of food, and let I be the income level. Then the consumer's problem involves maximization of the utility function U below (with parameter δ_m), subject to the budget constraint $I = p_m C_m + p_f C_f$:

(7.2) $$U = C_m^{\delta_m} C_f^{1-\delta_m}; \ \ 0 \leq \delta_m \leq 1$$

The problem is illustrated in Figure 7.2 for $p_m = p_f = 1$ and $\delta_m = 0.5$. The line 'Income = 2' depicts the budget constraint for the consumer if her income level is 2. Any consumption combination on this line or below (to the south-west) is feasible from a budget point of view. The consumer chooses the consumption combination giving maximal utility. Graphically, this occurs at the point of tangency of the budget constraint with an iso-utility curve, that is a curve depicting all consumption combinations giving rise to the same level of utility. In Figure 7.2 this occurs at point A, where the budget constraint is tangent to the U_1 iso-utility curve.

Remark 1: The marginal rate of substitution (MRS) is the absolute value of the slope of an iso-utility curve; that is, MRS $= |dC_f/dC_m| = [\partial U/\partial C_m)/(\partial U/\partial C_f)$. *It is a measure of the ease with which the consumer can substitute one good for another on the margin and still achieve the same utility level. If consumers take the final goods prices as given, utility maximization implies:* MRS $= P_m/P_f$

Figure 7.2 Consumer optimization problem, $p_m = p_f = 1, \delta_m = 0.5$

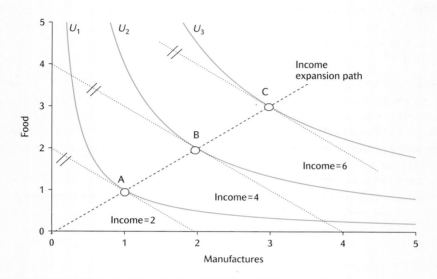

Box 7.1   Homothetic demand

The utility function specified in equation (7.2) is an example of a homothetic utility function. As illustrated in Figure 7.2, it gives rise to iso-utility curves that are radial blow-ups of one another, just like the isoquants are radial blow-ups if the production function exhibits constant returns to scale. So why do we distinguish between these two different concepts? Because it is customary to think of preferences as an ordinal concept. It is meaningful to speak of a doubling in output, as is the case if we double all inputs in a constant returns to scale production process, but not of a doubling of utility if we double the consumption levels. We cannot say we are 'twice as happy' if we consume twice as many of all goods, just that we prefer this consumption level over some other consumption combination.

The concept of the utility function is therefore a tool for explaining the optimal choices of consumers; it is a translation of the consumer's preference structure. The numbers attached to the iso-utility curves depicted in Figure 7.3 are arbitrary, only their magnitude is important. More specifically, it must be true that $U_1 < U_2 < U_3$, which holds for the numbers 1, 2, and 3, but also for the numbers 1, 6, and 400. If a utility function is homothetic, the iso-utility curves are radial blow-ups, as in Figure 7.3, and the two conclusions emphasized in the main text (C_m/C_f is a function of p_m/p_f and the distribution of income is not important) still hold.   »

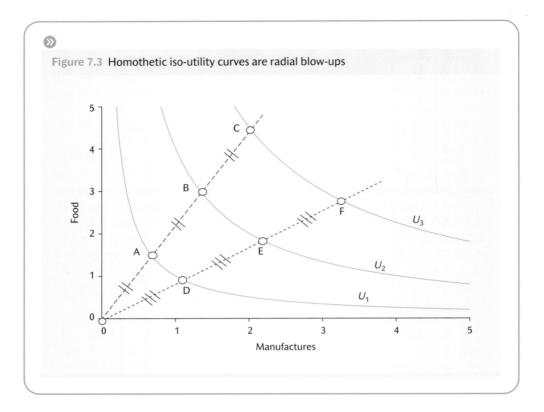

Figure 7.3 Homothetic iso-utility curves are radial blow-ups

Since the utility function (7.2) is of the Cobb–Douglas type, like the production functions (4.1), the reader of course realizes that the consumer's maximization problem is quite similar to the producer's problem of cost minimization. In the former problem, the budget constraint is given and the solution is a tangent iso-utility curve. In the latter problem the isoquant is given and the solution is a tangent isocost line. In Box 4.3 of Chapter 4, it was shown that the parameter α_m in the production function for manufactures represents the share of total cost in the manufacturing sector paid to the capital owners. Similarly, the parameter δ_m in the utility function (7.2) represents the share of income spent on manufactures as the solution to the maximization problem ($p_m C_m = \delta_m I$; see Technical Note 7.1).

Figure 7.2 also illustrates what happens if the consumer's income level increases from 2 to 4 or 6. Since the iso-utility curves are radial blow-ups of one another, any increase in the income level, for given final goods prices, leads to an equiproportional increase in the consumption of all goods, as illustrated by points B and C in Figure 7.2. This demand structure allows us to draw two main conclusions:

- The economy's optimal consumption ratio C_m/C_f is only a function of the final goods price ratio p_m/p_f. Obviously, an increase in p_m/p_f leads to a decrease in C_m/C_f. This is similar to the observation that under constant returns to scale the capital–labour ratios K_m/L_m and K_f/L_f only depend on the wage–rental ratio w/r.

- The economy's consumption level depends only on the final goods prices, and the aggregate income level I. The distribution of income over the different consumers in the economy is not relevant for determining the aggregate consumption levels.

The second observation is also clear from Figure 7.2. Suppose the aggregate income level is 8. If this income level is equally divided over two consumers, they both consume at point B. The aggregate consumption level is then 2B. If one of the consumers receives 6 income and the other consumer receives 2 income, then the first consumer consumes at point C and the second at point A. Aggregate income is then A + C = 2B. And similarly for any other distribution of income.

7.4 The production possibility frontier

We will illustrate and discuss the Heckscher–Ohlin proposition in the sequel using the production possibility frontier (PPF) introduced in Chapter 3. To do that we will first have to discuss some of the properties of the PPF in the neoclassical production structure. Recall that the frontier depicts all efficient production combinations in final goods space, that is the maximum output of food for any given feasible production level of manufactures. Similarly, in Chapter 6 we showed that the contract curve in the Edgeworth Box depicts all efficient input combinations. Since the contract curve was derived explicitly, see Technical Note 6.1, it is not hard to calculate all efficient output combinations, which is the PPF.[2] The result is depicted in Figure 7.4.

As the reader can see, in contrast to the Ricardian PPF of Chapter 3, which is a straight line, the PPF in the neoclassical trade model is curved. This arises from the difference in the degree of capital intensity between the two final goods sectors, which makes one sector more responsive to changes in capital input and the other sector more responsive to changes in labour input. As with the contract curve in the Edgeworth Box (illustrated in Figure 6.6), the

Figure 7.4 Production possibility frontier; $K = L = 5$; $\alpha_m = 0.8$; $\alpha_f = 0.1$

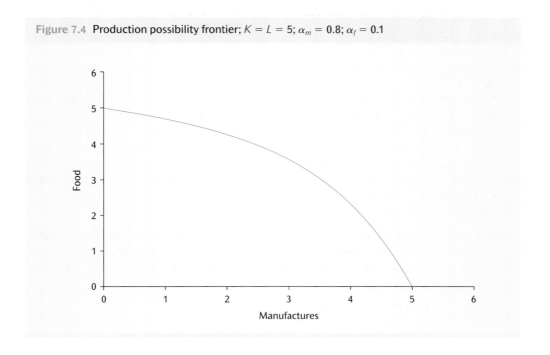

larger the difference in capital intensity, the more pronounced the curvature of the PPF, as illustrated in Figure 7.5.

Remark 2: The marginal rate of transformation (MRT) is the absolute value of the slope of the production possibility frontier |dF/dM|. It is a measure of the ease with which the producers can technically substitute the production of one good for another on the margin. If factor markets are perfectly competitive, and MC denotes marginal costs of production, the following relationship holds: $MRT = MC_m/MC_f$

The PPF of course also changes if the amount of the available inputs changes. Since the production of manufactures is capital intensive, an increase in the capital stock K, for a fixed value of the labour stock L, has a larger impact on the maximum production of manufactures than on the maximum production of food. Indeed, if we let M_{max} and F_{max} be the maximum attainable levels of output for manufactures and food, and use relative changes (see Technical Note 5.2) for the production functions, we get

(7.3) $$\tilde{M}_{max} = \alpha_m \tilde{K} + (1 - \alpha_m)\tilde{L}; \quad \tilde{F}_{max} = \alpha_f \tilde{K} + (1 - \alpha_f)\tilde{L}$$

Since $\alpha_m > \alpha_f$, the maximum production level for manufactures increases more rapidly than for food if the capital stock increases. Similarly, since $1 - \alpha_f > 1 - \alpha_m$, the maximum production level for food increases more rapidly than for manufactures if the labour stock increases. The fact that an increase in the amount of an available factor of production leads to a biased shift of the PPF is illustrated for increases in the capital stock in Figure 7.6.

Figure 7.6 also illustrates another aspect of changes in output that will be useful in the discussion below. Recall that the Rybczynski proposition relates changes in the available amount of a factor of production and changes in output for given final goods prices. We can illustrate

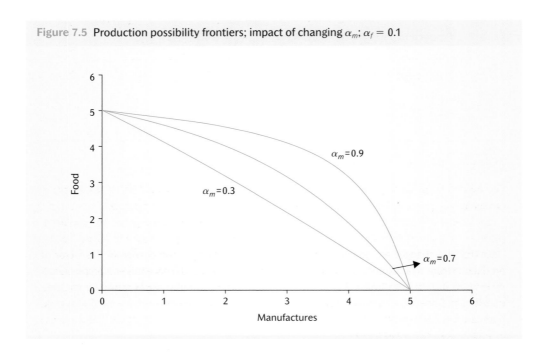

Figure 7.5 Production possibility frontiers; impact of changing α_m; $\alpha_f = 0.1$

the proposition in final goods space, for example by increasing the capital stock, as in Figure 7.6. If the capital stock is 2, the economy produces at point A for some ratio of final goods prices. For the same final goods prices, but a higher capital stock of 5, the economy produces at point B. The output of the capital-intensive manufactures has increased, that of the labour-intensive food has decreased. Similarly, if the capital stock is 8 for that final goods price ratio, the economy produces at point C. Since the changes in the Rybczynski proposition are equiproportional, the points A, B, and C are on a straight line. It is called the capital Rybczynski line and traces out all changes in output for changes in the capital stock from 2 to 8, for given final goods prices and labour stock (equal to 5 in Figure 7.6). If we analyse changes in the labour stock, we can derive a similar labour Rybczynski line.

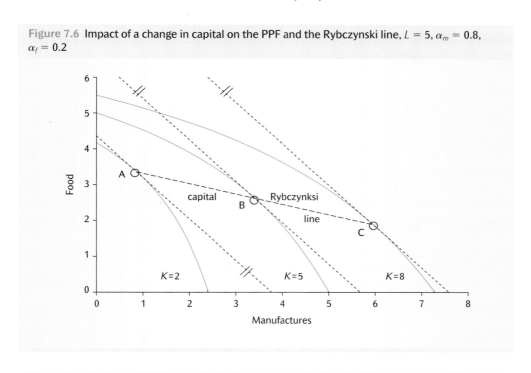

Figure 7.6 Impact of a change in capital on the PPF and the Rybczynski line, $L = 5$, $\alpha_m = 0.8$, $\alpha_f = 0.2$

 Box 7.2   Tool: Rybczynski lines

The Rybczynski proposition states that an increase in the available amount of one of the factors of production for given final goods prices leads to an increase in the output of the good that uses this factor intensively, and a fall in the output of the other good, provided both goods are produced. Moreover, the proof of the Rybczynski proposition in Chapter 6, using the Edgeworth Box, made it clear that the changes are equiproportional; that is, a doubling in the change of the factor of production leads to a doubling of the changes in output. In final goods space this equiproportionality leads to straight lines (called Rybczynski lines) connecting output changes starting from some equilibrium. Since there are two factors of production, capital and labour, there are two Rybczynski lines, a capital Rybczynski line and a labour Rybczynski line. This is illustrated in Figure 7.6 and further discussed in the main text.

Box 7.3   **The Leontief paradox**

The first, and most famous, empirical study of the neoclassical trade model was performed by Wassily Leontief (1956). Using trade data and factor intensities for the USA, Leontief computed the amount of capital and labour required to produce $1 million worth of US exports in 1951 and $1 million worth of US import-competing goods. Thinking that the USA was a capital-abundant country, he expected to show, on the basis of the Heckscher–Ohlin result discussed in this chapter, that US export production is more capital intensive than US import-competing production. Instead, he found that the capital–labour ratio was roughly $13,000 per worker year in the export sector, which was *lower* than the $13,700 per worker year in the import-competing sector. It appeared, therefore, that the USA was, on balance, importing capital services from abroad through its trade of goods and services. This has become known as the Leontief paradox.

Various explanations have been suggested to solve the Leontief paradox. First, it could be that there is a demand bias, in which case the USA would consume more capital-intensive products than other countries; see Chapter 17. Second, there could be a so-called factor-intensity reversal, in which case, for example, the production of manufactures is more capital intensive in the rest of the world while the production of food is more capital intensive in the USA, making it impossible to estimate the foreign factor intensities using US data, as Leontief did. More important, however, seems to be the third explanation, put forward by Jaroslav Vanek (1959), who argued that the 2 × 2 × 2 framework is too restrictive and we should distinguish between more types of goods and more factors of production. Theoretical work by Vanek showed that in a more general

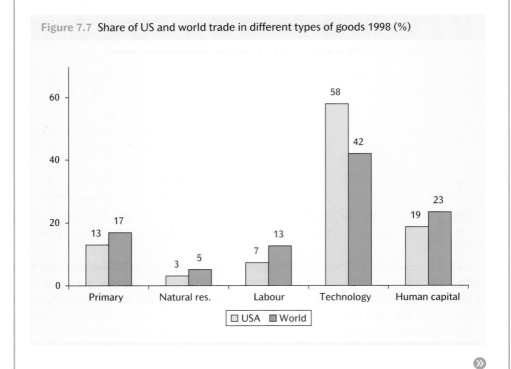

Figure 7.7 **Share of US and world trade in different types of goods 1998 (%)**

> ⟫ setting a weaker version of the Heckscher–Ohlin result holds; that is, a country tends to export goods and services which 'on average' make intensive use of the abundant factors of production. See section 7.9 for an empirical discussion.
>
> Figure 7.7 illustrates the argument that we should take more factors of production into consideration. Various special interest boxes in Chapters 4–8 briefly discuss the ITC data distinguishing between five types of products: primary, natural-resource-intensive, unskilled-labour-intensive, technology-intensive, and human-capital-intensive. Figure 7.7 shows that (i) by far the largest share of US exports is in technology-intensive and human-capital-intensive products, and (ii) when compared to the world average the USA has a revealed comparative advantage only in technology-intensive products (discussed further in Box 7.4). Neither observation is controversial.

7.5 Structure of the equilibrium

The Heckscher–Ohlin result concentrates on the structure of international trade flows in a trading equilibrium. It is therefore useful to review the general equilibrium structure of the neoclassical trade model, as summarized in Figure 7.8.

There are five types of economic agents: (i) labourers, (ii) capital owners, (iii) consumers, (iv) producers of manufactures, and (v) producers of food. Note that these are functional distinctions; the same person could be a producer of manufactures, a capital owner, and a consumer at the same time. Also note that Figure 7.8 distinguishes between two types of flows: the flows of goods and services, indicated by closed-point arrows, and money flows, indicated by open-point arrows. These two flows always move in opposite directions.

- The *labourers* supply their services to produce either manufactures or food. In return they receive a remuneration called the wage rate. Since labour is perfectly mobile between the two sectors, the wage rate is the same in the two sectors.

- The *capital owners* supply their services to produce either manufactures or food. In return they receive a remuneration called the rental rate. Since capital is perfectly mobile between the two sectors, the rental rate is the same in the two sectors.

- Both labourers and capital owners earn an income, which they use to spend on manufactures and food as *consumers*. Since production takes place under perfect competition and constant returns to scale, there are no profits generated in the economy. The only income available for consumption is therefore generated by supplying labour services and capital services.

- The *producers of manufactures* hire labour services on the labour market, for which they pay the wage rate, and capital services on the capital market, for which they pay the rental rate. They use these services in the most efficient way to produce manufactures, which they sell to consumers at the price p_m.

- The same applies for the *producers of food*.

Figure 7.8 Equilibrium structure

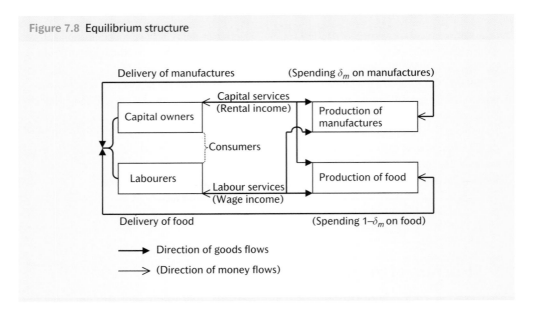

The economy is in equilibrium if six conditions are fulfilled: (i) consumers maximize their utility, (ii) producers maximize their profits, (iii) all labourers are employed, (iv) all capital is used, (v) the supply of manufactures is equal to the demand for manufactures, and (vi) the supply of food is equal to the demand for food. In the next two sections we will distinguish between two types of equilibria:

- The *autarky equilibrium*, in which the above six equilibrium relationships hold at the national level; there is no cross-border activity whatsoever.

- The *international trade equilibrium*, in which the above six relationships hold at the global level for the final goods markets, and at the national level for the factors of production. There is therefore no impediment to cross-border trade for final goods (at zero transport costs), while capital and labour services cannot move across borders.

7.6 Autarky equilibrium

Figure 7.9(a) illustrates the autarky equilibrium if there is an equal supply of capital and labour ($K = L = 5$), the cost share of capital in manufactures is 0.8 ($\alpha_m = 0.8$), the cost share of capital in food is 0.2 ($\alpha_f = 0.2$), and the share of income spent on manufactures is 0.6 ($\delta_m = 0.6$). As Figure 7.9 shows, the PPF is tangent to the income line generated by the autarky production point; that is, the marginal rate of transformation (*MRT*) is equal to the final goods price ratio p_m/p_f because producers maximize profits and markets are perfectly competitive. Similarly, the iso-utility curve is tangent to the income line generated by the production point; that is the marginal rate of substitution (*MRS*) is equal to the final goods price ratio p_m/p_f because consumers maximize utility and take prices as given. The autarky equilibrium is therefore characterized by (the sub-index '*au*' refers to autarky):

(7.4)
$$MRT_{au} = \left(\frac{p_m}{p_f}\right)_{au} = MRS_{au}$$

Figure 7.9 Autarky production and consumption (a) $K = L = 5$, $\alpha_m = 0.8$, $\alpha_f = 0.2$, $\delta_m = 0.6$; (b) $K = L = 5$, $\alpha_m = 0.9$, $\alpha_f = 0.2$, $\delta_m = 0.8$

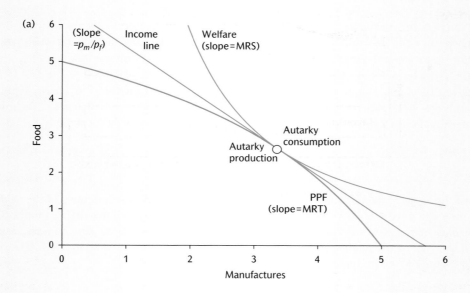

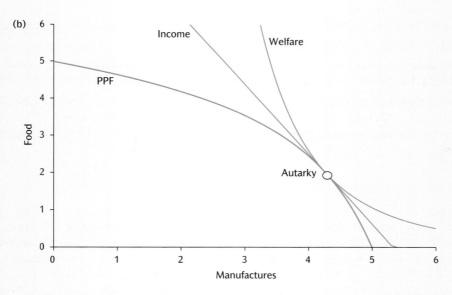

Clearly, given the restrictions facing the economy (no international contacts), the autarky equilibrium achieves the best possible outcome; at the equilibrium production point, which is also the equilibrium consumption point, welfare is maximized. The autarky equilibrium depends, of course, on the value of the parameters, the capital and labour stock available, the production functions, the utility function, etc. This is illustrated in Figure 7.9(b), with a higher value for the capital-intensity parameter for manufactures ($\alpha_m = 0.9 > 0.8$), which results in a more curved PPF, and a higher share of income spent on manufactures ($\delta_m = 0.8 > 0.6$), which results in a higher demand for manufactures relative to food.

Given the Cobb–Douglas production functions and utility function, the autarky equilibrium wage–rental ratio and final goods price ratio can be explicitly calculated; see Technical Note 7.2 (also for a definition of the parameter γ_{au}).

$$(7.5) \qquad \left(\frac{w}{r}\right)_{au} = \underset{\text{constant}}{\gamma_{au}} \frac{K}{L}; \quad \left(\frac{p_m}{p_f}\right)_{au} = \frac{\gamma_m}{\gamma_f}\left(\frac{w}{r}\right)_{au}^{-(\alpha_m-\alpha_f)}$$

Both the wage–rental ratio and the final goods price ratio are simple functions of the *relative* factor abundance K/L of the economy. If the capital stock increases relative to the labour stock, the wage–rental ratio rises since labour becomes relatively more scarce. This, in turn, results in a decrease of the relative price of manufactures, which uses capital relatively intensively (see Chapter 5). To summarize:

$$\frac{K}{L} \Leftrightarrow \frac{w}{r} \Leftrightarrow \frac{p_m}{p_f}$$

Since we are particularly interested in the effect of differences in relative factor abundance, Table 7.1 specifies the autarky equilibrium for 'Austria' and 'Bolivia'. The values *above* the double line in Table 7.1 are *exogenously specified* parameters. All values *below* the double line in Table 7.1 are *endogenously determined* by the conditions of the autarky equilibrium. Austria is capital abundant relative to Bolivia ($7/3 > 3/7$). Therefore, Austria's PPF is biased towards

Table 7.1 Autarky values for Austria and Bolivia

	Austria	Bolivia
Capital K	7	3
Labour L	3	7
Share of income δ_m spent manufactures	0.6	0.6
Capital parameter α_m manufactures	0.8	0.8
Capital parameter α_f food	0.2	0.2
Wage–rental w/r	1.83	0.34
Price manufactures/price food; (p_m/p_f)	0.70	1.92
Welfare level	2.96	2.67
Production of manufactures	4.03	2.42
Production of food	1.87	3.10

Figure 7.10 Autarky equilibrium

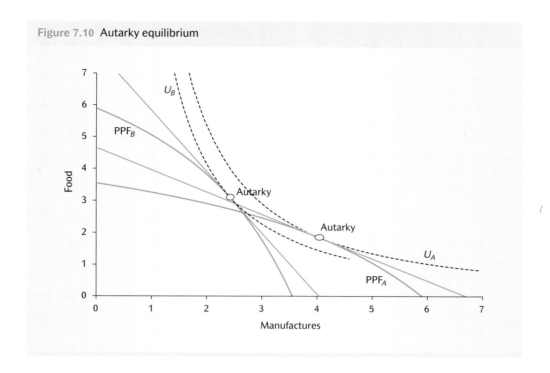

the production of manufactures, and it produces relatively more of manufactures in autarky. Note from Table 7.1 that the relative price of manufactures is higher in Bolivia in autarky, as illustrated in Figure 7.10.

7.7 International trade equilibrium

The international trade equilibrium is also characterized by utility maximization and profit maximization. Since the former leads to equality of the marginal rate of substitution and the final goods price ratio, and the latter leads to equality of the marginal rate of transformation and the final goods price ratio, the international trade equilibrium is summarized by (the sub-index 'tr' refers to trade):

(7.6)
$$MRT_{tr} = \left(\frac{p_m}{p_f}\right)_{tr} = MRS_{tr}$$

Since the same equalities between the marginal rate of substitution, the price ratio, and the marginal rate of transformation hold in the autarky equilibrium, the question may arise: what is the difference between the two equilibria? The answer is simple: international trade of final goods enables international arbitrage opportunities not previously available. The crucial aspect is to realize that although the autarky equilibrium is efficient given the imposed restriction of no trade, which leads to $MRT = p_m/p_f = MRS$ in both countries, it is not efficient if international trade is possible because the autarky prices are different in the two countries. Thus, in autarky $MRT = p_m/p_f = MRS$ holds *within* countries, but not *between* countries. It is this aspect that makes international trade and gains from trade possible.

Table 7.2 International trade values for Austria and Bolivia

	Austria	Bolivia
Wage–rental w/r	0.79	0.79
Price manufactures/price food; (p_m/p_f)	1.16	1.16
Welfare level	3.22	2.92
Production of manufactures	5.44	1.38
Consumption of manufactures	3.57	3.24
Export of manufactures	1.87	−1.87
Production of food	0.60	4.66
Consumption of food	2.75	2.50
Export of food	−2.16	2.16

The international trade equilibrium is summarized in Table 7.2 and illustrated in Figure 7.11.[3] International arbitrage opportunities arising from the costless trade of final goods ensures that the prices of food and manufactures must be the same in the two countries in the international trade equilibrium; the relative price with trade is in between the two autarky equilibrium prices:

$$(7.7) \qquad \left(\frac{p_m}{p_f}\right)^{Austria}_{au} < \left(\frac{p_m}{p_f}\right)_{tr} < \left(\frac{p_m}{p_f}\right)^{Bolivia}_{au}$$

For Austria the relative price of manufactures rises in trade relative to autarky. The production of manufactures therefore increases (and that of food falls); the production shifts from point aut_A in Figure 7.11 to point pr_A. Simultaneously, the higher relative price for manufactures in Austria results in a substitution away from manufactures on the consumption side in Austria; the consumption ratio C_f/C_m rises from the ratio in point aut_A to the ratio in point co_A. In the international trade equilibrium, the production point pr_A for Austria no longer coincides with the consumption point co_A for Austria. There is, of course, a link between these two points, since the total value of the expenditures on consumption cannot exceed the total value of income generated by the production level in the economy.[4] That is, the consumption point must be on the income line generated by the production point of Austria, with a slope equal to the international price ratio p_m/p_f; see Figure 7.11. Clearly, Austria now produces more manufactures than it consumes. It will therefore export manufactures in exchange for imports of food. Finally, we note that the welfare level achieved by Austria rises; the new consumption point co_A is on a higher iso-utility curve than at point aut_A.[5]

In Bolivia opposite changes take place. The relative price of manufactures falls, such that Bolivia produces less manufactures and more food. Simultaneously, the consumption mix in Bolivia moves in the direction of manufactures. Bolivia therefore produces more food than it consumes, which it will export in exchange for imports of manufactures. This allows Bolivia

Figure 7.11 International trade equilibrium

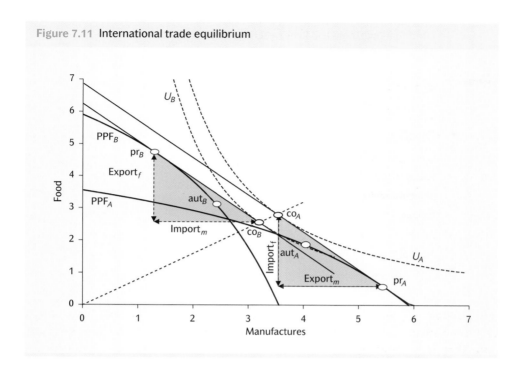

also to reach a higher welfare level. On a global scale the international trade flows improve efficiency. The world production of manufactures rises by 5.7 per cent from 6.45 to 6.82, and the world production of food rises by 5.8 per cent from 4.97 to 5.26. Note also that the international trade equilibrium requires that the excess demand for manufactures by Bolivia, that is its imports of manufactures, must be equal to the excess supply of manufactures by Austria, that is its exports of manufactures. The two *trade triangles* in Figure 7.11 must coincide.

Figure 7.12 proves the Heckscher–Ohlin proposition using Rybczynski lines. Let's again concentrate on Austria. Note that the global capital–labour ratio K/L is equal to $(7+3)/(3+7) = 1$. This is lower than Austria's capital–labour ratio, which is 7/3. If we now take away capital from Austria until its capital–labour ratio is equal to the global capital–labour ratio (in this case until its capital stock is 3), its output level will move along the capital Rybczynski line for given final goods prices until it reaches production point pr. In Figure 7.12 the PPF if $K = L = 3$ is also drawn, and labelled PPF. At point pr the demand for food is equal to the supply of food. Moving in the opposite direction, thus adding capital, we know that at given final goods prices the demand for food increases because the income level increases and (from the Rybczynski proposition) the supply of food decreases because food is labour intensive. Thus Austria, which is capital abundant, must import the labour-intensive food, and thus export the capital-intensive manufactures. A similar conclusion can be reached for Bolivia exporting the labour-intensive food using the labour Rybczynski line. Note that, to avoid cluttering the diagram, the distribution of capital and labour over the two countries was chosen such that Bolivia's labour Rybczynski line reaches the same production point pr. In general, of course, this is not the case.

Figure 7.12 International trade and Rybczynski lines

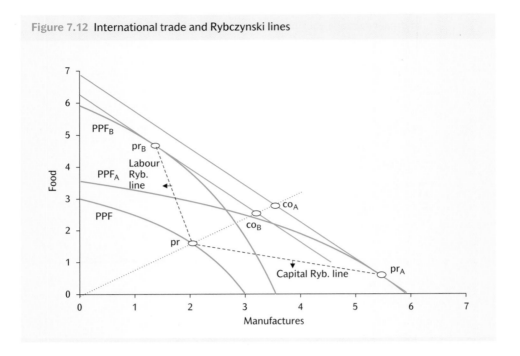

The ITC classifies 71 goods as 'technology-intensive manufacturing' products, incorporating various chemicals, medicaments, plastics, engines, generators, machines, tools, pumps, telecommunications and photo equipment, optical equipment, and aircraft. For the 151 countries for which the ITC provides data, total exports of technology-intensive manufactures in 1998 were equal to $2,022 bn, some 42 per cent of all exports. This makes technology-intensive manufactures by far the largest of the five categories identified by the ITC in terms of international trade flows. The left-hand side of Table 7.3 lists the top ten exporters of technology-intensive manufactures in absolute terms. With an impressive value of $354 bn, the USA is the world's largest technology-intensive manufactures exporter, including semiconductors, computers, and aircraft. The USA is followed by Germany ($240 bn; medicine and machinery) and Japan ($212 bn; semiconductors). With the exception of Taiwan, the other large exporters are all OECD countries.

   For the first time since we started to discuss the factor intensity of exports in these special interest boxes (see Chapters 4–6), some of the world's ten largest exporters in absolute terms also make it to the list of the world's ten largest exporters in relative terms. As the right-hand side of Table 7.3 indicates, this holds for Singapore, Taiwan, the USA, Japan, and the UK. The top three in relative terms are Singapore (computer chips and semiconductors), Ireland (computers and computer chips), and Malta (semiconductors). Figure 7.13 shows the relative dependence of countries on the exports of technology intensive manufactures. These are clearly concentrated in the rich OECD countries.   »

Table 7.3 Top ten technology-intensive manufacturing exporters, 1998

No.	Top 10 in absolute terms			Top 10 in relative terms		
	Country	Exports		Country	Exports	
		Value	%		%	Value
1	USA	354	58	Singapore	76	77
2	Germany	240	48	Ireland	70	43
3	Japan	212	56	Malta	69	1
4	UK	137	53	Philippines	69	20
5	France	124	43	Taiwan	59	70
6	Singapore	77	76	USA	58	354
7	The Netherlands	74	46	Switzerland	58	45
8	Italy	73	37	Japan	56	212
9	Taiwan	70	59	Malaysia	55	40
10	Belgium	54	33	UK	53	137

Source: WTO/UNCTAD International Trade Centre website http://www.intracen.org; value in bn US$. The % shares are relative to the country's total exports.

Figure 7.13 Technology-intensive manufacturing exports, shares 1998 %

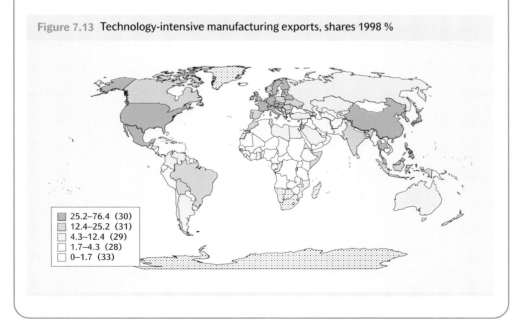

- 25.2–76.4 (30)
- 12.4–25.2 (31)
- 4.3–12.4 (29)
- 1.7–4.3 (28)
- 0–1.7 (33)

7.8 Application: the Summers–Heston data

We can use the empirical capital–labour ratio estimated for a range of countries in the Summers–Heston database, see Box 4.2, to better illustrate the functioning of the neoclassical model (and to show that complete specialization is possible). The illustrations below will use the observations for all countries for which data are available, but the discussion will focus on four relatively small countries: Norway, Austria, Bolivia, and Zambia. Of these four countries Norway had the highest capital per worker ($48,100), followed by Austria ($34,600), Bolivia ($5,700), and Zambia ($1,300); see Table 7.4. To illustrate the impact of the neoclassical model on the basis of the estimated capital–labour ratio for the 60 countries for which data are available, we measure the capital stock per worker in $10,000 and choose some values for the parameters: capital intensity for manufactures $\alpha_m = 0.8$, capital intensity for food $\alpha_f = 0.2$, and the share of income spent on manufactures $\delta_m = 0.7$.

Figure 7.14 shows the impact of the chosen parameter values for all countries in a situation of autarky, in which all countries will produce all goods. Since Norway has the highest capital stock per worker, it will have the highest wage–rental ratio in autarky, followed by Austria, Bolivia, and Zambia. Similarly, since the production of manufactures is capital intensive and Norway is capital abundant, the relative price of manufactures is lowest in autarky in Norway, followed by Austria, Bolivia, and Zambia. Both observations are illustrated in Figure 7.14(a). The impact of the capital stock per worker on the production of food and manufactures per worker in autarky is shown in Figure 7.14(b). Clearly, as the capital stock per worker increases countries produce relatively more capital-intensive manufactures. The autarky equilibrium is summarized in the top part of Table 7.4.

So what happens if all these countries start to trade with each other at zero costs? Let's assume that the equilibrium relative price of manufactures with trade is 0.98.[6] For Norway and Austria this is a higher price for manufactures than in autarky, such that the production of manufactures increases (and that of food decreases). For Bolivia and Zambia this is a lower

Table 7.4 The neoclassical model and the Summers–Heston data

	Norway	Austria	Bolivia	Zambia
Capital per worker	4.81	3.46	0.57	0.13
Autarky wage–rental	2.95	2.12	0.35	0.08
Autarky price manufactures/food	0.52	0.64	1.88	4.46
Autarky production manufactures	2.65	2.04	0.48	0.15
Autarky production food	0.59	0.56	0.39	0.29
Trade wage–rental	1.20	1.04	1.04	0.54
Trade price manufactures/food	0.98	0.98	0.98	0.98
Trade production manufactures	3.52	2.56	0.25	0.00
Trade production food	0.00	0.14	0.70	0.67

Note: Capital stock per worker $10,000, parameters: $\alpha_m = 0.8$; $\alpha_f = 0.2$; $\delta_m = 0.7$.

Figure 7.14 Autarky values

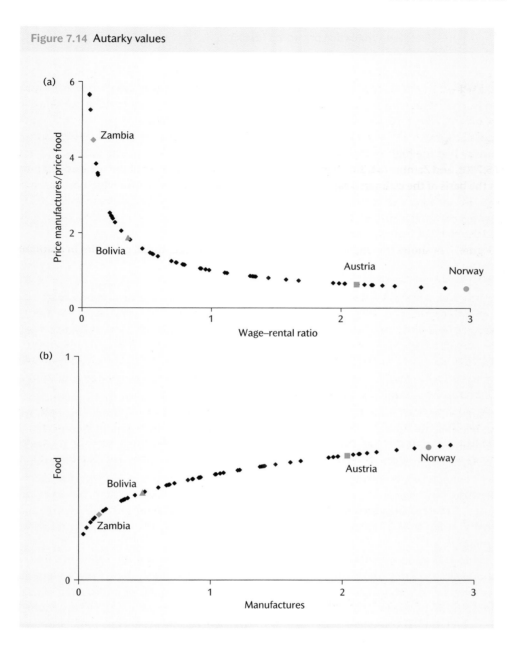

price for manufactures than in autarky, such that their production of manufactures decreases (and that of food increases). Norway and Austria will start to export manufactures, while Bolivia and Zambia will start to export food. Figure 7.15 shows the production pattern per worker with trade for all countries. It differs drastically from the autarky pattern in Figure 7.14(b). Note that some countries, such as Zambia, completely specialize in the production of

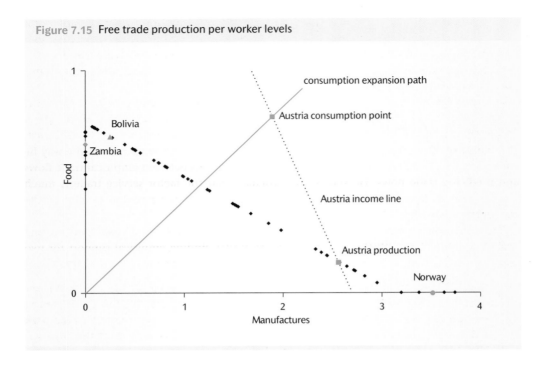

Figure 7.15 Free trade production per worker levels

food, while some other countries, such as Norway, completely specialize in the production of manufactures. Also note that the production pattern for the countries producing both food and manufactures is on a downward-sloping straight line. It is the capital Rybczynski line if the relative price of manufactures is 0.98. For all countries on this line, such as Austria and Bolivia, international trade leads to factor price equalization. This does not hold for the countries completely specializing in the production of one good, such as Norway and Zambia, where the wage rate and rental rate must clear the local factor markets. Note, however, from Table 7.4 that, as suggested by Ohlin, there is a tendency for factor prices to become more equal as a result of international trade (the wage–rental ratio falls in Norway and rises in Zambia).

Figure 7.15 also shows the consumption expansion path. All countries below this line will export manufactures, those above will export food. We have also drawn the income line generated by the production level per worker for Austria. The point of intersection with the consumption expansion path determines the Austrian consumption point. Clearly countries with a high capital stock per worker, such as Austria, will be able to generate more income per worker and consume more of both food and manufactures than countries with a low capital stock per worker. Differences in the capital stock per worker can therefore partially explain differences in welfare; see also Chapter 16.

7.9 The case of the missing trade

The first thorough analysis of the more general neoclassical trade model (more countries, more goods, and more factors) was performed by Bowen, Leamer, and Sveikauskas (1987). This section, however, discusses the more recent study of Daniel Trefler (1995), who analyses trade flows between 33 countries together accounting for 76 per cent of world exports and 79 per cent of world GNP. Trefler distinguishes nine factors of production: capital, cropland, pasture, and six labour categories (professional and technical workers, clerical workers, sales workers, service workers, agricultural workers, and production, transport, and unskilled workers).

The empirical success of the more general neoclassical trade model is modest: when the predicted sign of the net factor content of trade is weighted by size the model explains about 71 per cent. As Trefler (1995: 1031) puts it, this is 'uncomfortably close to the coin-toss alternative of 50 percent'. The important contribution of Trefler's work rests in the way he continues, by providing a detailed analysis of the deviations between empirical trade flows and predicted trade flows. He shows, in particular, that the factor service trade is much smaller than its factor-endowments prediction, a phenomenon referred to by him as 'the case of the missing trade'.

Trefler investigates several alternative hypotheses that may explain the case of the missing trade in conjunction with the neoclassical trade model, finding empirical support for two additions, namely (i) differences in technology and (ii) demand bias:

(i) The neoclassical model analysed in Part II.A of this book assumes that countries have access to the same technology. Trefler argues, however, that there are technology differences between countries, and that incorporating these differences (in a neutral way) increases the goodness-of-fit from 71 to 78 per cent. Obviously, we have already discussed the impact of technology differences on international trade in Chapter 3 of this book.

(ii) It is generally observed that consumers display a bias toward domestically produced goods; see Armington (1969). Allowing for Armington-type demand bias in the neoclassical model increases the goodness-of-fit from 71 to 87 per cent. The impact of demand differences on international trade is further discussed in Chapter 17. Incorporating both technology differences and Armington demand in the model increases the goodness-of-fit even further to 93 per cent.

7.10 Conclusions

We analyse the connection between the direction of international trade flows and the factor intensity of the production process in the general equilibrium structure of the neoclassical trade model. In autarky, countries with a high capital–labour ratio will have a high wage–rental ratio (since labour is relatively scarce) and a low relative price for the capital-intensive good. Allowing for free trade of final goods at no costs equalizes the final goods prices in the two countries, as well as the wage rate and the rental rate (provided both goods are produced in both countries; FPE proposition). Since the relative price of the capital-intensive good rises compared to autarky for the capital-abundant country (which raises the rental rate and reduces the wage rate; Stolper–Samuelson proposition), this country starts to produce more capital-intensive goods, which will be exported in exchange for the labour-intensive good. The opposite holds for the labour-abundant country (Heckscher–Ohlin proposition). As a result of improved efficiency at the global level, welfare increases in both countries in the international trade equilibrium compared to autarky. The model performs reasonably well empirically, provided we also take into consideration technology differences (See Chapter 3) and demand bias (see Chapter 17).

TECHNICAL NOTES

Technical Note 7.1 Utility maximization

The problem for a consumer who wants to maximize utility, given the income level I and the prices of final goods p_m and p_f, by choosing the consumption levels C_m and C_f is specified as:

(7.A1)
$$\max_{C_m, C_f} C_m^{\delta_m} C_f^{1-\delta_m} \quad s.t. \; I = p_m C_m + p_f C_f$$

To solve this problem we define the Lagrangean Γ using the Lagrange multiplier λ:

(7.A2)
$$G = C_m^{\delta_m} C_f^{1-\delta_m} + \lambda[I - p_m C_m - p_f C_f]$$

Derive the two first-order conditions $\partial\Gamma/\partial C_m = \partial\Gamma/\partial C_f = 0$ for an optimum and note

(7.A3)
$$\lambda p_m = \delta_m C_m^{\delta_m - 1} C_f^{1-\delta_m}; \quad \lambda p_f = (1 - \delta_m) C_m^{\delta_m} C_f^{-\delta_m}$$

Taking the ratio of these two conditions and simplifying determines the optimal spending ratio $p_m C_m / p_f C_f = \delta_m/(1 - \delta_m)$. Using this in the budget constraint gives

(7.A4)
$$I = p_m C_m + p_f C_f = p_m C_m + \frac{1 - \delta_m}{\delta_m} p_m C_m = \frac{1}{\delta_m} p_m C_m \Rightarrow p_m C_m = \delta_m I$$

Thus the share δ_m of income is spent on manufactures, and the share $1 - \delta_m$ on food.

Technical Note 7.2 Derivation of the autarky equilibrium

To derive the autarky equilibrium, we first note that the structure of the utility function ensures that the agents always want to consume a positive amount of both goods. Since these goods cannot be imported from abroad, both goods have to be produced in our own country. We can therefore use the factor price equalization proposition, the Stolper–Samuelson proposition, and the Rybczynski proposition whenever convenient, all of which require the economy to produce both goods in equilibrium. The demand for manufactures is given in equation (7.A4) as a function of income I and price p_m. Since the only income generated in the economy in equilibrium derives from the supply of labour or capital, total income is given by

(7.A5)
$$I = wL + rK = r\left(\frac{w}{r}L + K\right).$$

Furthermore, in Chapter 5 it was shown that there is a one-to-one correspondence between the rewards to factors of production and the price of final goods. In particular, if the wage rate w and the rental rate r are known, equation (5.3) gives the prices p_m and p_f. Using this equation, it follows that

(7.A6)
$$\frac{r}{p_m} = \frac{r}{\gamma_m r^{\alpha_m} w^{1-\alpha_m}} = \frac{1}{\gamma_m}\left(\frac{w}{r}\right)^{\alpha_m - 1}; \quad \frac{p_m}{p_f} = \frac{\gamma_m r^{\alpha_m} w^{1-\alpha_m}}{\gamma_f \; r^{\alpha_f} w^{1-\alpha_f}} = \frac{\gamma_m}{\gamma_f}\left(\frac{w}{r}\right)^{-(\alpha_m - \alpha_f)}$$

Using these results in the demand function for manufactures, we get

(7.A7)
$$C_m = \delta_m \frac{I}{p_m} = \delta_m \frac{r}{p_m}\left(\frac{w}{r}L + K\right) = \delta_m \frac{1}{\gamma_m}\left(\frac{w}{r}\right)^{\alpha_m - 1}\left(\frac{w}{r}L + K\right)$$

This gives us the demand for manufactures as a function of the wage–rental ratio w/r. If both goods are produced, the Rybczynski analysis of Chapter 6 and the full employment conditions determine the production level of manufactures, also as a function of the wage–rental ratio w/r; see Technical Note 6.2. Equating demand for and supply of manufactures gives us, after some algebra, the autarky equilibrium wage–rental ratio

(7.A8)
$$\left(\frac{w}{r}\right)_{au} = \gamma_{au}\frac{K}{L}; \quad \gamma_{au} \equiv \frac{(1 - \alpha_f) - \delta_m(\alpha_m - \alpha_f)}{\alpha_f + \delta_m(\alpha_m - \alpha_f)}$$

QUESTIONS

Question 7.1

Since Deng Xiaoping took over leadership of China in 1977, tariffs have decreased dramatically. In 2001, China even joined the WTO, sending a signal to the world that tariff reduction will continue in the future. The effects of the opening up of China to international trade are heavily debated within the media. Some commentators claim that trading with China is a good thing because products become cheaper. Others stress the negative effect it has on some Western industries, such as the clothes industry.

Let's analyse the integration of China in the world economy with the Heckscher–Ohlin model. Assume, to make things easy, that there are only two countries: China and the Western world (the Western world is considered to be one country). China is relatively labour abundant and the Western world relatively capital abundant. Furthermore, assume that only two goods are consumed and produced in China and the Western world. These are clothes (produced relatively labour intensively) and computers (produced relatively capital intensively).

7.1A Draw a consistent graph in which you indicate the autarky production and consumption points of China and the Western world with the help of production possibility frontiers and utility curves.

7.1B Explain intuitively whether the relative price of clothes in the Western world is higher or lower compared to the relative price of clothes in China when both China and the Western world are in autarky. How can you see this price difference in your graph?

7.1C Explain what will happen to the prices of clothes and computers in the Western world when the Western world and China start trading.

7.1D What effect will this have on the consumption of clothes and computers and on the production of clothes and computers in the Western world? Indicate the new consumption and production point in the graph with the help of a budget line and a new utility curve (if your graph becomes messy, please draw a new graph).

7.1E Is integration of China into the world economy a good thing for the Western world? Use the observations you made above in your analysis. Also comment on the distribution of welfare between industries and owners of production factors.

Question 7.2

Table 7.1 in the main text shows the autarky values for Austria. The values above the double line are exogenously specified parameters. The values below the double line are determined endogenously. If we change the parameter values above the line, we should be able to determine the endogenous values below the line. Determine the changes in (i) the wage–rental rate, (ii) the final goods price ratio, (iii) the welfare level, (iv) the production level of manufactures, and (v) the production level of food if:

7.2A The Austrian capital stock K increases.

7.2B The Austrian labor force L increases.

7.2C The capital intensity of manufactures α_m decreases.

7.2D The share of income spent on manufactures δ_m increases.

Question 7.3

Starting with Wasily Leontief, empirical research has shown that trade patterns cannot be explained by differences in factor endowments between countries alone. A simple thought-experiment can shed some light on this issue.

7.3A According to the Heckscher–Ohlin model, will there (other things equal) be more trade between developed countries or between developed and less developed countries?

7.3B Do trade data show more intensive trading between developed countries or between developed and less developed countries (see Chapter 1)?

7.3C What do you conclude from your answers to question 7.3A and 7.3B regarding the factor abundance model?

 See the Online Resource Centre for a Study Guide containing more questions
www.oxfordtextbooks.co.uk/orc/vanmarrewijk/

NOTES

1 See Allen (1965: 170).

2 The contract curve gives K_m as a function of L_m. The inputs for food can be calculated using $K_f = K - K_m$ and $L_f = L - L_m$. Using the production functions, the output levels can be determined. It is not possible to write the production possibility frontier as an explicit function.

3 We have made it easy for ourselves to calculate the equilibrium because both countries produce both goods in the international trade equilibrium. This is not necessary; see below and the *Study Guide*.

4 At least if there is no international borrowing or lending in the period under consideration, or if the values are measured in present-value terms.

5 The same conclusion follows from revealed preference.

6 This value would result if all countries were perfectly integrated (capital and labour mobility).

TRADE POLICY

Objectives/key terms

- Tariff/effective tariff
- Voluntary export restraints (VER)
- Double distortion
- Trade indifference curves

- Quota
- Harberger triangle
- Offer curve
- 'Optimal' tariff and retaliation

We analyse the impact of trade policy on the size of trade flows, focusing in particular on the distribution of winners (protected domestic producers) and losers (consumers, the country as a whole, and other countries). The distributional welfare aspects of trade policy make the demand for protection (lobbying) understandable.

8.1 Introduction

In the previous five chapters we have presented and analysed various economic forces giving rise to international flows of goods and services. We also demonstrated that these flows are beneficial for all countries involved, leading to higher efficiency in the Ricardian model based on technology differences and in the Heckscher–Ohlin model based on differences in factor abundance. This view of international trade flows benefiting society and increasing efficiency contrasts with a variety of different views from pressure groups frequently popularized in the media, blaming international economics, globalization, international trade flows, and international factor movements for virtually anything a specific group may dislike either at home or abroad, such as unemployment, low wages, environmental degradation, low development levels, unfair competition, etc. This leads to high-profile trade disagreements in the media, such as car imports from Japan in the 1980s, or the 'wars' between the European Union and the USA, such as the 'steel war', the 'cheese war', the 'meat war', and the 'banana war'.

It is not possible to evaluate precisely the quality of the arguments of all pressure groups leading to a specific position and policy recommendation, not only because such arguments are frequently lacking, or contradicting and inconsistent when they do exist, even within one group, but also because new pressure groups pop up and old ones disappear at a rate that is impossible to keep up with.[1] It is clear, however, that the many pressure groups give rise to a demand, whether successful or not, for action by government officials to impose trade restrictions, to limit 'unfair' competition, to save domestic jobs or the environment, etc. To a limited extent, this chapter gives some reasons for the existence of pressure groups or lobby groups. The majority of this chapter, however, analyses the consequences of imposing trade restrictions for production, consumption, and international trade flows. Arnold Harberger (1954), for example, argued that the monopoly power distortions in the USA impose a cost on society in the order of a few tenths of a per cent of GNP. A couple of years later, he estimated the costs of trade restrictions for the Chilean economy to be about 2.5 per cent of GDP; see Harberger (1959). How did he arrive at these estimates, and how accurate are they?

Famous economists	James Meade

Fig. 8.1
James Meade
(1907–95)

Meade studied and worked at both the University of Cambridge and Oxford University. He also worked at the London School of Economics and was active outside academia, for the League of Nations and for the British Cabinet Office, where he collaborated with Richard Stone on national income accounts for Britain. He incorporated the Keynesian framework in the textbook *An Introduction to Economic Analysis and Policy*, which appeared in 1936, only a few months after Keynes's *General Theory*. He systematically analysed internal and external balance in a general equilibrium framework. His work on trade policy and welfare analysis led to the 'theory of second best'. He shared the Nobel prize in economics in 1977 with Bertil Ohlin; see Chapter 7.

8.2 Tariffs, quotas, and other trade restrictions

Once a government body is convinced, for whatever reason, of the necessity to impose trade restrictions, there is an endless list of policy options to choose from. Suppose the European Commission decides that the domestic production of computers is of vital interest to the European Union, perhaps for security or strategic reasons, and decides to protect the computer industry from the hard and cold winds of global competition. Here are some options available to the European Commission:

- Impose a 100 euro tax per imported computer (specific tariff)
- Impose a 12 per cent tax per imported computer (*ad valorem* tariff)
- Restrict the number of imported computers (quota)
- Subsidize the production of European computers
- Subsidize the export of European computers
- Require a 'minimum content' before a computer may be labelled 'European'
- Prohibit the sale or import of computers to or from certain countries for safety reasons

All these policy measures will affect production, consumption, and trade flows in a different way. Clearly, therefore, we cannot provide an in-depth analysis of each policy measure in this introductory textbook. Instead, we restrict ourselves to providing a rather detailed analysis of the impact of tariffs on the international economic system, dealing more cursorily with the impact of some other trade restrictions (also in the Study Guide).

Despite the numerous eye-catching trade disputes mentioned in Section 8.1, trade restrictions, such as tariffs, have been falling on a global scale for a long time. This has undoubtedly contributed to the rapid increase in international trade and capital flows. To a large extent, the fall in trade restrictions can be attributed to the work of the General Agreement on Tariffs and Trade (GATT), a multilateral organization which has now transformed itself into the World Trade Organization (WTO); see Chapter 12. The GATT finished a long series of multilateral trade negotiation rounds in the complicated Uruguay Round, which lasted from 1986 to 1994. As illustrated in Figure 8.2, these successive GATT rounds substantially reduced the average tariff rates to approximately 15 per cent of the 1930 value.

Calculating an average tariff rate, as is done in the data underlying Figure 8.2, is actually quite complicated. We will not go into too much detail here, but an obvious first candidate for calculating an average tariff is, of course, weighing the imports of the various goods and services into the country by the value of the import flows. There are at least two disadvantages to that method. First, if a tariff on a specific good, say cheese, is very high, this may completely stop all imports of cheese into the country. This is called a *prohibitive* tariff. When import shares are used to calculate the average tariff, the prohibitive tariff for cheese imports receives a weight of zero, thus leading to a low estimate of average tariffs despite the fact that the tariff on cheese is so high as to stop all imports of cheese. Second, we should be careful to specify which activity we are protecting when calculating the impact of a combination of tariff rates. For this purpose, the *effective tariff* rate can be calculated; see Table 8.1.

Suppose the production of a final good is a simple process, requiring only the availability of some raw material and a processing stage to make the finished product. If the value of the finished product on the world market is $100 and our country imposes a 20 per cent tariff on

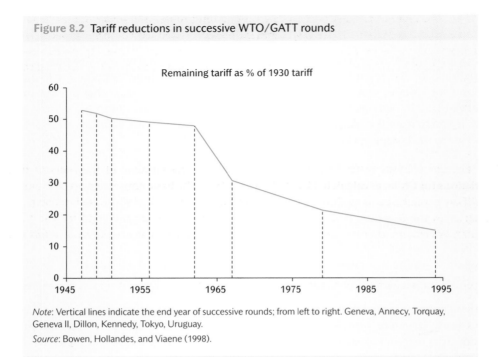

Figure 8.2 Tariff reductions in successive WTO/GATT rounds

Remaining tariff as % of 1930 tariff

Note: Vertical lines indicate the end year of successive rounds; from left to right. Geneva, Annecy, Torquay, Geneva II, Dillon, Kennedy, Tokyo, Uruguay.

Source: Bowen, Hollandes, and Viaene (1998).

Table 8.1 Calculating the effective tariff rate

Good	World price	Tariff (%)	Domestic price ($)
Finished product	100	20	120
Raw material	60	10	66
Available for processing stage	40	($100 \times (54 - 40)/40 = 35$)	54

the import of finished products, one could say that the tariff protection is 20 per cent. However, if the world market price for the raw material is $60, and our country imposes only a 10 per cent tariff on the import of raw materials, this implies that the entrepreneurs in our country can be remunerated for the processing stage to the extent of $100 \times 1.20 - $60 \times 1.10 = $54. If our country imposes no tariffs at all, there would only be $100 - $60 = $40 available for the processing stage of the production process. The effective rate of protection for the production process is therefore $100 \times (54 - 40)/40 = 35$ per cent, which is considerably higher than the nominal rates of 10 per cent and 20 per cent officially imposed by our country. The effective rate of protection is more cumbersome to calculate in a more complicated production process. In general, however, the effective rate of protection is higher the larger the share of raw materials in the production process, the lower the tariff on raw materials, and the higher the tariff on finished goods. Developed countries indeed have a tendency to put lower tariffs on the imports of raw materials than on the imports of finished products, leading to higher effective tariffs for the processing stage than the nominal tariffs suggest.

8.3 Tariffs and partial equilibrium

Small country

We start our analysis of tariffs with an explanation of the estimate of the costs of trade restrictions for Chile, as calculated by Harberger (1959). The basic consequences of imposing a tariff on a specific good, within a partial equilibrium framework, is illustrated in Figure 8.3, which gives the domestic demand and supply schedule for a specific good for the home country. We assume that the home country is a *small country*, that is its (net) demand is so

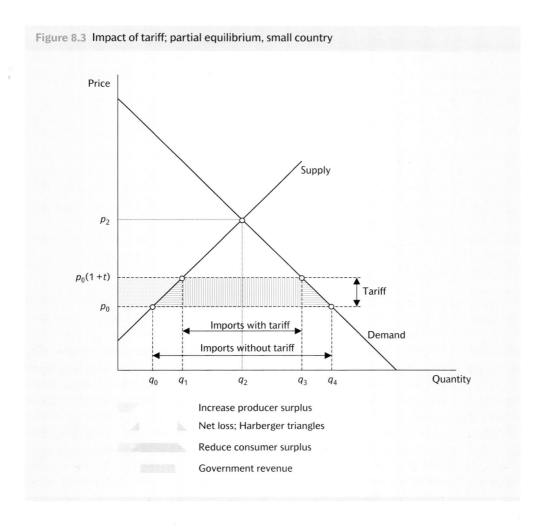

Figure 8.3 Impact of tariff; partial equilibrium, small country

Increase producer surplus

Net loss; Harberger triangles

Reduce consumer surplus

Government revenue

small that the country is not able to influence the price for the good on the world market, such that the *world price is given*. Moreover, we assume that the country imposes an *ad valorem* tariff t.

If the home country were not engaged in international trade, the market would clear at the price p_2 to ensure that domestic demand q_2 is equal to domestic supply. If the country, however, does not impose any tariff at all, the price for the good would be determined on the world market, equal to p_0. Since at the world price p_0 the quantity supplied q_0 is lower than the quantity demanded q_4, the difference $q_4 - q_0$ must be imported from abroad.

What happens if the home country imposes an *ad valorem* tariff of t? First of all, since the home country is small and cannot affect world prices, the world price p_0 of the good remains unchanged. When those goods are imported into the home country, however, the *ad valorem* tariff has to be paid, which increases the domestic price level to $p_0(1+t)$. Second, as a result of the increase in domestic price, home production increases from q_0 to q_1, and consumer demand falls from q_4 to q_3. Imports from abroad thus decrease from $q_4 - q_0$ to $q_3 - q_1$. Since domestic production has increased and imports have fallen, some people might argue that imposition of the tariff has the desired effect of protecting home production and jobs. These issues should be addressed in a general equilibrium setting, see the next section. Is the imposition of the tariff, within the structure of the partial equilibrium model, a good idea? No, it is not. To arrive at this conclusion, we have to investigate the welfare effects of the tariff, where we will distinguish between three types of agents, namely the producers, the government, and the consumers.

- Welfare for the domestic producers, as measured by the producer surplus, has *increased*. The size of this increase is measured left of the supply curve from the old price p_0 to the new price $p_0(1+t)$, as indicated by the dotted area in Figure 8.3.

- Welfare for the government, as measured by the government revenue, has *increased*. The size of the government revenue is equal to the difference between the domestic price $p_0(1+t)$ and the world price p_0, multiplied by the size of the imports q_3-q_1, as indicated by the area with vertical bars in Figure 8.3.

- Welfare for the consumers, as measured by the consumer surplus, has *decreased*. The size of this decrease is measured left of the demand curve from the old price p_0 to the new price $p_0(1+t)$, as indicated by all the shaded areas in Figure 8.3.

This analysis clarifies that there are winners and losers within the home country as a result of the imposition of the tariff, creating a conflict of interests within the country and thus explaining the frequently heated debates on imposing trade restrictions. The domestic producers are in favour of the tariff, as it increases the producer surplus. This explains why producers organize themselves into lobbying groups trying to convince government officials of the need to impose trade restrictions. Focusing attention strictly on revenue, the government is also in favour of the tariff. Within a broader perspective, the government will, of course, have to weigh the interests of the various groups within the country. Raising funds for the government to finance, for example, public schools, the construction of highways, and the like, is, however, a formidable problem for many developing nations, making the imposition of tariffs as an easy way to generate such funds an attractive option, see Box 1.2. The big losers are, however, the consumers, who are faced with a large decrease in the consumer surplus. The consumers more than completely finance the increase in producer surplus and the increase in government revenue. The difference is a net welfare loss to the home country, as measured by the so-called Harberger triangles indicated by the areas with horizontal bars in Figure 8.3. When estimating the welfare loss of trade restrictions in Chile, Harberger (1959) essentially estimated the size of these triangles. Note, finally, that the loss of the imposition of the tariff, the sizeable decrease in consumer surplus, is spread across many consumers, while the benefits, the increases in producer surplus and government revenue, are enjoyed by a limited number of producers and the government. This makes it much harder for consumers to organize themselves and defend the benefits of free trade, since there are many consumers and the interest of each individual consumer for this good is limited, than for the producers to organize vocal lobbying groups, since the interests of each producer are large. There is thus an organizational bias *against* free trade.

 Box 8.1   Quota equivalence and the attractiveness of VERs

The discussion in this chapter focuses attention on the analysis of tariffs. There are three reasons for this. First, there are many different types of trade restrictions and we cannot analyse them all in the same detail. Second, tariffs continue to present an important and visible obstacle to international trade flows, despite the reductions achieved over the years as a result of GATT/WTO efforts. Think, for example, of the role import duties play for tax collection in developing countries, see Box 1.2. Third, and most importantly, the impact of other trade restrictions, such as quota and voluntary export restraints (VERs), is largely *equivalent* to the impact of tariffs, at least in the framework analysed in this chapter. (This remark does not hold for the retaliation analysis at the end of this chapter.)

Consider, for example, the impact of imposing an import quota in the partial equilibrium framework analysed in Figure 8.3. If the size of this quota is equal to $q_3 - q_1$, the domestic market will clear at the price $p_0(1+t)$, and it is argued that the impact of a quota equal to $q_3 - q_1$ is equivalent to imposing a tariff t. This holds clearly for the loss in consumer surplus, the rise in producer surplus, and the net efficiency loss (the two Harberger triangles). The only distribution effect where the equivalence between tariffs and quota is questionable concerns the revenue the government will collect if it imposes a tariff. Who collects the potentially sizeable government revenue if a quota is imposed, rather than a tariff? To save the equivalence argument it is argued that the government can auction the import quota, and thus collect all this revenue. In practice, this does not occur, such that entrepreneurs who, through lobbying, historical accident, or otherwise, are able to get the licence to import the good with the quota restriction, can earn large profits.

The distribution of the tariff revenue can also explain the potential attractiveness of the so-called 'voluntary' export restraint for an exporting country. Suppose this country, let's say Japan, is convinced that a large importing country, say, the USA, is about to impose trade restrictions on the import of one of its goods, say cars. Obviously, Japan will be opposed to any trade restrictions on the import of cars into the USA. Convinced of the inevitability of American action, Japan may decide to 'voluntarily' limit the export of cars to the American market. The effect is equivalent to the USA imposing an import quota, except for the fact that the Japanese exporters are able to reap the tariff-equivalent government revenue. This makes a VER more attractive than an import quota.

Large country

The arguments above specifically stipulated that home is a small country. Apparently this is important, but why? The essential point is to realize in the above analysis that, other things being equal, the imposition of a tariff reduces imports of the good into the home country from $q_4 - q_0$ to $q_3 - q_1$; see Figure 8.3. If home is a *large* country, however, other things are not equal and the reduction in imports, which is a decrease in net demand by the home country on the world market, results in a lower price for the good on the world market. In Figure 8.4 this fall in the world price level as a result of the imposition of the tariff is indicated by the drop from p_0 to p_1. Essentially, then, the imposition of the tariff implies that the large home country uses its monopsony power to improve its terms of trade, as it can now import the good more cheaply. The rest of the analysis is similar.

- Producer welfare increases, as indicated by the dotted area in Figure 8.4.
- Government revenue increases, as indicated by the areas with vertical and diagonal bars in Figure 8.4.
- Consumer welfare falls, as indicated by the areas with dotted, horizontal and vertical bars in Figure 8.4.

Figure 8.4 Impact of tariff: partial equilibrium, large country

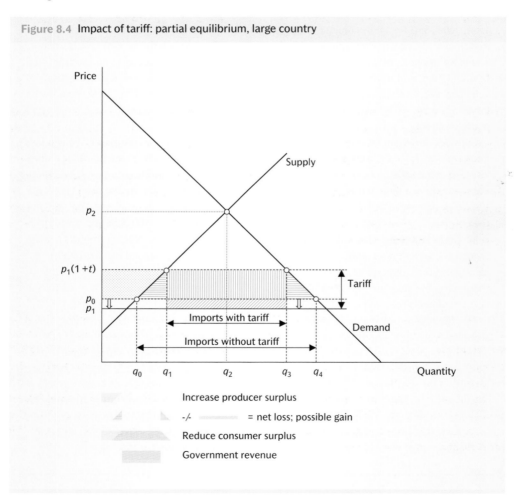

Increase producer surplus

-/- —————— = net loss; possible gain

Reduce consumer surplus

Government revenue

The main difference with the preceding analysis, in which home was a small country and could not influence the terms of trade, is that part of the government revenue, namely the area with diagonal bars in Figure 8.4, is not paid for by the domestic consumers but by the foreign producers. The net welfare gain for the home country is therefore the difference between the part (diagonal bars) of government revenue paid for by the foreign producers and the efficiency loss triangles (horizontal bars), which is potentially positive.

8.4 Tariffs and general equilibrium

We will now analyse the impact of a tariff in a general equilibrium setting. To do that, we use the neoclassical model explained in Chapters 4–7. We assume that the home country is relatively labour abundant, such that under free trade it will import the capital-intensive manufactures, and export the labour–intensive food. Moreover, we assume in this section that the home country is *small* and cannot influence its terms of trade. The price of manufactures relative to the price of food is therefore given. Section 8.7 below will analyse the general equilibrium impact of imposing a tariff if the home country is large.

If the home country engages in free trade, identified by the sub-index *tr*, the analysis in Chapter 7 shows that the production, consumption, and trade equilibrium is characterized by the following equalities; see also equation (7.6).

$$(8.1) \qquad MRS_{tr} = \frac{p_m}{p_f} = MRT_{tr}$$

The (given) world price of manufactures relative to food, that is the ratio at which the economy can trade with the rest of the world, is therefore equal to both the marginal rate of substitution on the consumption side of the economy and the marginal rate of transformation on the production side of the economy. If the country imposes an *ad valorem* tariff *t* on the imports of manufactures, however, this raises the domestic price of manufactures above the world price of manufactures. Producers and consumers in the home economy, facing domestic prices, therefore equate the marginal rate of transformation and the marginal rate of substitution to the *tariff-ridden* relative price level, which exceeds the ratio at which the economy can trade with the rest of the world.

$$(8.2) \qquad MRS_{tariff} = \frac{p_m(1 + t)}{p_f} = MRT_{tariff} > \frac{p_m}{p_f}$$

This equation characterizes the equilibrium if a tariff on the import of manufactures is imposed once we realize that the home country can still trade with the rest of the world at the world-relative price ratio p_m/p_f, and *not* at the domestic price ratio $p_m(1+t)/p_f$. The tariff-ridden consumption point of the economy must therefore be on the income line generated by the tariff-ridden production point, evaluated at world prices.[2]

The impact of the tariff is illustrated in Figure 8.5, where the closed square indicates production under free trade, the closed circle indicates consumption under free trade, the open square indicates the tariff-ridden production point, and the open circle indicates the tariff-ridden consumption point. Let's summarize the main conclusions.

Figure 8.5 Impact of tariff in general equilibrium

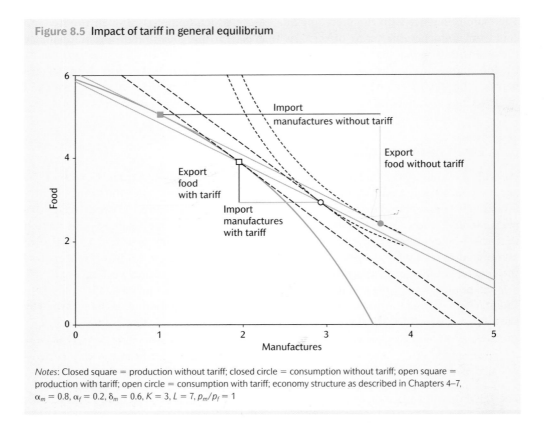

Notes: Closed square = production without tariff; closed circle = consumption without tariff; open square = production with tariff; open circle = consumption with tariff; economy structure as described in Chapters 4–7, $\alpha_m = 0.8$, $\alpha_f = 0.2$, $\delta_m = 0.6$, $K = 3$, $L = 7$, $p_m/p_f = 1$

- As in the partial equilibrium approach of Section 8.3, the production of manufactures increases because the relative price of manufactures rises, but it is clear that there is a simultaneous reduction in the production of food. This represents the opportunity costs of trade restrictions, as already identified by Adam Smith; see Chapter 3.

- There is a reduction of income generated by the economy (evaluated at world prices).

- The income loss and the deviation from world prices leads to a reduction in welfare (this is further explained below).

- The tariff leads to a reduction in the volume of trade.

The imposition of the tariff actually imposes a double distortion on the economy, as is implicit in equation (8.2) and made explicit in Figure 8.6. First, because the domestic price level deviates from the price level at which the economy can trade with the rest of the world, the economy produces at a sub-optimal production point, leading to an income loss. This reduction in income leads, of course, to a lower welfare level. Note, however, that at the income level generated by the tariff-ridden production point, the economy could consume at the open triangle in Figure 8.6, lowering the welfare level from U_3 to U_2. Second, the tariff also leads to a sub-optimal consumption point because the domestic price level deviates from the world price level, leading to consumption at the open circle and further reducing the welfare level from U_2 to U_1.

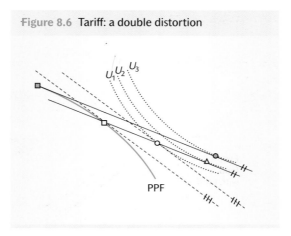

Figure 8.6 Tariff: a double distortion

 Box 8.3 Tool: the offer curve

Before we can continue with analysing the impact of imposing a tariff if the home country is large, such that it has market power and can influence its terms of trade, we have to introduce another economic tool of analysis, already used by Alfred Marshall, called the offer curve. Figure 8.7 depicts free trade production and consumption combinations for six different relative price levels of manufactures.[3] Going from top to bottom, we see that as the relative price of manufactures increases, the economy will produce more and more manufactures, until the economy is completely specialized in the production of manufactures. Simultaneously, we see that the consumption ratio of food to manufactures increases from top to bottom, because the relative price of manufactures is rising, and that the distance from the origin is determined by the income level of the economy generated by the production point.   »

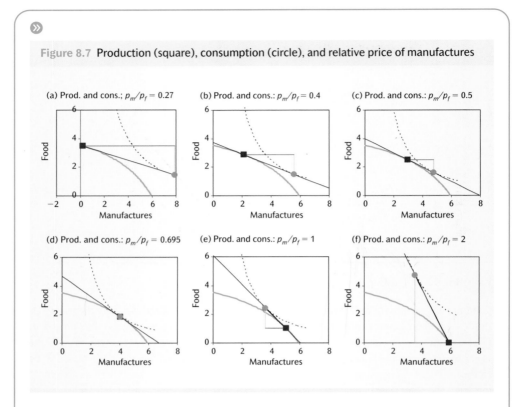

Figure 8.7 Production (square), consumption (circle), and relative price of manufactures

(a) Prod. and cons.; $p_m/p_f = 0.27$

(b) Prod. and cons.: $p_m/p_f = 0.4$

(c) Prod. and cons.: $p_m/p_f = 0.5$

(d) Prod. and cons.: $p_m/p_f = 0.695$

(e) Prod. and cons.: $p_m/p_f = 1$

(f) Prod. and cons.: $p_m/p_f = 2$

Figure 8.7 also draws the trade triangles at the different price levels, which make the inequality between production and consumption at the national level possible. Going again from top to bottom, we see that the economy initially exports food in exchange for imports of manufactures if the relative price of manufactures is very low. Once the relative price level of manufactures exceeds the autarky price (0.695), the economy starts to export manufactures in exchange for imports of food. The figure clearly demonstrates the connections that exist between the relative price of manufactures and the export–import combination the economy is willing to offer to the rest of the world at that price level.

Figure 8.8 depicts five of the six export–import combinations the economy is willing to offer to the rest of the world as illustrated in Figure 8.7. Point A in Figure 8.8, for example, depicts the export of manufactures the economy offers in exchange for the import of food if the relative price of manufactures is equal to 2. This relative price ratio is, of course, given by the slope of the line from point A to the origin in Figure 8.8. The five dots in Figure 8.8 give the export–import combinations for five different relative price levels. The offer curve, also depicted in Figure 8.8, connects these five points by depicting all possible export–import combinations for all possible relative price levels.

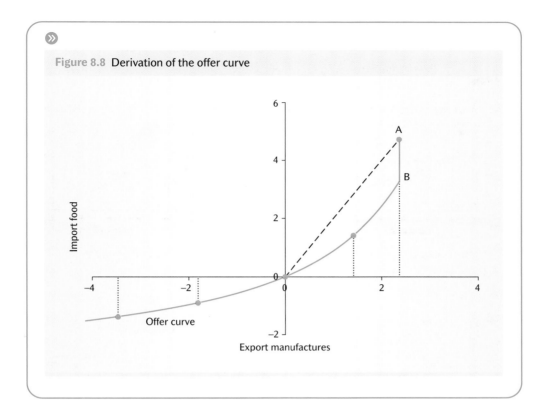

Figure 8.8 Derivation of the offer curve

8.5 General equilibrium with offer curves

Combining the offer curve of a country with the offer curve from the rest of the world allows us to determine the trading equilibrium in the economy, and the concomitant exports and imports. To illustrate this, we will use the economic structure also used in Chapter 7, where Austria was relatively capital abundant and Bolivia relatively labour abundant. For ease of reference we partly reproduce Table 7.1; see Table 8.2.

Using the procedure explained in Box 8.3, we can derive an offer curve for both countries. Actually, Section 8.4 already did this for Austria. We can repeat the procedure for Bolivia, and plot its offer curve in the same diagram. It will be convenient to measure Bolivia's import of manufactures in the same direction as Austria's export of manufactures, and similarly for imports and exports of food. This switches the orientation of Bolivia's offer curve relative to Austria, as illustrated in Figure 8.9.

The trading equilibrium of the two countries is given by the point of intersection of the two offer curves (not the origin), as indicated by the trade equilibrium point in Figure 8.9. The slope of the line from this point to the origin gives the trade equilibrium relative price of manufactures. At that price, the quantity of manufactures Austria is willing to offer in exchange for imports of food is equal to the quantity of manufactures Bolivia is demanding in exchange for exports of food. The world markets for both goods are thus in equilibrium.

Table 8.2 Parameter values for Austria and Bolivia

	Austria	Bolivia
Capital K	7	3
Labour L	3	7
Share of income δ_m spent on manufactures	0.6	0.6
Capital intensity α_m for manufactures	0.8	0.8
Capital intensity α_f for food	0.2	0.2

Figure 8.9 Determination of trade equilibrium with offer curves

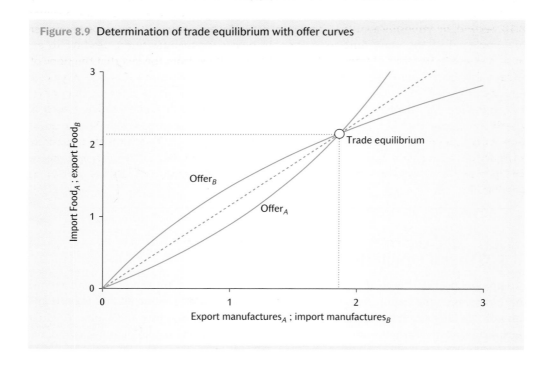

8.6 The 'optimal' tariff?

Given the preliminaries of Sections 8.4 and 8.5, we can now analyse the impact of imposing a tariff if the home country is large and can influence its terms of trade. Recall that the partial equilibrium analysis of Section 8.3 suggests that a large country might gain from trade under certain circumstances. As we will see below, this result carries over to a general equilibrium analysis.

If the country is able to benefit from imposing a tariff, this benefit must arise from the ability to influence its terms of trade, since Section 8.4 demonstrates that for any *given* terms of trade imposing a tariff always leads to a welfare loss. The analysis in Section 8.4 also shows that for any given terms of trade, imposing a tariff reduces the volume of trade; see Figure 8.5.

Since the offer curve derived in Box 8.3 depicts the combination of exports and imports for all possible terms of trade, and imposing a tariff reduces the volume of trade for any given terms of trade, we can conclude that the imposition of a tariff leads to an inward rotation of the offer curve. For the equilibrium derived in the previous section (see Table 8.2 and Figure 8.9), this inward rotation is illustrated in Figure 8.10 if the capital-abundant Austria imposes a 40 per cent tariff on the imports of food. Figure 8.10 also shows Austria's offer curve if it does not impose a tariff, which would lead to the free trade equilibrium point C. After the tariff is imposed by Austria, the tariff-ridden trade equilibrium point at which the export of manufactures by Austria is equal to the import of manufactures by Bolivia is at point D in Figure 8.10.

Figure 8.10 allows us to draw at least two conclusions. First, a tariff imposed by a large country also leads to a reduction in the volume of trade, as indicated by the arrows in Figure 8.10. Second, by imposing a tariff a large country can indeed exercise its monopsony power for food (and at the same time its monopoly power for manufactures), leading to an improvement in its terms of trade. In Figure 8.10 this follows from the fact that the slope of a line from the origin to the tariff-ridden equilibrium point D is steeper than the slope of a line drawn from the origin to the free trade equilibrium point C (these lines are not drawn in the figure). The tariff thus leads to a higher relative price of manufactures, which is Austria's export good and represents an improvement in Austria's terms of trade. The question remains whether or not Austria's welfare level has improved. To answer that question we make use of trade indifference curves, which essentially translate a country's preferences and production possibilities into export–import indifference curves. This is explained in detail in Box 8.4.

Figure 8.10 Trade equilibrium if Austria imposes a 40 per cent tariff

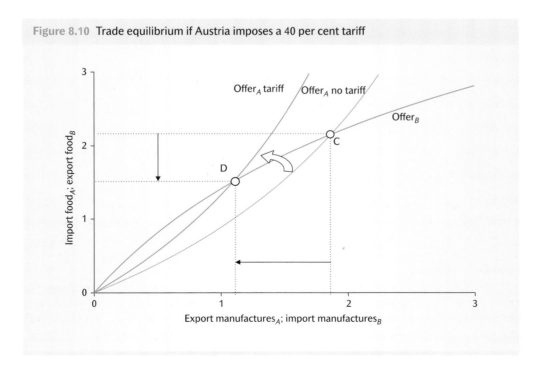

Box 8.4   Trade indifference curves

A country engaged in trade with the rest of the world is able to achieve a higher welfare level, as we have seen many times in previous chapters. There is thus a connection between the export–import combination of a nation and the welfare level this country is able to achieve. James Meade (1952) made this connection explicit by deriving trade indifference curves.

Point D_4 in the first quadrant of Figure 8.11 gives a specific combination of exports of manufactures in exchange for imports of food. To derive the maximum utility level the country can achieve with the export–import combination D_4, we take this point as the origin of the production possibility set, measured from right to left, rather than from left to right. In the second quadrant of Figure 8.11 we measure the consumption levels of manufactures and food. Given the export–import combination D_4, the country reaches its maximum utility level at point C_4, the point of tangency of the production possibility frontier and iso-utility curve$_4$ drawn in the second quadrant of Figure 8.11.

We can now ask ourselves which other export–import combinations allow the country to reach the same utility level. The procedure is similar to above, only in reverse order. First, we slide the production possibility frontier along iso-utility curve$_4$ in the second quadrant of Figure 8.11, preserving tangency. Second, the origin of the production possibility set depicts another export–import combination giving the same utility level as before. Three examples of this procedure, the consumption levels C_3, C_2, and C_1 and the concomitant export–import combinations D_3, D_2, and D_1, are given in Figure 8.11. The curve connecting the points D_4, D_3, D_2, and D_1 depicts a large range of other export–import combinations which allow the country to reach the same utility level. It is labelled trade indifference curve$_4$.

Figure 8.11 Derivation of trade indifference curves

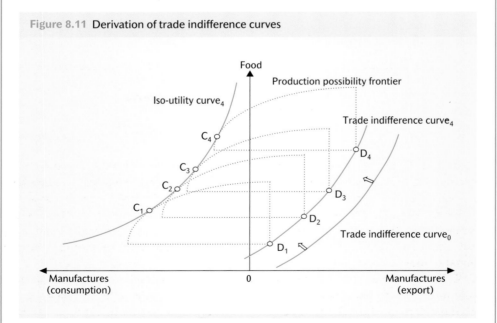

>> Three final remarks should be made. First, note that the trade indifference curve simultaneously reflects the curvature of the iso-utility curve and of the production possibility frontier. Second, we can in principle repeat this procedure for any arbitrary iso-utility curve, leading to an infinite number of trade indifference curves in the first quadrant of Figure 8.11. We have drawn one other example, labelled trade indifference curve$_0$. Third, note that the welfare level the economy can reach increases in the north-west direction in the first quadrant of Figure 8.11. In particular, trade indifference curve$_0$ depicts a lower welfare level than trade indifference curve$_4$.

Figure 8.12 The 'optimal' tariff

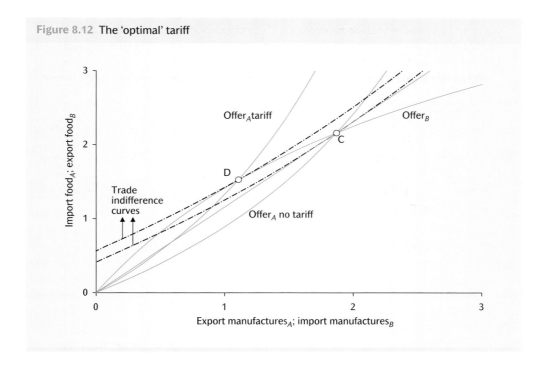

Figure 8.12 depicts two trade indifference curves. One curve is tangent at point C to the price line from the origin to point C, which depicts the free trade equilibrium. Tangency at that point is ensured by the perfectly competitive behaviour of the economic agents and the absence of distortions. The other trade indifference curve is tangent at point D to the offer curve of Bolivia. As explained in Box 8.4 , the trade indifference curve tangent at point D represents a higher welfare level for Austria. Can the government of Austria manipulate the international economic conditions to reach point D? The answer is yes, as also drawn in Figure 8.12. If the government of Austria imposes a tariff on the imports of food, this leads to an inward rotation of its offer curve and a concomitant change of the international trade equilibrium point. By carefully choosing its tariff rate, the government of Austria can in principle ensure that its tariff-ridden offer curve intersects Bolivia's offer curve at point D. Given the offer curve of Bolivia, the highest possible welfare level Austria can achieve is at point D. The tariff rate that ensures that Austria's tariff-ridden offer curve intersects Bolivia's offer curve at

point D is therefore known as the 'optimal' tariff. It is derived formally in Technical Note 8.1. If the country is large, in the sense that it can influence its terms of trade, this optimal tariff is always positive within this framework. See, however, the next section and Chapter 17.

8.7 Optimal tariffs and retaliation

In the analysis in the preceding section, the government of Austria is very smart. In fact, the government knows a lot and is able to perform extremely complicated calculations. It knows the production structure of its own economy, the preferences of its consumers, and the economic behaviour of its inhabitants. This allows it to calculate the production and consumption points for all possible relative prices of manufactures, and thus the concomitant export and import decisions at those prices. Using all this information, the government of Austria can then derive its own offer curve. In addition, the government can manipulate this offer curve by calculating the impact of imposing a tariff on the import of food for the above production, consumption, export, and import decisions. But that is not all. The government of Austria also knows all of this information on production, technology, preferences, consumption, exports, and imports for the economy of Bolivia, which allows it to derive Bolivia's offer curve. Finally, then, the government of Austria is able to combine all of this information into determining the point of tangency of its own trade indifference curves with Bolivia's offer curve, which enables it to calculate the 'optimal' tariff.

The above observations on the formidable informational requirements and supposed ability of the government of Austria to process detailed economic information in determining the optimal tariff raises two important questions. First, do we really think any government in the world has this information available, and is capable at the same time of performing the required calculations? The answer undoubtedly must be negative, putting the entire reasoning process of a country able to determine the optimal tariff into question. Second, even if we allow the government of Austria, within the setting of this economic structure, to be so smart as to calculate the optimal tariff, why shouldn't the same hold for the government of Bolivia?

The second question is addressed in Figure 8.13. If both countries engage in free trade, the trade equilibrium occurs at point C, the intersection of the two offer curves if neither country imposes a tariff on imports. As explained in the previous section, if Austria is very smart, it can calculate the point of tangency of Bolivia's offer curve and its trade indifference curves to determine the optimal tariff which will rotate its own offer curve inwards to ensure that the trade equilibrium moves from point C to point D to maximize its own welfare. If the government of Bolivia is as smart as the government of Austria, it will follow a similar procedure to calculate its own optimal tariff which will rotate its own offer curve inwards to ensure that its own welfare is maximized at the point of tangency of its own trade indifference curves and Austria's offer curve. In Figure 8.13 this is given by point E. Country B's optimal tariff is therefore calculated to rotate Bolivia's offer curve inward to move the trade equilibrium from point C to point E.

Where does all of this cleverness of Austria and Bolivia lead? Austria performs complicated calculations to try to move the international equilibrium from point C to point D. Bolivia performs complicated calculations to try to move the international equilibrium from point C to point E. The end result is that neither country gets what it wants, because the intersection of the two tariff-ridden offer curves occurs at point F. As drawn in Figure 8.13, this leads to lower trade and welfare levels for both countries. One can imagine that numerous game-theoretic

Figure 8.13 Tariffs and retaliation

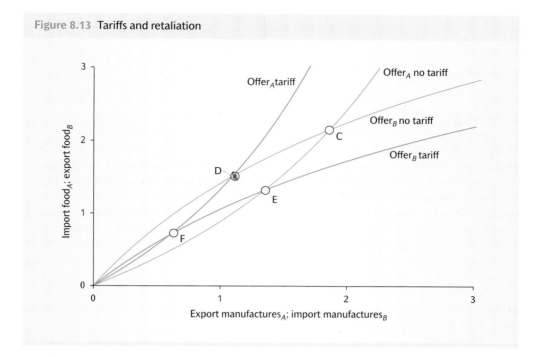

Box 8.5   **Human-capital-intensive manufacturing exporters**

The ITC classifies forty-three goods as 'human-capital-intensive manufacturing' products, incorporating synthetic colours, pigments, perfumes, cosmetics, rubber and tyres, tubes, pipes, various types of steel and iron, cutlery, televisions, radios, cars, watches, and jewellery. For the 151 countries for which the ITC provides data, total exports of human-capital-intensive manufactures in 1998 were equal to $1,127 bn, a sizeable 23 per cent of all exports. The left-hand side of Table 8.3 lists the top ten exporters of human-capital-intensive manufactures in absolute terms. With a value of $163 bn Germany is the world's largest human-capital-intensive manufactures exporter, followed by Japan ($125 bn) and the USA ($114 bn). In all three cases automobiles and parts for automobiles form the main component of these exports. The other large exporters are also OECD countries.

As indicated by the right-hand side of Table 8.3, three countries in the list of the world's ten largest exporters of human-capital-intensive manufactures in absolute terms also make it to the list of the world's ten largest exporters in relative terms, namely Spain, Canada, and Japan. The top three in relative terms is formed by Slovakia, Spain, and Slovenia. Automobiles and automobile parts are again the main component in all three cases. Figure 8.14 shows the relative dependence of countries on the exports of human-capital-intensive manufactures. These are concentrated in the rich countries, plus central Europe, Brazil, and Argentina.   »

Table 8.3 Top ten human-capital-intensive manufacturing exporters, 1998

No.	Top 10 in absolute terms			Top 10 in relative terms		
	Country	Exports		Country	Exports	
		Value	%		%	Value
1	Germany	163	32	Slovakia	44	4
2	Japan	125	33	Spain	41	43
3	USA	114	19	Slovenia	38	3
4	France	81	28	Canada	36	72
5	Canada	72	36	Finland	35	15
6	UK	61	24	Czech Republic	34	10
7	Belgium	51	31	Ukraine	34	3
8	Italy	50	25	Austria	34	19
9	Spain	43	41	Sweden	34	25
10	Mexico	36	31	Japan	33	125

Sources: WTO/UNCTAD International Trade Centre website http://www.intracen.org; value in bn US$. The % shares are relative to the country's total exports.

Figure 8.14 Human-capital-intensive manufacturing exports, share

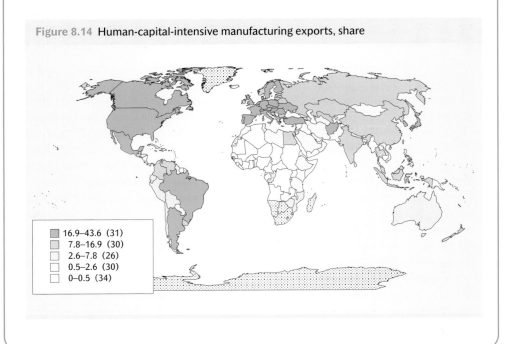

16.9–43.6 (31)
7.8–16.9 (30)
2.6–7.8 (26)
0.5–2.6 (30)
0–0.5 (34)

manoeuvres have been analysed by international economists within this framework, assuming that both countries move simultaneously in calculating 'optimal' tariffs in a sequence of steps, or that one country moves before the other country retaliates in a series of alternating steps in calculating 'optimal' tariffs, etc. In all cases, the end result of all this cleverness is the same. The international equilibrium moves in the wrong direction, leading to lower welfare levels for both countries than is achieved at the free trade equilibrium at point C in Figure 8.13. Traditionally, this is why we think there is an important role for multilateral trade negotiations, first in the GATT and now in the WTO (see Chapter 12), for moving the international economy into the direction of free trade, and away from retaliation and trade wars which reduce welfare for all countries involved.

8.8 Tariffs in the USA

For some important countries, such as the USA, the average tariff rate has reached historically low levels, as illustrated in Figure 8.15. At the beginning of the nineteenth century the tariff revenue was very high, about 50 per cent of the value of imports. In this period the southern part of the USA wanted to import cheap foreign manufactures (from Britain) while the northern part of the USA demanded protection of the domestic industry. The controversy over tariffs peaked in 1828 with the tariff of Abominations, when the southern congressmen made a strategic mistake by amending a bill to include high tariffs on raw materials in the hope that their northern colleagues would reject it (because northern manufacturers used those raw materials), which they did not.

With a compromise law in 1833 the average American tariff rate started to decline, although not coming down as far as European tariffs. The decline stopped in 1861 when the Morrill tariff was passed, raising rates on iron and steel products, followed by other duties in 1862 and 1864, also designed to finance the Civil War. At the beginning of the twentieth century tariff rates came down considerably when the Wilson administration put many items

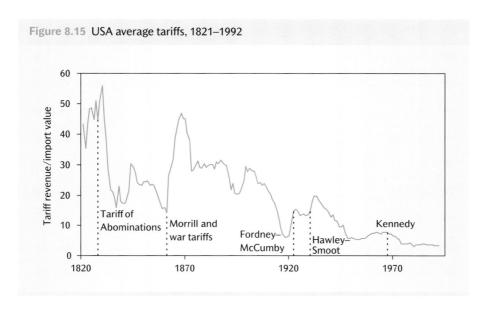

Figure 8.15 USA average tariffs, 1821–1992

on the 'free list'. This was reversed in the first recession after the First World War, when the Fordney–McCumby tariff was passed in 1922, intended to help the farmers. It was followed by the Hawley–Smoot tariff in 1930, which as Kenen (2000: 213) put it was 'once called the "Holy-Smoke Tariff" by a student with keener insight than memory'. After the Second World War a series of multilateral GATT negotiations, for example in the American-inspired Kennedy Round, eventually resulted in the current low average tariff rates, also for other countries in the world (see Figure 8.2).

8.9 Conclusions

We analyse the impact of trade policy on the size of trade flows and the distribution of welfare effects. In general, there are both winners and losers of imposing trade restrictions, which makes the demand for protection (lobbying) understandable. Among the winners are protected domestic producers and, in terms of tariff revenue, the government. The main losers are the domestic consumers, who pay for the increased profits of domestic producers and the tariff revenue, the country as a whole, in terms of an efficiency loss (Harberger triangles), and the foreign producers. The main difference between tariffs and quota rests in the question who receives the tariff-equivalent government revenue. The foreign country can try to reap this benefit by establishing a 'voluntary' export restraint. Imposing a tariff always leads to a net welfare loss for a small country, which cannot influence its terms of trade. Within a neoclassical framework, a large country, which can influence its terms of trade, might benefit from a net welfare gain by imposing an 'optimal' tariff based on its monopoly power. This argument breaks down under a system of retaliation leading to tariff wars, which clarifies the necessity of multilateral trade negotiations (WTO, see Chapter 12).

TECHNICAL NOTE

Technical Note 8.1 Derivation of the 'optimal' tariff

Using the standard optimal pricing rule for a monopolist $p(1-1/\varepsilon) = MC$, see Technical Note 9.1 in the next chapter, the 'optimal' tariff t_A for Austria can quite easily be derived as a function of the foreign excess demand elasticity ε_B^d once we realize that Austria acts as a monopolist, its marginal costs are its own price p_A, the price it charges indirectly through the tariff it imposes is the foreign price p_B, with elasticity $\varepsilon = \varepsilon_B^d$, and the two prices are related through $p_B = (1 + t_A)p_A$. Simple substitution gives:

$$\left.\begin{array}{l} p_B(1 - 1/\varepsilon_B^d) = p_A \\ p_B = (1 + t_A)p_A \end{array}\right\} \Rightarrow t_A = \frac{1}{\varepsilon_B^d - 1} \quad \text{('optimal' tariff)}$$

QUESTIONS

Question 8.1

The European Union (EU) is considered to be a 'large' country in this question. In the 1980s Japanese producers began to export many cars to the EU. To protect their domestic car industries, the governments of the EU countries pushed for protective tariffs. We analyse the impact of these tariffs in a partial equilibrium framework.

8.1A What makes a partial equilibrium analysis 'partial'?

8.1B Draw a partial equilibrium figure of the EU car market. Indicate clearly the volume of Japanese imports before and after the imposition of the tariff.

8.1C Is the tariff welfare improving for the EU? Why, or why not?

The Japanese car manufacturers were not happy with the EU protection and started a lobbying process in Brussels to abolish the EU tariffs. These lobbying efforts were not completely successful, such that the tariffs are abolished in return for a 'voluntary' restriction of car exports to the EU.

8.1D Why do the Japanese firms prefer the voluntary export restraints (VERs) to the tariffs?

8.1E What is the tariff-equivalent import quota (or rather VER in this question) for Japan in your figure of question 8.1B?

Question 8.2

A military coup in Zombio has overthrown the government. The new leaders, proud defenders of the national heritage, declare that all Western food imports will be subject to a tax of 10 per cent, to be paid at the customs office. Zombio produces and consumes two goods, namely copper and food. The figure below summarizes the free trade situation.

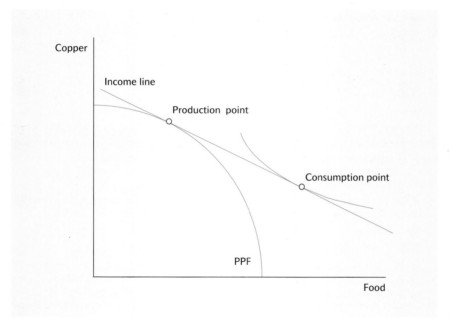

8.2A Is copper imported or exported in the free trade situation? Explain how you can derive this information from the graph above.

8.2B Explain what happens to the production of copper and food in Zombio if the military leaders impose a tariff τ on imports. Illustrate this in the graph and label the new production point P′.

8.2C What are the new consumption possibilities for Zombio (at world prices) generated by the production point P′? Indicate these possibilities in your graph.

8.2D Let C′ be the utility–maximizing consumption choice of consumers, given the consumption possibilities available to them (see question 8.2C). Illustrate point C′ in your graph.

8.2E Why do the consumers choose a different consumption point than your answer to question 8.2D? Denote the actual consumption point in your graph with C″.

8.2F Explain what the two distorting effects of the tariff are, and where you have illustrated them in this question.

Question 8.3

Suppose that the EU and the USA both produce bananas and steel, where the EU exports steel in return for American bananas.

8.3A Draw the offer curves of the EU and the USA in one figure. The trade of steel is measured on the horizontal axis and the trade of bananas is measured on the vertical axis. Indicate clearly which offer curve belongs to which country.

8.3B Illustrate the international trade equilibrium in your figure for question 8.3A, also showing the traded amounts of each product.

8.3C Draw two graphs in which you show the effects of a 'trade war' on welfare and trade. In your first graph, let the EU start the 'war' and in your second graph, let the USA start. Assume that, starting from free trade, one country imposes an 'optimal tariff' and the other country retaliates once.

Suppose now that, starting from free trade, the USA and the EU simultaneously impose 'optimal tariffs'.

8.3D Is the resulting outcome welfare maximizing for either country and/or for the world as a whole? What is this welfare situation called in game theory?

8.3E Is the above analysis relevant for the establishment and functioning of international trade organizations such as the WTO (World Trade Organization)?

See the Online Resource Centre for a Study Guide containing more questions
www.oxfordtextbooks.co.uk/orc/vanmarrewijk/

NOTES

1 The American economist Paul Krugman analyses the arguments of many influential pressure groups in an accessible style; see (at the time of writing) http://web.mit.edu/krugman/www/. Check the web links from www.oxfordtextbooks.co.uk/orc/vanmarrewijk/for the most up-to-date URL.

2 To be precise, this requires either a lump–sum redistribution of the government tariff revenue to the consumers, or government consumption preferences identical to private consumers.

3 The structure of the economy is explained in Chs 4–7; $\alpha_m = 0.8$, $\alpha_f = 0.2$, $\delta_m = 0.6$, $K = 7$, $L = 3$.

II.B

COMPETITIVE ADVANTAGE

Part II.B (Competitive Advantage) investigates the impact of imperfect competition, economies of scale, and product differentiation on the structure of the international economy and the size and type of its trade flows. This 'new trade' approach is the fruitful result of incorporating elements of the industrial organization literature in international economics. Part II.B also analyses the impact of new trade theory on (strategic) trade policy, discusses the main international organizations, and applies the economic insights on the structure of the world economy learned in Parts II.A and II.B to an investigation of the process of (European) economic integration.

IMPERFECT COMPETITION

Objectives/key terms

- Monopoly/oligopoly
- Cournot competition
- Pro-competitive effect of trade

- Mark-up pricing
- Reaction curves
- Reciprocal dumping

Acknowledging that many firms have market power, we discuss the effect of international trade, which increases competition, on production, consumption, and welfare.

9.1 Introduction

So far we have analysed perfectly competitive markets, that is markets in which the firms do not perceive they have any market power. More specifically, they do not think they can influence the price at which the market clears. All firms individually, therefore, take the market-clearing price as given in their profit maximization problem. Each firm determines how much it will produce at any given price level. The actions of all firms together determine the market supply. This is confronted with the demand of consumers to determine the price at which the market actually clears. Collectively, the firms therefore *do* influence the market-clearing price. If there are many firms, the impact of any individual firm on the market-clearing price is negligible; hence the assumption that each firm takes this price as given.

In many cases the assumption of perfect competition is a reasonable approximation. At the Dutch flower auction, for example, each night hundreds of growers deliver the flowers cut, selected, and packed that day to the auction to be sold off early the next morning at whatever price will clear the market. In many other cases, however, perfect competition is not a reasonable approximation. There may, for example, be only one company that delivers water to your house, or only one telephone company, or one electricity company, etc. If so, this company obviously has market power and will realize that an increase in its production level will reduce the market-clearing price. Or, equivalently, it will realize that if it raises the price level, the demand for its goods or services will fall. Alternatively, there may be only a few companies, rather than one. There are at the moment, for example, only two companies producing large wide-body commercial aircraft for the global market, namely the American Boeing company and the European Airbus consortium. Both companies realize that they have market power, and that their actions will influence the other company. They take this into consideration when determining the optimal strategy; see also Chapter 11.

If a firm does not take the price level on the market as given, but strategically interacts with other firms and the market to maximize its profits, we are no longer in the realm of 'perfect competition'. Instead, we say such a market is characterized by 'imperfect competition', a poorly chosen term indeed, certainly in those cases in which it gives a better description of the market. The world of perfect competition is attractive; it is well defined, its behavioural assumptions are clear and easy to understand; it leads to powerful conclusions; and in most

| **Famous economists** | Joseph Stiglitz |

Fig. 9.1
Joseph Stiglitz
(1942–)

Like Samuelson, Joe Stiglitz was born in Gary, Indiana. He received his PhD from MIT when he was only 24 years old. He has moved around from one prestigious university to another, never staying very long. Recently, he was chief economist of the World Bank before moving to Stanford University. His many contributions to economics focus on imperfect competition and the importance of costly information. Outside his own field the most influential contribution has undoubtedly been 'Monopolistic competition and optimum product diversity', published jointly with Avinash Dixit in the *American Economic Review* in 1977; see Chapter 10.

cases it substantially increases our knowledge and understanding of the workings of an economy. In contrast, the world of imperfect competition is a mess. Since there is an unlimited number of ways in which one can deviate from the 'perfect' world, there are many different 'imperfect' models, some of astounding complexity, leading to many different outcomes and policy prescriptions. To top things off, imperfect competition is hard to model in a general equilibrium setting, certainly in conjunction with production under increasing returns to scale (see the sequel). No wonder (international) economists have shied away from imperfect competition for a long time.

This does not mean that there has been no attention paid to the connections between monopoly power and international trade flows. As early as in 1701 Henry Martyn wrote a clear and concise tract, entitled *Considerations upon the East India Trade*, opposing monopoly restraints on the East India trade and restrictions on manufactured imports from India. Instead, such trade should be open to all merchants, not just to those licensed by the government:[1]

> In an open trade, every merchant is upon his good behavior, always afraid of being undersold at home, always seeking out for new markets in foreign countries; in the meantime, trade is carried on with less expense: This is the effect of necessity and emulation, things unknown to a single company.

Martyn therefore opposes monopoly power in trade flows, arguing that competition among companies improves efficiency. None the less, there may be good reasons why there are only a few firms, or one, in an industry. Many of the examples given above, such as power companies, telecommunications, or aircraft production, require large initial investments before production of goods and services can start: for example the construction of a power plant, the wiring of a city, or the development of new aircraft and construction of a factory to build them. After the initial investment, which can be seen as a fixed cost, production can start, involving high or low production costs. The larger the firm, as measured by the production level, the lower the costs of production per unit of output, because the large initial fixed investment costs can be spread across more goods. In other words, there are increasing returns to scale at the firm level. As we will argue in the next chapter, this is incompatible with perfect competition. The consequences of increasing returns to scale are analysed in more detail in the following chapters. This chapter analyses the impact of market power, and not the impact of increasing returns to scale, such that all production functions in this chapter exhibit constant returns to scale.

9.2 Monopoly

Suppose that there is only one firm active on a specific market. This firm is called a monopolist. Like any other firm, it will be interested in maximizing its profits, probably camouflaged in its brochures as a commitment to efficiency, service to society, and eagerness to deliver high-quality goods and services to its customers. Since it is the only firm active in the market, it will of course realize that its actions have a large impact on the market. In particular, the firm will realize that there is a negative relationship between the price charged for its products and the quantity sold on the market. The monopolist's profit maximization problem is therefore more sophisticated than the problem facing a perfectly competitive firm which treats the output price as a parameter. A monopolist must not only gather information about its own production processes and cost structure, but also about the market for its product and the responsiveness of this market to changes in the price charged by the monopolist. It is time for a quick review of the monopolist's profit maximization problem.

Figure 9.2 illustrates the monopolist's problem. The market demand curve is given by the downward-sloping solid line. It is assumed to be linear, which implies that the marginal revenue (*MR*) curve is also linear, with the same intercept and a slope twice as steep (see Box 9.1). The marginal revenue curve is steeper than the demand curve because the firm has to lower its price if it wants to sell more goods, which also lowers the revenue on the initial

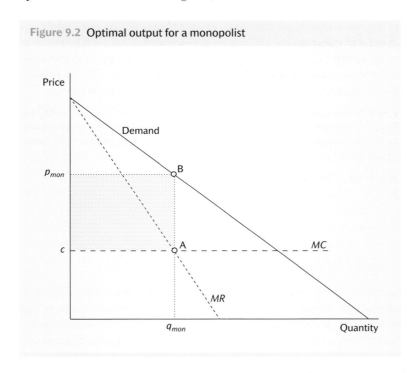

Figure 9.2 Optimal output for a monopolist

 Box 9.1   **Tool: microeconomics and markets**

The tools to be used in this chapter are taken from standard microeconomic theory. If a firm perceives it has market power, it will use this market power to the best of its advantage. We will analyse the case of a pure monopoly (one firm), of oligopoly (a few firms), and of monopolistic competition (many firms with individual market power; see Chapter 10). Let p be the price of a good, and q the quantity produced. If the demand curve is linear, that is, $p = a - bq$ for some positive parameters a and b, it follows that revenue R (price times quantity) equals

$$pq = (a - bq)q = aq - bq^2$$

This, in turn, implies that marginal revenue *MR* (increase in total revenue if more output is produced) is equal to $dR/dq = a - 2bq$.

We conclude, therefore, that if market demand is linear, then the marginal revenue curve is also linear, with the same intercept and a slope twice as steep as the demand curve.

output. We assume that the firm's marginal costs (MC) are constant, as indicated by the dashed horizontal line in Figure 9.2.

To maximize its profits, the firm will set its marginal costs equal to its marginal revenue, as indicated by point A. It will therefore produce the monopoly output indicated by q_{mon} in Figure 9.2. To determine the price the firm will charge at this output level, we have to go back to the demand curve, see point B, which gives us price level p_{mon}. The most important thing to note about Figure 9.2 is that the price charged by the monopolist is *higher* than the marginal cost of production. In determining the optimal price for its products, the monopolist thus charges a *mark-up* over the marginal cost of production. This mark-up depends on the price elasticity of demand $\varepsilon \equiv -(dq/dp)(p/q)$ as follows:

$$(9.1) \qquad p\left(1 - \frac{1}{\varepsilon(q)}\right) = c(q)$$

where $c(q)$ is the marginal cost of production; see Technical Note 9.1. The deviation between price and marginal cost of production is in stark contrast to a perfectly competitive market, in which the market-clearing price is always equal to the marginal cost of production. The fact that a monopolist's market power enables the firm to charge a higher price than the marginal cost of production also implies that the firm is able to make a profit. Since we assumed the marginal cost of production to be constant, the firm's profits are represented by the shaded rectangle in Figure 9.2 as $(p_{mon} - c)q_{mon}$, that is price minus cost times quantity sold.[2]

9.3 Monopoly in general equilibrium: autarky

As explained in Section 9.1, we focus on the consequences of market power in this chapter. Section 9.2 argued, in a partial equilibrium setting, that the most important implication of monopoly power is the fact that the price charged on the output market is a mark-up over the marginal cost of production. We now discuss the impact of monopoly power in autarky in a simple general equilibrium setting, based on James Markusen's (1981) analysis. The main assumptions are as follows:

- There is a single producer of manufactures; this is a monopoly market.
- There are many producers of food; the market is perfectly competitive.
- The markets for factors of production (capital and labour) are also perfectly competitive (the monopolist of manufactures therefore has no monopsony power on its input markets).
- All firms maximize profits.
- All consumers maximize utility, taking the final goods prices as given.

Without going into any further detail as to how the autarky equilibrium is determined exactly, we can draw some important conclusions based on the properties that must hold in this equilibrium. First, we know that the marginal rate of transformation must be equal to the ratio of marginal costs; see Chapter 7. Second, we know that the price charged by the monopolist is a mark-up over the marginal cost of production; see equation (9.1). Third, we know that the marginal rate of substitution must be equal to the ratio of final goods prices; see again Chapter 7. Fourth, we know that market-clearing in autarky implies that production must be equal to consumption in equilibrium. Combining this information leads to the following important conclusion:

(9.2)
$$MRT = \frac{MC_m}{MC_f} = \frac{p_m(1 - 1/\varepsilon_m)}{p_f} < \frac{p_m}{p_f} = MRS$$

where ε_m is the price elasticity of demand for manufactures.

The autarky equilibrium if there is a monopoly for manufactures is illustrated in Figure 9.3; see point Mon. Note that point Mon is in accordance with the four remarks made above. Perfect competition in the factor markets implies that the production point is efficient; that is, it must be on the production possibility frontier. Since the monopolist for manufactures charges a higher price than the marginal cost of production, the marginal rate of transformation deviates from the final goods price ratio, which in turn is equal to the marginal rate of substitution; see equation (9.2). Moreover, at the income level generated by the economy at point Mon, the consumers also want to consume at point Mon, such that production equals consumption in both sectors.

As is clear from Figure 9.2, the fact that there is a monopoly in manufactures implies that the economy is not producing at the social optimum; the utility level achieved at point Mon is equal to U_{mon}, which is strictly below the utility level U_{opt} which the economy can achieve in autarky at point Opt. The monopoly in manufactures, leading to a mark-up of price over marginal costs, therefore leads to a sub-optimal autarky equilibrium in which the production of manufactures is too low.

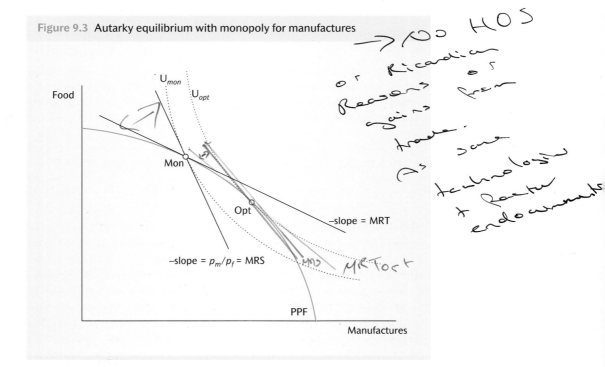

Figure 9.3 Autarky equilibrium with monopoly for manufactures

9.4 Oligopoly

Market power can, of course, also arise if there are only a few firms, rather than one, active in a market. This is called an oligopoly. If there are just two firms, say an Austrian firm (sub-index A) and a Bolivian firm (sub-index B), the market is called a duopoly. That case has already been analysed by Augustin Cournot (1838). He assumes that the two firms produce identical goods, such that there is only one market demand curve, and that both firms maximize their profits, given the demand curve and the output level of their opponent. Determining the equilibrium production levels, and concomitant price level, in this market is somewhat more involved than if there is only one firm. As in Section 9.2, we impose a linear demand curve; see, however, Technical Note 9.2.

Let p be the market price and $q = q_A + q_B$ be the total output in the market. We focus on the problem for the Austrian firm. Similar observations hold for the Bolivian firm. The basic problem for the Austrian firm is quite similar to the problem facing a monopolist. However, given the linear market demand $p = a - bq$ and the fact that total output is the sum of the Austrian firm's and Bolivian firm's output, it follows that the Austrian firm's profits π_A depend on the Bolivian firm's output level as follows:

$$(9.3) \qquad \pi_A = (p - c)q_A = [(a - c) - b(q_A + q_B)]q_A$$

where c is the marginal cost of production. Observe that

(i) Given the output level q_{B0} of the Bolivian firm, the Austrian firm maximizes profits π_A through a suitable choice of its output level, at say q_{A0}.

(ii) If the Bolivian firm changes its production level from q_{B0} to q_{B1}, the Austrian firm's profit maximization problem in point (i) is affected, which leads to a *different* optimal choice of its output level, say q_{A1}.

(iii) In general, therefore, each different output level of the Bolivian firm leads to a different optimal output level for the Austrian firm. The collection of all optimal output responses by the Austrian firm to the Bolivian firm's output level is called the *Austrian firm's reaction curve*.

This is illustrated in Figure 9.4. First, given that the Bolivian firm produces q_{B0} units of goods, the Austrian firm's optimal output choice must determine the optimal output combination on the dashed horizontal line generated by point q_{B0}. Since the Austrian firm maximizes profits, this dashed line must be tangent to one of its isoprofit curves, some of which are also drawn in Figure 9.4. The optimal production level for the Austrian firm, given that the Bolivian firm produces q_{B0}, is therefore equal to q_{A0}. Second, if the Bolivian firm increases its output level from q_{B0} to q_{B1}, this reduces the price level in the market and the Austrian firm's profitability. Consequently, the Austrian firm's optimal response is then a reduction in output, from q_{A0} to q_{A1}. Third, similar reactions by the Austrian firm to changes in the output level of the Bolivian firm are given by the dots in Figure 9.4. Connecting all such dots gives the reaction curve of the Austrian firm. Fourth, note that if the output level of the Bolivian firm is equal to zero, the Austrian firm's problem reduces to that of a monopolist. Clearly this leads to the maximum attainable profits for the Austrian firm,

Figure 9.4 Derivation of Austrian firm's reaction curve, $a = 8$, $b = c = 1$

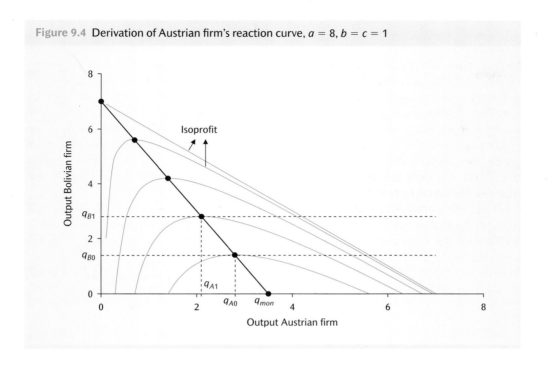

at point q_{mon} in Figure 9.4. The isoprofit curves of the Austrian firm in Figure 9.4 increase as they approach q_{mon}.

As already remarked above, the Bolivian firm faces a similar problem as the Austrian firm. This means that, taking the output level q_A as given, the Bolivian firm will derive its optimal (profit-maximizing) output level q_B. If we vary the Austrian firm's output level, we can derive all optimal responses by the Bolivian firm, which then obviously gives the Bolivian firm's reaction curve. This is illustrated in Figure 9.5, which also gives the Austrian firm's reaction curve and an isoprofit curve for each firm. Note that the isoprofit curve for the Bolivian firm is vertical at the point of intersection with its reaction curve because the Bolivian firm maximizes its profits at that point. The Cournot equilibrium is reached at the point of intersection of the two reaction curves, as indicated by point C in Figure 9.5. Why? Because, as the reader may wish to verify, it is the only point in the figure for which the Austrian firm maximizes its profits given the output level of the Bolivian firm, while simultaneously the Bolivian firm maximizes its profits given the output level of the Austrian firm. The duopoly price p_{duo} and quantity for each firm q_{duo} are derived in Technical Note 9.2, as given in equation (9.4).

$$(9.4) \qquad q_{duo} = \frac{a - c}{3b} = q_A = q_B; \quad p_{duo} = \frac{a + 2c}{3} < \frac{a + c}{2} = p_{mon}, \quad \text{because } a > c$$

Note, in particular, that the duopoly price is *lower* than the monopolistic price, which implies that the duopoly output level for the market ($2q_{duo}$) is higher than the monopoly output level.

Figure 9.5 Cournot equilibrium

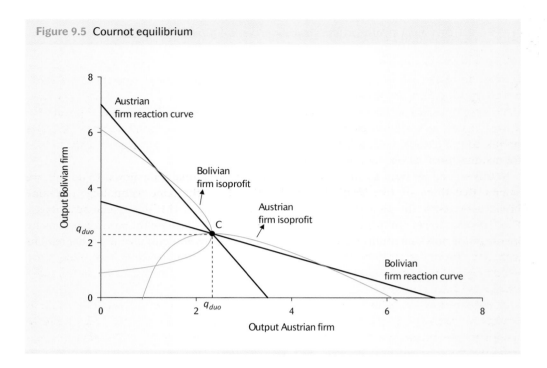

Apparently, more competition, as measured by an increase in the number of firms, leads to a lower price level. In fact, if the Austrian firm operates in a market with more than one firm, the following result holds in general; see again Technical Note 9.2:

$$\text{(9.5)} \qquad p\left(1 - \underbrace{\frac{q_A}{q}}_{\substack{\text{market} \\ \text{share}}} \frac{1}{\varepsilon(q)}\right) = c(q_A)$$

Equation (9.5) indicates that the marginal-revenue-equals-marginal-cost rule which the Austrian firm applies leads to a mark-up of price over marginal cost depending on:

• the price elasticity of demand $\varepsilon(q)$ prevailing in the market; and
• the Austrian firm's market share q_A/q.

More specifically, the higher the price elasticity of demand, the lower the mark-up, and the lower the Austrian firm's market share the lower the mark-up. In the limit, as the number of firms in the Cournot model becomes arbitrarily large and the Austrian firm's market share becomes arbitrarily small, the mark-up disappears and the price becomes equal to the marginal cost of production, as in the perfectly competitive model. One of the main attractions of the Cournot model is therefore that it reduces to the monopoly model if there is only one firm and to the perfectly competitive model if there are arbitrarily many firms.

9.5 The pro-competitive effect of international trade

We are now in a position to illustrate another benefit of international trade flows, namely the increase in market competition, which lowers the mark-up of price over marginal costs, which in turn increases efficiency. This benefit is called the pro-competitive gain from trade. To discuss this effect we use the Markusen (1981) framework analysed in Section 9.3 above. That is, we assume that the factor markets are perfectly competitive, firms maximize profits, consumers maximize utility, the food sector is perfectly competitive, while the market for manufactures has one monopoly producer.

In this section we want to analyse the impact of international trade flows. To do this, we assume that there are two *identical* countries; they have the same technology, the same homothetic tastes, the same stocks of capital and labour, etc. This has several advantages. First, it is easy to get our main point across. Second, we can illustrate the world economy by investigating only one country. Third, and most importantly, we neutralize any other reasons that may give rise to international trade flows, or that may lead to gains from trade; since technology is the same there is no Ricardian reason to trade, and since the capital–labour ratio is the same there is no Heckscher–Ohlin reason to trade.

The pro-competitive gains from trade are illustrated in Figure 9.6. In autarky both countries produce at the same distorted production and consumption point Mon, as discussed in Section 9.3. In autarky, the manufactures firm is a monopolist, which implies that the marginal rate of transformation is below the marginal rate of substitution, see equation (9.2). If trade of final goods is allowed, however, the monopoly producers for manufactures in both countries are confronted with an extra competitor, namely the previous monopolist in the other country. The market for manufactures has therefore become a duopoly, rather than a

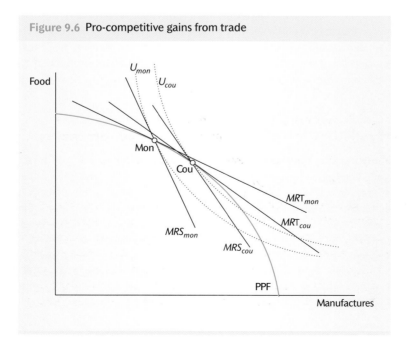

Figure 9.6 **Pro-competitive gains from trade**

monopoly, in both countries. As described in Section 9.4, and analogous to our reasoning in Section 9.3, we can therefore conclude:

$$(9.6) \qquad MRT_{duo} = \frac{MC_m}{MC_f}\bigg|_{duo} = \frac{p_m(1 - 1/2\varepsilon_m)}{p_f} < \frac{p_m}{p_f}\bigg|_{duo} = MRS_{duo}$$

As in the autarky equilibrium with a monopoly summarized in equation (9.2), the marginal rate of transformation is below the marginal rate of substitution in the trade equilibrium with a duopoly. Note, however, that in a duopoly firms only take the effect of their share of the market into consideration when determining the optimal production level; see equation (9.5). The wedge between the marginal rate of transformation and the marginal rate of substitution has therefore *reduced* from $1 - 1/\varepsilon_m$ to $1 - 1/2\varepsilon_m$ (because each firm in our example controls half the market). Consequently, the Cournot international trade equilibrium is illustrated by point Cou in Figure 9.6, in which the wedge between the marginal rate of transformation and the marginal rate of substitution has reduced, leading to more efficient production and higher welfare. This is known as the pro-competitive effect of international trade.

Remark: Note that the monopoly firms in both countries have a strong incentive to lobby with their respective governments *against* international trade flows. If they are successful in producing barriers to such flows, their profits will rise.

9.6 'Reciprocal dumping'

The power of the pro-competitive gains from trade is nicely illustrated in the Brander (1981) and Brander and Krugman (1983) 'reciprocal dumping' approach. It is based on the Cournot competition model of Sections 9.4 and 9.5, and therefore assumes a symmetric situation with two identical countries, but it allows for international trade to take place at positive transport costs. As we will see shortly, the model predicts that there is 'pointless' and costly trade in homogeneous products between the two countries, which none the less can increase welfare. The GATT 1994 defines 'dumping' as the sale of export below normal value. The term 'normal value' is operationalized either as (i) the comparable price of the product in the exporting country, (ii) the comparable price for export to a third country, or (iii) the cost of production in

---

 Box 9.2   Iceberg transport costs

'Iceberg' transport costs, introduced by Paul Samuelson (1952), imply that only a fraction of the goods shipped between locations actually arrives at the destination. The fraction that does *not* arrive represents the cost of transportation. The parameter T, defined as the number of goods that need to be shipped to ensure that one unit arrives per unit of distance, represents the transport costs. Suppose, for example, that the unit of distance is equal to the distance from Naaldwijk (a small town in the centre of the Dutch horticultural agglomeration) to Paris, and that 107 flowers are sent from Holland to France, while only 100 arrive unharmed in Paris and can be sold. Then $T = 1.07$. It is as if some goods have melted away in transit, hence the name iceberg costs. This way of modelling the transport costs without introducing a transport sector is very attractive in combination with the Chapter 10 price-setting behaviour of producers; see Chapter 14.

the country of origin plus a reasonable addition for selling cost and profit.[3] Since the firms in the model to be developed below sell goods in the other country at the same price as at home and do not recuperate the costs of transportation, it is called the 'reciprocal dumping' model.

We illustrate the reciprocal dumping model for linear demand functions using 'iceberg' transport costs; see Box 9.2. The parameter $T \geq 1$ denotes the number of goods that need to be shipped to ensure that one unit of the good arrives in the other country. If the marginal cost of producing the good is c for both firms, the marginal cost of delivering the good in the other country is therefore $Tc > c$. Let q_{AA} be the Austrian firm's supply in Austria and q_{BA} be the Bolivian firm's supply in Austria. With a linear demand curve, the price p_A in Austria can be written as a function of the total quantity supplied:

(9.7) $$p_A = a - b(q_{AA} + q_{BA})$$

Autarky

In autarky, the Austrian firm is a monopolist in Austria. As illustrated in Figure 9.7, the price is determined by the equality of marginal cost and monopoly marginal revenue at point A, leading to monopoly price p_{mon} and monopoly output q_{mon}.

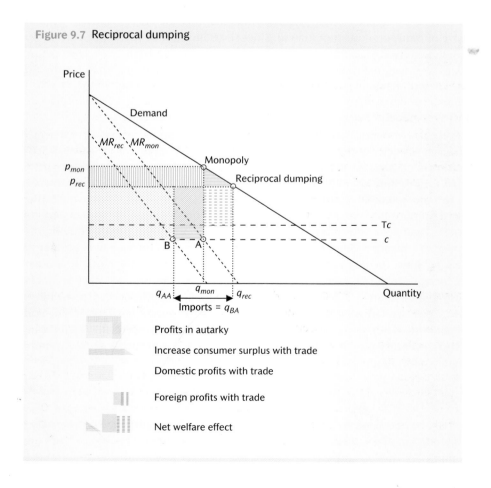

Figure 9.7 Reciprocal dumping

Profits in autarky

Increase consumer surplus with trade

Domestic profits with trade

Foreign profits with trade

Net welfare effect

Trade

With free international trade, the Austrian firm faces competition from the Bolivian firm, despite the fact that the Bolivian firm has higher marginal costs of delivering goods to the market of Austria as a result of the transport costs T. This gives the Austrian firm a natural advantage in the domestic market. None the less, as long as the price in Austria is above the Bolivian firm's marginal costs inclusive of transport costs Tc, the Bolivian firm will make a profit by selling goods in Austria's market. As shown in Technical Note 9.3, the reciprocal dumping equilibrium is given by:

$$(9.8) \qquad q_{AA} = \frac{a + Tc - 2c}{3b}; \quad q_{BA} = \frac{a + c - 2Tc}{3b}; \quad p_{rec} = \frac{a + c + Tc}{3}$$

Note that $q_{AA} > q_{BA}$; that is, the Austrian firm's market share in Austria is larger than the Bolivian firm's market share as a result of its lower marginal costs. The situation is illustrated in Figure 9.7. With imports equal to q_{BA}, the domestic market demand curve for the Austrian firm shifts inward (not drawn). The perceived marginal revenue curve therefore shifts down from MR_{mon} to MR_{rec}. The Austrian firm's output level is determined by the equality of the new marginal revenue curve with the marginal cost of production at point B. The Bolivian firm's demand curve in Austria is shifted further inwards (by the extent of q_{AA}) and its output level is determined by equality of its perceived marginal revenue curve with its marginal costs inclusive of transport costs (not drawn). Since the Bolivian firm sells fewer units in Austria's market, its perceived elasticity of demand is higher than the Austrian firm's, leading to a lower mark-up over marginal costs (which are higher for the Bolivian firm than for the Austrian firm, leading to the same price in equilibrium).

Reciprocal dumping and welfare

Note that this symmetric model gives rise to 'reciprocal dumping' as a result of the difference in perceived elasticity of demand: the Bolivian firm incurs high transport costs to sell goods in Austria's market at a lower mark-up over marginal costs than at home, and similarly for the Austrian firm in Bolivia's market. Despite this seemingly pointless and costly international trade, the pro-competitive effect of trade, leading to lower prices, higher quantities, and smaller deviations between price and marginal costs, may increase the welfare level of both countries. Figure 9.7 illustrates the welfare changes using the partial equilibrium tools developed in Chapter 8. Since trade reduces prices, there is an increase in consumer surplus. At the same time, the domestic firm's drop in profits at home is only partially compensated by an increase in profits abroad. In general, therefore, the welfare effect is ambivalent. As illustrated in Figure 9.8, however, for small and moderate transport costs the net welfare effects are positive. Only if transport costs are high (in this specific example if transport costs are 24 per cent; that is $T = 1.24$) is the net welfare effect negative. A further increase in transport costs eventually reduces this welfare loss as trade becomes too small and costly. Ultimately trade disappears (prohibitive transport costs).

9.7 Application: the Twaron takeover

Aramid fibres were made for the first time in the 1970s. These synthetic fibres are very strong and light, do not break or rust, and have a high chemical and heat resistance. They are used, for example, for friction and sealing, and the production of tyres, protective clothing, optical

Figure 9.8 Trade and welfare in the reciprocal dumping model, $a = 3.25$, $b = 0.65$, $c = 0.75$

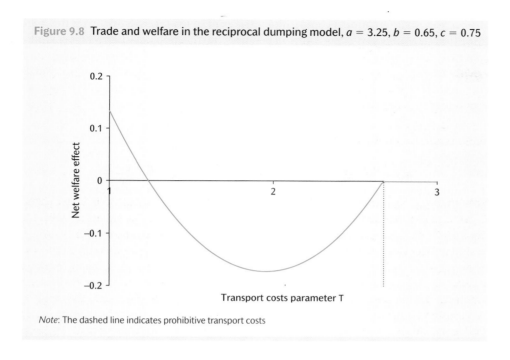

Note: The dashed line indicates prohibitive transport costs

Table 9.1 Implications of the Twaron takeover (%)

	Price elasticity of demand	
	$\varepsilon = 2$	$\varepsilon = 1$
Price rise after takeover	1.9	6.1
Rise in operating profits after takeover		
Kevlar	6.5	8.1
Twaron/Technora	9.5	15.6

cables, and bulletproof vests. Until recently there were three firms producing aramid fibres, namely an American firm (DuPont, producing 18,000 tons under the brand name Kevlar), a Dutch firm (Acordis, producing 10,300 tons under the brand name Twaron), and a Japanese firm (Teijin, producing 1,400 tons under the brand name Technora). In 2000 the Japanese firm Teijin bought the aramid fibre component from the Dutch firm Acordis. The impact of the takeover in this oligopolistic market structure, which changed from three suppliers to two suppliers as a result of the takeover, can be estimated using the Cournot model of Section 9.4. This is indicated in Table 9.1 for a demand structure with constant price elasticity (rather than the linear demand discussed in Section 9.4). After calibrating the model to ensure that the above distribution of market shares results (i.e. DuPont has the lowest and Teijin the highest marginal costs), the table reports the impact of the takeover for two demand elasticities, namely $\varepsilon = 2$ and $\varepsilon = 1$.

The decrease in international competition as a result of the takeover increases the market-clearing price by about 2–6 per cent, depending on the price elasticity of demand. All suppliers in the market benefit from the higher price, leading to higher operating profits. These rise for DuPont as a result of the higher price (an estimated effect of 6–8 per cent) and for the new combination Twaron/Technora as a result of the higher price and the better use of economies of scale (an estimated effect of 9–16 per cent).

 Box 9.3   A road map of things to come: China's ICT trade

Towards the end of 2005 the OECD (see Chapter 12) reported that China became the world's largest exporter of ICT goods, such as electronic components, telecommunication equipment, audio & video equipment and computer equipment. As illustrated in Figure 9.9, China's ICT trade has grown very rapidly, with exports increasing from $19 billion in 1996 to $180 billion in 2004, surpassing the EU and Japan in 2003 and taking over the lead from the USA in 2004. Similarly, imports of ICT goods into China grew from $17 billion in 1996 to $149 billion in 2004, but are still significantly smaller than imports into the EU and the USA.

A closer look at Figure 9.9 reveals that all countries simultaneously export *and* import ICT goods and that these trade flows are highly correlated. This, perhaps somewhat puzzling, phenomenon is known as *intra*-industry trade and is studied more closely in Chapter 10. It is puzzling because from

Figure 9.9 Exports and imports of ICT goods; selected countries, 1996–2004

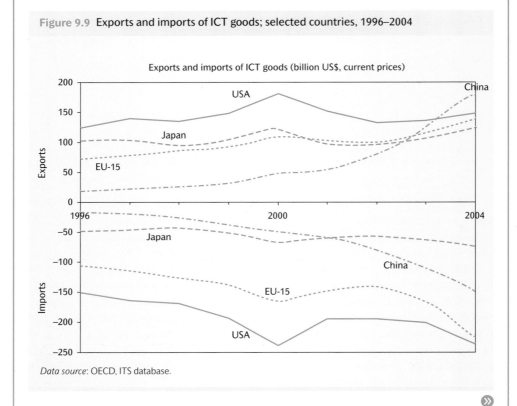

Data source: OECD, ITS database.

⟫ a technology or factor-abundance perspective we expect countries to *either* export *or* import certain types of goods. We may get some initial understanding by looking at the composition of China's trade in ICT goods. Table 9.2 shows the main ICT components and illustrates on the one hand that intra-industry trade also holds at the component level (simultaneous imports and exports) and on the other hand that the *net* trade flows differ substantially for the various components, where China is a net importer of electronic components and other ICT goods and a net exporter of telecommunication equipment, computer equipment, and audio & video equipment. The rapidly increasing net trade flows of the various components is illustrated in Figure 9.10. It shows that China is importing electronic components, processing these in local assembly plants

Table 9.2 China's exports and imports of ICT goods, 1996–2004

	Telecom eq.		Computer eq.		Electronic comp.		Audio & video eq.		Other ICT goods	
	Export	Import	Export	Import	Export	Import	Export	Import	Export	Import
1996	2,417	2,861	5,317	2,877	3,782	7,375	6,283	1,889	785	1,848
1997	2,685	2,453	7,513	3,864	4,922	9,664	7,168	1,989	906	1,618
1998	3,004	4,427	10,168	5,300	5,781	12,149	7,501	1,961	965	1,677
1999	3,738	4,904	11,697	6,968	7,766	18,386	8,453	2,345	1,009	2,169
2000	6,675	6,297	16,577	9,883	11,263	28,432	11,165	2,920	1,316	3,065
2001	8,759	7,416	21,076	11,607	11,371	31,333	12,616	2,796	1,483	4,117
2002	10,801	6,792	33,253	15,929	15,520	44,849	17,855	3,978	1,948	4,900
2003	14,558	7,812	59,245	22,890	22,879	67,442	24,289	5,438	2,332	6,949
2004	25,579	6,904	83,790	28,209	34,884	97,302	33,309	6,877	2,859	9,371

Data source: OECD, ITS database.

Figure 9.10 China's trade balance by ICT goods categories (export–import), 1996–2004

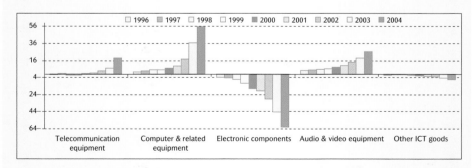

Data source: OECD, ITS database. bn $

>> to produce computers, telecommunication equipment, and audio & video equipment, and sells these final products to satisfy domestic demand and to export to the world market.

The various theories described in Parts II.A–C of this book help us to explain these trade flows. There are many different varieties of goods and various stages of the production process which help us to understand why we observe simultaneous imports and exports of the same category of products (Chapter 10). Since the various stages of the production process use different ratios of inputs (physical capital, human capital, skilled labour, and unskilled labour) it pays to locate different stages of the production process intensively using certain types of inputs in countries that are abundant in those inputses (Chapters 4–7). This explains why the labour-intensive assembly part of the production of ICT goods is increasingly located in China, as it opens up to the world economy (Chapter 17), since China is a relatively labour-abundant country. To enable this slicing-up-the-value-chain process, firms need to efficiently organize themselves in different countries of the world, making foreign direct investment decisions in the process (Chapter 15). This requires, in turn, large firms that have some market power (Chapter 9) and possess the necessary technology (Chapter 3) and local connections and market access (Chapter 14) to enable these increasingly complicated production processes (Chapter 16). These various aspects are reflected in Figure 9.11, depicting China's ICT trade balance relative to various countries. China imports electronic components mostly from nearby suppliers located in Taiwan, Korea, Japan, and Malaysia, with the available technology and large firms to produce and organize this process, leading to bilateral trade deficits relative to those countries. It then produces final goods in the labour-intensive-assembly part of the production process and exports to countries with a high demand for ICT goods in the USA, Europe, and Australia. Note that Hong Kong is listed as China's largest net export market of ICT goods. This is misleading, however, as a large part of China's trade is trans-shipped through Hong Kong, with the USA, Europe, and Australia as the ultimate destination markets.

Figure 9.11 China's trade balance in ICT goods (export–export), 2004

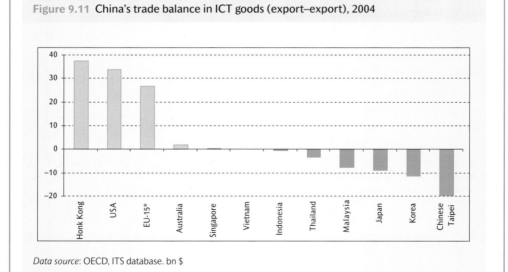

Data source: OECD, ITS database. bn $

9.8 Conclusions

Profit-maximizing firms in an imperfectly competitive market will charge a mark-up of price over marginal costs. The size of the mark-up depends on the price elasticity of demand and on the degree of competition, such that an increase in the number of firms reduces the mark-up. In a general equilibrium setting, imperfect competition leads to a sub-optimal outcome (a deviation between MRS and MRT). Since international trade increases market competition, as foreign firms start to compete on the domestic market and vice versa, international trade improves economic efficiency (by diminishing the deviation between MRS and MRT), the so-called pro-competitive gains from trade. This 'reciprocal' dumping may even increase welfare if international trade is costly.

TECHNICAL NOTES

Technical Note 9.1 Monopolist profit maximization

If a market's demand curve is given by $p(q)$, and a monopolist's cost function is given by $C(q)$, where q is the quantity of output, then the firm's profits π are given by

(9.A1)
$$\pi = p(q)q - C(q)$$

The first-order condition for profit maximization is

(9.A2)
$$p + \frac{dp}{dq}q = \frac{dC}{dq}$$

If we let $c(q)$ denote the marginal cost of production and, as is customary, measure the responsiveness of demand to price changes in relative terms, that is using the elasticity of substitution $\varepsilon(q) \equiv -(dq/dp)(p/q) > 0$, the first-order condition can be rewritten as

(9.A3)
$$p\left(1 - \frac{1}{\varepsilon(q)}\right) = c(q)$$

If demand is linear ($p = a - bq$), we have $\varepsilon(q) = (a - bq)/bq$ resulting in

(9.A4)
$$q_{mon} = \frac{a - c}{2b}; \quad p_{mon} = \frac{a + c}{2} > \frac{c + c}{2} = c, \quad \text{because } a > c$$

Technical Note 9.2 Cournot profit maximization

Suppose a market's demand curve is given by $p(q)$, where q is total output by all firms active in the market. If firm A is one of those firms, we can write market output as $q = q_A + q_{-A}$, where q_A is the output of firm A and q_{-A} is the output of all other firms. If firm A's cost function is given by $C(q_A)$, then firm A's profits π_A are given by

(9.A5)
$$\pi_A = p(q)q_A - C(q_A)$$

The first-order condition for profit maximization is

(9.A6)
$$p + \frac{dp}{dq}q_A = c(q_A)$$

where $c(q_A)$ is the marginal cost of production. Let $\varepsilon(q)$ be the price elasticity of demand, then the first-order condition can be rewritten as

(9.A7)
$$p\left(1 - \frac{q_A}{q}\frac{1}{\varepsilon(q)}\right) = c(q_A)$$

For a duopoly, linear demand curve $p = a - bq$, and $c(q) = c$, firm A's reaction curve is

(9.A8)
$$\frac{\partial \pi_A}{\partial q_A} = 0 \Rightarrow q_A = \frac{a - c}{2b} - \frac{1}{2}q_B$$

And similarly for firm B. The Cournot equilibrium is at the intersection of the reaction curves

(9.A9)
$$q_A = q_B = \frac{a - c}{3b}; \quad p_{duo} = \frac{a + 2c}{3} < \frac{a + c}{2} = p_{mon}, \quad \text{because } a > c$$

Technical Note 9.3 Reciprocal dumping model

Since the model is symmetric for the two countries, we concentrate on Austria. With a linear demand curve, the price p_A can be written as a function of firm A's supply in Austria q_{AA} and firm B's supply in Austria q_{BA}:

(9.A10)
$$p_A = a - b(q_{AA} + q_{BA})$$

Assuming that marginal cost of production is equal to c for both firms, and that there are iceberg transport costs, such that marginal cost for firm B for delivery of goods in Austria is equal to Tc, the profit functions π are

(9.A11)
$$\pi_A = [a - b(q_{AA} + q_{BA})]q_{AA} - cq_{AA}$$
$$\pi_B = [a - b(q_{AA} + q_{BA})]q_{BA} - Tcq_{BA}$$

First-order conditions for profit maximization, given the other firm's output level, are

(9.A12)
$$(a - bq_{BA}) - 2bq_{AA} = c; \quad (a - bq_{AA}) - 2bq_{BA} = Tc$$

Solving these two linear equations gives

(9.A13)
$$q_{AA} = \frac{a + Tc - 2c}{3b}; \quad q_{BA} = \frac{a + c - 2Tc}{3b}; \quad p_{rec} = \frac{a + c + Tc}{3}$$

QUESTIONS

Question 9.1

The national electricity markets in the Nordic countries (Denmark, Finland, Norway, Sweden) used to be protected from foreign competition and dominated by one power company. Between 1996 and 2000 far-reaching reforms were introduced establishing one integrated electricity market. A common power exchange was established (Nord Pool), international transmission links were opened to other players, and border tariffs were abolished. After 2000, the Nordic electricity market was even broadened by establishing trading links with Poland and Germany. We will analyse these developments using the imperfect competition framework of Markusen by concentrating on the Swedish national electricity market.

9.1A Illustrate the Swedish electricity market before 1996 in a graph, with the amount of electricity on the vertical axis and the amount of 'other products' on the horizontal axis. Draw the production possibilities frontier and the utility curve for which consumers maximize their utility. Indicate clearly the amount of electricity sold and its price.

9.1B Why can the Swedish monopolist charge an electricity price far above marginal cost? Is it 'fair' to charge a price above marginal costs?

9.1C Assume that Sweden first established an integrated electricity market with Norway.[4] Draw the new situation. What happens to the amount of electricity offered and the electricity prices on the Swedish market?

9.1D Explain who are the winners and who are the losers from the integrated electricity market with Norway.

9.1E What happens to the figure if more countries enter the common electricity market? Is this an attractive development?

Question 9.2

Let us analyse the gains and losses associated with the entry of the Norwegian electricity firm on the Swedish market more formally (see question 9.1D). Recall that there was initially only a Swedish monopoly producer on the Swedish electricity market. In the new situation a Norwegian firm is also allowed to sell electricity in Sweden. Assume that Figure 9.2 in the main text gives the demand for electricity in Sweden and the marginal revenue and cost curve for the Swedish monopolist in the initial situation.

9.2A Copy Figure 9.2 from the main text. What are the consumer surplus and producer surplus in a situation of monopoly?

9.2B Indicate in the same figure a possible total quantity of electricity supplied and the associated price level if the Norwegian firm is allowed to compete on the Swedish market, assuming that there are no transport costs. What is the consumer surplus and producer surplus in this new situation?

9.2C Who gains and who loses from the entry of the Norwegian firm? What are the pro-competitive gains from trade?

Assume now that the Norwegian firm faces positive transport costs when delivering electricity to the Swedish market. We suppose that it is still profitable for the Norwegian firm to supply electricity to Swedish consumers.

9.2D What is the quantity of electricity supplied and the associated price level if the Norwegian firm faces positive transport costs?

9.2E Who gains and who loses from the entry of the Norwegian firm if there are positive transport costs? Explain whether the gains and losses are equal to the situation without transport costs.

Question 9.3

The integration of the electricity markets in Nordic countries after 1996 should lead to pro-competitive gains from trade. The figure below, however, shows that Sweden's electricity imports do not show an upward trend after 1996.

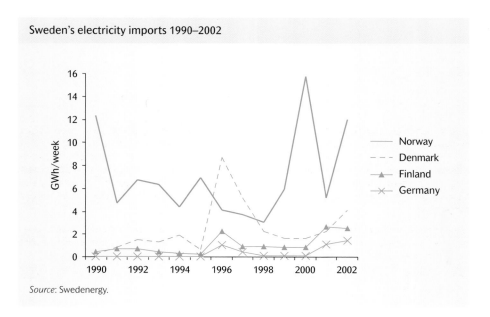

Source: Swedenergy.

9.3A Explain whether pro-competitive gains from trade may arise even though imports do not increase.

9.3B What alternative indicators can be used to evaluate whether Sweden has gained from the increase in competition in the electricity market?

 See the Online Resource Centre for a Study Guide containing more questions
www.oxfordtextbooks.co.uk/orc/vanmarrewijk/

NOTES

1 See Irwin (1996: 57).

2 The shaded area represents operating profits. This may be required to recuperate the initial (fixed cost) outlays if there are increasing returns to scale; see Chapter 10.

3 The normal value minus the export price is the margin of dumping. It must exceed 2 per cent to be actionable, in which case the importing country can levy an anti-dumping duty if the imports cause, or are likely to cause, injury to the domestic industry.

4 This is partly true because the existing electricity exchange in Norway (Stattnet Marked), which was later transformed into the common exchange Nord Pool, was first opened to Swedish players and only later to others.

INTRA-INDUSTRY TRADE

Objectives/key terms

- Aggregation level
- Intra-industry trade
- Dixit–Stiglitz demand
- Internal and external scale economies
- Mark-up pricing

- Grubel–Lloyd index
- (love-of-) variety
- Price elasticity of demand
- Monopolistic competition
- Zero profits

We extend the analysis of imperfect competition by including economies of scale, which in conjunction with the size of the market determines the number of different types of goods and services available. Trade increases the extent of the market, thus making more types of goods available. This can be used to explain the empirical phenomenon of intra-industry trade (two-way trade in similar types of goods).

10.1 Introduction

The phenomenon of intra-industry trade is a prime example of a widely known and accepted empirical regularity in the search for a satisfactory theoretical foundation for many years. For a long time the empirical researchers were therefore clearly ahead of the theoretical researchers. What is intra-industry trade? It refers to the fact that many countries simultaneously export and import very similar goods and services; intra-industry trade is therefore trade within the same industry or sector. Germany, for example, exports many cars to France and simultaneously imports many cars from France as well. Why does Germany do this? This chapter seeks to give an answer to this question based on aspects of a nation's demand structure, as well as its supply structure.

The intra-industry trade phenomenon was first noted empirically when a group of European countries formed the European Common Market, which has now grown into the European Union and currently consists of 25 countries; see Chapter 13. It was soon realized that intra-industry trade is a general characteristic of international trade flows. Path-breaking empirical research in measuring the size and importance of intra-industry trade was performed by Pieter Verdoorn (1960), Bela Balassa (1966), and Herbert Grubel and Peter Lloyd (1975); see Section 10.2.

Why did the realization that there is intensive intra-industry trade between nations embarrass theoretical economists? Because the theories of comparative advantage developed until then, based on Ricardian technology differences or Heckscher–Ohlin factor abundance, cannot explain this type of trade. Both types of models assume that firms in the same industry produce identical goods, such that consumers do not distinguish between the goods produced by different firms, nor care which firm produced the goods in making their demand decisions. A country will therefore either only export goods within the same industry, or only import these goods, but not simultaneously export and import goods within the same industry.

It was, of course, immediately realized that the goods and services produced by firms in the same industry are, in fact, not identical. Taking the simultaneous German exports of cars to France and imports of cars from France again as an example, everyone acknowledges that a

Famous economists	Avinash Dixit

Fig. 10.1
Avinash Dixit (1944–)

Born in Bombay, India, where he studied mathematics and physics, Dixit continued his studies at the University of Cambridge, where he got his BA, and at MIT, where he got his PhD before moving to Princeton in 1980. His theoretical work, characterizing market equilibrium and designing policies, covers various areas of economics, such as microeconomics, international economics, industrial organization, public economics, investment under uncertainty, and growth and development. Influential contributions are 'Monopolistic competition and optimum product diversity' published jointly with Joseph Stiglitz (see Chapter 9) in the *American Economic Review* in 1977, and two books, namely *Theory of International Trade*, with Victor Norman in 1980, and *Investment under Uncertainty*, with Robert Pindyck in 1994.

Volkswagen Golf is not the same as a Peugeot 206. They are similar products, delivering similar services, produced using a similar technology, such that they are classified in the same industry, but they are not the same. A satisfactory theoretical explanation should therefore be able to distinguish between goods and services that are close, but imperfect, substitutes. This requires a change in the demand structure of the economy, such that consumers demand many different varieties of similar, but not identical, products in the same industry.

Suppose that we are able to change the demand structure of the economy such that consumers have a preference for different varieties of similar products. Are we then able to explain intra-industry trade? Not yet, because we still have to explain why the domestic industry does not provide an arbitrarily large number of varieties to cater to the preferences of consumers. Going back again to the Germany–France car example, it is clear that Volkswagen has the ability and technology available to produce a car virtually identical to the Peugeot 206, and is thus able to fulfil demand for that type of product. Large initial investment costs, spread over several years, are required, however, before such a new type of car is designed, developed, tested, and can be produced. These large investment costs, giving rise to increasing returns to scale, are the primary reason for Volkswagen, or other German car manufacturers, to produce only a limited number of varieties. This also implies that a car manufacturer, being the only producer of a particular variety, has considerable market power, which it takes into consideration when maximizing profits.

 Box 10.1   Dixit–Stiglitz monopolistic competition

There is only one way for competition to be 'perfect'. In contrast, there is a bewildering range of models describing 'imperfect' competition, investigating many different cases and assumptions regarding market behaviour, the type of good, strategic interaction, preferences of consumers, etc. This was also the case with monopolistic competition, until Avinash Dixit and Joseph Stiglitz (1977) published 'Monopolistic competition and optimum product diversity' in the *American Economic Review*. This article was to revolutionize model building in at least four fields of economics: trade theory, industrial organization, growth theory, and geographical economics.[1]

The big step forward was to make some heroic assumptions concerning the symmetry of new varieties and the structural form, which allowed for an elegant and consistent way to model production at the firm level benefiting from internal economies of scale in conjunction with a market structure of monopolistic competition, without getting bogged down in a taxonomy of oligopoly models. These factors are responsible for the present popularity of the Dixit–Stiglitz model. Researchers in all fields now using the Dixit–Stiglitz formulation intensively were aware that imperfect competition is an essential feature of many empirically observed phenomena. The Dixit–Stiglitz model was therefore immediately accepted as the new standard for modelling monopolistic competition; its development was certainly very timely. In international trade theory, its introduction enabled international economists to explain and understand intra-industry trade; see Krugman (1979, 1980). In industrial organization it helped to get rid of many *ad hoc* assumptions, which hampered the development of many models; see Tirole (1988). The Dixit–Stiglitz model was also used to explore the role of intermediate differentiated goods in international trade models. This reformulation of the standard Dixit–Stiglitz model plays an important role in the link between international trade and economic growth; see Grossman and Helpman (1991a). Finally, the model is intensively used in geographical economics; see Brakman, Garretsen, and van Marrewijk (2001).

These considerations clarify why it took some time, and considerable ingenuity, to provide a solid theoretical explanation of intra-industry trade flows, since such an explanation has to incorporate:

- consumer preferences with a demand for different varieties of similar products;

- increasing returns to scale in production, limiting the diversity in production that the market can provide;

- a market structure of imperfect competition consistent with the phenomenon of increasing returns to scale.

The challenge is to incorporate these features in a simple general equilibrium setting, for which the industrial organization literature provided the most important stimulus with the Dixit and Stiglitz (1977) paper; see Box 10.1. The American economist Paul Krugman (1979, 1980) used the Dixit–Stiglitz variety specification combined with internal increasing returns to scale to analyse intra-industry trade in a Chamberlinian (Chamberlin, 1933) model of monopolistic competition. Simultaneously, Lancaster (1979) introduced consumer hetero-geneity, where consumers are distinguished by their most preferred product characteristics, in which differentiated products cater to different tastes. In both cases, increasing returns to scale limit the extent of diversity that the market can provide. We restrict attention to the Krugman variety approach, not only because it is the easiest framework to work with, but also because it has had a bigger impact on the rest of the international trade literature, and serves as a good introduction to geographical economics and endogenous growth theory; see Chapters 14 and 16.

10.2 Measuring intra-industry trade

How do we measure intra-industry trade, the extent of trade in similar goods? Although various options are available, the measure most often used is the Grubel–Lloyd index, which is simple and intuitively appealing. Let Ex_i be the exports of industry i and let Im_i be the imports of industry i, then the Grubel–Lloyd index GL_i for industry i is defined as

$$(10.1) \qquad GL_i = 1 - \frac{|Ex_i - Im_i|}{Ex_i + Im_i}$$

If a country only imports or only exports goods or services within the same industry, such that there is no intra-industry trade, the second term on the right-hand side of equation (10.1) is equal to 1 ($Ex_i/Ex_i = 1$ or $Im_i/Im_i = 1$), such that the whole expression reduces to 0. Similarly, if the exports of goods or services are exactly equal to the imports of those goods or services within the same industry ($Ex_i = Im_i$), the second term on the right-hand side of equation (10.1) is equal to zero, such that the whole expression reduces to 1. The Grubel–Lloyd index therefore varies between 0, indicating no intra-industry trade, and 1, indicating only intra-industry trade.

Which share of international trade is intra-industry trade? We first illustrate this question using data for the Philippines and Japan given in Table 10.1, and then report the results of a more detailed study in Table 10.2. International trade data are grouped at the 'digit' level. The first row of Table 10.1 gives exports and imports between the Philippines and Japan at the one-digit level, namely for SITC category 8, 'miscellaneous manufactured products'. Since the

Box 10.2   Tool: Grubel–Lloyd index

The most widely used tool in international economics for empirically determining the extent of intra-industry trade was developed by Herbert Grubel and Peter Lloyd, and is therefore known as the Grubel–Lloyd index. It is a simple index, explained in detail in the main text, which varies between 0 (no intra-industry trade) and 1 (complete intra-industry trade), or between 0 and 100 in percentage terms.

Table 10.1 International trade between the Philippines (RP) and Japan; 1998

SITC		Exports from RP	Imports into RP	GL index
8	Miscellaneous manufactured articles	383,167	576,412	0.80
81	Prefabricated buildings	4,147	2,186	0.69
82	Furniture and parts thereof	42,332	6,155	0.25
83	Travel goods, handbags, and similar containers	4,804	67	0.03
84	Articles of apparel and clothing accessories	115,627	3,255	0.05
85	Footwear	13,283	920	0.13
87	Prof. scientific and controlling instruments	24,091	175,018	0.24
88	Photographic apparatus	72,174	123,333	0.74
89	Miscellaneous manufactured articles	106,709	265,477	0.57

Source: OECD (Foreign trade by commodities) × $1,000; GL index = Grubel–Lloyd index; RP = Republica ng Pilipinas, the Republic of the Philippines.

Table 10.2 Intra-industry trade, GL index manufacturing sector 1995 (3-digit level, %)

Country	World	OECD 22	NAFTA	East Asia dev.	Latin America
Australia	36.6	17.5	16.0	39.2	41.6
Bangladesh	10.0	3.5	1.7	3.4	8.0
Chile	25.7	10.1	11.5	3.6	47.8
France	83.5	86.7	62.7	38.7	22.9
Germany	75.3	80.1	61.2	36.2	22.8
Japan	42.3	47.6	45.7	36.1	7.0
Malaysia	60.4	48.5	57.9	75.0	10.4
Hong Kong	28.4	20.2	25.2	19.9	13.6
UK	85.4	84.0	72.5	46.6	38.6
USA	71.7	74.0	73.5	41.4	66.0

Source: NAPES website, http://napes.anu.edu.au/

exports are $383 million and the imports are $576 million, applying equation (10.1) shows that according to the Grubel–Lloyd index 80 per cent of the trade in category 8 is intra-industry trade; see the last column in Table 10.1.

What are 'miscellaneous manufactured goods'? An indication is given in the other rows of Table 10.1, giving a breakdown at the two-digit level of category 8. Apparently, it consists of such diverse goods as prefabricated buildings, footwear, and photographic apparatus. The calculation in the above paragraph grouped all of this together at the one-digit level. The Grubel–Lloyd index of 80 per cent calculated above thus classifies trade of footwear in exchange for prefabricated buildings as intra-industry trade. This seems a bit far-fetched, and obviously leads to artificially high intra-industry trade estimates, such that it is preferable to analyse the goods classification and intra-industry trade at a more detailed level. For category 8 at the two-digit level in Table 10.1, the Grubel–Lloyd index of intra-industry trade varies from 0.03 for travel goods to 0.74 for photographic apparatus. The unweighted average of these eight two-digit categories is equal to 0.34, and the weighted average[2] is equal to 0.45. Both are considerably lower than the 0.80 value calculated at the one-digit level for category 8. We conclude, therefore, that analysing international trade flows at a lower, or more detailed, level of aggregation leads to a reduction in the estimated extent of intra-industry trade. The phenomenon of intra-industry trade, however, does not disappear if we do this; see Table 10.2.

Table 10.2 summarizes the extent of intra-industry trade in 1995 at the three-digit level for a selection of countries. Take the USA as an example. Averaged over all countries, no less than 71.7 per cent of US trade can be categorized as intra-industry trade. This is, however, unevenly distributed. US trade with the Asian newly industrialized countries (41.4 per cent intra-industry trade) and Latin America (66.0 per cent intra-industry trade) has a lower intra-industry trade component than US trade with the NAFTA countries (73.5 per cent) or the OECD countries (74.0 per cent). Similarly, the high overall level of intra-industry trade for France (83.5 per cent) is the combination of low intra-industry trade levels with respect to Latin

Figure 10.2 Evolution of intra-industry trade

Source: Siebert (1999).

America (22.9 per cent) and South-East Asia (38.7 per cent), and high intra-industry trade levels with respect to NAFTA (62.7 per cent) and the OECD (86.7 per cent). Table 10.2 also illustrates the lower intra-industry trade levels for developing nations (for example 10.0 per cent for Bangladesh), such that we may conclude that intra-industry trade is more prevalent among developed nations and that similar developed nations are largely engaged in trading similar types of goods between themselves.

Figure 10.2 depicts the evolution of the Grubel–Lloyd index for Germany, Japan, and the USA over a period of 35 years (1961–96), measured at the two-digit level. All three countries have experienced an increase in the extent of intra-industry trade; for Germany from 41 to 73 per cent, for Japan from 25 to 43 per cent, and for the USA from 47 to 67 per cent. Similar developments have occurred in most other nations. Apparently, intra-industry trade is becoming more important over time.

10.3 Dixit–Stiglitz demand

The Dixit–Stiglitz model of monopolistic competition acknowledges that consumers demand a large range of different varieties of similar, but not identical, products. Think, for example, of a range of varieties for mobile telephones, automobiles, televisions, etc. Although each producer of any individual variety has monopoly power in supplying its own variety, there is of course strong competition between firms in producing varieties of similar products. The demand structure of the Dixit–Stiglitz model allows for this strong competition. Let c_i be the level of consumption of a particular variety i of manufactures, and let N be the total number of available varieties. The Dixit–Stiglitz approach uses a constant elasticity of substitution (CES) function for the utility U derived from the consumption of manufactures as a function of the consumption c_i of the N varieties:[3]

(10.2)
$$U = \left(\sum_{i=1}^{N} c_i^\rho \right)^{1/\rho}; \quad 0 < \rho < 1$$

Note that the consumption of all varieties enters equation (10.2) symmetrically. This greatly simplifies the analysis in the sequel. The parameter ρ, discussed further below, represents the love-of-variety effect of consumers. If $\rho = 1$, equation (10.2) simplifies to $U = \Sigma_i c_i$ and variety as such does not matter for utility (100 units of one variety gives the same utility as one unit each of 100 varieties). Products are then perfect substitutes (one unit less of one variety can exactly be compensated by one unit more of another variety). We therefore need $\rho < 1$ to ensure that the product varieties are imperfect substitutes. In addition, we need $\rho > 0$ to ensure that the individual varieties are substitutes (and not complements) for each other, which enables price-setting behaviour based on monopoly power; see Technical Note 9.1 and Section 10.5.

It is worthwhile to dwell a little longer on the specification of equation (10.2). Suppose all c_i are consumed in equal quantities; that is, $c_i = c$ for all i. We can then rewrite equation (10.2):

(10.2′)
$$U = \left(\sum_{i=1}^{N} c^\rho \right)^{1/\rho} = (Nc^\rho)^{1/\rho} = N^{1/\rho}c = \underbrace{N^{(1/\rho)-1}}_{\text{love of variety}} \left[\underbrace{Nc}_{\substack{\text{claim on} \\ \text{resources}}} \right]$$

In many models, as in the model discussed here and in the endogenous growth model of Chapter 16, the term Nc in equation (10.2′) corresponds to a claim on real resources, requiring labour (and/or capital) to be produced. The number of available varieties N therefore represents an externality, or the extent of the market. Since $0 < \rho < 1$, the term $(1/\rho) - 1$ is larger than 0. This implies that an increase in the extent of the market N, which requires a proportional increase in the claim on real resources Nc, increases utility U derived from consumption of N varieties by more than the increase in the claim on real resources (since the term $N^{(1/\rho)-1}$ rises, it represents a bonus for large markets). In this sense an increase in the extent of the market, which increases the number of varieties N the consumer can choose from, more than proportionally increases utility; hence the term love-of-variety effect.

Now that we have briefly digressed on the love-of-variety effect, it is time to go back to the problem in hand: how does the consumer allocate spending on manufactures over the different varieties? Let p_i be the price of variety i for $i = 1, \ldots, N$. Naturally, funds $p_i c_i$ spent on variety i cannot be spent simultaneously on variety j, as given in the budget constraint with income I in equation (10.3):

$$(10.3) \qquad \sum_{i=1}^{N} p_i c_i = I$$

In order to derive a consumer's demand, we must now solve a somewhat more complicated optimization problem, namely maximize utility derived from the consumption of manufactures given in equation (10.2), subject to the budget constraint of equation (10.3). The solution to this problem is (see Technical Note 10.1):

$$(10.4) \qquad c_j = p_j^{-\varepsilon}[p^{\varepsilon-1}I], \quad \text{where } P = \text{price index}, \quad U = I/P, \quad \varepsilon \equiv 1/(1 - \rho) > 1$$

Note that the definition of the price index P apparently implies that $U = I/P$. The price index P thus gives an exact representation of the utility level derived from the consumption of manufactures; this utility increases if, and only if, the income level I increases faster than the price index P. Such a price index is called an exact price index; see Diewert (1981) for further details.

10.4 Demand effects; income, price elasticity ε, and the price index P

Section 10.3 derived the demand for manufacturing varieties. The demand for variety 1, for example, is influenced by four variables; see equation (10.4):

  (i) the income level I

  (ii) the price p_1 of good 1

  (iii) some parameter ε, and

  (iv) the price index P.

Let's go over these points in more detail.

Point (i) is straightforward. The higher the income level, the more the consumer spends on variety 1. In fact, this relationship is equiproportional: other things being equal, a 10 per cent rise in the income level results in a 10 per cent increase in the demand for all varieties of manufactures.

Point (ii) is also straightforward, but very important. It is straightforward in the sense that we obviously expect that the demand for variety 1 is a function of the price charged by the firm producing variety 1. It is very important in view of *how* demand for variety 1 depends on the price p_1. Note that the last part of equation (10.4) is written in square brackets. It depends on the price index for manufactures P and the income level I. Both are macroeconomic entities which the firm producing variety 1 will take as given; that is, it will assume to have no control over these variables (see below for a further discussion). In that case, we can simplify the demand for variety 1 by defining $\gamma \equiv [P^{\varepsilon-1}I]$ as $c_1 = \gamma p_1^{-\varepsilon}$. This in turn implies that the price elasticity of demand for variety 1 is constant and equal to the parameter $\varepsilon > 1$, i.e. $-(\partial c_1/\partial p_1)(p_1/c_1) = \varepsilon$. This simple price elasticity of demand is the main advantage of the Dixit–Stiglitz approach as it greatly simplifies the price-setting behaviour of monopolistically competitive firms; see Section 10.5. Figure 10.3 illustrates the demand for a variety of manufactures as a function of its own price for different values of ε. Note that the demand for a variety falls much faster as a result of a small price increase, say from 1 to 1.5, if the price elasticity of demand is high.

Point (iii) becomes clear after the discussion in point (ii). We have defined the parameter ε not only to simplify the notation of equation (10.4) as much as possible, but also because it is an important economic parameter as it measures the price elasticity of demand for a variety of manufactured goods. In addition, this parameter measures the elasticity of substitution between two different varieties; that is, how difficult it is to substitute one variety of manufactures for another variety of manufactures. Evidently, the price elasticity of demand and the elasticity of substitution are related in the Dixit–Stiglitz approach, a point that has been criticized in the literature. Be that as it may, our intuitive explanations of some phenomena in the remainder of this book will sometimes be based on the price elasticity of demand interpretation of ε, and sometimes on the elasticity of substitution interpretation, using what we feel is easiest for the problem at hand.

Point (iv), finally, indicates that the demand for variety 1 depends on the price index P. If the price index P increases, implying that on average the prices of the manufacturing varieties

Figure 10.3 Dependence of demand for a variety of manufactures on price and ε

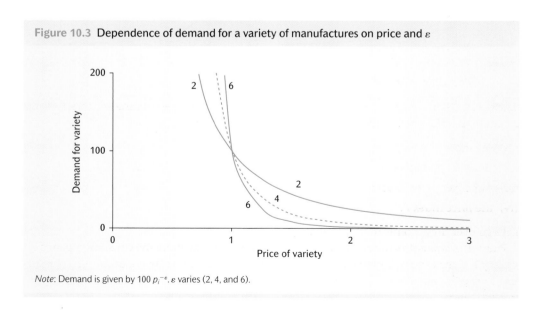

Note: Demand is given by $100\, p_i^{-\varepsilon}$. ε varies (2, 4, and 6).

competing with variety 1 are rising, then the demand for variety 1 is increasing (recall that $\varepsilon - 1 > 0$). The varieties are therefore economic substitutes for one another (if the price of a particular variety increases its own demand falls and the demand for all other varieties rises).

To finish our discussion of the demand structure of the core model, we want to make a final remark concerning point (ii) above, where we argued that the (own) price elasticity of demand for the producer of variety 1 is equal to ε. Recall the specification of the demand function: $c_1 = p_1^{-\varepsilon}[\, p^{\varepsilon-1}I\,]$. We argued that the term in square brackets is treated as a constant by the producer because these are macroeconomic entities. Although this is true, it overlooks a tiny detail: one of the terms in the specification of the price index of manufactures P is the price p_1. Thus, a truly rational producer would also take this minuscule effect on the aggregate price index into consideration.[4] For that reason it is often assumed that the number of varieties N produced is large; that is, if our producer is one of 80,000 firms we can safely ignore this effect. This is illustrated in Figure 10.4, where we have plotted the demand curve facing

Figure 10.4 Deviation between assumed demand and reality. (a) $N = 2$, (b) $N = 20$, (c) $N = 200$, (d) $N = 2000$, spending on manufactures = 100, price of other firms = 1, $\varepsilon = 5$

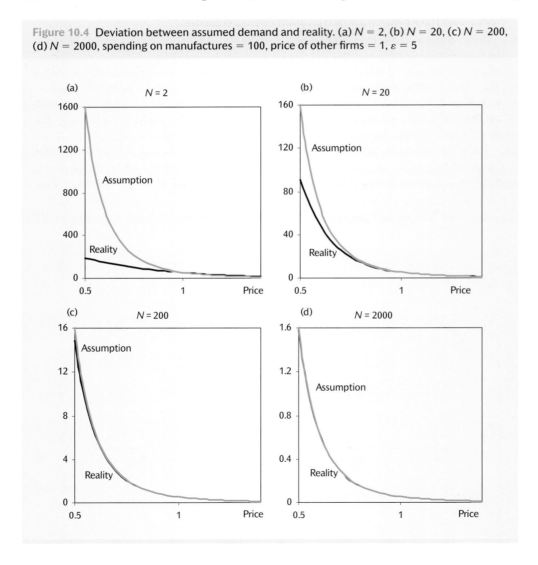

Box 10.3   External and internal economies of scale

The term 'economies of scale' or 'increasing returns to scale' refers to a situation in which an increase in the level of output produced implies a decrease in the average costs per unit of output for the firm. It translates itself into a downward-sloping average cost curve; see Figure 10.5. To identify the source of the fall in average costs Scitovsky (1954) distinguished between *internal* and *external* economies of scale. With internal economies of scale the decrease in average costs is brought about by an increase in the production level of the firm itself. The more the firm produces, the better it can profit from scale economies, and the higher its cost advantage over smaller firms. The market structure underlying internal scale economies must necessarily be one of *im*perfect competition as internal economies of scale imply market power. With external economies of scale, the decrease in average costs comes about through an output increase at the level of the industry as a whole, making average costs per unit a function of industry-wide output. Scitovsky distinguished here between *pure* and *pecuniary* external economies.

With *pure* (or *technological*) external economies an increase in industry-wide output alters the technological relationship between input and output for each individual firm. It therefore has an impact on the firm's production function. A frequently used example (dating back to Alfred Marshall) concerns information spillovers. An increase in industry output increases the stock of knowledge through positive information spillovers for each firm, leading to an increase in output at the firm level. The market structure can then be perfectly competitive since the size of the *individual* firm does not matter.

Pecuniary external economies are transmitted by the market through price effects for the individual firm, which may alter its output decision. Two examples, again based on Marshall, are the existence of a large local market for specialized inputs and labour market pooling. A large

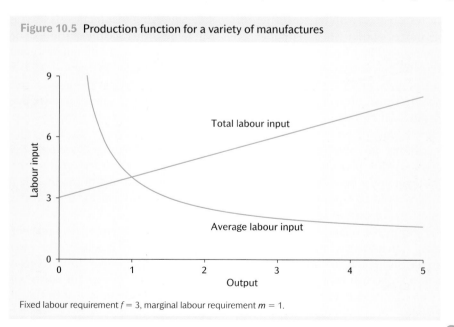

Figure 10.5 **Production function for a variety of manufactures**

Fixed labour requirement $f = 3$, marginal labour requirement $m = 1$.

> ❯❯ industry can support a market for specialized intermediate inputs and a pool of industry specific skilled workers, which benefits the individual firm. Contrary to pure external economies these spillovers do not affect the technological relationship between inputs and output (the production function). The price effects crucial to pecuniary externalities can only come about with imperfect competition.

the producer of a variety if she assumes she cannot influence the price index of manufactures, and the true demand taking this effect on the price index into consideration (details below Figure 10.4). Clearly, the assumption is a bad approximation if there are just two firms (panel a), but then nobody suggests you should use monopolistic competition in a duopoly. If there are twenty firms the approximation is already much better (panel b); if there are 200 firms the deviation is virtually undetectable (panel c); while it is unobservable if there are 2,000 firms (panel d). We can thus safely ignore this detail for a reasonably large number of varieties.

10.5 Increasing returns to scale

The Japanese companies Nikon and Canon, together with the Dutch ASM Lithography company, dominate the global market for chip machines, the vital tools for producing computer chips. The newest generation of ASM Lithography's machines, measuring 2 m^2 and weighing 7 tons, cost $7 million apiece. To give an indication of the size of the (fixed) costs required for the equipment of one chip-making factory, Doug Dunn, chairman of ASM Lithography, remarked (NRC, 2001a): 'It takes four years before a new factory is fully operational. It involves an investment of 2 billion dollars.' Clearly, then, chip makers are operative in a market with increasing returns to scale, implying that total costs increase, but costs per unit of output fall, as output expands. Numerous other sectors of the economy are also characterized by increasing returns to scale, usually because of initial investment costs before production can start; think of the automobile examples in Section 10.1, or the shipping industry, or the aircraft industry, or setting up an Internet site, or a law firm (where an initial investment in knowledge is required before legal services can be produced), etc.

We distinguish between external and internal increasing returns to scale; see Box 10.3. If there are increasing returns to scale, as in the examples given above, the firm will realize that its costs per unit of output fall if output expands. Internal returns to scale are therefore incompatible with perfect competition.[5] Therefore, if you think returns to scale are important, you must necessarily analyse a market of imperfect competition. In order not to overestimate the firm's power at the macroeconomic level, we will focus on a market of monopolistic competition.

Production in the manufacturing sector is characterized by internal economies of scale, which means that there is imperfect competition in this sector (see Box 10.3). The varieties in the manufacturing industry are all produced with the same technology. Internal economies of scale mean that each variety is produced by a single firm; the firm with the largest sales can always outbid a potential competitor. The economies of scale are modelled in the simplest way possible:

(10.5) $$l_i = f + mx_i$$

where l_i is the amount of labour necessary to produce x_i of variety i. The parameters f and m describe, respectively, the fixed and marginal labour input requirement. The fixed labour input f in (10.5) ensures that as production expands less labour is needed to produce a unit of x_i, which means that there are internal economies of scale. This is illustrated in Figure 10.5, showing the total labour required to produce a certain amount of output, and the average amount of labour required to produce that amount of output.

10.6 Optimal pricing and zero profits

Each manufacturing firm produces a unique variety under internal returns to scale. This implies that the firm has monopoly power, which it will use to maximize its profits. We will therefore have to determine the price-setting behaviour of each firm. The Dixit–Stiglitz monopolistic competition model makes two assumptions in this respect. First, it is assumed that each firm takes the price-setting behaviour of other firms as given; that is, if firm 1 changes its price it will assume that the prices of the other $N-1$ varieties will remain the same. Second, it is assumed that the firm ignores the effect of changing its own price on the price index P of manufactures. Both assumptions seem reasonable if the number of varieties N is large, as also discussed in Section 10.4. For ease of notation we will drop the sub-index for the firm in this section. Note that a firm that produces x units of output using the production function in equation (10.5) will earn profits π given in equation (10.6) if the wage rate it has to pay is W.

(10.6) $$\pi = px - W(f + mx)$$

Naturally, the firm will have to sell the units of output x it is producing; that is, these sales must be consistent with the demand for a variety of manufactures derived in Section 10.3. Although this demand was derived for an arbitrary consumer, the most important feature of the demand for a variety, namely the constant price elasticity of demand ε, also holds when we combine the demand from many consumers with the same preference structure. If the demand x for a variety has a constant price elasticity of demand ε, maximization of the profits given in equation (10.6) leads to a very simple optimal pricing rule, known as mark-up pricing; see Technical Note 9.1.

(10.7) $$p(1 - 1/\varepsilon) = mW$$

The term 'mark-up pricing' is obvious. The marginal costs of producing an extra unit of output is equal to mW, while the price p the firm charges is higher than this marginal cost. How much higher depends crucially on the price elasticity of demand. If demand is rather inelastic, say $\varepsilon = 2$, the mark-up is high (in this case 100 per cent). If demand is rather elastic, say $\varepsilon = 5$, the mark-up is lower (in this case 25 per cent). Note that the firm must charge a higher price than marginal cost in order to recuperate the fixed costs of labour fW. Because the price elasticity of demand ε is constant, the mark-up of price over marginal cost is also constant, and therefore invariant to the scale of production.

　　Now that we have determined the optimal price a firm will charge to maximize profits, we can actually calculate those profits. This is where another important feature of monopolistic competition comes in. If profits are positive (sometimes referred to as excess profits), it is

Box 10.4 The parameter ε as a measure of returns to scale?

The parameter ε is directly related to the consumer's preferences, as defined in equation (10.2). In equilibrium, however, it is also used as a measure of economies of scale. One specific measure of economies of scale is average costs divided by marginal costs; if marginal costs are lower than average costs an increase in production will reduce the cost per unit. We can calculate this measure for the equilibrium level of production. The production level is (eq. 10.8): $f(\varepsilon-1)/m$, which requires $f\varepsilon$ labour, so the average costs are $f\varepsilon/(f(\varepsilon-1)/m) = m\varepsilon/(\varepsilon-1)$. The marginal labour costs are simply m, so this measure of scale economies reduces to average costs/marginal costs $= \varepsilon/(\varepsilon-1)$. For a low value of ε this measure of scale economies is high, and vice versa. In equilibrium it only depends on the elasticity of substitution parameter ε, and not on the parameters f and m of the production function. This peculiar result, in which the measure of scale economies is related to parameters not of the production function but of the utility function, is an artifact of the Dixit–Stiglitz model of monopolistic competition, which makes average costs over marginal costs an unsuitable measure of scale economies.

apparently very attractive to set up shop in the manufacturing sector. One would then expect that new firms enter the market and start to produce a different variety. This implies, of course, that the consumer will allocate her spending over more varieties of manufactures. Since all varieties are substitutes for one another, the entry of new firms in the manufacturing sector implies that profits for the existing firms will fall. This process of entry of new firms will continue until profits in the manufacturing sector are driven to zero. A reverse process, with firms leaving the manufacturing sector, would operate if profits were negative. Monopolistic competition in the manufacturing sector therefore imposes as an equilibrium condition that profits are zero. If we do that in equation (10.6) we can calculate the scale at which a firm producing a variety in the manufacturing sector will operate; see Technical Note 10.2.

$$(10.8) \qquad\qquad x = \frac{f(\varepsilon-1)}{m}$$

Equation (10.8), giving the scale of output for an individual firm, may seem strange at first sight. No matter what happens, the output per firm is fixed in equilibrium. The constant price elasticity of demand in conjunction with the production function is responsible for this result. It implies that the manufacturing sector as a whole only expands and contracts by producing more or fewer varieties, as the output level per variety does not change. Since the scale of production is constant, as given in equation (10.8), it is easy to determine (i) how much labour is needed to produce this amount of output using the production function, and (ii) how many varieties N are produced in the economy by dividing the total labour force L by the amount of labour required per variety (which gives $N = L/f\varepsilon$); see Technical Note 10.2. Evidently, a larger market, as measured by the available amount of labour L, is able to support a larger number N of varieties, thus giving consumers more varieties to choose from.

10.7 Explaining intra-industry trade

How does all of the above help us to understand intra-industry trade flows, and possible gains from such trade flows? Let us first summarize the main conclusions derived in Sections 10.3–10.6:

- Consumers demand different varieties of similar goods. Other things being equal, the more varieties are available to cater to specific needs of the consumer, the higher the derived utility level.

- Consumer demand for any particular variety increases if (i) the price of the variety falls (with a constant price elasticity of demand ε), (ii) the price of any other variety increases, and (iii) the income level increases.

- Producers supply many different varieties of similar goods. Before production of any particular variety can start an initial investment cost is necessary (for invention of the variety, or to set up a production plant), such that there are internal increasing returns to scale. This gives market power to the individual producers.

- Producers maximize profits by choosing the optimal price level. Since the price elasticity of demand is constant, the mark-up of price over marginal costs is also constant.

- Firms enter and exit the market for producing new varieties until (excess) profits are equal to zero. In this setting, this results in a constant production level for each variety of manufactures, such that a change in total market supply is equivalent to a change in the number of varieties produced.

Given these preliminary results, it is straightforward to put two and two together and explain how intra-industry trade may arise, and what its benefits are. Consider two countries, Belgium and the Netherlands, with a demand and supply structure as laid out in Sections 10.3–10.6. We will assume these countries are identical in all respects, except in the size of their labour force; more specifically, we assume Belgium has 5 million labourers, and the Netherlands has 7 million labourers. Since technology is the same for the two countries, there is no Ricardian basis for international trade. Since there is only one factor of production (labour) it is impossible even to identify relative factor abundance, such that there is no Heckscher–Ohlin basis for international trade. None the less, international trade, of the intra-industry type, will arise in this model, and it will lead to gains from trade for both countries.

We start with a brief discussion of the autarky equilibrium. If we let the wage rate be the numéraire, all firms face the same marginal costs and the same price elasticity of demand. They therefore all charge the same price. If all workers are employed, the total income level is identical to the number of labourers, because firms enter and exit the market until profits are zero and the wage rate is the numéraire. As explained at the end of Section 10.6, and emphasized above, the number of varieties produced in each country is proportional to the size of the market (as measured by the total labour force):

$$(10.9) \qquad N_{Belgium} = \frac{L_{Belgium}}{f\varepsilon} ; \quad N_{Netherlands} = \frac{L_{Netherlands}}{f\varepsilon}$$

Suppose that the fixed costs f and the elasticity of substitution ε are such that 500 labourers are required in equilibrium for the production of one variety. As illustrated in Figure 10.6,

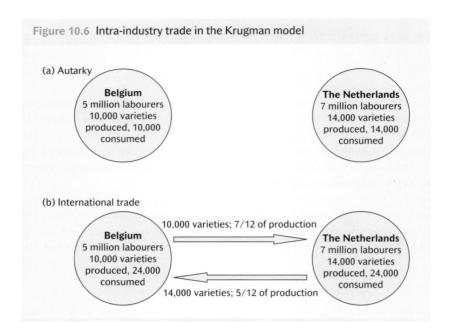

Figure 10.6 Intra-industry trade in the Krugman model

(a) Autarky

Belgium
5 million labourers
10,000 varieties
produced, 10,000
consumed

The Netherlands
7 million labourers
14,000 varieties
produced, 14,000
consumed

(b) International trade

Belgium
5 million labourers
10,000 varieties
produced, 24,000
consumed

10,000 varieties; 7/12 of production

14,000 varieties; 5/12 of production

The Netherlands
7 million labourers
14,000 varieties
produced, 24,000
consumed

Belgium will then produce and consume 10,000 varieties in autarky and the Netherlands will produce and consume 14,000 varieties in autarky.

What changes if these two countries start to trade with one another (at zero transport costs and in the absence of any other impediment to trade)? The answer is: virtually nothing and very much at the same time. The 'virtually nothing' part refers to the fact that the price for a variety does not change, nor does production size for any variety, or the number of varieties produced. The 'very much' part refers to the fact that we now have intensive trade flows between the two nations, because the consumers have a preference for variety and therefore want to consume all varieties produced in both countries. The total number of varieties consumed therefore increases from 10,000 in Belgium and 14,000 in the Netherlands to 24,000 in both countries. Since demand is proportional to the size of the market, a Belgian producer will export 7/12 of total production to the Netherlands, while a Dutch producer will export 5/12 of total production to Belgium. These intensive trade flows of similar types of goods, produced using similar technologies in both countries, can be classified as intra-industry trade.

In the Ricardian model, as in the Heckscher–Ohlin model, there are gains from trade through more efficient production at a global scale. In Chapter 9, where we discussed the pro-competitive gains from trade, the pressure of international competition reduces the domestic distortions, and therefore leads to efficiency gains. In the Krugman model, none of these factors is operative. The reader will have noticed that the production levels have not changed at all in either country. Since the Dutch are exporting 5/12 of their production level of each variety, the level consumed of those varieties falls by 5/12. In exchange the Dutch are now consuming 7/12 of the Belgian production level of the varieties produced in Belgium. The total consumption level has not changed ($10{,}000 \times 7/12 - 14{,}000 \times 5/12 = 0$). All we are doing is exporting manufactures in exchange for the import of an equal amount of manufactures. Are there any gains from these trade flows? The answer is: yes. Two remarks are in order.

First, note that the wage rate, and thus the consumer's income level, has not changed in trade relative to autarky, nor has the price of domestically produced varieties. If trade is possible, therefore, the consumer can still consume the same combination of goods as in autarky. The utility level cannot possibly decrease, while the fact that the consumer decides to consume a different basket of goods indicates that the utility level must rise.

Second, note that the varieties are imperfect substitutes for one another. Other things being equal, the marginal utility from consuming an extra unit of any particular variety falls. Recall that the consumer will equate the marginal utility per dollar for all goods in equilibrium. If trade is possible, therefore, the consumer will benefit by reducing the consumption level of domestically produced varieties with low marginal utility, in exchange for an increase in foreign-produced varieties with a high marginal utility.

International trade in this set-up thus leads to an increase in welfare because it allows consumers to enjoy the benefits of a larger market, which is able to sustain a large variety of goods and services produced to cater to specific preferences. Indeed, it is straightforward to show that the derived utility is a power function of the size of the market; see Technical Note 10.3.

10.8 An alternative interpretation: intermediate goods

So far, we have discussed the Krugman model of intra-industry trade, that is trade between countries of similar goods and services within the same industry, which is becoming more important, as measured by the Grubel–Lloyd index. The gains from trade in the Krugman setting derive from the ability to sustain a wider variety of goods and services in a larger market as a result of increasing returns to scale. A larger market therefore is better able to fulfil the preferences of consumers, who like variety. In short, the entire discussion and interpretation of the model is in terms of production and trade of *final* goods and services for the consumer market.

The Krugman interpretation of the model is illustrated in Figure 10.7. In autarky, country A produces N_A different varieties under increasing returns to scale and monopolistic competition.

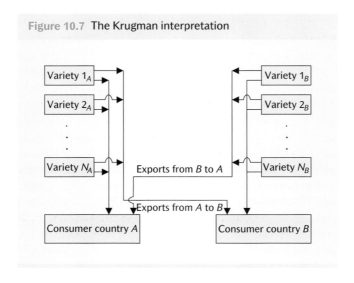

Figure 10.7 The Krugman interpretation

Similarly for country *B*. If the two countries engage in international trade with one another, the consumers in both countries purchase some goods from all domestic producers *and* import some goods from all foreign producers. The resulting trade flows are therefore intra-industry trade flows of final goods from producers to consumers.

The American economist Wilfred Ethier (1982) came up with an entirely different, and influential, interpretation of the same model. He pointed out (1982: 950–52) that: 'the largest and fastest growing component of world trade since World War II has been the exchange of manufactures between the industrialized economies. . . . (I cannot resist the temptation to point out that producers' goods are in fact much more prominent in trade than are consumer's goods).' One of the objectives of the Ethier article is therefore to explain the large intra-industry trade flows of *intermediate* goods, that is trade flows from one producer to another, rather than from producer to consumer.

Figure 10.8 illustrates how Ethier was able to explain those trade flows through a reinterpretation of the Krugman model. Instead of interpreting the various varieties produced in both countries as different final goods, he interpreted them as different, and new, intermediate goods in a complex final goods production process. This can refer to different types of capital goods, such as cars, printing machines, copiers, presses, etc., or to different types of services, such as accounting, engineering, cleaning, etc. The providers of intermediate goods, produced under increasing returns to scale, have market power and are operating in a market of monopolistic competition.

There is only one final good delivered to the consumers. The producers of the final good, say *Y*, combine the intermediate inputs from all variety producers in a perfectly competitive market, that is taking the prices of the intermediate goods providers as given, into the single

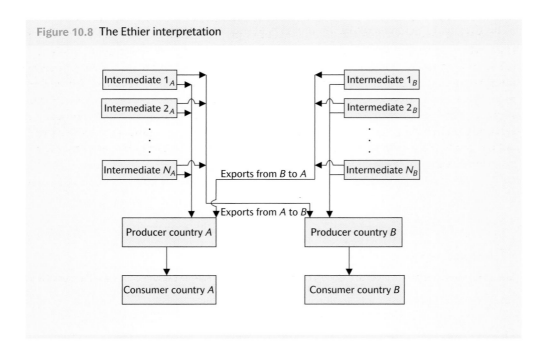

Figure 10.8 The Ethier interpretation

output. The final good production function is similar to the utility function in the Krugman approach; see equation (10.2):

$$(10.10) \qquad Y = \left(\sum_{i=1}^{N} x_i^{\rho} \right)^{1/\rho} ; \quad 0 < \rho < 1$$

In this interpretation, the x_i refer to intermediate goods deliveries. The price elasticity of demand for intermediate goods by final goods producers is, of course, again a constant, equal to $\varepsilon = 1/(1 - \rho)$. Once we impose a well-behaved utility function $U(Y)$ on top of this structure, the outcome is essentially the same as in the Krugman model. This time, as displayed in Figure 10.8, we have active international intra-industry trade flows of *intermediate goods* between nations.

It is also important to understand the difference of interpretation of an increase in the extent of the market in the Ethier model. First, recall that a larger market enables an increase in the number N of varieties produced. Second, remember that the increase in the number of varieties leads to higher utility levels in the Krugman model through a love-of-variety effect. In a similar way, a larger market leads to an increase in the number of intermediate goods available to final goods producers, which increases their total output level through a positive production externality. The different intermediate goods are imperfect substitutes for one another. Therefore, the more there are available to the final goods producer, the more efficiently the production process is organized, and the higher the production level.

10.9 Conclusions

The empirically observed prevalence of intra-industry trade (two-way trade in similar products), measured using the Grubel–Lloyd index, is hard to explain on the basis of differences in factor abundance or technology. Using the Krugman model, an extension of the Dixit–Stiglitz model, we provide an analysis of imperfect competition under economies of scale, which in conjunction with the size of the market determines the number of different varieties of goods and services available to consumers (or firms in the intermediate product interpretation of Ethier). International trade increases the extent of the market, thus making more types of goods available. This raises welfare through a love-of-variety effect for final goods or raises production through increased specialization leading to positive production externalities. In both cases the model can be applied to better understand intra-industry trade of final goods and intermediate goods. The general structure of this model will be the basis of more applications in the sequel of the book.

TECHNICAL NOTES

Technical Note 10.1 Dixit–Stiglitz demand

To maximize equation (10.2) subject to the budget constraint (10.3) we define the Lagrangean Γ, using the multiplier κ:

$$(10.A1) \qquad \Gamma = \left[\sum_{i=1}^{N} c_i^{\rho} \right]^{(1/\rho)} + \kappa \left[I - \sum_{i=1}^{N} p_i c_i \right]$$

Differentiating Γ with respect to c_j and equating to 0 gives the first-order conditions:

(10.A2)
$$\left[\sum_{i=1}^{N} c_i^\rho\right]^{(1/\rho)-1} c_j^{\rho-1} = kp_j \quad for \quad j = 1, \ldots, N$$

Take the ratio of these first-order conditions with respect to variety 1, note that the first term on the left-hand side cancels (as does the term κ on the right-hand side), and define $\varepsilon \equiv 1/(1-\rho)$ as discussed in the main text. Then:

(10.A3)
$$\frac{c_j^{\rho-1}}{c_1^{\rho-1}} = \frac{p_j}{p_1} \quad or \quad c_j = p_j^{-\varepsilon}p_1^\varepsilon c_1 \quad for \quad j = 1, \ldots, N$$

Substituting these relations in the budget equation gives:

(10.A4)
$$\sum_{j=1}^{N} p_j c_j = \sum_{j=1}^{N} p_j[p_j^{-\varepsilon}p_1^\varepsilon c_1] = p_1^\varepsilon c_1 \sum_{j=1}^{N} p_j^{1-\varepsilon} = p_1^\varepsilon c_1 P^{1-\varepsilon} = I, \quad or \quad c_1 = p_1^{-\varepsilon}P^{\varepsilon-1}I$$

$$P \equiv \left[\sum_{j=1}^{N} p_j^{1-\varepsilon}\right]^{1/(1-\varepsilon)}$$

This explains the demand for variety 1 as given in equation (10.4). The demand for the other varieties is derived analogously. The question remains why the price index P was defined as given in equation (10.A4). To answer this question we have to substitute the derived demand for all varieties in equation (10.2), and note along the way that $-\varepsilon\rho = 1 - \varepsilon$ and $1/\rho = -\varepsilon/(1-\varepsilon)$:

$$U = \left(\sum_{i=1}^{N} c_i^\rho\right)^{1/\rho} = \left(\sum_{i=1}^{N} (p_i^{-\varepsilon}P^{\varepsilon-1}I)^\rho\right)^{1/\rho} = IP^{\varepsilon-1}\left(\sum_{i=1}^{N} p_i^{-\varepsilon\rho}\right)^{1/\rho} = IP^{\varepsilon-1}\left(\sum_{i=1}^{N} p_i^{1-\varepsilon}\right)^{-\varepsilon/(1-\varepsilon)}$$

Using the definition of the price index P from equation (10.A4) this simplifies to:

(10.A5)
$$U = IP^{\varepsilon-1}\left(\sum_{i=1}^{N} p_i^{1-\varepsilon}\right)^{-\varepsilon/(1-\varepsilon)} = IP^{\varepsilon-1}P^{-\varepsilon} = I/P$$

Technical Note 10.2   Equilibrium scale of production

Put profits in equation (10.6) equal to zero and use the pricing rule $p(1-1/\varepsilon) = mW$:

(10.A6)
$$px - W(f + mx) = 0; \quad px = fW + mWx; \quad \left[\frac{\varepsilon}{\varepsilon-1}mW\right]x = fW + mWx$$

$$\left[\frac{\varepsilon}{\varepsilon-1} - 1\right]mWx = fW; \quad x = \frac{f(\varepsilon-1)}{m}$$

This explains equation (10.8). Now use the production function (10.5) to calculate the amount of labour required to produce this much output:

(10.A7)
$$l_i = f + mx = f + m\frac{f(\varepsilon-1)}{m} = f + f(\varepsilon-1) = f\varepsilon$$

Finally, determining the number N of varieties produced simply follows by dividing the total number of manufacturing workers by the number of workers needed to produce one variety: $N = L/l_i = L/f\varepsilon$.

Technical Note 10.3   Intra-industry trade and welfare

Since the price of all varieties is the same in equilibrium, the consumption level is the same for all varieties in equilibrium. From equation (10.2) it follows that the utility level is then equal to $U = N^{1/\rho}c$. The production level for any variety is given in equation (10.8) as $x = f(\varepsilon-1)/m$. Dividing this by the number of people L gives the per capita consumption c. Finally, recall that the number of varieties is proportional to the labour force, that is $N = L/f\varepsilon$, and combine the above information to get:

(10.A8)
$$U = N^{1/\rho}c = \left(\frac{L}{f\varepsilon}\right)^{1/\rho}\frac{f(\varepsilon - 1)}{mL} = \gamma_U L^{1/(\varepsilon-1)}; \quad \gamma_U \equiv \frac{\varepsilon - 1}{m}\left(\frac{1}{f\varepsilon}\right)^{1/\rho}$$

QUESTIONS

Question 10.1

Chapter 10 introduces the constant-elasticity-of-substitution (CES) utility function. It provided the breakthrough for intra-industry trade theory. Suppose that a consumer with this type of utility function (see equation 10.2) consumes three goods: coffee, tea and milk.

10.1A Use a numerical example to show that if $\rho = 1$, the consumer is indifferent to consuming three units of coffee or three units of a mix of the goods.

10.1B Use a numerical example to show that if $0 < \rho < 1$, the consumer prefers to purchase a combination of goods.

For the rest of this question we assume that each good is consumed in the same quantity. Section 10.3 then rewrites the utility function to distinguish between a love-of-variety effect and a claim on real resources (see equation 10.2'). Suppose that $\rho = 0.5$ and assume that one unit of each good is consumed.

10.1C Rewrite the utility function for coffee, tea, and milk to mimic equation (10.2'). How large is the claim on real resources? How large is the love-of-variety effect?

10.1D Use an example to illustrate how the love-of-variety effect represents a multiplier-like role in the utility function (use equation 10.2').

Question 10.2

'One definition of an economist is somebody who sees something happen in practice and wonders if it will work in theory.'

10.2A How does this joke relate to the theory of intra-industry trade?

Though the theory of intra-industry trade was an important breakthrough, much remains to be done. Several economists take issue with the parameter ε in the model.

10.2B Give two reasons why economists might be concerned about this parameter.

The merits of globalization are subject to fierce debates. One of the issues that anti-globalization advocates raise is the perceived decrease in the amount of variety in the world. Everybody buys the same brands and shops at the same stores.

10.2C What can the theory of intra-industry trade say about this issue?

Question 10.3

China and Australia both produce fireworks. The demand and supply structure in both economies is given by the Dixit–Stiglitz model, with an elasticity of substitution equal to 2 in both countries. Since continually firing the same crackers is quite boring, there is a love-of-variety effect for all consumers. The fireworks market is much larger in China than in Australia. In both countries the marginal labour input requirement is 1 and the fixed labour input per variety is 2.5. The Chinese labour employment in the fireworks industry is 10 million people. The Australian labour employment in the fireworks industry is 10 thousand people.

10.3A How many varieties will be supplied to the Australian and Chinese market in the autarky equilibrium?

10.3B How many varieties will be consumed in each country in the free trade equilibrium?

10.3C Does international trade increase the production efficiency in the two countries? Does international trade increase output?

10.3D What is the domestic market share of Australian producers if international trade is allowed?

10.3E Who benefits and who loses from international trade in this model? Are the benefits equally shared between Australia and China?

10.3F Describe how the Ethier interpretation would alter the analysis of international trade of fireworks. How does it affect the benefits of international trade, in comparison with the Krugman interpretation?

 See the Online Resource Centre for a Study Guide containing more questions
www.oxfordtextbooks.co.uk/orc/vanmarrewijk/

NOTES

1 The paper by Spence (1976) on a similar topic slightly pre-dates Dixit and Stiglitz (1977), but had considerably less influence. See Neary (2001) for a discussion on Dixit-Stiglitz monopolistic competition.

2 The sum of exports and imports as a share of the total is used as the relevant weight.

3 Many textbooks discuss the properties of the CES function. See also Brakman and van Marrewijk (1998), who compare it with the properties of other utility functions.

4 In fact, using equation (10.A4), the exact price elasticity of demand for a specific variety can be derived. Illuminating in this respect is the analysis in the neighbourhood of p if $p_i = p$ for all other varieties, in which case $-(\partial c/\partial p)(p/c) = \varepsilon[1-1/N]$. The second term on the right-hand side is inversely related to the number of varieties N, approaching 1 if N becomes large.

5 If a firm takes the price of output p as given and the costs per unit of output c fall as output expands, the firm would want to make an infinite amount of goods if c falls below p, which cannot be an equilibrium.

STRATEGIC TRADE POLICY

Objectives/key terms

- Strategic trade
- Brander–Spencer model
- Eaton–Grossman model
- Non-equivalence
- Bertrand competition
- Informational requirements

We analyse the impact of 'strategic' trade policy, designed to give domestic producers an advantage in a world characterized by imperfect competition.

11.1 Introduction

In Chapter 8 we discussed the effects of trade policy, that is tariffs, quotas, and the like, in a classical or neoclassical world of perfect competition. We concluded that trade restrictions are detrimental for small countries unable to influence the world price level, in both a partial and a general equilibrium setting. The analysis was somewhat less clear-cut for large countries, since their ability to influence the terms of trade suggested that a suitable restriction of trade (the 'optimal' tariff) would enable them to increase their welfare, be it at the cost of a deterioration of welfare in the other countries of the world. In a more general setting, taking retaliation by other countries through a suitable choice of their 'optimal' tariffs into consideration, we concluded again that free trade is the true optimal policy.

The optimal tariff argument is based on market power at the country level. Chapters 9 and 10 have discussed market power at the firm and industry level in a world of imperfect competition (monopoly, oligopoly, monopolistic competition), sometimes based on increasing returns to scale. This suggests, of course, that the analysis of trade policy in a world based on the models of Chapters 9 and 10 is more involved and potentially leaves more room for beneficial government intervention. As we will elaborate below, both suggestions are true in principle. An omniscient government *could* indeed potentially make the right 'strategic' choices by promoting the interests of certain sectors. This so-called strategic trade policy argument (see Sections 11.4 and 11.5) received a lot of attention for a fairly brief period of time, as explained in Section 11.6. We also explain why this attention did not last very long and give a number of reasons why the strategic trade policy arguments are not important in practice. Before addressing these issues, we explain the main economic implications of imposing a tariff or quota to protect a domestic industry characterized by market power; see Sections 11.2 and 11.3. The discussion in these two sections is based on Bhagwati (1965).

Famous economists	Jagdish Bhagwati

Fig. 11.1
Jagdish Bhagwati
(1934–)

Born and raised in India, Jagdish Bhagwati studied at Cambridge, MIT, and Oxford before returning to India in 1961 to work at the Indian Statistical Institute and the Delhi School of Economics. In 1968 he went back to MIT, where he worked for twelve years before moving to Columbia University. Currently, he is Special Adviser to the United Nations on Globalization and External Adviser to the World Trade Organization. Jagdish Bhagwati has published numerous articles and books on virtually all subfields of international economics, notably on trade, development, and trade policy. In 1971 he founded the *Journal of International Economics*, the foremost journal in the field today. Bhagwati's influence outside the academic community is steadily increasing. Among his better-known books are *Protectionism* (1988) and *The World Trading System at Risk* (1991).

11.2 Market power and tariffs

The analyses and discussions in Chapters 9 and 10 have demonstrated that international trade reduces the market power of domestic firms. Conversely, therefore, we expect protection to increase domestic market power. In contrast to the perfect competition analysis of Chapter 8, however, the effects of protection depend on the form it takes. In general, as first shown by Jagdish Bhagwati (1965) and demonstrated in this section and the next, quantitative restrictions such as quotas create larger distortions and generate more domestic market power than tariffs.

Figure 11.2 illustrates the case considered by Bhagwati. There is a single producer in the domestic market facing a downward-sloping demand curve, with concomitant marginal revenue curve (MR), and an upward-sloping marginal cost curve (MC). In the absence of international trade, the domestic supplier is a monopolist and output would be determined by equality of marginal cost and marginal revenue at point C, such that the firm would charge the monopoly price p_{mon}. Recall that, if this were a competitive industry, output would be determined by equality of price and marginal cost, that is at point B leading to price p_{comp}. If there is free international trade, and assuming that this is a small country facing competition from price-taking foreign suppliers[1] at the price p_{world}, the domestic firm would produce at the point where marginal cost is equal to the world price level, that is at point D. The difference between domestic demand at point E and domestic supply at point D would be imported from abroad.

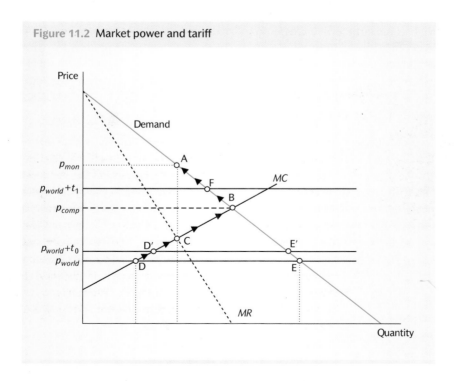

Figure 11.2 Market power and tariff

Imposing a tariff such that $p_{world} + t < p_{comp}$

If the government decides to protect the domestic firm by imposing a specific tariff t, the (welfare) consequences are initially similar to the analysis in Chapter 8. As long as the world price plus the tariff is below the competitive equilibrium price, as illustrated in Figure 11.2 for tariff t_0, the domestic firm increases output from point D to D', domestic demand falls from point E to E', and imports from abroad also decrease.

Imposing a tariff such that $p_{comp} < p_{world} + t < p_{mon}$

The analysis starts to deviate from the competitive analysis in Chapter 8 once the government imposes a 'prohibitive' tariff, such that the world price plus the tariff is above the competitive equilibrium price, as illustrated for tariff t_1 in Figure 11.2. If the domestic market were competitive, any tariff increase above the competitive price would have no further effects. The price equilibrium would remain at point B, price and quantity would be constant, and imports would be zero. If there is a single domestic firm, however, an increase of the tariff beyond the competitive price level enables the domestic firm to use its monopoly power by lowering output and increasing price and profits, up to the level $p_{world} + t_1$, that is at point F. Note that the *threat* of imports keeps the monopolist from exercising its monopoly power fully, even when no imports actually occur, such that raising an already prohibitive tariff leads to a domestic price increase and reduces domestic output.

Imposing a tariff such that $p_{mon} < p_{world} + t$

If the government raises the prohibitive tariff even further, such that the world price plus the tariff exceeds the monopoly price, the domestic firm maximizes profits at the monopoly price and does not raise the price any further; that is, the equilibrium remains at point A.

Note that, as the tariff level increases from 0 to $p_{mon} - p_{world}$, the domestic quantity and price combination first moves from point D to point B, and then from point B to point A. Any further tariff increases have no effect.

 Box 11.1   The strategic importance of sugar

After months of negotiations the EU Council (in the form of the Ministers for Agriculture; see Chapter 13) decided in May 2001 to reduce the EU support for the production of sugar. Because sugar is one of the most protected sectors in Europe, it is virtually impossible for developing countries to export it to the EU, with the exception of ex-colonies, which are given preferential treatment. The 300 million euro annual subsidy for the storage of sugar will be abolished. The EU buys sugar for €632 per tonne, almost three times the world price, and is levying import tariffs to keep foreign, more efficiently produced cane sugar from the market. Consequently, the European consumer is heavily subsidizing the 'strategically' important European sugar industry. In June 2005 the European Commission announced a drastic change in this system, reducing the price of sugar by 39 per cent in 2009, accompanied by subsidies to farmers to mitigate their loss. In addition, the EU will pay factories to stop producing sugar (starting with €730 per not-produced tonne initially, and a falling rate each subsequent year).

Information source: NRC Handelsblad (2001b) and *The Economist* (2005a).

11.3 The non-equivalence of tariffs and quotas

In Chapter 8 we briefly discussed how the imposition of a tariff and a quota leading to the same level of imports results in the same welfare effects and price level; see Box 8.1. This so-called equivalence between tariffs and quotas no longer holds if there is domestic market power. This is illustrated in Figure 11.3 for the Bhagwati framework explained in the previous section (one domestic firm and price-taking foreign suppliers). First, suppose the country imposes a tariff such that the world price plus the tariff is below the competitive price. As explained in Section 11.2, and illustrated in Figure 11.3, this leads to domestic production at point A, domestic demand at point B, and imports equal to the difference between points B and A. Second, suppose that *instead* of imposing a tariff, the government decides to impose a quantitative import restriction equal to the import level under the tariff (the difference between points B and A). Does this change the domestic equilibrium? Yes, it does. To understand this, we have to consider the strategic possibilities available to the domestic firm if either tariffs or the quota are imposed, as indicated by marginal revenue.

Under the tariff, the marginal revenue curve for the domestic supplier is equal to $p_{world} + t$. As a result of the quota, however, the domestic firm's demand curve essentially shifts to the left by the extent of the quota, as indicated by the arrows in Figure 11.3. Consequently, the domestic firm's marginal revenue curve is generated by this restricted demand curve. After allowing for the restricted foreign imports, the domestic firm can again exercise its monopoly power, leading to the equality of marginal revenue and marginal cost at point C and the price p_{quota}, as determined by point D.

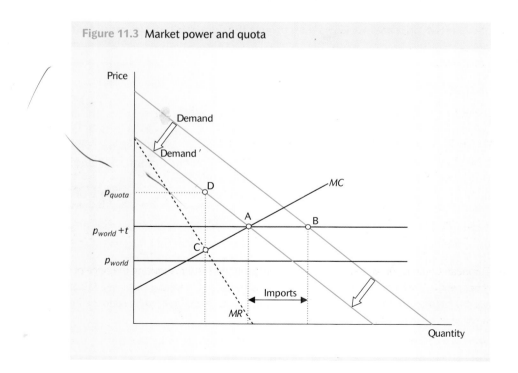

Figure 11.3 Market power and quota

Box 11.2   **The strategic importance of bananas**

After nine years of trade warfare the USA and the EU, led by Robert Zoellick and Pascal Lamy respectively, reached an agreement in April 2001 on a new regime for importing bananas into the EU. The warfare began in 1993 when the EU set up a mix of tariffs and quotas to help exports from former colonies. This system discriminated against bananas from Latin America, most of which are shipped by American companies, and was therefore ruled illegal by the WTO. The new system will consist of a tariff-only regime by 2006 (in line with WTO 'tariffication'; see Chapter 12). In the transitional period, starting 1 July 2001, quotas will be based on the import volume of 1994–6. This benefits the struggling, near-bankrupt Chiquita company relative to its rival Dole, which has diversified its sourcing of bananas. Personal contacts seem to be important in striking strategic trade deals; not only because Robert Zoellick and Pascal Lamy are personal friends, but also behind the scenes, as suggested by *The Economist* (2001a):

> If the banana accord survives it will also be a victory for Trent Lott, the Republican Leader of the Senate. Last year Mr Lott, who has received tens of thousands of campaign dollars thanks to the efforts of Chiquita's chief executive, made it clear that he would oppose any deal that hurt the company. This week Mr Lott is touring Europe. In Brussels, he should drop a thank-you note into Mr Lamy's letter box.

Information source: *The Economist* (2001a).

Clearly, if domestic firms enjoy some market power, protection of the domestic industry with quota rather than tariffs leads to higher prices and lower output. Using a similar partial equilibrium welfare analysis as in Chapter 8, quotas therefore lead to larger welfare losses. The clear policy message is therefore: if you *must* protect the domestic industry, use a tariff rather than a quota.

11.4 Strategic trade policy

One of the most controversial topics in the new trade literature is the suggestion that active government intervention, through tariffs, quotas, subsidies, or otherwise, may be able to raise domestic welfare by shifting oligopoly profits from foreign to domestic firms. The debate started in the 1980s, when there was great concern about American international competitiveness, with a series of papers by James Brander and Barbara Spencer (1983, 1985). The general idea is that government intervention can serve the 'strategic' purpose of altering the incentives of firms, thus deterring foreign competitors.

The main idea is conveyed quite easily in the Brander–Spencer analysis, which is based on the Cournot model of Section 9.4, by simplifying the international trade aspects of the model. There are two firms, an Austrian firm (index A) and a Bolivian firm (index B), producing a homogeneous good. Both firms export to a *third* market and do not face any domestic demand. Since there are no other distortions in this partial equilibrium analysis than the monopoly power in the industry, the marginal cost of each firm is also the social cost of the resources it uses. As a result, national welfare for each country can be measured by the profits earned by its firm. Details on the discussion below are given in Technical Note 11.1 at the end of this chapter.

In the absence of government intervention, the Austrian firm maximizes its profits taking the output level of the Bolivian firm as given. Similarly for the Bolivian firm. As explained in Section 9.4, this leads to two 'reaction curves' in (q_A, q_B)-space, giving the optimal response of each firm to the other firm's output level. The Cournot equilibrium is determined by the point of intersection of the reaction curves, where neither firm has an incentive to change its output decision; see Figure 11.4.

Does the Cournot equilibrium lead to the highest possible profits for the Austrian firm? No. As indicated in Figure 11.4, the Austrian firm's isoprofit curve is horizontal at the Cournot equilibrium, since it is the optimal response (maximizes profits) given the output level of the Bolivian firm. Taking the Bolivian firm's reaction curve as a restriction, the Austrian firm's profits are maximized at a point of tangency of the Bolivian firm's reaction curve with the Austrian firm's isoprofit curve; see the Brander–Spencer square in Figure 11.4.[2] Why does the Austrian firm not produce this level of output? Because it is lacking a credible pre-commitment. Given the output level of the Bolivian firm at the Brander–Spencer equilibrium, the Austrian firm has an incentive to produce a smaller level of output which would raise its profits even further.

The potential for beneficial active government intervention now becomes clear. If the Austrian government is somehow able to shift the Austrian firm's reaction curve to the right, such that it precisely intersects the Bolivian firm's reaction curve at the Brander–Spencer equilibrium, it will have made this point a credible equilibrium. In essence, the Austrian government would then give its firm a strategic advantage. Several options are available, but Technical Note 11.1 shows that one strategy that works for the Austrian government is giving an export *subsidy* of exactly the right amount to the production of goods in Austria.

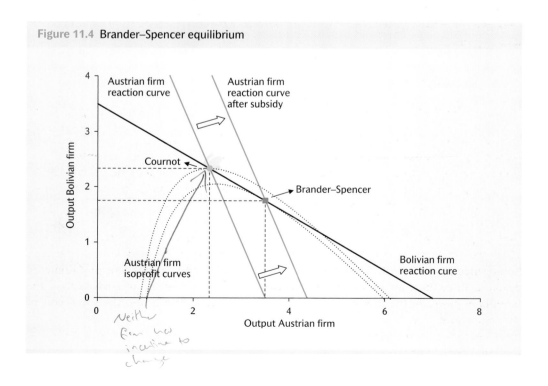

Figure 11.4 **Brander–Spencer equilibrium**

Box 11.3   The strategic importance of video recorders

Imposing tariffs and quantitative restrictions is not the only means to reduce imports. A noteworthy example in this respect is the decision of France in October 1982 to change its administrative procedure for the import of video recorders, after a period in which these imports, particularly from Japan, had rapidly increased. From then on, the recorders had to enter the country through an understaffed customs office in Poitiers, a small out-of-the-way place in the midwest of France. Carefully checking to see if the instructions were written in French and taking the recorders apart to verify the stated country of origin, the French rapidly succeeded in reducing the import of video recorders from 64,000 to 10,000 per month. After complaints from Japan and other European countries and an EC–Japan agreement to 'voluntarily' restrict exports of video recorders to Europe, the French government reversed the measure.

Information source: Lanjouw (1995: 11).

Technical Note 11.1 also shows that Austrian welfare (firm profit minus government outlays) is indeed maximized at the Brander–Spencer equilibrium.

11.5 The nature of competition

The Brander–Spencer model discussed in the previous section, leading to an export subsidy as the government's optimal policy, is based on strong assumptions (two firms exporting to a third market using Cournot competition). Naturally, this led to a series of responses from other economists investigating different strategic settings, based on price competition, more firms, domestic sales, entry and exit, differentiated goods, etc. The most important contribution in this respect is by Jonathan Eaton and Gene Grossman (1986). Before making a more general argument, they discuss the impact of a small change in the Brander–Spencer setting: rather than analysing Cournot-type quantity competition they analyse Bertrand-type price competition in an identical framework.

Consider, therefore, an Austrian and a Bolivian firm exporting to a third market, not facing any domestic demand. Since the firms are engaged in price competition we assume that the goods are imperfect substitutes to facilitate the analysis:[3] if the Austrian firm raises its price, this increases the demand for the Bolivian firm and vice versa. The absence of other distortions ensures that the marginal cost of each firm is also the social cost of the resources it uses, such that national welfare for each country is equal to the profits earned by its firm. Technical details on the discussion below are given in Technical Note 11.2 at the end of this chapter.

In the absence of government intervention, the Austrian firm maximizes its profits by choosing its price and taking the price level of the Bolivian firm as given, and similarly for the Bolivian firm. This leads to two 'reaction curves' in (p_A, p_B)-space, giving the optimal response of each firm to the other firm's price level. In contrast to Section 11.4, these reaction curves are upward sloping: if the Bolivian firm raises its price, the demand for the Austrian firm's product increases, which allows the Austrian firm to raise its price as well. Analogous to the analysis in Section 11.4, the Bertrand equilibrium is determined by the point of intersection

Figure 11.5 Eaton–Grossman equilibrium

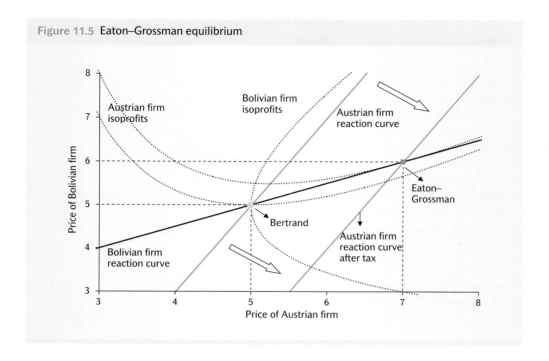

of the reaction curves, where neither firm has an incentive to change its pricing decision; see Figure 11.5.

The Bertrand equilibrium does not lead to the highest possible profit level for the Austrian firm, which is determined by the point of tangency of the Bolivian firm's reaction curve with the Austrian firm's isoprofit curve; see the Eaton–Grossman square in Figure 11.5. This time, however, the Austrian government can ensure that the Austrian firm's reaction curve is shifted to the right to intersect at the Eaton–Grossman point by levying an export *tax* of exactly the right amount. As Krugman (1990: 251) put it:

> So what Eaton and Grossman show is that replacing the Cournot with a Bertrand assumption reverses the policy recommendation. Given the shakiness of any characterization of oligopoly behavior, this is not reassuring.

Why do we have this reversal of the policy recommendation? Using terms introduced by Bulow, Geanokoplos, and Klemperer (1985), it is because with Cournot competition the choice variables are 'strategic substitutes' (higher output leads to lower marginal profitability of similar moves by the firm's rival), while with Bertrand competition the choice variables are 'strategic complements' (a higher price raises the marginal profitability of similar moves by the firm's rival). Eaton and Grossman show in a more general setting that the optimal policy recommendation depends on the choice variables being strategic substitutes (export subsidy) or strategic complements (export tax). Leaving aside the willingness of government officials who want to be re-elected to impose an export tax on an industry should the structural details demand such a policy response, it is time to evaluate the contribution of strategic trade policy.

11.6 Evaluation of strategic trade policy

For a fairly brief time period the idea of strategic trade policy, building on the framework of new trade theory, received a lot of attention, both from the international economics profession and from outside. The main reason for the outside attention is that any intellectually respectable case for intervention will quickly find support for the wrong reasons, namely as an excuse to impose arbitrary trade restrictions to protect sectors under competitive pressure from abroad. The special interest boxes in this chapter may give an idea how the Brander–Spencer idea can be misused in view of the 'strategic' importance of some protected sectors. The attention from the international economics profession is a response primarily based on this outside pressure for protection, namely to carefully scrutinize any idea that seems to support protection under some circumstances. Since the game-theoretic nature of the strategic trade policy argument makes the analyses of the scrutiny rather complex (involving the number of players, the number of time periods, the choice of strategic variables, who moves first, second, or third, the credibility of commitments, etc.), we will only briefly describe some of the main results in more general terms.

Competition for resources

The arguments in Sections 11.4 and 11.5 are based on a partial equilibrium framework. By now we have become accustomed in this book to value a general equilibrium framework for investigating international trade and trade policy, as it forces us to express our ideas in a consistent way and sometimes identifies the misleading nature of partial equilibrium results. As Dixit and Grossman (1986) argue, the export subsidy in the Brander–Spencer model works because it reduces the marginal costs for the Austrian firm in the subsidized sector, which deters exports to the third market by the Bolivian firm. In a general equilibrium framework, however, the subsidized sector can only expand by bidding away resources from other sectors, thus driving up the marginal costs in those sectors. This leads to reverse-deterrence in non-targeted sectors. Constructing a tractable general equilibrium model, Dixit and Grossman show that a subsidy to a specific sector only raises national income if the deterrent effect is higher in the subsidized sector than in the sectors that are crowded out as a result of the subsidy. Optimal policy therefore requires detailed knowledge of all sectors in the entire economy.

Entry and exit

The arguments in Sections 11.4 and 11.5 are based on the possibility of firms to earn supernormal profits over which firms (and countries) can compete. As argued in Chapter 10, the presence of supernormal profits will entice new firms to enter the market. This eliminates not only such profits, but also the arguments for strategic trade policy based on them. This line of reasoning is followed by Horstmann and Markusen (1986), who extend the Brander–Spencer framework by allowing for entry and exit of firms. The number of firms is determined by fixed costs leading to economies of scale. The authors show that a country providing a subsidy leads to a welfare loss through a reduction in scale economies or a worsening in the terms of trade.

Retaliation

There is an asymmetry in cleverness on the part of the governments in the Brander–Spencer model: the Austrian government gathers a lot of information and performs detailed calculations to determine the optimal export subsidy for its firm, while the Bolivian government does not. In an extended framework, many variants of which are analysed by Dixit and Kyle (1985), it is reasonable to assume that the Bolivian government is able to undertake similar Brander–Spencer policies. In this case the two countries end up in a prisoner-dilemma-type subsidy war, leading to a welfare loss for both countries (and a welfare gain for the third country).

Informational requirements

From a practical point of view, the most important objection to the ideas underlying strategic trade policy is the enormous informational requirement to carry out such a policy, certainly if the above objections are taken into consideration. Even in the partial equilibrium framework, the Austrian government must gather information about the production structure of the home and foreign firm, about the market demand in the third country, about the type of competition in the industry (Cournot or Bertrand), and about the interaction between firms. Then it must accurately undertake detailed calculations to determine the optimal policy. If it makes a mistake, either in size or direction of the policy, national income will fall rather than rise. In a more general setting, it must gather all of this information not only for the countries directly involved in this sector, but for all countries, all sectors, and all firms in the world. It must determine the nature of competition for all these sectors and countries, it must correctly weigh and calculate the benefits of taxing or subsidizing each sector, and it must correctly predict and evaluate the response for all sectors by governments from all countries in the world. Needless to say, all of this is quite impossible. Making mistakes along the way will reduce, rather than increase, national income. Moreover, it is evident that the entire process of gathering and processing so much information will put a claim on real resources that could have been used to produce goods and services.

11.7 Application: the aircraft industry[4]

The civil-aircraft industry is a prime example of an industry characterized by increasing returns to scale. Kenneth Arrow (1962), for example, cites the empirical regularity that after a new aeroplane design has been introduced, the time required to build the frame of the marginal aircraft is inversely proportional to the cube root of the number of aeroplanes of that model that have already been built, as illustrated in Figure 11.6. The aircraft industry is also a prime example of an industry that has been (mis)used for strategic trade policy reasons.

In view of the importance of economies of scale in the production process, attributed to learning-by-doing effects by Arrow, large companies, able to produce and sell an impressive number of similar type aircraft, enjoy a vital competitive advantage. At the same time, the development and implementation of a newly designed type of aeroplane is extremely costly (see below), making it doubly difficult to enter the market. In the late 1960s Boeing invented the 747 jumbo jet and the European politicians were worried that the big three American firms (Boeing, McDonnell Douglas, and Lockheed), which enjoyed the benefit of a huge home market, would close down the smaller and divided European industry, so they joined forces and began to pour government money into the Airbus industry, a consortium with four parent companies (France's Aérospatiale, Germany's Daimler-Benz Aerospace, British Aerospace, and CASA of Spain).

For a long time it looked like money down the drain. Eventually, however, Airbus industry has become successful enough to present the only challenge to the Boeing dominance

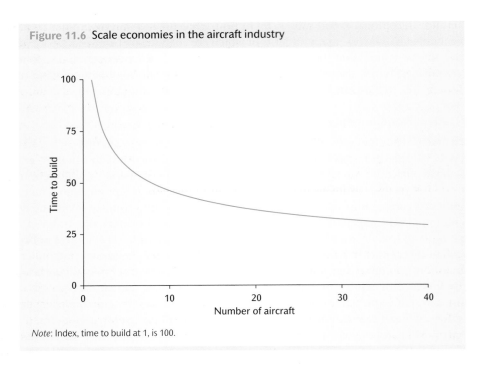

Figure 11.6 Scale economies in the aircraft industry

Note: Index, time to build at 1, is 100.

(Lockheed stopped producing civil aircraft in 1981 and McDonnell Douglas has merged with Boeing). Over the years, the battle between Boeing and Airbus has caused heated disputes between the American and European governments. The Americans see the struggle as a battle against subsidized competition, while the Europeans are fighting the American hegemony in a 'strategic' industry and argue that Boeing's aircraft are subsidized indirectly by the American defence budget. As *The Economist* (1997) put it: 'Any account of the civil-aircraft industry must begin with the caveat that it has never had free and fair competition. The civil-aircraft industry is the most politicised in the world–apart from the defence industry, to which it is joined at the hip.' A striking example occurred shortly after the Gulf War when the newly installed American president Bill Clinton called King Fahd of Saudi Arabia, urging him to buy $12 billion worth of Boeing and McDonnell Douglas aircraft (rather than Airbuses) made in the country that saved his hide. He did.

There have been two major attempts to force Boeing and Airbus to fight purely commercial battles. First, there was a special section written in the GATT's Tokyo Round in 1979, forbidding uneconomic pricing for airliners; see Chapter 12. Second, there was a bilateral European–American deal in 1992 limiting 'launch aid' (money to help develop a new model) to 33 per cent of the total development costs, to be repaid with interest within seventeen years. This put an end to most existing arguments on subsidized aircraft, opening up new problems for the super-jumbo market instead.

For decades Airbus looked enviously at Boeing's 747 jumbo jet, representing a very lucrative share of the civil-aircraft market, where Boeing holds a monopoly. As *The Economist* (1997) put it: 'Boeing's jumbo jet has been a licence to print money: the company makes $45m on each of the $150m-jets that it produces.' Since Boeing realized that Airbus was keen to develop an alternative to its ageing 747 jumbo jet, it came up with a rather successful delaying tactic in 1992 by starting talks with the four parent companies of Airbus to jointly develop a huge super-jumbo (to carry around 800 passengers). In 1995 the cooperation fell apart and Airbus started in earnest to develop the A380, able to carry 600 passengers and supposedly 20 per cent cheaper to operate than the 747. The total development costs for the A380 are estimated to be $10.7 billion, of which, in line with the 1992 agreement, the European governments will finance at 33 per cent. The A380 received a green light from Airbus officials at the end of 2000, with Singapore Airlines as launch customer, putting an end to Boeing's 32-year monopoly. In reaction, and after a failed attempt to sell a stretched version of the 747 which nobody wanted, Boeing tried, but failed to launch the 'sonic cruiser', a long-range jetliner flying just below the speed of sound, cutting an hour off transatlantic flights and three hours over the Pacific. The media fights continue untill this day.

11.8 Conclusions

We analyse the impact of trade policy in a world characterized by imperfect competition. Tariffs and quantitative restrictions are no longer equivalent. The imposition of tariffs in general leaves the forces of foreign competition intact, albeit at a lower level. This contrasts with the imposition of quantitative restrictions, which restrict more severely the strategic possibilities of foreign firms. It is therefore generally acknowledged that quotas are more restrictive than tariffs, which is one of the main reasons for the World Trade Organization to strive for 'tariffication' (the other being the clarity of the imposed trade restrictions). The so-called strategic trade policy tries to provide a competitive advantage to domestic firms by providing a credible pre-commitment. When evaluating the potential for strategic trade policy we noticed its weakness in a general equilibrium setting, the fragility of policy recommendations (type of strategic interactions, who moves first, strategic games, etc.), and most importantly from a practical perspective the enormous informational requirements for accurately performing such a policy.

TECHNICAL NOTES

Technical Note 11.1 The Brander–Spencer model

The Austrian firm produces quantity q_A and the Bolivian firm produces quantity q_B. This production is exported to a third country, with price p and a linear demand curve:

(11.A1)
$$p = a - b(q_A + q_B)$$

Both firms have marginal production costs c, but the Austrian government may give a production subsidy s per unit to the Austrian firm. The profit functions are therefore:

(11.A2)
$$\pi_A = pq_A - (c - s)q_A; \quad \pi_B = pq_B - cq_B$$

Both firms maximize profits taking the output level of the other firm as given, which leads to the following reaction curves (see Chapter 9):

(11.A3)
$$\text{firm } A: q_A = \frac{(a - c + s)}{b} - 2q_A; \quad \text{firm } B: q_B = \frac{(a - c)}{2b} - \frac{q_A}{2}$$

The intersection of the two reaction curves determines the equilibrium:

(11.A4)
$$q_A = \frac{a - c + 2s}{3b}; \quad q_B = \frac{a - c - s}{3b}$$

Taking the Bolivian firm's reaction curve into consideration, the Austrian government now has to decide how high the subsidy s should be. The government's objective is to maximize the Austrian firm's profits minus the subsidy it pays:

(11.A5)
$$\pi_A - sq_A = pq_A - cq_A$$

Note that this is equivalent to maximizing the Austrian firm's profits net of subsidies. The Austrian government should therefore ensure that the Bolivian firm's reaction curve is tangent to the Austrian firm's isoprofit curve net of subsidies, as illustrated in Figure 11.4. Note that for the profit level $\bar{\pi}_A$ the Austrian firm's isoprofit curve net of subsidies is given by all combinations q_A and q_B such that

(11.A6)
$$(p - c)q_A = (a - c - bq_B)q_A - bq_A^2 = \bar{\pi}_A$$

$$\text{so } q_B = \frac{a - c}{b} - q_A - \frac{\bar{\pi}_A}{bq_A}$$

The slope of an isoprofit curve is therefore $-1 + \bar{\pi}_A/bq_A^2$. Setting this equal to $-1/2$, the slope of the Bolivian firm's reaction curve, gives: $\bar{\pi}_A = bq_A^2/2$. Substitute this in the equation equalizing the Austrian firm's isoprofits and the Bolivian firm's reaction curve:

(11.A7)
$$\frac{a - c}{2b} - \frac{q_A}{2} = \frac{a - c}{b} - q_A - \frac{\bar{p}_A}{bq_A} = \frac{a - c}{b} - q_A - \frac{bq_A^2/2}{bq_A}$$

Solving this equation in q_A and substituting for the other variables in the other equations determines the Brander–Spencer optimum:

(11.A8)
$$q_A = \frac{a - c}{2b}; \quad q_B = \frac{a - c}{4b}; \quad s = \frac{a - c}{4}; \quad \bar{\pi}_A = \frac{(a - c)^2}{8b}$$

Technical Note 11.2 The Eaton–Grossman model

We discuss a simple version of this model, in which an Austrian and a Bolivian firm export to a third market and compete in prices, rather than quantities. The goods produced by the two firms are imperfect substitutes for one another, in which the demand for the good rises if the other firm raises its price. Naturally, the own-price effect is negative. Taking linear demand curves and constant marginal costs c, we get:

(11.A9)
$$q_A = a - p_A + p_B; \quad q_B = a - p_B + p_A$$

(11.A10)
$$\pi_A = (p_A - c)q_A; \quad \pi_B = (p_B - c)q_B$$

The remainder of this note follows the procedure of Technical Note 11.1. Maximizing profits, taking the competitor's price as given, leads to a firm's reaction curve in (p_A, p_B)-space. The intersection of the reaction curves gives the Bertrand equilibrium:

(11.A11)
$$p_A = p_B = a + c$$

The Austrian government, strategically maximizing domestic welfare, will decide to *tax* the production of the Austrian firm, leading to the Eaton–Grossman equilibrium:

(11.A12)
$$p_A = \frac{3a}{2} + c; \quad p_B = \frac{5a}{4} + c; \quad \bar{\pi}_A = \frac{9a^2}{8}; \quad \text{tax} = \frac{3a}{4}$$

QUESTIONS

Question 11.1

In the state of Alusia there is only one producer of olive oil. The producer is highly regarded by the government of Alusia because it has been producing olive oil for centuries using traditional methods which give the olive oil a typical Alusian taste. After a long period of autarky, the Alusian government decides to open the borders to international trade and allow its citizens to consume a larger variety of products. The government is, however, concerned about the consequences of this policy for the olive oil monopolist. The figure below gives the demand for olive oil in Alusia, the marginal cost curve of the monopolist, and the price of olive oil on the world markets.[5]

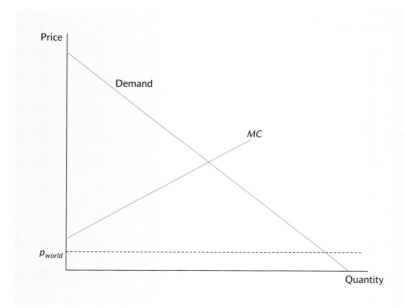

11.1A Indicate the autarky quantity supplied to the market and the price of olive oil in the figure above.

11.1B What would be the production level of olive oil for the Alusian producer, the quantity imported, and the price of olive oil in Alusia under free trade?

The Alusian government is considering protecting the olive oil industry by either imposing a tariff or introducing an import quota on the imports of olive oil.

11.1C Suppose that the government introduces a tariff such that the world price plus the tariff is below the competitive price and olive oil is produced domestically. Indicate the domestic production level, the import level, the price level, the consumer surplus, producer surplus and the government revenue for this tariff rate.

11.1D Determine what quota the government should impose which leads to the same level of imports as in 11.1C. Indicate the domestic production level, the import level, the price level, the consumer surplus, producer surplus and the government revenue for this import quota.

11.1E Explain whether you recommend the Alusian government to introduce a tariff or an import quota.

Question 11.2

The rapid economic growth in China is likely to be accompanied by growth in air travel. Large opportunities exist for both Boeing and Airbus to sell their planes in China. Let us analyse the market for large airplanes in China using the Cournot framework. The figure below gives possible reaction curves and isoprofit curves for both Airbus and Boeing.

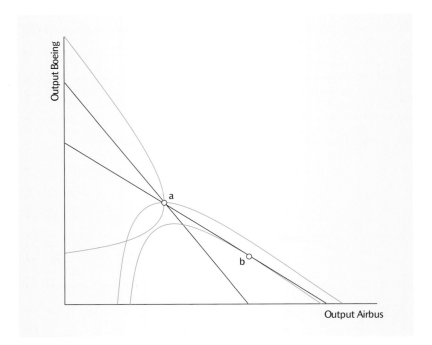

11.2A Indicate for each of the different curves if it is a reaction curve or an isoprofit curve and to which of the two firms it belongs.

11.2B Chapter 9 shows that the Cournot equilibrium outcome is reached at point a. However, at point b Airbus has a higher profit level. Explain why the equilibrium outcome is not at point b.

Suppose that the European Commission would like to give Airbus a strategic advantage in China. It therefore gives an optimal (total welfare-maximizing) subsidy for every airplane Airbus sells to China.

11.2C Draw the new situation in the figure above. What are the new output levels for both firms and how does the output of both firms change?

11.2D What will the US government think of this EU subsidy? Use the new figure to explain their position.

The US government looks enviously at the European subsidy and decides also to provide an optimal subsidy, given the EU subsidy.

11.2E Draw the situation that arises after the imposition of the US subsidy in the figure. What are the new output levels of both firms?

11.2F Assume that the European Commission sets a new optimal subsidy, followed by the US setting an optimal subsidy, followed by the EU again, etc. Will both countries eventually be better off or worse off?

Question 11.3

We could also imagine that Airbus and Boeing (see question 11.2) are competing with each other in a Bertrand framework (price competition), rather than a Cournot framework (quantity competition). Again the European Commission wants to stimulate the sales of Airbus in China.

11.3A Draw the reaction curves and some isoprofit curves for both Airbus and Boeing in a Bertrand framework. Put the price of an Airbus aircraft on the horizontal axis and the price of a Boeing aircraft on the vertical axis.

11.3B Should the European Commission subsidize or tax the aircraft Airbus sells to China? Draw the new situation in the figure when the European Commission optimally employs the instrument. How does the price demanded for aircraft change for both Airbus and Boeing?

11.3C What will the US government think of the EU policy?

11.3D Explain whether the Cournot or Bertrand framework is more appropriate to analyse competition between Airbus and Boeing.

 See the Online Resource Centre for a Study Guide containing more questions
www.oxfordtextbooks.co.uk/orc/vanmarrewijk/

NOTES

1 It is not explained why the market structure at home and abroad is different.

2 From your microeconomics course you may recognize this as the equilibrium that results if the Austrian firm is the Stackelberg leader.

3 With homogeneous goods Bertrand price competition would drive the price down to marginal costs, leaving no possibility of strategically transferring profits and effectively eliminating market power.

4 The information in this section is based on *The Economist* (1997, 2000b, 2001b).

5 Coming from non-Mediterranean countries we crudely assume that olive oil is a homogeneous good.

INTERNATIONAL TRADE ORGANIZATIONS

12

Objectives/key terms

- Beggar-thy-neighbour
- General Agreement on Tariffs and Trade (GATT)
- UN Conference on Trade and Development (UNCTAD)
- Organization of Economic Cooperation and Development (OECD)

- Central and Eastern European Economic Transition Process
- World Trade Organization (WTO)
- United Nations (UN)

We discuss the history and functioning of the main international trade organizations.

12.1 Introduction

The basis of the present international economic order was laid during and immediately after the Second World War. The primary concern in the consultations was not to repeat the disastrous experience of the international economic relations of the interwar period. During the Great Depression in the 1930s, the 'beggar-thy-neighbour' policies, in which each country tried to transfer its economic problems to other countries by depreciating its own currency and imposing high tariffs (see for example the Hawley–Smoot Act of the USA in 1930), led to an almost complete collapse of the international trade system, further exacerbating and prolonging the economic crisis. The impact of the beggar-thy-neighbour policies on international trade is aptly illustrated by the 'spiderweb spiral', measuring the size of world imports in each month by the distance to the origin; see Figure 12.1. In a period of only four years world trade flows dropped to one-third of their previous level (from January 1929 to January 1933, world imports fell from 2,998 to 992 million US gold $ per month).

The signing of the Charter in 1945 in San Francisco laid the foundations of the United Nations (UN) as an international organization. The system of international bodies developed afterwards is known as the United Nations family. Although consultations took place within

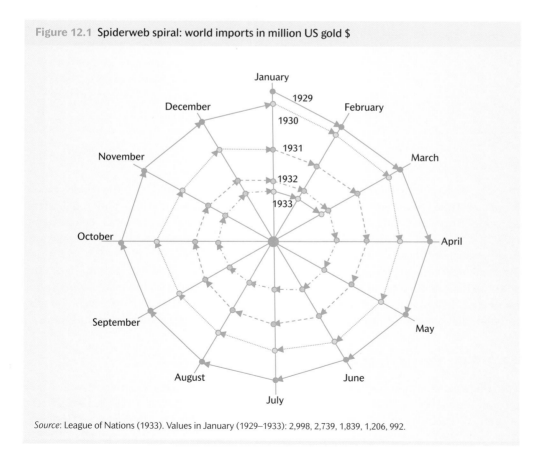

Figure 12.1 Spiderweb spiral: world imports in million US gold $

Source: League of Nations (1933). Values in January (1929–1933): 2,998, 2,739, 1,839, 1,206, 992.

Famous economists | **Jan Tinbergen**

The Dutch economist Jan Tinbergen was the first to receive the Nobel prize in economics in 1969 (together with Ragnar Frisch). He studied physics at the University of Leiden and wrote his thesis on extremum problems in physics and economics. Tinbergen became one of the founding fathers of econometrics in the 1930s. While working at the League of Nations, the predecessor of the United Nations, he was invited to test Haberler's business cycle theories, which resulted in *Statistical Testing of Business Cycle Theories* (1939). The first volume focused on investment activity, while the second volume constructed the first complete macroeconomic model for the USA.[1]

After the Second World War, Tinbergen became the first director of the Dutch Central Planning Bureau (a think-tank on economic problems for the Dutch government) and focused on policy making, which resulted in *Economic Policy: Principles and Design* (1956). Tinbergen argued that a government can only achieve several quantitative policy targets if it has an equal number of quantitative policy instruments available, the so-called 'Tinbergen rule'. Tinbergen held a part-time position at the Netherlands School of Economics (now Erasmus University Rotterdam) from 1933, but became a full-time professor of development planning in 1955, henceforth focusing on development problems. He gave advice to many countries and UN agencies, and lectured all over the world, which led *inter alia* to *Reshaping the International Order* (1976), a report to the Club of Rome coordinated by Tinbergen.

Fig. 12.2
Jan Tinbergen
(1903–94)

the UN, arguably the most important international organizations – the International Monetary Fund (IMF) and the World Bank (WB) on financial issues and the General Agreement on Tariffs and Trade (GATT), later to become the World Trade Organization (WTO), on international trade issues – were eventually located outside the UN. The postwar international economic order is therefore sometimes called the GATT/WTO – IMF/WB order. The remainder of this chapter briefly focuses attention on international organizations dealing with international trade and trade policies. Chapter 22 will deal with the main international monetary institutions. Lanjouw (1995) provides a more complete overview of the international trade institutions and Bakker (1996) of international financial organizations.

12.2 The World Trade Organization (WTO/GATT)

The original intention in the postwar period was to set up the International Trade Organization (ITO) for dealing with international trade issues (Havana Charter, 1948). In the end, the ITO was not set up, primarily because it was not ratified by the American Congress. As a result, the General Agreement on Tariffs and Trade (GATT), which was signed in 1947 in

Geneva in anticipation of the formation of the ITO, evolved in a *de facto* international organization with a secretariat in Geneva. Much later, on 1 January 1995, the GATT was converted to the World Trade Organization (WTO), thus becoming an official international organization.

The international GATT agreement is based on three principles:

1. *Non-discrimination*; as expressed in two sub-principles:

   (i) *Most favoured nation* (MFN) treatment; if a GATT country grants a trade concession to another GATT country, this concession automatically applies to all other GATT countries as well.

   (ii) *National treatment* of foreign products; apart from trade policy measures, imported goods must be treated the same as home-produced goods.

   There are two main exceptions to the non-discrimination principle:

   (i) *Free trade areas* and *customs unions*. If two or more countries decide to form a free trade area or a customs union, such as the countries of the European Union, discriminatory treatment is allowed, essentially because it is viewed as a move in the right direction of free trade. This is discussed in the next chapter.

   (ii) *Developing countries*. Preferential treatment for imports is allowed to assist developing countries since part IV, 'trade and development', was added to the GATT in 1965. This enables the Generalized System of Preferences; see UNCTAD below.

2. *Reciprocity*. If one GATT country makes a trade concession, other GATT countries should make equivalent concessions to balance the advantages and disadvantages of trade liberalization. As explained throughout this book, taking all static and dynamic gains of trade liberalization into consideration, it is probably optimal to allow free trade regardless of whether other countries do the same. In practice, however, countries regard trade liberalization as a concession that should be reciprocated by other countries. The most important exception to this principle is for developing countries, which are not required to reciprocate.

3. *Prohibition on trade restrictions other than tariffs*. In principle, trade restrictions other than tariffs, such as quotas, are prohibited. The main reason is that, although the imposition of a tariff influences the market, its operation does not affect the market mechanism. Moreover, it is easier to negotiate on tariff reductions than on the removal of other trade measures, which are more difficult to quantify. The most important exception to this principle applies in the case of balance-of-payments problems.

After the establishment of the GATT as an agreement, a series of trade liberalization rounds followed. Their successfulness in terms of the large reductions of imposed tariff rates was illustrated in Figure 8.2. Initially, the trade liberalization rounds rapidly succeeded each other, took a limited amount of time, and involved a limited number of countries, as illustrated in Figure 12.3. As time passed, more countries became members of the GATT, such that the negotiations became more complicated and took several years to complete; see Table 12.1.

The Kennedy Round (1964–7) is often taken as the dividing line, as it involved a change in negotiating technique. In the first five rounds, negotiations took place according to the principal–supplier rule; that is, there were bilateral negotiations for each product involving the principal suppliers to one another's markets. Under the MFN clause the results of the bilateral

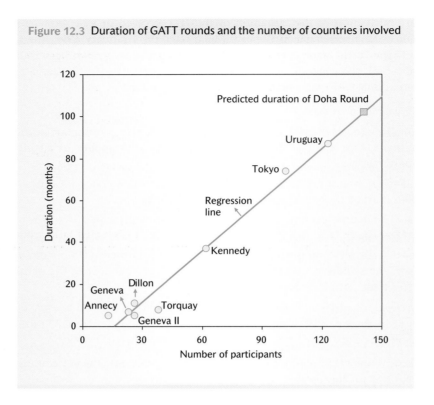

Figure 12.3 Duration of GATT rounds and the number of countries involved

Table 12.1 GATT/WTO rounds

Round	Start	Duration	Principal concern	# part.
Geneva	Apr. 1947	7 months	Tariffs	23
Annecy	Apr. 1949	5 months	Tariffs	13
Torquay	Sep. 1950	8 months	Tariffs	38
Geneva II	Jan. 1956	5 months	Tariffs, admission Japan	26
Dillon	Sep. 1960	11 months	Tariffs	26
Kennedy	May 1964	37 months	Tariffs, anti-dumping	62
Tokyo	Sep. 1973	74 months	Tariffs, NTBs, framework	102
Uruguay	Sep. 1986	87 months	Tariffs, NTBs, services, dispute settlement, textiles, agriculture, WTO	123
Doha	Nov. 2001	?	Tariffs, NTBs, labour standards, environment, competition, investment, transparency, patents	141

Notes: NTBs = non-tariff barriers; # part. = number of participants.
Source: Neary (2004).

negotiations also apply to the GATT partners. This connection between the bilateral negotiations made it difficult to get an overall picture of the granted and received concessions, which should be balanced under the principle of reciprocity. The Kennedy Round therefore started with the aim to achieve linear tariff reductions, making it necessary to negotiate only on the exceptions. In the end, the average tariff reduction was about 35 per cent, somewhat below the target of 50 per cent, primarily because countries with already low tariffs in absolute terms were not willing to apply the same percentage reduction as countries with high tariffs in absolute terms.

To avoid the difficulties of linear tariff reductions that became apparent in the Kennedy Round, the Tokyo Round (1973–9) used the so-called 'Swiss formula' for tariff reduction, based on the parameter A (14 in the original Swiss proposal); see Figure 12.4:

(12.1) $$\text{new tariff} = \frac{A \cdot \text{old tariff}}{A + \text{old tariff}}$$

As is clear from Figure 12.4, applying this formula leads to much higher tariff reductions for initially high tariffs, thus leading to a more rapid tariff harmonization. In addition, the Tokyo Round (which was called the Nixon Round until Nixon was forced to resign as president of the USA) involved negotiations on tropical products (concessions for some products, but not for sugar), non-tariff measures (agreement on codes of conduct), agriculture (restraint on export subsidies), specific sectors (total trade liberalization for civil aircraft), and safeguards (no agreement).

Attention in the negotiations clearly shifted towards the importance of non-tariff barriers. Initially, it was thought to be a result of the successfulness of the achieved tariff reductions. As Lanjouw (1995: 12) puts it:

> The metaphor applied here was of trade liberalisation representing the draining of a swamp. The reduction in tariffs symbolised letting the water level fall, uncovering what was below the surface

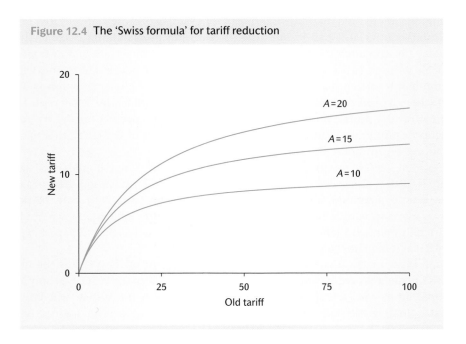

Figure 12.4 The 'Swiss formula' for tariff reduction

in the form of non-tariff barriers. However, it gradually became clear that protection by non-tariff measures was steadily increasing, so the expression 'new protectionism' became commonplace.

A clear example of the new protectionism is a 'voluntary' export restraint (VER), where a country limits the number of goods exported to another country, usually as a result of the pressure exerted by the government of the importing country. VERs are against GATT rules, but do not lead to complaints to the GATT as they are imposed by the exporting country. Perhaps the most noteworthy example of a VER is the decision of the Japanese car manufacturers in the 1980s, under severe pressure from the Japanese government, which in turn was pressured by the American government, to limit the number of cars exported to the USA. Lanjouw attributes the rise of the new protectionism to a combination of factors, such as structural shifts in the international division of labour (the rise of the newly industrialized countries: Hong Kong, South Korea, Singapore, and Taiwan), cyclical movements in economic activity (the economic slow-down at the beginning of the 1980s), a diminished willingness for structural adjustment, and a misinterpretation of the term reciprocity and the concept of trade balance surpluses and deficits (in particular in the USA, where some influential players seem to strive for bilateral trade balance with each other country, sometimes even for each good; thus trade is only 'fair' if the export of Japanese cars to the USA is of equal value as the export of American cars to Japan, leading to 100 per cent intra-industry trade).

The complications arising from the desire to stop the rise of the new protectionism and the increased number of countries involved in the GATT negotiations were responsible for the fact that the last completed GATT round, known as the Uruguay Round, lasted for seven years, from 1986 to 1993. In the end, substantial agreements were reached in several areas. First, the negotiations on liberalization of trade in services, an increasingly important part of world trade flows, led to the General Agreement on Trade in Services (GATS), a framework of principles and rules, such as MFN treatment of foreign suppliers, and for some sectors national treatment of foreign suppliers. Some subsectors were excluded (e.g. audio-visual, telecommunications, and maritime transport), for example because France feared impairing its 'cultural identity' if it had to liberalize its television programming. Second, the negotiations for the agricultural sectors eventually resulted in (i) conversion of non-tariff barriers to equivalent tariffs, (ii) tariffs to be reduced on average by 36 per cent in the next six years, (iii) a minimum foreign market share of 5 per cent after the implementation period, and (iv) reduction of export subsidies for seventeen agricultural products by 36 per cent. Third, an agreement on the protection of intellectual property rights (patents for twenty years and copyright for fifty years). Fourth, and finally, the conversion of the GATT to a full-fledged international organization, the WTO.

The current (2006) round of negotiations is called the Doha Round and started in November 2001. It discusses many issues, such as tariffs, non-tariff barriers, labour standards, environment, competition, investment, transparency, and patents, with many participating countries. Not surprisingly, therefore, progress is slow and the Doha Round was not finished at the initially planned 1 January 2005 deadline. As illustrated in Figure 12.3, past experience indicates that it may not be finished until April 2010.

An important practical consequence of the establishment of the WTO is the improved dispute settlement procedure after a complaint has been made to the WTO. Not only are there strict time limits for each stage in the procedure, but also the system will be virtually automatic, that is the panel report written by independent experts for the dispute is

Box 12.1   Globalization protests

Nowadays, international (trade) organizations tend to receive a great deal of media attention whenever they hold a large meeting. The media have, of course, always covered the most important discussions and decisions of such meetings in a low-key sophisticated way. Today, however, these meetings have become main events and are headline news on the television, the radio, in the newspaper, and on the Internet for weeks. Unfortunately, the media circus focuses attention on the issues surrounding the meeting rather than the meeting itself. Sometimes, the television cameras zoom in on the rioters among the 'globalization protesters', who are breaking windows, throwing bricks, spraying paint, turning over cars, setting buildings on fire, etc. At other times, they highlight the actions of the riot police, charging a building, beating up people who are lying on the ground, and, in an extreme case, shooting a protester.

Who are these globalization protesters and when did the massive violent protests start? The second part of the question is easy to answer. The first part is not. Although there had been earlier occasions on which protesters marched in the streets, the scale and aggression of the protests reached an unprecedented peak which shocked the world at the meeting of the World Trade Organization (WTO) in Seattle (USA) in December 1999. People chanted for example: 'Hey, hey, ho, ho, WTO has got to go', but they were also running through the streets, wearing masks and smashing shop windows, such that Seattle was put under a curfew, the mayor declared a civil emergency, and the governor sent in the National Guard.

Explaining who the protesters are is virtually impossible, as there are so many different groups, with different, usually conflicting, ideas. There were trade unionists attending a protest rally. There were colourful environmentalists in sea-turtle outfits. There were human-rights activists indicting Union Carbide for crimes against humanity. There was a French farm leader protesting against McDonald's with Roquefort cheese. As *The Economist* (1999) put it, there were 'students carrying Japanese cameras and drinking foreign coffee [who] railed that trade should be local, not global'.

Over time the protests have become even more aggressive, as for example at the European Union meeting in Gothenburg (Sweden) in June 2001 and at the G8 meeting (seven rich countries plus Russia) in Genoa (Italy) in July 2001, where the protester alluded to above was shot to death. In this respect the December 2005 WTO meeting in Hong Kong was relatively calm, with South Korean rice farmers furious at the prospect of freer trade as the most prominent demonstrators. Why the protests are getting so out of hand is not clear. Some say that the Internet makes it easier for the protesters to organize themselves. Others argue that the excessive media exposure generates interest from rioters around the world for the next meeting. Others still argue that the international organizations are bringing the protests upon themselves as they do not communicate the benefits of their actions to the public clearly; see for example *The Economist* (2001d):

> Hans Eichel, the German finance minister, is the latest European grandee to come out in favour of a directly imposed EU tax as a way of making the workings of the European Union more open and less mysterious. But if ordinary people notice a deduction on their payslips marked EU, is that really going to make the Union more popular? You need to have been locked up in a convention centre for a very long time to believe that.

Information source: *The Economist* (1999, 2001c, 2001d, 2001e, 2005c).

automatically accepted within a specified period, unless there is a consensus in favour of rejection. This contrasts sharply with the GATT procedure in which, rather remarkably, the accused party had veto power.

At the end of 2005, the WTO had 149 member countries and 32 observer governments waiting to become members; see Technical Note 12.1. Frenchman Pascal Lamy was appointed as director-general on 1 September 2005 for a four-year term. The WTO organization is located on rue de Lausanne 154, CH-1211 Geneva 21, Switzerland. The WTO website (http://www.wto.org) gives details of the history of the organization, provides many (trade) statistics, gives an overview of, and background information to, the current trade topics being discussed at the WTO, and contains the list of member countries.

12.3 The United Nations (UN) and UNCTAD

The signing of the Charter in 1945 in San Francisco laid the foundations of the United Nations (UN) as an international organization, becoming operative in October of the same year after ratification by sufficiently many countries. Under the guidance of the secretary general (at the time of writing Kofi Annan) and the secretariat located in New York City, the large UN system deals with many different aspects of human life and organization, such as human rights, international justice, security, military and peacekeeping operations, and economic, social, cultural, and development issues. In the economic sphere, the most important body is ECOSOC, the Economic and Social Council, which coordinates the work in the economic and social fields. In this respect, and to give an idea of the size of the UN family of organizations, ECOSOC's main involvement can be subdivided as follows:

* *Programs and funds*, such as the UN Conference on Trade and Development (UNCTAD), the UN Development Programme (UNDP), the Office of the UN High Commissioner for Refugees (UNHCR), the UN Children's Fund (UNICEF), etc.

* *Functional commissions*, such as the Commission for Social Development, the Commission on Human Rights, the Commission on Sustainable Development, the Commission on the Status of Women, etc.

* *Regional commissions*, such as the Economic Commission for Africa (ECA), the Economic Commission for Europe (ECE), the Economic Commission for Latin America and the Caribbean (ECLAC), the Economic and Social Commission for Asia and the Pacific (ESCAP), and the Economic and Social Commission for Western Asia (ESCWA).

* *Specialized (independent) agencies*, such as the International Labour Organization (ILO), the Food and Agriculture Organization of the UN (FAO), the UN Educational, Scientific and Cultural Organization (UNESCO), the World Health Organization (WHO), the World Bank group, and the International Monetary Fund (IMF).

For various reasons, the developing countries became increasingly dissatisfied with their role in the world economy during the 1950s and 1960s. One reason, forwarded by the development economists Raul Prebisch and Hans Singer, was the argument that over longer periods of time the terms of trade is turning against the developing countries, as these countries tend to be dependent for their export earnings on a limited number of primary products with falling relative prices. According to this argument, developing countries are forced to produce and export ever–increasing quantities of their primary products to finance the imports of manufactured goods from developed countries. There have been many empirical studies trying to test the Prebisch–Singer hypothesis of deteriorating terms of trade for developing countries. All in all, it is fair to say that the hypothesis is far from proven; see Box 12.2. A second reason for the dissatisfaction of developing countries with their role in the world economy was the phenomenon of 'tariff escalation', referring to the fact that developed countries tend to levy low tariffs for the imports of primary products necessary in the early stages of the production process, and high tariffs for the imports of processed goods, leading to high effective rates of protection for the later stages of the production process; see Chapter 8. A third reason for dissatisfaction was the GATT principle of non-discrimination, as the developing countries argued that they needed preferential treatment because they *are* less developed, a variant of the infant-industry argument. The developing countries, united in the Group of 77 (now containing more countries) wanted to set up an organization concentrating on their interests. This aim was realized at the first UNCTAD session in Geneva in 1964, establishing UNCTAD as a permanent international organization, with a secretariat and a secretary general (a post first held by Raul Prebisch). Plenary UNCTAD sessions take place every three or four years.

As an organization, UNCTAD does not have executive power. Instead, UNCTAD conference resolutions are recommendations for the UN General Assembly. After the confrontational approach at the first UNCTAD conference, which did not lead to any substantial results, the second UNCTAD conference at New Delhi in 1968 was more consensus based, which led to the Generalized System of Preferences (GSP). Under this system, OECD countries apply non-reciprocal preferential tariffs to imports of (primary) products from developing countries to raise export earnings and stimulate growth. To provide a legal basis for GSP, an addition (part IV) was made to the GATT system in 1965; see Section 12.2. UNCTAD and the GATT/WTO are therefore both concerned with trade and development issues, the main difference being that the GSP of UNCTAD is based on a unilateral decision by OECD countries (which can also be unilaterally withdrawn), while the GATT agreements are binding contractual obligations.

Multinational, or transnational, corporations, which have active branches in several countries, have become increasingly important in the world economy after the Second World War; see also Chapter 15. To analyse the impact of multinationals on international trade and investment flows and their general influence on the economic and social structure of (developing) nations, ECOSOC set up the Commission on Transnational Corporations in 1974, followed by the UN Centre on Transnational Corporation (UNCTC) in 1975 to support the work of the Commission. Over the years, there has been a remarkable shift in the general attitude towards the impact of multinationals on the economic system, particularly by developing countries, from a hostile and negative view in the 1960s and 1970s to a much more positive view in the 1980s and 1990s. The earlier negative picture was partly due to the political meddling of multinationals in the host countries, for example the active involvement of the American International Telephone and Telegraph Company (ITT) in attempts to bring down Salvador Allende, the Marxist president of Chile, because of fears of nationalization of ITT assets by the Allende government. The more recent positive picture on the impact of multinationals arises from the realization that the large investments by these companies, and the local knowledge and productivity spillovers created as a result of these activities, can be of vital importance for a successful development process, as explained in more detail in Chapters 14–16. Since 1991, the UN research in this area is summarized annually in UNCTAD's *World Investment Report*, at present arguably UNCTAD's most important publication.

Box 12.2   The terms of trade: are high export prices good or bad?

The ratio of export prices to import prices of a country is called the terms of trade. Now ask yourself if it is good or bad to have high export prices. If you have the interests of a firm in mind, you may be inclined to go along with the popular reasoning of businessmen in the newspaper: the dollar is overvalued, which implies that our export prices are too high, so that we can no longer compete effectively with foreign firms (followed by threats that factories will be closed down and jobs will be lost). The suggestion is that high export prices are bad. In Chapter 1, however, we argued that an important characteristic of international economics is the general equilibrium approach. We have to look at the complete picture, in which 'high' export prices reflect the interplay of economic forces on the supply side *and* the demand side, perhaps caused by the fact that we produce high-quality goods in popular demand. In this interpretation high export prices are good, as they lead to higher welfare levels. This is illustrated in Figure 12.5 in a neoclassical equilibrium framework in which the country, which exports manufactures, initially reaches welfare level U_0. If the price of manufactures, the export good, rises, the economy is able to reach the higher welfare level U_1. A simple analogy is to think of yourself as a country: you want the price of your export goods (labour services) which earns you an income to be as high as possible, and the price of your import goods (all goods and services you consume) to be as low as possible.

As discussed in the main text, the Prebisch–Singer hypothesis suggests that the terms of trade is deteriorating for developing countries. According to Krugman and Obstfeld (2000: 103), however, for the group of *advanced* countries as a whole the terms of trade deteriorated in the periods 1973–74 (first oil crisis) and 1979–80 (second oil crisis). Over a longer time period the net effects are minimal: in three decades (1970–97), the average terms of trade for the advanced countries deteriorated by only 6 per cent.

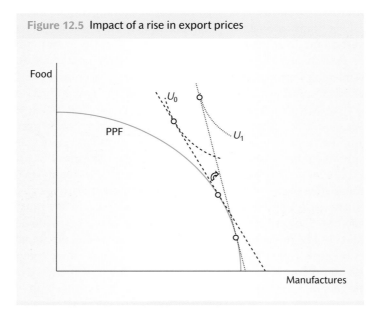

Figure 12.5 Impact of a rise in export prices

Virtually all people in the world now live in a country that is a member of the UN. At the time of rewriting this chapter (December 2005), the UN had 191 member countries; see Technical Note 12.2. The address of the spokesman for the secretary general is United Nations, S-378 New York, NY 10017, USA. The UN website (http://www.un.org) gives extensive information on the structure of the organization, its history, the current issues being discussed, and the list of member countries. The history and work of UNCTAD is available at the UNCTAD website (http://www.unctad.org). Since both UNCTAD and the WTO are active in the fields of international trade and development, these organizations work together, for which they established the International Trade Centre (ITC), 54–56 rue de Montbrillant, Geneva, Switzerland. The ITC website (http://www.intracen.org) contains trade documentation, detailed trade statistics per country, and the ITC magazine.

12.4 Organization for Economic Cooperation and Development (OECD)

The final international body to be briefly discussed in this chapter is the Organization for Economic Cooperation and Development (OECD), which was established in 1961 as the successor to the Organization for European Economic Cooperation (OEEC). The latter organization, comprising West European countries and Turkey, was established in 1948 to implement the Marshall Aid programme, by which the USA was assisting postwar recovery in Europe. At the end of the 1950s, the OEEC had attained its objectives. Its transition to the OECD, in part to coordinate aid to developing countries, allowed Canada and the USA to become full members. In the 1970s membership was extended to Japan, Finland, Australia, and New Zealand. At the end of the twentieth century, and partially as a result of the breakdown of the Iron Curtain, Mexico, South Korea, Poland, the Czech Republic, Slovakia, and Hungary joined the OECD; see Figure 12.6.

Figure 12.6 **OECD member countries**

The OEEC played an important role in the 1950s in reducing quantitative trade barriers (quotas) in Europe, leaving the reduction of tariffs to the GATT. Plans to form a free trade area were not successful, as there was a division between the countries that later formed the European Economic Community (EEC) and the countries that later formed the European Free Trade Area (EFTA). Eventually, many EFTA countries joined the EEC and formed the European Union (EU); see Chapter 13. The OECD plays an important role as a consultation forum on trade policy issues for the developed nations, without the necessity of coming to any direct agreements, which is a matter for the GATT/WTO. The OECD serves a mediating role in this respect, for example when (i) arguing in favour of positive adjustment policies in the OECD countries in the 1970s for those sectors of the economy that could no longer compete successfully with the newly industrializing countries, or (ii) when examining the agricultural question in the 1980s and producing a report in 1987 (later approved by the OECD council) with a method of reducing the effects of different national measures to a common denominator, making them comparable and negotiable, or (iii) when the OECD council adopted guidelines for multinationals (e.g. on transfer prices) and decided to apply the principle of national treatment to multinationals.

The OECD's Development Assistance Committee (DAC) plays an important role in coordinating national aid programmes to developing countries. The DAC strives for a reduction of tied aid, in which the recipient country is obliged to spend the development assistance in the donor country or in a group of countries linked to the donor country. In general, the effectiveness of development assistance diminishes if aid is tied rather than untied; see Brakman and van Marrewijk (1998) for a general overview of (unilateral) international transfers and tied aid.

 Box 12.3   General Agreement on Trade in Services

The General Agreement on Trade in Services (GATS) came into force in January 1995 (as a result of the GATT Uruguay Round) and is the first and only set of multilateral rules covering international trade in services. The total value of trade in services was about $1,350 billion in 1999, or about 20 per cent of total trade flows. It is generally agreed that this underestimates the true value of services trade, which has been rising faster than goods trade since at least 1980, since a large share of this trade takes place through establishment in the export market and is not recorded in balance-of-payments statistics. The largest component of services trade is tourism, the exports of which were estimated to be $443 billion in 1999, representing about 33 per cent of all services trade and about 6.5 per cent of total exports. The World Trade and Tourism Council estimates that tourism accounts for about one in ten workers globally. Other important services sectors are, for example, consulting, banking, software design, and telecommunications. The GATS defines four ways (modes of supply) in which a service can be traded:

- cross-border supply: services supplied from one country to another, such as telephone calls;
- consumption abroad: consumers from one country making use of a service in another country, such as tourism;
- commercial presence: a company from one country setting up subsidiaries or branches to provide services in another country, such as banking services;

- movement of natural persons: individuals travelling from one country to supply services in another country, such as consultants or maids.

The GATS covers all services with two exceptions, namely services provided in the exercise of governmental authority and air traffic rights (and all services directly related to air traffic rights). The negotiations regarding the liberalization of services trade were quite complex and led to a north–south controversy in the early years of the Uruguay Round. In the end these issues were resolved by agreeing to a minimal and flexible set of rules. The GATS consists of two parts, namely (i) the framework agreement containing the general rules and principles and (ii) the national schedules, which list individual countries' specific commitments on access to their domestic markets by foreign suppliers. The latter provides the required flexibility as follows:

- Each member chooses service sectors or subsectors on which they will make commitments to guarantee foreign suppliers the right to provide the service. There is no minimal coverage requirement.

- For the committed sectors, governments may set limitations regarding market access and the degree of national treatment.

- Governments may limit commitments to one or more of the above-listed modes of supply and they may withdraw or renegotiate commitments.

- Although the MFN treatment (see Section 12.2) applies to all services (whether scheduled or not), governments may take exemptions and provide more favourable treatment to certain trading partners for a maximum of up to ten years.

It is clear that this flexibility, which was necessary to come to an agreement, also limits the impact of GATS to those countries willing to liberalize their trade in services. A new round of trade negotiations to further liberalize trade in services was therefore started in January 2000.

Information source: www.wto.org

At the time of rewriting this chapter (December 2005), the OECD had thirty member countries; see Technical Note 12.3. The OECD secretariat is located on rue André Pascal 2, F-75775 Paris Cedex 16, France. The OECD website (http://www.oecd.org) gives details of the organization, provides many excellent statistics and reports, and contains the list of member countries with useful links to online data sources for each country.

12.5 Case study: economic transition in Central and Eastern Europe[2]

After the demolition of the Berlin Wall in 1989 and the subsequent dismantling of the Iron Curtain, the countries of Central and Eastern Europe (CEE) started to embark on a transition to reform their economic organizational structures, assisted by various international organizations and professional policy advisers. The economic organization of every society has to answer three basic questions, namely (i) what will be produced, (ii) how will this be produced, and (iii) to whom will the fruits of production be available? Schmidt (2001: 2) stresses the

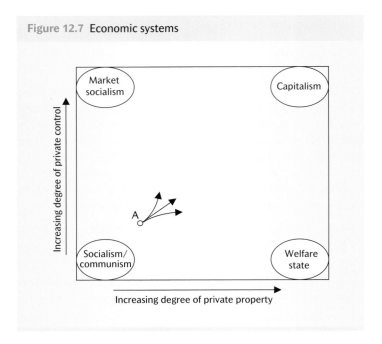

Figure 12.7 Economic systems

multidimensional properties of the transition process and distinguishes between at least two dimensions:

- Who owns the *property rights* to the available productive resources?
- Who *controls* the use of the available productive resources?

Since the property rights to the resources can vary from complete private ownership to complete state ownership and the control of the resources can vary from complete private control to complete government control, as illustrated in Figure 12.7, we can distinguish four benchmark extremes of different economic systems, none of which is to be found in the real world. At one extreme we have socialism/communism with state property and state control. At the opposite extreme we have capitalism ('*laissez-faire*') with private property and private control. On the other diagonal of the matrix in Figure 12.7 we have hypothetical extremes with state property and free markets, dubbed market socialism (see the China case study in Chapter 17), and private property with state regulation, dubbed 'welfare state'. The transition process in the CEE countries is multidimensional, if only because countries can choose a different mix of the more or less one-dimensional *privatization* (moving from state ownership to private ownership) and *deregulation* (moving from state control to private control) policies, even starting from the same initial conditions, as illustrated by point A and the (curved) arrows in Figure 12.7. Thus 'transition', which must be accompanied by institutional change, can mean different things to different countries at the same time or to the same country at different times.

The transition process also involves a change in the mix of output. This is illustrated in Figure 12.8, where we have drawn a production possibility frontier (PPF) of food and

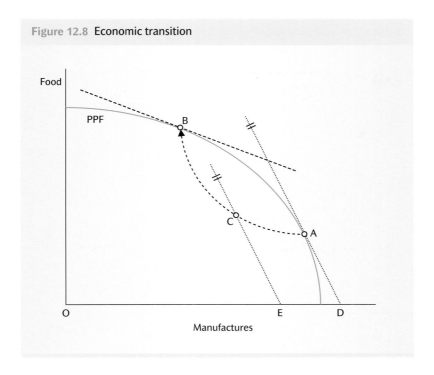

Figure 12.8 **Economic transition**

manufactures for a CEE country. Suppose that the government, which is initially in control of the productive resources, ensures that the economy is producing and consuming at point A on the PPF.[3] As a result of privatization and deregulation, the ultimate objective is for the economy to produce and consume at point B, which produces more food and less manufactures and better represents the people's preferences. During the transition phase from point A to point B, however, society has to reorganize itself. Capital has to be moved from one sector to another or completely discarded. People have to relocate, be educated for a new job, get used to the new organization of society and its institutional changes, etc. All of this implies that during the transition phase the economy will not be efficiently organized, such that it is producing *inside* the production possibility frontier. We therefore assume that, after a number of years, the CEE economy is producing at point C, rather than at point A. When measured at the initial equilibrium relative prices of point A, a standard procedure followed by statisticians, this implies a measured loss in real output from OD to OE. At the early stages of the transition process we can therefore expect a decline rather than a rise in measured output.[4] Moreover, depending on the speed and efficiency of the transition process, and the willingness and readiness for people to get used to the new environment, these early stages can last a long time. As Schmidt (2001: 7) remarks:

> When meeting and working with colleagues in CEE one cannot escape being struck by the extraordinary difficulties which the communist regime must have imposed on everyday life there (with an almost universal lack of personal freedom as its most poignant feature), and by the deep traces it has left in human attitudes even today. By their very nature privatization

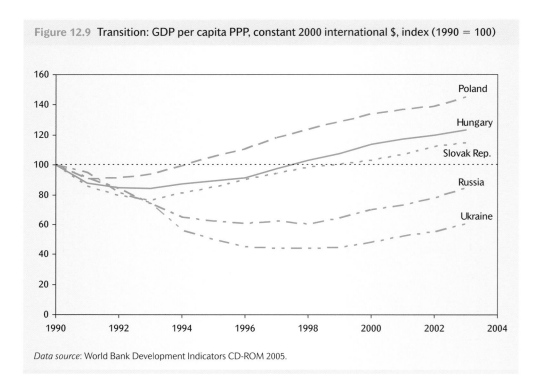

Figure 12.9 Transition: GDP per capita PPP, constant 2000 international $, index (1990 = 100)

Data source: World Bank Development Indicators CD-ROM 2005.

and deregulation are legal acts, the formalities of which can in principle be arranged on fairly short notice. But then? Then everybody has to get going in the new environment, but the adaptation (human and otherwise) required for that to happen in any effective way is a very complex process and takes much more time than was originally perceived, certainly in the West.

The extent of the decline in output and the length of time of the initial stage is illustrated for a selection of countries in Figure 12.9, using an index (1990 = 100) of per capita GDP measured in constant 2000 $. Poland, which followed a 'big bang' strategy of rapid reform, is the most successful CEE transition country. Per capita GDP dropped until 1991 (to 91 per cent) and started to rise thereafter (to 145 per cent in 2003). Hungarian GDP dropped until 1993 (to 84 per cent) before it started to rise (to 123 per cent in 2003), and similarly for the Slovak Republic, which just recovered to its 1990 level in 1999 and reached 115 per cent in 2003. The other two countries, Russia and the Ukraine, show just how dramatic the measured decline in output can be (to 61 per cent and 44 per cent, respectively), and how long the fall in output can last (up to 1998 for both countries).

. Figure 12.10, finally, illustrates the positive influence of foreign knowledge and capital in a successful transition process. Before 1990, there were virtually no foreign direct investments (see also Chapters 2 and 15) into the CEE countries, measured as net inflows relative to GDP in Figure 12.10. Hungary and Poland, both rather successful transition economies, are also

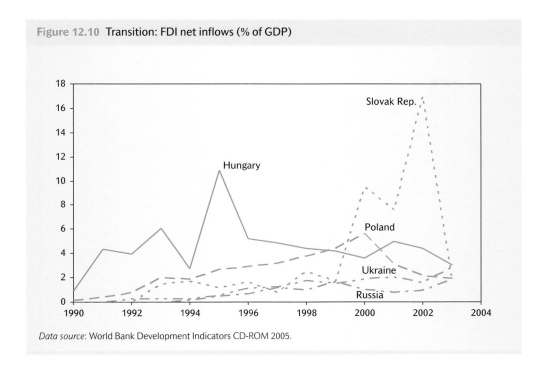

Figure 12.10 Transition: FDI net inflows (% of GDP)

Data source: World Bank Development Indicators CD-ROM 2005.

the most successful countries in attracting foreign direct investments, reaching levels above 4 per cent in 1998 and 1999 (for Hungary after an impressive, and clearly unsustainable, peak of more than 10 per cent in 1995). The other countries, in particular Russia and the Ukraine, were not nearly as successful in attracting foreign investors, who were not convinced of the commitment to the processes of privatization and deregulation. More recently, the Slovak Republic managed to attract formidable investment flows, particularly in the automobile sector.

12.6 Conclusions

We briefly discuss the history and functioning of the main international trade organizations. The GATT deals most directly with international trade problems and has been successful in reducing trade barriers in a series of complicated negotiation rounds. It was replaced by the WTO, which has a more effective dispute settlement mechanism. Of the many UN organizations, we reviewed the functioning of UNCTAD in particular, focusing on the problems of developing nations. The OECD, in contrast, is a club of advanced nations, also coordinating their interactions with developing countries. The process of CEE economic transitions illustrates the enormous and time-consuming problems of adjusting a country's economic organization and institutional framework.

Technical Note 12.1 WTO members

Table 12.2 WTO member countries, December 2005

	Country	Year		Country	Year
1	Albania	2000	31	Costa Rica	1995
2	Angola	1996	32	Côte d'Ivoire	1995
3	Ant. & Barb.	1995	33	Croatia	2000
4	Argentina	1995	34	Cuba	1995
5	Armenia	2003	35	Cyprus	1995
6	Australia	1995	36	Czech Rep.	1995
7	Austria	1995	37	D. R. Congo	1997
8	Bahrain	1995	38	Denmark	1995
9	Bangladesh	1995	39	Djibouti	1995
10	Barbados	1995	40	Dominica	1995
11	Belgium	1995	41	Dom. Rep.	1995
12	Belize	1995	42	Ecuador	1996
13	Benin	1996	43	Egypt	1995
14	Bolivia	1995	44	El Salvador	1995
15	Botswana	1995	45	Estonia	1999
16	Brazil	1995	46	Eur. Comm.	1995
17	Brunei	1995	47	Fiji	1996
18	Bulgaria	1996	48	Finland	1995
19	Burk. Faso	1995	49	Macedonia	2003
20	Burundi	1995	50	France	1995
21	Cambodia	2004	51	Gabon	1995
22	Cameroon	1995	52	Georgia	2000
23	Canada	1995	53	Germany	1995
24	C. Afr. Rep.	1995	54	Ghana	1995
25	Chad	1996	55	Greece	1995
26	Chile	1995	56	Grenada	1996
27	China	2001	57	Guatemala	1995
28	Taiwan	2002	58	Guinea	1995
29	Colombia	1995	59	G. Bissau	1995
30	Congo	1997	60	Guyana	1995

Table 12.2 (*Cont.*)

	Country	Year		Country	Year
61	Haiti	1996	95	Morocco	1995
62	Honduras	1995	96	Mozambique	1995
63	Hong Kong	1995	97	Myanmar	1995
64	Hungary	1995	98	Namibia	1995
65	Iceland	1995	99	Nepal	2004
66	India	1995	100	Netherlands	1995
67	Indonesia	1995	101	New Zealand	1995
68	Ireland	1995	102	Nicaragua	1995
69	Israel	1995	103	Niger	1996
70	Italy	1995	104	Nigeria	1995
71	Jamaica	1995	105	Norway	1995
72	Japan	1995	106	Oman	2000
73	Jordan	2000	107	Pakistan	1995
74	Kenya	1995	108	Panama	1997
75	South Korea	1995	109	Papua N. G.	1996
76	Kuwait	1995	110	Paraguay	1995
77	Kyrgyz. Rep.	1998	111	Peru	1995
78	Latvia	1999	112	Philippines	1995
79	Lesotho	1995	113	Poland	1995
80	Liechtenstein	1995	114	Portugal	1995
81	Lithuania	2001	115	Qatar	1996
82	Luxembourg	1995	116	Romania	1995
83	Macao	1995	117	Rwanda	1996
84	Madagascar	1995	118	Saudi Arabia	2005
85	Malawi	1995	119	Senegal	1995
86	Malaysia	1995	120	Sierra Leone	1995
87	Maldives	1995	121	Singapore	1995
88	Mali	1995	122	Slovak Rep.	1995
89	Malta	1995	123	Slovenia	1995
90	Mauritania	1995	124	Solomon Islands	1996
91	Mauritius	1995	125	South Africa	1995
92	Mexico	1995	126	Spain	1995
93	Moldova	2001	127	Sri Lanka	1995
94	Mongolia	1997	128	St Kitts & Nevis	1996

Table 12.2 (*Cont.*)

	Country	Year			Country	Year
129	St Lucia	1995		140	Tunisia	1995
130	St Vin. & Gren.	1995		141	Turkey	1995
131	Suriname	1995		142	Uganda	1995
132	Swaziland	1995		143	U.A. Emirates	1996
133	Sweden	1995		144	UK	1995
134	Switzerland	1995		145	USA	1995
135	Tanzania	1995		146	Uruguay	1995
136	Thailand	1995		147	Venezuela	1995
137	The Gambia	1996		148	Zambia	1995
138	Togo	1995		149	Zimbabwe	1995
139	Trin. & Tob.	1995				

Source: www.wto.org

Table 12.3 WTO observer governments, December 2005

	Country			Country
1	Afghanistan		17	Lebanese Rep.
2	Algeria		18	Libya
3	Andorra		19	Montenegro
4	Azerbaijan		20	Russian Federation
5	Bahamas		21	Samoa
6	Belarus		22	Sao Tomé Principe
7	Bhutan		23	Serbia
8	Bosnia & Herzeg.		24	Seychelles
9	Cape Verde		25	Sudan
10	Equatorial Guinea		26	Tajikistan
11	Ethiopia		27	Tonga
12	Holy See (Vatican)		28	Ukraine
13	Iran		29	Uzbekistan
14	Iraq		30	Vanuatu
15	Kazakhstan		31	Viet Nam
16	Lao People's D. Rep.		32	Yemen

Note: With the exception of the Holy See, observers must start accession negotiations within five years of becoming observers.

Source: www.wto.org.

Technical Note 12.2 UN members

Table 12.4 UN member countries, December 2005

	Country	Year		Country	Year
1	Afghanistan	1946	33	C. Afr. Rep.	1960
2	Albania	1955	34	Chad	1960
3	Algeria	1962	35	Chile	1945
4	Andorra	1993	36	China	1945
5	Angola	1976	37	Colombia	1945
6	Ant. & Barb.	1981	38	Comoros	1975
7	Argentina	1945	39	Congo Rep.	1960
8	Armenia	1992	40	Costa Rica	1945
9	Australia	1945	41	Côte d'Ivoire	1960
10	Austria	1955	42	Croatia	1992
11	Azerbaijan	1992	43	Cuba	1945
12	Bahamas	1973	44	Cyprus	1960
13	Bahrain	1971	45	Czech Rep.	1993
14	Bangladesh	1974	46	D. R. Korea	1991
15	Barbados	1966	47	D. R. Congo	1960
16	Belarus	1945	48	Denmark	1945
17	Belgium	1945	49	Djibouti	1977
18	Belize	1981	50	Dominica	1978
19	Benin	1960	51	Domin. Rep.	1945
20	Bhutan	1971	52	Ecuador	1945
21	Bolivia	1945	53	Egypt	1945
22	Bosnia Herz.	1992	54	El Salvador	1945
23	Botswana	1966	55	Equator G.	1968
24	Brazil	1945	56	Eritrea	1993
25	Brunei Dar.	1984	57	Estonia	1991
26	Bulgaria	1955	58	Ethiopia	1945
27	Burk. Faso	1960	59	Fiji	1970
28	Burundi	1962	60	Finland	1955
29	Cambodia	1955	61	France	1945
30	Cameroon	1960	62	Gabon	1960
31	Canada	1945	63	Gambia	1965
32	Cape Verde	1975	64	Georgia	1992

Table 12.4 (*Cont.*)

	Country	Year		Country	Year
65	Germany	1973	98	Liechtenstein	1990
66	Ghana	1957	99	Lithuania	1991
67	Greece	1945	100	Luxembourg	1945
68	Grenada	1974	101	Madagascar	1960
69	Guatemala	1945	102	Malawi	1964
70	Guinea	1958	103	Malaysia	1957
71	G.Bissau	1974	104	Maldives	1965
72	Guyana	1966	105	Mali	1960
73	Haiti	1945	106	Malta	1964
74	Honduras	1945	107	Marshall Islands	1991
75	Hungary	1955	108	Mauritania	1961
76	Iceland	1946	109	Mauritius	1968
77	India	1945	110	Mexico	1945
78	Indonesia	1950	111	Micronesia	1991
79	Iran	1945	112	Monaco	1993
80	Iraq	1945	113	Mongolia	1961
81	Ireland	1955	114	Morocco	1956
82	Israel	1949	115	Mozambique	1975
83	Italy	1955	116	Myanmar	1948
84	Jamaica	1962	117	Namibia	1990
85	Japan	1956	118	Nauru	1999
86	Jordan	1955	119	Nepal	1955
87	Kazakhstan	1992	120	Netherlands	1945
88	Kenya	1963	121	New Zealand	1945
89	Kiribati	1999	122	Nicaragua	1945
90	Kuwait	1963	123	Niger	1960
91	Kyrgyzstan	1992	124	Nigeria	1960
92	Laos	1955	125	Norway	1945
93	Latvia	1991	126	Oman	1971
94	Lebanon	1945	127	Pakistan	1947
95	Lesotho	1966	128	Palau	1994
96	Liberia	1945	129	Panama	1945
97	Libya	1955	130	Papua N. G.	1975

Table 12.4 (*Cont.*)

	Country	Year		Country	Year
131	Paraguay	1945	162	Suriname	1975
132	Peru	1945	163	Swaziland	1968
133	Philippines	1945	164	Sweden	1946
134	Poland	1945	165	Switzerland	2002
135	Portugal	1955	166	Syria	1945
136	Qatar	1971	167	Tajikistan	1992
137	Rep. Korea	1991	168	Thailand	1946
138	Rep. Moldova	1992	169	Macedonia	1993
139	Romania	1955	170	Timor-Leste	2002
140	Russian Fed.	1945	171	Togo	1960
141	Rwanda	1962	172	Tonga	1999
142	St Kitts & Nevis	1983	173	Trin. & Tob.	1962
143	St Lucia	1979	174	Tunisia	1956
144	St Vinc. & Gren.	1980	175	Turkey	1945
145	Samoa	1976	176	Turkmenistan	1992
146	San Marino	1992	177	Tuvalu	2000
147	S. Tomé Princ.	1975	178	Uganda	1962
148	Saudi Arabia	1945	179	Ukraine	1945
149	Senegal	1960	180	U. A. Emirates	1971
150	Serbia & Mont.	2000	181	UK	1945
151	Seychelles	1976	182	U. R. Tanzania	1961
152	Sierra Leone	1961	183	USA	1945
153	Singapore	1965	184	Uruguay	1945
154	Slovakia	1993	185	Uzbekistan	1992
155	Slovenia	1992	186	Vanuatu	1981
156	Solomon	1978	187	Venezuela	1945
157	Somalia	1960	188	Viet Nam	1977
158	South Africa	1945	189	Yemen	1947
159	Spain	1955	190	Zambia	1964
160	Sri Lanka	1955	191	Zimbabwe	1980
161	Sudan	1956			

Source: www.un.org

Technical Note 12.3 OECD members

Table 12.5 OECD member countries, December 2005

	Country	Year		Country	Year
1	Australia	1971	16	Korea	1996
2	Austria	1961	17	Luxembourg	1961
3	Belgium	1961	18	Mexico	1994
4	Canada	1961	19	Netherlands	1961
5	Czech Rep.	1995	20	New Zealand	1973
6	Denmark	1961	21	Norway	1961
7	Finland	1969	22	Poland	1996
8	France	1961	23	Portugal	1961
9	Germany	1961	24	Slovak Rep.	2000
10	Greece	1961	25	Spain	1961
11	Hungary	1996	26	Sweden	1961
12	Iceland	1961	27	Switzerland	1961
13	Ireland	1961	28	Turkey	1961
14	Italy	1962	29	UK	1961
15	Japan	1964	30	USA	1961

Source: www.oecd.org

QUESTIONS

Question 12.1

'If economists ruled the world, there would be no need for a WTO'.

12.1A Do you agree with the statement above? Explain.

12.1B Throughout the book we illustrate the benefits of free trade. Yet international trade negotiations are still steeped in terms such as concessions received and granted. Can you explain why this is so?

12.1C What is a beggar-thy-neighbour policy?

12.1D How is this related to the set-up of international trade organizations after the second World War?

12.1E On which three main principles is the GATT based?

12.1F Two main exceptions are given for the non-discrimination principle. Can you explain why these have been created?

12.1G Why did the successive trade rounds change their negotiating technique at the Kennedy Round?

12.1H Why do international trade negotiations give particular attention to non-tariff barriers?

12.1I What is the new protectionism?

12.1J Which concerns gave rise to the foundation of UNCTAD?

Question 12.2

The world has recently witnessed the rise of a new movement vehemently opposed to international bodies such as the World Bank, the IMF, and the WTO. As described in Box 12.1, this movement consists of many different groups of people, usually opposing different elements of the economic developments in the world. In view of this discontent, which apparently makes people so angry that they are willing to smash city centres, break windows, start fires, and fight with the police, it is good to discuss some of the many issues raised by the protestors. For clarity, we focus the discussion on the WTO as it is the most important trade organization and was the first target of the demonstrators. Give your view on the claims below.

- The WTO is an undemocratic organization.
- The WTO promotes international trade that is bad for the environment.
- The WTO represents exclusively the interests of the developed nations and the multinationals.
- The WTO leads to the development of a monotone global culture that destroys the diversity of other cultures.
- The WTO promotes 'unfair' trade.
- The WTO policies increase global inequality.
- The WTO policy of free trade destroys jobs.

Question 12.3

12.3A What are the terms of trade?

12.3B Does the corporate sector favour better (higher) terms of trade? Explain.

12.3C Do consumers favour better (higher) terms of trade? Explain.

The case study in Section 12.5 describes the transition process of Central and Eastern European countries. Figure 12.7 gives an overview of the possible economic systems countries may choose.

12.3D State for each of the countries below in which corner of Figure 12.7 you would place the country.

- Germany
- USA
- China
- Cuba.

Figure 12.8 describes the hypothetical transition of one of the Eastern European countries to capitalism.

12.3E Can you explain why the relative price is different before and after the transition process?

 See the Online Resource Centre for a Study Guide containing more questions
www.oxfordtextbooks.co.uk/orc/vanmarrewijk/

NOTES

1 Tinbergen earlier made a smaller model for the Netherlands. John Maynard Keynes did not like this work, as is evident from his book review in the *Economic Journal*. Tinbergen politely replied that Keynes had totally misunderstood his econometric methods.

2 The discussion in this section is based on Schmidt (2001).

3 Many experts argue that the CEE economies were not actually producing *on* the PPF, but somewhere *inside* the PPF as a result of various inefficiencies.

4 It is important to note that this measured decline will exaggerate the actual welfare loss if the economy was initially producing the wrong output mix, which does not reflect people's preferences.

ECONOMIC INTEGRATION

13

Objectives/key terms

- Preferential trade agreement
- Trade-creation/trade-diversion
- European Union (EU)

- Free trade area/customs union
- Regionalism/multilateralism
- EU enlargement

We review some of the many preferential trade agreements in the world, with special attention to Europe and EU enlargement. The rising popularity of economic integration, known as 'regionalism', is analysed in a neoclassical and new trade framework.

13.1 Introduction

Since a regional economic integration agreement gives preferential treatment to the members of the agreement, but not equal treatment to non-members as would be in line with the most favoured nation (MFN) clause of the GATT/WTO, any such agreement violates the non-discrimination principle of the GATT/WTO. As explained in Chapter 12, however, regional economic integration agreements can be exempted from the non-discrimination principle, either because a move towards uninhibited trade flows among a group of countries is seen as a step in the right direction of free trade, or because a preferential trade agreement provides an impulse to the growth and development process of less developed countries.

At the beginning of 2001, the European Union, under the guidance of Pascal Lamy, the European trade commissioner, decided to push through huge tariff reductions for 48 of the world's poorest countries. All goods, except arms, will be imported into Europe free of tariffs. Some goods, such as bananas, sugar, and rice, will be phased out later. Michael Finger, an economist at the World Bank, estimates that the 48 poorest countries' exports will grow by 15–20 per cent, or about $1.4 billion, per year. He also notes that the upsurge in exports will come at the expense of other developing countries, producing similar goods, which are not in the group of 48, such as Swaziland.[1] These two effects, the increase of trade for the countries receiving preferential treatment and the reduction of trade for countries that do not, were described for the first time by Jacob Viner (1950), referring to it as trade-creation and trade-diversion, respectively. This chapter discusses the welfare consequences of preferential trade policies in general and gives an overview of the most important regional trade agreements in the world. An overview of the empirical issues that play a role in estimating the impact of regional trade agreements will be given in Chapter 17.

Section 13.2 describes different types of regional economic integration agreements. Section 13.3 analyses the main economic consequences of economic integration based on the

Famous economists	Jacob Viner

Fig. 13.1
Jacob Viner
(1892–1970)

Born in Montreal, Canada, of Romanian immigrant parents, Jacob Viner was, according to Mark Blaug (1985: 256), 'a leading interwar price and trade theorist and quite simply the greatest historian of economic thought that ever lived'. He received his PhD in 1915 at Harvard University, written under the supervision of Frank Taussig, and worked at the University of Chicago, where he became editor of the *Journal of Political Economy*, before moving to Princeton in 1946. Viner's *Studies in the Theory of International Trade* (1937) provides the basis for much of our current views and knowledge on the history of international economics, particularly on the pre-scientific fallacies of the mercantilists in the seventeenth and eighteenth centuries. In 1950 Viner wrote *The Customs Union Issue*, identifying the trade-creation and trade-diversion effects, which became the basis for all subsequent work on customs unions and free trade areas.

neoclassical framework explained in Part II.A of this book. Section 13.4 gives a brief overview of some of the main regional economic integration agreements that are active today, from which it will be clear that there is an increasing tendency for the countries of the world economy to organize themselves in a decreasing number of large trading blocks. Section 13.5 analyses the consequences of this empirically observed tendency in a general equilibrium framework based on the imperfect competition and intra-industry trade models of Chapters 9 and 10 of Part II.B of this book. Section 13.6 describes the economic integration process after the Second World War of the countries currently forming the European Union, arguably the world's most successful economic integration agreement. Section 13.7 discusses the process of EU enlargement to accommodate the Central and Eastern European countries that wish to join or recently joined the EU after the fall of the Berlin Wall in 1989. Section 13.8 concludes.

13.2 Types of regional economic integration

Regional economic integration, in which a group of countries eliminates (artificial) barriers to international trade and competition on a regional rather than a global scale, has become increasingly popular since the Second World War. For the integration of final goods markets and factors of production, we can distinguish between the following types of economic integration agreements, possibly on a sectoral level only, or possibly excluding some sectors (the examples below are further discussed in the sequel of this chapter):

* *Preferential trade agreement (PTA)*. In such an agreement, tariffs or other trade restrictions are reduced among the members of the agreement for some goods or services, sometimes unilaterally. There is no general reduction of internal tariffs, nor a common external tariff. An example is provided by the preferential treatment given by the countries of the European Community to their former colonies in Africa, the Caribbean, and the Pacific (known as the ACP countries) under the Lomé Convention.

* *Free trade area (FTA)*. The members of a free trade area eliminate internal tariffs and other measures that restrict trade between its members, without any common trade policy relative to other countries. The lack of an external trade policy requires the use of certificates of origin for goods crossing the borders and other measures to prevent 'deflection' of trade; that is, taking advantage of arbitrage opportunities by importing goods from outside the free trade area via the country with the lowest barriers to imports. Examples are the European Free Trade Area (EFTA) and the North American Free Trade Area (NAFTA).

* *Customs union*. Like a free trade area, a customs union abolishes internal tariffs and other trade restrictions among the members of the union. In addition, the customs union develops a common trade policy, such as common external tariffs, relative to other countries. An example is provided by the European Economic Community (EEC).

* *Common market*. In this case, the member countries allow not only for the free movement of goods and services, but also for the free movement of factors of production, such as capital and labour. A common market gradually moves to an integrated (or internal) market if the member countries also eliminate other, more concealed barriers to trade arising from differences in national policy, for example regarding product standards or taxation. An example is provided by the European Union (EU).

* *Economic union*. An extension of the common/internal market is an economic union, in which case there is also harmonization of the institutional framework, regarding competition

policy, procurement, etc., and a fair degree of policy coordination. The economic union therefore provides the counterpart in the real sphere of a monetary union, in which case there is sufficient policy coordination to allow for one currency. A combined example is provided by the EU's Economic and Monetary Union (EMU).

13.3 Neoclassical theory of economic integration

Jacob Viner (1950) provided the first rigorous analysis of the ways in which a customs union can affect trade flows and resource allocations. He identified trade-creation and trade-diversion, see below, and argued that if trade-creation is dominant, the customs union raises welfare for the members of the customs union and world welfare. The main consequences of economic integration in a partial equilibrium framework are illustrated in Figures 13.2 and 13.3, depicting the demand and supply schedule for a specific good for Austria. We assume that Austria is a small country relative to two other countries, called Bolivia and Congo. The price for the good in Bolivia is equal to p_B, in Congo it is equal to p_C. We also assume that

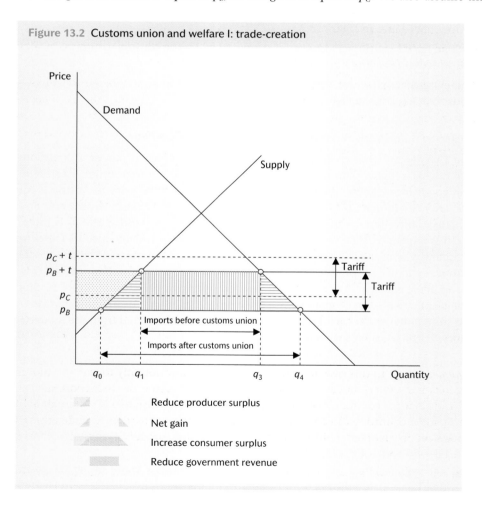

Figure 13.2 Customs union and welfare I: trade-creation

Austria initially imposes a specific tariff t on imports of the good from both Bolivia and Congo. We analyse the impact of economic integration if Austria decides to form a *customs union* with Bolivia, in which case the specific tariff t for imports from Bolivia is eliminated. Relative to Congo, for which the tariff is still in place, Bolivia therefore gets preferential treatment within the customs union with Austria.

I Customs union with the most efficient producer: trade-creation

Figure 13.2 depicts what happens if Bolivia is a more efficient producer than Congo, in which case p_B is lower than p_C. Before the formation of the customs union, Austria imports $q_3 - q_1$ goods from Bolivia, and the price in Austria is equal to $p_B + t$. After the formation of the customs union, the tariff t between Austria and Bolivia is eliminated, such that the price in Austria falls to p_B, quantity demanded increases from q_3 to q_4, quantity domestically supplied falls from q_1 to q_0, and imports from Bolivia rise from $q_3 - q_1$ to $q_4 - q_0$; hence the term trade-creation.

- Welfare for the producers in Austria, as measured by the producer surplus, falls by the dotted area in Figure 13.2.
- Welfare for the government in Austria, as measured by the government revenue, decreases by the shaded area in Figure 13.2.
- Welfare for the consumers in Austria, as measured by the consumer surplus, increases by the dotted, shaded and horizontal bar area in Figure 13.2.
- The net welfare effect for this particular good is therefore a *gain* for Austria equal to the horizontal bar areas in Figure 13.2.

II Customs union with an inefficient producer: trade-diversion

Figure 13.3 depicts what might happen if Bolivia is a less efficient producer than Congo, in which case p_B is higher than p_C. Before the formation of the customs union, Austria imports $q_3 - q_1$ goods from Congo, the more efficient producer, and the price in Austria is equal to $p_C + t$. After the formation of the customs union, the tariff t between Austria and Bolivia is eliminated. Since imports from Congo are still subject to the tariff t, and p_B is lower than $p_C + t$, this implies that the price falls from $p_C + t$ to p_B, quantity demanded increases from q_3 to q_4, quantity domestically supplied falls from q_1 to q_0, and there is trade-creation as imports rise from $q_3 - q_1$ to $q_4 - q_0$. As we saw above, this results in positive welfare effects. This time, however, there is a second, negative, welfare effect operative, called trade-diversion. Since the customs union with Austria gives Bolivia preferential treatment, Austria now starts to import goods from Bolivia rather than from Congo, that is trade is diverted from the more efficient producer to the less efficient producer.

- Welfare for the producers in Austria, as measured by the producer surplus, falls by the dotted area in Figure 13.3.
- Welfare for the government in Austria, as measured by the government revenue, decreases by the shaded and vertical bars area in Figure 13.3.
- Welfare for the consumers in Austria, as measured by the consumer surplus, increases by the dotted, shaded, and horizontal bars area in Figure 13.3.
- The net welfare effect for this particular good for Austria could either be positive or negative; it is equal to the horizontal bars area minus the vertical bars area in Figure 13.3.

Figure 13.3 Customs union and welfare II: trade-diversion

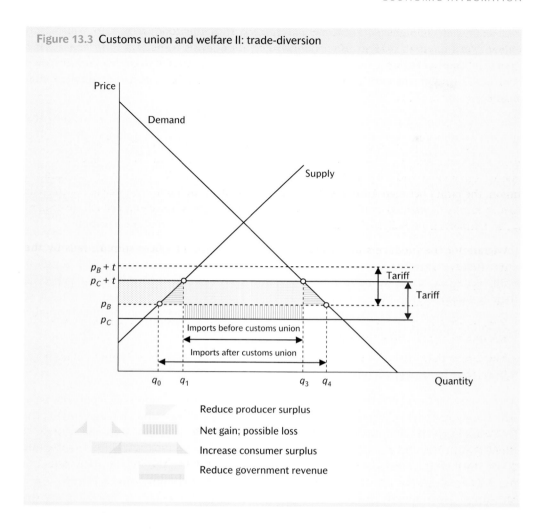

Reduce producer surplus

Net gain; possible loss

Increase consumer surplus

Reduce government revenue

III The welfare effects of a customs union: general equilibrium

In the above partial equilibrium analysis, the positive welfare effects arise from the Harberger triangles measuring the efficiency gains from trade-creation. The negative welfare effects arise from the reallocation of resources from the more efficient to the less efficient producer as a result of trade-diversion. As mentioned above, Jacob Viner therefore argued that the net welfare effect of creating a customs union is positive if the trade-creation effects dominate the trade-diversion effects. This topic was analysed in the literature that followed, see Lipsey (1960) and Lloyd (1982) for an overview. The potential positive welfare benefits of the formation of a customs union, which after all eliminates artificial barriers to trade, was convincingly demonstrated by Murray Kemp and Henry Wan Jr (1976).

Kemp–Wan proposition

Consider any competitive world trading equilibrium with a neoclassical production structure, with any number of countries and commodities, with no restrictions whatever on the tariffs and other

commodity taxes of individual countries, and with cost of transport fully recognized. Now let any subset of the countries form a customs union. Then there exists a common tariff vector and a system of lump-sum compensatory payments involving only members of the union, such that each individual, whether a member of the union or not, is not worse off than before the formation of the union.

The formal proof of the proposition is based on a fundamental theorem of neoclassical general equilibrium theory and beyond the scope of this book; see Debreu (1959).[2] This theory is able to derive very general results with respect to the number of goods and countries involved because it is based on two strong assumptions: perfect competition and a neoclassical production structure. This means that imperfect competition, economies of scale, knowledge spillovers, etc. are ruled out. Note that the partial equilibrium analysis above suggests that there may be negative welfare effects if trade-diversion dominates trade-creation, which requires a decline of international trade flows of the countries forming the customs union relative to the rest of the world. To rule out this possibility Kemp and Wan argue that it is possible for the countries forming the customs union to impose a common tariff vector that leaves world prices, and therefore the trade and welfare of non-members, at their pre-union prices. The elimination of trade barriers within the union then leads to efficiency gains, which in principle enables welfare gains for each union member through a system of lump-sum transfers.

13.4 Regional trade agreements

All members of the GATT/WTO are bound to notify the regional trade agreements (RTAs) in which they participate. Almost all members participate in at least one such agreement. The GATT has received 124 notifications of RTAs (relating to trade in goods). Since the creation of the WTO in 1995, 206 arrangements covering trade in goods or services were notified by July 2005. Since new agreements sometimes replace old agreements, the WTO estimates that of the 330 notifications 180 are currently in force. In July 2005 only one WTO member – Mongolia – was not party to a regional trade agreement. In this section we briefly discuss the main RTAs in the world, with the exception of Europe, which is dealt with separately in Section 13.6.

Africa (Figure 13.4)

At present, the most important regional trade agreement in Africa is the Common Market for Eastern and Southern Africa (COMESA), which was established in December 1994 and replaced a former preferential trade area, operative since 1981. COMESA currently consists of twenty member states, with a population of over 385 million people. Its task is to promote peace and security in the region and enhance economic prosperity through economic integration. It is therefore implementing a free trade area, and is scheduled to introduce a common external tariff schedule for third parties. The COMESA Centre is located on Ben Bella Road, PO Box 30051, Lusaka, Zambia. The COMESA website (http://www.comesa.int) provides background information to the organization, statistical data, and information by state.

Figure 13.4 COMESA countries

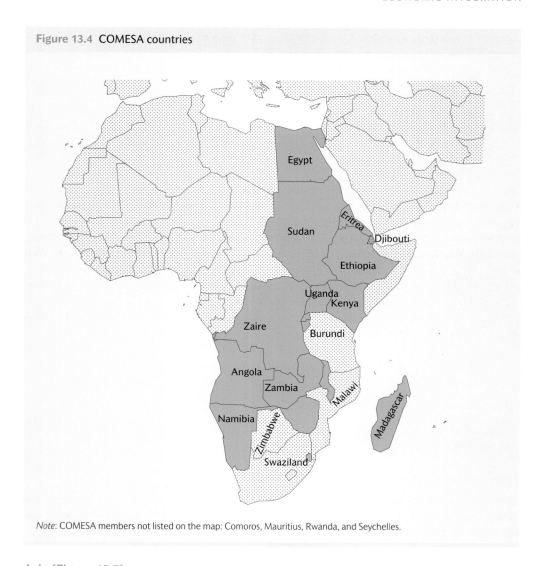

Note: COMESA members not listed on the map: Comoros, Mauritius, Rwanda, and Seychelles.

Asia (Figure 13.5)

The most important regional trade agreement in Asia is the Association of South-East Asian Nations (ASEAN), established by five countries in 1967, but currently consisting of ten countries, with about 500 million inhabitants. The ASEAN countries work together in several areas (political, economic, cultural, and social), and decided to form the ASEAN Free Trade Area (AFTA) in 1992, the establishment of which has now been moved forward to 2010 and 2015 (for new members). A commitment towards further economic integration was announced as ASEAN Vision 2020 at the 1997 Kuala Lumpur meeting, although many outside observers remain sceptical of the actual progress that will be made in the future. The ASEAN secretariat is located at 70A Jalan Sisingamangaraja, Jakarta 12110, Indonesia. The website (http://www.aseansec.org) provides up-to-date news of the organization, an overview of the

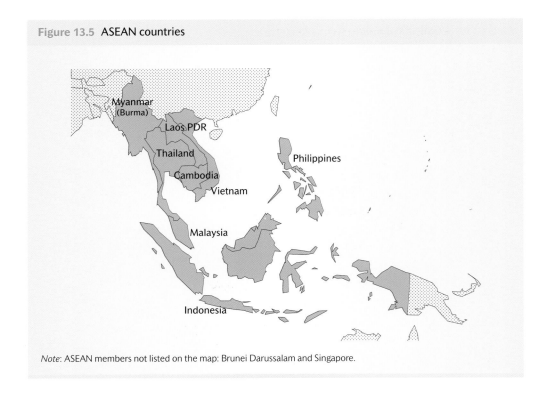

Figure 13.5 ASEAN countries

Note: ASEAN members not listed on the map: Brunei Darussalam and Singapore.

various areas of cooperation (political and security, economic, and functional), information on the ASEAN summits, and statistical information.

America (Figure 13.6)

The American continents have been very active in the formation of regional trade agreements, starting with Latin America in the 1950s. In the drive towards industrialization by import substitution, and realizing that for many countries in the region the domestic market was too small to allow for efficient production, regional free trade agreements were set up to increase the size of the local market. This resulted in, for example, the Central American Common Market (CACM), the Caribbean Community (CARICOM), the Andean Pact (ANDEAN), and the Mercado Commun del Sur (MERCOSUR), although some of these agreements were not energetically implemented.

In North America, the agreements started in 1965 with the USA–Canada Auto Pact, involving tariff-free trade in motor vehicles and parts. A few years later on the other side of the US border the *maquiladores* in Mexico, processing or assembling parts imported from the USA and subsequently exported to the USA, started to expand and develop, in part because import duties were only charged on the value added and not on the total value. After some years of negotiations these three countries, Canada, Mexico, and the USA, launched the North American Free Trade Agreement (NAFTA). The American fears of a rapid move of companies and loss of jobs to Mexico, called the 'giant sucking sound' by Ross Perot in the presidential election campaign (which he lost), were unsubstantiated in the years of rapid economic growth following the establishment of NAFTA.

Figure 13.6 Regional trade agreements in America

CARICOM members not listed on the map: Antigua and Borbuda, Bahamas, Bardados, Belize, Dominica, Grenada, Jamaica, St Kitts and Nevis, St Lucia, St Vincent and Grenadine, and Trinidad and Tabago; CACM members not listed on the map: El Salvador.

Since the Summit of the Americas in Miami, December 1994, talks are now under way to unite the economies of the western hemisphere in a single free trade agreement, the Free Trade Area of the Americas (FTAA). There are nine negotiating groups, on market access, investment, competition policy, etc. with the objective to establish the FTAA, see also the FTAA website (http://www.ftaa-alca.org). As is clear from Table 13.1, which gives the intra-regional and inter-regional trade flows between the various trading blocs, by far the largest trade flows in the FTAA area are the NAFTA intra-regional trade flows (73 per cent of the total), that is trade between Canada, Mexico, and the USA. For those countries, the

Table 13.1 FTAA intra- and inter-regional trade flows, bn US$ 1999 (% of total)

	NAFTA	MERCOSUR	ANDEAN	CACM	CARICOM
NAFTA	703 (73%)	43 (4%)	43 (2%)	16 (2%)	9 (1%)
MERCOSUR		18 (2%)	6 (1%)	0 (0%)	0 (0%)
ANDEAN			5 (1%)	1 (0%)	1 (0%)
CACM				3 (0%)	0 (0%)
CARICOM					1 (0%)

Source: Inter-American Development Bank.

establishment of the FTAA appears to be of relatively minor importance. For all other trading blocs, however, the largest trade flows derive from the inter-regional trade with the NAFTA countries, such that for all other countries establishment of the FTAA is a more important step towards free trade.

13.5 Regionalism and the new trade theory

In the course of the twentieth century, after the Second World War, the process of trade liberalization through multilateral negotiations within the GATT framework became increasingly difficult and time-consuming as more countries joined the GATT, see Chapter 12. At the same time, regional trade agreements, such as in Western Europe and North America, became increasingly popular and more powerful as many countries were organizing themselves in such agreements, which became known as 'regionalism'. On the basis of the Kemp–Wan proposition discussed in Section 13.3, one might think that this process, the apparent shift away from multilateralism towards regionalism, might be seen as a step in the right direction by trade policy experts, although worldwide liberalization would be better still. Instead, at the end of the 1980s and the beginning of the 1990s many trade policy experts and trade economists were worried about the shift from multilateralism towards regionalism. First, because of fears that countries that join a regional trade agreement might be more protectionist towards countries outside the trading bloc than they were before. Second, because the Kemp–Wan proposition in which no individual country is made worse off after the formation of a customs union is based on (i) the imposition of external tariffs that keep world prices and trade with non-members fixed, and (ii) a complicated internal transfer scheme among the members of the customs union, neither of which is observed in reality. Third, because the Kemp–Wan proposition is based on perfect competition and neoclassical production, such that it does not allow for imperfect competition, increasing returns to scale, and external effects.

Paul Krugman (1991) developed a simple, tractable, general equilibrium model based on the intra-industry trade framework of Chapter 10 to substantiate the fears of the trade policy experts regarding the shift from multilateralism to regionalism. As usual, his work illustrated the main issues involved, such that it received considerable attention and became the starting point of subsequent analysis and discussion; see for example De Melo and Panagariya (1993). In his first contribution Krugman assumes that a group of countries forming a trading bloc uses its monopoly power with respect to the rest of the world by imposing the 'optimal' tariff, as derived in Chapter 8. As a result, the tariff rate increases as the number of trading blocs falls. Since we do not observe increasing tariff rates in reality after the formation of a new trade bloc, which might start a process of retaliation, we discuss Krugman's model in this section for a given tariff rate, which is eliminated for those countries forming a trade bloc. This is not only closer to what we observe in reality; it also does not affect the main results and insights of the analysis and is easier to derive analytically; see also Krugman (1993).

Suppose the world consists of a large number N of 'provinces', each producing one unit of a unique good or variety.[3] Whether or not production takes place under increasing returns to scale or imperfect competition is unimportant. A collection of provinces may form a country, such that a large country may contain more provinces, each producing a unique good, than a small country, but the country level is basically irrelevant in the sequel. The price charged domestically is 1. If c_i is the consumption level for a good produced in province i, the identical utility function for all economic agents is given by (see also equation 10.2):

$$(13.1) \qquad U = \left[\sum_{i=1}^{N} c_i^\rho \right]^{1/\rho}; \quad 0 < \rho < 1, \quad \varepsilon \equiv 1/(1 - \rho) > 1$$

As explained in Chapter 10, this specification implies that consumers have a love of variety and that goods produced in different provinces are imperfect substitutes for one another, with the parameter ε as the elasticity of substitution. The world is divided into b symmetric trading blocs. There is free trade for all provinces within each trading bloc, such that the price charged for a good produced within the trading bloc is 1. Each trading bloc imposes a uniform *ad valorem* tariff t on all imports from outside the trading bloc, such that the price charged for such goods is $1 + t$. We are interested in the welfare effects in this simple set-up of the formation of a smaller number of larger trading blocs; that is, we are interested in the welfare effects of a fall in b.

Suppose, for example, that the world is initially divided into ten trading blocs of equal size. The inhabitants of any trading bloc then have access to 10 per cent of the world's varieties produced inside the trading bloc and freely traded at the price 1, and 90 per cent of the world's varieties imported from outside the trading bloc, subject to the tariff t, at the price $1 + t$. The income available to the inhabitants of a trading bloc derives from the income generated by the production of varieties inside the trading bloc and the tariff revenue levied on imports from outside the trading bloc.

A reduction of the number of trading blocs in the world to, say, eight implies that the inhabitants of any trading bloc have access to 12.5 per cent of the world's varieties produced inside the trading bloc and freely traded at the price 1, and 87.5 per cent of the world's varieties imported from outside the trading bloc at the price $1 + t$. At first sight this might seem beneficial as a larger fraction of goods is available at a lower price. However, we have seen in Section 13.3 that the total welfare effect depends on the balance between the trade-creation and the trade-diversion effect. Note that the term trade-diversion is not entirely appropriate in this set-up, since all goods are imperfect substitutes for one another. Instead, it should be interpreted in this framework as a diversion away from consumption of goods produced outside the trading bloc towards goods produced inside the trading bloc; that is, the increase from 10 to 12.5 per cent of the share of goods produced inside the trading bloc can be viewed as an increase in the fraction of goods whose *relative* price is distorted compared to the rest of the world. The latter interpretation makes the main effects derived in this model readily understandable. It can be shown, see Technical Note 13.1, that total world welfare (normalized to 1 for total free trade, that is if there is only one trading bloc) as a function of the tariff t, the elasticity of substitution between varieties ε, and the number of trading blocs b is equal to:

$$(13.2) \qquad \frac{[b^{-1} + (1 - b^{-1})(1 + t)^{1-\varepsilon}]^{\varepsilon/(\varepsilon-1)}}{b^{-1} + (1 - b^{-1})(1 + t)^{-\varepsilon}}$$

Figure 13.7 illustrates the total welfare level given in equation (13.2) as a function of the number of trading blocs b, in panel (a) for different values of the tariff rate t, and in panel (b) for different values of the elasticity of substitution ε. The main conclusions are:

1. Total welfare falls as the number of trading blocs b decreases for a large range of parameter settings. Only if the number of trading blocs is already fairly small, in Figure 13.7 ranging from three to six, is a further reduction in the number of trading blocs welfare improving.[4]

2. Total welfare is, of course, maximized if there is free trade (only one trading bloc). This welfare level is also approached in this set-up if the number of trading blocs becomes very large because then the relative price distortion disappears (the share of goods produced within the trading bloc then approaches zero).

3. An increase in the tariff rate t imposed on imports from outside the trading bloc leads to (i) a reduction in the welfare level and (ii) an increase in the number of trading blocs where the minimum welfare level is reached; see Figure 13.7(a). To some extent the connection between high tariffs and regionalism is ambivalent, where part (i) is the bad news and part (ii) is the good news (as a fall in b implies that the minimum is reached sooner if tariffs are high).

4. An increase in the elasticity of substitution ε leads to (i) a reduction in the welfare level and (ii) an increase in the number of trading blocs where the minimum welfare level is reached; see Figure 13.7(b). These results can be understood by realizing that if it is easier to substitute one variety for another, the distortive effect of the tariff is stronger. The connection between the elasticity of substitution and regionalism is therefore, like the connection between tariffs and regionalism, also ambivalent.

The advantage of the model in this section is that it highlights in a simple framework the main issues involved in the move towards regionalism and the fact that it provides a clear warning signal that this move could be detrimental to world welfare. Moreover, it shows how these issues depend on the elasticity of substitution between different goods and the tariff level imposed in the world economy. It should be noted, however, that the picture of the move toward regionalism emerging from the analysis in this section is somewhat too gloomy, as it does not take into consideration the costs of transporting goods and services. As repeatedly pointed out by Krugman (1991, 1993), in reality large trading blocs are formed between neighbouring countries, be it in Europe, America, Africa, or Asia, which account for a large share of a country's trade flows as the cost of transportation is low for neighbouring countries. Eliminating trade barriers within such 'natural' trading blocs, as Krugman calls them, therefore removes distorted relative prices to a larger extent than estimated on the basis of the share of income in the world economy of the countries in the trading bloc, therefore more rapidly leading to an increase in world welfare than suggested by the analysis in this section.

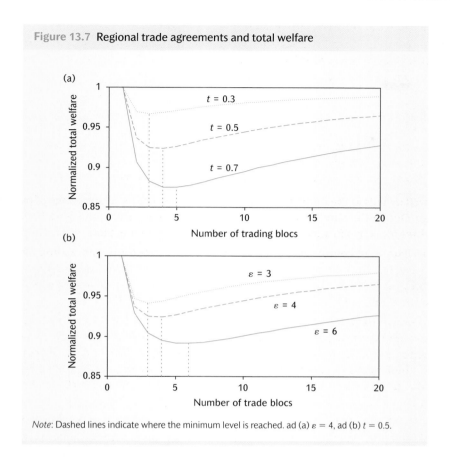

Figure 13.7 Regional trade agreements and total welfare

Note: Dashed lines indicate where the minimum level is reached. ad (a) $\varepsilon = 4$, ad (b) $t = 0.5$.

13.6 Europe and the European Union (EU)

The European economic integration process started after the Second World War with the European Coal and Steel Community, established in 1951 by the Treaty of Paris. As the name indicates, the ECSC was a sectoral agreement, establishing free trade among the member countries for the (at that time very important) coal and steel sectors only. Based on the devastating recent experience of the First World War and the Second World War, which cost the lives of millions of people and destroyed the economic, social, cultural, and historical fabric of many countries in Europe, one of the underlying ideas of strengthening the economic integration process of the major countries on the continent was to reduce the probability of future wars, particularly between France and Germany. Fortunately, there has been peace among the current EU member countries ever since, although the extent to which the economic integration process can take credit for this fact is of course open for discussion. Table 13.2 gives an overview of the continuation of the European economic integration process.

The Treaties of Rome in 1957 continued the sectoral integration process with the establishment of the European Atomic Energy Community (EURATOM), and started the total economic integration process with the establishment of the European Economic Community

Table 13.2 Overview of European Union economic integration

1951	ECSC	European Coal and Steel Community
	membership	Belgium, France, Luxembourg, the Netherlands, Italy, and W. Germany
1957	EURATOM	European Atomic Energy Community
1957	EEC	European Economic Community
1967	EC	European Communities, combining ECSC, EEC, and EURATOM
1973	Membership	+ United Kingdom, Ireland, and Denmark
1981	Membership	+ Greece
1986	Membership	+ Spain and Portugal
1990	Membership	+ East Germany (reunification of West and East Germany)
1993	EU	European Union
1995	Membership	+ Finland, Austria, and Sweden
1999	EMU	Economic and Monetary Union
2004	Membership	+ Cyprus, Czech Rep., Estonia, Hungary, Latvia, Lithuania, Malta, Poland, Slovenia, and Slovakia.

(EEC). The three organizations (ECSC, EEC, and EURATOM) were combined in the European Community (EC) in 1967. The Treaty of Maastricht (1991) established the European Union (EU, 1993) and provided the criteria for monetary integration in the Economic and Monetary Union (EMU, 1999). Over the years, the number of countries participating in the European integration process has increased from six to twenty-five, of which twelve countries (known as the euro area) have introduced the euro as their single currency; see Chapter 30.

The objective of the EEC Treaty was the establishment of a common market, which also allows for the 'four freedoms':

1. *Free movement of goods*. The common market requires not only the removal of tariffs and quantitative restrictions, but also the dismantling of other obstacles to free movement of goods. Most important in this respect was the Cassis de Dijon case in 1979. According to German regulations, Cassis de Dijon, a French fruit liqueur, did not contain enough alcohol (17 per cent rather than the minimum 32 per cent), and was therefore forbidden. The European Court of Justice ruled that a product legally brought to the market in one country of the EU also has to be accepted in another country. This principle ensures that different national regulations are mutually recognized, except for hazardous products, or for health, safety, or environmental reasons.

2. *Free movement of persons*. Workers have a right to work anywhere else in the EU (right of free movement) and individuals have the right to establish businesses anywhere else in the EU (right of establishment).

3. *Free movement of services*. The Cassis de Dijon verdict also holds for services, such that services offered in one EU country can also be offered in another EU country. The free

movement of persons and that of services are related, as the export of services frequently requires physical presence in the customer country.

4. *Free movement of capital*. Although capital controls were still operative in some countries until the late 1980s, restrictions on capital flows between EU countries have now been eliminated.

The main institutions of the European Union are:

- *The Council of the European Union*. Also known as the Council of Ministers, this central decision-making body meets in many different forms (as heads of states, or as ministers for Foreign Affairs, Agriculture, Transport, etc.).

- *The European Commission* administers and initiates policy in the EU. The Commission mediates between the member states and represents the EU in international negotiations.

- *The European Parliament*. This body, involved in decision and law making, is democratically chosen by the people of the EU member countries every four years, but has (too) limited power.

- *The European Court of Justice* provides judicial safeguards and is concerned with the interpretation of EU law, including actions brought before the court between member states and between the Commission and a member state.

- *The European Central Bank (ECB)*. A largely independent institution responsible for the monetary policy of the euro area, with price stability as the primary objective.

Two other European economic integration agreements outside the EU should be mentioned in this section. First, the Stockholm Convention established the European Free Trade Association (EFTA) in 1960. In the course of the twentieth century, many EFTA countries joined the EU, such that EFTA currently consists only of Iceland, Norway, Liechtenstein, and Switzerland. Second, the Central European Free Trade Area (CEFTA) was established in 1993 to reduce tariffs and other trade barriers and increase intra-regional trade. All CEFTA countries either have already joined the EU (Poland, Czech Republic, Slovakia, Hungary, and Slovenia) or want to join the EU (Bulgaria and Romania), which brings us to the next section on recent and future EU enlargement.

13.7 Recent enlargement of the European Union

Soon after the fall of the Berlin Wall in 1989, the EC established diplomatic relations with the countries of Central Europe, removed import quotas on a number of products, extended the Generalized System of Preferences (GSP; see Chapter 12), and concluded trade and cooperation agreements with many Central European countries. In 1993 at the Copenhagen European Council, the member states agreed that 'the associated countries in central and eastern Europe that so desire shall become members of the European Union'. All of this provided the candidate country meets the Copenhagen Criteria, that is:

- has achieved stability of institutions guaranteeing democracy, the rule of law, human rights, and respect for and protection of minorities;

- has achieved the existence of a functioning market economy as well as the capacity to cope with competitive pressure and market forces within the Union;

- has achieved the ability to take on the obligations of membership, including adherence to the aims of political, economic, and monetary Union;

- has created the conditions for its integration through the adjustment of its administrative structures, so that European Community legislation transposed into national legislation is implemented effectively through appropriate administrative and judicial structures.

As summarized in Table 13.3, no fewer than ten new countries joined the EU in 2004, while four more countries want to join the EU. It is generally expected that Bulgaria and Romania will be allowed to join in 2007. The prospects for the other two applicants (Croatia and Turkey) are less clear, partially in fear of the sheer (population) size of Turkey and its Muslim cultural background. The short-hand notation EU-15 is used to denote the EU members joining before 2004.

As suggested by the Copenhagen Criteria, there are substantial differences between the EU-15 countries and the candidate countries, which also differ substantially among themselves. The candidate countries, most of which were formerly centrally planned economies, are transforming into a more market-oriented economy, revising their laws and institutions, protecting human rights, and guaranteeing democracy. This does not mean that meeting the EU requirements will result in a straitjacket that makes all countries look alike; we certainly want to preserve the rich cultural, historical, and social diversity that makes Europe such a fascinating continent.

Table 13.4 provides details regarding the size in terms of land area, population, and GDP of the EU member countries, the EU applicants, and (for comparison purposes) of Japan and the USA. In addition, it provides details on the prosperity of these nations in terms of GDP per capita (corrected for differences in purchasing power). In terms of land area, France is the largest EU country, followed by Spain, Sweden, and Germany, while Malta is the smallest EU country. In terms of population, Germany is the largest EU country, followed by France, the UK, and Italy, while Luxembourg is the smallest EU country. In terms of total GDP, Germany is again the largest EU country, this time followed by the UK, France, and Italy, while Cyprus

Table 13.3 European Union: members and applicants, 2006

Member countries (EU-25)

- EU-15

Austria	Belgium	Denmark	Finland
France	Germany	Greece	Ireland
Italy	Luxembourg	Portugal	Spain
Sweden	The Netherlands	United Kingdom	

- 10 new members in 2004

Cyprus	Czech Rep.	Estonia	Hungary
Latvia	Lithuania	Malta	Poland
Slovakia	Slovenia		

Applicant countries

Bulgaria	Croatia	Romania	Turkey

Figure 13.8 The European Union, 2006

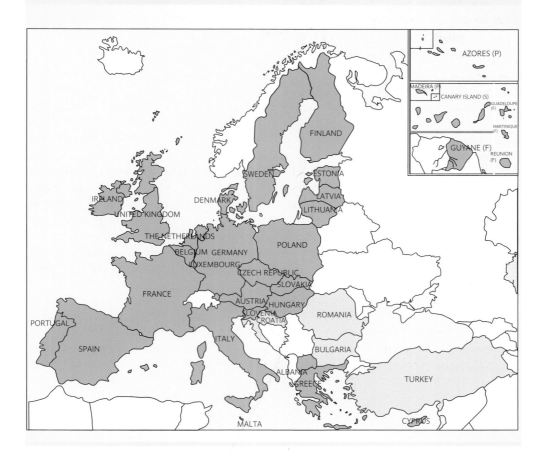

is the smallest EU country. In terms of prosperity, the differences between the EU countries are quite large. Luxembourg has by far the highest income per capita, followed by Ireland, Denmark, and Austria. The bottom nine places are occupied by new entrants in 2004, Latvia being the lowest at about 20 per cent of the per capita income level in Luxembourg. This diversity is illustrated in Figure 13.9 for land area, population, and income per capita.

As a whole, the EU-25 represents a formidable economic power, comparable to the USA. Although, with 457 million inhabitants, the EU-25 has more people than the USA (which has 292 million inhabitants), the American GDP level is slightly higher (+3 per cent) as a result of the about 61 per cent higher GDP level per capita (corrected for purchasing power) in the USA. When compared to Japan, the EU-25 has about 3.6 times as many people, earning a total income of about three times Japan's income level.

After long and painful negotiations which nearly failed and of which, according to *The Economist* (2000*a*), Germany's chancellor Gerhard Schröder complained that it 'makes me

Table 13.4 Economic statistics for the EU and selected countries

	GDP per capita	Population	Land area	Total GDP(bn)
EU-15				
Austria	28,000	8,140	82,730	228
Belgium	27,300	10,396	30,230	284
Denmark	28,300	5,397	42,430	153
Finland	26,900	5,220	304,590	140
France	25,600	59,900	550,100	1,533
Germany	24,600	82,531	348,950	2,030
Greece	19,200	11,041	128,900	212
Ireland	31,600	4,028	68,890	127
Italy	24,000	57,888	294,110	1,389
Luxembourg	50,700	452	2,586	23
Netherlands	27,400	16,258	33,880	445
Portugal	16,800	10,474	91,500	176
Spain	22,600	42,345	499,440	957
Sweden	27,100	8,976	411,620	243
United Kingdom	28,000	59,673	240,880	1,671
EU-15	25,100	382,722	3,130,836	9,606
EU entrants 2004				
Cyprus	19,000	730	9,240	14
Czech Rep.	16,800	10,211	77,280	172
Estonia	12,200	1,351	42,390	16
Hungary	14,600	. 10,117	92,100	148
Latvia	10,700	2,319	62,050	25
Lithuania	11,600	3,446	62,680	40
Malta	16,500	3,400	320	56
Poland	11,300	38,191	306,290	432
Slovakia	12,900	5,380	48,800	69
Slovenia	18,500	996	20,120	18
EU-25	23,100	456,863	3,852,106	10,554
EU applicants				
Bulgaria	7,500	7,801	110,630	59
Croatia	10,900	4,422	55,920	48
Romania	7,600	21,711	229,870	165
Turkey	6,800	70,712	769,630	481

Table 13.4 (*Cont.*)

	GDP per capita	Population	Land area	Total GDP(bn)
Japan	27,300	127,274	364,500	3,475
USA	37,100	291,685	9,159,000	10,822
Japan: index, EU-25 = 100	118	28	9	33
USA: index, EU-25 = 100	161	64	238	103

Notes: GDP per capita in pps (purchasing power standards; estimates for 2005); population in thousands (2004); size in km²; total GDP in billion pps.

Source: Eurostat and World Bank Development Indicators CD-ROM 2005.

Figure 13.9 EU diversity in size, population, and GDP per capita

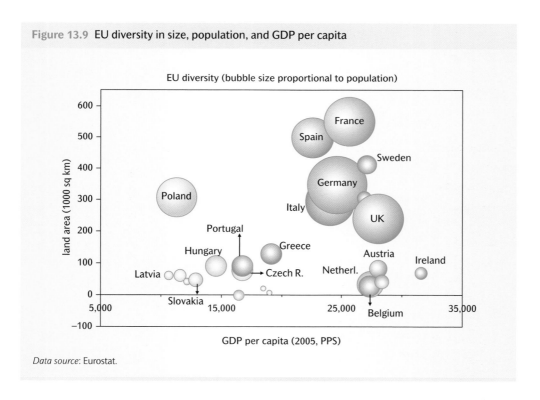

Data source: Eurostat.

sick', a major step forward in the EU enlargement process was taken in December 2000 in Nice, France. The Nice Treaty agreed on:

- *Majority voting*: more decisions can be taken with qualified majority, such as for trade negotiations in services. Other areas, such as tax and social-security policy, remain subject to national vetoes.

- *Rebalancing votes*: adjustment of the votes for the European Council, the European Parliament, and the Committees for the EU-15, the ten new entrants of 2004, and the potential entrants Bulgaria and Romania; see Table 13.5.

Table 13.5 Division of EU power after the Treaty of Nice

	European Council	European Parliament	Committees[a]
Germany	29	99	24
France	29	72	24
Italy	29	72	24
United Kingdom	29	72	24
Spain	27	50	21
The Netherlands	13	25	12
Belgium	12	22	12
Greece	12	22	12
Portugal	12	22	12
Sweden	10	18	12
Austria	10	17	12
Denmark	7	13	9
Finland	7	13	9
Ireland	7	12	9
Luxembourg	4	6	6
EU-15 total	237	535	222
Poland	27	50	21
Romania	14	33	15
Czech Rep.	12	20	12
Hungary	12	20	12
Bulgaria	10	17	12
Slovakia	7	13	9
Lithuania	7	12	9
Latvia	4	8	7
Slovenia	4	7	7
Estonia	4	6	7
Cyprus	4	6	6
Malta	3	5	5
Total	345	732	344

[a] This holds for (i) the Economic and Social Committee, and (ii) the Committee of the Regions.

- *European Commission*: the big countries give up the second commissioner from 2005. The maximum size of the commission may be put at twenty after 2007.
- *Flexibility*: groups of eight countries or more may pursue greater integration in certain areas (for example, the euro countries may decide on closer coordination of their financial and tax policies).

The rebalancing of the votes has given more power to the big EU countries, afraid of losing their power in an expanded EU with more countries. Most important in this respect is, of course, the number of votes in the Council, where many (i.e. more than 80 per cent) of the EU's decisions are now made by majority voting. A qualified majority requires not only about 74 per cent of the Council votes, but also the backing of at least 62 per cent of the population. The population rule ensures that Germany, as the most populous nation, becomes the EU's most powerful member, despite the fact that the big four countries all get 29 votes in the Council. None the less the small countries, that is all countries except the big four, have a disproportionately large influence in the Council as it requires a smaller population for them to get one vote in the Council than the EU average. The democratic principle of one man one vote does not hold here; in this respect one person from Luxembourg is about as important as five Irishmen, twelve Dutchmen, twenty Frenchmen (or Englishmen or Italians), or twenty-eight Germans.

13.8 Conclusions

There are many regional trade agreements in the world, in which countries are economically integrating by, for example, granting free access to their markets for the member countries (free trade area), in addition to pursuing a common external trade policy (customs union). We discuss some examples in Africa (COMESA), Asia (ASEAN), America (NAFTA, CACM, ANDEAN, CARICOM, MERCOSUR), and Europe (EU, EFTA, CEFTA). The rising popularity of economic integration is known as regionalism, to be contrasted with the multilateral WTO framework of removing trade barriers. Although a regional trade agreement in general increases welfare through increased trade flows (trade-creation), the discriminatory nature of the agreement that benefits insiders may reduce welfare through a shift towards less efficient producers (trade-diversion). A small new-trade general equilibrium model shows that the latter effect may be stronger for a fairly large range of trading blocs and elasticities of substitution, thus in general warning of a move away from multilateralism to regionalism. This argument seems to lose much of its force if the local nature of the regional agreements (and thus the high trade shares) are taken into consideration. The European Union presents the most powerful and successful economic integration scheme to date. Many Central and East European countries have recently joined the EU or want to join it. This requires large structural and political changes, both for the applicants and for the (rather undemocratic) political decision process of the EU. The monetary part of the European integration process, resulting in the Economic and Monetary Union (EMU), is discussed in Chapter 30.

Technical Note 13.1 Regionalism model

Using the exact price index P defined in equation (10.A4), in the regionalism model we get

$$P \equiv \left[\sum_{i=1}^{N} p_i^{1-\varepsilon} \right]^{1/(1-\varepsilon)}$$

(13.A1)

$$= \left[\sum_{i=1}^{N/b} 1 + \sum_{(N/b)+1}^{N} (1 + t)^{1-\varepsilon} \right]^{1/(1-\varepsilon)} = N \left\{ [b^{-1} + (1 - b^{-1})(1 - t)^{1-\varepsilon}] \right\}^{1/(1-\varepsilon)}$$

Thus, once we know the income level I in a trading bloc, equation (10.A4) gives us the demand for a particular variety, namely:

(13.A2)

$$c_j = p_j^{-\varepsilon} P^{\varepsilon-1} I = \begin{cases} \dfrac{I}{N(b^{-1} + (1 - b^{-1})(1 + t)^{1-\varepsilon})}, & \text{for } j \in \text{trading bloc} \\[3ex] \dfrac{(1 + t)^{-\varepsilon} I}{N(b^{-1} + (1 - b^{-1})(1 + t)^{1-\varepsilon})}, & \text{for } j \notin \text{trading bloc} \end{cases}$$

The income level I of a trading bloc is the sum of the production value N/b and the tariff revenue t levied per unit on the c_j goods sold of the $N(1-b^{-1})$ varieties imported from outside the trading bloc. Using the equation above, this implies:

(13.A3)

$$I = \frac{N}{b} + \frac{N(1 - b^{-1}) \, t \, (1 + t)^{-\varepsilon} I}{N(b^{-1} + (1 - b^{-1})(1 + t)^{1-\varepsilon})}$$

Solving this equation for the income level I gives

$$\left[1 - \frac{(1 - b^{-1}) \, t \, (1 + t)^{-\varepsilon}}{(b^{-1} + (1 - b^{-1})(1 + t)^{1-\varepsilon})} \right] I = \frac{N}{b}$$

(13.A4)

$$\left[\frac{(b^{-1} + (1 - b^{-1})(1 + t)^{1-\varepsilon}) - (1 - b^{-1}) \, t \, (1 + t)^{-\varepsilon}}{(b^{-1} + (1 - b^{-1})(1 + t)^{1-\varepsilon})} \right] I$$

$$= \left[\frac{b^{-1} + (1 - b^{-1})(1 + t)^{-\varepsilon}}{(b^{-1} + (1 - b^{-1})(1 + t)^{1-\varepsilon})} \right] I = \frac{N}{b}$$

$$I = \frac{N}{b} \left[\frac{(b^{-1} + (1 - b^{-1})(1 + t)^{1-\varepsilon})}{b^{-1} + (1 - b^{-1})(1 + t)^{-\varepsilon}} \right]$$

As shown in Chapter 10, the welfare of a trading bloc is equal to I/P. Since there are b trading blocs in the world, and using the above, total world welfare is equal to

(13.A5)

$$b \frac{I}{P} = b \frac{N}{b} \left[\frac{(b^{-1} + (1 - b^{-1})(1 + t)^{1-\varepsilon})}{b^{-1} + (1 - b^{-1})(1 + t)^{-\varepsilon}} \right] \frac{1}{N^{1/(1-\varepsilon)}(b^{-1} + (1 - b^{-1})(1 + t)^{1-\varepsilon})^{1-(1-\varepsilon)}}$$

$$= N^{\varepsilon/(\varepsilon-1)} \frac{[b^{-1} + (1 - b^{-1})(1 + t)^{1-\varepsilon}]^{\varepsilon/(\varepsilon-1)}}{b^{-1} + (1 - b^{-1})(1 + t)^{-\varepsilon}}$$

The figures in the text depict this total welfare level, normalized to unity if there is one trading bloc (global free trade).

Question 13.1

The European Union has some minor grapefruit producers (mostly in Cyprus, Italy, and Greece) and imports most grapefruit from the USA. On all imports of grapefruit the European Union levies a common tariff. Recently, Turkey has expressed ambitions to conquer the European grapefruit market by planting a high level of new grapefruit trees. These new farms are not yet as productive as their US counterparts (even when transport costs are taken into account) but will be cheaper once Turkey establishes a customs union with the European Union in agricultural products. Officials from the European Union worry about what will happen with the European grapefruit market and ask for your advice.

13.1A Draw a partial equilibrium framework of the European grapefruit market. Draw the demand and supply of grapefruit within Europe and the supply curves of the USA and Turkey. Indicate clearly the price of grapefruit in Europe, European production and European imports of grapefruit.

13.1B What happens to the imports, the production, and the price of grapefruit in Europe once it establishes a full customs union with Turkey?

13.1C What are the welfare effects of a full customs union with Turkey for consumers, producers and the EU governments? What is the total welfare effect?

13.1D If the European Union still wants to pursue a full customs union with Turkey, is there a loophole to increase welfare on the grapefruit market?

Question 13.2

A large number of papers has analysed the net welfare effect of regional trade agreements in a multi-country general equilibrium framework. Despite the analytical advances, however, the net welfare effect of regional trade agreements remains ambiguous. Two schools of economists have arisen. One school claims that regional trade agreements are likely to be more welfare enhancing. According to the other school, trade-diversion is likely to dominate trade-creation in most situations. Their disagreement is mainly on the importance of transport costs.

13.2A Explain how the results of the general equilibrium model of Krugman (see Section 13.5) change when transport costs are introduced.

13.2B Which regional trade agreements will economists mention when they want to stress that regional trade agreements are likely to be welfare enhancing?

13.2C Which regional trade agreements will economists name when they want to indicate that regional trade agreements are likely to deteriorate welfare?

Question 13.3

Most countries move from a relatively shallow type of economic integration to deeper types of economic integration. The main text describes, for example, that the European Union started out as a preferential trade agreement in 1951, a customs unions in 1968 and developed into a common market in 1993. Also for other regional trade agreements such a time line can be drawn. Search the Internet (or the main text) and do this for the regional trade agreements below.

13.3A COMESA

13.3B ASEAN

13.3C EAEC

13.3D CARICOM

See the Online Resource Centre for a Study Guide containing more questions
www.oxfordtextbooks.co.uk/orc/vanmarrewijk/

NOTES

1 *The Economist*, 3 March 2001, p. 77.

2 In this literature the weak phrase in the proposition that an individual 'is not worse off' after the formation of the customs union actually means that in general there is room for welfare improvement.

3 One 'unit' could, of course, refer to 1 billion, or 4 billion, or whatever the number of goods produced.

4 In Krugman (1991), which is based on the 'optimal' tariff approach, the minimum was reached at three trading blocs for a large range of elasticities of substitution.

II.C
TRADE
INTERACTIONS

Part II.C (Trade Interactions) brings the reader up to date with recent developments in international economics that have occurred in the last fifteen years or so. These are based on new interactions between international economics and other fields of economics; with economic geography, leading to a better explanation of location, with international business, leading to a better explanation of multinational firms, and with economic growth theory, leading to a better understanding of international differences in growth and development. Chapter 17 discusses the general implications of the insights that we have gained throughout this book for practical trade policy modelling.

GEOGRAPHICAL ECONOMICS

14

Blending some of the insights of the neoclassical trade model and the new trade model, in conjuction with factor mobility, allows us to provide a simple theory of location and agglomeration that is able to explain some empirical observations (such as Zipf's Law and the gravity equation).

14.1 Introduction

One of the most remarkable aspects of the global economic system is the unequal distribution of population and economic activity across the earth, see also Chapter 1. Millions of people are living close together in New York, Moscow, and Beijing. At the same time, there are large, virtually empty spaces available in the USA, Russia, and China. As we will illustrate in Section 14.2, the distribution of people and economic activity across space is not only remarkably unequal; it is also remarkably regular, both in terms of a pattern across space (Zipf's Law) and in terms of the interaction between economic centres (the gravity equation). The question arises, obviously, why economic activity is so unequally distributed, and why these regularities occur.

It has long been evident that these aspects cannot be adequately explained using a neo-classical framework. In particular, economies of scale and imperfect competition, interacting with some form of local advantages, are essential. This implies that it is rather complicated to *endogenously* determine the size of economic activity in different locations in a general equilibrium framework. It is therefore, in retrospect, not surprising that such an endogenous, general equilibrium determination of economic size was only fairly recently developed, in particular as it was awaiting the development of the appropriate tools for this endeavour in other fields of economics. The path-breaking contribution of the American economist Paul Krugman appeared in 1991. Since then many prominent researchers have published work on refinements, generalizations, and applications in this rapidly developing research area, which has become known as 'geographical economics' and combines elements from international economics, industrial organization, economic geography, spatial economics, urban economics, and endogenous growth.[1] The body of this chapter describes Krugman's original 'core' model. More recent alternative specifications, incorporating input–output linkages and factor abundance, are available leading essentially to the same conclusions; see Box 14.3.

Famous economists	James Peter Neary
 Fig. 14.1 James Peter Neary (1950–)	Born in Ireland and educated at University College Dublin (UCD) and Oxford, Peter Neary returned to UCD and used Dublin as a base to visit the world. He seems to be indefatigable in his economic analysis, organizational enthusiasm, and his travel explorations. Virtually all economists you meet know him (and like him). Amazingly, he also knows all of them personally. One of the first papers he published, on sector-specific capital (see Box 6.2), turned into a classic contribution almost instantly. Since then he has worked together with many economists on, for example, the Dutch disease, policy choice, and strategic commitment. Neary (2001) provides an excellent overview of the geographical economics literature, while Neary (2003) manages to succesfully tackle the problem of strategic interaction among firms in a general equilibrium setting.

14.2 Zipf's Law and the gravity equation

This section discusses two regularities in the unequal distribution of people and economic activity across space, namely (i) regarding the distribution pattern of centres of activity and (ii) regarding the interactions between these centres of activity.

Distribution pattern (Zipf's Law)

The regularity in the distribution pattern, known as Zipf's Law, is most easily illustrated using a concrete example. Take the largest urban agglomeration in India. In 1991, the most recent year for which we have reliable data, this was Bombay (now Mumbai), with more than 12.5 million inhabitants. Give this city rank number 1. Then take the second largest urban agglomeration (Calcutta, with more than 11 million inhabitants) and give this rank number 2. The third largest city (Delhi, with 8.4 million inhabitants) is given rank number 3, etc. Once you have arranged all 165 urban Indian agglomerations for which data are available in this way, you take the natural logarithm of the city size and the city rank. When the latter are plotted in a scatter diagram, the outcome is an almost perfect straight line; see Figure 14.2.

Obviously, there is a negative relationship between size and rank by construction. The puzzling feature is why this is an almost perfect log-linear straight line. A simple linear regression of the data plotted in Figure 14.2 gives (*t*-values in parentheses):

(14.1) $$\ln (population_i) = \underset{(528.4)}{16.94} - \underset{(-138.4)}{1.048} \ln (rank_i); \quad R^2 = 0.992$$

This regression explains 99.2 per cent of the variance in city size. Based on this estimate, we would predict the size of the population of urban agglomeration number 100, for example, to

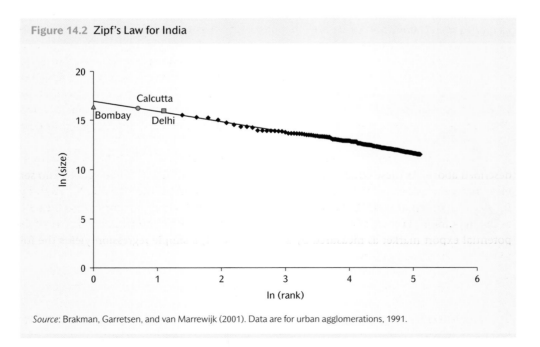

Figure 14.2 Zipf's Law for India

Source: Brakman, Garretsen, and van Marrewijk (2001). Data are for urban agglomerations, 1991.

be 182,000 people. This is very close to the actual size of number 100 (Tumkur), with a population of 180,000. This regularity in the distribution of city sizes holds not only for India, but also for the USA, Brazil, France, China, Russia, etc.[2] Apparently, hitherto poorly understood economic forces play an important role in determining the size distribution of cities, regardless of the economic structure, organization, wealth, and history of a nation. Ever since George Kingsley Zipf (1949) presented evidence on this regularity, scientists have been searching, rather unsuccessfully, for an adequate explanation.

Interaction (gravity equation)

There is also a pattern in the interaction between centres of economic activity. It is known as the 'gravity equation', and is related to Zipf's Law. The gravity equation, too, is most easily illustrated using a concrete example, for which we focus on the export flows of Germany, the dominant European economy. In 1998 France was the largest export market for Germany, with a value of $60.3 billion. The second largest German export market was the USA ($51.1 billion), followed by the UK, Italy, the Netherlands, Belgium, Austria, and Switzerland. The 'local' flavour of this top-export market list is immediately evident. Except for the USA, by far the world's largest economy, the most important German export markets are in Germany's direct vicinity. In this respect, its tiny neighbours, the Netherlands, Belgium, Austria, and Switzerland, are each more important to Germany than the mighty Japanese economy, which ranks as Germany's thirteenth export market. In fact, as an export market Japan is even less important for Germany than the Czech Republic, despite the fact that Japan's GDP is 67 times as large.[3]

The export of goods and services from one country to another involves time, effort, and hence costs. Goods have to be physically loaded and unloaded, transported by truck, train, ship, or plane, packed, insured, traced, etc. before they reach their destination. There they have to be unpacked, checked, assembled, and displayed before they can be sold to the consumer or an intermediate goods firm. A distribution and maintenance network has to be established, and the exporter will have to familiarize herself with the (legal) rules and procedures in another country, usually in another language and embedded in a different culture. All of this involves costs, which tend to increase with 'distance'. As indicated above, this can be both physical distance, which may be hampered or alleviated by geographical phenomena such as mountain ranges or easy access to good waterways, and political, cultural, or social distance, which also require time and effort before one can successfully engage in international business.

We use the term 'transport costs' as a shorthand notation for both types of distance described above. As these costs increase it will become more difficult to trade goods and services between nations. As a proxy for transport costs we calculated the 'distance to Germany' for all German export markets, taking the coordinates of the geographic centre of each nation as the hypothetical centre of economic activity. Also taking into consideration the size of the potential export market as measured by a country's GDP, a simple regression yields the following result (t-value in parentheses):

$$(14.2) \quad \ln (export_i) = \underset{(-0.40)}{0.281} + \underset{34.86}{1.033} \ln (GDP_i) - \underset{(-12.77)}{0.869} \ln (distance_i); \quad R^2 = 0.926$$

This simple relationship, which explains 92.6 per cent of the variance in German export size, is illustrated with respect to the distance to the German market in Figure 14.3, that is after

Figure 14.3 German exports and distance

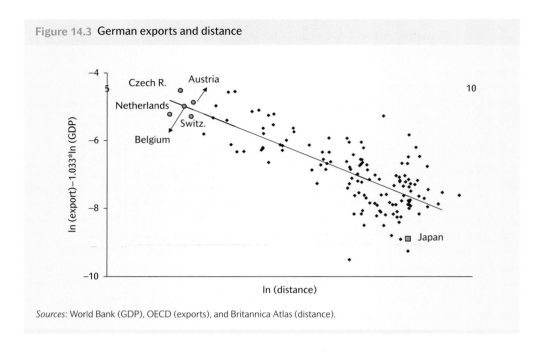

Sources: World Bank (GDP), OECD (exports), and Britannica Atlas (distance).

correcting the size of the export flow for the size of the destination market using the estimated coefficient of equation (14.2). The five small German neighbours mentioned above are in the top left corner and are all more important export markets than Japan, certainly after the GDP correction, which is in the bottom right corner. Since the actual German exports to Japan are below the regression line in Figure 14.3, the export flows from Germany to Japan are low even after correcting for the large distance. The empirical relationship known as the 'gravity equation', first applied to international trade between nations by Jan Tinbergen (1962), holds quite generally for all countries, irrespective of, but influenced by, wealth, development level, cultural, political, and sociological organization, and history. Since one of the main objectives of geographical economics is to provide a better understanding of the unequal distribution of economic activity across space and its regularities in terms of distribution pattern and interaction, it is time to have a closer look at the basic structure of this model.

14.3 The structure of the model

This section gives a non-technical overview of the general structure of the geographical economics model, as illustrated in Figure 14.4 (with so-called 'callouts' a–g). Our presentation will only identify two regions, labelled 1 and 2. There are two sectors in the economy, as usual manufactures and food. Consumers in region 1 consist of farm workers and manufacturing workers. Similarly for region 2. The farm workers earn their income by working for the farmers in their region. If they own the farm, it is as if they hire themselves. They then play a dual role, as both farmers and farm workers. The income stream of the farm workers is part of a bilateral transfer: they receive an income from the farmer (the farm wage rate) and in return they have to supply labour services to the farmer. All such bilateral transfers are indicated with

Figure 14.4 Structure of the geographical economics model

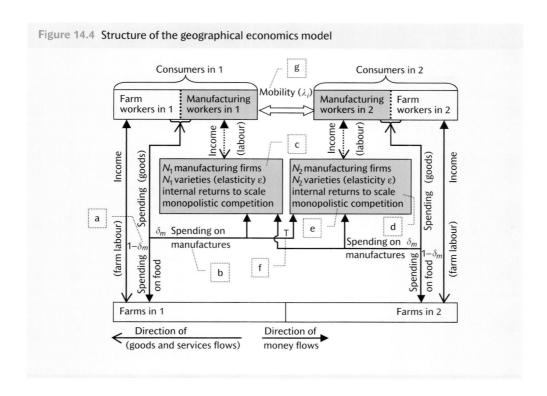

double-headed arrows in Figure 14.4. The closed-headed arrows refer to the direction of money flows, that is of income and spending. What the flow represents exactly is indicated along the lines connecting the arrow heads. The open-headed arrow refers to the direction of goods flows. These are indicated in parentheses along the lines connecting the arrow heads. The farmers in region 1 use the labour services of the farm workers from region 1 to produce food under constant returns to scale and perfect competition. They sell this food to the consumers, either in region 1 or in region 2. There are no transport costs for food.

The manufacturing sector consists of N_1 firms in region 1 and N_2 firms in region 2. Each manufacturing firm produces a differentiated good; that is, it produces a unique variety of manufactures, using only labour under internal economies of scale. This implies that the firms have monopolistic power, which they use in determining the price of their product. There are transport costs involved in selling a manufactured good in another region. These costs do not arise if the manufactured good is sold in the region in which it is produced. As a result of the transport costs involved in exporting manufactured goods to another region, firms will charge a higher price in the other region than at home. The manufacturing workers earn their income (the manufacturing wage rate) by supplying labour to the firms in the manufacturing sector of their region.

Demand

The consumers spend their income on food and manufactures. Since food is a homogeneous good they do not care if it is produced in region 1 or in region 2. As there are no transport costs for food it fetches the same price in both regions (implying that farmers earn the same wage in both regions). The optimal spending of income I is determined in two stages. At the first stage the consumers decide how much to spend on food and manufactures in general. Using the Cobb–Douglas utility function of Chapter 7 (Section 7.3), we already know the outcome: a constant share δ_m of income is spent on manufactures and $1-\delta_m$ on food (callout a). At the second stage the consumers decide how much of their income to spend on a particular variety of manufactures. Using the Dixit–Stiglitz approach of Chapter 10 (Section 10.3) gives demand as in equation (10.4), with $\delta_m I$ as the income term since income $(1 - \delta_m)I$ is spent on food (callout b). As discussed in Chapter 10, this results in a constant price elasticity of demand ε (callout c).

Supply

Food production is characterized by constant returns to scale and is produced under conditions of perfect competition. Workers in the food industry, which is used as numéraire, are assumed to be immobile. Given the total labour force, which we will normalize to 1, a fraction $1-\delta_m$ works in the food sector.[4] Production in the food sector equals, by choice of units, food employment: $F = (1- \delta_m)$. Since farm workers are paid the value of marginal product, their wage is 1. Production in the manufacturing sector is characterized by the internal economies of scale of Chapter 10: $l_i = f + mx_i$, where l_i is the amount of labour necessary to produce x_i units of variety i. The coefficients f and m are, respectively, the fixed and marginal labour input requirements (callout d). The market structure for manufactures is one of monopolistic competition (see Chapter 10), leading to a constant mark-up of price over marginal costs. Entry and exit into the manufacturing sector until (excess) profits are zero gives the constant optimal scale of production for each variety, see Technical Note 10.2. This production size per variety determines the number of varieties produced in a region (callout e).

Transport costs

Transport costs are modelled using *iceberg* transport costs, as discussed in Chapter 9. The parameter $T \geq 1$ denotes the number of goods that need to be shipped to ensure that one unit of a variety of manufactures arrives per unit of distance (i.e. the distance between regions 1 and 2). We assume that the distance of a location to itself is 0 (callout f).

 Box 14.1   The relevance of transport costs

Adam Smith noted the importance of locations near the coast with lower costs of transport, 'so, it is upon the sea-coast, and along the banks of navigable rivers, that industry of every kind naturally begins to sub-divide and improve itself, and it is frequently not till a long time after that those improvements extend themselves to the inland part of the country'.

Many measures, such as travel time, have been constructed to estimate transport cost. The most straightforward measure in international trade is the difference between the so-called CIF (cost, insurance, freight) and FOB (free on board) quotations of trade. CIF measures the value of imports from the point of entry, while FOB measures the value from a carrier in the exporting 'port'. ≫

≫ The difference between these two values is a measure of the cost of getting an item from the exporting country to the importing country. The ratio [(CIF/FOB) − 1] × 100%, reported in Table 14.1, thus provides an estimate of the transport costs, although it clearly underestimates the actual transport costs of international trade (note that products with very high transport costs are not traded at all). Different goods have, of course, different transport costs. Goods with a high value added have a relatively low CIF/FOB ratio, while perishable goods have a higher ratio. For the USA, for example, the *ad valorem* freight rate is 7.6 per cent for food and live animals, but only 2.25 per cent for machinery and transport equipment.

Table 14.1 **Estimated transport costs, based on CIF/FOB ratio, 1965–90**

Country	Transport costs (%)
Australia	10.3
Austria	4.1
Canada	2.7
Denmark	4.5
France	4.2
West Germany	3.0
Greece	13.0
Ireland	5.0
Italy	7.1
Japan	9.0
The Netherlands	5.6
New Zealand	11.5
Norway	2.7
Philippines	7.6
Portugal	10.3
Singapore	6.1
Spain	6.4
Sweden	3.5
Switzerland	1.8
Thailand	11.0
UK	6.0
USA	4.9

Source: Radelet and Sachs (1998).

≫

>> The shipping costs are higher for countries located far away from major markets (New Zealand) and for landlocked countries (Nepal). For example, the landlocked developing countries (not shown in the table) have on average 50 per cent higher transport costs than coastal developing economies. Since a doubling of trading cost appears to reduce economic growth by 0.5 per cent for developing countries and a large part of Africa is landlocked, this partially explains Africa's poor growth performance.

As a final indication of the importance of transport costs, we can compare freight costs with other trade costs, such as tariffs. For the USA, industry-level transport costs as a percentage of imports range from 1.9 to 8.5 per cent, with a mean of 4.8 per cent. Industry-level tariffs range from 0.5 to 14.4 per cent, with a mean of 4.1 per cent. Transport costs as such, therefore, seem to be at least as important as policy-induced trade barriers. Note, however, that the mnemonic transport costs T used in the main text are inclusive of such policy-induced trade barriers (as are cultural, sociological, etc. barriers). Although data are always subject to measurement error, the impression remains that trade costs are substantial, and cannot be ignored.

Information source: Radelet and Sachs (1998), Davis (1998), and Hummels (1999a,1999b).

Figure 14.5 Division of labour over the regions

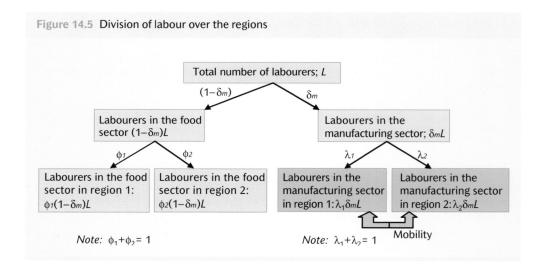

14.4 Multiple locations and equilibrium

Now that we have introduced two regions and transport costs, it becomes important to know where the economic agents are located. We therefore have to (i) specify a notation to show how labour is distributed over the two regions, and (ii) investigate what the consequences are for some of the demand and supply equations discussed in Section 14.3. To start with point (i), we have already introduced the parameter δ_m to denote the fraction of the labour force in the manufacturing sector, such that $1-\delta_m$ is the fraction of labour in the food sector. We now assume that of the labourers in the food sector a fraction $\varnothing_i$ is located in region i, and of the labourers in the manufacturing sector a fraction λ_i is located in region i. Figure 14.5 illustrates the division of labour. The boxes for the manufacturing sector are shaded, as in Figure 14.4, to indicate that their size can increase or decrease as a result of the mobility of the manufacturing workforce.

Point (ii) involves more work. We will concentrate on region 1. Similar remarks hold for region 2. It is easiest to start with the producers. Since there are $\varnothing_1(1- \delta_m)$ farm workers in region 1 and production is proportional to the labour input, food production in region 1 equals $\varnothing_1(1- \delta_m)$, which is equal to the income generated by the food sector in region 1 and the wage income paid to farm workers there. As a result of transport costs, the wage rate paid to manufacturing workers in region 1 will in general differ from the wage rate paid to manufacturing workers in region 2. We will identify these with a sub-index, so W_1 is the manufacturing wage in region 1. From now on, whenever we speak of 'the wage rate' we refer to the manufacturing wage rate. If we know the wage rate W_1 in region 1, we know from the mark-up pricing rule that the price charged in region 1 by a firm located in region 1 is equal to mW_1/ρ. The price this firm will charge in region 2 is T times higher than in region 1 as a result of the transport costs. Note that this holds for all N_1 firms located in region 1. Finally, since there are $\lambda_1\delta_m$ manufacturing workers in region 1, the number of firms N_1 located in region 1 is $N_1 = \lambda_1\delta_m/f\varepsilon$, which is proportional to the number of manufacturing workers in region 1 (see Chapter 10).

The price a firm charges to a consumer for a unit of a good depends both on the location of the firm (which determines the wage rate the firm will have to pay to its workers) and on the location of the consumer (which determines whether or not the consumer will have to pay for the transport costs of the good). As a result, the price index of manufactures will differ between the two regions. Again, we identify these with a sub-index, so P_1 is the price *index* in region 1. We can, however, be more specific since we have just derived the price a firm will charge in each region, and how many firms there are in each region. Substituting this in the demand function gives (see Technical Note 14.1):

$$(14.3) \qquad P_1 = \left[\underbrace{\lambda_1 W_1^{1-\varepsilon}}_{\substack{locally \\ produced}} + \underbrace{\lambda_2 T^{1-\varepsilon} W_2^{1-\varepsilon}}_{imported} \right]^{1/(1-\varepsilon)}$$

Thus, the price index in region 1 is essentially a weighted average of the price of locally produced goods and imported goods from region 2. Estimation of the impact of location on the consumption decisions of consumers requires us to know their income level, which brings us to the determination of equilibrium below.

We now have to establish the equilibrium relationships to tie up any loose ends. Together with the shaded boxes in Figure 14.4, referring to the mobility of firms and manufacturing workers, this determines the spatial distribution of economic activity. We proceed in three steps. First, we explain the *short-run* equilibrium relationships, that is for a given distribution of the manufacturing labour force. Second, we discuss the dynamics, that is how we move through a sequence of short-run equilibria (without factor mobility) over time to a *long-run* equilibrium (with factor mobility). Third, the *analysis* of both short-run and long-run equilibria is rather complex, so it is dealt with in Section 14.5.

Short-run equilibrium

In the short run, the distribution of the manufacturing workforce over the regions is given and cannot be changed instantaneously. We therefore want to establish the equilibrium relationships for an arbitrary distribution of the labour force. There are no profits for firms in the manufacturing sector (because of entry and exit), nor for the farmers (because of constant returns to scale and perfect competition). This implies that all income earned in the economy derives from the wages earned in the two sectors. This gives us the equilibrium relationship for income I_i in a region, which is equal to the sum of the farm wages ($\phi_i(1 - \delta_m)$ workers with a wage rate of 1) and the manufacturing wages ($\lambda_i \delta_m$ workers with a wage rate of W_i). For region 1 this is equal to:

(14.4)
$$I_1 = \underbrace{\lambda_1 \delta_m W_1}_{\substack{manufacturing \\ income}} + \underbrace{\phi_1(1 - \delta_m)}_{\substack{food \\ income}}$$

Demand in region 1 for products from region 1 is the sum of all individual demands by consumers in region 1. It depends on the aggregate income I_1, the price index P_1, and the price mW_1/ρ charged by a producer from region 1 for a locally sold good in region 1. Similarly, demand in region 2 for products from region 1 depends on aggregate income I_2, price index P_2, and the price TmW_1/ρ charged by a producer from region 1 for a good sold in region 2. Total demand for a producer in region 1 is the sum of the demand from region 1 and the demand from region 2, which depends on income in *both* regions, transport costs, and the price charged relative to the price index. Equating total demand to the supply determines equilibrium in the manufacturing sector (see Technical Note 14.2):

(14.5)
$$W_1 = [I_1 P_1^{\varepsilon-1} + I_2 T^{1-\varepsilon} P_2^{\varepsilon-1}]^{1/\varepsilon}$$

Intuitively, the equation makes perfect sense; wages in region 1 can be higher if this region is located close to large markets. The attractiveness of a region is related to the purchasing power of all regions and relative to the distance from the market. The advantage of using a general equilibrium approach is that the price indices and income levels, which play a crucial role, are determined endogenously.

Given the distribution of the manufacturing workforce λ_i, we have now derived the short-run equilibrium equations for region 1. They are equations (14.3), determining price index P_1, (14.4), determining income level I_1, and (14.5), determining the wage rate W_1. Similar equations hold for region 2, giving a total of six non-linear short-run equilibrium equations, discussed below and analysed in Section 14.5.

Discussion of symmetric example

We briefly discuss three possible short-run equilibria in a two-region version of the model. The two regions are identical in all respects, except possibly regarding the distribution of the manufacturing labour force. In particular, we also assume that the farm workers are equally divided over the two regions, that is $\phi_1 = \phi_2 = 1/2$. For clarity, we reiterate the short-run equilibrium equations for both regions.

(14.3′)
$$P_1 = [\lambda_1 W_1^{1-\varepsilon} + \lambda_2 T^{1-\varepsilon} W_2^{1-\varepsilon}]^{1/(1-\varepsilon)}; \quad P_2 = [\lambda_1 T^{1-\varepsilon} W_1^{1-\varepsilon} + \lambda_2 W_2^{1-\varepsilon}]^{1/(1-\varepsilon)}$$

(14.4′)
$$I_1 = \lambda_1 \delta_m W_1 + (1 - \delta_m)/2; \quad I_2 = \lambda_2 \delta_m W_2 + (1 - \delta_m)/2$$

(14.5′)
$$W_1 = [I_1 P_1^{\varepsilon-1} + I_2 T^{1-\varepsilon} P_2^{\varepsilon-1}]^{1/\varepsilon}; \quad W_2 = [I_1 T^{1-\varepsilon} P_1^{\varepsilon-1} + I_2 P_2^{\varepsilon-1}]^{1/\varepsilon}$$

Although we have now stripped the short-run equilibrium of the geographical economics model down to its bare essentials in its simplest version (two regions, identical in all respects except for the manufacturing labour force), it only yields to analysis in three special cases for the distribution of the manufacturing labour force, discussed below.

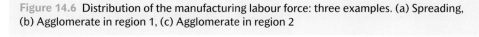

Figure 14.6 Distribution of the manufacturing labour force: three examples. (a) Spreading, (b) Agglomerate in region 1, (c) Agglomerate in region 2

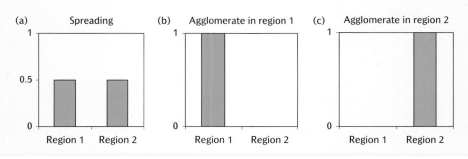

- *Spreading*: panel (a) of Figure 14.6. Suppose the two regions are identical in *all* respects, that is, the manufacturing workforce is also evenly distributed $\lambda_1 = \lambda_2 = 1/2$. Naturally, we then expect the wage rates of the short-run equilibrium to be the same for the two regions. Can we explicitly calculate this wage rate? Yes, if we're clever enough. One way to proceed is to guess an equilibrium wage rate, and then verify if we guessed right. This turns out to work if we guess that the equilibrium wage rates are $W_1 = W_2 = 1$ (use these values to calculate the price index in equation (14.3′) and the income level in equation (14.4′), then substitute the result in equation (14.5′) to verify that $W_1 = W_2 = 1$). Note that in the spreading equilibrium all variables are the same for the two regions; therefore the real wages are the same as well.

- *Agglomeration in region* 1: panel (b) of Figure 14.6. Suppose now that all manufacturing activity is agglomerated in region 1 ($\lambda_1 = 1$), such that there are no manufacturing labourers in region 2 ($\lambda_2 = 0$). Can we determine the equilibrium? Yes. Using the same procedure as above shows that $W_1 = 1$ is a solution.

- *Agglomeration in region* 2: panel (c) of Figure 14.6. This is the mirror image of the second situation described above.

We were able to derive the short-run equilibrium analytically for three separate cases: $\lambda_1 = 0$ (agglomeration in region 2), $\lambda_1 = 1/2$ (spreading), and $\lambda_1 = 1$ (agglomeration in region 1). Unfortunately, these are the only three cases. In all other circumstances, and recall that λ_1 can vary all the way from 0 to 1 so there are infinitely many other cases, one cannot derive the short-run equilibrium analytically. So we have to find another way to determine these equilibria, and explain what they mean in economic terms. We will do that numerically rather than analytically; see Section 14.5.

Dynamics and long-run equilibrium

The introduction of factor mobility implies that the shaded boxes in Figures 14.4 and 14.5, illustrating the structure of the model, can change in size over time, which in turn implies that the short-run equilibrium changes. Recall that labour is the only factor of production. We assume that the mobile workers react to differences in the real wage w, which adequately measures the utility level achieved. For different regions, the real wage is $w_r = W_r P_r^{-\delta}$; see the

Table 14.2 When is a long-run equilibrium reached?

Possibility 1	Possibility 2	Possibility 3
If the real wage for manufacturing workers in region 1 is the same as the real wage for manufacturing workers in region 2	All manufacturing workers are located in region 1 (agglomeration in region 1)	All manufacturing workers are located in region 2 (agglomeration in region 2)

Technical Notes. The adjustment of the short-run equilibrium over time is very simple. If the real wage for manufacturing workers is higher in region 1 than in region 2, we expect that manufacturing workers will leave region 2 and settle in region 1. If the real wage is higher in region 2 than in region 1, we expect the reverse to hold. We let the parameter η denote the speed with which manufacturing workers react to differences in the real wage, and use the simple dynamic system:

$$(14.6) \qquad \underbrace{\frac{d\lambda_1}{\lambda_1}}_{\substack{change \\ labour\ in\ 1}} = \underbrace{\eta}_{\substack{adj. \\ speed}} \underbrace{(w_1 - \overline{w})}_{\substack{wage \\ difference}}; \quad \text{where} \quad \overline{w} = \underbrace{\lambda_1 w_1 + \lambda_2 w_2}_{average\ real\ wage}$$

Note that $\overline{w}$ denotes the average real wage in the economy. A similar equation holds for region 2. Although this is essentially an *ad hoc* dynamic specification, it can be grounded in evolutionary game theory; see Weibull (1995), or otherwise justified, see Brakman, Garretsen, and van Marrewijk (2001). Now that we have specified how the manufacturing workforce reacts to differences in the real wage between regions, we can also note when a long-run equilibrium is reached. This occurs when one of three possibilities arises, as summarized in Table 14.2, namely (i) if the distribution of the manufacturing workforce between regions 1 and 2 is such that the real wage is equal in the two regions, not necessarily the symmetric equilibrium, (ii) if all manufacturing workers are located in region 1, or (iii) if all manufacturing workers are located in region 2.

14.5 Computer simulations: getting started

Table 14.3 did not specify the distribution of manufacturing workers, which is necessary for performing simulations. However, we not only want to use simulations to find *a* solution for *a* parameter setting of the model; we also want to learn something about the structure of the model, in this case, by investigating how the short-run equilibrium changes if the distribution of the manufacturing workers changes. Varying λ_1 between 0 and 1 gives a complete description of all possible distributions of the mobile workforce. We focus attention on the real wage in region 1 relative to the real wage in region 2, as it gives us an indication of the dynamic forces operating in the model, see equation (14.6). Once we find a short-run equilibrium for a distribution of the mobile labour force, it is easy to calculate the relative real wage w_1/w_2.

Figure 14.7 illustrates how the relative real wage in region 1 (w_1/w_2) varies as the share of the mobile workforce in region 1 (λ_1) varies. It is the result of 59 separate simulations in which the value of λ_1 is gradually increased from 0 to 1. Each time, the short-run equilibrium is calculated using the procedure described above. Then the relative real wage is calculated, giving 1 observation in the figure. What can we learn from it?

First, we argued that the mobile workforce has an incentive to move to regions with a higher real wage, such that a short-run equilibrium is also a long-run equilibrium if the real

Box 14.2 **Tool: Computer simulations**

In Section 14.4 we argued that the short-run equilibrium (for a given distribution of the manufacturing workforce) can be solved analytically in only three special cases. For all other situations, however, we can provide numerical solutions based on computer simulations to get a better grip on the economic forces active in the model. Simulations are becoming an increasingly popular tool in economics (see also Chapter 15) now that easy-to-use software has become widely available and personal computers are powerful and affordable enough to solve problems beyond the reach of mainframe computers only two decades ago. We first explain how computer simulations are performed.

Equations (14.3'–14.5') determine income I_r, price index P_r, and wage rate W_r in region r, respectively, given (i) the distribution λ_r of the manufacturing workforce, and (ii) the parameters of the model, that is the share of income δ_m spent on manufactures, the transport costs T, and the elasticity of substitution ε. If we have found a solution for these three equations for each region, we have found a short-run equilibrium in which world demand for food and each variety of manufactures is equal to world supply and no producer is earning excess profits. Five requirements must be met to perform simulations.

1. We must be clear what it is we are solving for. The short-run equilibrium determines the *endogenous* variables: income I_r, price index P_r, and wage rate W_r for each region r (and in doing so also gives us the real wages; see below). So we must determine numeric values of I_r, P_r, and W_r for which equations (14.3'–14.5') hold.

2. It must be realized that the solutions for the endogenous variables depend on the values of λ_r (the distribution of the mobile labour force, fixed in the short run) and the values of all the *parameters* (δ_m, ρ, ε, and T). This implies that we cannot start to find solutions for the endogenous variables before specifying values for the exogenous variables and parameters. Table 14.3 lists these for the 'base scenario', in which the share of income spent on manufactures δ_m is fairly low at 0.4, the substitution parameter ρ is 0.8, and the transport costs T are 1.7. The parameter σ will be discussed below.[5]

3. We must find a *solution method*, that is a well-specified procedure that will lead us to solving equations (14.3'–14.5') for numeric values of the endogenous variables, given the chosen levels of the exogenous variables and parameters. Several options are available at this point, but in this case the order of equations readily suggests a solution method, labelled 'sequential iterations'. It works as follows:

   (i) Guess an initial solution for the wage rate in the two regions, say ($W_{1,0}$, $W_{2,0}$), where 0 indicates the number of the iteration (we will use $W_{1,0} = W_{2,0} = 1$).
   (ii) Using ($W_{1,0}$, $W_{2,0}$) calculate the price indices ($P_{1,0}$, $P_{2,0}$) and the income levels ($I_{1,0}$, $I_{2,0}$) as implied by equations (14.3') and (14.4').
   (iii) Using ($I_{1,0}$, $I_{2,0}$) and ($P_{1,0}$, $P_{2,0}$) as calculated in step (ii) determine a new possible solution for the wage rate ($W_{1,1}$, $W_{2,1}$) as implied by equation (14.5').
   (iv) Repeat steps (ii) and (iii) until a solution is found.

4. We must specify a *stopping criterion*. The above description of the solution method casually mentioned in step (iv) to 'repeat steps (ii) and (iii) until a solution is found', but when is a ⟫

⟫ solution found? How close should we get to be satisfied that the numeric values we found are indeed a solution to equations (14.3'–14.5')? We used as a stopping criterion the condition that the absolute value of the relative change in the wage rate should not exceed some small value σ from one iteration to the next for all regions r :

$$(14.7) \qquad \left| \frac{W_{r,iteration} - W_{r,iteration-1}}{W_{r,iteration-1}} \right| < \sigma, \quad \text{for all } r.$$

5. Finally, we must choose a *programming language* and write a small program to actually perform the above calculations. Again, several options are available, but we used Gauss™, a widely used mathematical programming language, for our simulations.[6]

Table 14.3 Base-scenario parameter configuration

$\delta_m = 0.4$	$\rho = 0.8$	$T = 1.7$	$\sigma = 0.0001$

Figure 14.7 The relative real wage in region 1, base scenario

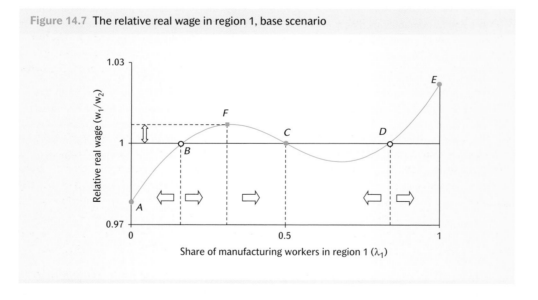

wage for the mobile workforce is the same in all regions. A long-run equilibrium therefore requires that the relative real wage is 1, as long as there are mobile labourers in both regions. It is only when a long-run equilibrium implies complete agglomeration (one region ends up with all mobile labourers, either $\lambda_1 = 0$ or $\lambda_1 = 1$) that the relative real wage is not equal to one (see points A and E).[7] In Figure 14.7 the long-run equilibria B, C, and D are reached for $w_1/w_2 = 1$. There are two types of long-run equilibria: (i) spreading of manufacturing production over the two regions (point C), and (ii) complete agglomeration of manufacturing production in either region (points A and E). The figure illustrates that there is a third type of long-run equilibrium in which manufacturing production is *partially* agglomerated in one of the two regions (points B and D), leading to a total of five long-run equilibria. It would have been very hard to find equilibria B and D analytically.

Second, the figure gives us a clear feel for the dynamics of the system, allowing us to distinguish between stable and unstable equilibria. Suppose, for example, that $\lambda_1 = F$ in Figure 14.7. Note that the mobile workforce is smaller in region 1 than in region 2. As illustrated, the associated short-run equilibrium implies $w_1/w_2 > 1$, as indicated by the double-headed arrow. The higher real wage in region 1 gives the mobile labourers an incentive to move from region 2 to region 1. This migration process into region 1 represents an increase of λ_1 in Figure 14.7. Migration will continue until the spreading equilibrium at point C is reached, where the real wages are equalized. Similar reasoning, leading to the spreading equilibrium at point C, would hold for any arbitrary initial distribution of the mobile labour force strictly in between points B and D, which could therefore be called the 'basin of attraction' for the spreading equilibrium. The spreading equilibrium is a stable equilibrium, in the sense that any deviation of the mobile labour force from point C within its basin of attraction will activate economic forces to bring us back to it. Similar reasoning holds for the two complete agglomeration equilibria, points A and E, each with its own basin of attraction (from point A to point B, and from point D to point E, respectively). These stable equilibria are indicated with closed circles in Figure 14.7. In contrast, the partial agglomeration long-run equilibria, points B and D, are *un*stable, indicated by open circles. If, for whatever reason, we are initially at point B or D, a long-run equilibrium is reached in the sense that the real wages are equal for regions 1 and 2. However, any small perturbation of this equilibrium will set in motion a process of adjustment leading to a different (stable) long-run equilibrium. For example, a small negative disturbance of λ_1 at point B leads to complete agglomeration of manufacturing activity in region 2, while a positive disturbance leads to spreading.

Computer simulations: stability

The main identifying characteristic of regions in the geographical economics model is the transport costs, assumed to be zero within a region, but positive between two different regions. The term 'transport costs' is a shorthand notation for many different types of obstacles to trade between locations, such as tariffs, language and culture barriers, and indeed the costs of actually getting goods or services at another location (see also Box 14.1). An important question is thus what the impact is of a change in the transport costs. To answer this question we repeat the simulation procedure giving rise to Figure 14.7 for both higher ($T = 2.1$) and lower ($T = 1.3$) transport costs. The results are summarized in Figure 14.8, which suggests the following conclusions:

1. If transport costs are large, the spreading equilibrium is the only stable equilibrium. It makes intuitive sense that if manufactures are difficult to transport from one region to another, the dynamics of the model lead to spreading of manufacturing activity; distant provision of manufactures is too costly, such that they need to be provided locally.

2. If transport costs are small, the spreading equilibrium is unstable while the two agglomerating equilibria are stable. An initial share of the mobile workforce λ_1 in between 0 and 0.5 serves as the basin of attraction for complete agglomeration in region 2, while an initial λ_1 in between 0.5 and 1 serves as the basin of attraction for complete agglomeration in region 1. Again this makes sense intuitively. With very low transport costs, the immobile market can be provided effectively from a distance, which therefore does not pose a strong enough force to counter the advantages of agglomeration.

3. For a range of intermediate values of transport costs (here for example if $T = 1.7$) there are five long-run equilibria. Three of those five, namely spreading and the two agglomeration equilibria, are stable. The other two equilibria are unstable. In this situation, the transport costs are high enough to allow for the local provision of manufactures (spreading). Simultaneously, the transport costs are low enough to allow for the provision of the immobile market from a distance (agglomeration).

The suggestions of the impact of a change in the transport costs on the stability of agglomeration and spreading in the geographical economics model, as discussed above on the basis of Figure 14.8, hold in fact quite generally. Fujita, Krugman, and Venables (1999) and Neary (2001) show that:

• For all transport costs *below* a critical level, labelled the *sustain point*, complete agglomeration of manufacturing activity in one region is a stable long-run equilibrium. If the transport costs exceed the critical sustain point level, agglomeration is not 'sustainable'; that is, agglomeration is an unstable equilibrium.

• For all transport costs *above* another critical level, labelled the *break point*, spreading of manufacturing activity over the two regions is a stable equilibrium. If the transport costs are lower than the critical break point level, the spreading equilibrium 'breaks'; that is, spreading is an unstable equilibrium.

• The sustain point occurs at a higher level of transport costs than the break point. There is thus *always* an intermediate level of transport costs at which agglomeration of manufacturing activity is sustainable while simultaneously spreading of manufacturing activity is a stable equilibrium. Note that the transport cost level chosen in Table 14.3 ($T = 1.7$) lies in between the break point and the sustain point, such that (i) the spreading equilibrium is stable, and (ii) the agglomeration equilibria are sustainable, as illustrated in Figure 14.8.

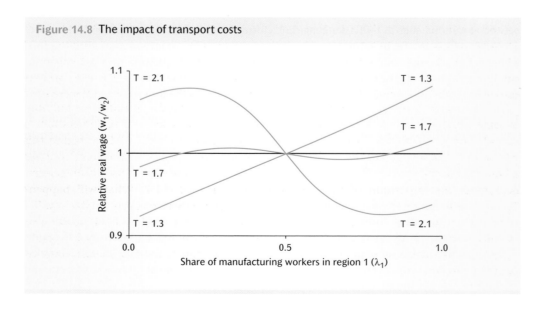

Figure 14.8 The impact of transport costs

Figure 14.9 Stability: sustain point and break points ('Tomahawk' diagram)

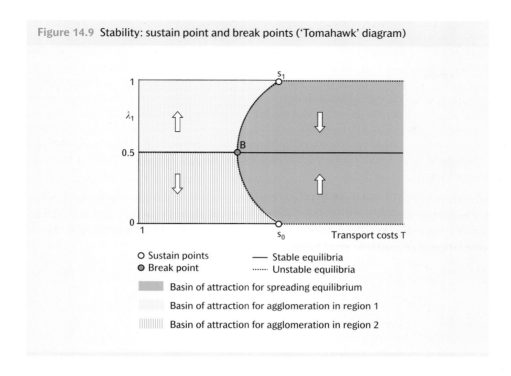

○ Sustain points   —— Stable equilibria
◉ Break point   ······ Unstable equilibria

▨ Basin of attraction for spreading equilibrium

▨ Basin of attraction for agglomeration in region 1

▥ Basin of attraction for agglomeration in region 2

The analysis is summarized in Figure 14.9 in (T,λ_1)-space, where the arrows indicate the direction in which the mobile manufacturing workforce will migrate as a result of differences in the relative real wage between the two regions. For each of the three stable equilibria the 'basin of attraction' is indicated, that is the area of initial parameter settings (T,λ_1) which will converge to this equilibrium; see the bottom of Figure 14.9.

It is important to point out the *hysteresis* or path-dependency aspect of the model; that is, history matters. Suppose that transport costs are initially high, say $T = 2.5$ in Figure 14.9. Then spreading of manufacturing activity is the only stable long-run equilibrium. Now suppose that transport costs start to fall given that the spreading equilibrium is established, say to $T = 1.7$. This will have no impact on the equilibrium allocation of manufacturing production since spreading remains a stable equilibrium. Only after the transport costs have fallen even further, below the break point B in Figure 14.9, will the spreading equilibrium become unstable. Any small disturbance will then result in complete agglomeration of manufacturing production in one region. It is not possible to predict which region this will be, but suppose that agglomeration takes place in region 1. Given that region 1 contains all manufacturing activity, assume now that the transport costs start to rise again, perhaps because of the imposition of trade barriers, say back to $T = 1.7$. What will happen? The answer is: nothing! Agglomeration of manufacturing activity remains a stable equilibrium. So for the same level of transport costs ($T = 1.7$) the equilibrium that becomes established depends on the way this level of transport costs is reached, on history. Obviously, predictions of parameters change are considerably harder in models characterized by path-dependency.

14.6 Welfare

Brakman, Garretsen, and van Marrewijk (2001) are the first to analyse in detail the welfare aspects of the geographical economics model. Here I only illustrate one of their findings, namely the link between stability and welfare maximization. As we have seen above, depending on the parameter configuration of the model, the active economic forces may drive the manufacturing workers towards agglomeration or spreading of economic activity. The obvious question arises whether the equilibrium thus established is 'good', in the sense that it is welfare maximizing.

Obviously, different allocations of manufacturing activity will have different welfare implications for different sets of people. Given transport costs T, it is, for example, clear that the mobile workforce usually achieves a higher welfare level in the complete agglomeration equilibrium than in the spreading equilibrium, since in the latter they have to import part of their consumption of manufactures from the other region. It is also obvious that the immobile workforce in region 2, given complete agglomeration in region 1, is worse off compared to the spreading equilibrium as they will have to import all their manufactures from the other region. It is impossible to argue *ex ante* which effect is more important, so we will have to weigh the importance of various groups, using their size as weight, after correcting the income level for the price index P_i in region i.

Figure 14.10 depicts the welfare level reached for different distributions of manufacturing activity and the three levels of the transport costs of Figure 14.9. If the transport costs are large ($T = 2.1$), we know that spreading is the only stable equilibrium. From Figure 14.10 it is clear that it is also welfare maximizing. If transport costs are low ($T = 1.3$), we know that complete agglomeration in either region is a stable equilibrium. Again, Figure 14.10 shows that it is welfare maximizing. Moreover, for the intermediate transport cost level, both spreading and agglomeration are stable equilibria, and they are local welfare maxima. Although the relationship is

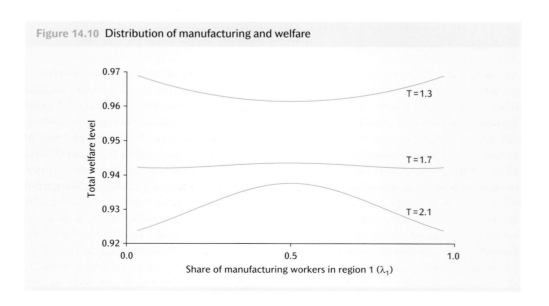

Figure 14.10 Distribution of manufacturing and welfare

Figure 14.11 Allocation of manufacturing production and total welfare

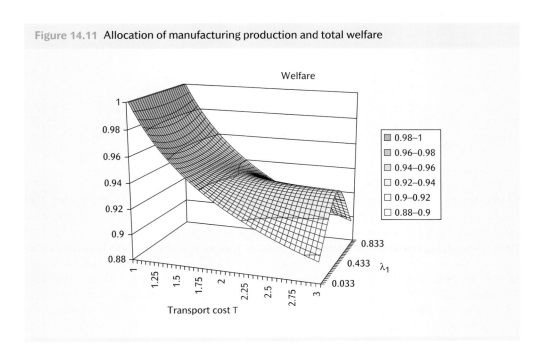

not exact, Brakman, Garretsen, and van Marrewijk (2001) find that there is a fairly strong tendency for stable equilibria also to be welfare maximizing. The policy implication is, of course, that there is only a limited incentive for government intervention, certainly once we take the lack of government knowledge on the precise economic structure and parameters into consideration. The link between the distribution of manufacturing activity and welfare is illustrated for a larger range of transport costs in Figure 14.11, which also shows, as was to be expected, that the maximum attainable welfare falls if transport costs increase.

14.7 Application: predicting the location of European cities

The geographical economics model has been succesfully modified in various ways to explain empirical phenomena, such as Zipf's Law and the gravity equation. One of the best applications, by the Dutch economist Dirk Stelder (2000), however, makes only a slight modification to the model described in this chapter to see to what extent it can be used to predict the location of European cities. Stelder defines a large grid of square locations on a truncated map of Europe. The distance between two locations is in principle calculated as the shortest path (that is 1 for horizontal and vertical neighbours, $\sqrt{2}$ for diagonal neighbours). Stelder's grid of Western Europe has more than 2,800 locations. Sea transportation is made possible at a few places, which are part of the network but do not act as potential locations for cities. The model allows for specific costs for transportation across land, across sea, and in hubs where (un)shipping can take place. The grid is also extended with a third dimension (height) to take the extra transportation costs into account when goods have to cross mountains.

The Stelder model starts with a flat initial distribution in which all locations on the grid are of equal size. The model simulations then calculate the redistribution of economic activity

Box 14.3 Linkages and factor abundance: alternative core models

The geographical economics model described in this chapter, referred to as the 'core' model of geographical economics by Brakman, Garretsen, and van Marrewijk (2001), analyses potential core–periphery structures by assuming that labour is the only input in the production process and that labour is mobile between regions in the long run (in response to differences in real wages). It could be argued, however, that labour mobility is probably only fairly large between regions within the same country or for particular types of labour between countries. One may therefore question the relationship between (falling) transport costs on the one hand and the appearance of multiple long-run equilibria and core–periphery structures on the other hand, as described in this chapter. These fears are, however, unfounded to the extent that we now have two widely used 'alternative core models' available in geographical economics that do not or only partially rely on labour mobility but still lead to the exact same type of relationship between transport costs and core–periphery structures. As an additional bonus, these alternative core models manage to incorporate aspects of factor abundance as discussed in Chapters 4–7 and of input–output linkages as discussed for the Ethier interpretation in Chapter 10. We briefly discuss both of these models.

- *Partial labour mobility*: the Forslid–Ottaviano (2003) factor abundance model. The core model of geographical economics presented in this chapter cannot be solved analytically, which explains the heavy use of computer simulations in geographical economics. The Forslid–Ottaviano model builds directly on the economic structure presented in this chapter by giving a different interpretation to the increasing-returns to scale production function. They assume that there are two types of inputs, namely mobile skilled labour and immobile unskilled labour. Food is produced under constant returns to scale using unskilled labour, while a variety of manufactures is produced under increasing returns to scale using both inputs. Unskilled labour is needed for the variable costs of the production process (proportional to the scale of output) and skilled labour is needed for the fixed costs of the production process (representing headquarter services and the costs of inventing the good). The production of manufactures is therefore relatively intensive in the use of skilled labour. If a region attracts more human capital and produces more manufactures (which also requires unskilled workers), the production of food decreases. The model not only has the advantage that it can analyse issues of factor abundance in a geographical economics framework, it also turns out to be an analytically solvable model, which ensures that it has become the most popular model to work with for answering applied policy questions.

- *No labour mobility*: the Krugman–Venables (1995) input–output model. It is even possible to do without labour mobility altogether and still derive the same relationship between transport costs and core-periphery structures. To this end, the Krugman–Venables model assumes that there is no labour migration between regions, so when a sector expands, the labour supply must come from other sectors in that region. Cumulative causation and the possibility of agglomeration in this model come from input–output linkages between firms, which are now assumed to use each other's output as an intermediate input. Firms benefit from being close to each other by not incurring transport costs on intermediate factors of production. In agriculture, produced under constant returns to scale, only labour is used, and the agricultural goods can be traded without trade costs. The latter assumption ensures that as long as both regions produce both goods the wage rate equals unity (by choice of units). Typically this model produces two types of equilibria. A spreading equilibrium arises for high trade costs of manufactures and a core–periphery equilibrium for low trade costs. For intermediate transportation costs, asymmetric but unstable equilibria are possible. So, without complete specialization this model produces in a qualitative sense the same type of equilbria as the core model.

Figure 14.12 Simulated location of European cities

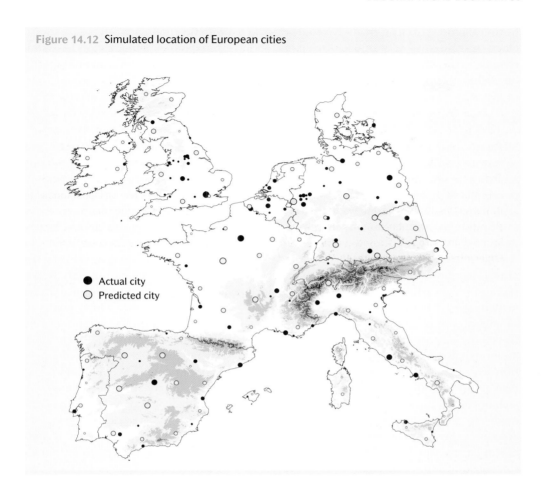

based on differences in real wages, given the parameter configuration. The location and size of the cities which emerge in the long-run equilibrium depend on the chosen parameter values and on the geographical shape of the economy. Figure 14.12 shows a model run that produces an equilibrium of 94 cities with $\delta_m = 0.5$, $\varepsilon = 5$ and $T = 1.57$.[8] The open circles are the simulated outcomes and the closed circles the 94 largest actual cities in 1996. As was to be expected with a flat initial distribution, the model produces an equilibrium city distribution that is more evenly spread than in reality. Large agglomerations such as Paris, London, Madrid, and Rome are not correctly simulated, because population density is for historical reasons higher in the North than in the South. The model predicts too many large cities in Spain and too few cities in the UK, the Netherlands, and Belgium. The results are nevertheless relatively good for Germany. The Ruhrgebiet, Bremen, Berlin, Frankfurt, Stuttgart, and Munich (and also Vienna) are not far from the right place. In the periphery of various countries some cities also appear correctly, such as Lille, Rouen, Nantes, Bordeaux, and Nice in France, Lisbon and Porto in Portugal, and Seville and Malaga in Spain.

Stelder points out that these kinds of model results of course *should be* wrong. A good fit would mean 'total victory of economics over all other social sciences because then the whole historical process of city formation would be explained with the three parameters δ_m, ε and T'. One of his objectives of the model is to clarify to what extent pure economic factors have contributed to the city formation process, concluding that even the basic model can produce city hierarchies if applied in spaces closer to geographic reality.

14.8 Conclusions

Blending some of the insights of the neoclassical trade model (perfect competition and constant returns to scale) and the new trade model (monopolistic competition, increasing returns to scale, and varieties of manufactures), combined with factor mobility (migration to regions with high real wages), allows us to provide a simple theory of location and agglomeration. The dynamic migration process implies that we distinguish between short-run equilibria (in which the distribution of manufacturing activity is given), and an adjustment path leading to a long-run equilibrium (either spreading of manufacturing activity or complete agglomeration). Using computer simulations to gain further insights into the model, we showed that for high transport costs spreading of manufacturing activity is a stable outcome, while for low transport costs agglomeration is a stable outcome. In an intermediate range, both agglomeration and spreading are stable outcomes, which points to some problems of predicting the effect of policy changes in view of the hysteresis aspect of the model (history matters). There is a positive, but not strict, association between stable long-run equilibria and the welfare maximum, suggesting limited need for policy intervention. The model has been modified to explain some important empirical observations and regularities (such as Zipf's Law concerning the distribution of city sizes, and the gravity equation concerning the size and direction of international trade flows). Applying the basic model to predict the location of European cities, taking the geographical context into account, turns out to be mildly successful. Finally, note that the model predicts that regions of similar size (spreading) will be involved in intra-industry trade and regions of different size (agglomeration) will be involved in inter-industry trade, roughly in line with empirical observations (see Chapter 10).

TECHNICAL NOTES

Some preliminary equations are given below. The first equation gives spending on food and manufactures, the second gives the demand for a particular variety, the third defines real income and wage, the fourth gives the notation for transport costs between regions r and s, depending on the parameter T and the distance D_{rs} between regions r and s.

(14.A1) $$F = (1 - \delta_m)I; \quad PM = \delta_m I$$

(14.A2) $$c_j = p_j^{-\varepsilon}[P^{\varepsilon-1}\delta_m I], \quad where \quad P = \left[\sum_{i=1}^{N} p_i^{1-\varepsilon}\right]^{1/(1-\varepsilon)} \quad for \ j = 1, \dots, N$$

(14.A3) $$real\ income:\ y = IP^{-\delta_m}; \quad real\ wage:\ w = WP^{-\delta_m}$$

(14.A4) $$T_{rs} = T^{D_{rs}}, \quad note:\ T_{rs} = T_{sr}, \quad and\ T_{rr} = T^0 = 1$$

Technical Note 14.1 Derivation of the price index

The number of firms in region s equals $\lambda_s \delta_m / f\varepsilon$.

The price of a firm located in region s charges in region r equals $mW_s T_{rs}/\rho$.

Substituting these two results in the price index for manufactures, see equation (14.A2), and assuming that there are $R \geq 2$ regions, gives the price index for region r:

$$(14.A5) \qquad P_r = \left[\sum_{s=1}^{R} \left(\frac{\lambda_s \delta_m}{f\varepsilon} \right) \left(\frac{mW_s T_{rs}}{\rho} \right)^{1-\varepsilon} \right]^{1/(1-\varepsilon)} = \left[\left(\frac{m}{\rho} \right) \left(\frac{\delta_m}{f\varepsilon} \right)^{1/(1-\varepsilon)} \right] \left(\sum_{s=1}^{R} \lambda_s W_s^{1-\varepsilon} T_{rs}^{1-\varepsilon} \right)^{1/(1-\varepsilon)}$$

It can be shown, see Brakman, Garretsen, and van Marrewijk (2001, ch. 4), that the parameter normalization $m = \rho$ and $f = \delta/\varepsilon$ does not essentially affect the dynamic behaviour of the model, although it does affect the welfare level. Applying this normalization considerably simplifies notation as it reduces the awkward constant in square brackets on the right-hand side of equation (14.A5) to 1. Using that normalization implies that equation (14.3) is a special case for $R = 2$ and $r = 1$.

Technical Note 14.2 Derivation of manufacturing equilibrium

Equation (14.A2) gives the demand for an individual consumer in a region. Replacing the income level I with the income level I_s of region s, the price index P with the price index P_s of region s, and the price p_j of the manufactured good with the price $mW_r T_{sr}/\rho$ which a producer from region r will charge in region s, we get the demand in region s for a product from region r:

$$(14.A6) \qquad \delta_m I_s (mW_r T_{sr}/\rho)^{-\varepsilon} P_s^{\varepsilon-1} = \delta_m (m/\rho)^{-\varepsilon} I_s W_r^{-\varepsilon} T_{sr}^{-\varepsilon} P_s^{\varepsilon-1}$$

To fulfil this consumption demand in region s note that T_{sr} units have to be shipped and produced. To derive the total demand in all $R \geq 2$ regions for a manufactured good produced in region r, we must sum production demand over all regions (that is, sum over the index s in the above equation and multiply each entry by T_{sr}):

$$(14.A7) \qquad \delta_m (m/\rho)^{-\varepsilon} \sum_{s=1}^{R} I_s W_r^{-\varepsilon} T_{sr}^{1-\varepsilon} P_s^{\varepsilon-1} = \delta_m (m/\rho)^{-\varepsilon} W_r^{-\varepsilon} \sum_{s=1}^{R} I_s T_{sr}^{1-\varepsilon} P_s^{\varepsilon-1}$$

In equilibrium this total demand for a manufactured good from region r must be equal to its supply $(\varepsilon -1)f/m$; see Chapter 10. Equalizing these two gives

$$(14.A8) \qquad (\varepsilon - 1) f/m = \delta_m (m/\rho)^{-\varepsilon} W_r^{-\varepsilon} \sum_{s=1}^{R} I_s T_{sr}^{1-\varepsilon} P_s^{\varepsilon-1}$$

which can easily be solved for the wage rate W_r in region r:

$$(14.A9) \qquad W_r = \left[\rho m^{-\rho} \left(\frac{\delta_m}{(\varepsilon - 1)f} \right)^{1/\varepsilon} \right] \left(\sum_{s=1}^{R} I_s T_{sr}^{1-\varepsilon} P_s^{\varepsilon-1} \right)^{1/\varepsilon}$$

As in Technical Note 14.1, the awkward constant in square brackets on the right-hand side disappears if we impose the normalization $m = \rho$ and $f = \delta/\varepsilon$. Doing that implies that equation (14.5) is a special case for $R = 2$ and $r = 1$.

QUESTIONS

Question 14.1

14.1A What is 'hysteresis' or 'path-dependency', and what is its importance for geographical economics?

14.1B What does this imply for empirical research?

The two-region geographical economics model predicts that manufacturing activity will spread over the two regions or agglomerate in one region depending on the size of three economic parameters:

- The (iceberg) transport cost (T)

- The elasticity of substitution (ϵ)
- The share of income spent on manufactures (δ_m)

14.1C Do high transport costs lead to spreading or agglomeration of manufacturing activity? Explain.

14.1D Does a high elasticity of substitution lead to spreading or agglomeration of manufacturing activity? Explain.

14.1E Does a high share of income spent on manufactures lead to spreading or agglomeration of manufacturing activity? Explain.

Question 14.2

This question reviews the general structure of the geographical economics model.

14.2A How do consumers decide how much to spend on food and manufacturing goods? What is the share of income they will spend on food?

14.2B Does every consumer spend an equal share of income on food? Why?

14.2C How do consumers decide on their consumption level for a particular variety of manufactures? What is the share of their income they will spend on one variety?

14.2D Is the wage rate for farm workers necessarily equal between the two regions?

14.2E Is the wage rate for manufacturing workers equal between the regions?

Question 14.3

Chapter 14 discusses the geographical economics model using graphs such as the one shown below.

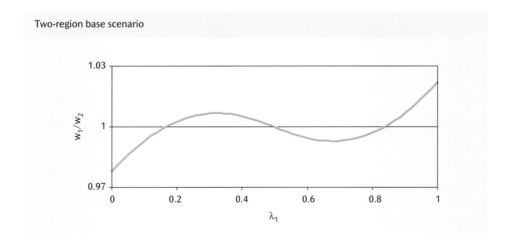

14.3A What does the line in the figure represent?

14.3B Identify the long-run equilibria in the figure. Explain.

14.3C How can you derive from the figure if a long-run equilibrium is stable or unstable?

14.3D Can your determine from the above figure if manufacturing activity will agglomerate in the long run?

14.3E Draw a new figure, similar to the one above but based on a different parameter setting, in which the agglomeration of manufacturing firms is the only stable long-run equilibrium.

14.3F Draw a new figure, similar to the one above but based on a different parameter setting, in which the spreading of manufacturing firms is the only stable long-run equilibrium.

See the Online Resource Centre for a Study Guide containing more questions
www.oxfordtextbooks.co.uk/orc/vanmarrewijk/

NOTES

1 For a while the term 'new economic geography' was popular. It was replaced by the term 'geographical economics', partly in order not to offend the older and respected economic geography literature.

2 The website for this book presents evidence for many countries in the world.

3 In 1998 Japan's GDP was $3,783 billion; the Czech Republic's GDP was $56 billion (The World Bank).

4 We imposed that the fraction of the workers in the manufacturing sector is equal to the fraction of income spent on manufactures and normalized the work force to 1. This eases notation without substantially affecting the (dynamic) equilibrium, as discussed in Brakman, Garretsen, and van Marrewijk (2001).

5 Note that ε can be determined from $\varepsilon = 1/(1 - \rho)$. Why did we choose this set of base-scenario parameters? To some degree, the choice is arbitrary. The share of income spent on manufactures δ_m and the elasticity of substitution $\varepsilon = 1/(1 - \rho)$ between goods have been chosen based on reasonable empirical estimates. Given the choice of δ_m and ρ, the value of the transport costs T is chosen to demonstrate an important aspect of the geographical economics model as illustrated in Figure 14.7 and discussed below.

6 The simulation exercises in the *Study Guide* are based on a more user-friendly Excel program.

7 If there is complete agglomeration the relative real wage cannot actually be calculated since there are no manufacturing workers in one of the regions. Points A and E in Figure 14.7 are therefore limit values.

8 The apparently peculiar choice of T results from a different parameterization used by Stelder, which we have respecified here using our parameterization.

MULTINATIONALS

15

Objectives/key terms

- Multinationals
- Foreign direct investment
- Horizontal/vertical mergers
- OLI framework

- Transnationality index
- Mergers and acquisitions
- Transfer pricing
- Hard-disk drives

Multinational firms, with increasing shares in world production, investment, and trade flows, represent the most visible part of the 'globalization' phenomenon. We evaluate some empirical evidence and analyse the economic forces behind multinational firms.

15.1 Introduction

When I start to get hungry from shopping in the centre of Europe's largest harbour, Rotterdam, I order a Big Mac at McDonald's, washing it down with Coca-Cola before driving back in my Toyota. If I fly eight hours to the west to visit my friend in Washington, DC, I rent a Toyota, after eating a Big Mac and drinking Coca-Cola at the airport. If I fly eighteen hours to the east to visit my in-laws in the Philippines, the Toyota taxi stops at McDonald's so that I can eat a Big Mac and drink Coca-Cola. In Holland, the USA, and the Philippines, and virtually everywhere else in the world, I can therefore consume the products of McDonald's, Coca-Cola, and Toyota. The fact that the same company is producing and selling products in more than one country – such a company is called a 'multinational corporation' (henceforth multinational, for short) – and sometimes virtually all over the world is probably the most visible aspect of the worldwide international economic links summarized under the label 'globalization'. Since multinational production, investment, and trade are becoming ever more important, see Sections 15.2 and 15.3, and none of the preceding chapters has devoted explicit attention to these phenomena, it is time to fill that gap in this chapter.

Table 15.1 lists the twenty largest multinational firms in 2003, ranked by foreign assets. Toyota is listed as number 8, but McDonald's and Coca-Cola, mentioned in the introduction above, do not make it to the top twenty (they are in the top 100). The top twenty list contains five French, five German, four American, two British, and two Japanese firms, plus one firm from Hong Kong and one Dutch/British firm. In the top twenty, there are five firms producing

---

Famous economists | **Joseph Schumpeter**

Fig. 15.1
Joseph Schumpeter
(1883–1950)

Born in Austria, where he was briefly Minister of Finance after the First World War, Schumpeter emigrated to the USA in 1932, where he worked at Harvard University. At the early age of 28 he wrote *Theory of Economic Development* (1912), which gave a pivotal role to the dynamic, innovating entrepreneur for achieving technical progress and a positive rate of profit on capital. As Blaug (1986: 215) puts it, Schumpeter 'stressed the fact that scientific and technical inventions amount to nothing unless they are adopted, which calls for as much daring and imagination as the original act of discovery by the scientist or engineer'. Moreover, he emphasized that economic progress consists not only of new machines and products, but also of new sources of supply, new forms of organization, and new methods of production. Schumpeter distinguished sharply between the entrepreneur, doing things in a new way and earning 'profit', and the capitalist, providing the capital required to finance a new venture and earning 'interest'. In 1942 he wrote *Capitalism, Socialism, and Democracy*, a book predicting the arrival of socialism. Another Schumpeter must-have in any economist's cupboard is *History of Economic Analysis* (1954), which appeared four years after his death, on the history of economic thought with many important remarks scattered about in hundreds of footnotes.

Table 15.1 Top twenty non-financial multinationals; ranked by foreign assets, 2003 ($bn and 1,000 employees)

Corporation	Home economy	Industry	Assets		Sales		Employment		TNI
			Foreign	Total	Foreign	Total	Foreign	Total	
1 General El.	USA	Electronics	259	647	54	134	150	305	43.2
2 Vodafone	UK	Telecom	244	263	50	60	47	60	85.1
3 Ford	USA	Motor veh	174	305	61	164	139	328	45.5
4 General Mot.	USA	Motor veh	154	449	52	186	104	294	32.5
5 British Petr.	UK	Petroleum	142	178	193	233	87	104	82.1
6 Exxon Mob.	USA	Petroleum	117	174	167	237	54	88	66.1
7 Shell	UK/Netherl.	Petroleum	113	168	130	202	100	119	71.8
8 Toyota	Japan	Motor veh	94	190	87	149	89	264	47.3
9 Total	France	Petroleum	88	101	95	118	61	111	74.1
10 France Tel.	France	Telecom	81	126	22	52	89	219	48.8
11 Suez	France	El gas water	74	88	34	45	111	172	74.7
12 El. de France	France	El gas water	67	186	16	51	52	167	32.9
13 E.On	Germany	El gas water	64	141	19	52	30	69	41.2
14 Deutsche Tel.	Germany	Telecom	63	147	24	63	75	249	37.0
15 RWE Group	Germany	El gas water	60	99	24	49	54	127	50.6
16 Hutchison	Hong Kong	Diversified	59	80	11	19	105	126	71.4
17 Siemens	Germany	Electronics	58	98	64	84	247	417	65.3
18 Volkswagen	Germany	Motor veh	58	150	71	98	160	335	52.9
19 Honda	Japan	Motor veh	53	78	54	70	93	132	72.0
20 Vivendi Un.	France	Diversified	259	647	54	134	150	305	65.2

Note: TNI = transnationality index = average of (%): foreign assets to total assets, foreign sales to total sales, and foreign employment to total employment.

Source: UNCTAD/Erasmus University database, WIR (2005).

motor vehicles, four petroleum firms, four firms in electricity, gas and water, three telecommunications firms, two electronics firms, and two firms classified as 'diversified'. The ranking based on foreign assets as a measure of multinationality is, of course, arbitrary. The largest firm in this respect, the American firm General Electric, has foreign assets valued at $259 billion, out of total assets of $647 billion. Its foreign sales are $54 billion, out of total sales of $95 billion, and it employs 150,000 persons abroad, out of a total of 305,000 employees. The UNCTAD/Erasmus University database in the World Investment Report therefore also calculates the relative average of these three indicators of multinationality, labelled the Transnationality index. For General Electric this calculation results in (see Table 15.1):

(15.1)
$$\frac{1}{3}\left(\frac{259}{647} + \frac{54}{95} + \frac{150}{305}\right) \times 100\% = 43.2\%$$

The Transnationality index for General Electric is much lower than for the British firm Vodafone (85.1 per cent) or the Japanese firm Honda (72 per cent). The highest Transnationality index (97.3 per cent), however, is achieved by the First Pacific Company from Hong Kong, not listed in Table 15.1. In general, the most international-oriented companies are to be found in the smaller developed countries.

15.2 The size and structure of multinationals

Multinationals are rapidly becoming more important in the global economic system. Sales of foreign affiliates of multinational firms have risen from 23.5 per cent of world GDP in 1982 to 46 per cent of world GDP in 2004; see Figure 15.2(a). This is, of course, not an entirely valid comparison since, unlike GDP, sales are not a value-added measure. As Figure 15.2(b) shows, however, the gross product of foreign affiliates relative to world GDP is also estimated to have increased substantially in this period, from 5.5 per cent in 1982 to 9.6 per cent in 2004. Similarly for assets of foreign affiliates, which increased from 18 per cent of world GDP in 1982 to 88.5 per cent in 2004, and for exports of foreign affiliates, which increased from 6.2 per cent in 1982 to 9.1 per cent in 2004; see Figures 15.2(c) and 15.2(d), respectively. Currently, about one third of all international trade flows are exports of foreign affiliates of multinational firms.

How does a company become a multinational? By operating and controlling foreign affiliates. This requires foreign direct investment (FDI) in either of two ways, namely through

Figure 15.2 Growing importance of multinationals: shares of foreign affiliates (% of world GDP)

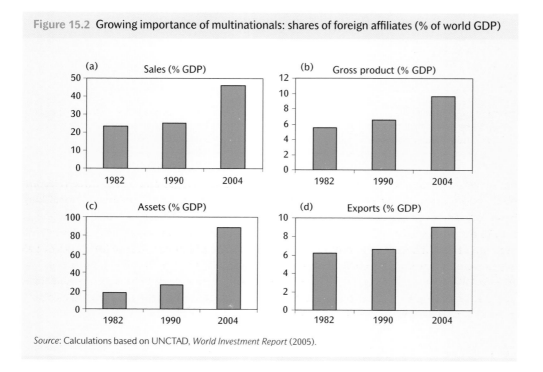

Source: Calculations based on UNCTAD, *World Investment Report* (2005).

(i) greenfield investments, that is setting up a new production location, or (ii) through mergers and acquisitions. In both cases, host-country assets are placed under the governance of multi-national firms, but greenfield investments also contribute to the growth of an international production system. The majority of FDI, some 78 per cent, is in the form of mergers and acquisitions, which, as the name suggests, can be subdivided into a small number of mergers (less than 3 per cent), with headquarters in both countries or in one country, and a larger number of acquisitions, with headquarters in the home country and the affiliate in the host country. Acquisitions, in turn, can be minority (with 10–49 per cent of a firm's voting shares), majority (foreign interest of 50–99 per cent), or full (foreign interest of 100 per cent). In terms of the number of deals, most acquisitions are full (65 per cent of all mergers and acquisitions). These distinctions are summarized in Figure 15.3. Acquisitions of less than 10 per cent of a firm's voting shares constitute portfolio investment.

Measured in constant 2000 dollars, foreign direct investment has increased from $33 billion in 1970 to $539 billion in 2003; see Figure 15.4. Partly as a result of the continuing process of economic and monetary integration within the European Union, the share of the EMU countries (see Chapter 30) has risen from 16 per cent in 1970 to 49 per cent in 2003. Simultaneously, and despite the increase in absolute terms, the share of North America dropped from 14 to 7 per cent, see Figure 15.4. It is equally clear from the figure that the evolution of FDI itself and the distribution of shares across different countries is not very stable because FDI flows and mergers and acquisitions (M&As) tend to come in waves, see Figure 15.5 for a selection of countries. Note, for example, that total FDI reached a peak of $1,511 bn in the year 2000, the USA reached a peak in its share of 45 per cent in 1987 and the EMU's share peaked at 50 per cent in 2002.

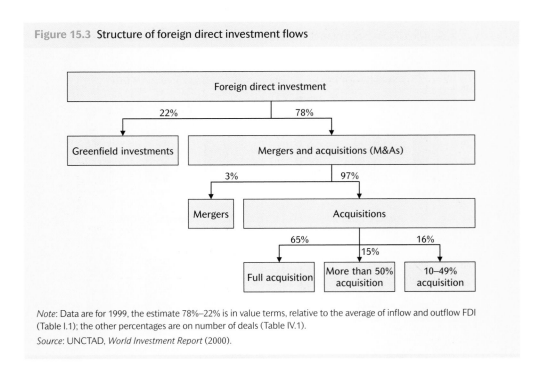

Figure 15.3 Structure of foreign direct investment flows

Note: Data are for 1999, the estimate 78%–22% is in value terms, relative to the average of inflow and outflow FDI (Table I.1); the other percentages are on number of deals (Table IV.1).

Source: UNCTAD, *World Investment Report* (2000).

Figure 15.4 Rapid increase in FDI until 2000

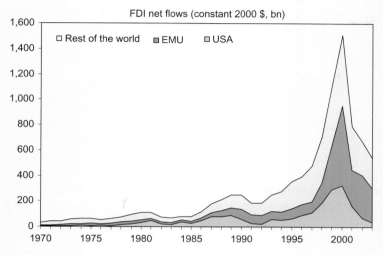

Source: Calculations based on World Bank Development Indicators CD-ROM 2005.

Figure 15.5 Volume of cross-border M&As; selected countries, 1980–2004

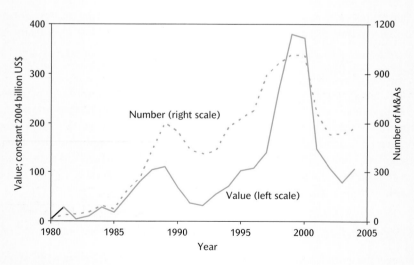

Note: Value is deflated using USA GDP deflator; sum for five countries: Australia, France, Netherlands, UK, and USA.
Source: Van Marrewijk (2005).

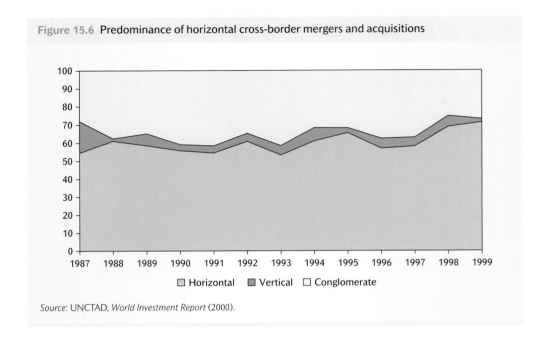

Figure 15.6 Predominance of horizontal cross-border mergers and acquisitions

Source: UNCTAD, *World Investment Report* (2000).

We can distinguish between three types of mergers and acquisitions.[1]

- *Horizontal* mergers and acquisitions between competing firms in the same industry. By consolidating their resources the merging firms aim to achieve synergies and often greater market power. Typical industries are pharmaceuticals, automobiles, petroleum, and several services industries.

- *Vertical* mergers and acquisitions between firms in client–supplier or buyer–seller relationships. The firms seek to reduce uncertainty and transaction costs as regards forward and backward linkages in the production process. Typical industries are electronics and automobiles.

- *Conglomerate* mergers and acquisitions between companies in unrelated activities. The firms seek to diversify risk and deepen economies of scope.

Horizontal mergers and acquisitions constitute the largest component of cross-border mergers and acquisitions. They have also become relatively more important over time, increasing from 55 per cent in 1987 to 72 per cent in 1999; see Figure 15.6. In contrast, conglomerate mergers and acquisitions have become relatively less important over time, falling from a high of 42 per cent in 1991 to 27 per cent in 1999, as firms tend to focus increasingly on their core business. The share of vertical mergers and acquisitions is limited, and tends to fluctuate wildly from year to year.

15.3 Foreign direct investment

A firm can become a multinational, that is, it can control by means of ownership of productive assets in more than one country, through foreign direct investment (greenfield investments and mergers and acquisitions). Data on foreign direct investment have been gathered systematically on a global scale for a surprisingly short period of time: UNCTAD started to produce the *World Investment Report* in 1990. This work has clearly demonstrated the growing importance of foreign direct investment and multinational production and trade (UNCTAD's preferred term is transnational, rather than multinational).

In the period 1970–2003 worldwide real GDP, measured in constant 2000 US\$, rose from \$12.2 trillion to \$33.5 trillion. This is an increase of 175 per cent, or roughly 3 per cent per year; see Figure 15.7(a). Measured similarly, worldwide international trade flows rose from

Figure 15.7 Development of world GDP, FDI, and trade, 1970–2003.

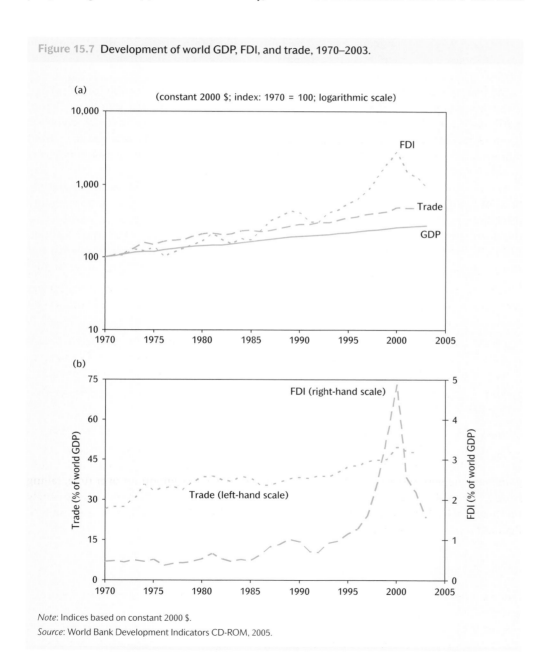

Note: Indices based on constant 2000 \$.

Source: World Bank Development Indicators CD-ROM, 2005.

$3.2 trillion in 1970 to $15.5 trillion in 2002, an increase of 380 per cent for the period, or almost 5 per cent per year. The steady growing importance of international trade flows, which as a share of world GDP increased from 26.5 per cent in 1970 to 47.6 per cent in 2002, is illustrated in Figures 15.7(a) and 15.7(b). Finally, also measured in constant 2000 US$, worldwide foreign direct investments rose from $55 billion to $514 billion, an increase of 833 per cent, or almost 7 per cent per year. As illustrated in Figure 15.7(a), therefore, foreign direct investments rose even more rapidly than international trade flows. It is also clear from the figure that foreign direct investments are much more volatile, with large peaks and troughs, than either trade flows or production levels. This is also evident from Figure 15.7(b), showing the volatile increase of foreign direct investments as a share of world GDP from 0.45 per cent in 1970 to 1.53 per cent in 2003, with a peak of 4.88 per cent in the year 2000.

The two panels of Figure 15.8 give a breakdown of the geographic distribution of foreign direct investments in inflows and outflows for six global regions: the European Union, North America, China, Africa, Latin America, and South-East Europe and CIS countries (Commonwealth of Independent States, which includes Russia). All data are in current billions of US dollars. Table 15.2 provides more details for this geographic distribution for the world as a whole.

As is evident from Figure 15.8 and Table 15.2, a large but falling part of the major destinations of foreign direct investment flows are to be found in the developed countries, mainly the European Union. Other sizeable inflows occur in North America and Asia. Within Asia, the distribution is rather skewed, with most recent flows going to East Asia, specifically to China. Latin America also receives a reasonable share of foreign direct investments, but Africa, Japan, and most countries in Eastern Europe and Central Asia receive rather limited inflows.

Figure 15.8 Foreign direct investment flows, 2002–2004 ($ bn)

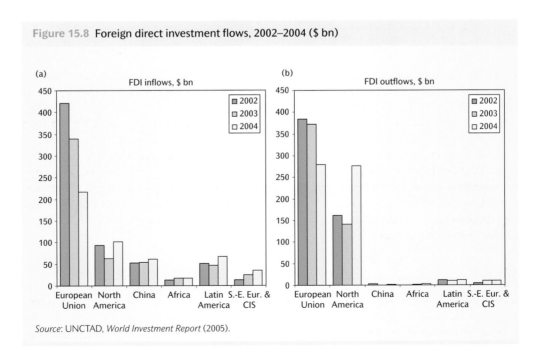

Source: UNCTAD, *World Investment Report* (2005).

Table 15.2 Geographical distribution of FDI flows, 2002–2004 (US$ bn)

	FDI inflows			FDI outflows		
	2002	2003	2004	2002	2003	2004
World	716.1	632.6	648.1	652.2	616.9	730.3
Developed economies	547.8	442.2	380.0	599.9	577.3	637.4
Europe	427.6	359.4	223.4	396.9	390.0	309.5
European Union	420.4	338.7	216.4	384.5	372.4	279.8
North America	92.8	63.2	102.2	161.7	140.9	276.7
Other developed countries	27.4	19.6	54.5	41.3	46.4	51.1
Developing economies	155.5	166.3	233.2	47.8	29.0	83.2
Africa	13.0	18.0	18.1	0.4	1.2	2.8
Latin America and the Caribbean	50.5	46.9	67.5	11.4	10.6	10.9
Asia and Oceania	92.0	101.4	147.6	36.0	17.2	69.4
Asia	92.0	101.3	147.5	36.0	17.2	69.4
South East and South-East Asia	86.3	94.8	137.7	35.1	21.2	69.4
East Asia	67.3	72.1	105.0	27.6	14.4	53.5
China	52.7	53.5	60.6	2.5	0.2	1.8
South-East Europe and CIS	12.8	24.1	34.9	4.5	10.6	9.7

Source: UNCTAD, *World Investment Report* (2005).

The developed countries are the main source of foreign direct investment flows, usually close to 90 per cent of the world total, with the European Union as the main source and North America as a close second source. On average, the developed countries were the source of about 91 per cent of the world foreign direct investment flows in 2002–2004, as well as the destination of almost 70 per cent of those flows. Finally, by combining the above information, the dominant source of *net* foreign direct investment flows is the developed countries in general and North America and the European Union in particular. The main net destinations of foreign direct investment flows are Latin America and East Asia, particularly China with an average net inflow of $55.6 billion in this period.

We conclude that the predominant source *and* destination of foreign direct investment flows are the high-income developed countries, a finding similar to the main intra-industry trade flows in the world. Although developing countries are relatively unimportant for foreign direct investment flows, it should be noted that these flows are very concentrated: only ten countries accounted for two-thirds of all inflows into developing countries; see Shatz and Venables (2000).[2] It is clear that the majority of the foreign direct investment flows into the developing countries go to the more advanced nations; very little goes to the least developed countries in Africa or Asia.

15.4 Explaining multinationals

Sections 15.2 and 15.3 show that multinationals are rapidly becoming more important in the global production, trade, and investment system. This poses two questions, namely (i) why do multinationals arise?, and (ii) what is the impact of multinationals on production, trade, and investment? The second question is the more difficult to answer, and will be briefly discussed in the next section. With respect to question (i), why multinationals arise, Bowen, Hollander, and Viaene (1998: 463) remark:

> That such a question is raised in the first place attests to the belief that familiarity with local business practices, consumer preferences and labour market conditions is an important asset which gives local firms an advantage over foreign transplants. From this it follows that a foreign firm, less familiar with the local terrain must, in order to sustain the rivalry of local enterprises, possess some other advantages, not shared by local firms.

Similar observations were made for the first time by John Dunning (1977, 1981) in what has become known as the OLI approach. According to Dunning three conditions need to be satisfied in order for a firm to become a multinational:

- *Ownership* advantages, which allow a firm to overcome the disadvantages of a foreign location. This can be a product or a production process to which other firms do not have access, such as a patent or a trade mark.
- *Location* advantages, such as input costs, strategic interaction, or trade policy, which make it more profitable to produce in a country than to export to it.
- *Internalization* advantages, which make it more profitable for a firm to undertake foreign production itself, rather than dealing with a foreign partner more familiar with the local environment.

The extensive empirical literature on firm characteristics associated with multinational firms, representing the sources of the ownership, location, and internalization advantages of Dunning, has recently been reviewed by Markusen (1995, 1998).[3] The latter study produces the following list of main firm and industry characteristics for multinationals.

1 Multinationals are associated with high ratios of R&D relative to sales.
2 Multinationals employ large numbers of scientific, technical, and other 'white-collar' workers as a percentage of their workforce.
3 Multinationals tend to have a high value of 'intangible' assets (market value minus the value of tangible assets, such as plant and equipment).
4 Multinationals are associated with new and/or technically complex products.
5 Evidence suggests that multinationality is negatively associated with plant-level scale economies.
6 Multinationals are associated with product-differentiation variables, such as advertising to sales ratios.
7 A minimum or 'threshold' level of firm size seems to be important for a firm to be a multinational, but above that level firm size is of minimal importance.
8 Multinationals tend to be older, more established firms.

In the international economics literature, the above firm and industry characteristics clearly lead us into the realm of imperfect competition, product differentiation, and increasing returns to scale; see Chapters 9 and 10. The discussion below can therefore build upon the main insights already derived in these chapters. Points 5 and 7 above, distinguishing between plant-level and firm-level economies of scale, have been crucial in understanding why and when multinationals arise in a general equilibrium framework.[4] Rather than elaborating on

Box 15.1 Transfer pricing

When firms are operative in more countries, each having different tariffs and different corporate income taxes, this raises the possibility of 'transfer pricing', that is the setting of prices on intrafirm transactions to minimize tax and tariff payments and maximize corporate profits; see Horst (1971). Although, according to international principles, the dutiable value of these transactions should be the arm's-length price, that is the price that would be charged to an outside buyer, exporters have some manoeuvring space when declaring a value for duty. Declaring a high import value increases the tariff payments to be made and at the same time shifts profits from the importing country to the exporting country. The latter will be beneficial if the importing country has a higher corporate tax rate than the exporting country. The overall payments of the firm therefore depend on the tariff duty relative to the difference in taxation rates.

In a small partial equilibrium model Bowen, Hollander, and Viaene (1998: 474–9) show that transfer pricing may also influence the firm's location decision. Assuming that the marginal production costs are the same in Home and Foreign, that the transfer prices may vary in a range with a minimum and a maximum, and allowing for the possibility to set up a production plant either in Home only or in both Home and Foreign, they show that a Home plant alone is optimal if the taxation of profits is low compared to the taxation of profits in Foreign. Otherwise, as the taxation rates become more equal, it is optimal to establish two production plants. Empirical studies, for example by Grubert and Mutti (1991), who study US multinational activity in 33 countries, found ample evidence of income shifting into countries with low tax rates. Moreover, host-country corporate taxes have a negative impact on export sales of local subsidiaries, but not on local sales.

the individual contributions in this area, the next section will explain in some detail the general structure and main results of a recent representative model of multinational activity by James Markusen and Anthony Venables.

15.5 Multinationals in general equilibrium

As argued in Chapter 1, international economists are not truly satisfied with an explanation of empirical observations until they can construct a general equilibrium model producing similar results. The last decade of the previous century has seen large improvements in this respect in trying to explain multinational firms and their impact on the international trading system in a general equilibrium framework. As pointed out above, we restrict attention to the Markusen and Venables (1998) model, which focuses on horizontal multinationals. As shown in Section 15.2, this comprises the majority of foreign direct investments. As in previous chapters, we analyse two countries, Austria and Bolivia, and two types of industries, manufactures and food. The food sector produces a homogeneous good under constant returns to scale, using capital K and labour L as inputs, in a perfectly competitive market. There are no transport costs for food, which will be used as numéraire. The production function for food is (compare equation (4.1)):[5]

(15.2)
$$F_A = K_A^{\alpha_f} L_{Af}^{1-\alpha_f} \quad F_B = K_B^{\alpha_f} L_{Bf}^{1-\alpha_f}; \quad 0 < \alpha_f < 1$$

Recall that α_f measures the capital intensity of the production process. Also note that the capital used in the production process of food in equation (15.2) does not have a sub-index f, in contrast to the labour used. This will be explained below. If we know the amount of capital and labour used in the food sector, we can derive the wage rate and the rental rate by equating them to the marginal product of labour and capital, respectively.[6]

Multinationals may arise in the production of manufactures, a homogeneous good, in a framework of imperfect competition using the Cournot model explained in Chapter 9. To model point 2 of Section 15.4, arguing that multinational production is (high-skilled) labour intensive, we assume that the production process of manufactures uses no capital.[7] The entire capital stock in both countries is therefore employed in the production of food, such that there is no need for a sub-index f in equation (15.2). In accordance with points 5 and 7 of Section 15.4, arguing that multinationals are characterized by firm-level and plant-level fixed costs, there are increasing returns to scale in the production process of manufactures. This will be modelled as a somewhat more complex version of the production process of Chapter 10.

The production of manufactures, which uses only labour, is characterized by the following parameters (identical in both countries).

- c – the (constant) marginal production costs in terms of labour. Together with the wage rate in the country of production, this determines the marginal costs of production.
- t – the amount of labour needed to transport one unit of manufactures from Austria to Bolivia, or vice versa. As argued by Dunning, it is necessary to have a location advantage for explaining multinationals, that is an incentive to produce in a country rather than to export to it, which is provided in this framework by the transport costs t.
- F – the firm-level fixed costs in terms of labour. Since each firm has to incur these costs only once, it provides the ownership advantage in Dunning's framework. Presumably, the firm-level fixed costs represent investments in R & D, employing white-collar workers for the technically more complex manufactures products, in accordance with points 1–4 of Section 15.4.
- G – the plant-level fixed costs in terms of labour. The firm can decide, at a cost, to set up more than one production plant, which enables the firm to avoid the transport costs t. Naturally, the firm only sets up multi-plant production if it is profitable to do so.

We can now distinguish between four different types of firms in the manufactures sector, as summarized in the decision process of Figure 15.9. First, the firm can decide in which country, Austria or Bolivia, it will establish its headquarters. In conjunction with the wage rate, this determines the level of the firm-specific and plant-specific fixed cost in the country of establishment. Second, the firm can decide whether or not to establish a production plant in the other country.[8] The advantage is, of course, that this allows the firm to avoid the transport costs of exporting goods to the other country. The disadvantage is that the firm has to incur extra fixed plant costs in the other country. If the firm does *not* establish a production plant in the other country we will call it a *national* firm, n_A if it is established in Austria and n_B if it is established in Bolivia. If the firm does establish a production plant in the other country we will call it a *multinational* firm, m_A if the headquarters are established in Austria and m_B if the headquarters are in Bolivia. If M_{AA}^n are the sales of manufactures in Austria of a national firm established in Austria, M_{AB}^n are the sales of manufactures in Bolivia of a national firm

Figure 15.9 Decision process and firm types

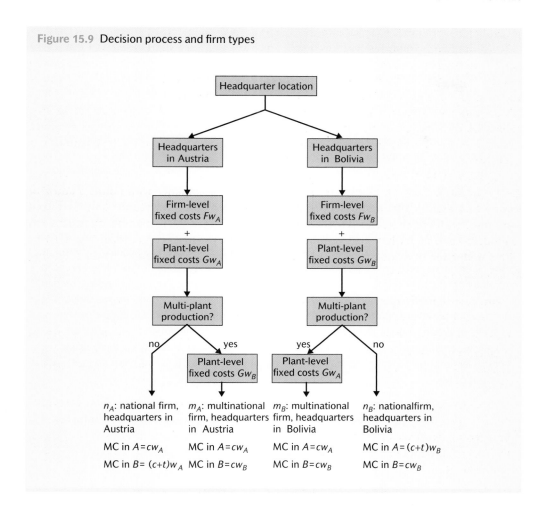

established in Austria, and similarly for M_{AA}^m and M_{AB}^m for multinational firms. The cost functions for firms with headquarters in Austria are therefore:

(15.3)   national firm: $(F + G)w_A + cw_A \overbrace{M_{AA}^n}^{\text{domestic sales}} + (c + t)w_A \overbrace{M_{AB}^n}^{\text{foreign sales}}$

multinational firm: $(F + G)w_A + Gw_B + cw_A \underbrace{M_{AA}^m}_{\substack{\text{domestic} \\ \text{sales}}} + cw_B \underbrace{M_{AB}^m}_{\substack{\text{foreign} \\ \text{sales}}}$

The remainder of the model is familiar from previous chapters. The utility function in both countries is as specified in Chapter 7 (Cobb–Douglas), with δ_m as the share of income spent on manufactures. This implies that the price elasticity of demand is equal to 1, such that the optimal pricing rule for a firm is equal to its market share; see Technical Note 9.2 for details. Firms will enter the market for manufactures in both countries until (excess) profits are equal to zero. Finally, general equilibrium obviously requires full employment of labour and capital, as well as market clearing for food and manufactures in both countries.

Box 15.2   Top business locations

Firms take many different factors into consideration before deciding where to locate their new business. The quality of the labour force is important, as is political and social stability, the quality of infrastructure (roads, telecommunications, railroads, air connections), the links to suppliers and demanders, unemployment, inflation, etc. To evaluate these various aspects, UNCTAD conducted a large survey among experts and multinational corporations in the 2005 *World Investment Report* in which China, India, and the USA constituted the top three locations on both lists.

The best location depends, of course, on the type of business the firm wants to establish. Japan, for example, does not make it to the top ten lists in Table 15.2, but is ranked fourth if a firm is looking for an attractive R&D location; see Figure 15.10. Suppose, similarly, that a firm wants to establish an efficient distribution centre with good links to other parts of Europe. Then, according to Buck Consultants International, the Netherlands is the best location, followed by Belgium and France. However, if a firm wants to establish a European headquarters, the UK is ranked first, followed by the Netherlands and (tied) Belgium and Germany. If a firm wants to establish a high-tech European production site, the UK is ranked first, followed by Ireland and France. Although these lists tend to draw a lot of media attention and may be flattering for high-ranked countries, we should not overemphasize their importance. Investment location decisions by firms may involve millions or billions of dollars and are therefore not taken lightly. Firms decide where to put up shop after carefully scrutinizing many possible locations for their advantages and disadvantages taking the particular firm situation into consideration, not on the basis of a list published by a magazine or a consulting firm.

Table 15.3 Most attractive global business locations, 2005

	Responses from experts		Responses from TNCs	
	Country	Score (%)	Country	Score (%)
1	China	85	China	87
2	USA	55	India	51
3	India	42	USA	51
4	Brazil	24	Russian Federation	33
5	Russian Federation	21	Brazil	20
6	UK	21	Mexico	16
7	Germany	12	Germany	13
8	Poland	9	UK	13
9	Singapore	9	Thailand	11
10	Ukraine	9	Canada	7

Source: UNCTAD, *World Investment Report* (2005).

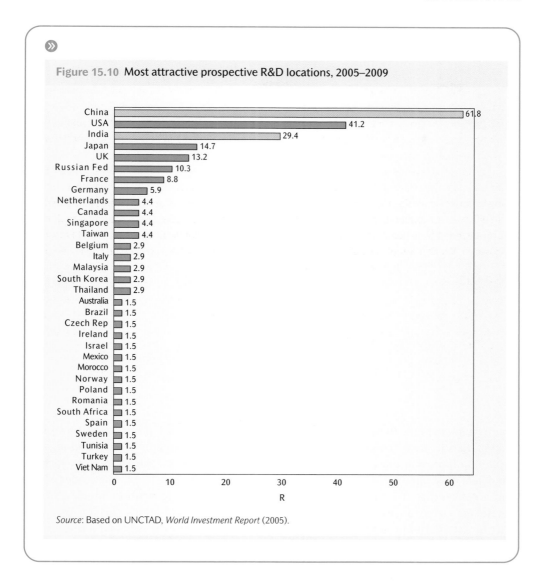

Figure 15.10 Most attractive prospective R&D locations, 2005–2009

Source: Based on UNCTAD, *World Investment Report* (2005).

15.6 Characterization of equilibrium

The main strong point of the current multinational models is the ability *endogenously* to determine the market structure. Firms may or may not decide to establish headquarters in a country. Similarly, they may or may not decide to establish another production plant in the other country. Whether or not they make these decisions is determined within the model, thus determining the nature of market competition endogenously. The market equilibrium outcome depends, of course, on the parameters and the size and distribution of the capital and labour stock.

Unfortunately, the main strong point of the current multinational models also constitutes its main weakness, as illustrated in Figure 15.11. The flexibility of the model, which enables a

Figure 15.11 Possible national/multinational regimes

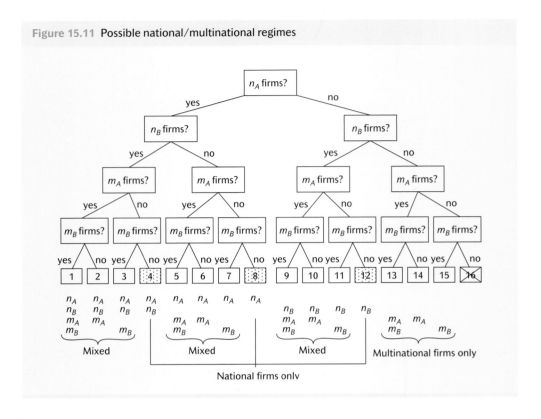

firm in manufactures to be a national firm in either country, or a multinational firm with headquarters in either country, opens up four logical possibilities: n_A, n_B, m_A, and m_B. This implies, in turn, that there are $2^4 = 16$ possible equilibrium market structures, of which we can delete only one (there has to be at least one firm); see Figure 15.11. The reader will of course realize that it is tiresome, if not virtually impossible, to analyse fifteen different regimes for a large range of parameter values or endowment distributions. Imagine the possibility of distinguishing between national firms, horizontal multinationals, *and* vertical multinationals, as some models do, in a world of five countries; it would increase the range of possible firms to $3 \times 5 = 15$, and the range of possible regimes to $2^{15} - 1 = 32,767$. It is clear that such a number of possibilities cannot be analysed without a powerful tool to assist the researcher.

To present the main results of the multinational model more clearly, we will group the fifteen regimes of Figure 15.11 into three aggregate types; (i) the shaded regimes in Figure 15.11 with *only national* firms, (ii) the three regimes on the right of Figure 15.11 with *only multinational* firms, and (iii) the other regimes with a *mixed* composition of firms (nationals and multinationals).

Figure 15.12 recalls the impact of different distributions of the world endowment of capital and labour between the two countries in a modified Edgeworth Box; see Chapter 6. At point C, in the centre of the box, the capital–labour ratio is the same in the two countries, and they are exactly equal in size. Going from point C to the north-east corner does not affect the capital–labour ratio in either country, but implies that Austria becomes larger than Bolivia.

Figure 15.12 Endowment distributions

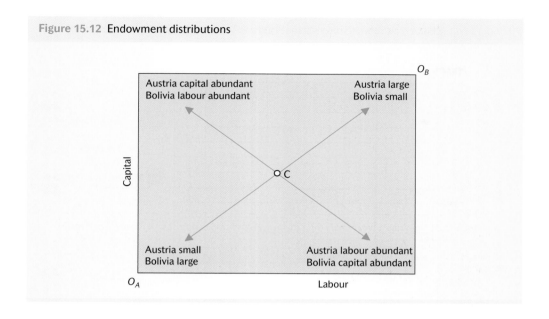

The reverse holds if we go in the opposite direction, to the south-west corner. Similarly, going from point C to the north-west corner implies that capital becomes more abundant in Austria and labour becomes more abundant in Bolivia. Again, the reverse effect holds if we go into the opposite direction.

Figure 15.13(a) shows the impact of all possible distributions of the world endowment of capital and labour between the two countries for the three main types of endogenous market equilibria of the multinational model in the base scenario, in which the transport costs are 15 per cent as a proportion of marginal costs and (if the wages in the two countries are equalized) the fixed costs for a multinational firm are 60 per cent higher than for a national firm.

The following observations are evident.

(i) If the two countries are *similar* in size and capital–labour ratio (in the neighbourhood of the centre of the box), the production equilibrium is dominated by *multinational* firms.

(ii) If the two countries are *different* in size and capital–labour ratio (in the corners of the box), the production equilibrium is dominated by *national* firms.

(iii) For *intermediate* endowment distributions, the production equilibrium is *mixed*, with both national firms and multinational firms.

All three observations are in striking correspondence with the empirical facts discussed in Sections 15.2 and 15.3, namely (i) large foreign direct investment flows between similar developed nations, (ii) virtually no foreign direct investment flows to the small least developed nations, and (iii) moderate investment flows to the Asian NICs (newly industrializing countries) and Latin America.

How can we explain these results? As the reader will recall from the description of the structure of the multinational model in Section 15.5, the decision to start multinational

Figure 15.13 Characterization of main regimes (a) base scenario, (b) smaller countries; 40%

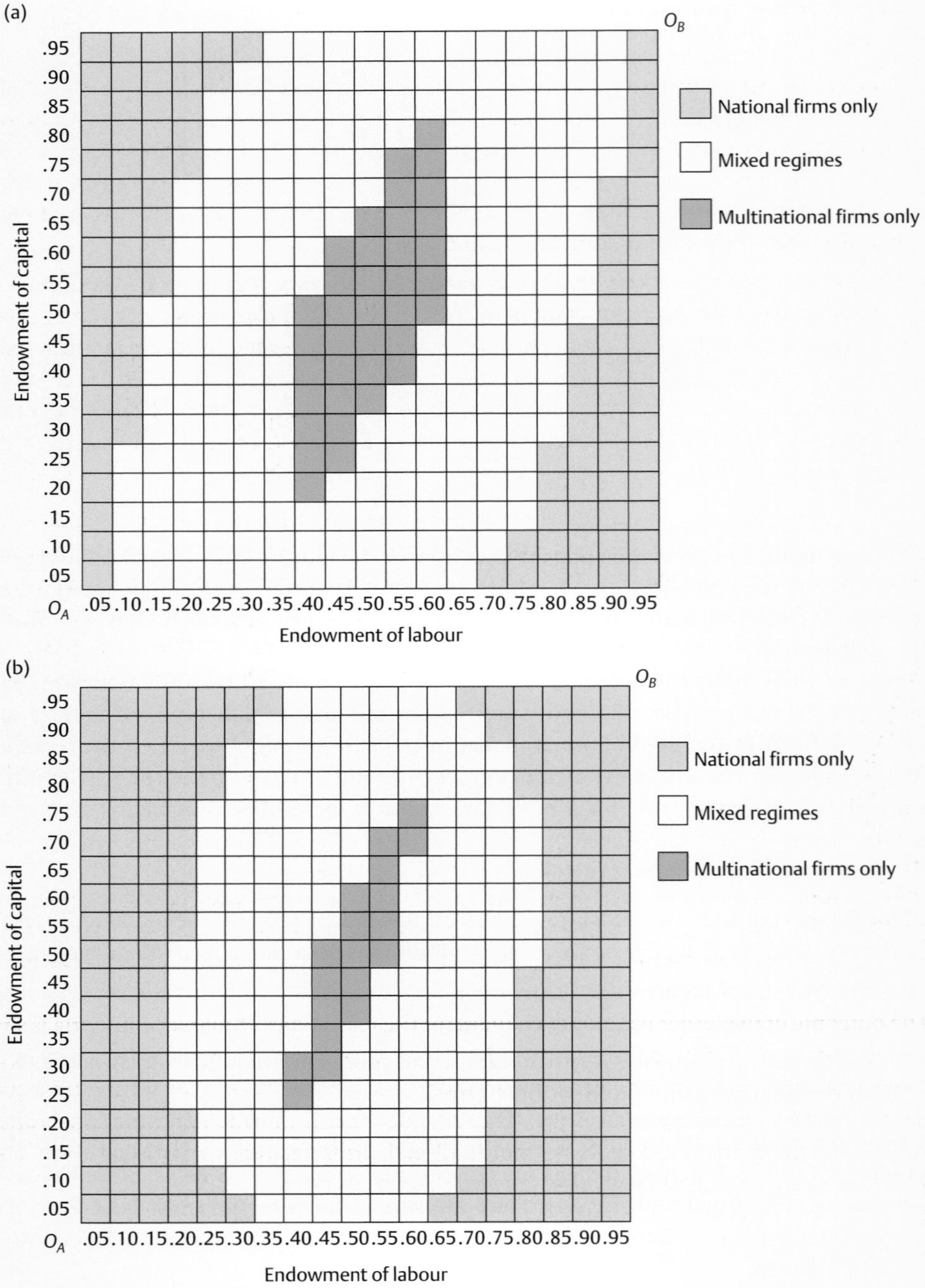

Source: Reprinted from *Journal of International Economics*, 46: Markusen and Venables, 'Multinational firms and the new trade theory', 194–5, copyright (1998), with permission from Elsevier Science.

production, that is set up a second production plant in the other country, depends on the size of the extra fixed plant costs relative to the size of the transport costs. Now suppose that we are close to one of the corners of the Edgeworth Box, that is either (a) the endowment ratio is very different between the two countries, or (b) one country is very small and the other country is very large:

(a) If the endowment ratio is very different, there is a strong incentive for Heckscher–Ohlin type inter-industry trade. The labour-rich country will specialize in the production of the labour-intensive manufactures. Since labour is expensive in the capital-abundant country it will be too expensive to incur the additional fixed costs of setting up an extra production plant, such that the production equilibrium is characterized by national firms producing manufactures in the labour-abundant country only.

(b) If one of the countries is very small, it is important to realize that there are economies of scale associated with the production of manufactures. This makes the small country unattractive as a home base for production (as it will be impossible to recuperate the fixed costs domestically) and as the basis for a foreign affiliate (the small market implies that the transport costs are fairly low if this market is serviced from abroad). The production equilibrium is therefore characterized by national firms producing manufactures in the large country only.

In both case (a) and case (b) of different countries the production equilibrium is characterized by national firms, which explains point (ii) above. At the same time, the above reasoning explains why multinationals arise if countries are similar, as in point (i) above, because similar countries imply similar wage rates (no specialization incentive) and similar market size (large transport costs to the other market which can be avoided by setting up a subsidiary abroad). The intermediate cases with the mixed results, point (iii) above, represent the transition from one extreme to the other.

The economic reasoning in cases (a) and (b) also enables us to understand the main impact of changing some of the parameters in the model. Since economies of scale are important for the production of manufactures, a decrease in the size of the global economy makes it more difficult to recuperate fixed costs investments. As fixed costs are larger for multinational firms than for national firms, a reduction in the size of the economy will reduce the range of endowment distributions in which multinationals arise, and increase the range of endowment distributions in which national firms arise, as shown in Figure 15.13(b). Growth in the world economy, as we have witnessed for many decades, therefore leads to the opposite effect of increasing the importance and occurrence of multinationals.

The outcome of two other parameter changes for the main types of market equilibria is similar to the situation depicted in Figure 15.13(b). First, a decrease in the transport costs of 10 per cent makes it relatively less attractive to incur the extra fixed costs of setting up a subsidiary abroad and therefore reduces the range of endowments in which multinationals arise. Second, increasing the fixed costs of multinational firms relative to national firms also reduces the range of endowments in which multinationals arise.

15.7 Case study: hard disk drives[9]

The manufacture of hard-disk drives (HDD), an essential component for the computer business, is a very dynamic industry, with revenues of more than $30 billion, product life cycles of less than eighteen months, and prices falling at more than 40 per cent per annum for more

Figure 15.14 The hard-disk drive value chain

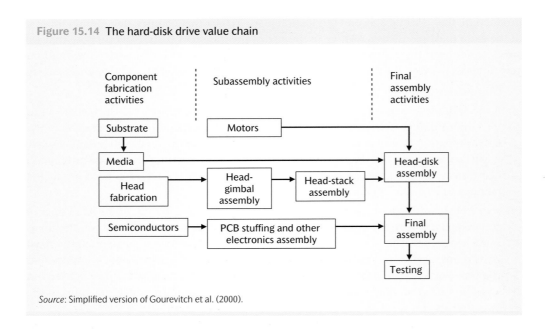

Source: Simplified version of Gourevitch et al. (2000).

than a decade. Twenty years ago not only 80 per cent of all drives production was done by US firms but the same was true for the assembly activities. As we will see, the pressure of globalization has rapidly changed the structure of doing business, as measured by the value chain, in this high-tech industry dominated by multinationals.

Figure 15.14 gives a simplified picture of the main steps in the HDD value chain, the sequence and range of activities that go into making a final product. Ignoring R&D, there are four major steps in the value chain: (i) electronics – this includes semiconductors, printed circuit boards (PCBs) and their assembly; (ii) heads – devices that read and write the data, which are manufactured in stages with labour-intensive subassembly activities, such as head-gimbal assembly (HGA) and head-stack assembly (HSA); (iii) media – the material on which the information is stored,[10] and (iv) motors – which spin the media with extreme precision.[11] Producers locate the production of the many discrete steps in the value chain around the world for various reasons. The final assembly of the disk, which gives it the 'Made in Singapore' or 'Made in Taiwan' label, is only one, and not necessarily the most important, aspect in this process. As Gourevitch, Bohn, and McKendrick (2000), discussing the structure of Seagate, the world's largest manufacturer of HDDs, put it:

> Although Seagate has kept control over almost all production, it has globally dispersed its operations to an extraordinary degree. A single component may be worked on in five countries and cross two oceans while Seagate is building it up through its value chain. Seagate develops new products (and processes) at seven locations in the United States and Singapore. It assembles disk drives in Singapore, Malaysia, Thailand, and China. In heads, the company fabricates its wafers in the United States and Northern Ireland, and cuts them into bars and assembles them into HGAs in Thailand, Malaysia, and the Philippines. It makes media in Singapore and motors in Thailand. It manufactures printed circuit cables in Thailand and assembles the electronics onto printed circuit boards in Indonesia, Malaysia, and Singapore. It is the largest nongovernment employer in Thailand and Singapore.

Table 15.4 Hard-disk drives: indicators of nationality of production

Measure[a]	USA	Japan	SE Asia	Other Asia	Europe	Other
Nationality of firm	88.4	9.4	0.0	2.2	0.0	0.0
Final assembly	4.6	15.5	64.2	5.7	10.0	0.0
Employment	19.3	8.3	44.0	17.1	4.7	6.5
Wages paid	39.5	29.7	12.9	3.3	8.5	6.1

[a] Nationality of firm (% of unit output); location of final assembly; employment in value chain; and wages paid in value chain, respectively.

Source: Gourevitch et al. (2000, table 2) (data for 1995). All numbers as percentage of world total.

Table 15.4 gives four different indicators of nationality of production for the HDD industry. The large majority (88.4 per cent per unit of output) of HDDs is made by US firms. But in sharp contrast to twenty years ago, only 4.6 per cent of the final assembly of HDDs is done in the USA. Most final assembly of disks now takes place in South-East Asia (64.2 per cent), which means the bulk of employment is in South-East Asia (44 per cent), rather than in the USA (19.3 per cent), although the value of wages paid is much higher in the USA (39.5 per cent) than in South-East Asia (12.9 per cent). Essentially, the HDD industry currently has two concentration clusters. The first is Silicon Valley in the USA, with a substantial share of research, design, development, marketing, and management (with a smaller counterpart in Japan). The second is in South-East Asia, which dominates final assembly, most labour-intensive subassemblies, and low-tech components, such as baseplates.

15.8 Conclusions

Multinational firms, with increasing shares in world production, investment, and trade flows, represent the most visible part of the 'globalization' phenomenon. The largest multinational firms are established in the OECD countries, with a concentration in certain sectors (electronics, petroleum, automotive, and chemical). Most foreign direct investment (FDI) arises from (majority) acquisitions, rather than from greenfield investments or mergers. Most FDI is horizontal, that is within the same industry, rather than vertical or conglomerate. Moreover, most FDI is from OECD countries to OECD countries, with Western Europe and Japan as the largest net sources and Latin America and Other Asia (non-NICs) as the largest net destinations (notably China). The OLI framework argues that a firm must have ownership, location, and internalization advantages before deciding to become a multinational. Empirical research finds that multinationals are R&D intensive, have a high value of intangible assets, produce differentiated goods, and make new or complex products.

An important accomplishment of the modern general equilibrium models of multinationals is the ability to determine the market structure endogenously; that is, the existence and distribution of national and multinational firms is determined by the production functions and the distribution of endowments. In general, and in accordance with the stylized facts, multinational firms dominate if countries are more similar, while national firms dominate if countries differ in size or relative factor endowment abundance. The main disadvantage of the modern general equilibrium models of multinationals is the rapidly increasing number of cases to be studied, which sometimes makes it hard to keep a clear overview of the results. When discussing the hard-disk-drive industry we saw that similar types of activity tend to cluster in certain regions (R&D in Silicon Valley and final assembly in South-East Asia), and that the 'nationality' of the final product depends very much on the indicator used.

Question 15.1

Several academics have wondered why a firm establishes a production plant abroad since this involves extra costs compared to home production (think, for example, of the cost of transferring people to a foreign country, of acquiring information, of overcoming language barriers, and of fighting cultural differences).

15.1A What is required according to Dunning before firms establish or purchase production plants abroad? Describe all the conditions carefully.

15.1B Give an example of every condition that is not mentioned in the main text.

15.1C How are the conditions modelled in the multinational model of Markusen and Venables (see Section 15.5)?

15.1D Why do all conditions have to be satisfied before a firm becomes a multinational?

Question 15.2

Chapter 15 first describes some empirical observations on the foreign direct investment flows between countries. The Markusen and Venables model (see Section 15.5) explains some of the most important empirical observations. This question reviews the empirical observations and their theoretical explanations.

15.2A Are the FDI flows into the least developed nations large or small? What is the theoretical explanation for this in the Markusen and Venables model?

15.2B Are the FDI flows into the developed nations large or small? What is the theoretical explanation for this in the Markusen and Venables model?

15.2C What other factors could explain FDI flows between countries?

Question 15.3

Imagine a machine manufacturer operating in East Germany. Before the fall of the Berlin Wall the manufacturer is only producing for the national market and prohibited from exporting to other countries. After the fall of the Berlin Wall, the manufacturer is allowed to sell machines to other countries. In contemplating how to deal with the new situation the manufacturer uses the model of Markusen and Venables. She wants to sell the machines in four countries with the following characteristics:

- *West Germany* is more advanced and capital abundant compared to East Germany. Because they are neighbouring countries, transport costs are low. Moreover, the German government provides a subsidy to East German firms establishing a plant in West Germany.

- *Poland* is also a neighbouring country with low transport costs. The Polish government does not provide a subsidy for the establishment of a plant. The level of development (measured by the endowment ratio) is more or less the same as in East Germany, but the Polish economy is considerably larger.

- As a result of newly introduced safety controls at the border, transport costs to the *Czech Republic* are very high. Like Poland, the Czech government does not provide a subsidy for the establishment of a new plant. East Germany and the Czech Republic are broadly equal in size and in level of development.

- *Slovakia* is not a neighboring country, such that transport costs are high. The establishment costs for a plant are high due to a tax. Also Slovakia and East Germany have the same level of development, but the Slovakian economy is smaller than the East German economy.

The manufacturer has to decide if she should establish a plant in the other country or produce the machines in East Germany and export the products.

15.3A At which node of the decision tree in Figure 15.9 is the manufacturer?

15.3B Consider for each of the four countries if it is likely that the manufacturer establishes a new plant according to the Markusen and Venables model. In which country is the producer most likely to establish a plant and in which least likely?

 See the Online Resource Centre for a Study Guide containing more questions www.oxfordtextbooks.co.uk/orc/vanmarrewijk/

NOTES

1 See UNCTAD (2000: 101).

2 Argentina, Brazil, Chile, China, Hungary, Indonesia, Malaysia, Mexico, Poland, Singapore.

3 See Markusen (1995) and Caves (1996) for further references.

4 Important early contributions are: Helpman (1984, 1985), Markusen (1984), and Ethier (1986).

5 The complete specification of the model is a bit too involved for this book, even in the Technical Notes section, so we refer the reader for details to Markusen and Venables (1998).

6 Which is equal to the value marginal product of labour and capital because food is the numéraire.

7 To emphasize the distinction between high-skilled versus low-skilled labour, the reader may reinterpret the capital stock K in this chapter as low-skilled labour and the labour stock L as high-skilled labour. The production of manufactures is then high-skilled labour intensive and the production of food low-skilled labour intensive.

8 The logical possibility of incurring firm-specific fixed costs in one country and one plant specific cost in the other country (vertical multinational) is not taken into consideration, see Markusen et al. (1996).

9 This section is based on Brakman, Garretsen, and van Marrewijk (2001).

10 According to Gourevitch, Bohn, and McKendrick (2000: 304): 'Typically, aluminum blank substrates are nickel-plated and polished before the platters are sputtered and finished. As with heads, media are a very high-technology aspect of HDD production'.

11 The Japanese Nippon Densan company has about a 75 per cent worldwide market share in motors.

NEW GOODS AND DEVELOPMENT

16

Objectives/key terms

- New goods
- Kaldor's stylized facts
- Solow residual
- Discount rate

- Variety/quality
- Neoclassical growth model
- Endogenous growth model
- Geography experiment

The stylized facts of economic growth, with ever-increasing welfare levels, cannot be adequately explained by the neoclassical growth model. Focusing instead on the importance of new goods (variety/quality), we stress the role of the profit-seeking entrepreneur for dynamic innovations. The geography approach may be useful in explaining the localization of and large swings in economic prosperity.

16.1 Introduction

After my alarm clock woke me up this morning, I made breakfast in the microwave oven. While driving to work in my car I called my wife on my mobile phone to remind her to buy Madonna's new compact disc. As soon as I arrived at work, I turned on the electric light and my computer, eager to check for new e-mails.

You probably didn't notice anything peculiar in the above three sentences, although you may have been wondering what a description of my morning activities is doing in a book on international economics. Two hundred years ago, however, the first three sentences would have been utter nonsense for everybody, even for a well-educated person. He or she would not know what an alarm clock was, or a microwave oven, nor be familiar with a car, a mobile phone, a compact disc, electric light, a computer, or e-mail. In fact, someone living 100 years ago, rather than 200, would also have been unaware of the above-mentioned goods and services, with the exception perhaps of cars and electric light. Indeed, come to think of it, I myself could not have imagined 30 years ago that I would be writing these words on a portable computer, that I would be able to reach my family with my mobile phone while walking around virtually anywhere in Europe, or that I would work together with other economists in the Netherlands, Cyprus, Italy, Luxembourg, Poland, the UK, and the USA by sending files back and forth as e-mail attachments.

Our lives have changed drastically over the past 200 years, 100 years, or even 30 years. It is much more comfortable than it has ever been in the past. We are able to do things (watch television, play laser tag games), visit places (Hawaii, Mount Kilimanjaro, the moon), and see things (even molecules, using a scanning tunnelling microscope) that were unheard of before. The quality of our lives has improved, in short, not only because we are now able to produce and consume *more* goods and services (larger houses, bigger cars, more hamburgers), but also, and probably more importantly, because we are now able to produce and consume

Famous economists	Paul Romer

Fig. 16.1
Paul Romer
(1955–)

After studying mathematics, physics, and economics at the University of Chicago, where he received his PhD in economics, Romer worked at Rochester, Chicago, and Berkeley, before settling at Stanford University. He was the instigator and most important developer of 'endogenous growth theory', which seeks to better understand the economic forces leading to innovation and improvements in standards of living. It all started with Romer's 'Increasing returns and long run growth', published in the *Journal of Political Economy* in 1986. His research in this area culminated in 'Endogenous technological change', published in the same journal in 1990. We should also mention his 1994 work 'New goods, old theory, and the welfare costs of trade restrictions' on the difficulty of comprehending, appreciating, and measuring the importance of *not* introducing new goods and services in an economy, published in the *Journal of Development Economics*.

entirely *new* goods and services, which better fit our preferences, or enable us to fulfil hitherto hidden needs and desires. All of this is an ongoing process. We can thus rest assured that only twenty years from now, we will have witnessed the birth of yet another large range of unknown, fascinating, useful, or otherwise interesting and worthwhile new goods and services, provided we last that long.

If new goods and services are so important for raising the standard of living and improving our well-being, the issues, problems, and policies affecting the creation and introduction of new goods and services will, of course, have been intensively and exhaustively analysed within the economic paradigm. Well . . . no, not exactly. These issues have, in fact, received only limited attention for a long time, with the noteworthy exceptions of Young (1928) and Schumpeter (1934). The main reason is probably, as pointed out by Paul Romer (1994: 9):

> Once we admit that there is room for newness – that there are vastly more conceivable possibilities than realized outcomes – we must confront the fact that there is no special logic behind the world we inhabit, no particular justification for why things are the way they are. Any number of arbitrarily small perturbations along the way could have made the world as we know it turn out very differently.

The issue is illustrated in Figure 16.2. Suppose the domestic production possibility frontier is given by the shaded area in Figure 16.2, and we have to decide whether it is better for the economy to produce at point A or at point B. The problem of acknowledging the importance of new goods starts exactly at the first word of the previous sentence: 'suppose'. As soon as we do that, and as soon as we draw a production possibility frontier, as we do in Figure 16.2, we already presuppose that both good X and good Y already exist, that is they have been invented and it is possible to produce them. The large majority of economic analysis focuses on efficiency and optimality considerations within this framework. This leads, of course, to important insights and policy prescriptions. What if, instead, good Y has not yet been invented and is not actually produced? This drastically changes the questions we must try to answer. Why has good Y not been invented? At what cost could it be invented and introduced? What are the gains for an individual firm and for society as a whole of inventing,

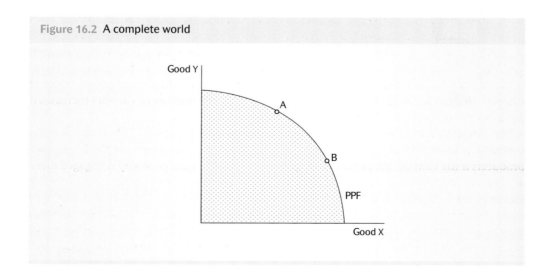

Figure 16.2 A complete world

producing, and introducing good Y? The starting point of the analysis is, therefore, supposing not that something exists, but that it does not. We return to this in the next chapter.

16.2 Modelling new goods

What is a new good? Well, if we say it is something that was not there before, any production activity undertaken by producers results in new goods. If the baker takes the loaves out of the oven, he has produced new goods. If I were to buy a Big Mac at McDonald's, it would also be classified as a new good. Clearly, this is not what we have in mind when we are talking of new goods, although at some point in time both examples could have been classified as such; the bread I buy (called 'Waldkorn') did not exist 30 years ago, and the Big Mac was invented by Jim Delligatti in 1968. Let's say a new good is something that was not there before, and which substantially deviates from any other good or service ever produced before.

Where does this leave us? Necessarily in a grey area. Mobile telephones are fairly new goods (although pre-dated by their bulkier ancestors for a longer time than you might think). In connection with an enormous antenna network, mobile phones are able to deliver services previously unavailable. You would probably also classify digital versatile disks (DVDs) and DVD players as fairly new goods. But are they? DVDs enable you to enjoy a movie on your television at home any time you want. But isn't that service already provided by VCRs? No, a DVD fan might say, the services of DVDs were not already provided by VCRs because a VCR cannot deliver the same clear image and high-quality sound as a DVD, which makes DVDs a new good. We do not want to go too deeply into this type of discussion, but it is at least clear that there are essentially two types of new goods. First, there are new goods that deliver (consumer) services previously unavailable, such as the ability to fly, to talk on a mobile phone, to play a computer game, etc. We have already called such new goods 'varieties' in Chapter 10. Second, there are new goods that deliver similar (consumer) services as before, but of a better quality, such as the introduction of colour television instead of black and white, the introduction of compact discs instead of the LP record, a more comfortable house because of better insulation, etc. We will call such new goods 'quality' improvements.

The variety approach

How do we model the introduction of new goods? Based on our classification, there are two possible roads to follow, namely the modelling of the introduction of new varieties and the modelling of quality improvements. We have already seen the variety approach in Chapter 10. The essence of the variety approach is based on the Dixit–Stiglitz specification by the term N, indicating the number of varieties available on the market. In the Krugman model of Chapter 10 and the Ethier interpretation of Section 10.8, the number of varieties increases if the extent of the market increases.

The Krugman and Ethier variety approach is illustrated in Figure 16.3. At time $t = 0$ the economy is in autarky and $N_{t=0}$ varieties are available to the consumers (or the final goods producers if the varieties are intermediate goods). At time $t = 1$ the economy is engaged more actively in international trade, which increases the extent of the market and therefore increases the number of available varieties to $N_{t=1}$. The variety approach is also used in a more dynamic setting of endogenous growth, in which case the number of available varieties may increase either as a result of an increase in the extent of the market, or as a result of active R&D efforts by firms to invent and introduce new varieties. In the latter case, Figure 16.3

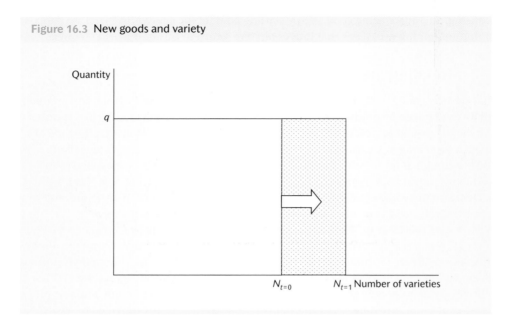

Figure 16.3 New goods and variety

depicts the evolution of the economy over time even in a stagnant population; see Romer (1990) and Grossman and Helpman (1991a).

The quality approach

The accumulated impact of quality improvements can be enormous. Take, for example, auto-mobile production. Cars have been around for more than 100 years. They first became a widely available popular means of transportation in the USA in 1908 when Henry Ford started building the Model T. Now millions of cars are produced and sold worldwide, the main mar-kets being Japan, Europe, and America. To many people, cars have therefore been available for decades. One could argue that cars today deliver similar services (transportation) as cars did 40 years ago. On the other hand, cars today are of so much better quality and deliver so much more power, comfort, safety, and pleasure that they are not at all comparable to the cars of 40 years ago. Most cars now have safety glass, anti-lock breaks, power steering, airbags, better fuel efficiency, more comfortable seats, and even navigational systems to help you find your way in a strange city. Indeed, it is no exaggeration to conclude that the most expensive Rolls-Royce available on the market 40 years ago, which only the happy few could afford, delivers worse transportation comfort and safety than the Volkswagen Golf does today, which more than half the population of the developed nations can afford.[1] All of this as a result of gradual improvements in quality.

The modelling of quality improvements is more complicated than the modelling of increases in product variety. Pioneering work was performed by Gene Grossman and Elhanan Helpman (1991a, 1991b) and Philippe Aghion and Peter Howitt (1992). The general modelling strategy, known as the 'quality ladder' approach, is illustrated in Figure 16.4, where we dis-tinguish between sixteen different varieties. Since we are concerned with quality improve-ments, the number of varieties will remain fixed. All goods can be produced at different quality levels. An increase in the quality level, as measured on the vertical axis in Figure 16.4,

Figure 16.4 Quality ladders

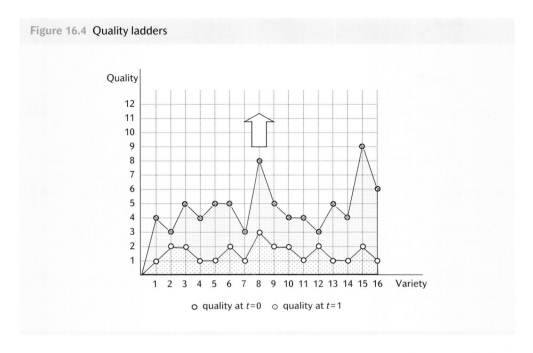

is able to better fulfil a consumer's preferences for the same quantity of output, or leads to higher productivity for the same quantity of output if it is an intermediate good.

Increases in the quality level are the result of R&D efforts by competing firms, trying to improve upon the current state-of-the-art technology. If a firm is successful in developing a quality improvement, this leads to a discrete increase in the quality level, which is therefore measured in integers $\{1, 2, 3, \ldots\}$ in Figure 16.4. A successful innovation allows the firm temporarily to drive its competitors out of the market and earn monopoly profits, until the firm itself is driven out of the market by the next successful innovator.

The open circles in Figure 16.4 illustrate the state-of-the-art technology at time $t = 0$. Variety number 8 is produced initially at the highest quality level ($q = 3$). The closed circles in Figure 16.4 illustrate the state-of-the-art technology at time $t = 1$. As drawn, all varieties have improved in quality, indicating that the R&D efforts led to successful innovations for all products. Variety number 8 has increased in quality from $q = 3$ to $q = 8$. Within the structure of this model, this indicates that there have been five successful innovations for variety 8 between time $t = 0$ and $t = 1$. Innovators in sectors number 2 and 12 have been less successful in that time period, since the quality improved only by one step in those two sectors. Most successful innovations have occurred in sector 15, where quality improved from $q = 2$ to $q = 9$, indicating seven successful innovations.

The R&D efforts in this approach are driven by the prospect of (temporarily) earning monopoly profits. Note that we discussed two distinct ways of modelling new goods, the variety approach and the quality approach. However, since both approaches lead to very similar economic outcomes, as clearly demonstrated by Grossman and Helpman (1991a), and the quality approach is analytically more complicated than the variety approach, we focus on the variety approach in the endogenous growth model of Section 16.6. First, however, we turn to dynamics, empirics, and the neoclassical growth model.

16.3 Kaldor's stylized facts of economic growth

After the discussion above on the importance of introducing new goods and services in an economy, an inherently dynamic issue, it is appropriate to investigate explicitly the economic forces underlying the evolution of the prosperity of nations. As we will see, the analysis of economic growth and international economics is closely linked. The neoclassical economic growth model uses a production structure similar to the neoclassical trade model of Part II.A. To overcome some of the shortcomings of neoclassical growth theory, the endogenous growth model was introduced in the 1980s, shortly after the arrival of the first new trade models, and using a similar structure as in Part II.B. Throughout this chapter, we present the most important empirical facts of economic growth and development, indicating how particular economic models may be useful in explaining these facts, and where support is lacking.

In an important contribution, Nicholas Kaldor (1961) suggests the following 'stylized facts' of economic change and development in capitalist societies as a starting point for the construction of theoretical models (see also Burmeister and Dobell, 1970: 65).[2]

1. The continued growth in the aggregate volume of production and in the productivity of labour at a steady trend rate.

2. A continued increase in the amount of capital per worker.

3. A steady rate of profit on capital.

4. Steady capital–output ratios over long periods.

5. A steady investment coefficient, and a steady share of profits and wages.

Two of these stylized facts are illustrated in Figure 16.5 for the USA (a) and France (b). The first, and most striking, fact is the steady trend rate increase in per capita output. Since Figure 16.5 (a) uses a logarithmic scale, the slope of the income graph represents the growth rate of the

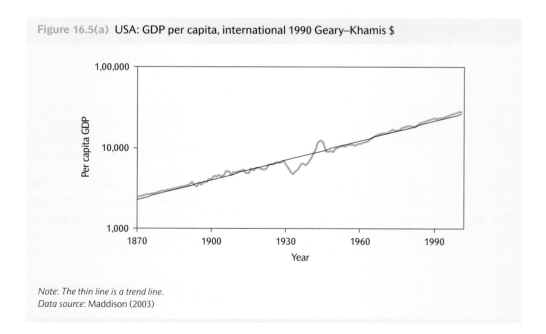

Figure 16.5(a) USA: GDP per capita, international 1990 Geary–Khamis $

Note: The thin line is a trend line.
Data source: Maddison (2003)

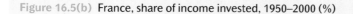

Figure 16.5(b) France, share of income invested, 1950–2000 (%)

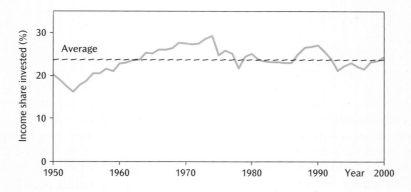

Data source: Penn World Table Version 6.1 (October 2002).

 Box 16.1   Tools: logarithmic graphs and a rule of thumb

To analyse graphically the impact of economic growth on the per capita income level we use a (natural) logarithmic scale in Figures 16.5, 16.8, and 16.9. The important advantage is that the *slope* of the income line reflects the *growth rate* of the economy, since:

$$y = ln(Y) \Rightarrow dy = d \, ln(Y) \; = \; \frac{dY}{Y} = \tilde{Y}$$

If the slope of the income graph is therefore relatively steady, as in Figure 16.5(a) for the USA, the *growth rate* of the economy is relatively steady. The reader must also realize that a one-unit increase in the income level in such a figure reflects a 2.72-fold increase in income level. A difference of two units in output therefore reflects a $2.72^2 = 7.39$-fold increase, a difference of three units reflects a 20.09-fold increase, etc. In evaluating the impact of seemingly small differences in growth rates it is useful to apply the following

Rule of thumb: a growth rate of x per cent implies a doubling in $70/x$ years.

According to the rule of thumb, which is surprisingly accurate, output doubles in 70 years if the growth rate is 1 per cent, whereas output doubles in 35 years if the growth rate is 2 per cent, etc.

---

economy; see Box 16.1. Over a longer time period, the slope of the income graph for the USA is indeed surprisingly steady. Using the Maddison data of Table 16.1, the compounded per capita growth rate for the USA in the period 1870–2001 has been 1.86 per cent. Applying a simple rule of thumb, see again Box 16.1, this implies a doubling in per capita output every $70/1.86 = 47.6$ years. On the remarkable stability of the American growth in output per capita Charles Jones (1995: 497) remarked:

an economist living in the year 1929 . . . 'fits a simple linear trend to the natural log of per capita GDP for the United States from 1880 to 1929 in an attempt to forecast per capita GDP today, say in 1987. How far off would the prediction be?' . . . the prediction is off by only about 5 percent.

Figure 16.5(b) shows part of Kaldor's stylized fact number 5 by depicting gross investment in France as a percentage of income. Arguing that the investment rate is steady, as Kaldor does, may be pushing it, but it is clear that over a longer time period there is no trend up or down in the relative investment level, but only fluctuations around the average rate.

Kaldor's other stylized facts are clearly related. If the investment level as a percentage of income is roughly steady, which must of course be driven by a fairly steady rate of profit, we are not surprised to find a steady capital–output ratio, such that capital per worker and output per worker will be rising over time. Section 16.5 will review some more evidence.

16.4 The neoclassical model and the Solow residual

The neoclassical model of economic growth was developed by Robert Solow (1956), for which he received the Nobel prize. It can, with some difficulty, explain Kaldor's stylized facts. The starting point of the analysis is a neoclassical aggregate production function, with constant returns to scale and the possibility of substituting between two factors of production, capital K and labour L, to produce output Y.

$$(16.1) \qquad Y_t = AK_t^\alpha L_t^{1-\alpha}$$

Increases in the output level can therefore be explained through an increase in one of the two factors of production. The capital stock increases through gross investment I, and decreases due to depreciation of capital μK, where μ is the rate of depreciation. The number of available labourers increases through the (exogenous) growth rate of the population n. If we let a sub-index t denote the time period, we get:

$$(16.2) \qquad K_{t+1} - K_t = I_t - \mu K_t; \quad L_{t+1} - L_t = nL_t$$

Entrepreneurs will, of course, invest in new capital only if it is profitable to do so. Frank Ramsey (1928) provides pioneering work in this area, and is therefore co-founder of the neoclassical growth model. We can, however, significantly simplify the analysis by positing, in accordance with stylized fact number 5, that the economic agents invest a constant fraction s of income into new capital goods, that is, $I_t = sY_t$. This simple framework suffices to show that the capital–labour ratio $k \equiv K/L$ evolves over time to a constant steady state rate, see Technical Note 16.1, given by

$$(16.3) \qquad sAk_t^\alpha = (\mu + n)k_t$$

The left-hand side of equation (16.3) represents the increase in the capital–labour ratio through gross investments, which depend on the savings rate s and the per capita output level Ak^α. It is a concave function, as illustrated in Figure 16.6, which reflects the decreasing marginal product of capital if more capital is used for a given level of labour. The right-hand side of equation (16.3) represents the required investment level to keep the capital–labour ratio constant, $(\mu+n)k$, by compensating for the rate of depreciation μk and the increase in labour nk. It is a linear function. The capital–labour ratio will increase if the investments are larger than what is required to keep the capital–labour ratio constant. This is illustrated for $k = 4$ in Figure 16.6, where the investment level at point G is larger than what is required to compensate for depreciation and labour force growth at point F, thus leading to an increase

Figure 16.6 Steady state equilibrium in the neoclassical growth model

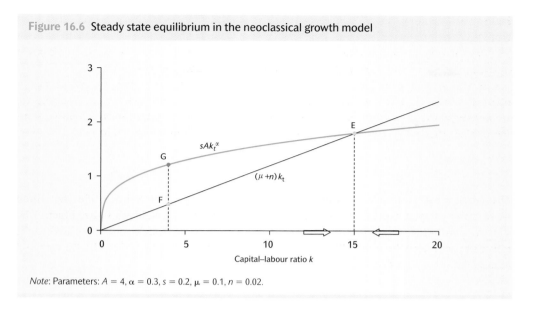

Note: Parameters: $A = 4, \alpha = 0.3, s = 0.2, \mu = 0.1, n = 0.02$.

in the capital–labour ratio. The economy will evolve over time to the steady state equilibrium point E.

Can the model sketched so far explain Kaldor's stylized facts? No, it cannot. The main difficulty is the fact that the economy evolves over time to a constant capital–labour ratio and a constant level of output per worker. To allow for an *increasing* level of output per capita, the neoclassical growth model imposes *exogenous* technological change. The easiest way to do this is by allowing the productivity constant A in equation (16.1) to increase over time, and thus be time dependent (A_t). Changing equation (16.1) accordingly and writing the result in relative changes, see Chapter 5, gives

(16.4)

$$\tilde{Y}_t = \underset{\substack{technical \\ change}}{\tilde{A}_t} + \underset{\substack{capital \\ increase}}{\alpha\tilde{K}_t} + \underset{\substack{labour\ force \\ increase}}{(1-\alpha)\tilde{L}_t} \Rightarrow$$

$$\tilde{A}_t = \underset{\substack{to\ be \\ explained}}{\tilde{Y}_t} - \underset{'explained'}{[\alpha\tilde{K}_t + (1-\alpha)\tilde{L}_t]} = \text{Solow residual}$$

The first part of equation (16.4) shows that increases in output $\tilde{Y}_t$ are the result of investments in capital $\alpha\tilde{K}_t$, changes in the labour force $(1-\alpha)\tilde{L}_t$, and improvements in technology $\tilde{A}_t$. Since improvements in technology are not explained within the model, it is called the Solow residual. It is calculated as given in the second part of equation (16.4).

Figure 16.7 shows the decomposition of economic growth into an 'explained' part from increases in the capital stock and the labour force, and the unexplained part of the Solow residual. As is evident from Figure 16.7(b), the Solow residual represents a sizeable part of the actual growth rate (usually more than one-third), which it follows closely. This fact and the fact that it is necessary to impose exogenous technological change to allow the economy to grow represent the major drawbacks of the neoclassical growth model.

Figure 16.7 'Explained' growth and Solow residual

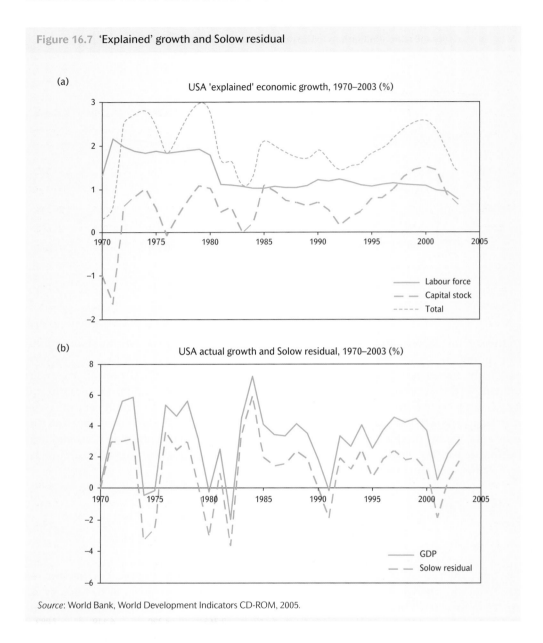

Source: World Bank, World Development Indicators CD-ROM, 2005.

16.5 Empirical pictures

Table 16.1 presents income per capita for a selection of currently developed and currently less developed countries for a longer time period (1870–2001), as pioneered by Angus Maddison (1991, 2003). The data are in constant 1990 international Geary–Khamis dollars, using a sophisticated aggregation method of calculating PPPs which facilitates comparing countries with each other. The evolution of income per capita as given in Table 16.1 is illustrated using a logarithmic scale in Figure 16.8 for the developed countries and in Figure 16.9 for the less developed countries.

Table 16.1 Income per capita levels (1990 Geary–Khamis $)

Country	1870	1890	1910	1930	1950	1970	1990	2001
(a) Currently developed countries								
Australia	3,273	4,458	5,210	4,708	7,412	12,024	17,106	21,883
Austria	1,863	2,443	3,290	3,586	3,706	9,747	16,905	20,225
Belgium	2,692	3,428	4,064	4,979	5,462	10,611	17,197	20,924
Canada	1,695	2,378	4,066	4,811	7,291	12,050	18,872	22,302
Denmark	2,003	2,523	3,705	5,341	6,943	12,686	18,452	23,160
Finland	1,140	1,381	1,906	2,666	4,253	9,577	16,866	20,344
France	1,876	2,376	2,965	4,532	5,271	11,664	18,093	21,092
Germany	1,839	2,428	3,348	3,973	3,881	10,839	15,929	18,677
Italy	1,499	1,667	2,332	2,918	3,502	9,719	16,313	19,040
Japan	737	1,012	1,304	1,850	1,921	9,714	18,789	20,683
Netherlands	2,757	3,323	3,789	5,603	5,996	11,967	17,262	21,722
Norway	1,432	1,777	2,256	3,712	5,463	10,033	18,466	24,580
Sweden	1,662	2,086	2,980	3,937	6,739	12,716	17,695	20,562
Switzerland	2,102	3,182	4,331	6,246	9,064	16,904	21,482	22,264
UK	3,190	4,009	4,611	5,441	6,939	10,767	16,430	20,127
USA	2,445	3,392	4,964	6,213	9,561	15,030	23,201	27,948
(b) Currently less developed countries								
Argentina	1,311	2,152	3,822	4,080	4,987	7,302	6,436	8,137
Bangladesh					540	629	640	897
Brazil	713	794	769	1,048	1,672	3,057	4,923	5,570
Chile			2,472	3,143	3,821	5,293	6,402	10,001
China	530	540		567	439	783	1,858	3,583
Colombia			1,162	1,474	2,153	3,094	4,840	5,087
India	533	584	697	726	619	868	1,309	1,957
Indonesia	654	660	834	1,164	840	1,194	2,516	3,256
South Korea	604			1,020	770	1,954	8,704	14,673
Mexico	674	1,011	1,694	1,618	2,365	4,320	6,119	7,089
Pakistan					643	952	1,597	1,947
Peru			975	1,417	2,263	3,807	2,955	3,630
Philippines	776		901	1,476	1,070	1,764	2,224	2,412
Taiwan	550			1,099	924	2,980	9,886	16,214

Source: Maddison (2003).

Figure 16.8 Log income per capita I, 1990 G–K $

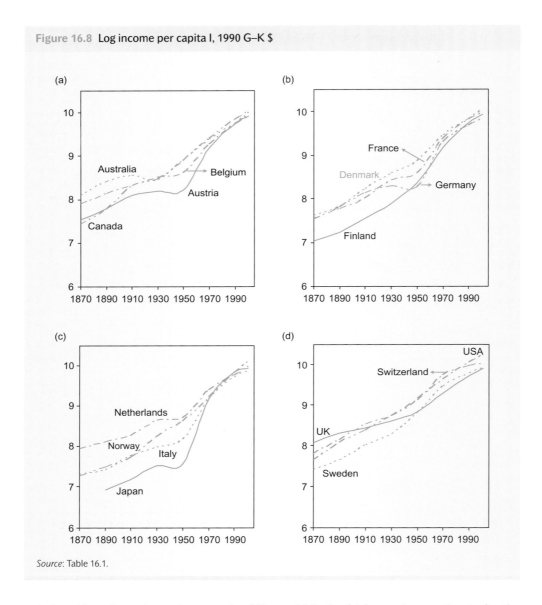

Source: Table 16.1.

As is evident from the various panels of Figure 16.8, the fairly steady growth rate for the USA, as also depicted in Figure 16.5 and in accordance with Kaldor's first stylized fact, is the exception for the currently developed countries rather than the rule. Among the countries experiencing large swings in the speed of economic development are Australia and Austria, with a period of stagnation from 1910 to 1950, Japan and the Netherlands, with a period of stagnation in the interbellum, and Italy and Japan, with a period of very rapid increase after the Second World War. Note the impressive performance of Japan, which managed to maintain per capita real GDP growth rates above 8 per cent for decades.

Studying the panels of Figure 16.8, the reader may be inclined to conclude that there is a convergence of income per capita levels over time, since all graphs move to a narrow range in 1990.

Figure 16.9 Log income per capita II, 1990 G–K $

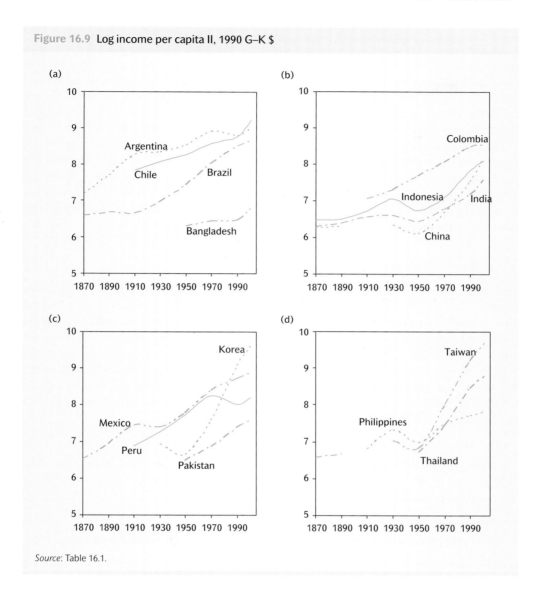

Source: Table 16.1.

That conclusion would be false, however, since the sampled countries depicted in Figure 16.8 are currently developed countries with similar income per capita levels. If we eliminate this 'sample bias', as we should according to De Long (1988), income per capita does not converge over time. The question of convergence or divergence of income per capita over time is rather complex and has resulted in numerous empirical studies.

We get a feel for De Long's argument if we inspect Figure 16.9, which depicts an impressive variation in the development of economic prosperity over time. Argentina, for example, was considerably wealthier in 1900 than Brazil, which has now caught up. Income per capita levels were stagnant in many countries, including Korea and the Philippines from 1910 to 1950, Indonesia, China, India, Pakistan, Thailand, and Taiwan from 1900 to 1950, and, worst of all,

Bangladesh which experienced stagnant or declining income per capita levels for almost the entire century. In contrast, South Korea, Taiwan, and more recently China have managed to maintain per capita real growth rates above 6 per cent for decades. The impact of such differences is mind-boggling. South Korea, for example, was estimated by Maddison to have real per capita GDP in 1870 of $604. Fifty years later, in 1920, this had increased to about $1,009, to fall back in the next 30 years to an income level of $770. Then, in the next 50 years, income increased very rapidly to $14,343, or an almost nineteen-fold increase in five decades.

The empirical evidence presented in this section leads to two conclusions. First, economic growth rates can differ drastically between nations for long periods of time. To be fair to Kaldor, we must note that he included this as his sixth stylized fact, not mentioned in Section 16.3. Second, history provides us with examples of countries with a steady development of income over time, such as the USA and Colombia, and with examples of stagnations and booms, such as Australia and Japan.

16.6 Endogenous growth

The large differences in economic development discussed in Section 16.5, the large Solow residual in empirically explaining economic growth rates as discussed in Section 16.4, and the fact that the neoclassical growth model depends on exogenous technical change to allow the economy to continue growing, together resulted in the desire to provide an alternative explanation for the dynamic forces underlying the variation in economic growth rates. The search for this alternative explanation, which is now known under the label 'endogenous growth', was led by Paul Romer (1986, 1990). In his review Romer (1994a) mentions five basic facts, in addition to Kaldor's stylized facts of Section 16.3, that should be accommodated in an economic growth model.

1. There are many firms in a market economy.
2. Discoveries differ from other inputs in that many people can use them at the same time (non-rival goods).
3. It is possible to replicate physical activities.
4. Technological advance comes from things that people do.
5. Many individuals and firms have market power and earn monopoly rents on discoveries.

A good is a rival good if only one person can use it at the same time. I can work on a computer, and so can you. But we cannot work on the same computer at the same time. A computer is therefore a rival good, as is a desk, a chair, a copier, etc. Knowledge is, in general, a non-rival good. I can apply the principles of addition, subtraction, or double- entry bookkeeping at the same time as you can. The combination of facts 2 (non-rivalness) and 3 (replication) implies that there must be increasing returns to scale. The argument is simple. Let $Y = F(K, L; A)$ be the production function, in which K is capital, L is labour, and A represents the state of technology. If I can in principle replicate the physical production process, there must be constant returns to scale in capital K and labour L; increasing these inputs by the factor $\lambda > 1$ must increase output by the same factor λ, that is $F(\lambda K, \lambda L; A) = \lambda F(K, L; A)$. If an increase in the state of technology or knowledge A, which is a non-rival good, by the same factor λ (however measured) has any positive productive influence on output, there must be increasing returns to scale at the aggregate level: $F(\lambda K, \lambda L; \lambda A) > F(\lambda K, \lambda L; A) = \lambda F(K, L; A)$.

Increasing returns to scale in production of course give rise to imperfect competition (fact 5), though to a limited extent as there are many firms in a market economy (fact 1). Since accumulating knowledge, testing and developing new products, and achieving scientific breakthroughs is costly and takes a lot of effort from talented individuals (fact 4), a proper model of economic growth should allow these efforts to be determined and remunerated within the model. Those, in a nutshell, are the requirements for an endogenous growth model. We will use a discrete version of the canonical model by Grossman and Helpman (1991a, ch. 3), giving it the Ethier (1982) intermediate goods interpretation (see Chapter 10) to explain the basic structure of endogenous growth models. There are N different varieties x_i which are imperfect substitutes of one another, with an elasticity of substitution equal to $\varepsilon = 1/(1-\rho) > 1$. The varieties are intermediate goods in the production process of one final good Y. If we let the sub-index t denote time and use the fact that the varieties will be produced in identical quantities, we get

$$(16.5) \qquad Y_t = \left(\sum_{i=1}^{N_t} x_{it}^{\rho}\right)^{1/\rho} = N_t^{(1/\rho)-1}\underbrace{[N_t x_t]}_{L_x/m}; \quad x_{it} = x_t \quad \text{for all } i$$

The model uses only labour as a factor of production, and distinguishes between two types of activity, labourers in the production process L_X and labourers in the research and development sector $L_{R\&D}$. In the equilibrium analysed below, the distribution of labourers over these two activities is stable over time. If m is the marginal labour required to produce one unit of a variety of intermediate goods, the total production level of intermediates $N_t x_t$, the term in square brackets in equation (16.5), must be equal to L_X/m. As is clear from (16.5), output Y_t can rise over time if N_t increases. To keep the term $N_t x_t$ constant, the production level per variety x_t must fall. This is illustrated for the three periods t_0, t_1, and t_2 if the term $N_t x_t = 10$ in Figure 16.10.

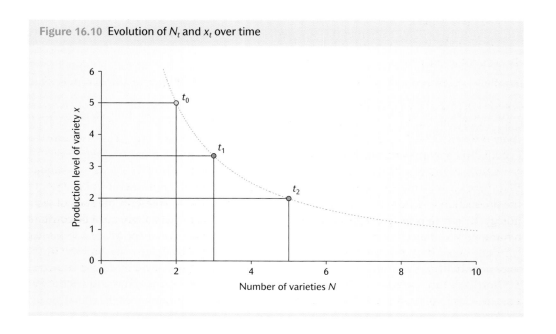

Figure 16.10 Evolution of N_t and x_t over time

We assume that the working population is constant; that is, $L_t = L$ for all t, and use the wage rate as numéraire, $W_t = 1$ for all t. This brings several simplifications. First, the income level in the economy is constant, because entry and exit in the R&D sector will ensure that (excess) profits are zero and the wage bill is constant, such that the income level is $W_t L_t = L$ for all t. Second, since the wage rate is constant, the price charged for a particular variety is also constant (use the optimal pricing rule of Chapter 9 to get: $p_t = mW_t/\rho = m/\rho$ for all t). Since the entrepreneur charges a higher price than the marginal costs of production, she earns an operating profit. Technical Note 16.2 shows that this operating profit π_t in period t is inversely related to the number N_t of varieties on the market as follows:

$$(16.6) \qquad\qquad\qquad\qquad \pi_t = (1 - \rho)\frac{L}{N_t}$$

Equation (16.6) clearly demonstrates the economic forces behind an endogenous growth model. A producer who has invented and patented a new variety of intermediate goods is able to derive an operating profit from the production of those goods by asking a higher price than marginal costs. These profits present a clear incentive to engage in R&D activities for inventing and developing new varieties. The profits are eroded in two ways.

- *Future* profits are evaluated using a discount rate θ; see Box 16.2. The higher the discount rate, the lower the present value of all future discounted profits, and therefore the smaller the incentive to invest in R&D.

- An increase in the number of varieties N_t increases competition and erodes future profits; see equation (16.6). If g is the growth rate of the number of varieties, which will be constant in this model, an increase in g erodes future profits faster and therefore, just like an increase in the discount rate θ, reduces the incentive to invest in R&D.

The benefits of investing in R&D have to be confronted with the costs of inventing a new variety. Essentially, these investment costs are equivalent to the fixed costs in the intra-industry trade model of Chapter 10. The costs in terms of labour of inventing a new variety in period t are assumed to be F/N_t. Note that the required amount of labour for inventing a new variety falls over time as the number of varieties increases. This represents a knowledge spillover, which makes it less costly to develop new varieties as the technical capabilities and knowledge level of the economy increase. Without these knowledge spillovers, the output level of the economy would eventually stop rising (once it is no longer profitable to invest in new varieties). With the knowledge spillovers, the economy will grow steadily forever, as shown in Technical Note 16.3. The growth rate of the economy is higher if

(i) the labour force is higher (increasing returns to scale ensure that size is important),

(ii) the fixed costs of investment F are lower, and

(iii) the discount rate is lower.

It is important to realize that the brief explanation of the endogenous growth model above has turned the appreciation in the economics profession for monopoly power and imperfect competition around, although not 180 degrees. We used to hammer into our students' heads that monopolies are bad and inefficient, and that imperfect competition should be viewed as a distortion. Once we acknowledge, however, that there are increasing returns to scale at the aggregate level, as explained above, we know the economic equilibrium must be characterized

Box 16.2   Discounting the future

Consumers care not only about current consumption levels, but also about future consumption levels. This is important to determine their savings decisions, that is the supply of funds that can be used by firms to finance investment decisions. To reflect the preference for current consumption by consumers, and take uncertainty about future developments into account, economic growth models assume that the agents value future consumption using the discount rate $\theta > 0$. Consumption t periods from now is then 'discounted' by the factor $[1/(1+\theta)]^t$. In most models, as here, the discount rate is equal to the interest rate. Suppose we take into consideration only three periods, in which profits are 10 in each period. Total discounted profits if the discount rate $\theta = 0.1$ are:

$$\left(\frac{1}{1.1}\right)^0 10 + \left(\frac{1}{1.1}\right)^1 10 + \left(\frac{1}{1.1}\right)^2 10 = 10 + 9.09 + 8.26 = 27.35$$

The weight given today to the profits two periods from today is therefore only 8.26, rather than 10. This effect is stronger if the discount rate rises. If $\theta = 0.2$, we get:

$$\left(\frac{1}{1.2}\right)^0 10 + \left(\frac{1}{1.2}\right)^1 10 + \left(\frac{1}{1.2}\right)^2 10 = 10 + 8.33 + 6.94 = 25.27$$

which shows that profits two periods from now are given a weight of only 6.94, rather than 10. A rise in the discount rate therefore reduces the present value of investments. To conclude, Technical Note 16.3 uses the fact that if the positive constant a is smaller than 1, the term $[1+a+a^2+a^3+\ldots]$ converges to $1/(1 - a)$.

by some form of imperfect competition. If we then also acknowledge that most economic progress derives from conscious and costly investment in R&D, which has to be recuperated somehow, it is only a small step to start to appreciate the fact that successful firms are able to exercise their monopoly power in a market of imperfect competition, thus generating operating profits that recuperate the costly investments in R&D. Without those monopoly profits, the economy would ultimately stop growing. It is the main contribution of Joseph Schumpeter to have pointed out these links.

16.7 An experiment in geographical economics

One important empirical characteristic of economic growth, namely the large swings in economic prosperity (long periods of stagnation or decline, followed by periods of rapid growth), is not explained by either the neoclassical growth model or the endogenous growth model, both of which focus on steady growth of income per capita. Brakman, Garretsen, and van Marrewijk (2001, ch. 10) argue that these large swings are better explained by the geographical economics model of Chapter 14. We illustrate this by briefly discussing a simulation dynamics experiment.

We extend the geographical economics model to twelve cities located, like a clock, at equal distances on a circle. This so-called racetrack economy is discussed in the *Study Guide* on the online resource centre. To allow for the simultaneous existence of economic centres of different size and avoid bang-bang[3] (corner) solutions, we introduce congestion costs, leading to higher production costs as economic activity concentrates in a certain location (for details, see Brakman, Garretsen, and van Marrewijk, 2001). We focus attention on the impact of a gradual, but step-wise, fall in the transport costs T (the other parameters of the model will remain fixed), as follows:

1. We set the transport costs at a very high level, namely $T = 3$.

2. We randomly select an initial distribution of manufacturing labour across the twelve cities.

3. Since the initial distribution is not a long-run equilibrium, manufacturing workers migrate to cities with higher real wages until a long-run equilibrium is reached.

4. Given the long-run equilibrium established in step 3, we now give a shock to the system by lowering the transport costs from $T = 3$ to $T = 2.9$.

5. The distribution of manufacturing activity over the twelve cities, which was a long-run equilibrium in 3, will, in general, no longer be an equilibrium after the change in transport costs in 4. This sets in motion a new process of labour migration to cities with higher real wages until a new long-run equilibrium is reached for the new level of transport costs (similar to 3).

6. We continue to shock the system along the lines of 4 and 5 by gradually, but step-wise, lowering transport cost to $T = 2.8$, $T = 2.7$, etc.

The fact that we analyse a twelve-city setting has the advantage that it allows for a much richer structure and more surprising economic interactions than the two-city setting. The disadvantage is, however, that it is more difficult succinctly to present and interpret the results of the simulations. We will therefore concentrate on the degree of agglomeration of economic activity by reporting a widely used empirical measure of industry concentration: the Herfindahl (1950) index, see for example Martin (1994), which is simply defined as the sum of the squared shares of manufacturing in each city. Thus, for example, if there are three cities and all manufacturing is located in one city, the Herfindahl index is: $1^2 + 0^2 + 0^2 = 1$. If manufacturing activity is equally divided over two of the three cities, the Herfindahl index is: $0.5^2 + 0.5^2 + 0^2 = 0.5$. If the manufacturing activity is equally divided over all three cities, the Herfindahl index is: $0.33^2 + 0.33^2 + 0.33^2 = 0.33$, etc. In general, the Herfindahl index is higher if economic activity is more agglomerated.

During the simulation experiment manufacturing activity is reallocated over the twelve cities 800 times. Figure 16.11 gives an overview of the evolution of the extent of agglomeration, as measured by the Herfindahl index. Initially, there does not appear to be much change in economic structure, say roughly up to reallocation number 130. Further reductions in transport costs start to set in motion a long process of increasing agglomeration of economic activity, reaching a peak at about 0.46, roughly from reallocation 480 to 580. As transportation costs continue to fall, the agglomeration of economic activity starts to decrease again, with a slight revival during the transition process from reallocation 650 to 730, as further discussed below. Eventually, as transport costs are virtually absent (in the end $T = 1.01$), manufacturing activity is roughly equally spread over the twelve cities.

In the initial phase, when transport costs are very high and manufacturing activity is relatively evenly spread, reductions in transport costs have very limited effects (roughly in the range from $T = 3.0$ to $T = 2.2$). This is illustrated by the low number of reallocations after a fall in transport costs needed to reach a new long-run equilibrium (sometimes only 1, 2, or 3

Figure 16.11 Evolution of agglomeration: the Herfindahl index

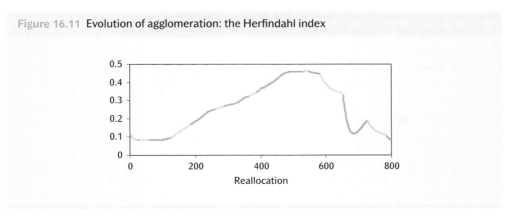

Figure 16.12 Dynamics of city size; cities 3, 6, and 9

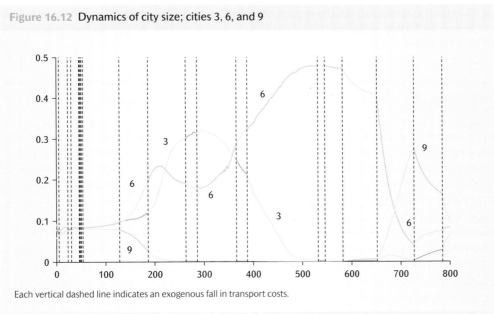

Each vertical dashed line indicates an exogenous fall in transport costs.

reallocations; in one case no reallocation is required). In this phase the Herfindahl index is about 0.085, only slightly above the minimum (0.083) if manufacturing activity is perfectly evenly spread over the twelve cities.

The evolution of manufacturing activity during the simulation is shown in Figure 16.12 for a selection of cities (3, 6, and 9). A vertical dashed line indicates an exogenous change in the transport costs, which sets in motion a new adjustment process to reach a new long-run equilibrium. Figure 16.12 dramatically illustrates the large swings in economic prosperity.

(i) There is an initial phase, in which all cities are roughly equal in size.

(ii) Then the process of agglomeration starts. City 6 rapidly attracts a lot of manufacturing activity, while city 3 increases in size more slowly. In contrast, manufacturing activity in city 9 disappears quite quickly.

(iii) There is an intermediate phase in which city 6 becomes smaller and city 3 takes over as the largest city.

(iv) The further reduction in transport costs causes a long gradual decline of manufacturing activity in city 3, and a simultaneous long-lasting rise of production in city 6, which for some time attracts almost half of all manufacturing activity.

 (v) When transport costs become very low, economic production in city 6 falls dramatically in a short period of time. Simultaneously, production in city 9 rapidly increases to a peak of almost 30 per cent of total production. This is remarkable since production in city 9 virtually disappeared when the process of agglomeration started.

(vi) Eventually, manufacturing production in all three cities is approximately of the same size as transport costs are virtually absent.

The simulation experiment gave many examples of 'leap-frogging' in which the economic size of cities changes drastically, and sometimes rapidly. This important empirical aspect of economic growth cannot be explained using either neoclassical or endogenous growth theories, but is more readily understood in a geographical economics framework.

 Box 16.3   Services, manufactures, agriculture, and development

At the end of Chapter 2 we briefly discussed the regularities in sector composition and prosperity at a specific point in time (the year 2003). In particular, we showed that high-income countries in general have a high share of employment in the services sectors and a low share of employment in the agricultural sectors. This box illustrates these issues for a selection of countries over several decades using the value added composition of services, manufacturing, and agriculture as a percentage of GDP.

As illustrated in Figure 16.13 for France and the USA, the share of income generated in the agricultural sectors in high-income countries was already very low in 1971 and has continued to decline until 2002 (from 7.2 per cent to 2.7 per cent in France and from 3.5 per cent to 1.6 per cent in the USA). Similarly, the share of income generated in the manufacturing sectors in the high-income countries also declines, an aspect of economic restructuring receiving wide attention in the media (referred to, for example, by Ross Perot as the 'giant sucking sound' of manufacturing being moved from the USA to Mexico during his failed presidential election campaign). In France the share of manufactuing declined from 27 per cent in 1978 to 18 per cent in 2002. In the USA it declined from 21 per cent in 1988 to 15 per cent in 2001. As we know, in both countries income levels have continued to rise despite (or perhaps thanks to) the reduced share of income generated in agriculture and manufacturing. As we have seen throughout Part II of this book, there are international welfare gains to be made for all participants if countries focus their production process on producing those goods and services or providing that part of the value chain for which they have a comparative advantage. Both France and the USA have a highly skilled and highly paid labour force. This indeed does make it hard to compete on the global market for more unskilled-labour-intensive parts of the production process, leading to a relative decline of manufacturing in the generation of income. The good news is that this frees up labour for other, more profitable types of production processes, leading to higher income levels. These are in the services sectors, where value added in the USA   ❯❯

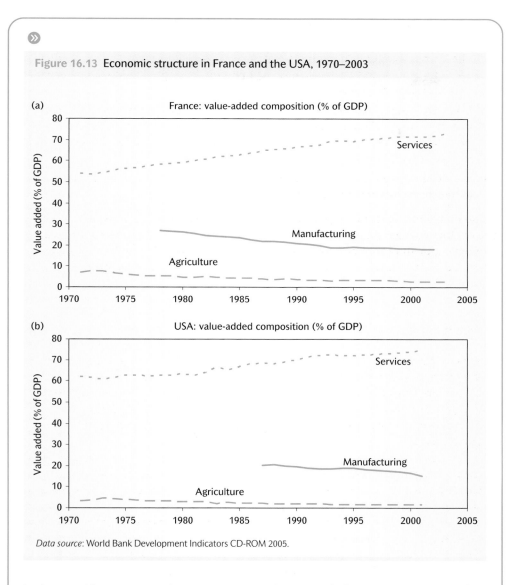

Figure 16.13 Economic structure in France and the USA, 1970–2003

(a)   France: value-added composition (% of GDP)

(b)   USA: value-added composition (% of GDP)

Data source: World Bank Development Indicators CD-ROM 2005.

has increased from 62 per cent in 1971 to 71 per cent in 2001 and in France even more rapidly from 54 per cent in 1971 to 73 per cent in 2003. Most of this increase is in producer services, such as management consulting, data processing, and financial services; see Grubel and Walker (1989) and van Marrewijk et al. (1997).

Figure 16.14 illustrates the value-added composition for some important developing countries, where things are quite different. Starting with India, the share of income generated in agriculture is much higher, but also rapidly declining (from a maximum of 49 per cent in 1967 to 22 per cent in 2003). The share of income in manufacturing rose fairly steadily from 13.7 per cent in 1960 to a peak of 18.1 per cent in 1995, to fall back to 15.8 per cent in 2003. The services sector rose from 34 per cent in 1960 to 51 per cent in 2003. In China, we see a similar decline of income generated

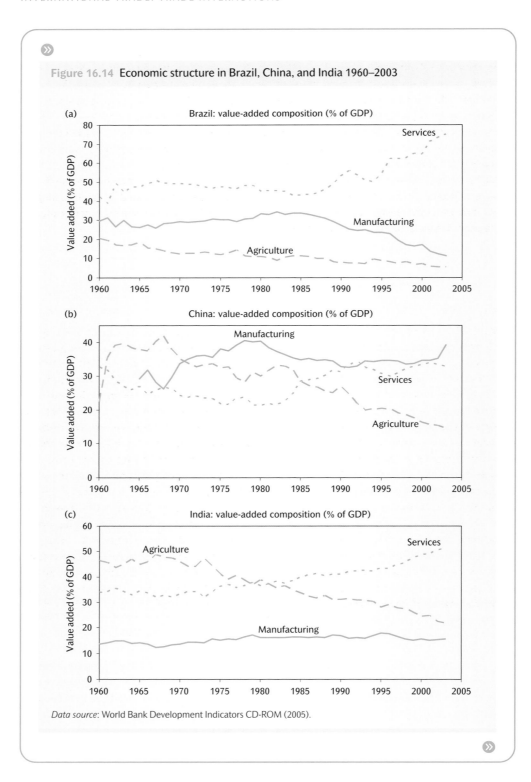

Figure 16.14 Economic structure in Brazil, China, and India 1960–2003

Data source: World Bank Development Indicators CD-ROM (2005).

>> in agriculture. The artificially low share in 1960 can be attributed to the 'Great Leap Forward' programme (with dire consequences; see Chapter 17). For the manufacturing sector, we see two peaks, the first in the late 1970s and early 1980s (about 40 per cent of income) and a second peak starting in the new millennium. We can relate the first peak to the more standard specialization process according to factor abundance theory and the second peak to the slicing-up-the-value-chain process requiring multinational enterprises and foreign direct investment to enable these processes; see Chapter 17 and Box 9.3. As a result of the succesful involvement of the Chinese economy in the global economy, the increase in the services sector has been fairly modest. Brazil, finally, provides us with a textbook example of economic development restructuring, where the share of income generated in agriculture generally declines, the share generated in manufacturing first increases, then reaches a peak and starts to decline, and the services share rises rapidly after the peak in manufacturing has been reached.

16.8 Conclusions

Most inhabitants of the OECD countries have become accustomed to ever-increasing per capita income levels. Historically, however, many countries have experienced long-lasting periods of stagnation as well as periods of extremely rapid increase. These and other stylized facts of economic growth cannot adequately be explained by the neoclassical growth model, which focuses on investment in capital goods as the main engine for growth, not only because it must rely on exogenous technical change to keep the economy growing, but also because of the large Solow residuals. To circumvent these shortcomings, we turn attention to endogenous growth models, in which entrepreneurial innovation in a world characterized by increasing returns to scale and imperfect competition is the main engine for economic growth. Innovation is modelled either as the invention of new goods and services or the development of quality improvements. In both cases Joseph Schumpeter has pointed out the essential role of monopoly profits to entice the entrepreneur to undertake innovative activities. The empirically observed large swings in economic growth cannot be explained by either neoclassical or endogenous growth theories. We argue that an elaboration of the geographical economics model might lead to better results in this respect. However, neoclassical theory is useful for understanding the importance of investment and capital accumulation, while endogenous growth is instrumental for understanding technical progress arising from the introduction of new varieties or quality improvements. Neither process can thrive without the other, as explained by van Marrewijk (1999).

TECHNICAL NOTES

Technical Note 16.1 Derivation of steady state

Recall the definition of the capital–labour ratio $k = K/L$; use the rate of change equation (16.2), the share of income invested, and the production function (16.1) to get:

$$\text{(16.A1)} \qquad k_{t+1} = \frac{K_{t+1}}{L_{t+1}} = \frac{I_t + (1 - \mu)K_t}{(1 + n)L_t} = \frac{sAK_t^\alpha L_t^{1-\alpha}}{(1 + n)L_t} + \frac{(1 - \mu)K_t}{1 + n \ \ L_t} = \frac{s}{1 + n}Ak_t^\alpha + \frac{1 - \mu}{1 + n}k_t$$

Now subtract k_t from both sides of the equation and simplify to derive the rate of change of the capital–labour ratio. Finally, put the resulting equation equal to zero to derive the steady-state capital–labour ratio, as given in equation (16.3) of the main text.

$$\text{(16.A2)} \qquad k_{t+1} - k_t = \frac{s}{1 + n}Ak_t^\alpha - \frac{\mu + n}{1 + n}k_t = 0 \Leftrightarrow sAk_t^\alpha = (\mu + n)k_t$$

Technical Note 16.2 Derivation of operating profit

First, note that the operating profit for a variety in period t is the difference between the price p_t charged and the marginal cost mW_t of producing one unit, times the number x_t of goods sold, that is $\pi_t = (p_t - mW_t)x_t$. Using the optimal pricing rule $mW_t = \rho p_t$, this reduces to $\pi_t = (1-\rho)p_t x_t$. The total value of production of manufactures $N_t p_t x_t$ must be equal to the income level L (see the main text), such that $p_t x_t = L/N_t$, which gives equation (16.6) in the main text.

Technical Note 16.3 Derivation of the endogenous growth rate

If the discount rate is θ, see Box 16.2, the growth rate of the number of varieties is g, such that $N_t = N_0(1+g)^t$, and we define $a^{-1} = (1+g)(1+\theta)$, then the present discounted value at time 0 of operating profits from time t using (16.6) is $(1-\rho)La^t/N_0$. The value at time 0 of developing a new variety is the sum of all future profits:

$$(1 - \rho)\frac{L}{N_0}[1 + a + a^2 + a^3 + \cdots] = \frac{1 - \rho}{1 - a}\frac{L}{N_0}$$

As explained in the main text, the cost of inventing a new variety at time 0 is equal to F/N_0. Equilibrium in the R&D sector requires equality of cost and benefits, which gives

$$1 - a = (1 - \rho)\frac{L}{F}, \quad or \ (1 + g) = \frac{F}{(1 + \theta)[F - (1 - \rho)L]}$$

The growth rate of the economy is therefore higher if (i) the labour force is higher (increasing returns to scale make the size of the economy important), (ii) the fixed costs of investment F are lower, and (iii) the discount rate is lower.

QUESTIONS

Question 16.1

Section 16.4 discusses the Solow model, which forms the starting point of economic growth theory. The central equation of the model is given by: $sAk_t^\alpha = (\mu + n)k_t$. This equation defines the steady-state equilibrium of the model.

16.1A What is a steady-state equilibrium?

16.1B What happens to output per capita if the capital–labour ratio is constant in the Solow model for a constant level of technology?

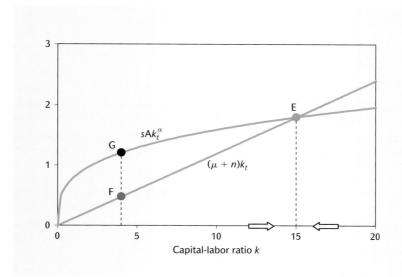

The graph above depicts the left-hand side and the right-hand side of equation (16.3).

16.1C What is measured on the vertical axis of the diagram?

16.1D Draw the effect of an increase in the population growth rate n in the graph. What happens to the steady-state equilibrium and why?

16.1E Draw the effect of an increase in the savings rate s in the graph. What happens to the steady-state equilibrium and why?

Question 16.2

Section 16.6 of the book discusses the structure and implications of the endogenous growth model.

16.2A What is the main difference between this growth theory and that of Solow?

16.2B What seems to be the key factor for a growing income per capita if you look at these two classes of growth models?

In the endogenous growth model, the rate of innovation in the economy is determined within the model. The explicit solution, derived in Technical Note 16.3, is:

$$1 + g = \frac{F}{(1 + \theta)(F - L/\varepsilon)}$$

where g is the rate of innovation, F is a parameter for the fixed cost of inventing a new variety, L is the labour force, θ is the rate of time preference, and ε is the elasticity of substitution between varieties.

16.2C Based on the equation above, determine what happens to the rate of innovation if:

- F, the fixed cost of inventing a new variety, increases
- L, the labour force, increases
- θ, the rate of time preference, increases.

16.2D Based on your knowledge of the structure of the endogenous growth model, explain intuitively why each of the effects in question 16.2C arises.

The US government has launched a series of investigations into the abuse of market power by Microsoft, a producer of computer software. The company claims that its market power actually benefits its customers, as it is the best way to fulfil their needs.

16.2E Explain how the endogenous growth model is related to the discussion of the Microsoft case.

Question 16.3

Section 16.7 of the book evaluates the outcome of a number of computer simulations for the racetrack economy of the geographical economics model, introducing congestion costs to mitigate the economic incentives for agglomeration.

16.3A Explain why the endogenous growth model and the Solow model cannot explain the empirically observed large swings in prosperity.

16.3B Explain how the experiment in Section 16.7 results in large swings in prosperity.

16.3C If we use the simulation results on the distribution of income for the world today, with very high transport costs in earlier times and rapidly dropping transport costs now, what does this imply for the future?

The simulations of Section 16.7 illustrate the snowball effect of economic forces, for example by showing that the clustering of firms in a region as a result of increasing returns to scale make this region attractive for other firms in surrounding regions.

16.3D What does the above comment imply for the development of Africa? Do you think that there is a link with the 'brain-drain' phenomenon?

 See the Online Resource Centre for a Study Guide containing more questions www.oxfordtextbooks.co.uk/orc/vanmarrewijk/

NOTES

1 Driving a 40-year-old Rolls-Royce will give you other types of enjoyment than driving a brand new Volkswagen Golf.

2 Kaldor mentions a sixth stylized fact; see below.

3 See van Marrewijk and Verbeek (1993).

APPLIED TRADE POLICY MODELLING

17

Objectives/key terms

- Demand bias
- Linder hypothesis
- Applied general equilibrium
- Dynamic costs of trade restrictions

- Armington assumption
- Applied partial equilibrium
- Dupuit triangle
- Case study: China

We briefly discuss some of the problems and procedures of applied trade policy modelling, on both the demand and the supply side of the economy, and in both a partial and a general equilibrium framework. Next, we turn to the problem of measuring the hidden costs of trade restrictions, illustrated by a case study of China.

17.1 Introduction

We have almost come to the end of the international trade part of this book. In the preceding chapters we presented many theories on international economic phenomena, developed in reaction to and illustrated by empirical information on the world economy. Moreover, we reviewed various implications of these theories for international economic policies. Readers with a practical orientation may wonder at this stage if they have learned enough and are ready to start working on applied trade policy problems at ministries, research institutes, consulting firms, banks, and the like. In this respect, I am afraid we have to be modest and give a dual answer: (i) you have learned a lot, but (ii) there is a lot more to learn before you can start working on applied trade policy:

 (i) All the material presented to you in the previous chapters is essential information before you can start working on applied trade policy. We have given a fairly complete, thorough, and up-to-date overview of the most important international economic theories. When working in applied trade policy *all* these elements will come back to you: perfect competition, constant returns to scale, factor abundance, technology differences, imperfect competition, increasing returns to scale, multinationals, geographic concentration, the international economic order, new goods, development, etc. It is all used and combined in many different ways in applied trade policy.

(ii) After finishing their PhDs Joseph Francois and Kenneth Reinert, the editors of *Applied Methods for Trade Policy Analysis: A Handbook*, started working at the US International Trade Commission (USITC) in Washington, DC where they discovered (1997: 3): 'Within a few weeks of our arrival at the USITC, it became apparent that there was a broad set of tools required for our jobs that were rather different from those emphasized in academia.' Since they continue to argue that their 560-page handbook only represents an *introduction* to the tools needed for applied trade policy analysis, it is obvious that the remainder of this chapter cannot adequately cover and teach these tools.

The sequel of this chapter gives a brief overview of the main problems and procedures of applied trade policy modelling, first partial equilibrium and then general equilibrium, and concludes with a discussion on the hidden costs of trade restrictions that are not measured in any applied trade policy model. Before we get started, however, we list the main characteristics of applied trade policy analysis (see Francois and Reinert, 1997):

1. *Detailed policy orientation*. This indicates a commitment by the applied researcher to sectoral and institutional details of a policy, and thus the willingness to learn about trade data nomenclatures, input-output relationships, industrial classification schemes, and details on imposed trade and domestic policies (quotas, tariffs, VERs, subsidies, etc.).

2. *Non-local changes in policy parameters from distorted base equilibria*. Theoretical models frequently analyse the impact of small changes starting from an initial non-distorted equilibrium. Applied trade policy models, instead, start from a base equilibrium with the relevant distortions from government policy built into it and analyse the impact of the policy changes actually under consideration.

3. *Accurate and current data*. The outcome of policy experiments in a model depends on the functional forms used to describe technology and agents' behaviour, the base data used to

Famous economists	Léon Walras

Fig. 17.1
Léon Walras
(1834–1910)

Born in a small town in Normandy, France, Léon Walras studied in Paris and was active in various fields (journalism, clerk at a railway company, director of a bank) before he was appointed as a professor of political economy at the University of Lausanne in 1870. There he finished his work on the two-part *Elements of Pure Economics* (1844–70), which he revised several times. It was largely neglected in his own time, inaccessible as it was to contemporary readers. Using marginal utility theory and maximization, he was the first to write down and solve a multi-equation model of general equilibrium in all markets. For this he now receives wide recognition. As Schumpeter remarked (quoted in Blaug, 1986: 264): 'As far as pure theory is concerned, Walras is in my opinion the greatest of all economists.'

describe the initial equilibrium, and the behavioural elasticities of the functional forms. The analyst must choose the share and elasticity parameters accurately, and use current data for 'calibration' (a procedure to ensure that the model fits the data), which usually involves a trade-off between accuracy and currency of data.

4. *Model structure determined by the data.* Since the applied researcher is trying to answer practical questions, the model structure is to a fair extent determined by the data. In a homogeneous-goods, perfect-competition framework, for example, it is hard to explain two-way trade in similar goods. None the less, this is what we observe in the data. Applied researchers therefore sought a practical way of modelling two-way trade, which they found on the demand side of the economy, to which we now turn.

17.2 Demand

In their theories international economists pay, in general, little attention to the demand side of the economy, focusing instead on supply factors, such as differences in technology, endowments, increasing returns to scale, and imperfect competition, to explain international trade flows. Applied trade policy modellers have long recognized that the demand side plays a crucial role for better understanding empirically observed trade flows, for example to explain the phenomenon of intra-industry trade (two-way trade in identical or similar products). This section briefly discusses three aspects of the demand side: demand bias, the Linder hypothesis, and the Armington assumption.

Demand bias

To derive the Heckscher-Ohlin result in the factor abundance model discussed in Part II.A of this book we assumed that all consumers in all countries have identical homothetic preferences. Figure 17.2 illustrates what may happen if this assumption is not valid. Consider again the case of Austria and Bolivia, producing food and manufactures using capital and labour as factors of production. If the production of manufactures is capital intensive and Austria is

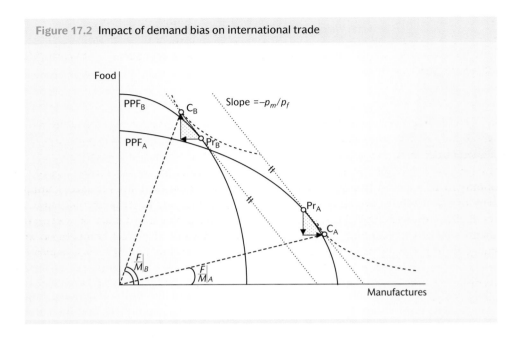

Figure 17.2 Impact of demand bias on international trade

relatively capital abundant, the production possibility frontier for Austria is relatively biased towards the production of manufactures, as explained in Chapter 7 and illustrated in Figure 17.2. Let p_m/p_f be the relative price of manufactures in the international trade equilibrium. Austria then produces at point Pr_A and Bolivia at point Pr_B in Figure 17.2, such that, in accordance with the Rybczynski result, Austria produces relatively more manufactures. This time, however, we assume that Austrian consumers have a demand bias towards the consumption of manufactures, that is at the price ratio p_m/p_f Austrians want to consume relatively much less food than Bolivians. As illustrated in Figure 17.2 with the two coinciding trade triangles, this demand bias can result in Austria importing manufactures and exporting food, despite the fact that Austria produces relatively more manufactures than Bolivia and in contrast to the Heckscher-Ohlin result. Demand bias may therefore also explain the Leontief paradox, see Chapter 7, if American consumers have a preference for capital-intensive products.

Linder hypothesis

Linder (1961) presents a different explanation for the direction of trade in differentiated manufactures. He argues that producers in each country manufacture goods to satisfy the needs of the consumers in that country. Since not all consumers are alike and some prefer goods with different characteristics, international trade provides a means to obtain these other goods and benefit from a wider variety of goods. This part is similar to Krugman's formalization of the intra-industry trade model explained in Chapter 10. Linder continues, however, by arguing that countries with similar standards of living will consume similar types of goods. The high-income countries, with large amounts of capital per worker, will therefore have similar tastes and largely trade with other high-income countries. This is also what we observe in the data. The other side of the coin of the Linder hypothesis is, of course, that poor countries will consume similar types of goods and trade largely with other poor countries. In contrast, the data show that poor countries tend to trade with rich countries. According to Linder this can be explained by assuming that trade in raw materials and agricultural products is based on the neoclassical factor abundance theory, while Linder's theory applies to trade in differentiated manufactures.

Armington assumption

One of the problems of applied research in international economics is the phenomenon of two-way trade in the same product category, which cannot adequately be explained by perfect competition models with homogeneous goods. Part II.B of this book, which discusses literature developed in the 1980s and 1990s, seeks an explanation on the supply side of the economy in an imperfectly competitive environment in which each *firm* produces a unique variety of manufactures, which is an imperfect substitute for any other variety of manufactures. Earlier, however, applied research has addressed this problem in a practical way on the demand side of the economy, keeping intact the framework of perfect competition and homogeneous goods, by using the 'Armington (1969) assumption' in which each *country* (or region) produces a unique good. These country goods, say x_1 and x_2 for countries 1 and 2, are imperfect substitutes and combined to produce a composite utility good, say U_1 for country 1, for example as follows:

(17.1)
$$U_1 = \left[\underbrace{a_{11}x_1^\rho}_{\substack{domestic\\good}} + \underbrace{a_{21}x_2^\rho}_{\substack{imported\\good}} \right]^{1/\rho} ; \quad 0 < \rho < 1$$

The approach can easily be extended to accommodate more countries, while the parameter ρ and the constants a_{ji}, which may vary per country, are chosen to reproduce the actual trade flows between countries. Note the similarity between the (CES) Armington assumption and the Ethier interpretation of the Krugman model in Chapter 10.

17.3 Partial equilibrium models

The basic disadvantage of partial equilibrium models in applied trade policy modelling, the fact that such models do not take many economic factors into consideration, is simultaneously the most important advantage of these models. If the trade policy question the researcher is trying to address is limited in scope, perhaps concerning one or only a few sectors in a single country and a few policy variables, applied partial equilibrium models allow for a rapid and transparent analysis. The methodology used is quite similar to the theoretical approach explained in Chapter 8. The applied researcher, however, is not interested in the potential theoretical costs of trade restrictions, but in actually estimating the size of these costs for a specific set of policies in a specific set of markets.

To estimate these costs the applied researcher has to calculate the actual size of the Harberger triangles in a market structure for which the observed prices and quantities (produced, imported, and consumed) and the imposed trade restrictions are consistent with the empirically observed data (an example of point (ii) in the introduction to this chapter). She is therefore operating in a 'second-best' world in which the initial equilibrium is influenced by the currently imposed trade restrictions. A simple example is given in Figure 17.3, in which the researcher has to estimate the effect of increasing the imposed tariff rate from the current level t_0 to the newly suggested level t_1 for a small country which cannot influence the price p_0

of the good on the world market. We know from Chapter 8 that the net welfare loss to society of imposing the tariff rate t_0 relative to free trade is equal to the sum of the Harberger triangles A in Figure 17.3. Now note that increasing the tariff rate from t_0 to t_1 not only leads to an extra welfare loss equal to the triangles C in Figure 17.3 but also magnifies the impact of the initial distortion, leading to an additional welfare loss equal to the rectangles B in Figure 17.3. Moreover, when compared to a policy of free trade, the net welfare loss of imposing a tariff t_1 is equal to the sum of triangles A and C and rectangles B.

Before calculating the size of the Harberger triangles, which as we saw do not actually have to be triangles, the researcher has to undertake a few actions. She has to collect data on observed prices and quantities. She has to estimate the slope of the demand and supply functions, perhaps by using estimated elasticities for demand and supply based on econometric studies. She has to accommodate and quantify the type of trade policy imposed on the market; see Laird (1997) for further details. Finally, she has to decide if domestic goods and imported goods are perfect substitutes (as in Figure 17.3) or imperfect substitutes (based on the Armington assumption); see Box 17.1 for an example.

Figure 17.3 Partial equilibrium and second-best

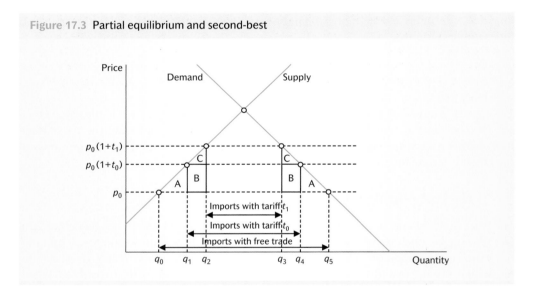

 Box 17.1   US steel protection

Francois and Hall (1997) use partial equilibrium methods to estimate the impact of US steel protection in 1992. After a period in which the US steel industry threatened to file hundreds of anti-dumping and countervailing duty complaints, negotiations began in the 1980s on voluntary export restraints (VERs), which led to agreements with nineteen countries and the European Community. By the end of the 1980s, after the dollar had reduced considerably in value, the quotas had largely ceased to be binding. The US president announced in 1989 the phasing out of the VERs by 1992. Renewed search for protection by the US steel industry did not lead to new VERs, but to anti-dumping and countervailing duties. This episode allows Francois and Hall to compare the transition from bilateral quotas to bilateral tariffs.

⟫ The estimated costs of protection for the US steel industry are illustrated in Figure 17.4 for three types of products: cut-to-length steel plate, cold-rolled products, and corrosion-resistant products. Depending on the type of trade policy and the methodology used, the sum of the estimated costs varies from $305 million to $877 million. We can draw two main conclusions. First, the costs of protection are higher if imports are imperfect substitutes for domestic products. Compare, for example, the $121 million estimated costs of tariffs for cut-to-length steel plate in the imperfect substitutes case with the $42 million in the perfect substitutes case. The size of these differences depends crucially, of course, on the elasticity of substitution between domestic and imported goods. Second, within each methodology the estimated costs of protection are higher for quotas than for tariffs. Compare, for example, the $73 million estimated costs of quotas for cold-rolled products with the $50 million of tariffs in the perfect substitutes case. These differences arise from the distribution of the tariff equivalent government revenue (see Chapter 8).

The WTO ruled America's 'safeguard' steel tariffs illegal in November 2003 and allowed Europe to threaten with retaliatory duties of $2.2 billion on various products (ranging from motor boats to orange juice). America caved in to the threats a little while later for two reasons. First, the structure of Europe's WTO-sanctioned tariffs was designed to particularly hurt products made in states that were crucial for president Bush's re-election campaign. Second, because China became President Bush's unlikely ally: thanks to its rapid economic development and high demand for raw materials, the world price for steel, and thus also prices in the USA, started to increase again, giving Bush sufficient grounds for lifting the tariffs; see *The Economist* (2003a, 2004).

Figure 17.4 US steel industry: estimated costs of protection, $ million

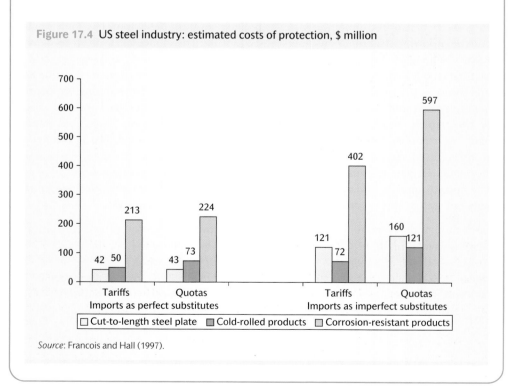

Source: Francois and Hall (1997).

17.4 General equilibrium models

If an applied researcher is trying to answer more ambitious questions, involving a range of trade policy measures, a range of sectors, and/or a range of different countries, she will use applied general equilibrium models (AGE; also known as computable general equilibrium models, CGE) which take into consideration the simultaneous effects of all proposed policy measures for all sectors and countries. The use of such models, which in general should give better and more detailed answers to the posed questions, has become much more popular over the last two decades as a result of improved data availability, more readily available computing power, and the development of user-friendly software to use this computing power. Some questions to be answered in this way are:

- What is the impact of the formation of the North American Free Trade Area (NAFTA) for wages, employment, and production in Mexico, Canada, and the USA?

- What is the impact of the GATT's Uruguay Round on trade and welfare for the OECD countries and the developing countries?

- What will be the consequences of EU enlargement for the sectoral distribution of production, trade, and GDP for both the EU countries and the EU candidate countries?

General remarks

On the basis of the first (NAFTA) question posed above, Drusilla Brown (1992) discusses the use of applied general equilibrium models. All such modelling begins with basic general equilibrium international trade theory. The researcher must specify the stocks of factor endowments, the nature of technology, consumer preferences, firm behaviour, etc. for a range of products, endowments, firms, consumers, and countries. The model takes into consideration the flows of goods and (factor) services, the payments for those goods and services, and the actual trade policy conditions imposed by the various countries. The parameters of the functional forms in the model are then estimated, partly on the basis of (econometric) work of other researchers and partly based on the ability of the model to reproduce as closely as possible the actually observed data on production, prices, consumption, trade, and imposed (policy) restrictions. After this preliminary work has been completed, the researcher can perform counterfactual experiments by solving the model again after changing one or several policy parameters to determine the economic impact of the policy changes.

The applied models deviate from the theoretical models not only by identifying a large number of sectors and factors of production, but also in some other ways:

- Most models differentiate industry sales by destination, frequently using a constant elasticity of transformation (CET) aggregation procedure, making the production possibility frontier between the exportable variety and the domestic variety concave rather than linear. Increasing returns to scale are usually modelled as a fixed investment in capital and labour before production can begin, with variable costs proportional to output.

- Factor markets are modelled in different ways. Sometimes capital and labour can move freely between sectors within a country, but not between countries. Sometimes a Keynesian approach is used in which the real wage is fixed and employment may vary. Sometimes the labour supply is fixed, but capital can move freely to or from the rest of the world at an exogenous world rental rate.

- In many cases an Armington-type assumption is used.
- The researcher models the economic structure of some, but not all, countries in the world. Countries that are not explicitly modelled are usually captured with *ad hoc* excess demand functions depending on relative prices.

The historical development of the applied general equilibrium models has largely coincided with the theoretical developments in Parts II.A, II.B, and II.C of this book. Brown (1992) distinguishes three main applied general equilibrium policy approaches:

1. *Static models with perfect competition and constant returns to scale.* The first models were based on the neoclassical approach of Part II.A, static in nature with constant returns to scale and perfect competition, the main difference being the incorporation of the Armington assumption to allow for two-way trade. Estimating the impact of NAFTA is then largely an exercise in calculating trade-creation and trade-diversion effects, although this time taking the factor supply restraints into consideration; see Chapter 13. In evaluating five type (1) studies on the impact of NAFTA, Brown (1992: 56–7) concludes: 'the differentiated product-CRS models show small welfare gains of less than 1 percent of GNP, though the welfare effects are positive for the participating countries'.

2. *Static models with imperfect competition and increasing returns to scale.* The second set of applied general equilibrium models is based on the various approaches discussed in Part II.B of this book, static in nature, but incorporating imperfect competition and increasing returns to scale. They were developed in part in reaction to points of critique of the applied models in (1) above, in particular with respect to the necessity to incorporate (Armington) country-specific production differentiation to explain two-way trade. As Brown (1992: 41) puts it: 'the fact that it is a convenient assumption does not make it a good assumption for empirical analysis'. She argues that a framework of product differentiation at the firm level, based on increasing returns to scale, is more suitable in many cases, not only because firms will incorporate the elasticity of demand in their pricing decisions, but also to allow greater intersectoral specialization. As discussed in Part II.B, potential gains from trade then also arise from increased competition, more efficient use of scale economies, productivity increases as a result of increased specialization, and love of variety. In evaluating four type (2) studies on the impact of NAFTA, Brown (1992: 57) concludes: 'models that . . . incorporate IRS . . . show welfare gains for Mexico in the range of 2 to 4 percent'.

3. *Dynamic models.* The third generation of applied general equilibrium models is dynamic in nature and based on the work discussed in Part III.C of this book, incorporating labour migration, investments, capital movements, and multinational firms. This can be done by specifying the time path for one of the exogenous variables (as in the geographical economics experiment of Section 16.7), by endogenizing the growth of some of the variables of the system (as in the Solow model of Section 16.4), or by explicit intertemporal optimization by firms and consumers (as in the endogenous growth model of Section 16.6). In evaluating three type (3) studies on the impact of NAFTA, Brown (1992: 57) concludes: 'The addition of international capital flows suggests . . . welfare gains for Mexico of 4 to 7 percent. Finally, endogenizing productivity growth produces much larger welfare effects, possibly in the range of 10 percent of Mexican GNP.'

As the above description on the use of applied general equilibrium models suggests, the theoretical developments in international economics, prompted by the search for models

Box 17.2   Assessing the dynamic impact of the Uruguay Round

Using a Korea-based model, Francois, McDonald, and Nordström (1997) analyse the difference between static and dynamic effects of the GATT's Uruguay Round for six groups of countries: (i) Korea, (ii) Japan, (iii) Other Asia, (iv) North America, (v) Europe, Australia, and New Zealand, and (vi) the rest of the world. Their analysis is based on three different hypotheses. First, the regional capital stocks are assumed to be fixed. Second, capital can accumulate in each region with a fixed savings rate. Third, capital can accumulate in each region with an endogenous savings rate (in which the real return to capital is equal to the benchmark level in the long run).

In line with the discussion in Section 17.4, and as illustrated in Figure 17.5, the estimated impact of the Uruguay Round for the different regions is small if the capital stock is fixed, ranging from 0.1 per cent of GDP for North America, Europe, and the rest of the world to 2.1 per cent of GDP for Korea. In general, the Uruguay Round turns out to be 'capital friendly'; that is, the imposed policy changes lead to increased capital accumulation and larger welfare gains for most regions (Japan and North America are the exception). Korea's GDP, for example, is estimated to increase by 2.7 per cent rather than 2.1 per cent. Finally, if we consider a more complete dynamic model, with endogenous determination of savings using the simple closure rule given above, welfare gains are substantially larger for all regions, even for Japan (from 0.4 to 0.9 per cent) and North America (from 0.1 to 0.4 per cent). The most dramatic improvement is for Korea (an estimated increase of 9.2 per cent).

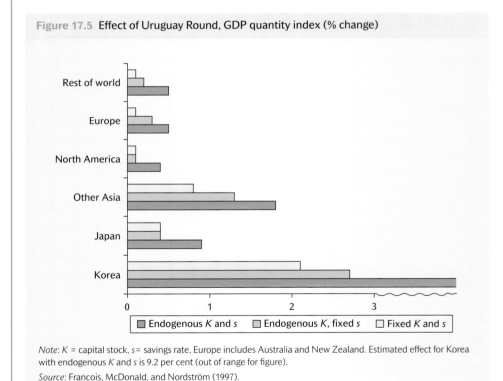

Figure 17.5 Effect of Uruguay Round, GDP quantity index (% change)

Note: K = capital stock, s = savings rate, Europe includes Australia and New Zealand. Estimated effect for Korea with endogenous K and s is 9.2 per cent (out of range for figure).

Source: Francois, McDonald, and Nordström (1997).

that are better able to explain the empirical observations, have gradually led to an increase in the estimated costs of trade restrictions. The earlier constant returns-perfect competition models used for evaluating major policy changes, such as NAFTA or the Uruguay Round (see Box 17.2), estimated the potential gains in a range below 1 per cent of GNP. The second generation of models, based on imperfect competition and increasing returns to scale, estimated the potential gains in a range up to about 4 per cent of GNP. Finally, the third generation of models, taking some dynamic issues into consideration, estimate the potential gains in a range up to 10 per cent of GNP. The estimated costs of trade restrictions has thus gradually increased over time to more substantial importance. None the less, as the rest of this chapter argues, there are good reasons to believe, and there is supporting evidence in favour of this belief, that for all their sophistication these models *still* underestimate the importance of international access through trade, foreign direct investment, capital flows, etc.

17.5 Measuring what is not there: the Dupuit triangle

As far as we know, the first analysis of the value of a new good to society, that is the first attempt to try to measure the value of something that does not yet exist, was provided by the French engineer Jules Dupuit in 1844. As head of an engineering district, he was responsible for building roads, bridges, and canals. He was therefore interested in developing practical rules for determining if a specific project should be built, for which he described a demand curve and a revenue curve, which allowed him to identify an important problem associated with the introduction of new goods.

The main issue is illustrated in Figure 17.6, depicting a downward-sloping demand curve for a good, say a bridge, that has not yet been introduced. The vertical axis represents the price

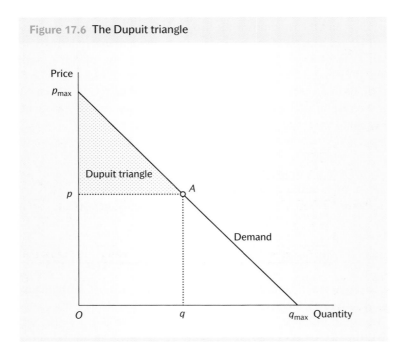

Figure 17.6 The Dupuit triangle

Box 17.3   Tool: the Dupuit triangle

The French engineer Jules Dupuit tried to measure the surplus value for society of the introduction of new goods. If firms enter new markets until profits are driven to zero, as in the monopolistic competition model of Chapter 10, total firm revenue must be equal to total costs. Since the area under the demand curve is a measure of the value to consumers of a new good, and total revenue generated by the firm is a measure of the costs to the firm, and thus to society, of producing this new good if profits are zero, the difference between these two areas is a measure of the surplus to society as a whole generated by introducing the new good. If the demand curve is linear, as in Figure 17.6, this difference is a triangle; hence the name Dupuit triangle.

to be paid each time the bridge is crossed. If the price is too high (above p_{max}), nobody will use the bridge. If the price is zero, the bridge will be used most intensively at q_{max}. As we know from standard microeconomic theory, the area under the demand curve measures the value of the bridge to the consumers at any given quantity. At a price of 0, for example, the total value of the bridge to consumers is equal to the area $Op_{max}q_{max}$.

Suppose, then, that a private company is interested in building this bridge, and evaluates whether or not it is worthwhile to go ahead with the project. In Figure 17.6, we assume that the firm charges price p, resulting in q crossings of the bridge and total revenue pq, equal to the area $OpAq$ in Figure 17.6. How the firm determines the price p it charges for one crossing of the bridge is immaterial for our argument. What is important is the fact that the total area under the demand curve at q, that is the area $Op_{max}Aq$, is strictly *larger* than the revenue generated by the firm from the crossings of the bridge, the area $OpAq$. The difference between the value to consumers and the revenue for the firm, that is the triangle $p_{max}Ap$, represents a welfare gain for which the firm building the bridge is not compensated in terms of revenue. If the firm decides that the total revenue generated by the bridge is not enough to compensate it for the costs of building and maintaining the bridge, for argument's sake because the revenue is exactly equal to the total costs, it will decide not to build the bridge. Paul Romer (1994b), who labels $p_{max}Ap$ the Dupuit triangle, then argues that the *welfare loss* to society of *not* building the bridge is equal to the Dupuit triangle in Figure 17.6.

In general, the above reasoning makes clear that there are costs involved, in terms of a welfare loss to society as a whole, of *not* introducing a good on the market. The Dupuit triangle can be interpreted as a measure for this welfare loss.[1] Moreover, it is evident that we cannot rely on market forces to ensure that all new goods that are valuable to society will actually be introduced, because the firm introducing a new good can only appropriate part of the surplus it generates.[2]

17.6 More on the dynamic costs of trade restrictions

In Chapter 8 we analysed the impact of imposing trade restrictions, both in a partial equilibrium framework and in a general equilibrium framework. To calculate the costs of such trade restrictions, we try to estimate the size of the Harberger triangles, see also Section 17.3. In general, such estimated costs of trade restrictions are in the neighbourhood of 1 per cent of

GDP, or 2–4 per cent of GDP in a framework of imperfect competition and increasing returns to scale; see Section 17.4. Despite the fact that this amounts to the sizeable sum of $290–1,170 *billion* on a global scale in 1997, the costs of trade restrictions appear to be moderate in relative terms. The endogenous growth model of Section 16.6 argues that increases in economic welfare arise primarily from developing new varieties and producing quality improvements of existing varieties. As argued in Section 17.5, the costs of *not* introducing a new good on the market can be measured by the Dupuit triangle.

Romer (1994b) combines these insights by pointing out that one of the most important consequences of imposing trade restrictions is the fact that they might lead to new goods and services *not* being available on the market, leading to an underestimation of the actual costs of trade restrictions. This is illustrated in Figure 17.7 for a country that does not produce the good in question. Without trade restrictions, the equilibrium is at point E_0, leading to quantity demanded q_0 at the world price level p. If the country imposes an import tariff t, we should distinguish between two possibilities.

(i) The good is still imported from abroad. The price rises to $p + t$, which leads to a welfare loss for the economy equal to the Harberger triangle in Figure 17.7.

(ii) The good is no longer imported from abroad, perhaps because the foreign producer can no longer recuperate its fixed costs. The welfare loss for the economy is equal to the Dupuit triangle in Figure 17.7.

Romer essentially argues that when we are estimating the costs of trade restrictions we tend to focus our attention almost exclusively on the small Harberger triangles in Figure 17.7, rather than on the large and much more important Dupuit triangles. This practice is understandable, since it is easier to measure the costs of something you can observe (the Harberger

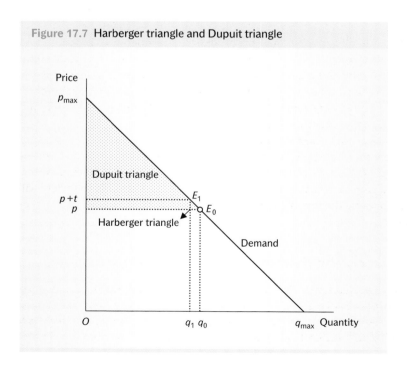

Figure 17.7 Harberger triangle and Dupuit triangle

triangles) than something that is not there (the Dupuit triangles of the goods and services not introduced on the market).

Using a model quite similar to the framework presented in Section 16.6, Romer (1994b) illustrates his argument for a small developing economy, say Developia, which does not invent its own capital goods. Instead, those intermediate capital goods and services are invented abroad. After a successful innovation, the foreign inventors face the decision whether or not to introduce the intermediate good on Developia's market, which gives them an operating profit as the price they charge will be higher than the marginal costs of production and transport. They will only introduce the new intermediate good on Developia's market if the operating profits are higher than the fixed costs of introduction, say for setting up a local consulting office. This criterion determines the number of varieties introduced on the market. Romer discusses the impact of 'expected' versus 'unexpected' tariffs for Developia's market, but I prefer to give it the 'static' versus 'dynamic' interpretation of Brakman and van Marrewijk (1996).

Suppose the government of Developia imposes an *ad valorem* tariff τ on the purchases of all foreign goods. The *static* effect of this tariff policy is an increase in price, leading to inefficiency and a welfare loss calculated as the sum of all Harberger triangles, as illustrated in Figure 17.7. When measured as the percentage reduction in output relative to the output level without tariffs, this leads to a welfare loss of τ^2 per cent in Romer's model.[3] The *dynamic* effect of this tariff policy also takes into consideration the fact that the reduction in operating profits for the foreign entrepreneurs will induce some of them not to introduce the intermediate good on Developia's market. Calculation of the dynamic welfare loss therefore also includes the Dupuit triangles of Figure 17.7. In Romer's model, the dynamic welfare loss is equal to a $2\tau - 2\tau^3 + \tau^4$ per cent reduction in output. Figure 17.8 illustrates the difference between static and dynamic loss. For example, if $\tau = 0.2$ the static welfare loss in output is 4 per cent (at point E_0),

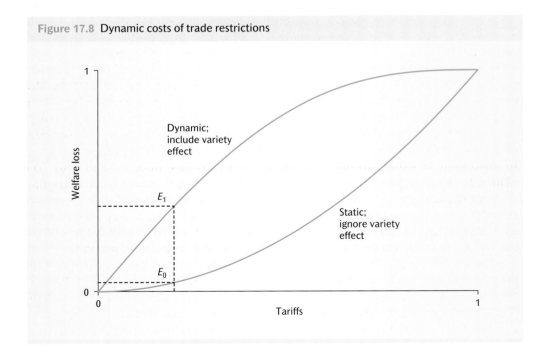

Figure 17.8 Dynamic costs of trade restrictions

while the dynamic welfare loss is 39 per cent (at point E_1)! This suggests a huge underestimate of the costs of trade restrictions using Harberger triangles. See van Marrewijk and Berden (2007) for a true dynamic analysis.

17.7 China, a case study

The main difficulty of calculating the dynamic costs of trade restrictions as explained in Section 17.6 is the fact that even if you think that the dynamic costs are much more important than the static costs, it is almost impossible to estimate their size. Again, how do you estimate the size of the welfare loss as a result of goods and services that are not introduced using a generally accepted methodology? It is virtually impossible, at least for the moment. None the less, we can provide circumstantial evidence that the dynamic costs are more important than the static costs. My favourite example is the difference in economic development between North Korea and South Korea after the Korean ceasefire in 1953. North Korea isolated itself economically from virtually all outside influences, thus not benefiting from the knowledge increases and inventions of new goods and services in the rest of the world. The result was a stagnant, or slowly deteriorating, North Korean economy for more than five decades, eventually resulting in large famines. The developments in North Korea contrast sharply with those in South Korea, which focused aggressively on expansion on the world market, using knowledge and capital goods from all over the world, leading to an enormous rise in living standards; see Figure 16.9(c). Unfortunately, lack of reliable data on the North Korean economy prevents me from going into further detail here.[4] Instead, we will briefly focus attention on the developments in mainland China.

China is a very large country, with an impressive cultural, economic, and military history, dating back thousands of years. According to recent estimates, there are some 1.3 billion Chinese. Since we want to get a feel for the importance of international trade and capital flows, and openness to the outside world, even for such a large country as China, we will measure economic progress in China relative to the outside world. To this end, Figure 17.9 depicts China's GNP per capita as a percentage of world average GNP per capita.

In 1949 Mao Zedong proclaimed the founding of the People's Republic of China and installed a new political and economic order modelled on the Soviet example. In 1958, Mao broke with the Soviet model and started a new economic programme called the Great Leap Forward. Its aim was to raise industrial and agricultural production by forming large cooperatives and building 'backyard factories'. The results of the market disruption and poor planning, leading to the production of unsaleable goods, were disastrous. Within a year, starvation appeared even in fertile agricultural areas, resulting in famine from 1960 to 1961. The relationship with the Soviet Union deteriorated sharply, leading to the restriction of the flow of scientific and technological information to China, and the withdrawal of all Soviet personnel in 1960. When compared to the world average, the impact of the Great Leap Forward shows up in Figure 17.9 as a deterioration of China's living standards from an already low 4.05 per cent in 1960 to an even lower 2.42 per cent in 1962 (a relative decline of 40 per cent!).

In the early 1960s Liu Shaoqi and his protégé Deng Xiaoping took over direction of the party and adopted pragmatic economic policies at odds with Mao's revolutionary vision. In 1966, when the Chinese economy had almost recuperated from the consequences of the Great Leap Forward and Chinese per capita GNP had bounced back to 3.16 per cent of the world average, Mao started the Cultural Revolution, a political attack on the pragmatists who

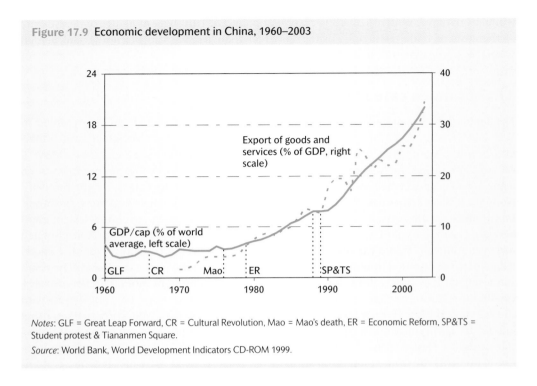

Figure 17.9 Economic development in China, 1960–2003

Notes: GLF = Great Leap Forward, CR = Cultural Revolution, Mao = Mao's death, ER = Economic Reform, SP&TS = Student protest & Tiananmen Square.

Source: World Bank, World Development Indicators CD-ROM 1999.

were dragging China back towards capitalism. The Red Guards, radical youth organizations, attacked party and state organizations at all levels. Again, Mao's insightful ideas were disastrous to the Chinese standard of living, which dropped to 2.56 per cent of the world average in 1968; see Figure 17.9 (this time a relative decline in position of 'only' 20 per cent). The Chinese political situation stabilized after some years along complex factional lines, stabilizing the Chinese living standards to slightly above 3 per cent of the world average and leading to the reinstatement of Deng Xiaoping in 1975, who was stripped of all official positions only a year later by the Gang of Four (Mao's wife and three associates).

Mao's death in September 1976 set off a scramble for succession, leading to the arrest of the Gang of Four and the reinstatement of Deng Xiaoping in August of 1977. In a pivotal meeting in December 1978 the new leadership adopted economic reform policies to expand rural incentives, encourage enterprise autonomy, reduce central planning, open up to international trade flows with the outside world, establish foreign direct investment in China, and pass new legal codes in June of 1979.

The positive consequences of the economic reforms for the Chinese standard of living were enormous, dramatically illustrating the dynamic costs of trade restrictions. The policy of openness is illustrated in Figure 17.10 for the net foreign direct investment flows into China as a percentage of GNP. There are no data available before 1971, but as illustrated by Figure 17.10 there were *no* foreign direct investments into China from 1971 to 1979 (we can be sure that this also held for a long period preceding 1971). After the economic reforms, foreign direct investments into China rose rapidly to a stagnating level of about 1 per cent of GNP in the period 1988–91, followed by a continued rise to a peak of more than 6 per cent of GNP in 1993 and 1994, and stabilizing at around 4 per cent of GNP thereafter (remember that these are percentages of a rapidly increasing GNP level; see Figures 16.9(b) and 17.9).

Figure 17.10 Capital inflows into China, net foreign direct investment (% of GNP), 1970–2003

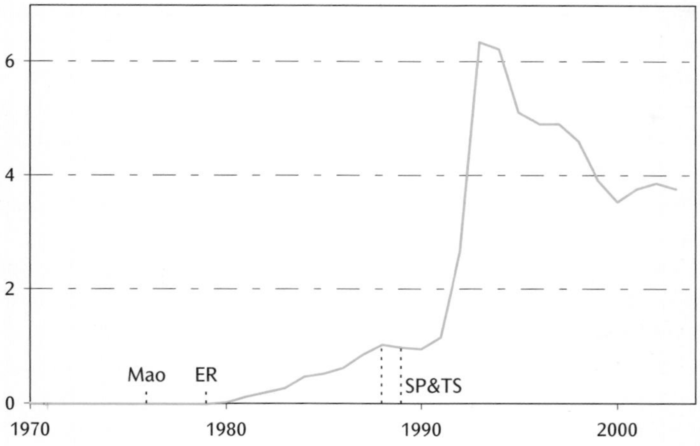

Notes: GLF = Great Leap Forward, CR = Cultural Revolution, Mao = Mao's death, ER = Economic reform, SP&TS = Student protest & Tiananmen Square.

Source: World Bank, World Development Indicators CD-ROM 1999.

The period of temporary stagnation in 1988–90 is indicated by the term 'Student Protest & Tiananmen Square' in Figures 17.9 and 17.10. At the end of the 1980s party elders feared, in reaction to student demonstrators, that the reform programme was leading to social instability and called for greater centralization of economic controls. The political debate culminated in university students in Beijing camping out at Tiananmen Square to protest against those who would slow reform. Martial law was declared and military force was used against the protesters, leading to hundreds of casualties. Eventually, this only temporarily stopped the reform process as younger, reform-minded leaders began their rise to top positions and Deng Xiaoping renewed his push for a market-oriented economy, as sanctioned by the Party Congress in 1992.

The impact of the economic reform programme, interrupted temporarily by the events surrounding Tiananmen Square, is clearly visible in Figure 17.9. As a percentage of the world average, the Chinese standard of living rose from 3.8 per cent in 1978 to 7.8 per cent in 1988, where the increase was interrupted for a year, to continue rising to 20 per cent in 2003 (a relative increase of 430 per cent in 25 years!). As far as economic prosperity is concerned, Deng Xiaoping, who died in 1997, has been extremely important for the Chinese people.

17.8 Conclusions

As explained in the introduction to this chapter, we can only scratch the surface in describing the many issues at stake in applied trade policy modelling, which in general involves the use of accurate and current data, a model structure determined by the data, a detailed policy orientation, and the analysis of non-local changes in policy parameters from distorted base equilibria. Applied researchers have used the demand side of the economy to solve some practical problems in matching models and data, for example by incorporating demand bias, the Linder hypothesis, and the Armington assumption.

If the trade policy question the researcher is trying to address is limited in scope, perhaps concerning one or only a few sectors in a single country and a few policy variables, applied partial equilibrium models, based on estimating the size of the Harberger triangles, allow for a rapid and transparent analysis. If the researcher is trying to answer more ambitious questions, involving a range of trade policy measures, a range of sectors, and/or a range of different countries, she will use applied general equilibrium models which take into consideration the simultaneous effects of all proposed policy measures for all sectors and countries. There are roughly three types of applied general equilibrium models: (1) constant returns and perfect competition, (2) increasing returns and imperfect competition, and (3) dynamic models. In general, the estimated costs of trade restrictions increases as we move from type (1) to type (2), and from type (2) to type (3) models.

We conclude the chapter by arguing that none of the applied general equilibrium models can really measure the importance of international economic contacts through the exchange of goods, capital, foreign direct investment, knowledge, ideas, etc. The main reason is that imposing trade restrictions may result in goods and services *not* being introduced on the market. We use the Dupuit triangle to estimate the costs of goods that are not introduced, which is a tricky procedure even in a theoretical framework. Using a simple model, we show that such costs can be substantial (and much larger than the empirically estimated costs in applied general equilibrium models). A case study of China's recent history gives at least some suggestive evidence in favour of this view.

QUESTIONS

Question 17.1

An American tractor producer considers introducing a new type of tractor in Kenya. It costs 1 million Kenyan shillings to produce and transport one tractor to Kenya. However, before the tractor can be introduced, the Kenyan dealer needs to stock spare parts and train new personnel to sell and repair the new machine. These fixed costs amount to 10 million Kenyan shillings. At the request of the American tractor producer, a consultant has estimated the demand curve for the new type of tractor in Kenya. The figure on the next page shows this demand curve. Furthermore, the consultant notes that Kenya is currently levying an import tariff of 20 per cent over the value of tractors (both production and transportation).

17.1A If the fixed costs are ignored, what is the optimal price the American tractor producer will charge on the Kenyan market? Remember that the American producer is a monopolist.

17.1B Indicate in the figure what the consumer surplus, producer surplus, and government revenue are at this optimal price.

17.1C Explain why the American tractor producer will not introduce the new tractor on the Kenyan market. What is the welfare loss for the Kenyan economy?

17.1D How can the tractor producer convince the Kenyan government that action is needed? What kind of action should the tractor producer recommend?

Question 17.2

In March 2001 some of the world's largest pharmaceutical companies brought the South African government before the High Court in Pretoria. Their complaint was that the Medicines Act, which had not come into effect at that time, would undermine the patent rules of the World Trade Organization. An important part of the dispute was the provision that allowed for the parallel imports of patented AIDS medicines from other countries where these medicines are sold at a lower price. We analyse this court case using the following data for the market of AIDS medicines in South Africa.

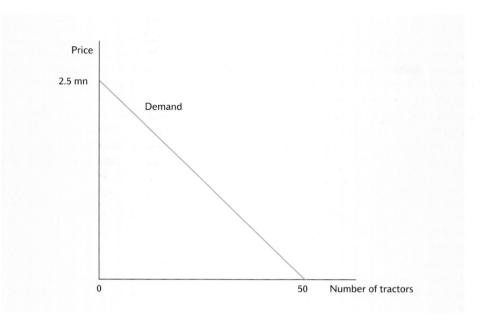

Market data on AIDS medicine in South Africa	
Number of medicines currently sold in South Africa	1,000,000
Current price of the medicine in South Africa	US$9.34
Price of the medicine in Thailand	US$0.60

Initially, the South African AIDS patients have to buy their medicines from the large pharmaceutical companies for US$9.34. If the Medicine Act is activated, cheaper medicines can be imported from Thailand, such that the price drops to US$0.60. Assume that the demand for AIDS medicines in South Africa is given by:

$$p = a - bQ$$

where p is the price for the medicine, Q the quantity demanded, and a and b are parameter constants. Normally, when conducting a policy study, one has to estimate this demand function. As this is beyond the scope of this question, we quantify the demand function in a non-rigorous way.

17.2A What would be a reasonable value for the constant 'b'? Explain your choice.

17.2B Using the value for 'b' from question 17.2A, what is the value of the constant 'a' in the demand function?

17.2C Draw the demand function for AIDS medicines in South Africa. Draw in the same figure the change in welfare if the South African government passes the Medicines Act.

17.2D What are the dynamic problems arising from the introduction of the Medicines Act?

17.2E Do you advise the South African government to introduce the Medicines Act or not? Why?

Question 17.3

The fast growth and integration into the world economy of China is seen by some people as a threat. They are afraid that other economies will suffer from China's fast growth. Researchers of the IMF have taken up this issue in the *World*

Economic Outlook of April 2004. For their analysis they use a general equilibrium model that captures in detail the geographic and sectoral structure of trade flows. With this model they estimate what the world will look like in 2020 when the Chinese economy stagnates and what it will look like when the Chinese economy grows fast. The difference between these two scenarios shows who are the winners and who are the losers of fast economic growth in China. The figure below presents the results. The figure shows the difference in GDP both under the assumption that output and labour markets adjust instantly and under the assumption of structural rigidities.

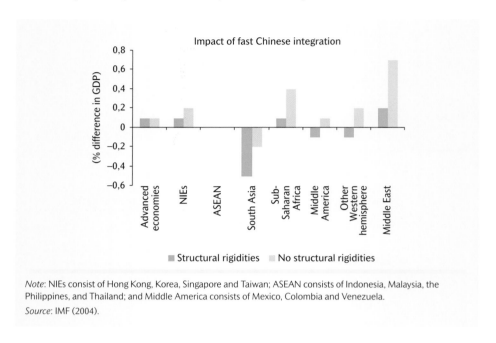

Note: NIEs consist of Hong Kong, Korea, Singapore and Taiwan; ASEAN consists of Indonesia, Malaysia, the Philippines, and Thailand; and Middle America consists of Mexico, Colombia and Venezuela.
Source: IMF (2004).

17.3A Why do you think the Middle East and Sub-Saharan Africa in particular gain from fast growth of the Chinese economy?

17.3B Why do you think South Asia in particular loses from fast growth of the Chinese economy?

17.3C The model used by the IMF researchers takes into account only changes in trade. Through which other channels can the world be affected? Are countries likely to gain or lose through these channels?

17.3D What do you recommend the governments of South Asia to do based on this analysis?

 See the Online Resource Centre for a Study Guide containing more questions
www.oxfordtextbooks.co.uk/orc/vanmarrewijk/

NOTES

1 As a student of mine noted, the Dupuit triangle probably overestimates this loss. If the bridge is not built, an alternative means of crossing the river, such as a ferry, will be viable. The ferry will have a similar Dupuit triangle which mitigates the welfare loss of not building the bridge.

2 Price discrimination cannot solve this problem, as explained in Romer (1994b).

3 For details on these calculations see Romer (1994b).

4 Similar examples of neighbours with different openness of economic systems, and corresponding differences in economic development, are: East versus West Germany, and Thailand versus Myanmar.

PART III
INTERNATIONAL MONEY

III.A
MONEY BASICS

Part III.A provides a brief review of the money market (Chapter 18) and then discusses the size and structure of foreign exchange markets (Chapter 19), purchasing power parity (Chapter 20), and interest rate parity (Chapter 21). This part concludes with an overview of the main international money organizations and institutions (Chapter 22).

THE MONEY MARKET

18

We start the monetary part of this book with a basic review of the money market, describing the functions of money, different types of money, the demand for money, the money supply process, and monetary equilibrium.

18.1 Introduction

The money market plays a crucial role in the economy through its unique position relative to all other markets. A smoothly operating money market allows an economy to function properly by conveying (changes in) relative prices of different goods and services (and thereby relative scarcity) as clearly as possible. This chapter gives a brief review of the main aspects of the money market by discussing the functions of money, listing different types of money, describing money demand and supply, and analysing the monetary equilibrium.

18.2 The functions of money

The easily posed question 'What is money?' has turned out notoriously difficult to answer, particularly given the variety of financial instruments used on today's financial markets. A useful starting point is given by John Hicks (1967), who focuses on the functions of money for a definition:

> Money is what money does. Money is defined by its functions.

Even so, it is hard to determine what should and what should not be classified as money. We can safely conclude that at this moment there is no commonly accepted answer. In a sense, money is like a chair: fairly easy to recognize, but hard to define. In practice, economists distinguish between three primary functions of money:

- *Means of payment* Without 'money' as a generally accepted means of payment, exchange would be only possible if there is a 'double coincidence of wants': I can buy your pig only if you will take my five sacks of rice in return. Alternatively, we could look for indirect means of exchange: I sell my five sacks of rice to John, who gives you two kegs of beer, while you give me your pig. Obviously, the transaction costs for this type of barter exchange are very high,

Famous economists	Milton Friedman

Fig. 18.1
Milton Friedman
(1912–)

Born in New York and educated at Rutgers, Chicago, and Columbia, Milton Friedman spent most of his academic career at the University of Chicago. He is widely regarded as the leader of the Chicago School of monetary economics, which stresses the importance of the quantity of money as a policy instrument and a determinant of business cycles and inflation. Friedman argues against government economic controls and dismisses Keynesian theories of consumption, prices, and inflation. Together with Anna Schwartz he wrote an influential empirical study in 1963 entitled *A Monetary History of the United States, 1867–1960*. In 1976 Friedman won the Nobel prize in economics for his 'achievements in the fields of consumption analysis, monetary history and theory, and for his demonstration of the complexity of stabilization policy'. Many people remember him as the enthusiastic person emphasizing the importance of individual freedom in the ten-part television series *Free to Choose*, for which he wrote a book in 1980 with the same title (jointly with Rose Friedman).

seriously limiting the efficiency of economic interaction. The most important function of money is therefore undoubtedly its use as a means of payment. Historically, precious metals, such as gold and silver coins, have been used for this purpose. More prosaic means, such as shells on certain islands and cigarettes in Second World War prisoner-of-war camps, have also been used. Nowadays, it is either paper bills and coins in your wallet or digital numbers on your bank account.

- *Store of value* If money is accepted as a means of payment, it automatically also functions as a store of value, at least during the time period in which the person receiving the money holds on to it before paying someone else. This time period tends to be shorter if the inflation rate is high, since the usefulness of money as a store of value diminishes if the value of money falls rapidly.

- *Unit of account* Money also provides the more abstract function of a unit of account as the legal currency for a certain area, such as dollars in the USA, yen in Japan, and euros in the Economic and Monetary Union (EMU) in Europe. It functions as a numéraire to compare prices of different goods, which greatly reduces information and transaction costs. Without a unit of account it is hard to say if a stapler that costs five handkerchiefs in one shop is more expensive than in another shop where it costs four batteries, particularly if we realize the possible number of comparisons. If there are n goods, there are $(n/2)(n-1)$ relative prices; so 1,000 goods implies 499,500 relative prices and one million goods implies 500 billion relative prices. Expressing all prices in the same unit of account makes comparisons much easier. The unit of account is also used for legal documents, for borrowing and lending, as a standard for measuring wealth and a means for aggregation, etc.

18.3 Different types of money

National currencies (coins, banknotes and electronic money) tend to be the most successful at the functions listed above. They are often the only 'money' accepted generally as a means of payment. That is why we will focus on them here. But we are not completely out of the woods yet. For if you put your national currency on a bank deposit for ten years, it no longer functions as a means of payment for ten years. Where do we draw the line? Not surprisingly, several solutions are available for the *classification problem* – defining the borderline between money and other less liquid financial assets. As a result of financial innovations, which have made it increasingly easy to use bank deposits as a means of payment (credit cards, electronic banking), the policy emphasis has shifted over time towards broader monetary aggregates that include more financial assets. From narrow to broad, the four most common definitions of money are (see also Section 18.6 for the symbols used below):

- *Monetary base* (B) consists of currency in circulation (C) and reserves (R) that commercial banks hold at the central bank (which can be converted to currency at negligible transaction costs): $B = C + R$

- *Money stock* M_1 consists of currency in circulation (C) and private non-banks' overnight deposits (OD, which can be converted to currency at negligible transaction costs, for example using cash dispensers, also called sight deposits): $M_1 = C + OD$

- *Broader money stock* M_2 consists of M_1 + time deposits (TD, that is deposits with agreed maturity up to two years) + savings deposits (SD, that is deposits redeemable at notice up to three months): $M_2 = M_1 + TD + SD$.

- *Broader money stock M_3 consists of M_2 + other short-term liabilities (*OSL*) of the banking system (repurchase agreements, money market fund shares/units and money market paper, and debt securities with maturity up to two years): $M_3 = M_2 + OSL$*

Unfortunately, these definitions and measurements of the monetary aggregates are not entirely the same in all countries. Table 18.1 summarizes some of these differences for Japan, Europe, the USA, and the UK.

Table 18.1 Definitions of money in Japan, the UK, the USA, and euro area

Country	M1	M2	M3
Euro area (ECB) and the UK	Currency in circulation + overnight deposits	M_1 + deposits with agreed maturity up to 2 years + deposits redeemable at notice up to 3 months	M_2 + repurchase agreements + money market fund shares/units and money market paper + debt securities up to 2 years
Japan	Currency in circulation + deposit money	M_1 + quasi-money	Not reported, but: M_2 + certificates of deposits
USA	Currency + checkable deposits	M_1 + household holdings of savings deposits, time deposits, and retail money market funds	M_2 + institutional money funds + managed liabilities of depositories, namely large time deposits, repurchase agreements, and eurodollars

Source: Bofinger (2001, p. 16).

Figure 18.2 Australia: different types of money

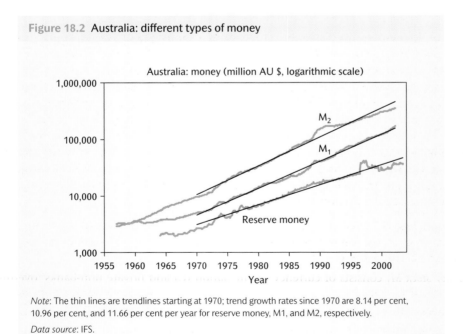

Note: The thin lines are trendlines starting at 1970; trend growth rates since 1970 are 8.14 per cent, 10.96 per cent, and 11.66 per cent per year for reserve money, M1, and M2, respectively.

Data source: IFS.

Figure 18.2 depicts the volume of some different types of money stock in Australia since the 1950s. As the figure uses a logarithmic scale, the slopes of the various lines give the growth rates of the money stocks; see Box 16.1. As is evident from the trendlines summarizing the behaviour over longer time periods in Figure 18.2, the broader money stocks increased faster in Australia. Although this is generally the case for most economies, it is not a universal phenomenon; see also Figure 18.3(a).

18.4 The money market

Before we review the supply and demand for money, we discuss the five main players on the money market. This will help us to understand the demand and supply process. The main players are:

- *The central bank* In modern countries the central bank is guaranteed a monopoly over the supply of banknotes and coins and is responsible for a smoothly operating monetary system. Examples are the Bank of Japan (BoJ), the Bank of England (BoE), and the Federal Reserve system (Fed) in the USA and the European Central Bank (ECB) for the European countries that participate in the Economic and Monetary Union (EMU).

- *Commercial banks* Through their role as an intermediary between borrowers and lenders, commercial banks are at the centre of the (international) money and capital markets. Their liabilities consist mainly of deposits and their assets of loans (to firms, households and the government), deposits at other banks, and bonds. The *banking system* consists of the central bank together with the commercial banks. Table 18.2 lists the top ten commercial banks in

Table 18.2 Top ten commercial banks in the USA as of 31 March 2004

Rank	Bank name	Consol. assets (Mn $)	Domestic assets(Mn $)	Dom. as % cons.	Cuml. as % cons.	% fgn own.
1	Bank of America	690,573	647,499	94	10	0
2	JP Morgan Chase	648,692	382,594	59	19	0
3	Citibank	606,191	274,283	45	28	0
4	Wachovia	364,474	343,056	94	33	0
5	Wells Fargo	347,560	347,045	100	38	0
6	Bank One	256,701	236,246	92	42	0
7	Fleet National	195,323	178,566	91	45	0
8	US Bank	191,606	191,606	100	47	0
9	Suntrust	124,298	124,298	100	49	0
10	HSBC USA	99,867	89,724	90	50	100

Notes: Ranked by consolidated assets; consol assets = consolidated assets; dom. as % cons. = domestic assets as a percentage of consolidated assets; cuml. as % cons. = cumulative consolidated assets as a percentage of the sum of consolidated assets for all banks; % fgn own. = percentage of foreign ownership; total number of banks = 1,376; total cons. assets = 6,982,131 million.

Source: www.federalreserve.gov

the USA as of 31 March 2004, ranked by consolidated assets. It shows, for example, that the largest bank has assets worth almost $700 billion, that some banks have large assets abroad, that the top ten banks own about 50 per cent of the total consolidated assets for all banks (of which there are 1,376), and that only one bank in the top ten (HSBC) is of non-American origin.

- *Government sector* Although the central bank is a government organization, it is useful to distinguish clearly between the central bank and other government organizations, since they play different roles in the money market and have different responsibilities regarding the macroeconomic performance of an economy.

- *Private non-bank public* The majority of the activities of the commercial banks relate to the private non-bank public, that is consumers and firms who hold deposits at the banks or borrow money from the banks.

- *Foreign sector* International organizations and foreign consumers, firms, and governments are grouped under the heading foreign sector. Changes in a country's net position relative to the foreign sector often play a crucial role for understanding international money and capital markets.

18.5 The demand for money

The demand for money is obviously related to the functions of money described in Section 18.2. Since its primary use is as a medium of exchange, the first theory of the demand for money, the quantity theory of money based on Irving Fisher (1911), focuses on this function. On the straightforward assumptions that the number of transactions increases as the size of the economy (as measured by real income Y) increases and that the need for money (M) per transaction rises if the price level (P) increases, the standard specification of the *quantity theory of money* is:

(18.1) $$MV = PY,$$

where V is the income velocity of money (the number of transactions).

A few remarks on this specification are in order. First, as stated, equation (18.1) does not give the demand of money, but merely *defines* the income velocity of money. It only becomes an indication for the (transactions) demand for money once we make auxiliary assumptions concerning the behaviour of the income velocity of money. Initially, a popular, but questionable, assumption used in this respect was a constant velocity of money, say $\overline{V}$, in which case equation (18.1) implies: $M^d = PY/\overline{V}$. Since that specification ignores the other functions of money and is empirically refuted (see, for example, Figure 18.3(b)), it is hardly used anymore. Second, since there are different types of money identified in practice (see Section 18.3), we also have different types of income velocities of money associated with these different types of money as specified by equation (18.1). This is illustrated for the USA in Figure 18.3.

Figure 18.3 illustrates that a broader money stock does not necessarily grow faster than a more narrowly defined money stock. Moreover, it is evident from Figure 18.3(b) that the income velocity of money is not constant and may move in opposite directions for different types of money. Needless to say, this makes the central bank's policy choices aimed at

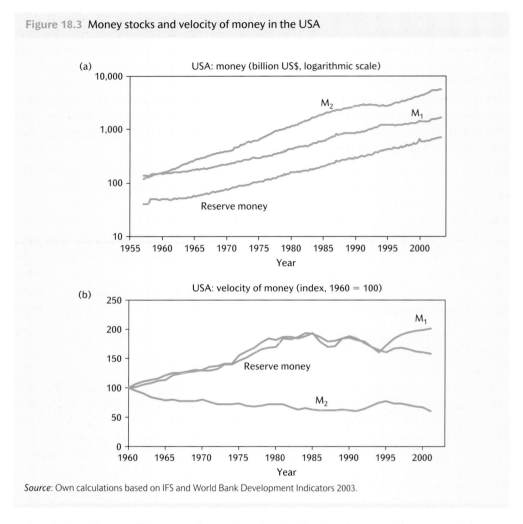

Figure 18.3 Money stocks and velocity of money in the USA

Source: Own calculations based on IFS and World Bank Development Indicators 2003.

maintaining price stability more challenging than if the signals it received were all pointing in the same direction.

Individuals holding money face a simple trade-off: liquidity versus return. Basic forms of money holdings earn no interest (i), but can be used immediately, if necessary, as a means of payment. Parts of broader money stocks earn a (low) interest rate at the expense of a somewhat lower liquidity. Both compete with still less liquid financial assets earning a higher rate of return. Most theories of money demand focus on this trade-off between liquidity and return in addition to the use of money as a medium of exchange. Keynes's (1936) theory of liquidity preference, for example, identifies a transactions motive (facilitating trade in goods), a precautionary motive (store of value), and a speculative motive for holding money (return on investment). Money demand is therefore not only influenced by the level of production in an economy, but also by the interest rate, representing the opportunity cost of holding money. Similarly, in Baumol (1952) and Tobin's (1956, 1958) inventory model, individuals determine the number of trips to the bank as a function of the income level and the interest rate (so-called shoe-leather costs). A basic theoretic money demand function is therefore given by (see also Boxes 18.1 and 18.3):

(18.2) $$M^d/P = M^d(\underset{-}{i}, \underset{+}{Y})$$

In view of the specification in equation (18.1), this can be interpreted as an attempt to explain how the interest rate influences the income velocity of money.[1] Most empirical estimates of money demand functions use a log-linear specification. If we let i denote the interest rate, the real money demand is either specified as:

(18.3a) $$ln(M_t/P_t) = b_0 + b_1 \, ln(Y_t) + b_2 \, ln(i_t) + \varepsilon_t,$$

or as:

(18.3b) $$\ln(M_t/P_t) = \beta_0 + \beta_1 \ln(Y_t) + \beta_3 i_t + \varepsilon_t,$$

where ε_t is an error term. The parameters β_1 and β_2 are the income and interest rate elasticities of money demand, respectively, as they indicate by what percentage the real demand for money changes per percentage change in the income level or interest rate. The specification in (18.3b), where the interest rate term is non-logarithmic, is more popular in empirical work. In that case the parameter β_3 is called the *semi-interest elasticity* of money demand, as it shows

---

Box 18.1   **Wealth and the demand for money**

Milton Friedman (1956) emphasizes that the demand for money should be treated like the demand for goods and services. In this respect an individual's wealth plays an important role. Friedman identifies five components of wealth: money, bonds, shares, real assets, and human capital. Money is therefore just one of the components of wealth and, as in the usual theory of consumer choice, the demand for money depends on: (i) the budget constraint (total wealth to be held in various forms), (ii) the price and return of wealth and alternatives, and (iii) an individual's preferences. In general, therefore, the demand for money depends on the return to all individual components of wealth, the income level, the wealth level, and preferences. Obviously, it is very difficult to quantify all possible types of real assets and human capital and their respective returns, which makes the theory hard to apply empirically. However, it is clear that the wealth component plays a role in the determinants of the demand for money. Coenen and Vega (1999), for example, estimate the following demand for money (M_3) in the euro area:

(18.4) $$\ln(M_t) = 1.140 \ln(Y_t) - 0.820(i_{bond,t} - i_{money,t}) - 1.462\pi_t + \varepsilon_t,$$

where π_t is the inflation rate. The fact that the income elasticity of money demand is above unity can be attributed to the wealth effect (since in the period under investigation nominal wealth rose more quickly than nominal income). The estimated semi-interest elasticity for the broad money stock M_3 in equation (18.4) is negative, as expected, and based on the difference between the long-run and the short-run interest rate (since some components of M_3 do earn interest). Finally, the inflation rate in the economy has a negative influence on the demand for money as inflation erodes the value of the money stock; see also Box 18.3.

the percentage by which the real demand for money changes if the interest rate changes by one percentage point. See also Box 20.1.

18.6 The money supply process

To understand the money supply process we will study the balance sheets of the central bank and the banking system. It is important to realize that this process is a two-step procedure: the central bank directly controls the monetary base and thereby indirectly influences broader money stocks M_1, M_2, and M_3. This occurs through its control of the monetary base and other instruments affecting the behaviour of commercial banks, such as the interest rate for reserves and the minimum reserve ratio. By influencing the money supply process the central bank hopes to maintain price stability. Table 18.3 summarizes the financial statement of the euro system (ECB plus central banks participating in the euro; see Chapter 30).

Table 18.3 Consolidated weekly financial statement of the euro system, 20 August 2004

Assets	Balance	Liabilities	Balance
Gold and gold receivables	127,382	Banknotes in circulation	462,185
Claims on non-euro area residents denominated in foreign currency	173,010	Liabilities to euro area credit institutions related to monetary policy operations denominated in euro	140,356
Claims on euro area residents denominated in foreign currency	17,104	Other liabilities to euro area credit institutions denominated in euro	125
Claims on non-euro area residents denominated in euro	7,261	Debt certificates issued	1,054
Lending to euro area credit institutions related to monetary policy operations denominated in euro	320,998	Liabilities to other euro area residents denominated in euro	56,132
Other claims on euro area credit institutions denominated in euro	1,415	Liabilities to non-euro area residents denominated in euro	9,016
Securities of euro area residents denominated in euro	67,862	Liabilities to euro area residents denominated in foreign currency	244
General government debt denominated in euro	42,086	Liabilities to non-euro area residents denominated in foreign currency	11,869
Other assets	114,858	Counterpart of Special Drawing Rights allocated by the IMF	5,896
		Other liabilities	55,123
		Revaluation accounts	70,205
		Capital and reserves	59,771
Total assets	871,976	Total liabilities	871,976

Note: Amounts are in millions of euro.

Source: www.ecb.int

Like all other balance sheets, Table 18.3 is organized according to the principles of double-entry bookkeeping. The sum of all assets is therefore necessarily equal to the sum of all liabilities. The assets are central bank holdings of claims to future payments, by its citizens, commercial banks, the government sector, or the foreign sector. The majority of the domestic assets held by the central bank are loans to domestic commercial banks and domestic government bonds. The foreign assets constitute the central bank's official international reserves. Their level changes if the central bank intervenes in the foreign exchange market by buying or selling foreign exchange (or alternatively by changes in exchange rates that influence the balance sheet valuation of international reserves). Table 18.3 shows that on 20 August 2004 the total value of all assets of the euro system was 871,976 million euro. The liabilities side of the central bank balance sheet lists currency in circulation and deposits of commercial banks. The latter are largely deposits required by law as partial backing for the liabilities of the commercial banks. Individuals and non-bank firms can, in general, not deposit money at the central bank. Table 18.4 simplifies the information given in Table 18.3 to highlight the position of the central bank relative to other players on the money market.

Using Table 18.4, the properties of the balance sheet, and the definition of the monetary base (B) given in Section 18.3, it follows that:

$$(18.5) \qquad B = C + R = NPFor + NPGov + CrBank - BalCB$$

Ignoring changes in the central bank's balance of other assets and liabilities (BalCB) for simplicity, equation (18.5) shows that changes in the monetary base come about through changes in the central bank's net position relative to the foreign sector, its net position relative to the government sector, or credit extended to the commercial banks. We discuss examples of each of these possibilities in turn.

1. If the central bank intervenes in the foreign exchange market by purchasing foreign currency from a commercial bank, the central bank's net position relative to the foreign sector (and its official reserves) increases. In general, the purchase is paid for by crediting the commercial bank's account at the central bank by the same amount, such that the deposits of the banking sector (R), and therefore the monetary base, increase by the same

Table 18.4 **Simplified financial balance sheet of the central bank**

Assets	Balance	Liabilities	Balance
Net position *vis-à-vis* the foreign sector (including gold holdings)	NPFor	Currency in circulation	C
		Deposits of the domestic banking sector	R
Net position *vis-à-vis* the domestic government sector	NPGov	Balance of other assets and liabilities	BalCB
Credits to the domestic banking sector	CrBank		
Total net assets		Total net liabilities	

amount. However, the central bank can take countervailing measures, such as 2 or 3 below, to prevent changes in the monetary base occurring as a result of foreign exchange intervention. This is called *sterilization* of interventions; see also Chapter 28.[2]

2. If the central bank grants a loan to the state, its net position relative to the government, and hence the monetary base, changes as soon as the state starts to spend the funds by paying firms or individuals (credited to an account at a commercial bank). Similarly, if the central bank purchases or sells government bonds (open-market policy), the monetary base increases or decreases, respectively. In many European countries, the direct purchase of government bonds (from the government) is forbidden, so that the central bank can only buy government bonds in the secondary market. This is not frequently done in Europe, but it is in Japan (as a means to change the monetary base).

3. If the central bank grants a loan to a commercial bank, for example under a credit facility, the monetary base increases by the same amount.

To discuss changes in the money stocks M_1, M_2, and M_3, we have to focus on the second step of the money supply process, in which the monetary base can be seen as an input. It is most useful to look at the consolidated balance sheet of the banking system as a whole; that is, by aggregating the balance sheet of the central bank and all commercial banks into a single balance sheet. This means that all claims between commercial banks and between the central bank and commercial banks are netted out. Table 18.5 presents a simplified version of this consolidated balance sheet similar to Table 18.4 for the central bank. The asset side consists of three entries: the net position of the banking system relative to foreigners (NEA), credits of the banking system to the domestic government sector (CrGov), and credits to the domestic private non-bank sector (CrDom). The liabilities side of the consolidated balance sheet distinguishes between the various assets included in the different types of money discussed in Section 18.3; see equation (18.6).

Table 18.5 Simplified consolidated financial balance sheet of the banking system

Assets	Balance	Liabilities	Balance
Net external assets (including gold holdings)	NEA	Currency in circulation	C
		Overnight deposits	OD
Credits to the domestic government sector	CrGov	Time deposits (with agreed maturity up to 2 years)	TD
Credits to the domestic private non-bank sector	CrDom	Savings deposits (redeemable at notice up to 3 months)	SD
		Other short-term liabilities of the banking system	OSL
		Balance of other assets and liabilities	BalBS
Total net assets		Total net liabilities	

(18.6a) $M_1 = C + OD$

(18.6b) $M_2 = M_1 + TD + SD$

(18.6c) $M_3 = M_2 + OSL = NEA + CrGov + CrDom - BalBS$

Ignoring changes in the banking system's balance of other assets and liabilities (BalBS) for simplicity, equation (18.6c) shows that changes in the money stock M_3 come about through changes in the banking system's net external assets, credit extended to the government sector, or credit extended to the private non-bank sector. The mechanics of changing the broad money stock M_3 are therefore quite similar to the mechanics of changing the monetary base. In general, money is created when a bank purchases claims from a non-bank. The broader money stocks M_2 and M_3 include (interest-bearing) credits (time deposits, savings deposits, and other short-term liabilities of the banking system). The general money supply model to be discussed below is also valid for these broader money stocks. However, for ease of exposition we will henceforth focus our discussion on the money stock M_1.

   Note: In the remainder of the book, the term 'money' will refer to the money stock M_1, unless explicitly stated otherwise.[3]

   Box 18.2 explains how the supply of monetary base is equivalent to the supply of money if commercial banks behave like automatons. As any other firm, however, commercial banks strive for profit maximization, which depends on the demand for credit, their market position, and their cost structure. Although we will not go into the details of this process, it is

---

 Box 18.2   Mechanistic money multiplier

The simplest way to link the two steps of the money supply process, from the monetary base to the money stock, is by assuming mechanistic behaviour on the part of the commercial banks, as summarized in the following two ratios:

• $c \equiv C/OD$, the cash holding ratio

• $r \equiv R/OD$, the reserve ratio.

The first indicates that there will be some constant ratio of cash to overnight deposits and the second that there will be a constant ratio of deposits of the banking sector at the central bank to overnight deposits, dictated by the central bank's minimum reserve requirements. The money multiplier (*mult*) is defined as the ratio between the money stock and the monetary base. From the above it follows that:

(18.7) $$mult \equiv \frac{M}{B} = \frac{OD + C}{C + R} = \frac{(OD/OD) + (C/OD)}{(C/OD) + (R/OD)} = \frac{1 + c}{c + r}$$

Although this multiplier process can be embellished using a quasi-dynamic story, the end result is that there is a one-to-one correspondence between the monetary base and the money stock. If the central bank controls the monetary base, it therefore also controls the money stock. The discussion in the text explains how the behaviour of commercial banks, which depends on (differences in) interest rates, complicates this process, and thus makes the money multiplier a function of, for example, interest rates.

clear that two interest rates play a crucial role for the commercial bank's profitability; see Klein (1971) and Bofinger (2001, ch. 3):

- i, the interest rate on credit extended by the bank
- i_{res}, the interest rate for reserves held by the bank at the central bank.

If the interest rate i on credit extended by the bank, henceforth referred to as 'the' interest rate, increases, it becomes more attractive for the bank to extend credit. It is identical to the effect of a price increase for the supply of goods or services for any regular firm. The interest rate for reserves held by the bank at the central bank i_{res}, known as the refinancing rate, is paid on the minimum reserve ratio, which is determined by the central bank. A single bank takes its level of deposits as given, depending on stochastic flows. The supply of reserves is perfectly elastic at the refinancing rate i_{res} set by the central bank, which represents the costs of refinancing an unexpected drain of deposits (at the central bank or other banks). Acknowledging that the money supply process also depends on general economic conditions, as measured by real income Y, we get:

$$(18.8) \qquad\qquad M^s = M^s(\underset{+}{i}, \underset{-}{i_{res}}, \underset{+}{Y})$$

Having thus derived a simple money demand function in Section 18.5 and an elementary money supply function in this section, the next section discusses how these two interact to determine the monetary equilibrium.

18.7 Monetary equilibrium

The demand for money, equation (18.2) must, in macroeconomic equilibrium, be equal to the supply of money, equation (18.8). Monetary equilibrium is therefore given in equation (18.9), where the demand for money is equal to the supply of money. Together these forces determine the interest rate and the money stock in an economy as a function of, *inter alia*, the refinancing interest rate and the income level. This is illustrated in Figure 18.4, where i^* and M^* are the equilibrium interest rate and money stock.

$$(18.9) \qquad\qquad M^d(\underset{-}{i}, \underset{+}{Y}) = M^s(\underset{+}{i}, \underset{-}{i_{res}}, \underset{+}{Y})$$

So how does the central bank influence the monetary equilibrium? This is illustrated in Figure 18.5 if the central bank uses interest (refinance) rate targeting. Suppose the initial refinance rate is $i_{res,old}$. The monetary equilibrium is then at point E_{old} with interest rate i_{old}^* and money stock M_{old}^*. If the central bank thinks this level of the money stock is too high and the economy might become overheated, it can increase the refinance rate, to $i_{res,\,new}$, say.[4] This increases the costs of refinancing for commercial banks, which therefore shift their money supply schedule to the left, as indicated in Figure 18.5. A new monetary equilibrium results from the interaction of the money demand schedule and the new money supply schedule at point E_{new}, resulting in a lower equilibrium money stock M_{new}^* and a higher equilibrium interest rate i_{new}^*. A tighter monetary policy by the central bank, in this case a higher refinance rate, therefore causes a higher interest rate in monetary equilibrium and a lower money stock through the interaction of market behaviour by banks, firms, and consumers.

As an alternative to interest rate targeting, the central bank might be using monetary base targeting; that is it might determine the level of the monetary base rather than the level of the

Figure 18.4 Monetary equilibrium

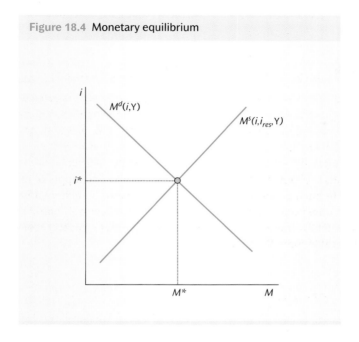

Figure 18.5 An increase in the reserve interest rate and monetary equilibrium

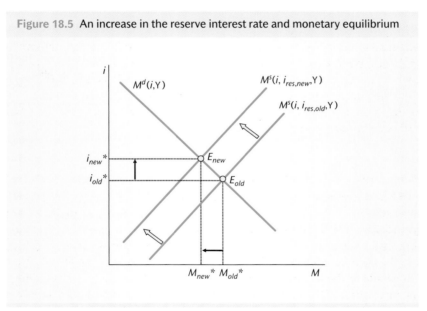

refinance rate. Since commercial banks, through their profit-maximizing behaviour, ensure a negative relationship exists between the monetary base and the refinance rate, these two policies lead to similar outcomes in a deterministic setting: a higher monetary base is associated with a lower refinance rate; either policy leads to a lower interest rate and a higher money stock in monetary equilibrium (see also Chapter 27).[5]

Box 18.3   **Money and prices under hyperinflation**

Under extreme circumstances, such as hyperinflation, the impact of the real interest rate and real income level on the demand for money may become negligible. The term hyperinflation refers to periods of very high inflation rates in which money loses its value very rapidly. Philip Cagan (1956) identified hyperinflation as a period in which the inflation rate is at least 50 per cent per month. This happened, for example, in Bolivia in 1984 and 1985, with a monthly peak of 183 per cent inflation from January 1985 to February 1985. In September of 1985 prices were 600 times as high as they were in April of 1984. Under these conditions, Cagan argued that the demand for money simplifies to:

(18.10) $\ln(M_t) = -\gamma \pi_t^e,$

where γ is a semi-elasticity parameter and π_t^e is the expected inflation rate. To estimate such a function, one would of course need a theory of expectation formation. However, the growth rate of the money stock and the rate of inflation can be effectively illustrated in a logarithmic graph as the slope of the money stock and the slope of the price index, respectively (see Box 16.1). This is illustrated in Figure 18.6. As is evident from the slopes of the curves in Figure 18.6, the expectations are initially lagging a bit behind realizations as the money stock is growing more rapidly than the price level (May–August 1984). Then expectations are rapidly catching up with realizations (inflation is higher than money growth) until the inflation peak in February 1985 shows that prices have increased too rapidly. The Bolivian government introduced a drastic stabilization plan at the end of August 1985, reducing the increase in the money stock from 70 per cent to 57 per cent to 39 per cent and to 28 per cent in the months July–October 1985. With some lag the price level followed suit, with inflation rates of 66 per cent, 66 per cent, 57 per cent, and −2 per cent in that same period. Apparently, the Bolivians became convinced by October 1985 that the government was serious in its efforts to reduce hyperinflation.

Figure 18.6 **Money and prices under extreme circumstances**

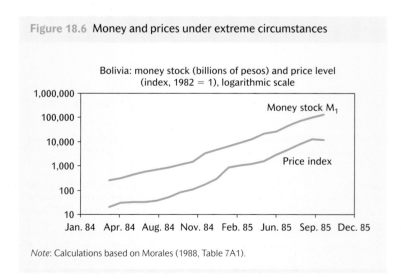

Note: Calculations based on Morales (1988, Table 7A1).

18.8 Conclusions

We briefly discussed the basics of the money market. Money is used as a means of payment, a store of value, and a unit of account. We identified different types of money (from narrow to broad: monetary base, M_1, M_2, and M_3), but will henceforth focus on the money stock M_1 in our discussions unless explicitly stated otherwise. Money is supplied by the banking system (central bank plus commercial banks), which in the aggregate responds to price signals, notably the interest rate. The demand for money depends positively on income (transactions demand) and negatively on the interest rate (opportunity cost or the price for holding money). The interaction of these forces determines the monetary equilibrium, that is the interest rate and the money stock. The central bank can use various policies to influence this equilibrium; a tighter monetary policy implies higher interest rates and a lower money stock. The building blocks of monetary equilibrium discussed in this chapter will be used throughout the sequel.

QUESTIONS

Question 18.1

18.1A In the fifteenth and sixteenth centuries, Spanish galleons brought large quantities of gold and silver from the Americas. This had a profound monetary impact in Europe. Use the quantity theory of money to describe the impact of this gold inflow, given that the velocity of money is constant.

18.1B Suppose now that we turn to the nineteenth century and the Industrial Revolution in the USA. Assume that the velocity of money and money stock are constant and that output increases quickly due to productivity increases. Use the quantity theory of money to describe the monetary impact of this productivity increase.

18.1C It is the end of the twentieth century and developments in information technology promise great productivity increases. The central bank, which directly controls the money stock, wishes to maintain price stability. Which variables does it take into account when determining the optimal money stock according to the quantity theory of money?

18.1D It is shown in the text that the velocity of money is not constant. Can you explain why this may be the case? What gives rise to increases or decreases of the velocity of money?

Question 18.2

18.2A Section 18.3 describes various monetary aggregates and Section 18.5 describes the money supply process. Which aggregate is directly determined by the central bank? Which aggregates are indirectly determined by the central bank?

18.2B Draw a basic central bank balance sheet consisting of the following six balance sheet components: foreign reserves, currency in circulation, lending to commercial banks, deposits of commercial banks, domestic government bonds, and central bank capital.

18.2C The People's Bank of China (PBOC) maintains a fixed exchange rate between the yuan (the Chinese national currency) and the US dollar. In order to do so, it buys or sells US dollars to clear the money market at the desired exchange rate. Indicate what happens on the central bank balance sheet if the PBOC buys dollars in exchange for yuan.

18.2D According to the quantity theory of money, with money velocity and output constant, what happens to the price level after the intervention? What can the PBOC do to prevent its interventions from influencing the price level? Indicate the effect of this operation on your central bank balance sheet.

18.2E Suppose that the Chinese government runs a huge budget deficit. It no longer wishes to finance this by borrowing from commercial banks. It decides to borrow directly from the central bank. Show the effect of this operation on your central bank balance sheet. What is the likely effect on the price level of this operation?

Question 18.3

18.3A Changes in the monetary base induce changes in the broader monetary aggregates. Suppose that the money multiplier is 2. What will happen to the money stock if the Japanese central bank allows a 1 million yen increase of base money? What policy instruments do central banks use to induce changes in the money supply?

18.3B The money multiplier is not fixed in practice, but fluctuates according to economic conditions. Can you think of a variable that directly affects the money multiplier (think about the incentives of commercial banks)?

18.3C Show in a graph the effect of the monetary loosening by the Japanese central bank on the monetary equilibrium.

18.3D Suppose that income increases. How does this affect the monetary equilibrium?

18.3E The central bank of Japan has the objective of price stability. Unfortunately, prices have been falling in Japan for much of the 1990s. In response, the central bank has increased the monetary base. Yet prices have continued to fall. Changes in the monetary base fail to fully translate into broader monetary aggregates. Can you explain how this is possible?

 See the Online Resource Centre for a Study Guide containing more questions
www.oxfordtextbooks.co.uk/orc/vanmarrewijk/

NOTES

1 Note that other factors, such as financial innovations, also influence the demand for money.

2 The central bank usually intervenes to attain some sort of exchange rate target and might sterilize these interventions to prevent changes in the domestic money stock.

3 This implies, retro-actively, that we discussed the demand for money stock M_1 in Section 18.5.

4 Note that we use the terms 'old' and 'new' here to avoid confusion that might arise from the standard use of '0' and '1' in view of their association with different types of money stocks; see Section 18.3.

5 It should be noted that the economic implications of the two policies are in general different in a stochastic setting in which demand and supply can shift up and down because the impact of shocks on the monetary system may vary.

FOREIGN EXCHANGE MARKETS

19

Objectives/key terms

- Spot exchange rate
- Appreciation and depreciation
- Black and parallel markets
- Plain vanilla
- Effective exchange rates
- Intervention

- Bid, ask, and spread
- (Triangular) arbitrage
- Forward, swap, option, and swaption
- Hedging and speculation
- Trading volume
- Brokers

We provide an introduction to foreign exchange markets by discussing different types of exchange rates and instruments (spot, forward, swap, and option), the main players on the foreign exchange markets (commercial banks, firms, other financial institutions, and central banks), and the size and composition of these markets.

19.1 Introduction

After discussing national money in the previous chapter, we now turn to the international aspects of money. Most international transactions, such as the international trade of goods and (tourist) services or international investment activities, involve the exchange of one currency for another. The most noteworthy, and rather recent, exception to this rule is the international exchange between the countries of Europe's euro area (Austria, Belgium, Finland, France, Germany, Greece, Ireland, Italy, Luxembourg, the Netherlands, Portugal, and Spain), which decided to introduce one common currency on 1 January 1999: the euro. The trade of different currencies takes place on the foreign exchange markets, at prices called exchange rates. This rarely involves the exchange of banknotes between citizens, except in the case of tourism or illegal (drugs) trade. Instead, most foreign exchange involves the trade of foreign-currency-denominated deposits between large commercial banks in international financial centres, such as London, New York, and Tokyo. There are different types of exchange rates and instruments, such as spot rates, forward rates, swaps, and options. We begin our discussion with the spot exchange rate market.

19.2 Spot exchange rates

It is important to realize that an exchange rate is a price, namely the price of one currency in terms of another currency. This price is determined simply by demand and supply in the foreign exchange market. As there are many countries with convertible currencies, there are many exchange rates, such as the exchange rate of a Singapore dollar in terms of European euros or the exchange rate of a Japanese yen in terms of British pounds. Since the exchange rate is a price, a rise in the exchange rate indicates that the item being traded has become more expensive, just as is indicated by any other price rise. Therefore, if the exchange rate of a Singapore dollar in terms of European euros rises, this indicates that the Singapore dollar has become more expensive. Various specialized symbols have been introduced to identify

Famous economists	Kenneth Rogoff

Fig. 19.1
Kenneth Rogoff
(1953–)

Born in Rochester (upstate New York) and educated at Yale and MIT, Kenneth Rogoff is one of the most versatile and productive scholars in international finance. As a talented chess player, he devoted much of his time when he was young to this game. So much so, in fact, that he missed two years of high school and temporarily dropped out at MIT too. He became international grandmaster in 1978 (only the thirteenth American to achieve this at the time). Since he took positions at the IMF and the Federal Reserve before returning to the academic community (Wisconsin, Berkeley, Princeton, and eventually Harvard), it is perhaps not surprising that his main contributions are both theoretical and empirical. Of this we should certainly mention his work with Meese on out-of-sample exchange rate forecasting (see Chapter 26) and his work with Obstfeld on the new open economy macroeconomics (see Chapter 31).

Table 19.1 **Some international currency symbols**

Country	Currency	Symbol	ISO code
Australia	dollar	A$	AUD
Canada	dollar	C$	CAD
China	yuan	–	CNY
EMU countries	euro	€	EUR
India	rupee	Rs	INR
Iran	rial	RI	IRR
Japan	yen	¥	JPY
Kuwait	dinar	KD	KWD
Mexico	peso	Ps	MXP
Saudi Arabia	riyal	SR	SAR
Singapore	dollar	S$	SGD
South Africa	rand	R	ZAR
Switzerland	franc	SF	CHF
UK	pound	£	GBP
USA	dollar	$	USD

Table 19.2 **Some spot exchange rates on 13 September 2004, at 1.39 a.m. ET**

Price of	Bid spot rate	Ask spot rate	In terms of currency	Country	Spread %
1 USD	1.2905	1.2908	CAD	Canada	0.0232
1 USD	1.2575	1.2581	CHF	Switzerland	0.0477
1 USD	6.52	6.57	ZAR	South Africa	0.7669

Source: http://finance.yahoo.com

specific currencies, such as $ to denote (US) dollars, € to denote European euros, £ to denote (British) pounds, and ¥ to denote (Japanese) yen. Table 19.1 lists some of these international currency symbols. The table also lists the three-letter international standard (ISO) code to identify the currencies.

As discussed below, there are various types of exchange rates, but we first focus attention on the *spot* exchange rate, the price of buying or selling a particular currency at this moment. Table 19.2 lists some spot exchange rates as recorded on 13 September 2004, at 1.39 a.m. ET. The fact that we have to be so precise by listing not only the day on which the spot exchange rates were recorded, but also the exact time and the time zone, signals an important general property of exchange rates: they are variable. In fact, exchange rates are *extremely variable*: only a few minutes later all quoted prices for the spot exchange rates deviated from the values reported in Table 19.2. This makes exchange rates rather special prices, as the variability in the quoted prices is much higher than for goods and services traded on the marketplace, although generally of the same order of magnitude as many other prices in financial markets. In the chapters to follow, we will on the one hand have to explain the high variability of exchange rates relative to most other prices, and on the other hand use this information for macroeconomic modelling.

Table 19.2 lists the exchange rate of the US dollar in three countries, namely Canada, Switzerland, and South Africa. There are actually two rates quoted: (i) the *bid* rate, that is the price at which banks are willing to buy one US dollar (what they are bidding for one dollar), and (ii) the *ask* rate, that is the price at which the banks are willing to sell one US dollar (what they are asking to sell you one dollar). These quotes are for large amounts only (1 million dollars or more). The difference between the buying and selling rate is called the *spread*. It generates revenue for the currency trading activities of the banks. In practice, the spread is quoted relative to the bid price. So, based on Table 19.2, a Swiss bank might quote USD 1.2575–81, indicating the bank is willing to buy dollars at 1.2575 and willing to sell dollars at 1.2581. Obviously, banks from other countries can also buy and sell US dollars for Swiss francs; that is, trading in these currencies is not only limited to Swiss and American banks. Note that the spread between the bid price and the ask price, the margin for the banks, is very small. For the US dollar–Swiss franc in our example it is only 0.0477 per cent ($=100\% \times (1.2581 - 1.2575)/1.2575$). As shown in Table 19.2, the spread is even smaller for trade in the US–Canadian dollar (0.0232 per cent), but larger for trade in the US dollar–South African rand (0.7669 per cent). In general, the spread is quite small and decreases with the intensity with which the two currencies involved are traded, suggesting that the American dollar and Canadian dollar are more frequently traded than the American dollar and the Swiss franc, which are in turn more frequently traded than the American dollar and the South African rand.[1] Since the spread is so small, most of the remainder of this book will assume that the bid price is equal to the ask price (such that the spread is zero) and speak of *the* exchange rate of the US dollar in terms of Canadian dollars, Swiss francs, or South African rands.

Figure 19.2 illustrates the variability of exchange rates for a longer time period (1971–2004) for the exchange rate of the US dollar in Canada, South Africa, and Switzerland using monthly data. There are clearly big differences in the price of the US dollar over time, as well as big differences in variability between countries. In Canada, for example, the US dollar exchange rate varied from a low of 0.9596 on 1 May 1974 to a 67 per cent higher value of 1.5995 on 1 April 2002 (see the dashed vertical lines in Figure 19.2). In South Africa, on the other hand, the US dollar exchange rate varied from a low of 0.6678 on 1 August 1974 to a 1,697 per cent higher value of 12 on 1 January 2002. Over the period as a whole, the US dollar has *appreciated*, that is has become more expensive, relative to the Canadian dollar and the South African rand. There are, however, sub-periods within this time frame in which the US dollar *depreciated*, that is became less expensive, relative to the Canadian dollar and South African rand, most notably in South Africa after 1 January 2002. Similarly, for the period as a whole the US dollar has depreciated relative to the Swiss franc, although there are (long) sub-periods in which the US dollar appreciated relative to the Swiss franc, notably in the period 1979–85.

We have seen that exchange rates vary considerably over time, even within one day. The same is *not* true for the exchange rate at different locations for a given point in time. Since currencies are homogeneous goods (a yen is a yen, no matter where it comes from) and the spreads are very small, if the Japanese yen exchange rate were high in one location, say

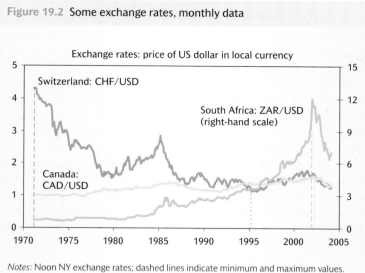

Figure 19.2 **Some exchange rates, monthly data**

Notes: Noon NY exchange rates; dashed lines indicate minimum and maximum values.
Data Source: IFS.

Table 19.3 **Cross exchange rates: spot, 1 February 2004**

Price of 1	(country)	In terms of			
		CAD	CHF	USD	ZAR
CAD	(Canada)	1.0000	0.9434	0.7471	5.2671
CHF	(Switzerland)	1.0599	1.0000	0.7919	5.5828
USD	(USA)	1.3385	1.2628	1.0000	7.0500
ZAR	(South Africa)	0.1899	0.1791	0.1418	1.0000

Note: Based on price of US dollar (shaded).

Data Source: see Figure 19.2; for ISO code see Table 19.1.

New York, and low in another location, say London, at the same point in time, traders could make a profit by (electronically) rapidly buying yen in London (where they are cheap) and selling them in New York (where they are dear). As a result of this *arbitrage* activity, the price of yen would rise in London and fall in New York. Profit opportunities exist until the price is equal in the two locations. In view of the small spreads, the ability to move large funds swiftly around the globe electronically, and the huge trading volume (see Section 19.6), equality occurs almost instantaneously. This not only holds for direct arbitrage for a particular exchange rate, but also for so-called *triangular arbitrage* for different pairs of exchange rates. This is illustrated in Table 19.3. Suppose we know the price of one US dollar at noon on 1 February 2004 in terms of Canadian dollars (1.3385), Swiss francs (1.2628), and South African rand (7.0500). In view of arbitrage opportunities, this suffices to calculate all cross exchange

Figure 19.3 Some implied cross exchange rates: Canadian dollar, monthly data

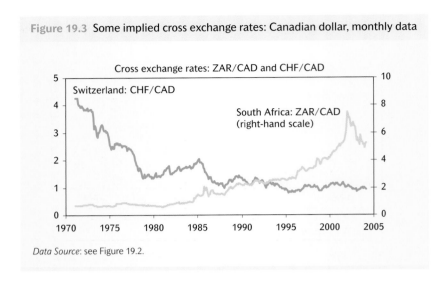

Data Source: see Figure 19.2.

rates as given in Table 19.3. We know, for example, that one Swiss franc must cost 5.5828 South African rand, because 7.0500 rand is worth one US dollar, which in turn is worth 1.2628 Swiss francs, so that 7.0500 rand is worth 1.2628 Swiss francs, or one Swiss franc is worth 7.0500/1.2628 = 5.5828 rand. Similarly for the other entries in Table 19.3. Figure 19.3 illustrates the evolution of the implied cross exchange rate of the Canadian dollar in terms of the Swiss franc and South African rand based on the data used for Figure 19.2.

19.3 Players and markets

The main players on the foreign exchange market are commercial banks, firms, non-bank financial institutions, and central banks. Individuals, such as tourists, may of course also participate on the foreign exchange market, but these transactions constitute only a very small fraction of the total market. We therefore concentrate on the other players:

- *Commercial banks* All major international transactions involve the debiting and crediting of accounts at commercial banks; that is, most transactions relate to the exchange of bank deposits (in different locations and denominated in various currencies). This puts commercial banks at the centre of the foreign exchange market. Banks perform the role of intermediary for their clients (mostly firms) by bringing together their demands and supplies, either directly or indirectly through trade with other banks (interbank trading). The latter accounts for most of the market activity; see Figure 19.4.

- *Firms* The international exchange of goods and services by firms, either related to inputs, final goods, or intermediate (capital) goods and services, almost always involves foreign exchange trading to pay for these activities. Firms contact their banks to take care of these payments.

- *Non-bank financial institutions* As a result of financial deregulation, foreign exchange transactions are also offered to the public by non-bank financial institutions. Large pension funds and other institutional investors are active participants on the foreign exchange market.

Figure 19.4 Foreign exchange market turnover by counterparty (% of total turnover)

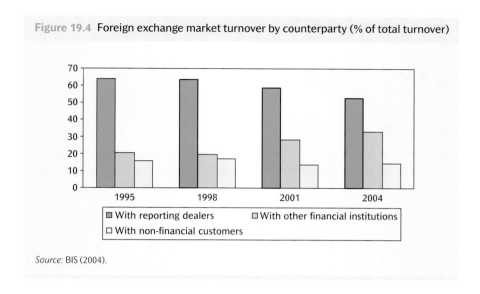

Source: BIS (2004).

- *Central banks* Depending on various macroeconomic circumstances, such as the unemployment rate, the growth rate of the economy, the inflation rate, and explicit or implicit government policies, the central bank of a country may decide to buy or sell foreign exchange. Although the size of these central bank *interventions* is usually relatively modest, their impact can be substantial as the other players in the market may view them as indicative of other future macroeconomic policy changes.

The Bank for International Settlements (BIS; see Chapter 22) conducts a triennial survey of the foreign exchange market by gathering detailed information every three years for the month of April. Based on this information, Figure 19.4 illustrates that most trading activity on the foreign exchange market takes place between the reporting traders (brokers). Its share in the total is, however, gradually declining (from 64 per cent of the total in 1995 to 53 per cent in 2004). Trade with other financial institutions has increased (from 20 per cent in 1995 to 33 per cent in 2004). The rest of the trading activity is relative to non-financial customers. Its share in the total is relatively stable.

Although currencies can be bought and sold openly on the foreign exchange market in many countries, many other (mostly developing) countries impose a range of restrictions on currency trading. Sometimes you need a government licence to trade, sometimes the amount you can trade is limited, sometimes there is a time limit within which received foreign currency must be sold to the central bank, and sometimes it is simply forbidden for individuals and firms to use foreign currency. As a result of these legal restrictions on foreign exchange transactions, it is almost inevitable for illegal *black markets* for currency trading to develop and meet the demand of individuals and firms. Obviously, the exchange rate on the black market will deviate from the official exchange rate on the market permitted and controlled by the government, which creates a powerful (illegal) arbitrage incentive for those allowed to trade on the official market. Quite frequently, the black market rate, which fluctuates daily, is a better indicator of the 'appropriate' (market-clearing) exchange rate than the official rate, which tends to be fixed for longer time periods. This was the case, for example, in Guatemala, with an artificial official exchange rate of one quetzal per dollar for more than three decades. In the case of Guatemala, however, the government allowed the black market to operate quite openly (next to the post office) as an alternative to the official exchange market. Such a market is called a *parallel market*.

19.4 Forward-looking markets

The large variability of exchange rates illustrated in Figure 19.2 potentially poses problems for agents active on the foreign exchange market. Suppose, for example, that you represent a Japanese firm and have sold a thousand watches for delivery and payment in France in three months time at a total price of €150,000. At the current exchange rate of ¥133.49 per euro, the payment of €150,000 is worth ¥20,023,500. Since the total cost of producing and delivering the watches for your company is about 19 million Japanese yen, you stand to make a profit of about 1 million yen on this transaction, so your boss will be pleased. However, payment (in euro) takes place only three months later. To your surprise and dismay, the euro turns out to have considerably depreciated relative to the Japanese yen in this period, such that three months later the spot exchange rate for the euro is only ¥120.34. The payment of €150,000 is now worth only ¥18,051,000, which means that your company made a loss of about one million yen, rather than a profit of one million yen. Your boss is not pleased.

Could you have avoided the 1 million yen loss? Yes, you could have, but it required you to take action three months earlier on a forward-looking market using a forward-looking instrument. In this case, for example, you could have sold the €150,000 on the forward-exchange market three months earlier at a then-agreed-upon forward price of, say ¥131.24 per euro. This would have *guaranteed* you a revenue of ¥19,686,000 upon payment and ensured a profit of about ¥700,000. That is, you could have *hedged* your foreign exchange risk exposure on the forward exchange market. Since many other economic agents face exposure to similar or opposite foreign exchange risks (which they would like to hedge) and other economic agents would like to take a gamble (*speculate*) on the direction and size of changes in the exchange rate, a whole range of forward-looking markets has developed, with associated rather exotic terminology. We can distinguish, for example, between three so-called *plain vanilla* instruments, namely *forwards*, *swaps*, and *options*. According to the BIS (2002, p. 34), the term plain vanilla refers to instruments 'which are traded in generally liquid markets according to more or less standard contracts and market conventions'. Combinations of the basic instruments can then be used to construct tailor-made financial instruments, such as currency *swaptions* (options to enter into a currency swap contract), etc.

The spot exchange rate is the price at which you can buy or sell a currency today. The forward exchange rate is the price at which you agree upon today to buy or sell an amount of a currency at a specific date in the future.[2] A swap involves the *simultaneous* buying and selling of an amount of currency at some point in the future and a *reverse* transaction at another point in the future. A currency swap applies this to a stream of profits. Finally, an option gives you the right to buy or sell a currency at a given price during a given period. Formal definitions of these instruments are given in Technical Note 19.1.

Figure 19.5 illustrates the movement of the spot and forward exchange rates of the US dollar relative to the Australian dollar in the period 1986–2004. Obviously, the forward rate

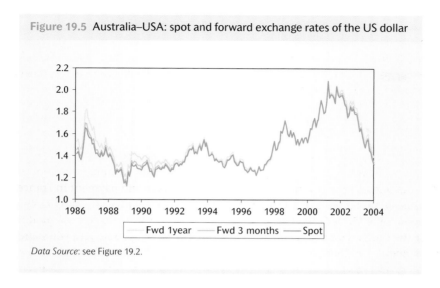

Figure 19.5 Australia–USA: spot and forward exchange rates of the US dollar

| Fwd 1year — Fwd 3 months — Spot |

Data Source: see Figure 19.2.

and the spot rate move, in general, quite closely together. However, there are times (such as 1997–2001) in which spot and forward rates are very close together and other times (such as 1986–93) at which they are pretty far apart (particularly for the longer one-year forward rate). Most of the time, the forward rate of the US dollar was higher than the spot rate; that is, the US dollar was selling at a *premium*. If the opposite holds, that is if the forward rate is below the spot rate, the currency is said to be selling at a *discount*. We will later emphasize that the existence of a forward premium is driven by an expected appreciation of the currency, while a forward discount is driven by an expected depreciation of the currency. To get a better (and comparable) view of the degree to which the US dollar was selling at a premium or a discount in this period, we can calculate the annualized forward premium for different maturities. Let S denote the spot exchange rate, F the forward rate, and let the duration be measured in months. Then this is given by:

$$(19.1) \qquad Forward\ premium\big|_{annual,\%} = \frac{(F - S)/S}{duration/12}$$

Figure 19.6 illustrates the forward premium for different maturities. It shows that the variability of the one-month-forward premium is much higher than the forward premium for three months or one year. It also shows that the changes from one period to the next can be quite large, that the predicted percentage change of appreciation or depreciation (as measured by the forward premium) can be substantial (up to 10 per cent per year, with a peak of 18 per cent for the one-month rate), and that the forward premium is in general in the same direction for different times to maturity. The latter indicates that it is in general not expected for a currency to depreciate in the short-run and appreciate in the long-run, or vice versa.

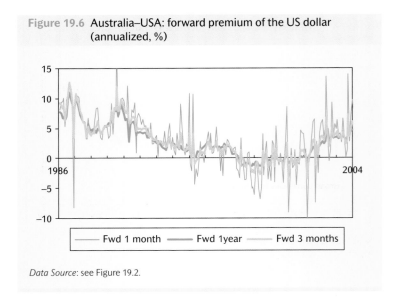

Figure 19.6 Australia–USA: forward premium of the US dollar (annualized, %)

Data Source: see Figure 19.2.

19.5 Effective exchange rates

As illustrated in Figure 19.2 for the US dollar relative to the Canadian dollar, the South African rand, and the Swiss franc, most of the time a currency is appreciating relative to some currencies and simultaneously depreciating relative to some other currencies.[3] The question then arises whether the currency has actually become more valuable or less valuable over time. The precise and correct, but cumbersome, answer is, of course, that it depends on the currency used for comparison. It is, however, frequently useful to distil the divergent movements in (bilateral) exchange rates into a key (index) number summarizing the overall movement of a country's exchange rate. Such an index is called an *effective* exchange rate. As with the design of any index number, its construction (involving decisions on which currencies to include and how to weigh them) depends on the specific purpose for which it is used. The US Federal Reserve, for example, calculates six effective exchange rates for various policy purposes on a regular basis. There is: (i) a 'broad' index, focusing on the value of the dollar relative to all foreign countries with a share in US trade of at least 0.5 per cent, (ii) a 'major' index, focusing on the value of the dollar relative to the major international currencies from the euro area, Canada, Japan, the UK, Switzerland, Sweden, and Australia, and (iii) an 'OITP' index, focusing on the value of the dollar relative to other important trading partners (OITP). For all three indices, a *nominal* and a *real* effective exchange rate are calculated. The real exchange rate involves (changes in) the price levels in different countries. Since this is extensively discussed in the next chapter, this section focuses on the nominal effective exchange rate.

Figure 19.7 illustrates the value of the US dollar relative to the major international currencies (using daily data) and relative to the broad index of major US trading partners (using monthly data). Clearly, the nominal broad index moves quite differently from the major currency index. The latter moves up and down over time without a clear trend, whereas the former moves up most of the time. This difference is caused by the inclusion of some high-inflation countries in the broad index (see also Chapter 20). As Leahy (1998: 812) puts it: 'The inclusion of such countries restricts the usefulness of the nominal versions of these

Figure 19.7 USA: nominal effective exchange rate

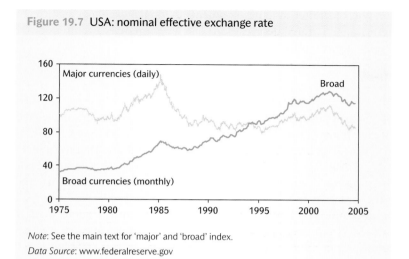

Note: See the main text for 'major' and 'broad' index.
Data Source: www.federalreserve.gov

Figure 19.8 USA: third-market competitiveness weights, 2004

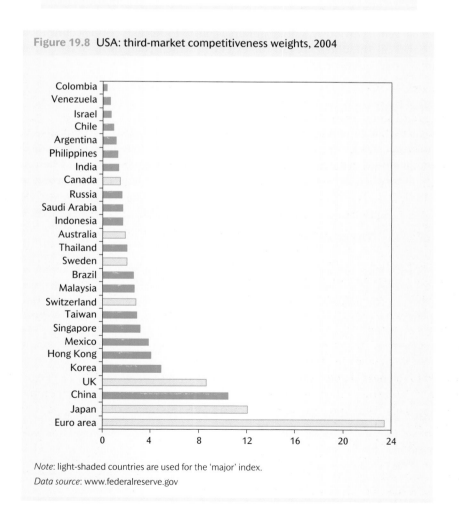

Note: light-shaded countries are used for the 'major' index.
Data source: www.federalreserve.gov

indexes to analysis of shorter-term developments in foreign exchange markets because, over the longer term, large nominal depreciations of a few currencies swamp information on the value of the dollar against other currencies.'

The exchange rate indices illustrated in Figure 19.7 are calculated as follows:[4]

$$(19.2) \qquad I_t = I_{t-1} \Pi_j (S_{j,t} / S_{j,t-1}) \, w_{j,t},$$

where I_t is the value of the index at time t (usually put equal to 100 for some benchmark year), $S_{j,t}$ is the spot rate (price) of the US dollar in terms of currency j at time t, and $w_{j,t}$ is the weight of currency j at time t. An increase of the index therefore indicates that the dollar is becoming more expensive 'on average'; that is, it appreciates 'on average'. Various methods are used to construct the (time-varying) weights $w_{j,t}$. A simple method would just use the share of a currency in the country's exports, imports, or total trade. The Federal Reserve uses a more complicated procedure based on the share of a foreign country's goods in all markets that are important to US producers to derive third-market competitiveness weights; see Leahy (1998) for details. Figure 19.8 illustrates these weights for the year 2004 (see also Chapter 20). By far the greatest weight (23.4 per cent) is given to the euro area countries (see Chapter 30), followed by Japan (12.1 per cent), China (10.4 per cent), the UK (8.6 per cent), and South Korea (4.9 per cent). Obviously, similar nominal effective indices for other countries use other weights, based on the differences in the extent to which changes in other currencies are important for that specific country.

19.6 Trading volume

The foreign exchange market is the largest financial market in the world. In April 2004, average turnover was $1,900 billion *per day*. Just pause for a moment to appreciate the enormous sums of money being transferred daily on the foreign exchange market when compared to $9,273 billion, the total value of world exports of goods and services in the whole *year* 2003

 Box 19.1 **The power of foreign exchange markets**

In the popular press you will sometimes see comparisons of the daily turnover on the foreign exchange market or of multinationals with the GDP levels of some countries, usually with the intention to suggest that individual countries are small and powerless compared to global financial market forces. To a fair degree that is, of course, nonsense, not only because sovereign states have enormous (legislative) powers beyond those of any individual firm, but also because GDP is a *value-added* measure that should not be compared with turnover in financial markets. The total production value of the financial services sector in the Netherlands in 2003, for example, was equal to only 6.7 per cent of Dutch GDP (CBS, 2004: 46). This number includes the entire banking sector, the insurance companies, and other financial services. The value added created on the foreign exchange market is therefore only a fraction of that 6.7 per cent. Obviously, the capital flows on the foreign exchange markets are large and, as we will see in the sequel, can be powerful at times, but we should keep the fraction of the financial services sector in the economy in general (and the fraction of the foreign exchange market in particular) in proper perspective.

Figure 19.9 Global foreign exchange market turnover (daily average in April (billion US$))

Data Source: BIS (2004), triennial central bank survey.

(World Bank Development Indicators, 2005). This large volume is one of the main reasons for the low spreads, as illustrated in Table 19.2.

Figure 19.9 illustrates the changes in the composition of the foreign exchange turnover for the six triennial BIS surveys. Foreign exchange swaps are the most traded instruments, over-taking the spot transactions market volume sometime between 1992 and 1995. Outright for-wards constitute a relatively small market by comparison. The figure also illustrates that the traded volume on the foreign exchange market fell for the first time since the surveys started in 2001, most notably in the spot market. This reduction, followed by a rapid increase of 57 per cent in the period 2001–2004, can be attributed largely to the introduction of the euro, which eliminated intra-EMS trading (see Chapter 30).

The US dollar is the most traded currency on the foreign exchange market, followed by the euro, the Japanese yen, the pound sterling, and the Swiss franc. Figure 19.10 illustrates the changes in the shares of these five most traded currencies, taking the share of the Deutsche Mark as indicative of the importance of the euro before its introduction. The dollar–euro pair was by far the most traded currency pair in 2004, capturing 28 per cent of global turnover, followed by dollar–yen (17 per cent) and dollar–sterling (14 per cent); see BIS (2004, p. 1). For historical reasons that provided a first-mover advantage, the UK (London) is by far the largest foreign exchange market, capturing 31.3 per cent of total turnover, followed by the USA (New York: 19.1 per cent) and Japan (Tokyo: 8.3 per cent). This is illustrated in Figure 19.11 for the twenty largest foreign exchange markets in the world.

Finally, we should point out that the over-the-counter (OTC) derivatives market involves transactions between two financial institutions outside of the regular market, for example if the Dutch ABN AMRO bank calls the American Citibank to make a deal. This market consists of interest rate derivatives contracts and non-traditional foreign exchange derivatives (such as cross-country currency swaps and options). It has been growing very rapidly for quite some time now, to reach an average daily turnover of $1,200 billion in April 2004.[5]

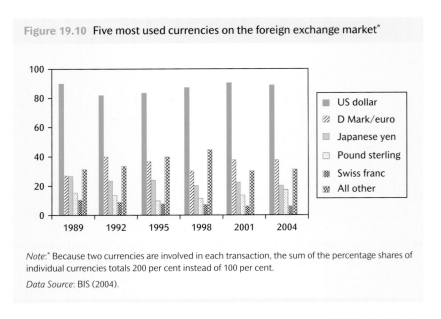

Figure 19.10 Five most used currencies on the foreign exchange market*

Note: * Because two currencies are involved in each transaction, the sum of the percentage shares of individual currencies totals 200 per cent instead of 100 per cent.

Data Source: BIS (2004).

Figure 19.11 Twenty largest foreign exchange markets, April 2004 (% of total)

Data Source: BIS (2004).

19.7 Conclusions

With a daily turnover of $1,900 billion in 2004, the foreign exchange markets are the world's largest financial markets. The largest foreign exchange markets are located in London, New York, and Tokyo, respectively. The most important players are commercial banks (through intermediaries called *brokers*), firms, non-bank financial institutions, and central banks. The most traded currencies are the US dollar, the euro, the Japanese yen, and the British pound sterling.

There are different types of exchange rates and instruments, such as spot rates, forward rates, swaps, and options. The difference between the banks's buying (bid) and selling (ask) exchange rate is called the spread. In view of the large traded volume, the spread is usually quite small. We will mostly put the spread equal to zero in the forthcoming chapters, speaking of *the* (bilateral) exchange rate between two currencies, which is the price of one currency in terms of another currency. Exchange rates are characterized by a high variability, changing from one day to the next, and even from minute to minute. On the one hand this variability will have to be explained. On the other hand it will be used for macroeconomic modelling.

As a consequence of the high variability of exchange rates, a given currency (such as the euro) usually appreciates relative to some currencies and simultaneously depreciates relative to some other currencies. To summarize these divergent bilateral movements, it is useful for policy purposes to calculate an index, called an effective exchange rate, of that currency relative to a weighted basket of a range of other currencies. As a result of international arbitrage, the same currency sells for (virtually) the same price at different locations at the same point in time. This also holds for cross exchange rates as a result of triangular arbitrage, involving the exchange of three currencies. If the forward rate of a currency, which is the forward price of the currency, is higher than the spot rate, the currency is sold at a premium. Otherwise, it is sold at a discount. After this chapter introducing the various foreign exchange markets, we are ready to investigate some of the underlying economic forces governing these markets (namely purchasing power parity and interest rate parity) in the next two chapters.

TECHNICAL NOTE

Technical Note 19.1 Formal definitions

The Bank for International Settlements gives the following definitions for the main instruments in its triennial survey (BIS, 2002: 35):

- *Spot transaction*: single outright transaction involving the exchange of two currencies at a rate agreed on the date of the contract for value or delivery (cash settlement) within two business days.

- *Outright forward*: transaction involving the exchange of two currencies at a rate agreed on the date of the contract for value or delivery (cash settlement) at some time in the future (more than two business days later).

- *Foreign exchange swap*: transaction which involves the actual exchange of two currencies (principal amount only) on a specific date at a rate agreed at the time of conclusion of the contract (the short leg), and a reverse exchange of the same two currencies at a date further in the future at a rate (generally different from the rate applied to the short leg) agreed at the time of the contract (the long leg).

- *Currency swap* (including cross-currency swap): contract which commits two counterparties to exchange streams of interest payments in different currencies for an agreed period of time and to exchange principal amounts in different currencies at a pre-agreed exchange rate at maturity.

- *Currency option/warrant*: option contract that gives the right to buy or sell a currency with another currency at a specified exchange rate during a specified period.

QUESTIONS

Question 19.1

Suppose you want to buy a car. You either want to buy a Chevrolet for US$23,000, a Volkswagen for €15,900, a Honda for ¥2.2 million or a Hyundai for 22 million Korean won. The following exchange rates are given.

	Foreign currency per dollar	Foreign currency per euro
American dollar	1.0	1.3
European euro	0.8	1.0
Japanese yen	106.0	135.9
Korean won	1120.9	1437.1

19.1A Which car is cheapest when all prices are expressed in American dollars?

19.1B Do relative prices change when expressed in euros? Explain why this is the case.

19.1C Which currency has to appreciate for the cheapest car to become more expensive?

19.1D Which currencies have to depreciate for the cheapest car to become more expensive?

Question 19.2

Imagine you have € 100,000 and want to invest it in the foreign exchange market. After an extensive analysis you conclude what the exchange rates will be one year ahead. The table below gives both the spot exchange rate of the amount of foreign currency per euro and the expected exchange rate in one year.

	Spot rate	Expected future rate
Australian dollar	1.71	1.77
British pound	0.69	0.72
Japanese yen	135.2	130.0
US dollar	1.27	1.24

19.2A Explain in which currency you want to invest.

19.2B How much euro do you expect to have in one year?

Question 19.3

Since June 2002 the value of the euro has increased rapidly against the dollar. The figure below shows that the nominal effective exchange rate of the dollar has decreased during the same period.

19.3A Is an appreciation of the euro favorable for the competitiveness of American exporters?

19.3B What does the decrease of the nominal exchange rate of the dollar indicate about the competitiveness of the American industry?

19.3C Do your observations of 19.3A and 19.3B contradict each other? How can you explain these observations?

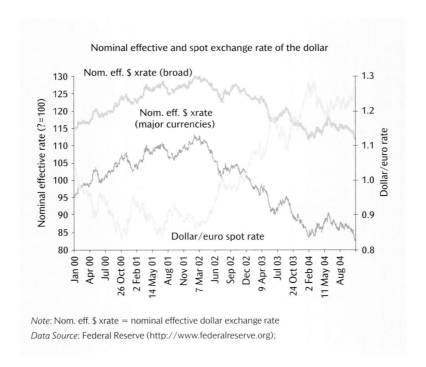

Nominal effective and spot exchange rate of the dollar

Note: Nom. eff. $ xrate = nominal effective dollar exchange rate

Data Source: Federal Reserve (http://www.federalreserve.org);

See the Online Resource Centre for a Study Guide containing more questions
www.oxfordtextbooks.co.uk/orc/vanmarrewijk/

NOTES

1 In the most recent BIS triennial survey using data of April 2001 this was, in fact, the case. Trading volume in million US dollars per day of local currency relative to the US dollar was 25,177 for Canada, 18,644 for Switzerland, and 7,775 for South Africa; see BIS (2002, Table E.7, p. 64) and Section 19.6. Other factors, such as the expected variability of the exchange rate, also affect the spread.

2 The *futures* market is slightly different from the forward market in that only a few currencies are traded, with standardized contracts at certain locations (such as the Chicago Mercantile Exchange, the largest futures market) and specific maturity dates.

3 Obviously, at any moment in time there is always at least one currency non-appreciating relative to all other currencies and at least one currency non-depreciating relative to all other currencies.

4 The symbol Π_j denotes the product over the index j; so, for example, $\Pi_{j=1}^{4} a_j = a_1 \cdot a_2 \cdot a_3 \cdot a_4$. It is therefore similar to the summation symbol Σ_j, but used for products.

5 Activity in the foreign exchange and OTC markets cannot be directly compared as a result of differences in characteristics and uses of products.

PURCHASING POWER PARITY

- Law of One Price
- Purchasing power parity (PPP)
- Real effective exchange rate
- Differentiated goods
- Non-traded goods
- PPP corrections

- Absolute and relative version
- Real (bilateral) exchange rate
- Transaction costs
- Fixed investment and thresholds
- Harrod–Balassa–Samuelson effect
- Endogenous and exogenous

We discuss absolute and relative versions of the Law of One Price (for individual goods) and purchasing power parity (PPP, for price indices). There can be substantial short-run deviations from PPP, but in the long run relative PPP holds remarkably well because fundamentals and arbitrage are dominant long-run economic forces.

20.1 Introduction

According to the Law of One Price identical goods should (under certain conditions) sell for the same price in two different countries at the same time. It is the foundation for purchasing power parity (PPP) theory, which relates exhange rates and price levels. The absolute PPP exchange rate equates the national price levels in two countries if expressed in a common currency at that rate, so that the purchasing power of one unit of a currency would be the same in the two countries. Relative PPP focuses on changes in the price levels and the exchange rate, rather than the level. Although the term purchasing power parity was apparently first used by Cassel (1918), the ideas underlying PPP have a history dating back at least to scholars at the University of Salamanca in the fifteenth and sixteenth centuries; see Officer (1982). As we will see, long-run relative PPP holds remarkably well, even though there can be substantial short-run deviations from relative PPP. Many structural models that seek to explain exchange rates and exchange rate behaviour are based on this presumption, leading Rogoff (1992) to conclude that most international economists 'instinctively believe in some variant of purchasing power parity as an anchor for long-run real exchange rates'.

20.2 The Law of One Price and purchasing power parity

Suppose that the exact same product, say a computer chip, is freely traded in two different countries, say America (sub-index A) and Britain (sub-index B). Suppose, furthermore, that there are no transportation costs, no tariffs, no fixed investments necessary for arbitrage, and no other impediments to trade flows between these two countries of any type whatsoever. Should not, under those conditions, the (appropriately measured) price of the computer chip in Britain be the same as in America? According to the Law of One Price, it should. Obviously, we have made a range of assumptions before we came to the conclusion that arbitrage should ensure that the Law of One Price holds. Any violation of these conditions can, in principle, cause a violation of this law. We discuss these issues in the second part of this chapter.

Famous economists	Karl Gustav Cassel

Fig. 20.1
Karl Gustav Cassel
(1866–1945)

The Swedish economist Gustav Cassel was a founding member of the Swedish School of economics, together with Knut Wicksell and David Davidson. He earned a degree in mathematics at the University of Uppsala and studied economics in Germany before returning to the University of Stockholm, where he worked from 1903 to 1936. Two of his most prominent students were later Nobel laureates, Gunnar Myrdal and Bertil Ohlin (see Chapter 7). Some of his most important work is on the theory of interest rates (*The Nature and Necessity of Interest*, 1903), which he conceived of as a regular price, namely the price of the input 'waiting'. He also popularized the notion of purchasing power parity, as discussed in this chapter. Supposedly, his dying words were: 'A world currency!'

There are, actually, different versions of the Law of One Price. There is a strong *absolute* version and a weaker *relative* version. Both can be applied to individual products and to price indices. Let's start with the strongest version of all. Suppose we have a large number N of individual products consumed and produced in America and Britain (computer chips, flour, cars, movies, etc.). We let the sub-index i denote the type of product (so i ranges from 1 to N) and the sub-index t denote time (which could, for example, be quarters, months, or days). Then the absolute version of the Law of One Price for each individual good i implies:

$$(20.1) \qquad P_{Bi,t} = S_t\, P_{Ai,t}\,, \quad i = 1, \ldots, N.$$

where $P_{Ai,t}$ is the price of good i in America at time t (in dollars), $P_{Bi,t}$ is the price of the same good in Britain at the same time (in pounds sterling), and S_t is the nominal exchange rate of the US dollar (the price in pounds sterling for purchasing one dollar).

Equation (20.1) imposes a restriction on the price levels of the same good in different countries. Instead, the relative version of the Law of One Price imposes a restriction on the changes in these price levels, more specifically:

$$(20.1') \qquad \frac{S_{t+1} P_{Ai,t+1}}{P_{Bi,t+1}} = \frac{S_t P_{Ai,t}}{P_{Bi,t}}, \quad i = 1, \ldots, N.$$

In essence, the relative version argues that the deviation, if any, between the prices of some good in the two countries in one time period also holds in the next period. The relative version of the Law of One Price is weaker than the absolute version, simply because equation (20.1) implies equation (20.1'), but not vice versa. That is, if there is a constant deviation from the Law of One Price, the relative version holds while the absolute version does not.

To get from the Law of One Price to purchasing power parity (henceforth PPP), we have to go from the microeconomic to the macroeconomic level and look at price indices. Virtually all countries publish several types of price indices, such as the consumer price index, the producer price index, the GDP deflator, etc. All of these are constructed in different ways, emphasize different aspects of the economy and can be used for PPP comparisons; see also Box 20.2. The exposition below focuses on the consumer price index (CPI). The CPI is usually constructed as a weighted average of the prices of individual (groups of) products, with the weights representing the share of income spent by households on a particular product in some reference year. Let α_i be the weight of product i and let $P_{A,t}$ denote America's price index in period t, given by

$$(20.2) \qquad P_{A,t} = \sum_{i=1}^{N} \alpha_i P_{Ai,t}, \quad \text{with} \quad \alpha_i \geq 0, \quad \sum_{i=1}^{N} \alpha_i = 1$$

Now suppose that Britain's price index $P_{B,t}$ is constructed identically (this need not be the case, which is a potential cause for PPP deviations, see Sections 20.4 and 20.5). If the absolute version of the Law of One Price (equation 20.1) holds for individual products, this means there is a clear relationship between the exchange rate and the price indices in Britain and America:

$$(20.3) \qquad P_{B,t} = \sum_{i=1}^{N} \alpha_i P_{Bi,t} = \sum_{i=1}^{N} \alpha_i (S_t P_{Ai,t}) = S_t \sum_{i=1}^{N} \alpha_i P_{Ai,t} = S_t P_{A,\,t}\,,$$

where the second term from the left is simply the definition of Britain's price index, the third term follows from the absolute Law of One Price for individual products, the fourth term takes

Figure 20.2 Different versions of the Law of One Price and PPP*

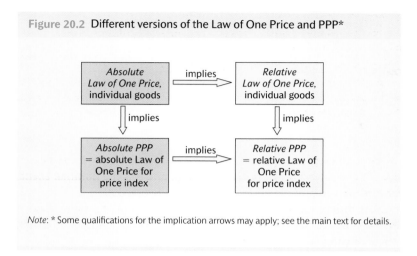

Note: * Some qualifications for the implication arrows may apply; see the main text for details.

the (common) exchange rate out of the summation sign, and the fifth term follows from the definition of America's price index. The first and last terms of equation (20.3) can be more conveniently written in logarithmic form. As this is the case more generally in the monetary parts of this book, we henceforth agree to the following:

Convention: a lower-case letter x of a variable X in general denotes its natural logarithm, that is $x = \ln(X)$. *So, for example,* $s_t = \ln(S_t)$, $p_{A,t} = \ln(P_{A,t})$, *etc.*

Using this convention, a slight re-arrangement of equation (20.3) gives us the absolute version of PPP in logarithmic terms; see equation (20.4). Writing the latter in time differences gives us the relative version of PPP; see equation (20.4′).

(20.4)
$$s_t = p_{B,t} - p_{A,t}$$

(20.4′)
$$(s_{t+1} - s_t) = (p_{B,t+1} - p_{B,t}) - (p_{A,t+1} - p_{A,t})$$

The relative version of PPP (eq. 20.4′) can be derived either from the absolute version of PPP (eq. 20.4) or from the relative version of the Law of One Price (eq. 20.1′).[1] Both of these can, in turn, be derived from the absolute version of the Law of One Price. Figure 20.2 schematically summarizes the strongness of these 'laws' and their relationships. The absolute version of the Law of One Price for individual goods is the strongest condition and, under some qualifications, implies all other versions without being implied by any of them. Similarly, the relative version of PPP is the weakest of all assumptions: it is implied by all other versions and does not imply any of them.

20.3 Prices and exchange rates

Is there an empirical relationship between exchange rates and price indices, as suggested by the PPP conditions in Section 20.2? There certainly is! A very simple, but quite convincing, demonstration of this relationship is based on the (weakest) relative PPP version (eq. 20.4′), as illustrated in Figure 20.3. As we will argue below, the PPP relationship is actually a long-run

Figure 20.3 Exchange rates and prices, 1960–2001

Note: Calculations based on World Bank Development Indicators CD-ROM 2003; 55 observations; the line has a 45-degree slope; see the main text for details.

relationship, with substantial deviations from PPP 'equilibrium' in the short run. To find supporting evidence of relative PPP, we therefore have to look at a long enough time period to ensure that the deviations between developments in price indices in two different countries are big enough, and the associated economic arbitrage forces strong enough, to allow for these differences to have an impact on the exchange rate. Using World Bank data, we can analyse a time period of 41 years. At this stage, we are not interested in the details of the developments over time, just in the extremes, that is the first year of observation (1960) and the last year of observation (2001). We will use the USA as benchmark country. Under those circumstances, the (logarithmic) relative PPP equation (20.4') translates into:

(20.5) $\qquad s_{2001} - s_{1960} = (p_{cj,2001} - p_{cj,1960}) - (p_{US,2001} - p_{US,1960}); \quad cj = 1, \ldots, 55,$

where s is the US dollar exchange rate in foreign currency and p_{cj} is the consumer price index for the 55 countries for which both exchange rates and price indices were available. Figure 20.3 depicts the left-hand side of equation (20.5) on the horizontal axis and the right-hand side on the vertical axis for 55 data points. They are nearly all on a straight line through the origin with a 45-degree slope (also depicted in the figure), as would be predicted by equation (20.5), providing visual support for the relative PPP hypothesis. The largest deviations from the 45-degree line are some (mostly Latin American) countries at the upper-right hand of the diagram which have had very high inflation rates relative to the USA and concomitant high increases in the US dollar exchange rate.

(20.5') $\qquad s_{2001} - s_{1960} = \underset{(0.0875)}{0.235} + \underset{(0.0174)}{0.993} \times [(p_{cj,2001} - p_{cj,1960}) - (p_{US,2001} - p_{US,1960})]$

Equation (20.5') reports the econometric estimate of equation (20.5) based on the empirical observations depicted in Figure 20.3. See Box 20.1 for an explanation of this procedure. The

Box 20.1   Basic econometrics

When we are developing different theories to try to better understand various economic phenomena, we often assume that the relationships between the economic variables we are analysing are exact. In principle, our theories should lead to results, that is, propositions or predictions that should hold empirically if the theory is true. If we gather economic data to test if the theoretical implications do indeed hold in reality, we need a method to determine if a theory is refuted or not. This is the work of econometricians. In practice, things are, as usual, not quite that simple for four main reasons.

1. We must recast the theory in a manner suitable for empirical evaluation and testing. This means we have to acknowledge the fact that the relationships between the economic variables of our theories are not exact due to simplifications and disturbances. There may, therefore, be deviations from the exact relationships that we can attribute to other phenomena, such as measurement errors or the weather, which do not immediately refute the theory. The point is, of course, that these deviations should not be 'too large'.

2. It can be very complicated, even after overcoming the first problem, to actually test the implications of a theory for technical or econometric reasons. Numerous examples can be given of the many hurdles econometricians sometimes have to take and traps to avoid, before they can devise an adequate test of what may at first look like a simple implication of a theory. Section 20.6 discusses some of these problems when testing for purchasing power parity.

3. It can be virtually impossible, even after overcoming the first and second problems, to pinpoint the nature of an observed friction between theory and empirics. Remember that our theories are usually based on a range of assumptions. In many cases, economic theorists may be convinced by the arguments of econometricians that an implication of a theory does not hold in practice, but disagree strongly on the particular assumption on which the theory was based which caused this friction. It can take several decades of scientific research, involving the development of new theories and new tests, etc., before some, if any, consensus on the nature of the problem is reached.

4. Even if an empirical test confirms our theory, this does not necessarily prove it. Maybe some other theory can also explain the observations; we are never really sure.

The remainder of this box focuses on the simplest version of the first problem. Suppose we have an economic theory that predicts a linear relationship between the economic variables y and x: $y = a + bx$. Since all theories are simplifications of reality (which is what makes it theory), there is always a range of phenomena that might influence the actual relationship between the variables y and x. There can be other, more complicated, economic forces not modelled in the theory that could affect the relationship; there can be forces outside of economics (such as the weather, volcanic eruptions, or political changes) that could affect it; there can be errors in measurement, etc. This leads us to posit that the observed relationship is as follows:

(20.6)
$$y_t = a + bx_t + u_t,$$

where the sub-index t denotes different observations (for example different time periods or different countries) and the variable u_t denotes the deviation between the structural linear part of an observation and the actual value of the observation. This deviation should not be 'too large', so   »

⟫ when we average it over many observations its value should be zero (it is, for example, normally distributed with mean 0 and variance σ^2).

An econometrician is, of course, not given the 'true' parameters a and b of the structural linear equation (although there may be 'implied' theoretical values, as discussed in this chapter). Instead, she is given a number of observations, that is joint pairs (x_t, y_t) of the economic variables x and y. These are depicted as the dots (or balls) in Figure 20.4. Her task is then to find the best line to fit these empirical observations, that is estimate an intercept, say $\bar{a}$, and a slope, say $\bar{b}$, to minimize the (quadratic) distance from the observations to the line. We are not concerned with how this is done here. Instead, we briefly discuss how hypotheses can be tested using this procedure.

Figure 20.4 was artificially constructed based on a 'true' model with intercept 2 and slope 1 ($a = 2$, $b = 1$) by adding (normally distributed) disturbances u_t using a random number generator. Since the econometrician is only given the observations and not the true parameters, she tries to estimate these ($\bar{a}$ and $\bar{b}$) based on the observations. The terminology is to 'run a *regression*', where y is the *endogenous* variable (the variable to be explained) and x is the *exogenous* variable (the explanatory variable). She finds:

(20.7)
$$y = \underset{(0.4730)}{2.776} + \underset{(0.0744)}{0.872 \cdot x}$$

The numbers in parentheses in equation (20.7) are estimated standard errors of the estimated coefficients, see below. Instead of the true parameter 2, the econometrician therefore estimates the intercept to be 2.776, and instead of the true parameter 1, she estimates the slope to be 0.872. Well, we do not expect her to find the exact parameters, but how far off is she, is this within acceptable limits, and how good is the 'fit' of the estimated line? To start with the last point, it is clear that the fit is better the closer the observations are to the estimated line. A popular measure for this fit is the

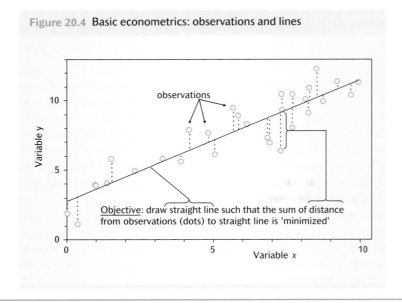

Figure 20.4 Basic econometrics: observations and lines

⟫

> share of the variance of the variable y explained by the estimated line, the so-called R^2. In this case, 83.1 per cent of the variance is explained by the regression ($R^2 = 0.831$). In general, the higher R^2, the better the fit. It should be noted, however, that the share of the variance that can be explained differs widely per application, with some areas of economics where researchers are happy if they can explain 20 per cent of the variance and others where less than 90 per cent is considered bad. In this respect, the standard errors reported in equation (20.8) are more useful as they indicate the reliability of the estimated coefficients. They can be used for hypothesis testing. Based on the so-called t-distribution, we can calculate the probability that the true parameter has a particular value, given the observations on the pairs (x_t, y_t) available to us and the associated regression line. As a rough rule of thumb: hypotheses within two standard deviations away from the estimated coefficient are accepted (in this case: slope in between 0.7232 and 1.0208 and intercept in between 1.830 and 3.722). Alternatively, the rule of thumb implies that an absolute t-value larger than 2 denotes a 'significant' parameter as the estimated coefficient differs from the hypothesis 'equal to zero' by more than two standard deviations.

estimated standard errors are denoted in parentheses immediately below the estimated coefficients. The overall goodness-of-fit is quite high, as 98.4 per cent of the variance is explained by the regression ($R^2 = 0.984$). Some simple hypotheses tests would show that the estimated slope coefficient does not differ significantly from one (as would be implied by relative PPP theory) and that the estimated intercept is (just) significant (in contrast to this theory).[2] A more thorough discussion of these issues is deferred to Section 20.6.

20.4 Real effective exchange rates

Section 20.2 derived the nominal exchange rate between two countries consistent with absolute or relative PPP; see equations (20.4) and (20.4'). On that basis, we can now define (in logarithmic terms) the *real* (bilateral) exchange rate, say q_t, as the difference between the nominal effective exchange rate and the price indices of the two countries:

(20.8) $$q_t \equiv s_t - (p_{B,t} - p_{A,t}).$$

This real exchange rate then provides a measure of the deviation from PPP between the two countries. We can, of course, also calculate the relative counterpart of the bilateral real exchange rate by taking the first difference of equation (20.8). In both cases, developments in the nominal exchange rate are corrected for developments in the price levels of the two countries, implying that the real exchange rate is a measure of the evolution of one country's competitiveness relative to another country. More specifically, if the real exchange rate in equation (20.8) increases, this implies that the higher price of the US dollar (s_t) is only partially offset by differences in price developments between Britain and America ($p_{B,t} - p_{A,t}$), so that America has become less competitive compared to Britain.

In practice, countries are more interested in the general development of their competitive position, not just relative to one country in particular. The *real effective exchange rate* does just that, by calculating a weighted average of the bilateral real exchange rates (see also

Section 20.5). It plays an important role in policy analysis as an indicator of the competitiveness of domestic relative to foreign goods and the demand for domestic and foreign currency assets. As the real effective exchange rate is an index, the focus is on changes of the index relative to some base year; that is, the policy focus is on relative and not absolute PPP.

The Federal Reserve has changed its weighting procedure from the earlier used share of total trade to a third-market competitiveness index, based on the share of a foreign country's goods in all markets that are important to US producers (see Box 20.2 for the European Central Bank's method in this respect). Figure 20.5 illustrates the difference between these two procedures for the six largest trading partners of the USA. Note that for the competitiveness index: (i) the developments tend to be more stable over time (see e.g. Japan), (ii) the importance of neighbouring states (Canada and Mexico) is reduced, as is (to a smaller extent) the importance of Japan, and (iii) the importance of Europe is increased. The developments

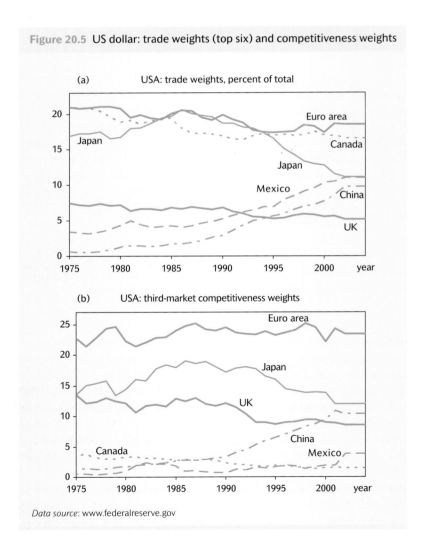

Figure 20.5 US dollar: trade weights (top six) and competitiveness weights

Data source: www.federalreserve.gov

Figure 20.6 US dollar: real effective exchange rates

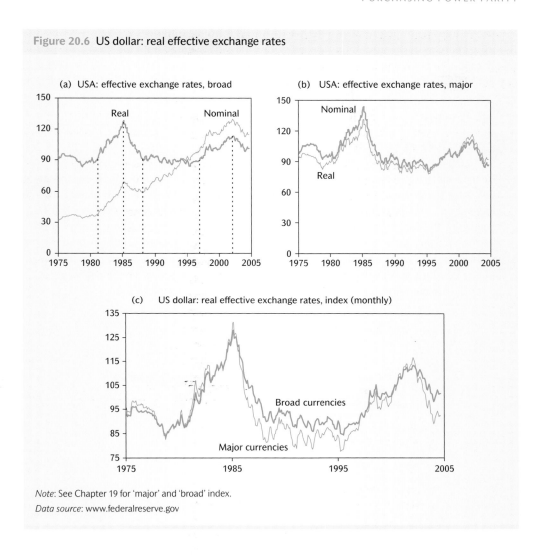

Note: See Chapter 19 for 'major' and 'broad' index.
Data source: www.federalreserve.gov

for China are similar using either trade weights or competitiveness weights, rising from less than 2 per cent in 1980 to about 10 per cent in 2004.

Figure 20.6 shows the evolution of the real and nominal effective exchange rates for the USA in the period 1975–September 2004. As panel (a) makes clear, there is a big difference in the development of the real versus the nominal effective exchange rates for the broad range of currencies. There is, in particular, no consistent increase in the real value of the US dollar. The developments for the nominal and real exchange rates using the major foreign currencies as a benchmark are much more similar; see panel (b). As already explained in Section 19.5, this difference is caused by the inclusion of high-inflation countries in the broad index, compared to the absence of such countries in the major index. As panel (c) illustrates, there is little deviation in the developments of the real index for the major and broad index.

Can we infer from Figure 20.6 whether or not PPP holds empirically? Well, yes and no. Ignoring changes in the underlying weights, if relative PPP were to hold for every time period and for all countries, the real effective exchange rate would have to be a horizontal line. If absolute PPP holds, the level of this line would be determined. Taking the broad index in

Box 20.2   Effective exchange rates of the euro

Like the Federal Reserve, the European Central Bank (ECB) regularly publishes effective exchange rates, namely both real and nominal effective index rates of the euro (1999-Q1 = 100) relative to two groups of countries (EER 23 = a benchmark group of 23 countries; EER-42 = a broader group of 42 countries).[3] The September 2004 issue of the ECB's *Monthly Bulletin* introduced this new set of effective exchange rates, following an update of the associated trade weights and an extension of the list of the euro area's trading partners. The weights are based on exports and imports (excluding intra-euro area trade), where the exports are double-weighted to capture the competition faced by euro area exporters in foreign markets (third-market effects); see Figure 20.7.

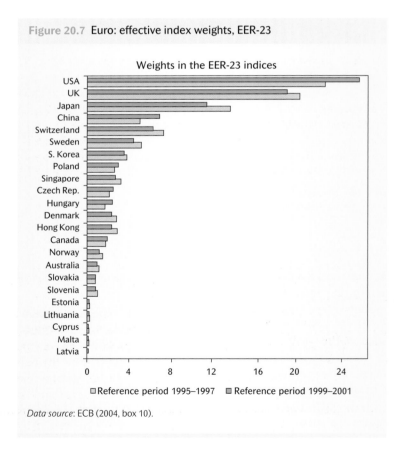

Figure 20.7 Euro: effective index weights, EER-23

Data source: ECB (2004, box 10).

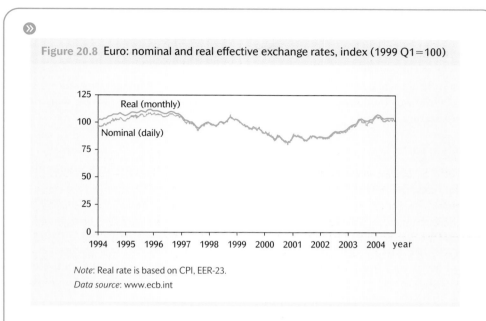

Figure 20.8 Euro: nominal and real effective exchange rates, index (1999 Q1=100)

Note: Real rate is based on CPI, EER-23.

Data source: www.ecb.int

Figure 20.8 depicts the evolution of the real and nominal effective exchange rates of the euro since 1994. Obviously, euro data were not available before the formation of the euro, so in that period the data are based on a basket of euro legacy currencies.[4] Perhaps in view of the more limited time period, the value of the euro has not fluctuated as substantially (nor as abruptly) as the value of the US dollar. In addition, and similar to the major index of the USA, the deviation between the nominal and real index rate is relatively small. Again similar to the USA, the deviation between the nominal and real index is more substantial for the broader group of EER-42 countries. This is not shown in the diagram; see however ECB (2004, box 10).

panel (a) as our point of reference, the US real effective exchange rate clearly is not a horizontal line. Relative PPP therefore does not hold for all time periods. There is not, however, a consistent upward or downward movement. Instead, compared to a baseline of roughly 90 points, there are two large upward deviations (as indicated in panel (a)) namely in the period 1981–88 (with a peak in March 1985) and in the period 1997–2004 (with a peak in February 2002). Both these periods and their relationships with economic policy will be discussed in forthcoming chapters. For now, it suffices to note that on the basis of the US experience, short-run relative PPP does not hold. Indeed, there can be large and prolonged deviations from short-run PPP. However, we do not see a consistent upward or downward movement. Instead, relative PPP tends to return to some base level. This suggests that in the long run relative PPP does hold. A formal analysis to substantiate this claim is beyond the scope of this book, but Section 20.6 provides a discussion of empirical literature that supports this claim.

20.5 Causes of deviations from PPP

Section 20.4 has shown that there can be substantial and prolonged periods of deviation from relative PPP exchange rates. To understand some of the potential causes for these deviations, it is most fruitful to take a closer look at the more important of the many assumptions we had to make before we could invoke the Law of One Price for individual goods on which PPP is based; see Section 20.2.

Transaction costs

An obvious reason for a failure of the Law of One Price is the existence of transaction costs, including shipping costs, insurance costs, tariffs and non-tariff barriers, etc. Any such transaction costs will impose a band width around the Law of One Price rates within which arbitrage is not profitable. Only substantial deviations of the exchange rate enable agents to benefit from arbitrage opportunities. Acknowledging that the band width will vary from one good to another, this suggest that the arbitrage forces will gradually become stronger as the deviation of the exchange rate from PPP increases. One measure for the extent of these types of transaction costs is the deviation between cost, insurance, and freight (CIF) and free on board (FOB) quotations of trade, see Box 14.1 for a further discussion.

Differentiated goods

In deriving the Law of One Price, we assumed we were dealing with homogeneous goods. In practice, very few goods are perfectly homogeneous. Wines differ not only from one country to another, but even per region and vineyard; a Toyota differs from a Mercedes; there are many different varieties of tulips, etc. In fact, the more knowledgeable you are about specific commodities, the better you usually realize that these are differentiated products, even for such basic items as types of flour, qualities of oil, or grades of iron ore. Since we lump all these different goods together under one heading when constructing our price indices, it is no surprise that absolute PPP does not hold, nor that there can be prolonged deviations of relative PPP. None the less, the various types of differentiated goods are to some extent substitutes for one another. Again, this implies that the arbitrage forces will gradually become stronger as the deviation of the exchange rate from PPP increases.

Fixed investments and thresholds

Before they can take advantage of arbitrage opportunities, economic agents usually have to incur a fixed investment cost, such as establishing reliable contacts, organizing shipping and handling, setting up a distribution and service network, etc. Based on earlier work of the theory of investment under uncertainty, Dixit (1989) and Dumas (1992) therefore argue that in addition to the transaction costs imposing a band width, the sunk cost of investment associated with engaging in arbitrage ensures that traders wait until sufficiently large opportunities open up before entering the market. As Sarno and Taylor (2002, p. 56) put it: 'Intuitively, arbitrage will be heavy once it is profitable enough to outweigh the initial fixed cost, but will stop short of returning the real rate to the PPP level because of the . . . arbitrage (CvM: i.e. transaction) costs.' Since the investment costs will vary for different types of goods, this yet again implies that the arbitrage forces will gradually become stronger as the deviation of the exchange rate from PPP increases.

Non-traded goods

When invoking the Law of One Price to derive PPP, we implicitly assumed that all goods entering the construction of the price index were tradable. In fact, a large share of our income, perhaps as much as 60–70 per cent, is spent on non-tradable goods, that is on products or (more frequently) services that effectively cannot be traded between countries and for which arbitrage, which drives PPP, is not possible. Important examples are housing services, recreational activities, health care services, etc. Although one could argue that the existence of non-tradable goods is just an extreme (namely infinite) case of transaction costs, there is a long tradition in international economics to devote special attention to the distinction between tradable and non-tradable goods, and for good reasons. These issues, and the degree to which non-tradable goods introduce a bias in PPP deviations, are therefore discussed separately in Section 20.7 below.

Composition issues

Related to the above point is the observation that in deriving the PPP exchange rate in Section 20.2, we assumed that the price indices in the two countries are constructed in an identical way. In practice, this is not the case. Not only do the weights for different categories differ per country, but so also do the types of goods associated with each category. Obviously, these

 Box 20.3   **Exchange rates, and prices under hyperinflation**

The case of Bolivian hyperinflation in 1984 and 1985 already discussed in Box 18.3 also provides a good test for the validity of PPP under extreme circumstances. The monthly Bolivian inflation rate peaked at 183 per cent (from January to February in 1985). At the same time, the exchange rate of

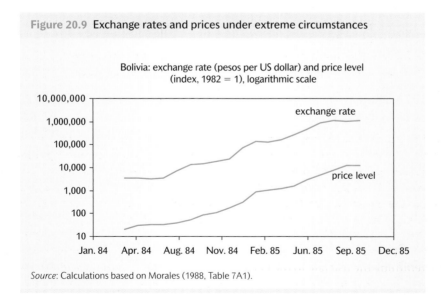

Figure 20.9 Exchange rates and prices under extreme circumstances

Source: Calculations based on Morales (1988, Table 7A1).

⟫ foreign currencies measured in Bolivian pesos (the price of foreign currencies) increased very rapidly. The monthly increase in the price of the US dollar, for example, peaked at 198 per cent (from December 1984 to January 1985). Obviously, with such high inflation rates, which dwarf the importance of the foreign inflation rates (in this case in the USA), we expect (on the basis of PPP) that changes in the exchange rate are dominated by changes in the Bolivian price level; see equation (20.4). In fact, this is what happened: from April 1984 to July 1985, Bolivian prices increased 230-fold, while in that same period the US dollar exchange rate increased 247-fold. Figure 20.9 uses a logarithmic graph of the exchange rate and the price level in this period to illustrate this. The slope of the price level curve therefore represents the inflation rate and the slope of the exchange rate curve the growth rate of the price increase of the US dollar. The similarities in the two curves, and therefore the suggested validity of long-run PPP, are obvious. See Box 18.3 for further details. Moreover, see Figure 20.3 for Bolivia's performance on exchange rates and prices in the period 1960–2001.

construction differences can cause deviations from PPP, even when the absolute Law of One Price holds for every individual good. When dealing with many countries, as is the case when we calculate real effective exchange rates, these problems are exacerbated.

20.6 Testing for PPP

There have been many empirical tests of PPP in the last four decades and an enormous evolution of the proper underlying procedures for these tests. This section gives a brief overview of the empirical findings; see Sarno and Taylor (2002, ch. 3) for an excellent and more detailed review. Early empirical tests of PPP (until the late 1970s) were essentially directly based on equation (20.4). More specifically, one would estimate the equation (see Box 20.1 for some econometrics and testing basics):

$$(20.9) \qquad\qquad s_t = \gamma_1 + \gamma_2\, p_{at} + \gamma_3\, p_{bt} + u_t$$

A test of the hypothesis $\gamma_2 = 1, \gamma_3 = -1$ would be interpreted as a test of absolute PPP. Using this test for first differences in equation (20.9), that is replace s_t by $s_{t+1} - s_t$, etc., would be interpreted as a test of relative PPP. In general, this early literature, which did not use dynamics to distinguish between short-run and long-run effects, rejected the PPP hypothesis. A clear exception is the influential study by Frenkel (1978), who analyses high-inflation countries and gets parameter estimates very close to the PPP values, suggesting that PPP holds in the long run.

As it turns out, there are many econometric problems associated with the early testing procedure. An economic issue is the so-called endogeneity problem, referring to the fact that in equation (20.9) it is not simply prices that determine exchange rates, but both prices and exchange rates are determined simultaneously in a larger economic system.[5] The most important problem is, however, purely technical (that is: econometric) in nature. See Granger and Newbold (1974) and Engle and Granger (1987) for so-called cointegration and stationarity problems.[6]

The early studies of the next generation of tests addressing the econometric problems of PPP testing were rather mixed in their support for PPP; see for example Taylor (1988) and Taylor and McMahon (1988). Once it was realized that these early cointegration studies, which tended to focus on rather short time periods, had very low power of the tests, that is, low precision with which definite conclusions could be drawn, it was clear that one final econometric problem had to be overcome. Two methods were devised to address this power problem, namely analysing really long time series data and analysing panel data. Both methods generally support long-run (relative) PPP. As the name suggests, the really long time series method extends the period of observation, which introduces an exchange rate regime-switching problem (from gold standard to Bretton Woods to floating exchange rates; see Chapter 22–note that the exchange rate may behave differently under different regimes, which is an issue that must be addressed by an econometrician). Frankel (1986) analyses dollar–sterling data from 1869 to 1984. See also Edison (1987), Glen (1992), and Cheung and Lai (1994). Panel data studies avoid the regime-switching problem by focusing on a short time period of analysis (usually the more recent floating exchange rates), but combine evidence from many different countries simultaneously in one test. The most powerful test used in Taylor and Sarno (1998), for example, provides evidence supporting long-run PPP during the recent float period.

20.7 Structural deviations: PPP corrections

The above discussion focused on the empirical validity of *relative* long-run PPP. A related problem is the phenomenon of PPP *corrections*. The correction problem focuses on the fact that there is a consistent bias in real income measures for different countries when the nominal exchange rate is used as a basis for comparison. As such, it argues that there is a consistent bias in *absolute* PPP deviations. As mentioned in Section 20.5, the argument is based on the distinction between traded and non-traded goods. It goes back to Harrod (1933), Balassa (1964), and Samuelson (1964), and is therefore known as the *Harrod–Balassa–Samuelson effect*. The effect plays a role in policy discussions for new entrants to the European Union; see Chapter 30 (in particular Technical Note 30.1).

The ranking of production value using current US dollars, that is converted at the going exchange rate, is deceptive because it tends to overestimate production in the high-income countries relative to the low-income countries. To understand this we have to distinguish between *tradable* and *non-tradable* goods and services. As the name suggests, tradable goods and services can be transported or provided in another country, perhaps with some difficulty and at some costs. In principle, therefore, the providers of tradable goods in different countries compete with one another fairly directly, implying that the prices of such goods are related and can be compared effectively on the basis of observed (average) exchange rates. In contrast, non-tradable goods and services have to be provided locally and do not compete with international providers. Think, for example, of housing services, getting a haircut, or going to the cinema.

Since (i) different sectors in the same country compete for the same labourers, such that (ii) the wage rate in an economy reflects the average productivity of a nation (see also Chapter 3), and (iii) productivity differences between nations in the non-tradable sectors tend to be smaller than in the tradable sectors, converting the value of output in the non-tradable sectors on the basis of observed exchange rates tends to underestimate the value of production in these sectors for the low-income countries. See Box 20.4 for details. For example, on the basis of observed exchange rates, getting a haircut in the USA may cost you $10 rather than the $1 you pay in Tanzania, while going to the cinema in Sweden may cost you $8 rather than the $2 you pay in Jakarta, Indonesia. In these examples the value of production in the high-income countries relative to the low-income countries is overestimated by a factor of 10 and 4, respectively.

To correct for these differences, the United Nations International Comparison Project (ICP) collects data on the prices of goods and services for virtually all countries in the world and calculates 'purchasing power parity' (PPP) exchange rates, which better reflect the value of goods and services that can be purchased in a country for a given amount of dollars. Reporting PPP GNP levels therefore gives a better estimate of the actual value of production in a country.

Figure 20.10 illustrates the impact on the estimated value of production after correction for purchasing power by comparing it to the equivalent value in current dollars. The USA is still the largest economy, but now 'only' produces 21.4 per cent of world output, rather than 30.3 per cent. The estimated value of production for the low-income countries is much higher than before. The relative production of China (ranked second) is more than three times as high as before (rising from 3.9 per cent to 12.5 per cent), and similarly for India (rising from 1.6 per cent to 6.0 per cent), Russia (rising from 1.2 per cent to 2.5 per cent), and Indonesia (rising from 0.5 per cent to 1.3 per cent).[7] The drop in the estimated value of output is particularly large for Japan (falling from 12.0 per cent to 7.1 per cent), reflecting the high costs of living in Japan. Of course, when estimating the importance of an economy for world trade or capital flows, it is more appropriate to use the actual exchange rates on which these transactions are based, rather than PPP exchange rates.

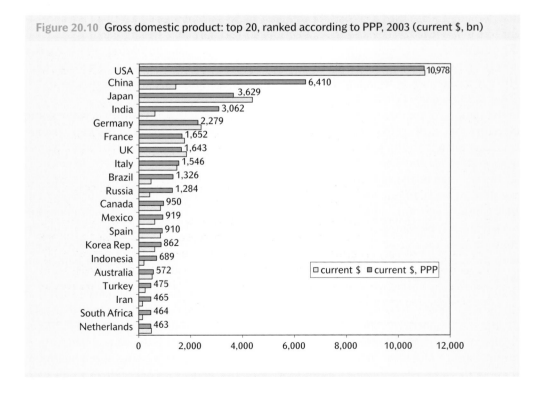

Figure 20.10 Gross domestic product: top 20, ranked according to PPP, 2003 (current $, bn)

Box 20.4   **Purchasing power parity (PPP) corrections**

Suppose there are two countries (Australia and Botswana) each producing two types of goods (traded goods and non-traded goods) using only labour as an input in the production process. This box is based on the Ricardian model; see Chapter 3. All labourers are equally productive within a country (homogeneous labour and constant returns to scale), but there are differences in productivity between countries. As illustrated in Table 20.1, we assume Australian workers to be five times more productive in the traded goods sector and only twice as productive in the non-traded goods sector.

Table 20.1 Labour productivity in Australia and Botswana

	Number of products produced per working day	
	Traded goods	Non-traded goods
Australia	20	20
Botswana	4	10

- Between-country arbitrage.   Assuming there are no transport costs or other trade restrictions, arbitrage in the traded goods sector will ensure that the wage rate in Australia will be five times as high as the wage rate in Botswana because Australian workers are five times more productive. Taking this as the basis for international income comparisons leads us to think that per capita income is 400 per cent higher in Australia than it is in Botswana.

- Within-country arbitrage.   Assuming labour mobility between sectors within a country, arbitrage for labour between the traded and non-traded goods sector will ensure that the price of traded goods in local currency is the same as the price of non-traded goods in Australia (because labour is equally productive in the two sectors), whereas the price of traded goods in local currency is 2.5 times as high as the price of non-traded goods in Botswana (because labour is 2.5 times less productive in the traded goods sector than in the non-traded goods sector). In local currency, therefore, non-traded goods are much cheaper compared to traded goods in Botswana than in Australia.

- Real income comparison.   Suppose that 40 per cent of income is spent on non-traded goods in both countries. Some calculations (based on a Cobb–Douglas utility function) then show that the real per capita income is 247 per cent higher in Australia than in Botswana. Although substantial, this is significantly lower than our earlier estimate of 400 per cent because non-traded goods are relatively much cheaper in Botswana than in Australia. The 153 per cent (= 400 per cent – 247 per cent) overestimated difference between income in current $ and real income is larger, (i) the larger the share of income spent on non-traded goods, and (ii) the larger the international deviation between productivity in traded compared to non-traded goods.

20.8 Conclusions

If there are no impediments whatsoever to international arbitrage, an identical good should sell for the same price in two different countries at the same time. This absolute version of the Law of One Price for individual goods can be used to derive a relative version of the Law of One Price (focusing on changes rather than levels) and a (relative and absolute) version relating exchange rates and price indices, referred to as purchasing power parity (PPP). The derivation is based on assumptions which, if they do not hold exactly, can cause deviations from PPP. The most important causes of such deviations are transaction costs, composition issues (the way in which indices are constructed), and the existence of differentiated goods, fixed investments, thresholds, and non-traded goods. Empirical studies do, indeed, find substantial and prolonged short-run deviations from relative PPP as measured by real effective exchange rates. In the long run, however, relative PPP holds remarkably well, certainly in view of the strict assumptions necessary for deriving PPP. The majority of the remaining chapters will focus on structural models invoking long-run (relative) PPP. There is, therefore, a bias in our analysis to try to understand the long-run equilibrium implications of economic policies and developments. It should be noted, finally, that there is a structural bias in deviations from absolute PPP based on observed differences between countries of traded relative to non-traded goods. This so-called Harrod–Balassa–Samuelson effect makes PPP corrections necessary when comparing, for example, the real income levels of different countries. Such corrections are now widely available.

QUESTIONS

Question 20.1

20.1A If relative PPP holds, does this also imply that the absolute Law of One Price holds? And what about the relative Law of One Price? Explain.

20.1B Suppose that a laptop costs 1,000 dollars in the USA and 800 euros in the Eurozone. If absolute PPP holds, and Europe and the USA trade only laptops, what is the dollar–euro exchange rate?

20.1C Due to changes in demand, the price of a laptop in the USA increases to 1,200 dollars. If absolute PPP holds, what happens to the exchange rate?

20.1D Suppose that Europe and the USA trade a broad basket of goods. The prices of these goods are measured by the consumer price index and the rate of inflation in the USA is persistently higher than in Europe. What happens to the exchange rate according to PPP theory?

20.1E Given the discussion in Chapter 19 about the relationship between money growth and prices, what impact do you expect of monetary tightening by the ECB (lowering money growth) on the exchange rate?

Question 20.2

Politicians often claim that the value of the currency of some other country is too low, which gives the firms of that country an unfair competitive advantage. Econometric evidence, such as that in Figure 20.3, indicates that relative PPP does not hold in the short run, while it does hold in the long run.

20.2A What does this imply for countries with a fixed exchange rate that is 'unfairly low'?

20.2B Can a country maintain an 'unfair' competitive advantage in the long run by somehow manipulating its exchange rate?

Question 20.3

20.3A The real *effective* exchange rate can be measured in many different ways. Can you name the choices you would have to make if you would like to present a graph of the real *effective* exchange rate of the British pound?

20.3B Suppose the real exchange rate of the pound *vis-à-vis* the euro is stable at 2. Does absolute PPP hold? Why (not)? Does relative PPP hold? Why (not)?

20.3C Suppose that the real exchange rate of the pound *vis-à-vis* the euro increases to 3. What does this mean for the competitive position of British firms? What does this imply for the validity of relative and absolute PPP?

See the Online Resource Centre for a Study Guide containing more questions
www.oxfordtextbooks.co.uk/orc/vanmarrewijk/

NOTES

1 The latter is based on a similar argument as going from (20.1) to (20.4).

2 As a clear outlier caused by its dollarization, Ecuador was deleted from the data. This did not materially affect the analysis, although inclusion would have made the new estimated intercept (0.195) insignificant.

3 The ECB calculates no fewer than five real rates, using as deflators: consumer price indices (CPI), producer price indices (PPI), gross domestic product (GDP deflator), unit labour costs in manufacturing (ULCM) and unit labour costs in the total economy (ULCT).

4 The euro area is assumed fixed for the whole period, so it includes Greece throughout the period even though Greece only joined on 1 January 2001.

5 Krugman (1978) constructs a simple model to address this endogeneity problem in which the monetary authorities intervene against real shocks with monetary policies, thus influencing both exchange rates and prices. His parameter estimates are indeed closer to the PPP hypothesis.

6 The early literature did not properly investigate the residuals of the estimated equation to verify the stochastic properties on which the estimates, and hence the associated PPP tests, are based.

7 These percentages are not listed in Figure 20.10. More details are provided on the book's website.

INTEREST RATE PARITY

Objectives/key terms

- Nominal and real interest rates
- Inflation and deflation
- Term structure of interest rates
- Perfect substitutes
- Uncovered interest parity
- Rational expectations
- Simple efficiency hypothesis
- Risk aversion
- Fisher equation

- Maturity
- Rising, flat, and falling term structure
- Covered interest parity
- Risk neutrality
- Market efficiency
- Exposure (translation, transaction, economic)
- Risk premium

After discussing nominal and real interest rates and the term structure of interest rates, we derive the covered and uncovered interest parity conditions, relating differences in international interest rates with the forward exchange market premium and the expected rate of appreciation, respectively. As these conditions are crucial for understanding the foreign exchange markets, we evaluate them empirically in conjunction with risk premia.

21.1 Introduction

Chapter 20 established a clear, long-run relationship between exchange rates and price levels known as purchasing power parity. In this chapter we will establish a clear short-run and medium-run relationship between exchange rates and interest rates. Obviously, this provides an indirect long-run link between interest rates and prices and ensures that exchange rates, interest rates, and prices are all interconnected and determined simultaneously within the economic system. Such systems are analysed in Parts III.B and III.C of this book. The driving force behind the links between interest rates and the foreign exchange markets is arbitrage. We have already seen in Chapter 19 that arbitrage is a powerful force on the foreign exchange market for ensuring that the same currency is traded at the same price in different locations at the same time. Here, we will focus on arbitrage relating markets in different time periods. Depending on the type of arbitrage (either hedged or unhedged), we derive two important relationships between interest rates and exchange rates, both of which will be evaluated empirically. First, however, we take a closer look at the structure of interest rates.

21.2 Interest rates

In addition to the more indirect, long-run link between interest rates and prices through the exchange rate discussed in the introduction to this chapter, there is also a direct link between interest rates and the price level. When you invest some money, say €1 million, for some time period in a eurozone country, such as the Netherlands, the *nominal* interest rate, which we will denote by the letter *i*, represents the reward to you in terms of euros. However, as a consumer you are not interested in this nominal value, but in the real goods and services you can purchase with these funds. To calculate the real return on your investment, that is the *real*

Famous economists	Irving Fisher

Fig. 21.1
Irving Fisher
(1867–1947)

Born in upstate New York, Irving Fisher studied science and philosophy at Yale university, where he stayed for the rest of his career (he actually actually earned the first PhD in economics ever awarded by Yale). He was one of the greatest mathematical economists of all time, a topic on which he wrote (quite remarkably in this field of specialization) very clearly. Of his many contributions to economics we should at least mention his work on (i) interest rates (distinguishing between stocks and flows as well as nominal and real interest rates), (ii) index numbers (on which he was 'the greatest expert of all time', according to James Tobin), and (iii) the quantity theory of money (formulating the equation of exchange: $MV = PT$, where M is money, V is velocity, P is the price level, and T is the volume of transactions). He made a fortune when his firm with a patent for a visible card index system merged and later became Remington Rand and then Sperry Rand. He lost most of this during the stock market crash of 1929.

interest rate which we will denote by the letter *r*, you will have to correct your nominal return for increases in the price level. If we let the Greek letter π denote the inflation rate in the economy, we can simply do this by using the (Irving) *Fisher equation*:[1]

(21.1) $r = i - \pi$

As a reminder, we will use the following notation in the sequel:

  i = nominal interest rate
  π = inflation rate
  r = real interest rate

Figure 21.2 illustrates the relationship between nominal and real interest rates and inflation in the Netherlands in the period 1979–2004. It is clear that the nominal interest rate tends to be high when the inflation rate is high, indicating that investors demand a high nominal return for their funds in order to compensate them for the loss in value due to the high inflation rate. This concern about real rather than nominal returns implies that nominal interest rates are in general more volatile than real interest rates. As shown in Figure 21.2, however, the real interest rate also varies considerably over time. Note, in particular, that (i) the real interest rate can be higher than the nominal interest rate, as happened in a period of negative inflation (deflation) in 1987, and (ii) the real interest rate can be negative if inflation is higher than the nominal interest rate, as happened in 2001 and 2003.

There is, of course, not a single interest rate within a country. There are different interest rates for customers with varying reliability (see also Section 21.6) and there are different interest rates for varying time periods, that is with varying terms to maturity. In the bond market we observe, for example, interest rates for 3 months, 6 months, 1 year, etc. Fortunately, as

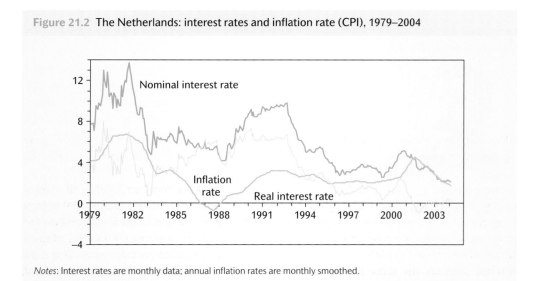

Figure 21.2 The Netherlands: interest rates and inflation rate (CPI), 1979–2004

Notes: Interest rates are monthly data; annual inflation rates are monthly smoothed.

Data sources: IFS (interest rate, 6-month interbank middle rate), World Bank Development Indicators CD-ROM (inflation 1960–2001), and Dutch Central Bureau of Statistics (www.cbs.nl; inflation 2001–2004).

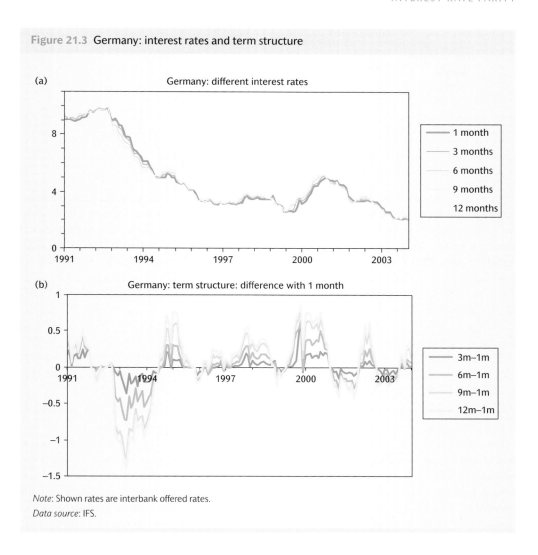

Figure 21.3 Germany: interest rates and term structure

Note: Shown rates are interbank offered rates.
Data source: IFS.

illustrated for Germany in panel (a) of Figure 21.3, the different national interest rates move up and down very closely together. In this respect it is not too far-fetched to refer to *the* national interest rate, as most of what follows will do.

None the less, interest rates do not move rigidly up and down together, as illustrated more clearly in panel (b) of Figure 21.3 by subtracting the 1-month interest rate at any point in time from the 3-, 6-, 9-, and 12-month interest rates to highlight changes in these differences. The structure of interest rates over time to maturity is known as the *term structure* of interest rates. If the interest rates rise with the term to maturity, the term structure is said to be *rising*; if the interest rates are the same for all terms to maturity, the term structure is said to be *flat*, etc. This is illustrated for a particular point in time in Figure 21.4, namely for the US term structure on 10 January 2006. In this case, the interest initially rises with time to maturity

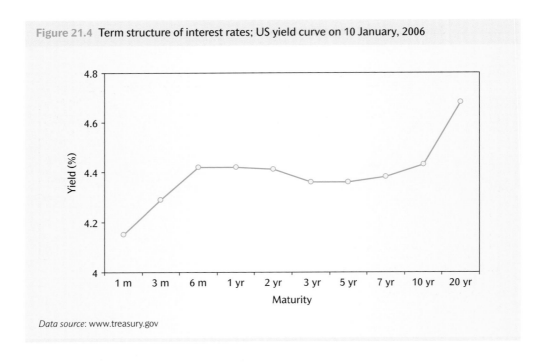

Figure 21.4 Term structure of interest rates; US yield curve on 10 January, 2006

Data source: www.treasury.gov

(1 month to 6 months), then is (virtually) flat (6 months to 2 years), then falls (2 years to 3 years), is flat again (3 years to 5 years), and eventually rises (5 years to 20 years).

According to the liquidity premium theory, risk-averse investors prefer to lend short term and therefore put a premium on long-term bonds, resulting in interest rates rising with the holding period of the bond and thus a *rising* term structure. In panel (b) of Figure 21.3, this would translate into larger positive differences relative to the 1-month interest rate with increasing maturity. This rising term structure was actually observed in Germany in the period 1991–2004 most of the time. The figure also illustrates, however, that a falling term structure also occurred frequently, namely in 1992–94, 1995/96, 1999, 2001, and 2002/3. Other demand and supply factors for individual segments of maturities are therefore strong enough to invert the liquidity premium theory's presumption of a rising term structure. Figure 21.5 shows that similar results hold for Japan in the period 1986–2004, where panel (a) illustrates that the various national interest rates move up and down very closely together and panel (b) that the term structure can be either rising or falling. In addition, the figure illustrates a phenomenon specific to Japan in the second half of 1999 and since May of 2001: there is a lower bound of zero on the nominal interest rate.

21.3 Covered interest parity

The discussion in Section 21.2 focused on investments by Europeans in bonds in euros. There are, of course, many other (international) investment options open. For clarity, we will consider only one other option, namely buying an American bond rather than a European bond.

Figure 21.5 Japan: term structure of interest rates

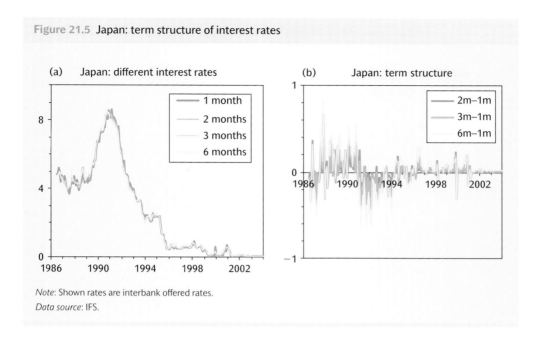

(a)   Japan: different interest rates

Legend:
- 1 month
- 2 months
- 3 months
- 6 months

(b)   Japan: term structure

Legend:
- 2m–1m
- 3m–1m
- 6m–1m

Note: Shown rates are interbank offered rates.
Data source: IFS.

We will assume that the two assets are *perfect substitutes*, implying in particular that there is no difference in perceived riskiness of one asset relative to the other (see Section 21.6). Suppose, for concreteness, that you have a large sum L of euros to invest for one time period and care only about the return in euros. Figure 21.6 shows two possible investment options.

- Option I: you can purchase a European bond. If the European interest rate is equal to i_{EU}, you will receive $(1 + i_{EU})L$ euros by the end of the period.

- Option II: you can purchase an American bond. Since these are denominated in dollars, you will have to be active on the foreign exchange market: first, by exchanging your L euros on the spot market for L/S US dollars, where S is the spot exchange rate of the US dollar (its price in euros), second, by investing these L/S dollars in American bonds. If the American interest rate is equal to i_{US}, you will receive $(1 + i_{US})$ (L/S) dollars by the end of the period. You are not, however, interested in the return in dollars, but only in the return in euros, so you will have to convert these dollars at the end of the period back to euros. This poses a problem because at the moment you are making your investment decision (option I or option II); you do not yet know what the future spot exchange rate of the dollar will be. This is where the forward exchange market provides a solution. Since you know exactly how many dollars you will receive one time period from now if you choose option II (namely $(1 + i_{US})(L/S)$ dollars), you will also know exactly how many euros you will receive if you sell these dollars before making your investment decision at the forward exchange rate F on the forward exchange market, namely $(1 + i_{US})(F/S)L$ euros.

In short, you know exactly the return on your investment if you choose option I and the return on your investment if you choose option II. Obviously, many other economic agents make similar calculations as you do (possibly trying to benefit from arbitrage opportunities) and all of you will invest in the asset with the highest return. If the two assets are perfect

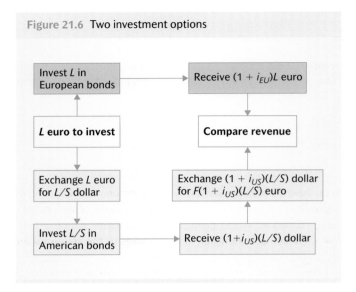

Figure 21.6 Two investment options

substitutes and both are held in equilibrium, the return to the two assets must therefore be the same to ensure that the market does not prefer one asset over the other; that is, we have the following equilibrium condition:

(21.2)
$$\frac{F(1 + i_{US})}{S} L = (1 + i_{EU})L \implies \frac{F}{S} = \frac{1 + i_{EU}}{1 + i_{US}}$$

Obviously, the time frame for equation (21.2) must be consistent, so if F is, for example, the 3-month forward rate, than i_{EU} and i_{US} must be 3-month interest rates. Recalling the convention introduced in Chapter 20 that lower-case letters of symbols in general refer to the natural logarithm of upper-case letters, you may have noted that we have right away used a lower-case letter i to denote the interest rate. This is not a mistake, but a

Convention exception: lower-case letters for interest rates are not natural logarithms.

There is a good reason for this exception, as we will now see. The second equality of condition (21.2) can be written more tersely by taking the natural logarithm and using the approximation ln $(1 + x) \approx x$ (where the symbol $\approx$ should be read as 'is approximately equal to') as discussed in Box 21.1, to get (see Technical Note 21.1 and Box 21.2):

(21.2′)
$$f - s \approx i_{EU} - i_{US}$$

Equation (21.2′) states that the logarithmic difference between the forward rate and the spot rate must be equal to the difference between the domestic and the foreign interest rate. It is known as the *covered interest parity condition*, because you have fully covered your exposure to your return in foreign currency on the forward exchange market. It provides a powerful and crucial relationship between interest rates and (spot and forward) exchange rates in international money and finance analysis. Its counterpart, *un*covered interest parity, will be discussed in Section 21.5.

Box 21.1 Linear approximation

Recall from your analysis class that if $g(x)$ is a smooth function, which means that it can be differentiated as many times as necessary, then the value of the function can be approximated by a Taylor series expansion around any point x_0 as follows:

(21.3) $$g(x) = g(x_0) + g'(x_0)(x - x_0) + (1/2)g''(x_0)(x - x_0)^2 + \cdots$$

A linear approximation ignores all terms after the first derivative:

(21.3') $$g(x) \approx g(x_0) + g'(x_0)(x - x_0)$$

Suppose we want to have a linear approximation of the function $g(x) \equiv \ln(1 + x)$ around the value $x_0 = 0$. According to (21.3') we must then first determine the value of the function g and the value of the derivative g' evaluated at the point $x_0 = 0$. This gives us $g(0) = \ln(1 + 0) = 0$ and $g' = 1/(1 + 0) = 1$. Using that information in (21.3') gives us the approximation $\ln(1 + x) \approx x$ discussed in the text. Figure 21.7 shows that this approximation is very accurate for small values of x. Since the covered interest parity condition (21.2') uses it to approximate the natural logarithm of interest rates, which are usually quite small (say smaller than 10 per cent), the approximation is usually fairly accurate. Only under extreme conditions, such as under periods of hyperinflation, is it better to focus on the original condition (21.2) and not to use the approximation.

Figure 21.7 Accuracy of linear approximation of ln(1+x)

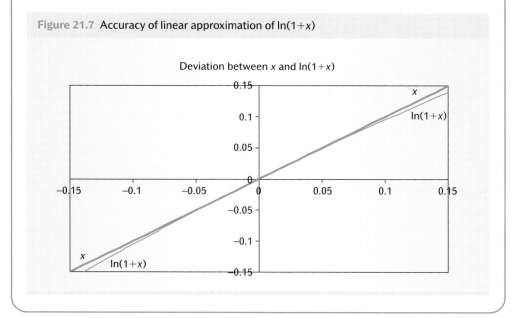

21.4 The empirics of covered interest parity

In deriving the covered interest parity condition we assumed that the assets involved were perfect substitutes. Moreover, the derivation ignored transaction costs. If either assumption is not met in practice, this may cause a deviation from the covered interest parity condition.

None the less, this section will argue that the covered interest parity holds almost perfectly, that is within a very narrow range for very similar types of international assets. To illustrate this, we will continue with our Australia–USA example already discussed in Section 19.4. In the analysis below we will measure time periods in months. To indicate this, f_{12} will denote the 12-month forward rate of the US dollar (measured, of course in Australian dollars), i_{12} will denote the 12-month interest rate, etc.

We already know that exchange rates are very volatile. Panels (a) and (b) of Figure 21.8 confirm this volatility for forward and spot rates by depicting the change in f and s, that is $f_{12,t} - f_{12,t-1}$ and $s_t - s_{t-1}$. Box 21.2 explains that this actually gives a (very good) approximation of the relative change of the level variable, so for the spot rate we have $s_t - s_{t-1} \approx (S_t - S_{t-1})/S_{t-1}$ and similarly for the forward rate. Interest rates are also pretty volatile if we focus on relative changes. However, the covered interest parity condition is $f - s \approx i_{EU} - i_{US}$; that is, it relates the log difference in forward and spot rates with the difference in interest rates (and not their

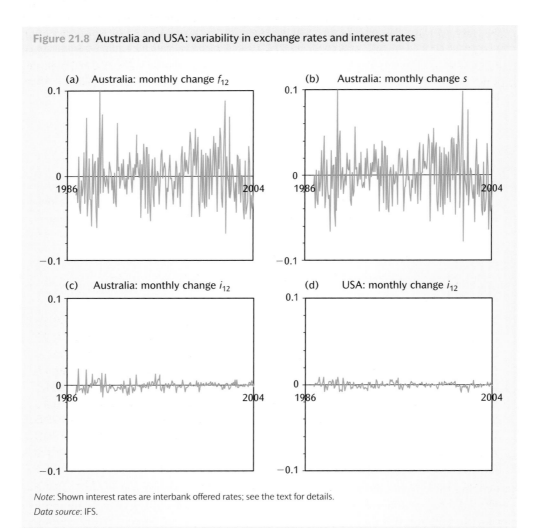

Figure 21.8 Australia and USA: variability in exchange rates and interest rates

Note: Shown interest rates are interbank offered rates; see the text for details.
Data source: IFS.

relative changes). Using the same vertical scale as for panels (a) and (b), panels (c) and (d) of Figure 21.8 show that changes in the levels of the interest rate are not of the same order of magnitude as changes in the log of the forward and spot rates. At first sight, this difference in changes may make it hard to see how covered interest parity can hold. However, the parity condition relates *differences* in *f* and *s* with *differences* in interest rates. This implies that the condition may still hold if most of the change in *f* is usually absorbed by a change in *s* (and not by a change in interest rates), or vice versa. As we will see, this is indeed the case.

Figure 21.9 suggests that the covered interest parity condition does hold empirically. It is not, of course, a proper econometric test, which would have to make sure that (i) the home and foreign assets are indeed comparable in terms of maturity and default and political risk (hence euro-currency deposits are frequently used; see Levich, 1985), (ii) econometric problems as discussed in Chapter 20 are avoided, and (iii) transaction costs are taken into consideration. In view of the sophisticated computer and communication equipment used today in modern foreign exchange dealing rooms, which makes transaction costs small and covered interest parity indeed riskless, it should come as no surprise that covered interest parity holds almost perfectly. In an analysis of five major currencies against the US dollar, Clinton (1988), for example, finds that the neutral band, which is determined by transaction costs, should be within 0.06 per cent per annum from parity. Before the advanced computing and communication equipment was available, the margins were, of course, considerably larger.

Box 21.2   **Basic properties of (natural) logarithms**

Logarithms are used frequently in financial research, mainly because they make the analysis of products, ratios, and powers simpler by transferring these into sums, differences, and products, respectively, through their three basic properties:

- the log of the product ab is the sum of the logs: $\ln(ab) = \ln(a) + \ln(b)$
- the log of the ratio a/b is the difference of the logs: $\ln(a/b) = \ln(a) - \ln(b)$
- the log of the power a^b is the product of b and log a: $\ln(a^b) = b \ln(a)$

Another advantage of using logarithms is that their change represents the *relative* change of the original variable since the derivative of $\ln(X)$ is $1/X$. So, if we use our convention and define $x \equiv \ln(X)$, we get $dx = (1/X)dX$, that is the growth rate of the variable X. It is this property that underlies the fact that the slope of a time variable represents its growth rate when a logarithmic scale is used. If time is continuous, as in the theory chapters to follow, the change in natural logs is actually equal to the growth rate. If time is discrete, as in empirical work, the growth rate can be approximated using the difference in logs. Table 21.1 shows how accurate the approximation is using the monthly 2003 US dollar exchange rates in Australia as an example. This represents a tough test because exchange rates are extremely volatile. None the less, the maximum error is only 0.2 per cent, namely in October 2003 when the actual relative change is -6.196 and the logarithmic approximation gives -6.396. Panels (a) and (b) of Figure 21.8 therefore give the monthly relative change of the forward and spot rate. »

Table 21.1 Approximation accuracy: Australia–US $ spot exchange rates, 2003

| 2003 | Exchange rate US$ | | Relative changes and errors (in %) | | |
	S_t	$s_t \equiv \ln(S_t)$	(a) exact $100 \cdot (S_t - S_{t-1})/S_{t-1}$	(b) approximation $100 \cdot (s_t - s_{t-1})$	error $a - b$
January*	1.78078	0.577051	−0.267	−0.268	0.000
February	1.70794	0.535288	−4.090	−4.176	0.086
March	1.62880	0.487844	−4.634	−4.744	0.111
April	1.65330	0.502773	1.504	1.493	0.011
May	1.58353	0.459657	−4.220	−4.312	0.092
June	1.51964	0.418473	−4.035	−4.118	0.084
July	1.47896	0.391339	−2.677	−2.713	0.036
August	1.53480	0.428400	3.776	3.706	0.070
September	1.55231	0.439744	1.141	1.134	0.006
October	1.45613	0.375782	−6.196	−6.396	0.200
November	1.43379	0.360321	−1.534	−1.546	0.012
December	1.37381	0.317588	−4.183	−4.273	0.090

Note: * the January change is relative to the 1 Dec. 2002 exchange rate: 1.78555.
Source: Calculations based on IFS data:

Figure 21.9 Australia–USA: 12-month covered interest parity

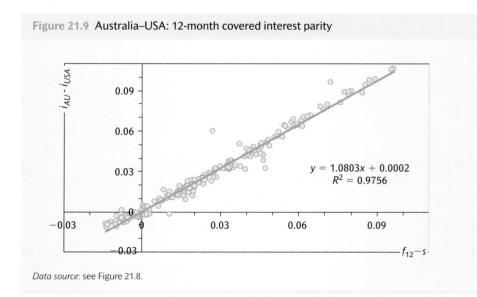

$y = 1.0803x + 0.0002$
$R^2 = 0.9756$

Data source: see Figure 21.8.

21.5 Uncovered interest parity

In Section 21.3 we compared two options available to you if you had a large sum L of money available for investment for one period, namely buying European or American bonds. After calculating the return on each option, we concluded that both assets were going to be held in equilibrium only if the return on each asset was the same, which resulted in the derivation of the covered interest parity condition. In that discussion we realized that if you purchased the American bond, you were exposed to foreign exchange risk. To avoid this risk we decided to hedge it on the forward exchange market by selling the dollars to be received next period for a price agreed upon today. In comparing the revenue from the two options, there was therefore no difference in riskiness involved since we assumed explicitly that the default and political risk of the two assets was the same. Hence we were justified in demanding the same return.

There are, of course, under the circumstances described above, more options available to you. One of these options (called option III below) is *not* to hedge your risk on the forward exchange market. For clarity of exposition, it is better to now explicitly add a sub-index t to denote time. Let's compare your revenue from option I, that is buy the European bond, with the revenue from option III: buy the American bond and do not hedge on the forward exchange market. Nothing has changed for option I, so:

- revenue from buying European bond: $(1 + i_{EU,t})L$.

Before you can purchase the American bond you have to convert your euros to dollars at the exchange rate S_t, which will give you L/S_t dollars. In the next period your revenue will therefore be $(1 + i_{US,t})(L/S_t)$ dollars. You have decided not to hedge your foreign exchange risk, so in the next period you will have to exchange your currency on the spot exchange market. In this period, when you have to make your investment decision, you obviously do not know next period's spot exchange rate. To make your decision you will therefore have to form some expectation today about the future spot exchange rate. This can be a simple (single number) or complicated (distribution function) expectation. Let's denote the expected value of your forecasting process by S_{t+1}^e; then we conclude:

- *expected* revenue from buying American bond: $\dfrac{S_{t+1}^e(1 + i_{US,t})}{S_t}L$

We cannot draw immediate conclusions from comparing these two revenues, because you know the return to investing in the European bond for sure, whereas the return to investing in the American bond is uncertain. Only under the additional assumption of *risk-neutral* economic agents, hypothesizing that agents just focus on the expected value of the return and do not care at all about the underlying distribution of risk, should the sure return to the European bond be equal to the expected return of the American bond. Under that assumption, then, and after a similar logarithmic transformation and approximation as discussed in Section 21.3, we arrive at the *uncovered interest parity condition*:

(21.4) $$s_{t+1}^e - s_t \approx i_{EU,t} - i_{US,t}$$

Equation (21.4) says that the difference in home and foreign interest rate must be equal to the expected appreciation of the foreign currency. As such, the equation is pretty useless for empirical testing because it contains the expectation of the future exchange rate and

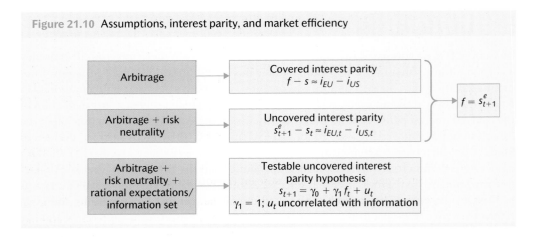

Figure 21.10 Assumptions, interest parity, and market efficiency

expectations cannot be directly measured.[2] Alternatively, you can view it as a simple method to define these expectations under the assumption of risk neutrality. In combination with the covered interest parity condition (21.2'), however, it is trivial to see that the forward exchange rate should be equal to the expected value of the future spot exchange rate:

$$(21.5) \qquad\qquad f = s_{t+1}^e$$

Equation (21.5) still does not give us a testable hypothesis, unless we are willing to go one step further, namely by assuming *rational expectations*. Under rational expectations economic agents make no systematic forecast errors. They will not, of course, be able to predict the future exchange rate exactly, but their prediction should reflect all information available to them at the time they are making the prediction. Any forecasts errors must therefore be uncorrelated (that is, not systematic) with the information set available at the time of the prediction. Under the additional assumption of rational expectations, the uncovered interest parity condition can therefore be tested by estimating a regression similar to (see Box 20.1 and Frenkel, 1976):[3]

$$(21.6) \qquad\qquad s_{t+1} = \gamma_0 + \gamma_1 f_t + u_t,$$

where u_t is the (forecast) error term. Under the hypothesis of risk neutrality and rational expectations, we expect the parameter γ_1 to be equal to unity and the forecast error to be uncorrelated with the information available at time t. Empirical estimates of equations such as (21.6) are frequently called tests of *market efficiency*. There are different types of market efficiency, where the joint hypothesis of risk neutrality and rational expectations is dubbed the *simple efficiency hypothesis* by Sarno and Taylor (2002: 10). Figure 21.10 schematically summarizes this discussion.

21.6 Risk premium and transaction costs

When comparing the revenue from purchasing a European bond with the revenue from purchasing an American bond in the previous section, we noted that the European agent was exposed to foreign exchange risk when purchasing the American asset. In general, we can identify three types of exchange risk exposure.

- *Translation exposure.* This accounting exposure arises from assets and liabilities denominated in foreign currency. Suppose, for example, that a German firm has a foreign subsidiary in Thailand, with the assets and liabilities denominated in Thai baht. The translation process expresses financial statements measured in one currency in terms of another currency. Using the current exchange rate to do this, as is for example required in the USA, implies that the net value of the foreign subsidiary changes in terms of euros, even if it does not change in terms of baht.

- *Transaction exposure.* This arises from engaging in transactions denominated in foreign currency, such as a Japanese firm selling watches to a French firm with payment on delivery in three months' time. This example was discussed in Section 19.4, where it was pointed out that the firm can hedge transaction exposure on the forward exchange market.

- *Economic exposure.* This focuses on the exposure of changes in a firm's value to changes in the exchange rates. If a firm is active in many countries, with associated receipts and payments in different foreign currencies, and the value of the firm is equal to the present value of all future after-tax cash flows in these countries translated into the base country currency, then it is clear that economic exposure is the most comprehensive measure of exposure to foreign exchange risk (and far from easy to calculate).

In deriving the uncovered interest parity condition (eq. 21.4), we assumed that the economic agents were risk neutral; that is, in comparing the revenue from purchasing the European versus the American bond they just focus on the expected value of the return and do not care at all about the underlying distribution of the risk. In practice, however, we expect individuals and organizations to exhibit *risk aversion*: other things equal, they prefer less risk to more risk. This does not mean that risky assets will not be held in equilibrium, just that risk-averse investors will demand a compensation for holding these assets. This is called a *risk premium*. It implies that firms, individuals or countries with bad credit (considered to be a more risky investment) must pay a higher interest rate than those with good credit. The risk premium will rise if: (i) the degree of risk aversion rises and (ii) the perceived riskiness increases. Note in addition that the derivation of the uncovered interest parity condition ignored transaction costs, including capital controls (such as a tax on capital in- or outflows) and market transaction costs. Including both a risk premium and acknowledging transaction costs, instead of (21.4) we would expect:

$$(21.7) \qquad i_{EU,t} = i_{US,t} + (s^e_{t+1} - s_t) + \text{risk premium} + \text{transaction costs}$$

Equation (21.7) indicates that the return from investing at home ($i_{EU,t}$) is equal to the return from investing abroad ($i_{US,t}$) *plus* the expected appreciation of the dollar if investing abroad ($s^e_{t+1} - s_t$) *plus* a risk premium to compensate for the exposure to foreign exchange risk if investing abroad *plus* any transaction costs involved in foreign investments. In short, there is ample reason to expect the uncovered interest rate parity condition (21.4) not to hold perfectly. We should, however, point out three reasons why it may hold approximately for some markets. First, broad transaction costs, both capital controls and market transaction costs, have declined considerably over time. As indicated by equation (21.7), this narrows the band within which uncovered interest parity should hold. Second, for the major, regularly traded currencies we should expect the risk premium to be within reasonable (but non-zero) limits, which again narrows the band within which uncovered interest parity should hold. Third, and perhaps most importantly, equation (21.7) was derived from a *European* perspective.

For an American individual or firm, Europe is the foreign country demanding a risk premium and involving transaction costs. Since the actual exchange rate is based on the aggregate behaviour of both Europeans and Americans, the deviation from uncovered interest parity caused by equation (21.7) and its American counterpart should at least to some extent cancel in the aggregation process, yet again narrowing the band within which uncovered interest parity should hold. This does not mean that risk premia and transaction costs are not important for explaining aggregate behaviour. They certainly are important, as will be demonstrated in Chapters 29 and 30 and in the next section.

21.7 The empirics of uncovered interest parity

The condition of uncovered interest parity is clearly much more difficult to appropriately test empirically than the condition of covered interest parity, in particular because such tests involve joint hypotheses of risk neutrality and rational expectations, where the latter also implies that proper attention has to be given to analyse which information was available to the economic agents at the time they were forming their expectations. None the less, Figure 21.11 tries to provide some heuristic support for uncovered interest rate parity by continuing our Australia–USA example, based on equation (21.6). Panel (a) of the figure shows the spot exchange rate and the concommittant forward exchange rate that should be viewed as its predictor (appropriately moved forward in time, so by one month for f_1, by two months for f_2, etc.). Forward and spot rates clearly move up and down together, but there is, equally clearly, considerable deviation between them.

Panels (b)–(f) of Figure 21.11 show the (in)accuracy of the forward rate as a predictor of the future spot rate in level terms. Clearly, and not surprisingly, the deviation between the forecast and the realization increases if the forecast horizon becomes larger: the observations are much closer to the line for the 1-month forecast than for the 2-month forecast, which are in turn closer than the 3-month forecast, etc. (as reflected in the R^2, the share of the variance that is explained). In addition, for short forecast horizons the prediction seems to be fairly efficient in the sense that the estimated slope coefficient is very close to 1 and the estimated intercept is very close to 0, as should be the case based on equation (21.6).[4] What is more problematic, however, is the fact that the estimated slope coefficient is substantially smaller than 1 and the estimated intercept is substantially larger than 0 if the forecast horizon increases, suggesting that the forward rate is a structurally biased predictor of the future spot rate if the time horizon increases. A possible explanation for this effect may be that investors are not risk neutral and/or there are transaction costs, as both assumptions are needed to derive equation (21.6); see the previous section (equation 21.7).

There have been numerous empirical tests of the simple efficient market hypothesis based on the joint hypothesis of risk neutrality and rational expectations. Proper econometric testing in this area is, however, notoriously difficult. Frenkel's (1976) test using levels (eq. 21.6) was criticized for econometric reasons and replaced by tests in deviation from s_t unfavourable for the simple efficiency hypothesis; see for example Fama (1984). However, the non-linear nature of risk premia makes econometric tests based on linearity questionable; see Bekaert and Hodrick (1993). As pointed out by Hansen and Hodrick (1980), an important characteristic of the forward exchange market is its 'overlapping contract' nature: there are contracts with many different times to maturity, which creates serial correlation in the forecast errors (and therefore econometric problems).

Figure 21.11 Australia–USA: prediction accuracy of forward rates

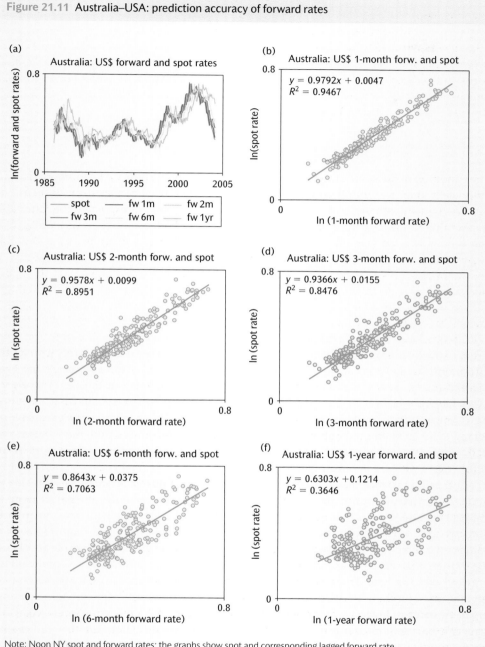

(a)

Australia: US$ forward and spot rates

ln(forward and spot rates)

1985   1990   1995   2000   2005

— spot   — fw 1m   ⋯ fw 2m
— fw 3m   — fw 6m   — fw 1yr

(b)

Australia: US$ 1-month forw. and spot

$y = 0.9792x + 0.0047$
$R^2 = 0.9467$

ln(spot rate)

ln (1-month forward rate)

(c)

Australia: US$ 2-month forw. and spot

$y = 0.9578x + 0.0099$
$R^2 = 0.8951$

ln (spot rate)

ln (2-month forward rate)

(d)

Australia: US$ 3-month forw. and spot

$y = 0.9366x + 0.0155$
$R^2 = 0.8476$

ln (spot rate)

ln (3-month forward rate)

(e)

Australia: US$ 6-month forw. and spot

$y = 0.8643x + 0.0375$
$R^2 = 0.7063$

ln (spot rate)

ln (6-month forward rate)

(f)

Australia: US$ 1-year forward. and spot

$y = 0.6303x + 0.1214$
$R^2 = 0.3646$

ln (spot rate)

ln (1-year forward rate)

Note: Noon NY spot and forward rates; the graphs show spot and corresponding lagged forward rate.
Data: IFS.

Table 21.2 Australia–USA: statistical properties of forward and spot rates

	f_1-s_{-1}	f_2-s_{-2}	f_3-s_{-3}	f_6-s_{-6}	$f_{12}-s_{-12}$
Average	0.0031	0.0061	0.0087	0.0152	0.0264
Standard error	0.0021	0.0030	0.0036	0.0051	0.0079
Minimum	−0.1013	−0.1464	−0.1720	−0.1668	−0.2423
Maximum	0.0734	0.1141	0.1295	0.2035	0.3275
Correlation coefficients	f_1-s_{-1}	f_2-s_{-2}	f_3-s_{-3}	f_6-s_{-6}	$f_{12}-s_{-12}$
f_1-s_{-1}	1				
f_2-s_{-2}	0.720	1			
f_3-s_{-3}	0.579	0.820	1		
f_6-s_{-6}	0.419	0.573	0.719	1	
$f_{12}-s_{-12}$	0.367	0.493	0.599	0.787	1

Data source: Calculations based on IFS monthly data; 217 observations, February 1986–February 2004.

The correlation problem is illustrated in Table 21.2, which summarizes the statistical properties of the forecast errors, where s_{-1} denotes the one-month lagged spot rate, s_{-2} denotes the two-month lagged spot rate, etc. It shows that the average error becomes larger and significantly positive if the time horizon increases.[5] The second part of Table 21.2 shows the (very high) correlation coefficients between the forecast errors. This should come as no surprise, since exchange rates are heavily influenced by new information becoming available on changes in economic conditions and policy. As time progresses and more news that influences the exchange rate becomes available, the overlapping forward contracts are affected in a similar way, creating serial correlation.

Another way to look at the correlation problem is by realizing that the errors in shorter terms to maturity contracts provide information on the future errors in the longer terms to maturity contracts. This is illustrated in Figure 21.12 for the extent to which the one-month forecast error provides information for the two-month forecast error next month (panel (*a*)) and for the three-month forecast error two months from now (panel (*b*)). Clarida and Taylor (1997) use this structure in a flexible framework to test the information content of the forward exchange rate. They conclude (p. 360): 'forward foreign exchange premiums contain significant information regarding subsequent movements in the spot foreign exchange markets. Independently of whether or not foreign exchange markets are characterized by risk aversion or a failure of the rational expectations hypothesis, it appears that the market mechanism is relatively successful in imparting information into the term structure of forward premiums in this respect.'

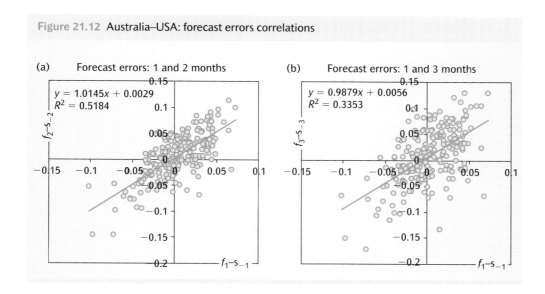

Figure 21.12 Australia–USA: forecast errors correlations

21.8 Conclusions

The Fisher equation provides a direct relationship between interest rates and prices through the decomposition in nominal and real interest rates, where the latter are equal to the nominal interest rate minus the inflation rate. Although nominal interest rates rise with rising inflation rates to compensate for this high inflation, the real interest rate also varies considerably over time and can be both negative and higher than the nominal interest rate. If interest rates increase for longer terms to maturity, the term structure of interest rates is said to be rising. Empirically, it can also be flat or falling.

Hedged international arbitrage between two assets that are deemed perfect substitutes gives rise to the covered interest parity condition: the difference between the home and foreign interest rate is equal to the log difference between forward and spot exchange rates. Empirically, covered interest arbitrage holds almost perfectly. If such international arbitrage between two assets is not hedged on the forward exchange market *and* investors are risk neutral, it is possible to derive the uncovered interest parity condition: the difference between the home and foreign interest rate is equal to the expected appreciation of the foreign currency. In conjunction with covered interest parity, this implies that the forward rate is equal to the expected future spot rate.

Tests of uncovered interest parity are based on the additional assumption of rational expectations. These tests, which are frequently rejected empirically, are therefore based on a range of assumptions, including risk neutrality and rational expectations (together forming the simple efficient market hypothesis). Apart from the notoriously difficult econometric problems involved in the testing procedure, this may be caused by transaction costs and risk aversion leading to (time-varying) risk premia. Advanced empirical work shows that the term structure of forward premiums contains significant information regarding subsequent movements of spot exchange rates.

TECHNICAL NOTE

Technical Note 21.1 Covered interest parity

Before showing how to get from equation (21.2) to (21.2′) it is useful to recall the second basic property of (natural) logarithms (see Box 21.2):

• the log of the ratio a/b is the difference of the logs: $\ln(a/b) = \ln(a) - \ln(b)$

We also use the linear approximation $\ln(1+x) \approx x$ described in Box 21.1. The transformation of the second equality in (21.2) to (21.2′) is then as follows:

(21.A1)
$$\frac{F}{S} = \frac{1 + i_{EU}}{1 + i_{US}} \Leftrightarrow \ln\left[\frac{F}{S}\right] = \ln\left[\frac{1 + i_{EU}}{1 + i_{US}}\right]$$

Since the log of the ratio is the difference of the logs, we know that:

(21.A2)
$$\ln\left[\frac{F}{S}\right] = \ln(F) - \ln(S); \quad \text{and} \quad \ln\left[\frac{1 + i_{EU}}{1 + i_{US}}\right] = \ln(1 + i_{EU}) - \ln(1 + i_{US})$$

Using the linear approximation, we know that $\ln(1 + i_{EU}) \approx i_{EU}$ and $\ln(1 + i_{US}) \approx i_{US}$. Moreover, by our convention we have defined $f \equiv \ln(F)$ and $s \equiv \ln(S)$. Using (21.A2) and this respective information in the second equation of (21.A1), we get:

(21.A3)
$$\ln\left[\frac{F}{S}\right] = \ln(F) - \ln(S) \equiv f - s = \ln\left[\frac{1 + i_{EU}}{1 + i_{US}}\right] = \ln(1 + i_{EU}) - \ln(1 + i_{US}) \approx i_{EU} - i_{US}$$

This is equation (21.2′) in the main text: $f - s \approx i_{EU} - i_{US}$.

QUESTIONS

Question 21.1

An investor in London has two investment opportunities. He can invest in two-year UK government bonds with an annual nominal interest rate of 4.5 per cent, or he can invest in two-year US government bonds with an annual nominal interest rate of 2.6 per cent . Currently the spot exchange rate is 1.8 US dollar/UK pound and the two years forward exchange rate is 1.7 US dollar/UK pound.

21.1A Should the investor hold his money in UK or US government bonds?

21.1B Does the covered interest parity hold? Do you think this situation will exist for a long time?

Question 21.2

The same London investor now looks to Europe and notices that the annual nominal interest rate on two-year German government bonds is 2.7 per cent. Remember that two-year UK government bonds give an annual nominal interest rate of 4.5 per cent. The spot exchange rate is 0.7 UK pound/European euro.

21.2A Do financial markets expect the pound to appreciate of depreciate against the euro?

21.2B What is the two-year forward rate of the euro against the pound for the covered interest parity to hold?

21.2C If the London investor is risk neutral and decides not to hedge the exchange rate risk, what should the expected euro/pound spot exchange rate in two years be at least in order for this investor to hold German bonds?

21.2D What should the expected euro/pound spot exchange rate in two years be at least if the London investor is risk averse?

Question 21.3

The covered and uncovered interest parity condition constitute powerful tools for predicting exchange rate movements. Below we have listed a number of events. Predict with the covered or uncovered interest parity condition what will happen with the European euro/US dollar spot exchange rate.

21.3A The Federal Reserve announces that the discount rate will be lowered.

21.3B GDP figures of the euro area turn out to be better then expected, raising expectations that the European economy is coming sooner out of its slump.

21.3C The ECB president hesitates before he says 'strong euro'.

21.3D Most large American companies unexpectedly raise their profit prospects.

See the Online Resource Centre for a Study Guide containing more questions
www.oxfordtextbooks.co.uk/orc/vanmarrewijk/

NOTES

1 Equation (21.1) is the approximation of the exact equation: $(1 + r) = (1 + i)/(1 + \pi)$; see Box 21.1.

2 We can, of course, get indirect measures from surveys, derived from asset prices, consensus forecasts, etc.

3 For econometric reasons the actual test is now usually in deviation from s_t; see also below and Chapter 20.

4 A statistical t-test as explained in Box 21.1 would show that the slope coefficient is significantly different from 1 if the forecast horizon is longer than 2 months and the intercept is significantly different from 0 if the forecast horizon is longer than 3 months.

5 The falling estimated slope coefficient is thus not fully compensated by the rising intercept in Figure 21.11.

MONEY
ORGANIZATIONS AND
INSTITUTIONS

Objectives/key terms

- Fixed and flexible exchange rates
- Gold standard and gold points
- Bretton Woods
- Parity, devaluation, and revaluation
- International Monetary Fund (IMF)
- Bank for International Settlements (BIS)

- Policy trilemma
- World wars and recession
- Floating rates
- $(n-1)$ problem
- World Bank
- Appreciation and depreciation

We present the so-called policy trilemma to better understand the policy choices made in recent history regarding the international monetary system, including the gold standard, Bretton Woods, and the recent floating rates era. We also briefly discuss the main international monetary organizations (IMF, BIS, and the World Bank).

22.1 Introduction

Before presenting an overview of the history, structure, and functions of the most important current international monetary organizations, namely the International Monetary Fund, the World Bank, and the Bank for International Settlements, we offer a general picture of more recent international monetary history. We focus on four main periods in particular, namely the gold standard era (1870–1914), the world wars and recession era (1914–45), the Bretton Woods era (1945–71), and the floating rates era (1971–now). To better understand the policy choices made in these periods regarding the structure of the international financial system, it is useful to have a grasp of the so-called policy trilemma, which argues that out of three specific policy objectives only two can be reached simultaneously at the expense of the third objective. This discussion is related to a choice between a fixed exchange rate regime and a flexible exchange rate regime. Our explanation of the policy trilemma in the next section is based on the uncovered interest rate parity condition derived in the previous chapter. We conclude by reviewing a number of important international monetary institutions.

22.2 Exchange rate regimes and the policy trilemma

In theory, we can distinguish between two types of exchange rate regimes, namely *fixed* exchange rates and *flexible* exchange rates. In practice, there is a sliding scale (with associated colourful typology) from one hypothetical extreme to the other; see Section 22.6. As the names suggest, the difference between fixed and flexible exchange rates is the extent to which the exchange rate is allowed to change in response to market pressure. Under fixed exchange rates, the central bank of a country has set the exchange rate at a particular level and it will not allow the currency to appreciate or depreciate relative to that level. To maintain the fixed exchange rate, the central bank must be ready to intervene in the foreign exchange market by buying or selling reserves or by increasing or reducing the interest rate (see Chapter 19). Under flexible exchange rates, on the other hand, the central bank does not intervene in the foreign exchange market and allows the currency to freely appreciate or depreciate in

Famous economists	Barry Eichengreen

Fig. 22.1
Barry Eichengreen
(1952–)

Born in Berkeley, California, Barry Eichengreen studied at UC Santa Cruz and Yale, where he received his PhD in 1979. He worked at Harvard for six years before moving to Berkeley and was also a senior policy adviser for the IMF. He is one of the most prolific experts on all aspects of the international monetary system, including its institutions, history, theory, and empirics. Some of his most important books cover the history of the gold standard (see this chapter), the impact of financial crises (see Chapter 29), and the European monetary unification process (see Chapter 30); on all of this see, for example, *Golden Fetters: The Gold Standard and the Great Depression, 1918–1939* (1992), *European Monetary Unification* (1997), and *Capital Flows and Crises* (2003).

response to changes in market demand and supply. These issues are discussed further in Parts III.B and III.C of this book.

The history of the international economic order relating to exchange rate regimes and capital market integration is closely connected; see Mundell (1968), Eichengreen (1996), and Obstfeld and Taylor (2003). To better understand this connection, it is useful to distinguish between three possible policy objectives that a nation might try to achieve:[1]

(i) Monetary policy independence

(ii) A fixed exchange rate

(iii) International capital mobility.

The first objective is desirable as it allows a country to determine its monetary policy independently of other countries, based on its own economic circumstances. The second objective is desirable as it provides price stability for international transactions and a clear point of reference. The third objective is desirable as it allows spreading of investment risks and access to the most profitable projects internationally.

It turns out that only two of these three policy objectives can be achieved at any one point in time, at the expense of the third objective. Focusing on the EU and the USA, this can be illustrated most effectively by recalling the uncovered interest rate parity condition with transaction costs (using a zero risk premium, see equation (21.7)):

$$(22.1) \qquad i_{EU,t} = i_{US,t} + (s_{t+1}^e - s_t) + transaction\ costs,$$

where the sub-index t denotes time, $i_{EU,t}$ is the EU interest rate, $i_{US,t}$ is the US interest rate, s_t is the (log) US dollar exchange rate (price of one dollar in terms of euros), and s_{t+1}^e is the (log) expected value of next period's US dollar exchange rate.

If there is complete international capital mobility (objective (iii) holds), the transaction costs are very low, such that equation (22.1) reduces to the uncovered interest parity condition itself: $i_{EU,t} = i_{US,t} + (s_{t+1}^e - s_t)$. This implies that expected changes in the exchange rate are the only reason for an interest rate differential between the EU and the USA. With full international capital mobility, policy makers must therefore *choose* between monetary policy independence (reaching objective (i), as measured by a possible deviation between EU and US interest rates) and a fixed exchange rate (reaching objective (ii). If, for example, they decide to fix the exchange rate ($s_{t+1}^e - s_t = 0$), this automatically implies $i_{EU,t} = i_{US,t}$, making monetary policy independence impossible. Similarly, if they decide to strive for monetary policy independence, this automatically makes a fixed exchange rate impossible ($s_{t+1}^e \neq s_t$) when $i_{EU,t} \neq i_{US,t}$. The only way in which objectives (i) and (ii) can be achieved simultaneously is by giving up objective (iii), in which case equation (22.1) with fixed exchange rates reduces to $i_{EU,t} = i_{US,t} + transaction\ costs$. A country can then steer its own interest rate (retain policy autonomy) and have a fixed exchange rate at the cost of immobile capital, which prevents portfolio investors from making direct capital flows to or from the EU so as to benefit from the interest rate differential. Although intermediate solutions are possible for monetary policy independence and capital controls (some capital controls buy you some monetary independence; see also Table 22.1), this does not hold for fixed exchange rates, see Chapter 28.

The incompatibility between objectives (i)–(iii) was pointed out by Nobel laureate Robert Mundell in the early 1960s. It is called the *incompatible trinity, incompatible triangle,* or *policy*

Figure 22.2 The policy trilemma

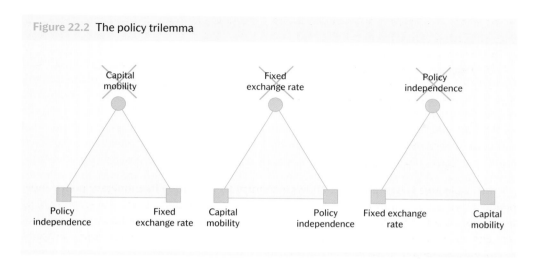

Figure 22.3 Overview of international monetary regimes

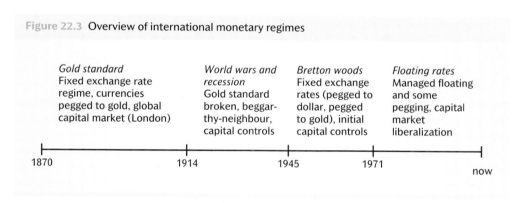

trilemma and provides us with a categorization scheme that helps us to understand the changes in the international economic order over time. Figure 22.2 illustrates the trilemma. In each triangle of the figure the two squares indicate the objectives pursued by the government, whereas the circle at the top of the triangle indicates the policy objective that cannot be met. The trilemma indicates that there is a price to pay for policy makers when they want to achieve full capital mobility, fixed exchange rates, or policy autonomy. The next four sections discuss how the choices have changed over time by focusing on the most recent main international monetary regimes, see also Eichengreen (1996) and Obstfeld and Taylor (2003).[2] Figure 22.3 gives an overview of these regimes, their duration, and a summary of their main characteristics. They are:

- gold standard (±1870–1914)
- world wars and recession (1914–45)
- Bretton Woods (1945–71)
- floating rates (1971–now).

22.3 Gold Standard (±1870–1914)

Towards the end of the nineteenth century, when the UK was the world's leading economy and London the undisputed global financial centre, an increasing share of the world economy moved to the gold standard. This was a stable and credible fixed exchange rate regime in which countries valued their currency in terms of gold. It started in Britain in 1844 when the Bank Charter Act established that Bank of England notes, fully backed by gold, were the legal standard. It became an international standard in 1871 when Germany established the Reich Mark on a strict gold standard, soon followed by many other European nations, and eventually by Japan (1897), India (1898), and the USA (1900). With countries issuing banknotes directly backed by gold, and by allowing gold to be freely imported and exported across borders according to the gold standard rules, the exchange rates between the currencies became fixed. Suppose, for example, that the Federal Reserve pegs the price of gold at $35 per ounce and the Bank of England at £7, then the exchange rate of the British pound in terms of US dollars must be 35/7 = 5, otherwise profitable arbitrage opportunities arise. In practice, taking the costs of shipping and insuring gold in transit into consideration, the exchange rates could fluctuate within narrow margins called *gold points*. The gold standard functioned as a disciplining device for countries, which led to a convergence of interest rates and a global capital market centred in London (see also Chapter 2), in exchange for a reduction in policy autonomy.

The gold standard worked quite well at the end of the nineteenth and the beginning of the twentieth century, but there are also several drawbacks to the gold standard. First, although currency backed by gold generally leads to relatively stable prices (see Box 22.1), the rate of inflation is not only determined by macroeconomic conditions but also by the random discoveries of new gold supplies. There have been considerable fluctuations linked to these events; see Cooper (1982). Second, the international payments system requires gold as reserves. As economies are growing, central banks strive for an increase in the buffer stock of their gold reserves (else there would be deflation; recall $MV = PY$; see Chapters 18 and 21). Simultaneous competition for gold by central banks might bring about unemployment through a reduction in their money supply; see also Part III.B. Third, the gold standard gives countries with a large gold supply, such as Russia and South Africa, the ability to influence the world's macroeconomic conditions by selling gold. Fourth, and perhaps most importantly, the gold standard puts undue restrictions on the use of monetary policy as a means for fighting unemployment under special circumstances, such as a worldwide recession (this is true for any fixed exchange rate regime).

22.4 World wars and recession (1914–45)

The pillars of the international economic system – the gold standard, multilateral trade, and the interchangeability of currencies – crumbled down one by one during the First World War (1914–18), the Second World War (1939–45), and particularly during the Great Depression, which started in October 1929 and lasted throughout the 1930s. To finance its war efforts, Britain ended the convertibility of Bank of England notes in 1914. Nations printed more money than could be redeemed in gold, hoping to win the First World War and redeem the excess out of reparations payments. Losing the war, Germany was indeed required by the

Treaty of Versailles to pay large punitive damages, of which in the end it could only effectively transfer a fraction; see Brakman and van Marrewijk (1998, ch. 1). To deal with these difficulties the Bank for International Settlements was established in 1930 under the Young Plan; see Section 22.9. Many nations, including the USA and the UK, instituted capital controls to prevent the movement of gold. Britain returned to the gold standard at the pre-war gold price in 1925, which entailed a significant deflation for the economy, much to the dismay of British economist John Maynard Keynes, who called the gold standard a 'barbarous relic'.

The credibility of the gold standard was broken by the First World War, such that countries were no longer willing to give up their policy autonomy for a well-functioning international

 Box 22.1   Price stability under the gold standard

Some historians argue that Britain moved to the gold standard as early as 1717, when Sir Isaac Newton was master of the Royal Mint. However, since both a gold and a silver standard were used simultaneously, this is technically a bimetallic standard. During the 1700s and early 1800s a general shortage of silver put pressure on this bimetallic standard, which was officially replaced by a gold standard in 1844. One of the advantages of the gold standard, when adhered to consistently for a long time period, is price stability. This is demonstrated most effectively by Twigger (1999), who uses various sources to calculate a price index for Britain during a 250-year period. Figure 22.4 shows its inverse, the value of the British pound, using a logarithmic scale. Until the start of the First World War, the long-run value of the pound is remarkably stable, although fluctuating considerably from year to year as a result of the quality of harvests, wars, etc. Only after the Second World War, that is in the Bretton Woods and floating rates era, does a steady price increase cause a steady decline in the value of the pound.

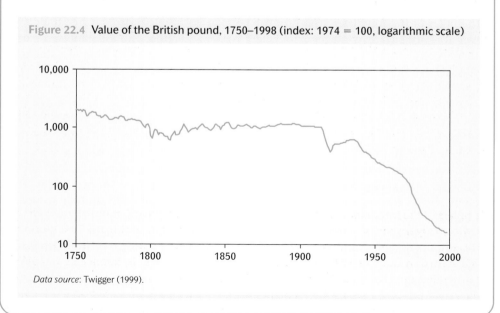

Figure 22.4   **Value of the British pound, 1750–1998 (index: 1974 = 100, logarithmic scale)**

Data source: Twigger (1999).

economic system, focusing instead on domestic political goals. Consequently, when the Great Depression hit in 1929, countries engaged in non-cooperative, competitive beggar-thy-neighbour devaluations and instituted capital controls. This greatly exacerbated the crisis, caused the international trade system to collapse, and put millions of people out of a job, with unemployment rates of more than 30 per cent, see also Chapter 12. Both the punitive damages required from Germany in the Treaty of Versailles and the economic consequences of the nationalistic policies imposed during the Great Depression are seen as major contributing factors in causing the outbreak of the Second World War. While the war was raging, politicians and advisers started to work on a plan to prevent this from happening again.

22.5 Bretton Woods (1945–71)

The foundations for a new international economic order were laid at the Mount Washington Hotel in Bretton Woods, New Hampshire, when the delegates of 44 allied nations signed the Bretton Woods Agreement in July 1944. The delegates set up a system of rules, institutions, and procedures and established the International Monetary Fund (see Section 22.7) and the World Bank (see Section 22.8). Planning for the new order had been under way some three years since the American president Franklin Roosevelt and the British prime minister Winston Churchill signed the Atlantic Charter in August 1941. There was no question towards the end of the Second World War that the balance of power had shifted towards the USA, politically, economically, as well as militarily. This meant that, although there was some compromise towards the British plan designed by John Maynard Keynes, the structure of the Bretton Woods system was based on the plans designed by American Harry Dexter White, who would remain a powerful initial influence at the IMF as the first US executive director.

The pillar of the American vision for the postwar economic order was free trade and a prevention of beggar-thy-neigbour policies. William Clayton, the assistant secretary of state for economic affairs, apparently summed up this point by saying: 'we need markets—big markets—around the world in which to buy and sell'. Free trade involved lowering tariffs and other trade barriers, a task for the GATT/WTO (see Chapter 12), and a stable international monetary system to foster the development of trade and capital flows. To do this the gold standard was re-established indirectly through the role of the US dollar as international reserve currency. The US government fixed the price of gold at $35 per ounce and made a commitment to convert dollars to gold at that price (for foreign governments and central banks). In conjunction with the strength of the US economy, this made dollars even better than gold as international reserves, since dollars earned interest and gold did not. Other countries pegged their currency to the US dollar at a *par value* and would buy and sell dollars to keep exchange rates within a *band* of plus or minus 1 per cent of parity. To avoid the beggar-thy-neighbour devaluation problem, member countries could only change their par value with IMF approval, which required a decision by the IMF that the balance of payments was in 'fundamental disequilibrium'. A decrease in the value of a currency was called a *devaluation*, an increase a *revaluation*. This terminology still holds for all fixed exchange rate regimes. For floating regimes we use *appreciation* and *depreciation* respectively.

Box 22.2 The *n*−1 problem

If there are *n* countries participating in a fixed exchange rate regime with a dominant reserve currency, such as in the Bretton Woods system, there are only *n*−1 independent exchange rates. The good news is that only *n*−1 countries have to use their monetary policy to fix the exchange rates, leaving one degree of monetary freedom in the system to tackle macroeconomic policy problems. Take the example of two countries committing to fix their exchange rates. As long as one country anchors its currency to the other, the latter has complete freedom in its policies. The bad news is that the country with the dominant reserve currency, which in the Bretton Woods system was the USA, will be tempted to use this degree of freedom to tackle its own macroeconomic problems and not those of the other *n*−1 countries involved in the system. This is known as the *n*−1 problem. Note that the gold standard did not have this asymmetric position of a reserve currency, since all countries were pegging their exchange rate to gold.

We should note that in the Bretton Woods system the other *n*−1 countries in principle had the power to discipline the USA by threatening to convert their dollar holdings to gold, to which the USA had pegged the dollar. In practice, with the exception of France, very few countries actually used this disciplinary device. During the 1960s, Germany and Japan, the key other countries involved in the system, were too dependent on the USA (politically and militarily) to afford a confrontation with that country. This implied that although the dollar was legally convertible to gold, in practice it was not.

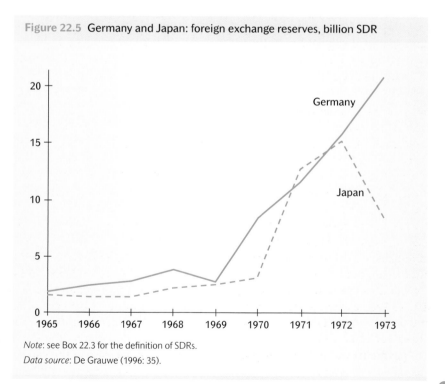

Figure 22.5 Germany and Japan: foreign exchange reserves, billion SDR

Note: see Box 22.3 for the definition of SDRs.
Data source: De Grauwe (1996: 35).

>> The USA used its degree of freedom to try to maintain high growth rates and keep unemployment rates low. This implied expansionary fiscal and monetary policy, leading to high inflation rates and budgetary and current account deficits, particularly in conjunction with the escalating involvement of the USA in the Vietnam War. Although Germany and Japan, keen on keeping inflation rates low, were trying to avoid importing the US inflation rate, they were forced to do so because of their pegged exchange rates in the Bretton Woods system. Speculators realized this dilemma and were betting massively on a revaluation of the German mark and the Japanese yen by purchasing these currencies, which forced the German and Japanese authorities to intervene in the foreign exchange market and accumulate dollar reserves in unprecedented amounts; see Figure 22.5. It was this pressure that eventually forced the collapse of the Bretton Woods system; see Section 22.6. These problems are further analysed in Chapter 28.

22.6 Floating rates (1971–now)

Increasing pressure on the Bretton Woods system caused by the $n-1$ problem (see Box 22.2) during the 1960s and early 1970s caused its collapse. Massive sales of gold by the Federal Reserve and European central banks led to the instalment of a two-tier gold market on 17 March 1968. Private traders could buy and sell gold at a price determined by market forces on the London gold market, while central banks would continue to transact with one another at the (lower) official gold price of $35 per ounce. The latter was only used to a limited extent. Speculation against the dollar forced the German Bundesbank to purchase $1 billion during a single day on 4 May 1971, and another $1 billion during the first hour of the next trading day alone; see Krugman and Obstfeld (2003: 560). Germany gave up and allowed the mark to float. It became clear that the dollar had to be devalued. This was, however, very difficult under the Bretton Woods system because it implied that all other currencies, which were pegged to the dollar, had to be revalued with approval from the IMF and all other countries, many of which were reluctant to do so. Richard Nixon, the American president, forced the issue on 15 August 1971 by formally ending the convertibility of US dollars to gold and imposing a 10 per cent tax on all imports into the USA until an agreement was reached. Although this *Smithsonian agreement* to devalue the dollar by about 8 per cent came in December of 1971 (at the Smithsonian Institution in Washington, DC), it was unable to save the Bretton Woods system. After renewed speculative attacks, there was another 10 per cent devaluation of the dollar on 12 February 1973, followed by a decision to float the exchange rate of the US dollar relative to the most important international currencies on 19 March 1973.

Although the present international monetary system is called the floating rates era, this does not mean that all currencies are freely determined by market forces. On the contrary, almost all countries at some time or another engage in some type of foreign exchange market intervention, either through their legal framework, direct intervention, or their interest rate policy. As illustrated in Figure 22.6, on the sliding scale from fixed exchange rate regimes to flexible exchange rate regimes, the IMF (2004: 118) identifies:

- *No separate legal tender* The currency of another country circulates as the sole legal tender (formal dollarization), or the member belongs to a monetary or currency union in which the same legal tender is shared by the members of the union.

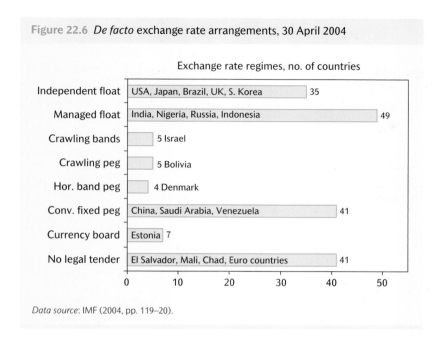

Figure 22.6 *De facto* exchange rate arrangements, 30 April 2004

Exchange rate regimes, no. of countries

Independent float	USA, Japan, Brazil, UK, S. Korea — 35
Managed float	India, Nigeria, Russia, Indonesia — 49
Crawling bands	5 Israel
Crawling peg	5 Bolivia
Hor. band peg	4 Denmark
Conv. fixed peg	China, Saudi Arabia, Venezuela — 41
Currency board	Estonia 7
No legal tender	El Salvador, Mali, Chad, Euro countries — 41

Data source: IMF (2004, pp. 119–20).

- *Currency board arrangements* A monetary regime based on an explicit commitment to exchange domestic currency for a specified foreign currency at a fixed exchange rate. The domestic currency will be issued only against (fully backed) foreign exchange.

- *Conventional fixed-peg arrangements* The country (formally or *de facto*) pegs its currency at a fixed rate to another currency or a basket of currencies. The exchange rate may fluctuate within narrow margins and the parity rate may be adjusted.

- *Pegged exchange rates within horizontal bands* The value of the currency is maintained within certain (wider) margins of fluctuation around a fixed central rate.

- *Crawling pegs* The currency is adjusted periodically in small amounts at a fixed rate or in response to changes in selective quantitative indicators, such as past inflation differentials *vis-à-vis* major trading partners, etc.

- *Crawling bands* The currency is maintained within certain (wider) fluctuation margins and the central rate or margins are adjusted periodically.

- *Managed floating* The monetary authority attempts to influence the exchange rate without having a specific exchange rate path or target.

- *Independently floating* The exchange rate is market determined, with any official foreign exchange market intervention aimed at moderating the rate of change and preventing undue fluctuations in the exchange rate, rather than establishing a level for it.

Table 22.1 summarizes the policy choices made by most countries concerning the policy trilemma explained in Section 22.2 for each of the four most recent international monetary systems. During the gold standard era there was broad consensus to give up policy autonomy in exchange for capital mobility and maintaining fixed exchange rates. This broke down during the world wars and recession era, as most countries pursued activist monetary policies to

Table 22.1 The policy trilemma and the international economic order

| Era | Resolution of trilemma – countries choose to sacrifice: | | | Notes |
	policy autonomy	capital mobility	fixed exchange rate	
Gold standard	most	few	few	Broad consensus
World wars and recession	few	several	most	Capital controls especially in Centr. Europe, Lat. America
Bretton Woods	few	most	few	Broad consensus
Floating rates	few	few	many	Some consensus; currency boards, dollarization, etc.

Source: Obstfeld and Taylor (2003).

try to solve domestic problems at the cost of either imposing large capital controls or on giving up fixed exchange rates. In the Bretton Woods era there was again broad consensus to maintain fixed exchange rates, this time by sacrificing capital mobility (which was limited directly after the Second World War and then gradually increased). For the floating rates era, the table depicts the more recent policy choices as they have evolved over time, in which many countries have been willing to give up fixed exchange rates in return for policy autonomy and capital mobility. See Chapter 1 for information on the two waves of globalization regarding capital mobility.

22.7 International Monetary Fund (IMF)

As one of the Bretton Woods institutions, the International Monetary Fund (IMF) is located in Washington, DC and is the central institution of the international monetary system. It came into existence in 1946 and started operations one year later. With 184 member countries it covers virtually all countries in the world. The IMF's stated objectives are fourfold:

- the balanced expansion of world trade,
- stability of exchange rates,
- avoidance of competitive devaluations, and
- orderly correction of balance of payments problems.

The third of these stated objectives clearly points to the devastating experiences during the Great Depression; see Section 22.4.

The IMF employs about 2,800 people from many countries, with two-thirds of its professional staff economists. The highest IMF authority is the *Board of Governors*, which meets once a year with a representative from each of the member countries (usually the minister of finance or the president of the central bank). Key policy issues relating to the international monetary system are considered in the *International Monetary and Financial Committee* (IMFC), which meets twice per year. The day-to-day work is carried out by the *Executive Board*,

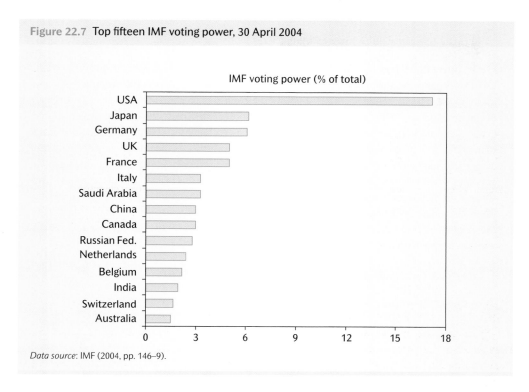

Figure 22.7 Top fifteen IMF voting power, 30 April 2004

Data source: IMF (2004, pp. 146–9).

consisting of 24 executive directors; with eight permanent members (USA, Japan, Germany, France, UK, China, Russia, and Saudi Arabia) and sixteen rotating members appointed for two years. Unlike some other international organizations, the IMF has a weighted-voting system, equiproportional to a country's quota in the IMF, which is determined broadly by its economic size and importance in international trade. See Figure 22.7 for the fifteen countries with the largest quota as of 2004.

The IMF gets its resources from the quota countries pay when they join the IMF and from periodic increases in these quota, of which countries pay 25 per cent in Special Drawing Rights (SDRs; see Box 22.3) or in major currencies. The quotas determine a country's voting power and the amount of financing it can receive from the IMF. The total quota increased to SDR 212 bn in 1999. In addition, the IMF has standing arrangements to borrow up to SDR 34 billion if there is a threat to the monetary system, namely under the General Arrangements to Borrow (GAB, set up in 1962 with eleven participants) and the New Arrangements to Borrow (NAB, set up in 1997 with 25 participants).

To perform its tasks, the IMF employs three main functions:

• *Surveillance* This is the annual regular consultation with and policy advice to IMF members regarding policies to promote economic growth and stable exchange rates. The IMF views are published in the *World Economic Outlook* and the *Global Financial Stability Report*. Moreover, all member states are annually reviewed on their macroeconomic policies through so-called Article IV consultations.

• *Technical assistance* This consists of training and assistance for fiscal, monetary, and exchange rate policies, supervision of the banking system, financial regulation, and statistics

Box 22.3   Special Drawing Rights (SDRs)

Under the Bretton Woods system, the international monetary system largely depended on gold and US dollars to provide it with the international reserves necessary to support the expansion of world trade. To avoid the dependence of the supply of reserve assets on gold production and US balance of payments deficits (which were needed to provide US dollar reserves), the IMF introduced Special Drawing Rights (SDRs) in 1969, an artificial international reserve asset which the IMF could allocate to members as a percentage of their quotas when the need arose. As the IMF's unit of account, this 'paper gold' has no physical form but is used as a bookkeeping entry for transactions among member countries or with the IMF. The latest allocation, to a total of SDR 21.4 billion, took place in 1981. The value of the SDR is set using a basket of four major currencies, the composition of which is reviewed every five years. In October 2004, one SDR was a composite of euros, yen, pounds, and dollars (approximately 36, 13, 12, and 39 per cent, respectively) and worth about US$ 1.47; see Table 22.2.

Table 22.2 Composition and value of one SDR on 8 October 2004

(a). Composition of one SDR

Currency	Weight (units)	Value in USD	Per cent of total
Euro	0.4260	0.524576	36
Japanese yen	21.0000	0.190097	13
Pound sterling	0.0984	0.175831	12
US dollar	0.5770	0.577000	39
Total value of SDR in US dollar		1.467504	100

(b). Value of one SDR in selected currencies

Euro	1.19164	Australian dollar	2.01636
Japanese yen	162.277	Chinese yuan	12.1462
Pound sterling	0.821254	Indian rupee	67.2558
US dollar	1.4675	Swiss franc	1.84964

provision. See Figure 22.8 for the regional distribution of this assistance. After the collapse of the Soviet Union, for example, the IMF helped the Baltic states and Russia set up treasury systems for their central banks.

- *Financial assistance* This is provided in particular to countries with balance of payments problems, conditional on implementation of a policy programme designed in conjunction with the IMF to correct these problems. For example: (i) during the 1997–98 Asian financial crisis the IMF pledged $21 billion to Korea to reform its economy and (ii) in October 2000 the IMF approved a $52 million loan (part of a three-year $193 million loan) to help Kenya cope with the effects of a severe drought.

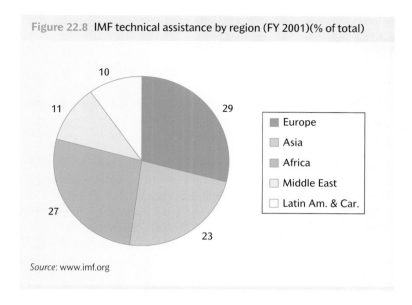

Figure 22.8 IMF technical assistance by region (FY 2001)(% of total)

Source: www.imf.org

IMF loans are in principle temporary, usually at low interest rates, and conditional on economic policy implementations. In most cases, IMF approval provides a lending signal to other institutions and investors, enabling the country to attract additional funds.

22.8 World Bank

The World Bank is the sister organization of the IMF. Like the IMF, it is located in Washington, DC and has 184 member countries. It came into existence in 1945 and started operations in 1947. Its primary objective is to fight poverty and assist less developed countries in their efforts to improve standards of living and reduce poverty. The World Bank Group consists of the following five institutions:[3]

- *International Bank for Reconstruction and Development* (IBRD; established 1945, fiscal 2004 lending: $11 billion for 87 new operations in 33 countries). The IBRD aims to reduce poverty in middle-income and creditworthy poorer countries. It is able to borrow at low cost and offer its clients good borrowing terms.

- *International Development Association* (IDA; established 1960, fiscal 2004 commitments: $9 billion for 158 new operations in 62 countries). The IDA provides interest-free credits and grants to the world's 81 poorest countries (with 2.5 billion inhabitants) that otherwise have little or no capacity to borrow on market terms.

- *International Finance Corporation* (IFC; established 1956, fiscal 2004 commitments: $4.8 billion for 217 projects in 65 countries). Working with business partners and without government guarantees, the IFC promotes economic development through the private sector by providing equity, long-term loans, finance and risk management products, etc.

- *Multilateral Investment Guarantee Agency* (MIGA; established 1988, fiscal 2004 guarantees issued: $1.1 billion). The MIGA helps promote foreign direct investment in developing countries by providing guarantees to investors against non-commercial risks, such as expropriation, currency inconvertibility, war and civil disturbance, etc.

- *International Centre for Settlement of Investment Disputes* (ICSID; established 1966, fiscal 2004 cases registered: 30). The ICSID helps encourage foreign investment by providing international facilities for conciliation and arbitration of investment disputes, thereby helping foster an atmosphere of mutual confidence between states and foreign investors.

The World Bank employs about 10,000 people (of whom 3,000 in country offices) from many countries, including economists, educators, environmental scientists, financial analysts, anthropologists, engineers, etc. The World Bank is run like a cooperative with the member countries as shareholders, where the weight is determined by the size of a member's economy; in 2004 the USA had 16.41 per cent of the votes, Japan had 7.87 per cent, Germany had 4.49 per cent, etc. The highest authority is the *Board of Governors*, which meets once a year with a representative from each of the member countries (usually the minister of finance or the minister of development). The day-to-day work is carried out by the *Executive Directors*, with five permanent members (USA, Japan, Germany, France, and UK). According to an unwritten rule, the Bank's president is an American, while the managing director of the IMF is a European.

Both the IMF and the World Bank have been under a lot of criticism in the past decade regarding the efficacy of their policies. The advice given to the IMF and the World Bank is as diverse as its critics are, where some so-called 'supply-siders' argue that the policies are too 'Keynesian' and others that they are too 'neo-liberal', thinking that free competition and market forces will automatically bring prosperity.[4] Some think that the Bretton Woods institutions undermine the national sovereignty of recipient countries and see these institutions as the political tools of Western nations and multinational enterprises.

We should keep in mind, however, that the processes of improving living standards and fighting poverty, the primary tasks of the World Bank, are enormously complicated and time consuming. Adequate evaluation of policy recommendations should be done on a case-by-case basis, taking the country-specific circumstances into consideration. There is no simple panacea for all problems. Like all other institutions and individuals, the World Bank is not infallible and has made plenty of mistakes. At the same time, its assistance and aid have been extremely valuable for alleviating poverty, sometimes under the most difficult of circumstances. In response to its critics, the World Bank has switched from economic growth in the aggregate to poverty reduction and supporting small local enterprises. It is investing in clean water, education, and sustainable development, while adopting a range of safeguard policies to ensure that their projects do not harm certain individuals or groups. It provides detailed information on its analysis and policy recommendations on its website: www.worldbank.org.

Similarly, we should keep in mind that by its very nature the IMF usually enters the public arena only once a country is in dire financial straits, sometimes after years of mismanagement or outright theft invisible to the outside world. Local nationals, politicians in particular, are more than willing to point to the IMF as an easy target to blame for the economic hardship associated with trying to overcome these years of mismanagement and theft. Like the World Bank, the IMF is not infallible and can point at both success and failure in its policy

Table 22.3 **IMF voting power and the economy: selected countries, 2003**

Country	Country share in world total (%)		
	Population	GDP, PPP	IMF voting power
China	20.54	12.47	2.94
India	16.97	5.96	1.92
Belgium	0.17	0.58	2.13

Sources: World Bank Development Indicators CD-ROM 2005 and www.imf.org

recommendations. Of course, countries can always choose not to borrow from the IMF in the first place. In response to its critics, the IMF has greatly increased its transparency in recent years. Its reports, board discussions, consultations, and the staff's analysis is now public information, largely available at the IMF's website: www.imf.org. One important point of criticism, regarding the lopsided distribution of voting rights, remains. Developing countries are in general underrepresented and developed countries (Europe in particular) are overrepresented, either when compared to the size of the population or their share in world income. This is illustrated in Table 22.3 for China, India, and Belgium. As the economic clout of the Asian countries is increasing relative to that in the rest of the world, the IMF faces the challenge of reflecting this increased influence in its distribution of voting power.

22.9 Bank for International Settlements (BIS)

Located in Basel, Switzerland, the Bank for International Settlements (BIS) was established in 1930 and is the oldest international financial institution. Initially, the BIS dealt with German reparations issues (hence its name), but its focus quickly shifted to central bank cooperation in pursuit of financial and monetary stability. After the Second World War, the BIS focused on implementing the Bretton Woods system until this system collapsed in 1971. During the oil crises in the 1970s and 1980s the focus was on managing cross-border capital flows and eventually on regulatory supervision of internationally active banks. This led to the Basel Capital Accord in 1988, an agreement among the Group 10 central banks to apply minimum capital standards to their banking sectors (by defining capital and the structure of risk weights). As a result of advances in risk management and technology, a revision of these standards, known as Basel II, is under way (2001–2006), leading to more risk-sensitive minimum capital requirements for banking organizations.

The BIS has a modest staff of fewer than 600 persons and in 2004 had 55 member central banks, including the OECD countries (see Chapter 12), but for example also Brazil, India, China, Indonesia, Mexico, and the Philippines. Voting power is proportional to BIS shares issued in the country of each member. The BIS also performs traditional banking functions, such as foreign exchange and gold transactions, and trustee and agency functions. It was, for example, the agent for the European exchange rate arrangements such as the European Monetary System (EMS, 1979–94) before the introduction of a single currency, see Chapter 30. Finally, the BIS is instrumental in collecting, compiling, and disseminating economic and financial statistics, such as the triennial central bank survey of foreign exchange and derivatives market activity (see Chapter 19). This information is available on its website: www.bis.org.

22.10 Conclusions

The policy trilemma argues that of the three policy objectives (i) fixed exchange rates, (ii) capital mobility, and (iii) policy autonomy, it is only possible to simultaneously achieve two objectives at the expense of the third objective. We reviewed the main choices made in history for the four most recent international monetary systems: (a) the gold standard, (b) world wars and recession, (c) Bretton Woods, and (d) the floating rates era. During the gold standard era there was broad consensus to give up policy autonomy in exchange for capital mobility and maintaining fixed exchange rates. This broke down during the world wars and recession era, as most countries pursued activist monetary policies to try to solve domestic problems at the cost of either imposing large capital controls or on giving up fixed exchange rates. In the Bretton Woods era there was again broad consensus to maintain fixed exchange rates, this time by sacrificing capital mobility (which was limited directly after the Second World War and then gradually increased). In the floating rates era, many countries have been willing to give up fixed exchange rates in return for policy autonomy and capital mobility. The International Monetary Fund is the central institution of the international monetary system, providing surveillance, technical assistance, and financial assistance in case of problems. Special Drawing Rights are artificial international reserves created by the IMF. The World Bank Group consists of five institutions focusing on poverty reduction. The Bank of International Settlements is an organization for central bank cooperation.

QUESTIONS

Question 22.1

22.1A A nation might try to achieve three main policy objectives, namely monetary policy independence, a fixed exchange rate, and international capital mobility. What are the merits of each of these objectives? Why are they desirable?

22.1B Since the year 2000, US policy makers have grown concerned about the exchange rate between the US dollar and the Chinese yuan. Effectively, the yuan was fixed to the dollar at a rate they considered to be inappropriate. Moreover, China was able to maintain some monetary independence. What does this imply for capital mobility?

22.1C The buoyant growth of the Chinese economy in the twenty-first century has attracted a great deal of capital towards China. Given that capital restrictions are hard to enforce perfectly, Chinese money growth has been rapid. What does this imply for monetary policy independence?

22.1D As the Chinese economy integrates ever more tightly into the global economic system, capital restrictions will become ever harder to enforce. What policy options do the Chinese monetary authorities have in light of this development?

Question 22.2

22.2A At the end of the nineteenth century many industrialized nations moved to a gold standard. Several drawbacks to this standard are discussed in the text. One is that the rate of inflation is influenced by the discovery of gold supplies. Explain why this is so.

22.2B The IMF has various classifications for different exchange rate regimes. How would you classify the gold standard? Explain.

22.2C The First World War effectively ended the gold standard era. Can you explain, with the help of the policy trilemma, why the start of the First World War caused policy makers to change their monetary arrangements?

22.2D When the Great Depression hit in 1929, countries often engaged in beggar-thy-neighbour policies. Can you explain how this works?

22.2E The Bretton Woods Agreement sought to enact a new and stable international monetary order. This order eventually broke down due to diverging economic policy interests. Explain with the policy trinity (for the USA, Germany, and Japan) how this came about.

22.2F The Bretton Woods Agreement was brought down by the $n-1$ problem. Is the $n-1$ problem typical for all exchange rate regimes?

Question 22.3

22.3A In the past decades a significant number of Latin American countries have moved towards dollarization. What is dollarization and how would you classify this arrangement?

22.3B What motivations could these governments have to dollarize? Why didn't they yennize, or rupeeize?

22.3C Some economic analysts have argued that only corner solutions for exchange rate regimes are sustainable in the long run. They believe that only a fully floating currency or a very solid fixed arrangement (currency board or separate legal tender) is durable. Explain why this might be so.

22.3D Do we observe the corner solutions argument in practice?

22.3E Of the rich industrialized economies (USA, Japan, euro area), none has a fixed exchange rate regime relative to each other. Explain why this is so, using the policy trilemma.

 See the Online Resource Centre for a Study Guide containing more questions
www.oxfordtextbooks.co.uk/orc/vanmarrewijk/

NOTES

1 See Brakman et al. (2006) for a similar analysis.
2 General historical information in the next four sections is based on the Wikipedia encyclopaedia; see http://en.wikipedia.org
3 The term 'World Bank' refers only to IBRD and IDA.
4 See any standard macroeconomics textbook on this terminology.

III.B
EXCHANGE RATES

Part III.B provides an overview of basic exchange rate theories. We discuss the elasticity and aborption approach (Chapter 23), the (long-run) monetary approach (Chapter 24), the (short-run) effects of monetary and fiscal policy (Chapter 25), and the transition from short-run to long-run in a sticky-price model with rational expectations (Chapter 26).

ELASTICITIES AND ABSORPTION

23

Objectives/key terms

- Marshall–Lerner condition
- Volume effect and value effect
- Pricing to market
- Domestic and external equilibrium
- Tinbergen rule
- Principle of effective market classification

- Elasticities approach
- Pass-through analysis
- Absorption approach
- Swan diagram
- Assignment problem

The elasticities approach focuses on the relationship between exchange rates and the current account balance. The absorption approach extends this framework to include income effects, which enables the analysis of some simple policy adjustment problems.

23.1 Introduction

Our discussion on the economic consequences of (changes in) exchange rates first focuses on their impact on the current account. It is important to keep in mind that this chapter will therefore basically ignore the capital account of the balance of payments and any role it may have on influencing exchange rates and exchange rate equilibrium. One reason for this neglect of the capital account, which will be remedied in the chapters to come, is the tight capital controls that were in place during the time period the theories discussed below were put forward. An advantage of this neglect is that it allows us to build up our knowledge on the impact of exchange rates gradually, thus making it easier for us to understand at a later stage how the capital account will influence our earlier acquired insights. The remainder of this chapter will start with an analysis of changes in the real exchange rate, which is the price of foreign goods relative to domestic goods. We then incorporate basic income effects into this analysis, which allows us to analyse simple adjustment problems.

23.2 Elasticities and the Marshall–Lerner condition

In Chapter 20 we defined the real exchange rate Q as the product of the nominal exchange rate S and the ratio of the price indices P for the two countries; see Section (20.4). Suppose the EU is the home country and the US is the foreign country. We let S denote the nominal exchange rate of the US dollar, so it is the number of euros we have to pay in order to purchase one dollar, and we let P_{EU} and P_{US} be the price level in the EU and the USA, respectively. Obviously, the price level is measured in *euros* in the EU and in *dollars* in the USA. The real exchange rate is defined as:

$$(23.1) \qquad Q = S \frac{P_{US}}{P_{EU}}$$

Note that the real exchange rate is a *relative* price (the exchange rate measured in €/$ multiplied by the price ratio in $/€), namely the price of American goods relative to European

---

Famous economists	Alfred Marshall

Fig. 23.1
Alfred Marshall
(1842–1924)

Born into a middle-class family in London and raised to enter the clergy, Alfred Marshall instead became the dominant academic figure in economics after the publication of *Principles of Economics: An Introductory Text* (1890). In this book he emphasized that the price and output of a good are determined by both demand and supply. This concept is still used today to understand if changes in either demand or supply cause changes in observed prices and quantities. Marshall also introduced the concepts of price elasticity, consumer surplus, and producer surplus, thus laying the foundations of welfare economics. In economic dynamics he favoured what he referred to as economic biology, arguing that technology, institutions, and preferences evolve over time, along with the behaviour of people in response to those changes.

goods. The real exchange rate increases, that is American goods become more expensive relative to European goods, if:

- the nominal exchange rate S increases (say from 0.80 to 1.20 euros per dollar),
- the price level in America increases, or
- the price level in Europe decreases.

For a consumer, whether she is living in Europe or America, any of these three changes indicates that American goods become more expensive relative to European goods. In general, therefore, we expect an increase in the real exchange rate to cause a substitution of consumption away from American goods towards European goods in both countries.

The *elasticities approach* focuses on the relationship between the (real) exchange rate and the flow of goods and services as measured by the current account balance. Let X denote the exports of European goods to America and let M denote the imports of American goods into Europe. As argued above, these export and import levels are functions of the real exchange rate, which is the price of American goods relative to European goods. If the real exchange rate Q increases, American goods become more expensive, which not only reduces the European demand for imports M but also increases the demand for European exports X. We can summarize both effects in the current account balance CA, which measures our net exports. Suppose we use European goods as numéraire, then the current account balance is given as:

$$(23.2) \qquad CA(Q) = X(\overset{+}{Q}) - Q \cdot M(\overset{-}{Q})$$

Note that we must pre-multiply our imports M from America, which is measured in American goods, with the real exchange rate Q, the relative price of American goods, to ensure that all our measurements are in European goods. The equation summarizes how our export and import levels, and hence our current account balance, depend on the real exchange rate.

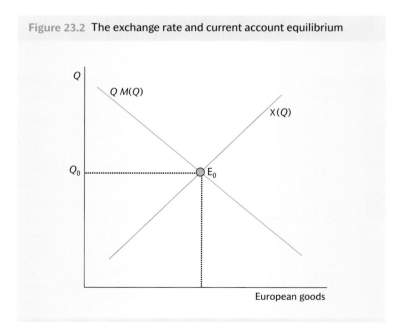

Figure 23.2 The exchange rate and current account equilibrium

If we ignore the capital account of the balance of payments or if capital flows are severely restricted or very limited, as they have been in the past for currently developed countries and are at present for some developing countries, equation (23.2) can be viewed as a simple equilibrium condition for the real exchange rate Q, namely by requiring equilibrium on the current account $(CA = 0)$. This is illustrated in Figure 23.2, where the current account is in equilibrium at the point of intersection of the X and QM curves (point E_0), leading to the equilibrium real exchange rate Q_0. Moreover, as is evident from equation (23.1), if we assume that the price levels in Europe and America are constant (or their ratio is constant), then equation (23.2) is tantamount to an equilibrium condition for the nominal exchange rate S; see Box 23.1. Under that additional assumption, then, the analysis below on the real exchange rate also holds for the nominal exchange rate.

A rise in net exports is frequently referred to as an *improvement* of the current account and a fall as a *deterioration*. Although this terminology is confusing from a welfare perspective (as there is nothing particularly good or bad about such changes in the current account; see Chapter 2), it does make sense from a stability perspective in this framework. Note that the curve QM is drawn downward sloping in Figure 23.2, which implicitly assumes that the *value effect* of a rise in Q, which given the import level ($\overline{M}$, say) raises the term $Q\overline{M}$, is more than compensated by the *volume effect* of the fall in imports M caused by the increase in the real exchange rate. In general, this need not be the case, which led Marshall (1923) and Lerner (1944) to analyse under which conditions an increase in the real exchange rate leads to an improvement of the current account. To do this they defined the price elasticity of export demand $\varepsilon_x = (Q/X)X' > 0$ and the price elasticity of import demand $\varepsilon_m = -(Q/M)M' > 0$ to derive what is now known as the Marshall–Lerner condition (starting from initial equilibrium; see Technical Note 23.1):

(23.3) $$CA'(Q) > 0 \Leftrightarrow \varepsilon_x + \varepsilon_m > 1$$

Figure 23.3 The Marshall–Lerner condition and stability

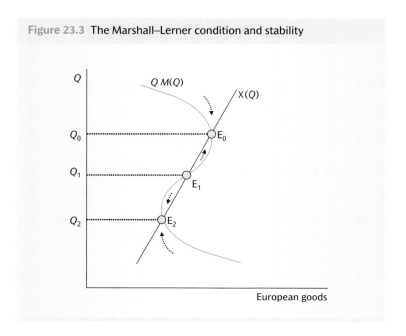

European goods

Suppose there is a surplus on the European current account ($X > QM$), indicating that the value of European exports of goods and services to America is higher than the value of European imports from America. If we see that as an indication that American goods are too expensive (or European goods are too cheap), we should expect the relative price of American goods to decline ($Q\downarrow$). Similarly, if there is a deficit on the European current account we should expect the relative price of American goods to increase. Under this, admittedly rather simple, adjustment mechanism, the Marshall–Lerner condition determines whether or not the equilibrium real exchange rate is stable. This is illustrated in Figure 23.3 in which, in contrast to Figure 23.2, there is a range of real exchange rates for which the value effect dominates the volume effect of QM. This gives rise to multiple equilibria, denoted E_0, E_1, and E_2, with concomitant real exchange rate Q_0, Q_1, and Q_2. The dashed arrows in the figure indicate whether the real exchange rate is rising or falling, showing that equilibria E_0 and E_2 are stable, whereas equilibrium E_1 is not. Equivalently, the Marshall–Lerner condition is satisfied for equilibria E_0 and E_2, and not for equilibrium E_1.

 Box 23.1   Fixed exchange rates and intervention

The framework of Section 23.2 can easily be used to illustrate the fundamentals of fixing exchange rates if we, as suggested in the main text, assume that the price levels in Europe and America are fixed. For simplicity, we normalize the ratio of the price levels to unity, such that equation (23.1) simplifies to $Q=S$ and equation (23.2) becomes:

(23.2′) $CA(S) = X(S) - S \cdot M(S)$

This is illustrated in Figure 23.4, with the initial equilibrium at point A and the associated exchange rate equal to S_0.

Figure 23.4 Fixed exchange rates and intervention

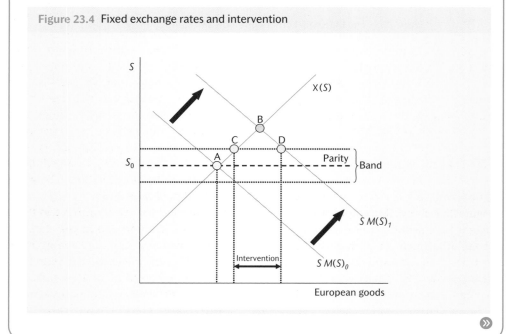

> » Now suppose that the *SM (S)* curve shifts to the right, perhaps because Europeans have developed an extra taste for American goods and want to import more of these goods for any given exchange rate. Under flexible exchange rates this shift would lead to a new equilibrium at point B in Figure 23.4 and a concomitant appreciation of the US dollar (and equivalent devaluation of the euro). If the ECB wants to fix the value of the euro at the old equilibrium level S_0, however, it will not allow the dollar to appreciate by that much. As illustrated in Figure 23.4, fixed exchange rate regimes usually allow for a band width around the parity rate S_0, which implies that the dollar exchange rate will appreciate to $S_0 + band / 2$ with the difference between the demand and supply of dollars, as given by the points D and C in Figure 23.4, supplied by the ECB. See also Chapter 20.

23.3 Elasticities and time: the J-curve

The analysis in Section 23.2 shows under which condition an appreciation of the US dollar (which is a depreciation of the euro) leads to an improvement of the European current account balance. We did not say anything about the time required to achieve this improvement. Here we have to distinguish between the value effect of the real exchange rate appreciation of the dollar, which is instantaneous, and the volume effect that the change of the relative price of American goods has on our export and import levels, which requires time to adjust.

Let's first focus on the value effect, starting from an initial current account equilibrium, say $0 = \overline{X} - \overline{Q}\,\overline{M}$. If the real exchange rate rises at time t_1 to $\hat{Q} > \overline{Q}$ and there is no instantaneous adjustment of the export and import levels, the *impact effect* of the dollar appreciation is a deterioration rather than an improvement of the European current account since $\overline{X} - \hat{Q}\overline{M} < \overline{X} - \overline{Q}\,\overline{M} = 0$. As illustrated in Figure 23.5, this follows from the simple fact that the price increase of American goods has made our imports more expensive, leading to an immediate deterioration of the current account at the old export and import levels.

Turning now to the volume effects of the real exchange rate change, it is clear that the substitution away from American to European goods requires time to adjust. Consumers need time to substitute between different goods and adjust their consumption patterns, and producers need time to attract new capital, install new plants, hire workers, build new distribution channels, etc. We should expect, therefore, that the price elasticities of export and import demand are gradually increasing over time, leading only gradually to the required improvement of the current account balance. As illustrated in Figure 23.5, the current account balance is only back to its initial position at time t_2, leading to an improvement thereafter as denoted by the long-run effect. Since the shape of the initial deterioration in between the time periods t_1 and t_2 resembles the letter J, this is called the *J-curve* effect.

Figure 23.6 shows IMF empirical estimates of the J-curve effect for five countries and three different time periods. It provides estimated price elasticities of export and import demand after an adjustment of six months (short run), one year (medium run), and the ultimate effect when the adjustment is complete (long run). In all cases, the estimated elasticities increase when the adjustment period increases. With the exception of Denmark, the Marshall–Lerner condition is not satisfied for the short run, indicating an initial deterioration of the current account balance after a real depreciation of the domestic currency in

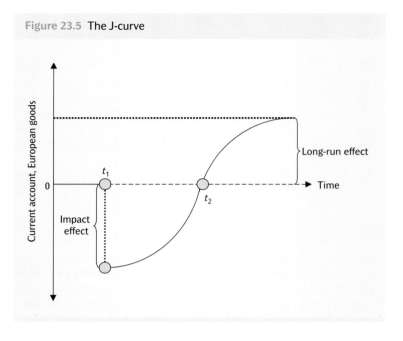

Figure 23.5 The J-curve

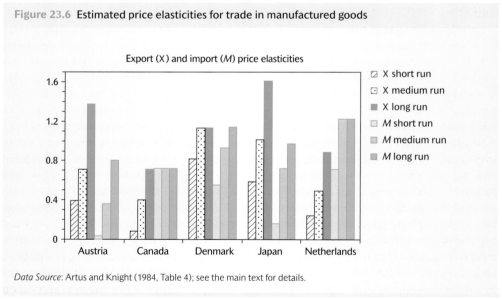

Figure 23.6 Estimated price elasticities for trade in manufactured goods

Data Source: Artus and Knight (1984, Table 4); see the main text for details.

accordance with the J-curve effect. For all countries in the figure, the medium- and long-run estimated elasticities do satisfy the Marshall–Lerner condition, indicating that an adjustment lag of one year is usually sufficient to ensure that a depreciation of the domestic currency leads to an improvement of the current account. The next section discusses the J-curve for the USA in the 1980s.

Box 23.2   Pass-through analysis and pricing to market

As noted and analysed in Box 23.1, the economic consequences of changes in the real exchange rate are identical to those of changes in the nominal exchange rate if the domestic and foreign price levels are fixed in the short run. This remark, however, implicitly assumes that exporters and importers completely pass through changes in the nominal exchange rate to changes in the price level charged in the foreign country, as well as implicitly assuming that either the Law of One Price holds or some version of PPP; see Chapter 20. In practice, this is not the case, as studied in *pass-through analysis*.

Suppose, for example, that the Word™ program sells for $100 in the USA. If the exchange rate is €1 per dollar, it should sell for €100 in Europe according to the Law of One Price. If the dollar appreciates to €1.10 per dollar, the Word program should be selling for €110 if Microsoft® decides to completely pass through the increase in the dollar exchange rate. And it should be selling for €90 if one week later the dollar depreciates to €0.90 per dollar. There are two good reasons why Microsoft may decide not to do this. First, changing the price in local currency (in this case in euros) is costly, so rather than announcing daily changes in its price level, Microsoft will rather change its prices less frequently, reflecting somewhat longer-term changes in the exchange rate. Second, Microsoft will realize that changes in its European price level will affect its competitive position. Since it has the power to determine its own price, it will take into consideration how changes in its European price level will alter its competitive position. This *pricing-to-market* behaviour will make it unlikely that Microsoft will completely pass through an appreciation of the US dollar to higher European prices (at least in the short run); see Dornbusch (1987) and Krugman (1987).

23.4 Application: Plaza, Louvre, and the J-curve

The fall of the Shah of Iran in 1979 initiated a second oil shock, with prices rising rapidly from $13 to $32 per barrel.[1] This led to high inflation rates and a sharp recession, with high unemployment rates in the oil-importing countries, including the USA. In October 1979 Paul Volcker, chairman of the Federal Reserve, announced a tightening of monetary policy to fight inflation. Ronald Reagan was elected president in November 1980 and kept his promise to lower taxes starting in 1981 (he also promised to balance the budget, but that is another matter). The combined effects of the tight monetary policy, high interest rates, and the fiscal expansion started to drive the value of the US dollar up on the foreign exchange markets from 1981 onwards; see Figure 23.7. The appreciation of the dollar made it easier to fight inflation, so monetary policy could be relaxed. Together with the continued fiscal expansion, the American economy started to grow rapidly and unemployment fell (see the next section on connections between exchange rates and unemployment), which in turn led to a further appreciation of the dollar.

The American current account balance was −0.01 per cent of GDP in 1979. In accordance with the J-curve effect, it improved slightly in 1980 and 1981 (to 0.08 and 0.16 per cent, respectively) before it started to deteriorate with a delay from 1982 onwards. Since the dollar was continuing to appreciate in real terms, the current account continued to deteriorate with a delay. Eventually, the dollar would reach its maximum real value in February 1985, about

Figure 23.7 USA: Plaza, Louvre, and J-curve

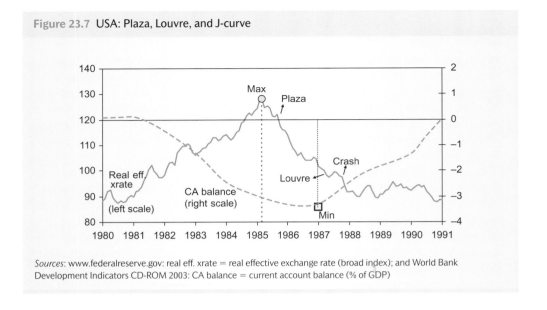

Sources: www.federalreserve.gov: real eff. xrate = real effective exchange rate (broad index); and World Bank Development Indicators CD-ROM 2003: CA balance = current account balance (% of GDP)

46 per cent higher than it had been in June 1980. The lowest value on the current account balance of −3.42 per cent of GDP was reached in 1987.

In the course of 1985 it was clear that the dollar was overvalued, which contributed to the American economic slowdown which had started in 1984 and to mounting protectionist pressure in America. On 22 September 1985 the Reagan Administration no longer ignored this link between the strong dollar and mounting protectionism, and announced at a meeting in the Plaza Hotel in New York that the Group of Five (G-5 = USA, Japan, Germany, Britain, and France) countries would jointly intervene in the foreign exchange market to reduce the value of the dollar. This led to a sharp fall the next day, which continued for about one and a half years until February 1987, when the real value of the dollar had reached a level about 30 per cent below its peak level of two years earlier. In a new meeting at the Louvre in Paris the G-5 declared that the dollar was 'broadly consistent with underlying economic fundamentals'. For a while there was an implicit agreement to intervene in the foreign exchange market if the dollar moved outside a band of plus or minus 5 per cent of certain parity rates relative to Germany and Japan. This period ended with the US stock market crash in October 1987, driving the real value of the dollar down until it reached a level in March 1988 roughly similar to the level it had been in December 1980.

23.5 Absorption approach

The elasticities approach discussed in Section 23.2 focuses exclusively on the effect of changes in relative prices on imports, exports, and the current account balance. This implies that it ignores the influence of income effects for determining these variables. After all, if the European income level rises, we should expect an increase in the level of European imports

Figure 23.8 Domestic equilibrium

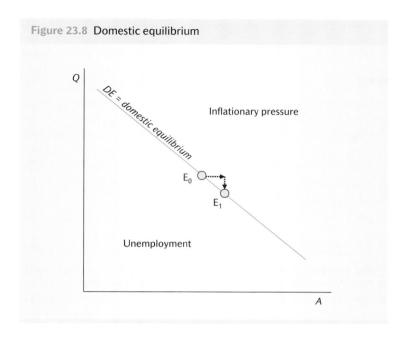

from America for any given relative price of American goods. The *absorption approach*, see Alexander (1951) and Black (1959), remedies this shortcoming of the elasticities approach in a simple Keynesian framework. The term absorption, which we will denote by A, refers to the total spending level in an economy and is equal to the sum of consumption spending C, investment spending I, and government spending G. Let Y denote income. Recall the simple income equation:

(23.4) $$Y = \underbrace{C + I + G}_{absorption \equiv A} + (X - M) \Leftrightarrow Y - A = X - M$$

The second part of equation (23.4) clarifies that if income exceeds absorption there is a current account surplus, while if absorption exceeds income there is a current account deficit. The absorption approach thus emphasizes that the excess of domestic demand over domestic production will have to be met by imports.

We are now in a position to describe macroeconomic equilibrium and characterize different types of disequilibria. Let's start with the *domestic equilibrium*, defined as that level of output corresponding to the natural rate of unemployment, that is the rate of unemployment that does not lead to an accelerating rate of inflation; see Friedman (1968). In this simple framework output depends on the level of absorption A and on the real exchange rate of the US dollar Q:

(23.5) $$Y = Y(\overset{+}{A}, \overset{+}{Q})$$

As indicated by equation (23.5), the influence of both variables on output is positive. This leads to a negatively sloped curve representing domestic equilibrium in (A,Q)-space, as illustrated in Figure 23.8. Suppose we start from point E_0, a point of initial domestic equilibrium, and the level of absorption increases. At a given real exchange rate Q, this increased demand for domestic goods lowers unemployment and therefore leads to inflationary pressure in the economy. To restore equilibrium, the relative price of American goods Q will have to decline such that the reduced demand in America for European export goods and the increased demand in Europe for American import goods reduces the European output level and returns us back to the natural rate of unemployment. As also illustrated in Figure 23.8, everywhere above the curve representing domestic equilibrium the economy will experience inflationary pressure, while everywhere below the line the economy will experience unemployment.

We turn now to the *external equilibrium*, that is combinations of absorption A and the real exchange rate Q for which the current account is in equilibrium.[2] The current account balance depends negatively on the level of absorption because an increase in domestic spending leads to an increased demand for import goods. It depends positively on the real exchange rate Q, provided the Marshall–Lerner condition is fulfilled:

$$(23.6) \qquad\qquad CA = CA(\bar{A},\overset{+}{Q})$$

Figure 23.9 depicts combinations of absorption and the real exchange rate with external equilibrium. On the basis of equation (23.6), the curve is upward sloping in (A,Q)-space. Starting from point E_0, a point of initial external equilibrium, an increase in the level of absorption for a given real exchange rate will lead to additional import demand and therefore a current account deficit. To restore external equilibrium the relative price of American goods Q will have to increase, so as to increase the demand in America for European exports and reduce the demand in Europe for American imports and eliminate the European current account deficit. As also illustrated in Figure 23.9, everywhere below the curve representing external equilibrium Europe experiences a current account deficit, while everywhere above this curve it experiences a current account surplus.

Figure 23.9 External equilibrium

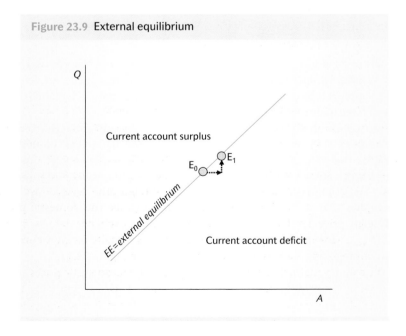

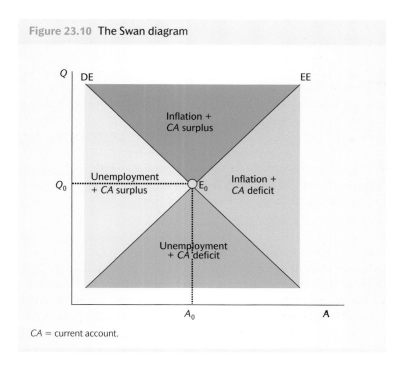

Figure 23.10 The Swan diagram

CA = current account.

Figure 23.10 combines the information on domestic equilibrium and external equilibrium in one graph. It is named after the Australian economist Trevor Swan. There is a unique combination of absorption and the real exchange rate (A_0, Q_0) for which the economy is both in domestic equilibrium and in external equilibrium; see Swan (1955). For any other combination of absorption and the real exchange rate the economy is in one of four disequilibrium regimes, namely (i) unemployment + *CA* deficit, (ii) unemployment + *CA* surplus, (iii) inflation + *CA* deficit, or (iv) inflation + *CA* surplus.

23.6 Adjustment problems

On the basis of the absorption–elasticity framework developed in Section 23.5 and summarized by the Swan diagram we can illustrate several types of adjustment problems. In this section we will focus on two of these problems, namely the *Tinbergen rule* and the *assignment problem*. The former can be illustrated using the dilemma analysed by Meade (1951). Suppose we are investigating a small country with a fixed exchange rate regime and sticky prices (see Chapter 24 on sticky prices). It cannot influence the foreign price level, so we take that as given. This implies that the real exchange rate is fixed (since the domestic price level is sticky, the foreign price level is given, and the nominal exchange rate is fixed), say at $Q_0 = S \cdot P_{foreign} / P_{home}$. Moreover, suppose that the country is initially facing a current account deficit and unemployment, such as illustrated by point E_0 in Figure 23.11.

As long as the country maintains it fixed exchange rate and its domestic prices are sticky, the economy cannot move away from the horizontal line at $Q = Q_0$ in Figure 23.11. The policy makers now face the following dilemma. To alleviate the domestic unemployment problem they may try to stimulate an increase in absorption, thus moving the economy from point E_0

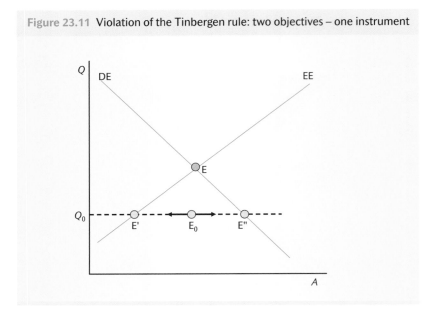

Figure 23.11 Violation of the Tinbergen rule: two objectives – one instrument

into the direction of point E″. Although this movement lowers the level of unemployment, it comes at a price, namely an increase in the current account deficit because the economy is simultaneously moving away from the external equilibrium curve. Alternatively, the policy makers may decide to alleviate the current account deficit by trying to stimulate a reduction in absorption, thus moving the economy from point E_0 into the direction of point E′. Although this movement lowers the current account deficit, it again comes at a price, namely an increase in unemployment because the economy is simultaneously moving away from the domestic equilibrium curve. In short, the policy makers face a choice: they can either try to achieve domestic equilibrium *or* external equilibrium, but not both simultaneously. The problem arises because the policy makers violate the Tinbergen rule; that is, they try to achieve two objectives (domestic and external equilibrium) with one policy instrument (the level of absorption). According to Tinbergen (1952) this is not possible. This is formulated in the

Tinbergen rule: a government can only achieve any number of policy objectives if it has at least the same number of independent policy instruments available.

In this case, the government can reach both domestic and external equilibrium if it adjusts both the level of absorption and the exchange rate.[3]

This brings us to the second adjustment problem. Suppose the government decides to give up on fixing the exchange rate and uses the level of absorption and the exchange rate to achieve both domestic and external equilibrium. Which instrument should it use for which policy target? To answer this *assignment problem* Mundell (1962) developed the:

Principle of effective market classification: each policy instrument should be assigned to the target variable on which it has the greatest relative effect.

A simple illustration of this principle is given in Figure 23.12 in an admittedly rather restrictive framework (see, however, the discussion below). Suppose we start again at a point

Figure 23.12 The assignment problem

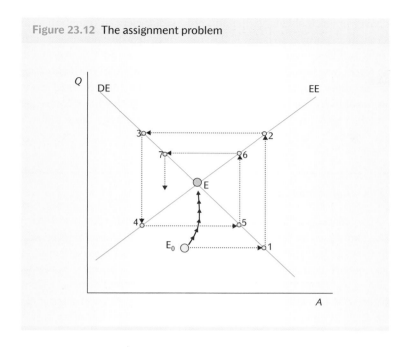

of unemployment and current account deficit, such as point E_0 in the figure. Furthermore, suppose the policy makers can somehow sequentially adjust the level of absorption and the real exchange rate to achieve domestic and external equilibrium, where they decide to use the level of absorption to achieve domestic equilibrium and the real exchange rate to achieve external equilibrium. The hypothetical path the economy would then follow if we first try to achieve domestic equilibrium is indicated by the points 1, 2, 3, 4, . . . It is clear that the economy will eventually reach both domestic and external equilibrium at point E if this path is followed indefinitely.[4] If, however, we were to reverse the instrument – target selection in this case–that is, use the absorption level to achieve external equilibrium and the real exchange rate to achieve domestic equilibrium, then we would move *away* from full equilibrium at point E rather than towards it. This is most easily seen in Figure 23.12 by starting at point 7 and reversing the arrows to points 6, 5, 4, etc., moving further and further away from full equilibrium. The latter pairing of instruments and targets is thus a violation of the principle of effective market classification. Clearly, which instrument should, according to this rule, be used for which target depends crucially on the relative slopes of the domestic and external equilibrium curves.

   Although this procedure is useful to discuss the principle of effective market classification, we should, of course, note that no actual economy adjusts to market disequilibria in the way illustrated by the cobweb 1, 2, 3, 4, . . . in Figure 23.12, not only because no policy maker has complete control over the level of absorption and the real exchange rate such as to enable this adjustment path, but also because it appears to be very inefficient to reach full equilibrium in such a roundabout way. In practice, some gentler steering and gradual simultaneous adjustment of both the level of absorption and the real exchange rate, as indicated by the arrows leading more directly from point E_0 to point E, seems to be preferable. It remains, of course, questionable whether any government is able to gather and process sufficient information so as to steer the economy directly from point E_0 to point E. It is, moreover, also questionable whether it actually needs to do this. If prices, wage rates, and exchange rates are not sticky or fixed but react to regular market forces, we should expect simultaneous adjustment of the level of absorption and the real exchange rate to the disequilibria as depicted in Figure 23.12 more or less in accordance with the arrows as drawn from point E_0 to point E. The exact path will, of course, depend on the speed with which wages, prices, expenditure levels, and exchange rates adjust, see Chapters 24–26.

 Box 23.3   Adjustment problems in Italy, 1986–93

At the end of the 1980s and in the early 1990s Italy was a member of the European Monetary System (EMS). This system of fixed exchange rates, a forerunner of EMU, used regular small realignments in the parity rates before 1987 to avoid a build-up of economic tension in the system arising from different macroeconomic and monetary policies. After 1987, however, it evolved in a system of rigidly fixed exchange rates, despite the fact that the Italian inflation rate remained much higher than the German inflation rate (the EMS benchmark country); see Figure 23.13. As a result of the higher inflation rate, coupled with a rigidly fixed exchange rate, the lire became increasingly overvalued. This caused competitiveness problems for the Italian economy, resulting in increasing current account deficits. It became clear that the Italian government would have to start using both instruments at its disposal to try to achieve both domestic and external equilibrium; that is, it would have to devalue the Italian lire. Speculators realized this dilemma and took action accordingly, which led Italy to drop out of the EMS altogether in September 1992. The lire started a sharp decline in value and the current account balance started to improve one year later.

Figure 23.13 Italian adjustments, 1986–93

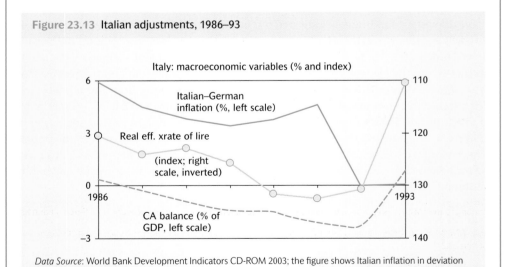

Data Source: World Bank Development Indicators CD-ROM 2003; the figure shows Italian inflation in deviation from the German inflation rate; note that the real effective exchange rate of the lire (domestic currency) is depicted on an inverted scale to make movements commensurate to changes in Q in the text.

23.7 Conclusions

The elasticities approach focuses on the relative price effects on the current account balance. According to the Marshall–Lerner condition, which states that the sum of the price elasticities of export and import demand must exceed unity, a depreciation of the domestic currency will improve the current account balance. Empirical estimates show that the Marshall–Lerner condition is fulfilled for most countries, but only after a sufficiently long period of time has elapsed to ensure that the export and import quantitities can adjust to the change in relative prices. According to this J-curve effect, the initial response to a depreciation of the domestic currency is to deteriorate the current account balance, leading to an improvement only after an adjustment period of about one year. The absorption approach incorporates income effects into the analysis of the current account balance. This allows for a typology of types of disequilibria and the analysis of some simple adjustment problems. We discussed the Tinbergen rule (to achieve a certain number of economic objectives you need the same number of policy instruments to reach these objectives) and the assignment problem (each instrument should be used on the target for which it has the greatest relative effect).

TECHNICAL NOTE

Technical Note 23.1 Derivation of the Marshall–Lerner condition

Equation (23A.1) recalls the definition of the current account balance, where X is exports, M is imports, and Q is the real exchange rate. Totally differentiating this equation with respect to Q gives equation (23A.2).

(23A.1) $$CA(Q) = X(\overset{+}{Q}) - Q \cdot M(\bar{Q})$$

(23A.2) $$CA'(Q) = X' - QM' - M$$

Divide both sides by M, use the initial current account balance condition $X = QM$, and the elasticity definitions $\varepsilon_x \equiv (Q / X)X' > 0$ and $\varepsilon_m \equiv -(Q / M)M' > 0$ to get:

(23A.3) $$\frac{CA'(Q)}{M} = \frac{X'}{M} - \frac{QM'}{M} - 1 = \frac{QX'}{X} - \frac{QM'}{M} - 1 \equiv \varepsilon_x + \varepsilon_m - 1$$

Clearly, $CA' > 0$ if and only if, $\varepsilon_x + \varepsilon_m > 1$, as stated in the main text.

QUESTIONS

Question 23.1

According to the elasticities approach the real exchange rate determines the current account via different channels.

23.1A Which are the three channels through which the real exchange rate influences the current account (see equation 23.2)?

23.1B Through which channels does the real exchange rate influence the current account in the short run and through which channels in the long run? Explain these differences.

23.1C Do you think the Marshall–Lerner condition is more likely to hold in the short run or the long run?

23.1D How do your observations of 23.1B explain the J-curve?

Question 23.2

The graphs below show the development of the real effective exchange rate and the current account during particular events in Italy, Mexico, Japan, and South Korea.

- From 1987 onwards Italy participated in the European Monetary System, which fixed the exchange rate of the Italian lira to the currencies of other EMS members. The Italian inflation rate was, however, consistently higher than the inflation rate in other members of the EMS. After heavy speculation the authorities were therefore forced to devalue the lira in September 1992.

- In 1994 foreign investors and Mexican citizens lost their confidence in the value of the Mexican peso. Although the Mexican government defended the fixed exchange rate with the American dollar for some time, in December 1994 the authorities announced that the peso would float, leading to the so-called 'Tequila crisis'.

- In spring 1995 the Japanese yen reached its highest value against other currencies and depreciated markedly afterwards.

- During the Asian crisis of 1997 investors lost faith in the health of the so-called tiger economies. This also affected the prospects of the South Korean economy and as a consequence the Korean won depreciated rapidly.

Analyse whether the four countries experienced a J-curve effect during these four episodes. If not, why do you think the current account did not behave according to the J-curve theory?

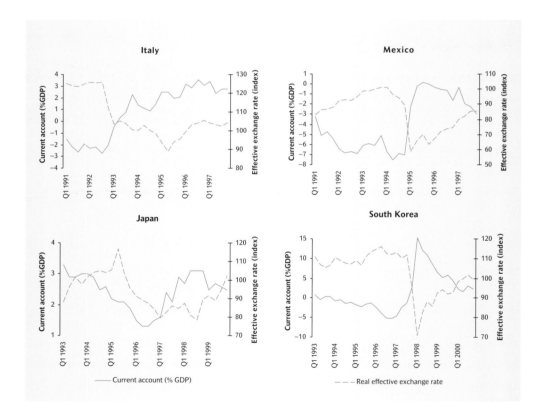

Question 23.3

During the 1960s France tried to keep a fixed exchange rate with other industrialized nations participating in the so-called Breton Woods system. In 1968 this fixed exchange rate arrangement came under severe pressure. Forced by violent protests, the French government granted large wage increases in 1968. Let's analyse the effect of these wage increases with the Swan diagram.

23.3A Assuming that the French economy was first in equilibrium, which disequilibrium regime did the French economy move into after the wage increases? What is the state of the current account and the domestic economy in this regime?

23.3B If wages and prices are flexible, does the French government face a problem? Explain.

The French economy, like most economies, is characterized by downward wage and price rigidity. The French government therefore either has to choose between external or domestic equilibrium.

23.3C Explain why the French government faces this problem.

23.3D Why is domestic equilibrium unsustainable and external equilibrium undesirable in the disequilibrium regime?

23.3E President de Gaulle declared in 1968 that he would never devalue the French franc. Do you think he kept his word?

 See the Online Resource Centre for a Study Guide containing more questions www.oxfordtextbooks.co.uk/orc/vanmarrewijk/

NOTES

1 The first oil shock was in 1973.

2 The discussion in the text assumes that external equilibrium implies that $CA = 0$. If there are steady capital inflows or capital outflows in the economy, these can be accommodated for an external equilibrium with a steady current account deficit or surplus.

3 Note that this discussion is a special case of the policy trilemma; see Chapter 22. There we have two instruments (monetary policy and capital controls) and three objectives (free capital flows, a fixed exchange rate, and independent monetary policy).

4 Note that starting from point E_0 we would reach E quicker if we first tried to achieve external equilibrium. This depends, of course, on the initial situation and does not materially affect the remainder of the analysis.

THE MONETARY APPROACH

24

Objectives/key terms

- Monetary approach
- Price flexibility
- Stocks and flows
- Expectations

- Price specie flow mechanism
- Hoarding and dishoarding
- Asset approach
- Exchange rate corrections

The monetary approach emphasizes the fact that the exchange rate is the relative price of two monies. The demand for money therefore plays an important role in the adjustment process and in determining exchange rate levels. We also discuss the degree of price flexibility and the role of expectations formation.

24.1 Introduction

The elasticities approach and the absorption approach discussed in Chapter 23 were popular theories for the balance of trade for a couple of decades. As we have seen, these theories emphasize the current account (trade in goods and services), but have little to say about capital flows. Since international interactions in the world today are also characterized by large capital flows in well-developed financial markets, we must go beyond the role of trade flows and incorporate the role of financial assets for a better understanding of the balance of payments. This is what the monetary approach does.

24.2 Money, price flexibility, and the modelling of exchange rates

Suppose we draw two lines in the balance of payments, one to determine the current account and one to determine the private capital account, such that the remainder directly affects the money supply (through changes in official holdings of gold, foreign exchange, Special Drawing Rights, and reserves at the IMF); see Chapter 2 and equation (24.1). According to the monetary approach, a balance of payments disequilibrium is a monetary disequilibrium, that is a disequilibrium between the amount of money supplied and the amount of money people wish to hold. Simply stated: if the domestic demand for money is higher than what is supplied by the central bank, the excess demand for money will be satisfied by an inflow of money from abroad and vice versa if the demand for money is lower than what is supplied by the central bank. This principle and the so-called price specie flow mechanism of disequilibrium adjustment (see the next section) had already been formulated by the Scottish philosopher David Hume in the eighteenth century (1752; II V 9):

> Suppose four-fifths of all the money in Great Britain to be annihilated in one night, and the nation reduced to the same condition, with regard to specie, as in the reigns of the Harrys and the Edwards, what would be the consequence? Must not the price of all labour and commodities sink in proportion, and everything be sold as cheap as they were in those ages?

Famous economists	David Hume

Fig. 24.1
David Hume
(1711–76)

Born in Edinburgh, David Hume was one of the most important figures in the Scottish Enlightenment. As a contemporary of Adam Smith, he was a philosopher, essayist and historian who is now best known for *A Treatise of Human Nature* (1739–40), which was not well received at the time and, according to Hume, 'fell dead-born from the press'. He noted that when we observe one event always following after another event, we think there is a connection between the two that makes the second event follow from the first. However, we can never be sure that one event causes the other. Associated with this problem of causation is his rejection of the principle of induction. His most important contribution to economics is on the price specie flow mechanism; see Section 24.3.

What nation could then dispute with us in any foreign market, or pretend to navigate or to sell manufactures at the same price, which to us would afford sufficient profit? In how little time, therefore, must this bring back the money we had lost, and raise us to the level of all neighbouring nations? Where, after we have arrived, we immediately lose the advantage of the cheapness of labor and commodities; and the farther flowing in of money is stopped by our fulness and repletion.

In short, Hume argues that a sudden drop in England's money supply will lower prices, such that exports rise and imports fall. This current account surplus leads to an inflow of money from abroad, that is an inflow of gold and silver in Hume's days, which raises prices until equilibrium is restored.

We have repeatedly emphasized in the previous chapters that the exchange rate is a price, namely the price of one currency relative to another currency, or equivalently the price of foreign money expressed in domestic money. The most direct explanation of the relative price of money then comes from analysing the money market, which is what the monetary approach to the balance of payments does. Based on simple accounting identities, the analysis *ex post* must lead to the same answers as given by other (e.g. the elasticities and absorption) approaches. However, since exchange rates are a monetary phenomenon, it seems more appropriate and direct to include an analysis of the money market, as most of the remaining chapters will do. Suppose, for example, that we analyse an economy in which there are goods, bonds, and money. The balance of payments flows will be constrained as follows:

$$(24.1) \qquad (X_{goods} - Im_{goods}) + (X_{bonds} - Im_{bonds}) + (X_{money} - Im_{money}) = 0,$$

where X denotes exports and Im denotes imports. The three accounts – for goods, bonds, and money – must sum to zero. An analysis of the balance of payments can, of course, focus on the current (goods and services) and capital (bonds) account, but that implies that the nature of the money market is ignored, which seems unwarranted (and rather roundabout) if one wants to explain the relative price of money.

The above does not mean, of course, that the price of goods is not important for determining equilibrium, if only because it affects the nominal demand for money; see Chapter 18. This

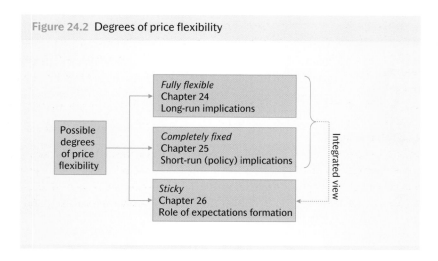

Figure 24.2 **Degrees of price flexibility**

brings us to an important topic, namely the degree of price flexibility in determining the balance of payments, possibly relative to exchange rate flexibility. We can distinguish between three main possibilities, each of which has been analysed separately for good reasons (and we will do so too; see Figure 24.2), namely:

- Prices are *fully flexible* and determined by equilibrium conditions. This possibility is analysed in this chapter, focusing on the monetary approach to the balance of payments. Although full price flexibility is assumed to hold at any point in time in this analysis, for both fixed and floating exchange rate regimes, it is probably best to interpret the analytic results as providing insights into long-run economic relationships.

- Prices are *completely fixed* and exogenously given throughout the analysis. This possibility allows for disequilibrium situations on the goods market (unemployment) and is analysed in Chapter 25, which focuses on the (short-run) implications of fiscal and monetary policy under various circumstances.

- Prices are *sticky*; that is, they are fixed in the short run and gradually adjust over time towards their long-run equilibrium level. This possibility is analysed in Chapter 26, where it is assumed, more specifically, that prices are sticky whereas exchange rates are fully flexible. This turns out not only to allow us to integrate the insights gained in Chapters 24 and 25 into a single framework, but also to focus on the issue of expectations formation and the empirically observed degree of exchange rate variability relative to price variability; see also Box 24.1.

 Box 24.1   **Price and exchange rate flexibility in Europe**

It is quite clear that prices of goods and services change over time, as does the exchange rate. We have already noted in Chapter 19 that exchange rates change very frequently, not only from month to month, but even from week to week, day to day, and hour to hour. We are not used to such frequent changes in prices of goods and services. The IKEA catalogue in the Netherlands, for example, is published in August of every year with prices that are valid for one year. The prices of magazines, haircuts, etc. are changed regularly, but rather infrequently. The degree of price flexibility relative to the degree of exchange rate flexibility is, of course, an empirical question. Figure 24.3 uses monthly European data and the US dollar–euro exchange rate to show that, indeed, exchange rate changes are much larger from one period to the next than are price changes, providing some support for the argument that prices are sticky relative to exchange rates. One important explanation for this observed price stickiness is the fact that the wages of workers, which represent a large fraction of the costs of providing goods and services, are written into long-term contracts and negotiated only periodically.

Figure 24.3 is, of course, somewhat biased as it depicts changes in the overall price index, which is a composite of several individual prices (such that increases in one price may cancel decreases in another price) relative to a single exchange rate. A similar picture emerges, however, if we use nominal effective exchange rates, see Chapter 19. Alternatively, we can analyse the variability of individual

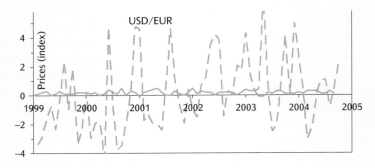

Figure 24.3 Price and exchange rate flexibility (% change, monthly data)

Data source: http://www.ecb.int (HICP, 14 November 2004).

Table 24.1 Summary statistics of monthly changes, Europe (%)

| | Changes in prices | | | | | |
	Overall	Proc. food	Food	Ind. goods	Energy	Services
Mean	0.18	0.21	0.19	0.07	0.42	0.20
St. dev.	0.14	0.19	0.55	0.12	1.38	0.12
Min.	−0.10	−0.10	−0.60	−0.30	−2.90	−0.10
Max.	0.50	1.20	2.50	0.50	4.20	0.60
	Changes in exchange rates					
	USA	Australia	S. Korea	Hong Kong	Japan	S. Africa
Mean	0.14	−0.08	0.11	0.15	0.09	0.28
St. dev.	2.55	2.35	3.07	2.53	2.77	4.23
Min.	−4.33	−5.79	−5.74	−4.29	−6.42	−6.86
Max.	6.77	6.72	9.99	6.76	8.91	20.03

Notes: St. dev. = standard deviation; Min. = Minimum; Max. = Maximum; Proc. = Processed; Ind. = Industrial; data range: February 1999–September 2004.

Data source: www.ecb.int.

components of the European harmonized index of consumer prices (HICP) relative to the variability of some other exchange rates. This is done in Table 24.1, which shows that the individual consumer price components (food, processed food, industrial goods, energy, and services) have a much lower variability, that is a lower standard deviation and a lower range of changes (= maximum−minimum) than the exchange rate changes. It also shows that in this particular period energy is by far the most variable component of consumer prices, but not quite as variable as the exchange rates reported in the second part of the table.

24.3 The monetary model and the price specie flow mechanism

This section presents a simple version of the monetary model with fully flexible prices under fixed exchange rates to highlight the role of money in payments adjustment, also known as the (price) specie flow mechanism.[1] Since exchange rates are fixed, the central bank has to intervene by buying or selling international reserves to maintain the fixed exchange rates; see Box 23.1. This implies that the money supply becomes an endogenous variable. Using a simple mechanistic money supply process, see Box 18.2, money supply is equal to a money multiplier (which we set equal to one for convenience) times high-powered money, that is domestic credit D plus net foreign assets R.

$$(24.2) \qquad M = D + R$$

A change in the money supply is then caused by a change in the domestic component D or a change in the reserves R, where the latter is equal to the sum of the current and capital account balance in a system of fixed exchange rates; see Chapter 18.

We distinguish between two countries, called Home and Foreign. Variables without any subscripts will refer to Home, whereas variables with a subscript f will refer to Foreign. Throughout the analysis, we will focus attention on Home although similar functions and remarks also hold for Foreign. Assuming that, as a result of fully flexible prices, output is always at its full employment level we pose the simplest possible money demand function in equation (24.3), where nominal money demand M is equal to the velocity V times the price level P.[2] The homogeneity of money in prices implies that there is no money illusion, such that money is neutral in the long run.

$$(24.3) \qquad M^d = VP; \quad M_f^d = V_f P_f$$

One of the implications of the monetary approach to the balance of payments is that it focuses attention on the stock of money as an equilibrium condition; that is, it is a *stock approach* rather than, for example, the elasticities approach which focuses on the flow demand of goods and services. Any stock approach is simultaneously also a flow approach to the extent that the change of a stock variable over time is a flow variable. For that reason, it is convenient to have a clear, separate notation for the change of a variable over time, for which we will use a dot. That is, we henceforth use the following

Convention: a dot over a variable denotes its derivative with respect to time t, that is its change over time, so $\dot{x} = dx/dt$.

Equation (24.3) gives the long-run implications of the money demand function, but as discussed above, individuals in an open economy can only adjust the money stock gradually through the balance of payments. This short-run money market adjustment mechanism is given in equation (24.4), where individuals believe that at current prices they can adjust the money stock by hoarding (spending less than income) or dishoarding (spending more than income) and α is the speed of adjustment. Our simple model is completed in equation (24.5) by invoking the Law of One Price in this one-good world.

$$(24.4) \qquad \dot{M} = \alpha(VP - M); \qquad \dot{M}_f = \alpha_f(V_f P_f - M_f)$$

$$(24.5) \qquad P = SP_f$$

Figure 24.4 shows the equilibrium rate of hoarding $\dot{M}$ for the Home economy. As the price level rises, the nominal demand for money increases, which creates a stock excess demand for money and thus an incentive for hoarding to adjust the money stock. Since the exchange rate is fixed, we can depict Foreign's rate of *dishoarding*, $-\dot{SM}_f$ in the same diagram, as a decreasing function of the price level for similar reasons. Equilibrium in the figure is reached at point E_0, where the domestic rate of hoarding is equal to the foreign rate of dishoarding. This determines the equilibrium price level P_0 and the equilibrium rate of hoarding $\dot{M}_0$ as a function of the demands for money and the *current* distribution of the world money stock $M+SM_f$ over the two countries. Note, however, that the equilibrium at point E_0 affects the distribution of the world money stock. More specifically, Home is hoarding money, so its money stock is increasing, while Foreign is dishoarding, so its money stock is decreasing. This change in the distribution of the world money stock affects the equilibrium depicted in the figure.

Figure 24.5 illustrates this price specie flow adjustment process over time. The equilibrium rate of hoarding resulting from domestic income being larger than domestic spending leads to an increase in assets, that is an increase in the domestic money stock, which shifts Home's equilibrium hoarding schedule up and to the left over time. Similarly, the decrease in the money stock abroad shifts Foreign's dishoarding schedule down and to the left. As the world money stock is redistributed across the two countries the equilibrium therefore shifts to the left (in the figure from E_0 to E_1) and reduces the degree of hoarding and dishoarding until a long-run equilibrium is reached along the vertical axis (not shown). During this process the price level may either rise or fall. Figure 24.5 illustrates a situation in which the price level is rising as the world money stock is redistributed from Foreign to Home, which occurs if, and only if, Home's adjustment parameter is larger than Foreign's, that is if $\alpha > \alpha_f$. If these two parameters are the same, a redistribution of the world money stock will not affect the equilibrium price level; see Technical Note 24.1.

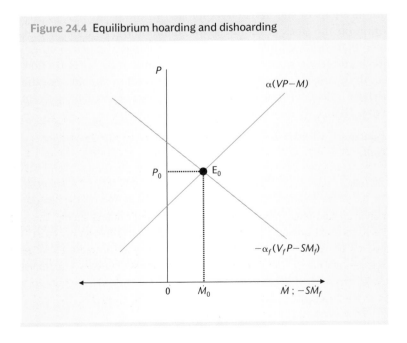

Figure 24.4 Equilibrium hoarding and dishoarding

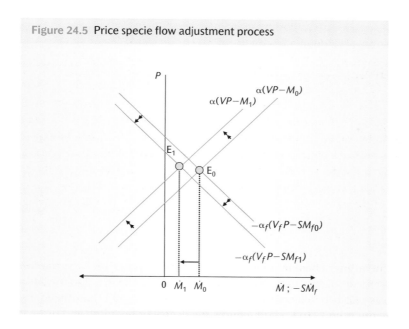

Figure 24.5 Price specie flow adjustment process

Box 24.2   **Effect of a devaluation in the basic monetary model**

What is the effect of a devaluation of the Home currency in the model of Section 24.3? Suppose the exchange rate (the price of the foreign currency in terms of domestic currency) rises from S_0 to S_1. Since there is only one good and the Law of One Price holds, a devaluation cannot change the relative price of goods. Moreover, since there is full employment, there are no income and employment effects. As Dornbusch (1980a: 125–6) puts it: 'What then can a devaluation do? In the present model a devaluation is a change in the relative price of two monies. (This is always true. Here it is the *only* aspect of a devaluation.)'

At initial prices in terms of Home currency it follows from $P=SP_f$ that foreign prices would fall proportionally to the devaluation. Foreign's money demand $M_f^d = V_f P_f$ would therefore fall, see equation (24.3), which results in an incentive to dishoard in Foreign at current domestic prices. This is illustrated in Figure 24.6 by the shift to the right of Foreign's dishoarding schedule. The new short-run equilibrium is at point E_1 with higher prices in terms of domestic currency. The prices measured in foreign currency must have fallen since the domestic prices are increased from E_0 to P_1 while the increase in the exchange rate was proportional to the rise from E_0 to E'. The Home country thus creates a surplus on the current account in response to the devaluation of the domestic currency, setting in motion an adjustment process to increase the domestic money supply. This is caused by the fact that at constant domestic prices the devaluation causes foreign prices to fall and the purchasing power of cash balances abroad to increase. Foreigners increase their spending as a result of this excess real balance, leading to a price rise in domestic currency. Over time the current account balance implies a redistribution of the world money stock, leading to rising expenditure in Home and a falling expenditure in Foreign until equilibrium is restored. The effects of the devaluation of the Home currency are therefore transitory.   ⟫

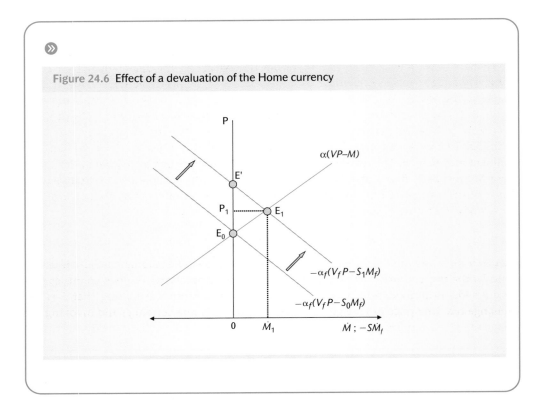

Figure 24.6 Effect of a devaluation of the Home currency

24.4 Flexible price monetary approach (floating exchange rates)

Section 24.3 introduced the basic monetary model and discussed the price specie flow adjustment mechanism in a system of fixed exchange rates. Since the early 1970s, however, most large trading blocs have moved to a system of floating exchange rates relative to one another (while they might maintain fixed exchange rates within the trading block, as is the case for most European countries); see Chapter 22. This section therefore discusses how the monetary approach can be used to determine the exchange rate in a system of floating exchange rates.

As already emphasized in Chapters 19–21, one of the most important empirical characteristics of the floating exchange rate experience is the high volatility of exchange rates. To a considerable extent this high volatility was not expected, because Friedman (1953) argued that stability of a flexible exchange rate regime was ensured by the stabilizing behaviour of speculators. In general, the *asset approach* to the exchange rate (of which the monetary approach is a special case, such that this section provides a simple example) explains this high volatility by emphasizing that the exchange rate is an asset price (namely the relative price of monies). To determine the exchange rate, we should therefore use the tools for the determination of asset prices, such as bond prices or share prices; see Mussa (1976, 1979). A strong point of this view is that we observe that exchange rate volatility is similar in magnitude to the volatility of other asset prices. The price of an asset, such as a share of ING Bank, changes because the market changes its view of what the asset is worth, presumably something like the expected discounted value of future profits. This means that in the asset approach substantial changes in the exchange rate can take place without it being observed that substantial underlying trade is taking place. It also means that in the asset approach expectations formation is important for understanding exchange rate levels and changes. The expectations issue is touched upon in Box 24.3, but we reserve a more thorough analysis of expectations formation for Chapter 26.

As in Section 24.3, we analyse a two-country world, where Foreign variables are identified by the sub-index f. Prices are fully flexible and instantaneously adjust to ensure equilibrium on the money market. The real demand for money M/P is more complete than in the analysis of Section 24.3; it is a standard positive function of the income level y (transactions demand) and a negative function of the interest rate i (opportunity costs). Using a logarithmic specification, equilibrium on the money market is given by:

$$(24.6) \qquad m - p = \alpha y - \beta i; \quad m_f - p_f = \alpha y_f - \beta i_f$$

Note that we have assumed for simplicity that the money demand parameters α and β are the same for the two countries, although this is by no means necessary. The two countries produce an identical good, which is viewed as a perfect substitute. Recalling that S is the exchange rate (the price of Foreign currency in terms of Home currency) and invoking the Law of One Price implies:

$$(24.7) \qquad p = s + p_f$$

Combining the information given in equations (24.6) and (24.7) determines the exchange rate; see Technical Note 24.2 and equation (24.8). Box 24.3 discusses some potential complications of (24.8) regarding uncovered interest parity and expectations formation.

$$(24.8) \qquad s = (m - m_f) - \alpha (y - y_f) + \beta(i - i_f)$$

The results of this flexible price monetary approach for determining the exchange rate as reflected in equation (24.8) are straightforward:

- A more rapid increase in the Home money supply than in the Foreign money supply increases the exchange rate one for one (and thus leads to a Home currency depreciation). Like all other prices, the exchange rate (which is the price of Foreign currency) increases proportionally with the money stock.

- An increase in the domestic income level reduces the exchange rate (and thus leads to a domestic currency appreciation). The increase in income increases the transactions demand for money. Given the nominal money supply, equilibrium on the money market can only be restored if the domestic price level falls, which, given the Law of One Price, requires a reduction in the exchange rate.

Box 24.3 **Expectations**

Equation (24.8) gives a first indication of the relationship between exchange rates, money stocks, income levels, and interest rates. As discussed in Chapter 21, however, the interest rates in the two countries are related to one another through a simple mechanism of arbitrage under risk neutrality by the uncovered interest arbitrage condition; see equation (22.4). More specifically, the expected change in the exchange rate must be equal to the difference between Home and Foreign interest rates:

(24.9) $$s_{t+1}^e - s_t = (i_t - i_{f,t})$$

Taking this additional relationship into consideration means that equation (24.8) is not the end of the flexible price monetary approach story, because substituting the uncovered interest parity condition (24.9) into the equilibrium relationship (24.8) gives rise to an interdependence between expectations and realizations, as illustrated in Figure 24.7 (where we have added a time sub index t to be specific about the timing of each variable). Note that there is a nested reasoning in which the exchange rate today depends on the expected exchange rate tomorrow, while the exchange rate tomorrow will depend on the expected exchange rate as of tomorrow for the day after tomorrow, etc. We must have some method to solve this infinitely nested problem. As this is an important and non-trivial expectations issue, we postpone its analysis until Chapter 26.

Figure 24.7 **Interdependencies between expectations and realizations**

$$S_t = (m_t - m_{f,t}) - \alpha\,(y_t - y_{f,t}) + \beta\,(S_{t+1}^e - S_t)$$

24.5 Money, income, and exchange rates

In a continuation of our discussion in Section 21.3, where we argued that there is indeed a long-run relationship between exchange rates and prices (relative PPP), we will now argue that there is indeed a long-run relationship between exchange rates, money stocks, and income levels. The monetary approach, as summarized in equation (24.8), can in this respect essentially be viewed as providing the main reasons why price levels in different countries may change, namely because the money stock changes or because the income level changes. For reasons explained in Box 24.3, we will ignore the influence of changes in the interest rate in the remainder this section.

As the monetary approach is an extension of the PPP approach discussed in Chapter 20 and we already know that relative PPP is a long-run and not a short-run relationship, we will use the same procedure as used in Section 21.3 by analysing changes over a long enough time period. More specifically, using World Bank data and the USA as a benchmark, we take the time difference of equation (24.8) from 2001 to 1960 to estimate changes in the US dollar foreign exchange rate as a function of changes in the domestic money stock (M_2) relative to the US money stock and changes in the domestic income level (measured in constant 1995 US dollar) relative to the US income level. This gives:

(24.10)
$$s_{2001} - s_{1960} = -\underset{(0.283)}{0.557} - \underset{(0.294)}{0.898} \times [(y_{cj,2001} - y_{cj,1960}) - (y_{US,2001} - y_{US,1960})]$$
$$+ \underset{(0.060)}{0.936} \times [(m_{cj,2001} - m_{cj,1960}) - (m_{US,2001} - m_{US,1960})]$$

The estimated equation (24.10) explains about 84 per cent of the variance in exchange rates ($R^2 = 0.84$) and indicates that the exchange rate depends positively on relative changes in the money stock and negatively on relative changes in output. Simple hypothesis tests would show that the estimated coefficient for differences in the money stock (0.936) does not differ significantly from one while the estimated coefficient for differences in output does differ significantly from zero, all of which is in accordance with the flexible price monetary approach discussed in Section 24.4 (see Box 20.1 for some information on econometrics and hypothesis testing).

Figure 24.8 illustrates the impact of differences in changes in the money stock on the exchange rate, after the latter is corrected for differences in output (see Box 24.4). Countries such as Uruguay, which have experienced a large increase in the money stock relative to the USA, were confronted with a large increase in the US dollar exchange rate. The opposite holds for countries that experienced a decline in the money stock relative to the USA, such as Switzerland. Similarly, Figure 24.9 illustrates the impact of differences in changes in

---

 Box 24.4   Exchange rate corrections

If we want to illustrate the empirical results of equation (24.10), we have to overcome an elementary obstacle. Since the exchange rate depends both on differences in the money stocks *and* on differences in output, if we were to draw a picture with changes in the exchange rate on the vertical axis and the difference in changes of the money stock on the horizontal axis, part of the depicted observed change in the exchange rate should actually be attributed to the change in output (and not to the change in money depicted on the horizontal axis). To overcome this graphical obstacle, it is customary to calculate *corrected* changes in the exchange rate before depicting them in a graph; that is, if we want to illustrate the relationship between exchange rates and the money stock we first neutralize the effect of output on the exchange rate, while if we want to illustrate the relationship between exchange rates and output we first neutralize the effect of money on the exchange rate. So how do we perform this neutralization or correction? Well, that is actually quite simple. Once we have an empirical estimate of the influence of one variable on another, the correction simply subtracts this influence from the observations. More specifically, using the empirical estimates of equation (24.10) we get:

$$(s_{2001} - s_{1960})_{corrected\ for\ output} = s_{2001} - s_{1960} + 0.898 \times \left[(y_{cj,2001} - y_{cj,1960}) - (y_{USA,2001} - y_{USA,1960}) \right]$$

$$(s_{2001} - s_{1960})_{corrected\ for\ money} = s_{2001} - s_{1960} - 0.936 \times \left[(m_{cj,2001} - m_{cj,1960}) - (m_{USA,2001} - m_{USA,1960}) \right]$$

It is these exchange rates corrected for other influences which best illustrate the influence of a specific variable. This is used to produce Figures 24.8 and 24.9.

Figure 24.8 Money and exchange rates (corrected for output)

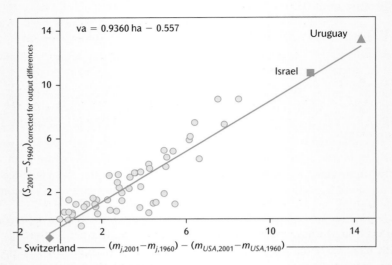

$va = 0.9360\,ha - 0.557$

Vertical axis: $(S_{2001} - S_{1960})$ corrected for output differences

Horizontal axis: $(m_{j,2001} - m_{j,1960}) - (m_{USA,2001} - m_{USA,1960})$

Note: va = vertical axis, ha = horizontal axis.

Data source: World Bank Development Indicators CD-ROM 2003; va = vertical axis, ha = horizontal axis.

Figure 24.9 Output and exchange rates (corrected for money)

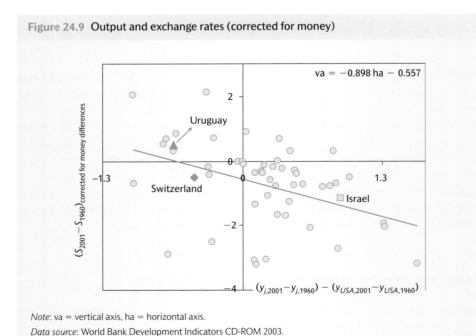

$va = -0.898\,ha - 0.557$

Vertical axis: $(S_{2001} - S_{1960})$ corrected for money differences

Horizontal axis: $(y_{j,2001} - y_{j,1960}) - (y_{USA,2001} - y_{USA,1960})$

Note: va = vertical axis, ha = horizontal axis.

Data source: World Bank Development Indicators CD-ROM 2003.

output on the exchange rate, after the latter is corrected for differences in money. Countries such as Israel, which have experienced an increase in output relative to the USA, are confronted with a decrease in the exchange rate of the US dollar (an appreciation of the domestic currency) after the latter is corrected for the change in the money stock. The opposite holds for countries such as Switzerland, which experienced a decrease in output relative to the USA. As a comparison of the two figures indicates, the impact of the money stock on the exchange rate seems to be more convincing than the impact of output on the exchange rate. This suggestion, which can be corroborated by statistical tests, is not surprising as the exchange rate is a monetary phenomenon. None the less, the impact of output on the demand for money does have a noticeable and significant impact on long-run changes in the exchange rate.

24.6 Conclusions

The monetary approach to the balance of payments stresses the fact that the exchange rate is the relative price of two monies. Accordingly, a disequilibrium results if the demand for money differs from the amount supplied by the monetary authorities. In the basic monetary model with fixed exchange rates (see Section 24.3), such a disequilibrium gives rise to an adjustment process (Hume's price specie flow mechanism) that redistributes the world's money stock between the two countries until a new (stock) equilibrium is reached. In the flexible price monetary approach under flexible exchange rates (see Section 24.4), such a disequilibrium gives rise to an immediate adjustment of the exchange rate to equilibrate the demand for and supply of money. The latter approach indicates that the domestic currency depreciates one for one if the money supply increases and appreciates if the income level increases. Both of these effects are supported by (long-run) empirical evidence. The degree of price flexibility has important consequences for the modelling of exchange rate behaviour. Assuming, as we have done in this chapter, that prices are fully flexible is probably best interpreted as indicative of long-run exchange rate behaviour. We analyse the consequences of (short-run) fixed and (medium-run) sticky prices in the next two chapters. The modelling of expectations formation also has important consequences for understanding exchange rate behaviour. This issue is further analysed in Chapter 26.

TECHNICAL NOTES

Technical Note 24.1 Equilibrium price in the basic monetary model

The equilibrium in the basic monetary model of Section 24.3 requires that the domestic rate of hoarding is equal to the foreign rate of dishoarding; that is, $\dot{M} = -S\dot{M}_f$. Using equation (24.4), this gives the equilibrium condition:

(24A.1)
$$\alpha(VP - M) = -\alpha_f(V_f SP_f - SM_f)$$

Substituting the Law of One Price (24.5) and solving for the equilibrium price level gives:

(24A.2)
$$P = \frac{\alpha M + \alpha_f SM_f}{\alpha V + \alpha_f V_f}$$

Technical Note 24.2 Flexible price monetary approach

By solving equations (24.6) for the respective price levels and subtracting, we obtain:

(24A.3) $$p - p_f = [m - (\alpha y - \beta i)] - [m_f - (\alpha y_f - \beta i_f)]$$

Solving (24.7) for the exchange rate and substituting (24A.3) gives

(24A.4) $$s = p - p_f = (m - m_f) - \alpha(y - y_f) + \beta(i - i_f)$$

QUESTIONS

Question 24.1

24.1A Of which theory is the monetary approach an extension?

24.1B Look at the example of David Hume in paragraph 24.2. What would happen to the British pound if the exchange rate were fully flexible and fully accommodated the described economic shock?

The assumptions about price adjustments are important for exchange rate analysis. You can imagine that in practice different economies have different degrees of flexibility.

24.1C What economy would you expect to have relatively flexible prices? Which economy do you expect to have relatively sticky prices?

Question 24.2

The basic monetary model allows us to analyse money hoarding in Australia (home) and South Korea (foreign), who have tied their currencies (the Australian dollar and the won) together. Suppose at first that the equilibrium rate of money hoarding is zero.

24.2A Draw in a graph the equilibrium rate of hoarding for Australia and South Korea as a function of money demand.

Now suppose that a new South Korean government is elected. This government wants to improve its competitive position and devalues the won with respect to the Australian dollar.

24.2B Draw in your graph the short-run effects of this policy measure and explain the changes. What are the effects on Australian and South Korean output?

24.2C Assume that the South Korean adjustment parameter is higher than that of Australia. Show in your graph the long-run effects of the South Korean devaluation. What has happened to the price level in Australia and South Korea? Why?

Tired of the South Korean devaluations, the Australians belatedly accept to enter into a monetary union. This however entails a revaluation of the Australian dollar.

24.2D What are the eventual effects of this revaluation on the Australian and South Korean price levels?

Question 24.3

24.3A Suppose you are a currency trader specializing in euros and US dollars. You believe that the asset approach to exchange rates is correct and can earn you money. What would your reaction be to the following news items (explain):

- The IMF predicts that the US economy will grow faster than the eurozone
- The ECB unexpectedly hints that it will raise interest rates
- Newly released figures indicate that money growth in the USA is faster than in the eurozone
- Inflation in the US is higher than expected

24.3B What is the role of expectations in the monetary model as presented in this chapter?

24.3C What can empirical research tell us about the monetary model?

 See the Online Resource Centre for a Study Guide containing more questions
www.oxfordtextbooks.co.uk/orc/vanmarrewijk/

NOTES

1 Whitman (1975) calls it a global monetarist model.

2 Given the fixed income level, this is a so-called 'Cambridge' money demand function.

SHORT-RUN ECONOMIC POLICY

25

Objectives/key terms

- Fixed exchange rates
- Instantaneous adjustment
- Monetary expansion
- Short run
- Offset coefficient

- Perfect substitutes
- Capital mobility
- Fiscal expansion
- Mundell–Fleming model
- Crowding out

We analyse the short-run implications of monetary and fiscal policy for small and large countries, under different exchange rate regimes and varying degrees of capital mobility.

25.1 Introduction

The previous chapter focused on the long-run determination of the money stock (fixed exchange rates) or the exchange rate (flexible exchange rates), using the monetary approach to the balance of payments if prices are fully flexible. Monetary and fiscal authorities and politicians are, however, frequently more interested in the short-run implications of policy changes, in an effort, for example, to reduce unemployment, boost output, and increase the chance of being re-elected. Consequently, this chapter focuses on the short-run implications of monetary and fiscal policy under various economic circumstances. We take the price level as fixed and do not consider the implications of price adjustment, changes in wealth, or expectations formation. These issues are analysed in Chapter 27.

The fundamental insights exposed in this chapter were developed by Robert Mundell (1962, 1963, and 1968) and Marcus Fleming (1962). The framework of analysis is therefore known as the Mundell–Fleming model. A thorough understanding of the main implications of this framework is crucial for policy makers up to this day, to know what they can and cannot do in particular circumstances. This derives mainly from the contributions of Robert Mundell, who, as Dornbusch (1980: 4–5) notes:

> created models and concepts that rapidly became the Volkswagens of the field – easy to drive, reliable, and sleek. Mundell drew on the Canadian experience to point out the striking implications of capital mobility for the conduct of stabilisation policy . . . his innovation went beyond imposing important new questions in that he created simple, forceful models to serve as organizing frameworks for thought and policy and as springboards for posing new problems.

Famous economists	Robert Mundell

Fig. 25.1
Robert Mundell
(1932–)

The Canadian Robert Mundell studied at MIT and the London School of Economics. He joined Columbia University in 1974, but also worked *inter alia* at the IMF, the University of Chicago, and the Graduate Institute in Geneva. Using formal analysis and intuitive interpretation of the results, he provided the foundations for the analysis of the implications of monetary and fiscal policy under different exchange rate regimes and various degrees of capital mobility. Similar work in the 1960s by Marcus Fleming, a long-time deputy director of the IMF research department, ensured that textbooks refer to the Mundell–Fleming model, although it is clear that Mundell's influence and contribution predominate, as is evident from the Dornbusch quote in the main text. Mundell had a keen eye for answering questions with important policy implications, as he also did when analysing the theory of optimum currency areas, which greatly influenced the policy debate on Europe's EMU many years later. This influence was clearly acknowledged when he was awarded the Nobel prize in economics in 1999, where the press release states: 'At a given point in time academic achievements might appear rather esoteric; not long afterwards, however, they may take on great practical importance.'

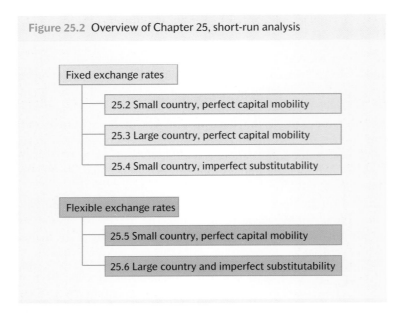

Figure 25.2 Overview of Chapter 25, short-run analysis

The Mundell–Fleming model analyses the interactions of output, money, and interest-bearing assets in an open economy. The effectiveness of fiscal and monetary policy is influenced by three factors: (i) the exchange rate regime; (ii) the size of the country; and (iii) the degree of capital mobility. As summarized in Figure 25.2, we analyse these influences sequentially in the remainder of this chapter, starting with a fixed exchange rate regime for a small country under perfect capital mobility. This setting finds fiscal policy to be very effective and monetary policy entirely ineffective, due to the endogeneity of the money stock under fixed exchange rates. These strong policy conclusions are mitigated for large countries (Section 25.3) and under imperfect capital mobility (Section 25.4). The effectiveness of fiscal and monetary policy for a small country under perfect capital mobility is reversed under a regime of flexible exchange rates (Section 25.5), in which case monetary policy is very effective and fiscal policy is entirely ineffective. These conclusions are again mitigated for large countries and under imperfect capital mobility (Section 25.6).

25.2 Fixed exchange rates (small country, perfect capital mobility)

We analyse a setting in which there are two assets: money and bonds, where money holdings do not earn an interest rate whereas bond holdings do. There are both domestic and foreign bonds, which we assume to be *perfect substitutes*. Economic agents are therefore indifferent between holding either domestic or foreign bonds, such that their yields must be equalized. Since exchange rates are fixed and there is no exchange rate uncertainty, this implies that the domestic and foreign interest rates must be the same. Moreover, we assume that portfolio *adjustment* is *instantaneous*. The combination of perfect substitutability and instantaneous portfolio adjustment is called *perfect capital mobility*. It implies that yields are continuously equalized and asset holders are always in portfolio equilibrium. As we will discuss in the sequel, the degree of capital mobility has important implications for the ability to conduct monetary policy.

In this section we analyse a small open economy which is not able to influence economic conditions in the rest of the world economy. As we focus on the short run and prices are fixed, we will normalize the domestic and foreign price level and the fixed exchange rate equal to 1 (taking logs therefore means that they do not show up in the equations). Consequently, the demand for money m depends positively on transactions demand from changes in output y and negatively on the opportunity cost from increases in the interest rate i, see equation (25.1). We label this the *LM* equation. In the short run, given fixed prices and a fixed exchange rate, demand in the economy is determined by a simple open economy *IS* equation, where output depends negatively on the interest rate (associated with the costs of investment) and positively on output in the rest of the world, see equation (25.2). As in Chapter 24, variables without any subscripts will refer to Home, whereas variables with a subscript f will refer to Foreign. The term u in equation (25.2) is a demand shift parameter, reflecting other factors affecting the demand for domestic goods. Note that the real exchange rate, as analysed in Chapter 23, does not yet play a role in equation (25.2) since prices and the nominal exchange rate are fixed (its impact is therefore subsumed in the parameter κ_1). This will change when we analyse a flexible exchange rate regime in Sections 25.5–6. Equation (25.3), finally, indicates that perfect capital mobility implies that the domestic interest rate is equal to the foreign interest rate. Since we are analysing a small country which cannot influence economic conditions in the rest of the world, the foreign interest rate is fixed, as is the foreign output level.

(25.1)
$$m = \alpha y - \beta i$$

(25.2)
$$y = \kappa_1 - \kappa_2 i + \kappa_3 y_f + u$$

(25.3)
$$i = i_f$$

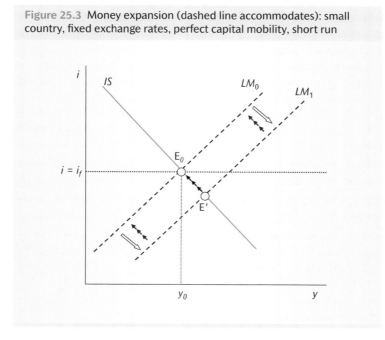

Figure 25.3 Money expansion (dashed line accommodates): small country, fixed exchange rates, perfect capital mobility, short run

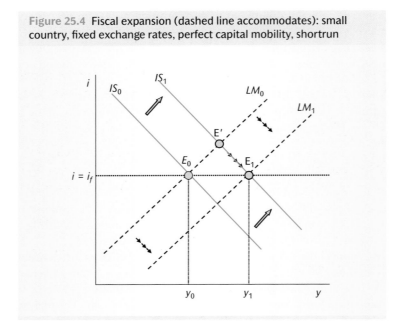

Figure 25.4 Fiscal expansion (dashed line accommodates): small country, fixed exchange rates, perfect capital mobility, shortrun

As illustrated in Figure (25.3), at the initial equilibrium point E_0, the model is solved quite easily. First, perfect capital mobility (equation 25.3) determines the interest rate. Second, using this information, the *IS* curve (equation 25.2) determines output. Third, using these interest rate and output levels, the *LM* curve (equation 25.1) determines money demand. As already explained in Chapter 24, under a fixed exchange rate regime money supply is endogenous with perfect capital mobility (since the central bank has to intervene by buying or selling international reserves to maintain the fixed exchange rate). The *LM* curve therefore accommodates to whatever level of money demand ensures equilibrium in the economy. This implies that if the monetary authorities conduct monetary policy by increasing domestic credit, indicated by the outward shift of the *LM* curve from LM_0 to LM_1 in Figure 25.3, the impact of this monetary policy is completely reversed by an offsetting contraction of the international reserves, which shifts the *LM* curve back from LM_1 to LM_0. Thus, for a small country with fixed exchange rates under perfect capital mobility, monetary policy is entirely ineffective.

Figure 25.4 illustrates what happens in these circumstances if there is a fiscal expansion in Home. First, the fiscal expansion shifts the *IS* curve to the right, from IS_0 to IS_1. Point E′ in Figure 25.4 cannot be an equilibrium as it would imply a higher interest rate in Home than in Foreign. Consequently, there is an inflow of international reserves and an accommodating expansion of the domestic money supply which shifts the *LM* curve to the right, from LM_0 to LM_1. The new equilibrium is therefore at point E_1, where output has expanded considerably as a result of fiscal policy, not only from the fiscal expansion itself, but also because of the accomodating monetary expansion. We therefore arrive at the following strong

Policy conclusion I: for a small country with fixed exchange rates under perfect capital mobility, fiscal policy is very effective whereas monetary policy is entirely ineffective.

25.3 Fixed exchange rates and large countries (perfect capital mobility)

The strong policy conclusions for a small country faced with a fixed exchange rate and perfect capital mobility derived in Section 25.2 are mitigated if the country is 'large' instead of 'small', indicating that its economic policies are influential enough to affect equilibrium conditions in the rest of the world economy. We analyse this in our two-country setting by adding an LM curve and an IS curve for Foreign; see equations (25.1′) and (25.2′), respectively. Foreign's money demand rises from an increase in transactions demand if its output level rises (the term $\alpha_f y_f$ in 25.1′) and falls as a result of an increase in opportunity costs if the interest rate rises (the term $-\beta_f i_f$ in 25.1′). Similarly, Foreign's output level falls with an increase in the interest rate (the term $-\kappa_{2f} i_f$ in 25.2′) and rises if demand from abroad increases as a result of an increase in Home's output (the term $\kappa_{3f} y$ in 25.2′). With perfect capital mobility, the interest rate must be the same in the two countries; that is, equation (25.3) must hold. Together these five equations determine money demand in Home and in Foreign, the output level in Home and in Foreign, and the interest rate.

(25.1′) $$m_f = \alpha_f y_f - \beta_f i_f$$

(25.2′) $$y_f = \kappa_{1f} - \kappa_{2f} i_f + \kappa_{3f} y$$

Note that an increase in Foreign's output level would increase Home's output (25.1), which in turn would increase Foreign's output (25.1′), which would increase Home's output, etc. As shown in Technical Note 25.1, these types of interconnections in the world economy can be summarized by deriving equilibrium IS and LM equations. These are shown in equations (25.1″) and (25.2″), where a prime (′) indicates a newly defined (positive) parameter and m_w denotes the world demand for money ($m_w \equiv m + m_f$).

(25.1″) $$LM_e: \quad m_w = \alpha' y - \beta' i + \alpha_f \kappa_{1f}$$

(25.2″) $$IS_e: \quad y = \kappa_1' + u' - \kappa_2' i$$

All newly defined parameters in (25.1″) and (25.2″) are larger than their counterparts in (25.1) and (25.2); that is, $\alpha' > \alpha$, $\beta' > \beta$, $u' > u$, $\kappa_1' > \kappa_1$, and $\kappa_2' > \kappa_2$. These two equilibrium relationships jointly determine Home's output level and the world interest rate, as illustrated at the initial point of intersection E_0 of the upward-sloping LM_e curve and the downward-sloping IS_e curve in Figure 25.5. The IS curve is flatter than in the small-country case (since $\kappa_2' > \kappa_2$), indicating that a decline in interest rates is more expansionary as a result of the mutual international repercussion effects.

Figure 25.5 illustrates that the ineffectiveness of monetary policy under fixed exchange rates exposed in Section 25.2 is mitigated if such a policy is conducted by a large country able to influence the world interest rate. A credit expansion in Home increases the world money stock and shifts the LM_e curve to the right. The new equilibrium is at point E_1, where the interest rate has fallen and Home's output has increased. Output in Foreign also increases, both as a result of the fall in the interest rate and as a result of the output expansion in Home. A similar analysis of a fiscal expansion in Home would shift the IS curve to the right (not shown in the figure), increase Home's output, and increase the interest rate. In that case, the effect on Foreign's output is ambivalent. On the one hand foreign output will expand as a

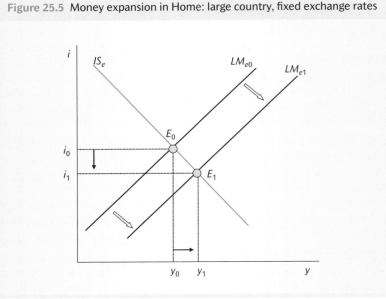

Figure 25.5 Money expansion in Home: large country, fixed exchange rates

result of the increase in Home's output. On the other hand, foreign output will contract as a result of the rise in interest rates. The net effect is uncertain. To conclude: once mutual repercussion effects are taken into consideration, both fiscal and monetary policy are effective. The main difference is that a domestic fiscal expansion may lower income abroad, whereas a domestic monetary expansion will always increase income abroad.

25.4 Imperfect substitutability (small country, fixed exchange rates)

A second possibility to mitigate the strong policy conclusions for a small country faced with a fixed exchange rate and perfect capital mobility, as derived in Section 25.2, is to allow for imperfect substitutability between domestic and foreign assets. Retaining the small-country assumption, that is taking Foreign's interest rate and level of output as given, the domestic interest rate is determined by equilibrium in the home securities market. Since they are imperfect substitutes for foreign securities, irrespective of whether or not domestic securities are internationally traded, their equilibrium yield is determined endogenously. Capital market equilibrium is therefore given in equation (25.3'), where K is the stock of domestic securities held by the private sector and σ is the demand for domestic securities.[1] Obviously, the demand for our securities rises with an increase in the domestic interest rate and falls with an increase in the foreign interest rate.

(25.3') $K = \sigma(i, i_f, y, y_f)$

Equilibrium in Home's financial markets is determined by money market equilibrium (25.1) and equilibrium in the security market (25.3'). In view of the fixed exchange rate regime, which makes the money supply process endogenous, financial equilibrium determines the money stock or, for given domestic credit D, the stock of international reserves R (see Section 24.3) and the yield on domestic securities. So what happens if there is a domestic credit expansion, such that the central bank buys domestic debt and creates money $(-dK = dD > 0)$? The reduction in the stock of securities creates an excess demand and thereby lowers Home's interest rate. The extent of this reduction depends on the degree of asset substitutability. If Home and Foreign securities are almost perfect substitutes, the domestic interest rate will remain very close to the foreign interest rate. If they are very imperfect substitutes, however, there must be a large change in Home's interest rate in order to accept the shift in portfolio composition.

As explained earlier, if Home and Foreign securities are perfect substitutes, there will be *no* change in Home's interest rate and consequently no change in the demand for money. In those conditions, in view of the endogeneity of the money supply under fixed exchange rates, the domestic credit expansion must be completely offset by a contraction of international reserves; that is, $dR = -dD$. If Home and Foreign securities are imperfect substitutes, however, the domestic credit expansion will result in a fall in the domestic interest rate. This reduction in the interest rate is more substantial if the degree of substitutability falls. Associated with the fall in the domestic interest rate is a rise in the demand for money; see equation (25.1). Consequently, in view of the rising demand for money, the domestic credit expansion is no longer completely offset by a contraction of international reserves; that is, $-dR/dD < 1$. Again, this effect is larger if it is harder to substitute between domestic and foreign securities. One method for determining the degree of assets substitutibility is therefore to empirically estimate the *offset coefficient* dR/dD. Our discussion on the degree of asset substitutability is summarized in equation (25.4), whereas Box 25.1 discusses some empirical estimates of offset coefficients.

(25.4)
$$-\frac{dR}{dD} = \begin{cases} 1, & \text{if perfect asset substitutability} \\ <1, & \text{if imperfect asset substitutability} \end{cases}$$

Figure 25.6 Monetary expansion: small country, fixed exchange rates, imperfect substitutability, short run

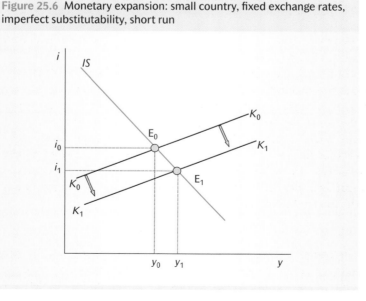

Box 25.1   Empirically estimated offset coefficients

The offset coefficient measures the degree to which a domestic credit expansion is offset by a contraction of international reserves in a system of fixed exchange rates; see equation (25.4) and the discussion in the main text. With some caveats, it can be interpreted as a measure of the degree of asset substitutability. Early work on estimating offset coefficients was done by Kouri and Porter (1974), soon followed by Bean (1976), Connoly and Taylor (1976), Genberg (1976), Guittan (1976), and Zecher (1976). Using these studies, as reported and discussed in Hallwood and MacDonald (2000), Figure 25.7 illustrates some estimated offset coefficients. In four cases, identified by the shaded bars in the figure, the estimate is not statistically significantly different from (minus) 1, suggesting perfect substitutability between domestic and foreign assets. In the five other cases the offset coefficient is smaller than 1 in absolute terms, suggesting imperfect asset substitutability or (in the cases of Germany and Japan) a large-country effect.

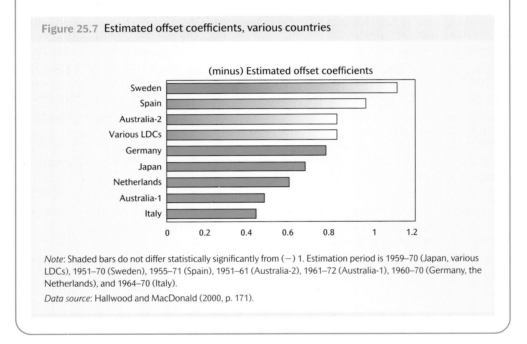

Figure 25.7 Estimated offset coefficients, various countries

Note: Shaded bars do not differ statistically significantly from (−) 1. Estimation period is 1959–70 (Japan, various LDCs), 1951–70 (Sweden), 1955–71 (Spain), 1951–61 (Australia-2), 1961–72 (Australia-1), 1960–70 (Germany, the Netherlands), and 1964–70 (Italy).

Data source: Hallwood and MacDonald (2000, p. 171).

The implications for our discussion on the effectiveness of monetary policy are illustrated in Figure 25.6, which shows the downward-sloping *IS* curve along with the *KK* curve with equilibrium in the market for domestic securities. The slope of the *KK* curve is determined by the degree of asset substitutability. Under perfect capital mobility, the *KK* curve is horizontal. The initial equilibrium is at point E_0. As explained above, a domestic credit expansion shifts the *KK* curve down from K_0K_0 to K_1K_1. The extent of the downward shift depends on the degree of asset substitutability or the offset coefficient. With imperfect substitutability, the interest rate falls and output expands to reach the new equilibrium E_1. Monetary policy now works, while the effects of fiscal policy will be dampened (not shown). With perfect substitutability, the *KK* curve is flat, the downward shift is zero, and monetary policy is entirely ineffective.

25.5 Flexible exchange rates (small country, perfect capital mobility)

The remainder of this chapter analyses the short-run impact of fiscal and monetary policy under a *flexible* exchange rate regime in which payments are balanced and the money stock is fully controlled by the monetary authorities. This section focuses on a small country facing perfect capital mobility to arrive at effectiveness conclusions diametrically opposed to those derived in Section 25.2 under fixed exchange rates. More specifically, we show that under flexible exchange rates monetary expansion is very effective for raising output, whereas fiscal expansion leads to full crowding out through a deterioration of the current account balance and is therefore entirely ineffective. The next section again mitigates these conclusions for large countries and imperfect substitutability.

Although we assume, as before, that domestic and foreign prices are fixed in this short run analysis, the fact that the nominal exchange rate S is fully flexible implies that the real exchange rate SP_f/P, which is the price of Foreign relative to Home goods, can change. Since the real exchange rate plays a crucial role in the ensuing analysis, we do not normalize the domestic and foreign price levels to unity (so the log terms p and p_f show up in the equations below), while realizing that any change in the real exchange rate is only brought about by a change in the nominal exchange rate. Moreover, we restrict attention in this chapter to static expectations regarding the exchange rate, such that with an integrated world capital market nominal interest rates are equated internationally. The more interesting (and more complicated) analysis of expectations formation is postponed until Chapter 26.

Monetary equilibrium is given in the *LM* equation (25.5), where the real money stock $m–p$ is equal to money demand, which depends positively on output (transactions demand) and negatively on the interest rate (opportunity costs). Output is demand determined, as given in the *IS* equation (25.6). We distinguish four different factors influencing demand. First, net exports are determined by the real exchange rate, where an increase (a rise in the relative price of foreign goods) leads to an improvement of the current account (provided the Marshall–Lerner condition holds; see Chapter 23). Second, an increase in the interest rate reduces investment demand. Third, an increase in foreign output increases demand for our goods. Fourth, and finally, the term u is a demand shift parameter. Equation (25.7) closes the model by requiring that the domestic interest rate is equal to the foreign interest rate.

$$(25.5) \qquad\qquad m - p = \alpha y - \beta i$$

$$(25.6) \qquad\qquad y = \kappa_1(s + p_f - p) - \kappa_2 i + \kappa_3 y_f + u$$

$$(25.7) \qquad\qquad i = i_f$$

As illustrated in Figure 25.8 at the initial equilibrium point E_0, the model is solved quite easily. First, perfect capital mobility (equation 25.7) determines the interest rate. Second, using this information and given the money stock completely controlled by the monetary authorities, the *LM* curve (equation 25.5) determines output. Third, using these interest rate and output levels, the *IS* curve (equation 25.6) determines the nominal exchange rate. In this setting, therefore, the *IS* curve accommodates to whatever level of the exchange rate ensures equilibrium in the economy.

The effectiveness of monetary policy in this setting is also illustrated in Figure 25.8. A monetary expansion shifts the *LM* curve to the right, from LM_0 to LM_1, because the fixed price level

Figure 25.8 Money expansion (dashed line accommodates): small country, flexible exchange rates, perfect capital mobility, short run

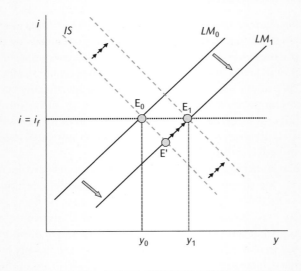

Figure 25.9 Fiscal expansion (dashed line accommodates): small country, flexible exchange rates, perfect capital mobility, short run

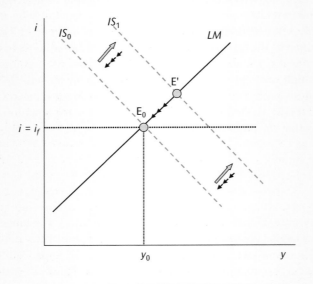

Box 25.2   The fi – fi – fi rule

To remember the effectiveness of fiscal and monetary policy for a small country under fixed and flexible exchange rates and perfect capital mobility can sometimes be difficult for students. The Dutch–American economist Richard Gigengack, who works at the University of Groningen, devised an amusing mnemonic to assist his students. We can make three bilateral choices, regarding

- Policy: fiscal – monetary
- Exchange rates: fixed – flexible
- Effectiveness: fine – not fine

The fi – fi – fi rule consists of two parts. First, it notes that *fi*scal policy under *fi*xed exchange rates works *fi*ne (i.e. is effective). Second, it argues that the student (starting from fi – fi – fi) can change any *two* bilateral choices to arrive at the correct conclusion. By switching, for example, the policy and effectiveness choices it follows that monetary policy under fixed exchange rates does not work fine, etc.

---

implies that a rise in nominal balances also increases real balances. This shift leads to a fall in interest rates and an expansion of output. In the absence of capital mobility, the new equilibrium would be at point E', where the goods and money markets clear and the current account balance has deteriorated. Taking capital mobility into consideration, however, implies that point E' cannot be an equilibrium because the domestic interest rate has fallen below the foreign interest rate, creating a tendency for capital to flow out and thus causing a depreciation of the domestic currency (a rise in S). This depreciation, in turn, lowers the relative price of domestic goods and shifts the accommodating *IS* curve up and to the right, leading to a further increase in domestic output, but this time accompanied by a rise in the domestic interest rate (closing the gap with the foreign interest rate). The depreciation of the domestic currency continues until monetary equilibrium is restored at the foreign interest rate (point E_1). In these circumstances, therefore, monetary policy is very effective: first because output increases as a result of the monetary expansion, and subsequently as a result of the accommodating depreciation of the domestic currency which improves the current account balance.

Figure 25.9 illustrates the effects of a fiscal expansion which, given the initial exchange rate, shifts the *IS* curve up from IS_0 to IS_1. Again, in the absence of capital flows the new equilibrium would be at E', where output and the interest rate have increased. Taking capital mobility into consideration, this cannot be the final equilibrium since the domestic interest rate is higher than the foreign interest rate, creating a tendency for capital to flow in and thus causing an appreciation of the domestic currency (a fall in S). This appreciation shifts demand away from domestic to foreign goods. Since the appreciation of the domestic currency will continue until the initial equilibrium (determined by the foreign interest rate and the *LM* curve) is reached, the *IS* curve shifts all the way back from IS_1 to IS_0. The appreciation of the domestic currency therefore leads to complete *crowding out*, that is a current account deterioration which completely offsets the initial demand expansion. To summarize (see also Box 25.2), we arrive at the following strong:

Policy conclusion II: for a small country with flexible exchange rates and perfect capital mobility, monetary policy is very effective whereas fiscal policy is entirely ineffective.

25.6 Flexible exchange rates, large countries, and imperfect substitutability

The strong policy conclusions derived in the previous section on the effectiveness of monetary and the ineffectiveness of fiscal policy under a flexible exchange rate regime are again mitigated if we analyse large countries or allow for imperfect substitutability. As we will see, the analysis of large countries that are able to influence economic conditions in the rest of the world is a bit more involved than in the case of fixed exchange rates discussed in Section 25.3. We can analyse international repercussions in a two-country setting by adding an *LM* curve and an *IS* curve for Foreign analogous to those for Home; see equations (25.5′) and (25.6′), respectively. Note that the impact of a change in the real exchange rate $s + p_f - p$ for Foreign's demand is, of course, opposite to the impact on Home's demand, compare (25.6) and (25.6′).

(25.5′)
$$m_f - p_f = \alpha_f y_f - \beta_f i_f$$

(25.6′)
$$y_f = -\kappa_{1f}(s + p_f - p) - \kappa_{2f} i_f + \kappa_{3f} y$$

With perfect capital mobility, the interest rate must be the same in the two countries; that is, equation (25.7) must also hold. Together these five equations determine the output level in Home and Foreign, the interest rate in Home and Foreign, and the nominal exchange rate. For comparative static purposes it is most convenient to reduce this system to two equilibrium equations, which we do in two steps.

First, we substitute (25.7) into the other equations and note that income demand at home depends in part on the income level abroad (25.6), while income demand abroad depends in part on the income level at home (25.6′). These two equations therefore jointly and simultaneously determine the income level in each country as a function of the real exchange rate and the interest rate. As shown in Technical Note 25.2, which also defines the positive parameters κ_1', κ_{1f}', κ_2', κ_{2f}', and u', the net effect of these interactions is:

(25.8)
$$y = \kappa_1'(s + p_f - p) - \kappa_2' i + u'$$
$$y_f = -\kappa_{1f}'(s + p_f - p) - \kappa_{2f}' i + \kappa_{3f} u'$$

Other things equal, therefore, the real exchange rate has a positive effect on the income level at home and a negative effect on the income level abroad. For both countries, an increase in the interest rate reduces output, while an increase in the domestic demand shift parameter increases income at home more strongly than income abroad.

Second, we realize that general equilibrium in both countries requires that the income levels determined in equation (25.8) be consistent with the income levels for monetary equilibrium; see equations (25.5) and (25.5′). Full equibrium for the Home economy can therefore be derived by substituting Home's output level from (25.8) into (25.5). This gives us combinations of the world interest rate i and the real exchange rate $s + p_f - p$ with full equilibrium in the Home economy; see Technical Note 25.2 and equation (25.9) below. As illustrated in Figure 25.10, it is an upward-sloping curve since an increase in the real exchange rate, which is a depreciation of the Home currency, raises income in Home after taking into account international repercussion effects. A higher interest rate is therefore required to restore equilibrium. Similarly, full equibrium for the Foreign economy can be derived by substituting Foreign's output level from (25.8) into (25.5′). This gives us combinations of the world

Figure 25.10 Fiscal expansion in Home: large country, flexible exchange rates

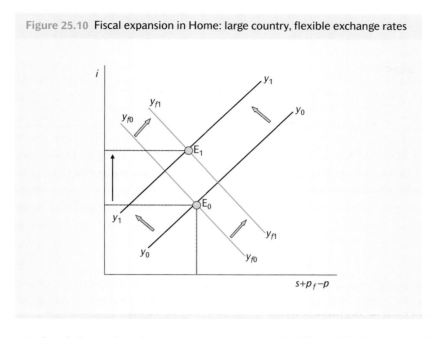

interest rate i and the real exchange rate $s + p_f - p$, with full equilibrium in the Foreign economy. This curve is downward sloping since an increase in the real exchange rate, which is an appreciation of the Foreign currency, reduces income in Foreign after taking into account international repercussion effects. A lower interest rate is therefore required to restore equilibrium. Taken together, this gives us two curves in interest rate and real exchange rate space determining full equilibrium in the world economy. The details of this derivation are given in Technical Note 25.2, which also defines the positive parameters γ_1, γ_{1f}, γ_2, and γ_{2f}. Equation (25.9) summarizes the resulting full equilibrium relationships for the Home and Foreign economy. As illustrated by the initial equilibrium at point E_0 in Figure 25.10, the two curves jointly determine the equilibium interest rate and real exchange rate.

(25.9)   Home: $i = \gamma_1(s + p_f - p) + \gamma_2(\alpha u' - (m - p))$

          Foreign: $i = -\gamma_{1f}(s + p_f - p) + \gamma_{2f}(\alpha_f \kappa_{3f} u' - (m_f - p_f))$

Figure 25.10 illustrates the effects of a fiscal expansion in Home on the world economy. The initial equilibrium is at E_0, the point of intersection of the upward-sloping $y_0 y_0$ curve (depicting combinations of interest rate and real exchange rate with equilibrium in the Home economy) and the downward-sloping $y_{f0} y_{f0}$ curve (depicting combinations of interest rate and real exchange rate with equilibium in the Foreign economy). At the initial real exchange rate, the fiscal expansion in Home (the term u' in equation 25.9), taking international repercussions into account, will raise income in both countries. To restore equilibrium the interest rate must rise, shifting the $y_0 y_0$ curve up to $y_1 y_1$ and the $y_{f0} y_{f0}$ curve up to $y_{f1} y_{f1}$. The interest rate must therefore unambiguously rise as a result of the fiscal expansion. The net effect on the real exchange rate is uncertain as it depends on the relative shifts of the equilibrium schedules. The effects of the fiscal policy on income can be deduced from the money market equilibrium conditions (25.5) and (25.5'). Since the money supply has not changed and the interest rate has increased, the income level must have increased in both countries. In short, since a large country can affect the interest rate it faces in the world economy, fiscal policy under a regime of flexible exchange rates is no longer ineffective. There is, therefore, no complete crowding out.

The effect of monetary policy can be analysed similarly. A monetary expansion in Home would shift the *yy* curve down and to the right (not shown in the figure) and leave the foreign

 Box 25.3   **Japan's economic slump**

For many years since the Second World War, Japan was the shining economic example for other countries to follow. Its economy grew rapidly and unemployment was low (certainly by Western standards) for several decades. Toyota's just-in-time production process set the standard for all other car producers in the world and the popular media that feared that Japan's ingenuity and relentless drive forward would soon dwarf production levels in the rest of the world. All of this changed after Japan's stock market crash in 1991 and after it became clear that the phase of rapid catch-up had ended for good. For the next fourteen years Japan's economic performance was rather mediocre and unemployment levels increased; see Figure 25.11(a). In response, the Japanese government did what it had done for a long time when the economy was slowing down: it gave a fiscal stimulus. The government budget deficit was high and rising. In contrast, the money growth rate declined drastically, such that the inflation rate also dropped, even to deflation levels (falling prices); see Figure 25.11(b). In view of the standard policy recommendation as explained in this chapter, this policy response is quite surprising. Under a system of flexible exchange rates and with high capital mobility, monetary policy is more effective than fiscal policy. In this respect, the prominent economist Paul Krugman has pointed out in a number of papers (see e.g. Krugman, 1998) that a *permanent* monetary expansion (to overcome the so-called liquidity trap) is necessary to put Japan's economy back on track.

Figure 25.11 **Economic developments in Japan, 1980–2003**

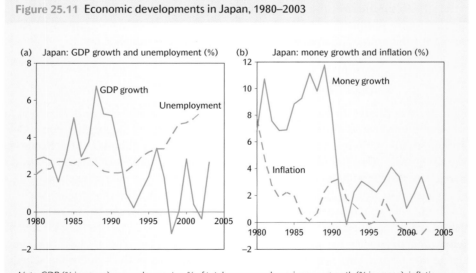

Note: GDP (% increase); unemployment as % of total; money and quasi money growth (% increase); inflation, consumer prices (annual %).

Data source: World Bank Development Indicators CD-ROM 2005

equilibrium schedule $y_f y_f$ unaffected. It therefore results in a decrease in the world interest rate and an increase in the real exchange rate, that is a depreciation of the Home currency. This raises income in Home. Remarkably, the opposite is true in Foreign. Again, using the monetary equilibrium condition (25.5′) and noting that the foreign money supply has not changed, it is clear that the decline in interest rate must be offset by a decrease in foreign income to restore monetary equilibrium.

It has become clear from the above analysis that both fiscal and monetary policy can be effective if a country can influence the interest rate it faces. Since this is also possible in the case of imperfect asset substitutability, which is more completely analysed in Section 25.4, it should come as no surprise that fiscal policy can be effective even for a small country under flexible exchange rates if domestic and foreign assets are imperfect substitutes. Obviously, the extent of this effectiveness is influenced by the degree of asset substitubility. In the limit, with perfect substitutes, a small country cannot influence its own interest rate and fiscal policy is ineffective under flexible exchange rates.

25.7 Conclusions

We analysed the effectiveness of fiscal and monetary policy in various conditions, namely for small and large countries, under fixed and flexible exchange rates, and for varying degrees of capital mobility. As summarized in Table 25.1, we arrived at very strong policy conclusions for small countries under conditions of perfect capital mobility, namely that fiscal policy is very effective and monetary policy entirely ineffective under fixed exchange rates, whereas monetary policy is very effective and fiscal policy is entirely ineffective under flexible exchange rates. Although these strong conclusions are mitigated for large countries able to influence the world interest rate and in the case of imperfect capital mobility, there is broad consensus that, in view of the generally high degree of international capital mobility, fiscal policy is

Table 25.1 Effects of fiscal and monetary policy under perfect capital mobility (short-run)

(a) Fixed exchange rate regime

Home is	Monetary expansion in Home Effect on output in		Fiscal expansion in Home Effect on output in	
	Home	Foreign	Home	Foreign
Small country	0	0	+	0
Large country	+	+	+	?

(b) Flexible exchange rate regime

Home is	Monetary expansion in Home Effect on output in		Fiscal expansion in Home Effect on output in	
	Home	Foreign	Home	Foreign
Small country	+	0	0	0
Large country	+	−	+	+

more effective in the short run under fixed exchange rates and monetary policy is more effective in the short run under flexible exchange rates.

Table 25.1 also summarizes the international spillover effects of short-run fiscal and monetary policy. It shows a clear international conflict of interests. Under fixed exchange rates a small country can only boost output through a fiscal expansion, which if the country is large may reduce output abroad. Similarly, under flexible exchange rates a small country can only boost output through a monetary expansion, which if the country is large will reduce output abroad for sure. In this respect, when facing unemployment the rest of the world will always support the less effective policy expansion in Home, as it will never hurt and may benefit the Foreign output level.

TECHNICAL NOTES

Technical Note 25.1 Large-country solution, fixed exchange rates

Imposing perfect capital mobility, the interest rates in the two countries must be the same ($i=i_f$). If we now substitute (25.2′) in (25.2) and rearrange, we get the large-country full equilibrium IS_e equation; see (25A.1). Note that we assume $1 - \kappa_3\kappa_{3f} > 0$

(25A.1)
$$y = (\kappa_1 + u - \kappa_2 i) + \kappa_3 y_f = (\kappa_1 + u - \kappa_2 i) + \kappa_3(\kappa_{1f} - \kappa_{2f} i + \kappa_{3f} y)$$

$$(1 - \kappa_3\kappa_{3f})y = \kappa_1 + u + \kappa_3\kappa_{1f} - (\kappa_2 + \kappa_3\kappa_{2f})i$$

$$y = \frac{\kappa_1 + \kappa_3\kappa_{1f}}{(1 - \kappa_3\kappa_{3f})} + \frac{u}{(1 - \kappa_3\kappa_{3f})} - \frac{(\kappa_2 + \kappa_3\kappa_{2f})}{(1 - \kappa_3\kappa_{3f})}i = \kappa_1' + u' - \kappa_2' i$$

where
$$\kappa_1' = \frac{\kappa_1 + \kappa_3\kappa_{1f}}{(1 - \kappa_3\kappa_{3f})}; \quad u' = \frac{u}{(1 - \kappa_3\kappa_{3f})}; \quad \kappa_2' = \frac{(\kappa_2 + \kappa_3\kappa_{2f})}{(1 - \kappa_3\kappa_{3f})}$$

Similarly, world money demand is the sum of the demand from the individual countries (25.1) and (25.1′). Substituting now gives us the large-country equilibrium LM_e equation; see (25A.2).

(25A.2)
$$m_w = m + m_f = (\alpha y - \beta i) + (\alpha_f y_f - \beta_f i)$$

$$m_w = \alpha y - (\beta + \beta_f)i + \alpha_f(\kappa_{1f} - \kappa_{2f} i + \kappa_{3f} y)$$

$$m_w = (\alpha + \alpha_f\kappa_{3f})y - (\beta + \beta_f + \alpha_f\kappa_{2f})i + \alpha_f\kappa_{1f} = \alpha' y - \beta' i + \alpha_f\kappa_{1f}$$

where
$$\alpha' = \alpha + \alpha_f\kappa_{3f}; \quad \beta' = \beta + \beta_f + \alpha_f\kappa_{2f}$$

Technical Note 25.2 Large-country solution, flexible exchange rates

We combine equations (25.6) and (25.6′) in matrix notation; see (25A.3). We invert this system (using for example Cramer's rule) to get (25A.4). Multiplication then gives (25A.5). We assume $1 - \kappa_3\kappa_{3f} > 0$ and that the direct income effect dominates the indirect effect; that is, $\kappa_1 - \kappa_3\kappa_{1f} > 0$ and $\kappa_{1f} - \kappa_{3f}\kappa_1 > 0$. Consistency of the solutions (25A.5) for income with monetary equilibrium, see (25.5) and (25.5′), gives (25A.6).

(25A.3)
$$\begin{bmatrix} 1 & -\kappa_3 \\ -\kappa_{3f} & 1 \end{bmatrix} \begin{bmatrix} y \\ y_f \end{bmatrix} = \begin{bmatrix} \kappa_1(s + p_f - p) - \kappa_2 i + u \\ -\kappa_{1f}(s + p_f - p) - \kappa_{2f} i \end{bmatrix}$$

(25A.4)
$$\begin{bmatrix} y \\ y_f \end{bmatrix} = \left(\frac{1}{1 - \kappa_3\kappa_{3f}}\right) \begin{bmatrix} 1 & \kappa_3 \\ \kappa_{3f} & 1 \end{bmatrix} \begin{bmatrix} \kappa_1(s + p_f - p) - \kappa_2 i + u \\ -\kappa_{1f}(s + p_f - p) - \kappa_{2f} i \end{bmatrix}$$

(25A.5)
$$\begin{bmatrix} y \\ y_f \end{bmatrix} = \begin{bmatrix} \kappa_1'(s + p_f - p) - \kappa_2' i + u' \\ -\kappa_{1f}'(s + p_f - p) - \kappa_{2f}' i + \kappa_{3f} u' \end{bmatrix}$$

where
$$\kappa_1' = \frac{\kappa_1 - \kappa_3\kappa_{1f}}{1 - \kappa_3\kappa_{3f}}; \quad \kappa_2' \equiv \frac{\kappa_2 + \kappa_3\kappa_{2f}}{1 - \kappa_3\kappa_{3f}}; \quad u' = \frac{u}{1 - \kappa_3\kappa_{3f}}$$

$$\kappa_{1f}' = \frac{\kappa_{1f} - \kappa_{3f}\kappa_1}{1 - \kappa_3\kappa_{3f}}; \quad \kappa_{2f}' = \frac{\kappa_{2f} + \kappa_{3f}\kappa_2}{1 - \kappa_3\kappa_{3f}}$$

(25A.6)

Home: $\kappa_1'(s + p_f - p) - \kappa_2'i + u' = (1/\alpha)(m - p + \beta i)$

or $\quad i = \gamma_1(s + p_f - p) + \gamma_2(\alpha u' - (m - p))$

where $\quad \gamma_1 = \dfrac{\alpha\kappa_1'}{\beta + \alpha\kappa_2'}; \quad \gamma_2 = \dfrac{1}{\beta + \alpha\kappa_2'}$

Foreign: $\quad -\kappa_{1f}'(s + p_f - p) - \kappa_{2f}'i + \kappa_{3f}u' = (1/\alpha_f)(m_f - p_f + \beta_f i)$

or $\quad i = -\gamma_{1f}(s + p_f - p) + \gamma_{2f}(\alpha_f\kappa_{3f}u' - (m_f - p_f))$

where $\quad \gamma_{1f} = \dfrac{\alpha_f\kappa_1'}{\beta_f + \alpha_f\kappa_{2f}'}; \quad \gamma_{2f} = \dfrac{1}{\beta_f + \alpha_f\kappa_{2f}'}$

QUESTIONS

Question 25.1

Suppose the citizens of a small open economy with a fixed exchange rate suddenly realize that the future is not as bright as they had imagined. To prepare for the hard times ahead, they suddenly save more and consume less.

25.1A Suppose for a moment that the central bank does not intervene (the exchange rate is flexible). Indicate how this shock changes the IS and LM curve of the small economy. What happens to GDP and trade? How do the interest rate and exchange rate change without central bank intervention?

25.1B How will the central bank of the small economy act in order to keep the exchange rate fixed? What is the effect of this policy response on GDP and trade?

The government and central bank of our small economy are not happy with the negative consumer sentiment and wish to give a boost to the economy.

25.1C Explain whether the authorities can better boost the economy with fiscal policy, monetary policy, or a combination of both.

25.1D Should the government and central bank consider abolishing the fixed exchange rate regime before they give a stimulus to the economy?

Question 25.2

The citizens of a large open economy with a fixed exchange rate may also lose confidence. As a result they save more and consume less.

25.2A Draw the IS and LM curve of a large open economy. Explain in what way and why these curves differ from the IS and LM curves of a small open economy.

25.2B Indicate on the graph what the effects are of the loss of confidence. How do GDP and the interest rate change? What is the effect on the rest of the world?

25.2C What can the authorities (central bank and government) do to counter the negative effects of the loss of confidence? Can foreign authorities do something?

25.2D Discuss which policy measure is best to take.

Questions 25.3[2]

From 2003 onwards the world economy, most notably the USA, started to grow again. In 2004 and 2005 the American Federal Reserve system raised short-term interest rates several times in order to cool down the economy. Despite these developments, the real bond yields remained unusually low. The media voiced two alternative theories to explain these low real bond yields. One group of economists explained the low real bonds yields by excess saving and another by excess liquidity. Use the IS–LM model (in which both curves represent the world economy) to explain how excess saving and excess liquidity can lead to low bond yields. Which theory is most likely to explain the economic phenomenon?

 See the Online Resource Centre for a Study Guide containing more questions
www.oxfordtextbooks.co.uk/orc/vanmarrewijk/

NOTES

1 The impact of changes in wealth on the demand for securities is ignored in equation (25.3′).

2 Based on *The Economist*, 'Is the world experiencing excess saving or excess liquidity', 13 August 2005.

EXPECTATIONS AND STICKY PRICES

26

Objectives/key terms

- Dornbusch–overshooting model
- Rational expectations
- Adaptive expectations
- Mathematical–statistical expectations
- Chartists and fundamentalists
- Sticky prices
- Phase diagram
- Individual expectations
- Bubbles and sunspots
- Random walks

The Dornbusch–overshooting–sticky-price model provides a bridge between short-run and long-run analysis. We also evaluate the crucial role of expectations formation.

26.1 Introduction

This chapter focuses on a crucial aspect in international monetary economics, namely the role of expectations formation in determining the exchange rate. At the same time, the chapter provides a bridge between the short-run fixed price analysis of Chapter 25 and the long-run flexible price analysis of Chapter 24, by investigating exchange rate formation in a sticky-price model. Created by Dornbusch (1976), this model assumes that prices cannot adjust instantaneously, but instead respond to discrepancies in long-run equilibrium fundamentals. As it was the first model to explain the important empirical phenomenon of exchange rate overshooting and is still central to international monetary analysis today, it is referred to both as the *Dornbusch* model and the *overshooting* model.

The chapter consists of two main parts. The first part, Sections 26.2–26.5, focuses on the bridge between short-run and long-run equilibrium by analysing the transition process from the short-run equilibrium (with a given price level) to the long-run equilibrium (with fully flexible prices). The role of the expectations formation process turns out to be vital for determining this transition path. The second part of the chapter, Sections 26.6–26.8, then analyses the expectations formation process in more detail using the flexible price monetary model; see Chapter 24. We will discuss some problems, such as indeterminacy, and some fascinating possibilities, such as rational bubbles.

Famous economists	Rudiger Dornbusch

Fig. 26.1
Rudiger Dornbusch
(1942–2002)

The German economist Rudiger Dornbusch studied at the Graduate Institute in Geneva, Switzerland, and the University of Chicago. He briefly worked at Rochester, the London School of Economics, and Chicago before moving to MIT. As a good debater with a lively personality he had a profound impact on many prominent disciples, policy issues, and the intellectual climate. His most influential contribution on policy and research in international finance, which appeared in 1976, explains why exchange rates fluctuate so markedly. Expectations formation and price stickiness played an important role in this so-called 'overshooting' model, on which Kenneth Rogoff (2002) remarked: 'His justly celebrated 'overshooting' paper is, indeed, arguably the most influential article written in the field of international economics since World War II.' In a contribution to commemorate the 25th anniversary of the paper, a few months earlier while Dornbusch was still alive, he also noted (Rogoff, 2002b): 'There is little question that Dornbusch's rational expectations reformulation of the Mundell–Fleming model extended the latter's life for another twenty-five years, keeping it in the forefront of practical policy analysis.'

26.2 Rational expectations and financial equilibrium

As explained in Box 24.3, the uncovered interest parity condition, a crucial building block in international monetary economics, automatically ensures that the way in which economic agents form expectations is an important determinant of the equilibrium exchange rate at each point in time. If economic agents have forward-looking behaviour, we have to somehow solve the nestedness problem, because the exchange rate today depends on the expected exchange rate tomorrow, while the exchange rate tomorrow will depend on the expected exchange rate as of tomorrow for the day after tomorrow, etc. We return to these issues in Section 26.6. For now, we will assume that agents have *rational expectations*; that is, individual agents must form expectations in a way consistent with the economic model itself. In Sections 26.2–26.5, in the absence of any uncertainty, this hypothesis amounts to *perfect foresight*; that is, individuals know the exact future path of the exchange rate and all other relevant economic variables when making their decisions.

The Dornbusch model is one of the first papers in international finance to incorporate rational expectations, only pre-dated in this respect by Black (1973). It is based on four under-lying assumptions: (i) in the long run the quantity theory of money and purchasing power parity (PPP) holds, (ii) in the short run goods prices are sticky and there is slow adjustment to disturbances, (iii) uncovered interest rate parity always holds, and (iv) the economic agents are endowed with rational expectations (here: perfect foresight). This section discusses the financial equilibrium. Section 26.3 introduces price stickiness and the phase diagram. Section 26.4 then analyses rational expectations and equilibrium dynamics, which are used in Section 26.5 to discuss exchange rate overshooting.

The building blocks for determining the financial equilibrium are given in equations (26.1)–(26.3). The real demand for money M/P depends positively on the income level y (transactions demand) and negatively on the interest rate i (opportunity costs). Using a log-arithmic specification, equilibrium in the money market is given by equation (26.1). The assets held by individual agents in the economy are deflated by the weighted average of domestic prices p_h and foreign prices, where the latter are equal to p_f denominated in foreign currency and $s + p_f$ denominated in domestic currency (s denotes the spot exchange rate); see equation (26.2).[1] Finally, the uncovered interest rate parity condition as discussed in Chapter 21 relates the expected change in the exchange rate to the difference between Home and Foreign inter-est rates ($i_h - i_f$). In combination with imposing rational expectations (such that the actual change in the exchange rate is equal to the expected change), and using continuous rather than discrete time (such that the change over time is equal to $\dot{s}$, using the convention intro-duced in Chapter 24), the uncovered interest parity condition is given in equation (26.3).

$$(26.1) \qquad\qquad m - p = \alpha y - \beta i_h$$

$$(26.2) \qquad\qquad p = \gamma p_h + (1 - \gamma)(s + p_f)$$

$$(26.3) \qquad\qquad \dot{s} = i_h - i_f$$

By combining equations (26.1)–(26.3) we can determine the financial equilibrium as a first-order differential equation of the exchange rate s and the domestic prices p_h:

$$(26.4) \qquad\qquad \dot{s} = \left[\gamma p_h + (1 - \gamma)s + \underbrace{(\delta - m)}_{exogenous} \right](1/\beta),$$

where the constant δ is a combination of the exogenous variables (p_f, y, and i_f) and the parameters (α, β, and γ); see Technical Note 26.1.

Equation (26.4) describes the motion of the exchange rate in a rational expectations environment. It is illustrated in Figure 26.2 by taking two steps.

- The first step is to determine combinations of the exchange rate s and the domestic price level p_h for which the exchange rate does not change. This gives the downward–sloping $\dot{s} = 0$ curve in Figure 26.2. The reasoning is as follows. It is evident from equation (26.3) that the exchange rate does not change if the domestic interest rate is equal to the foreign interest rate, which is given. Plugging this domestic interest rate in the money demand function (26.1) gives, other things equal, the equilibrium price level. Since the price level is a weighted average of domestic and foreign prices, see equation (26.2), an increase in the domestic price p_h must be accommodated by a decrease in the exchange rate s to restore financial equilibrium.

- The second step is to determine whether the exchange rate increases or decreases above and below this curve; that is, whether $\dot{s}$ is larger or smaller than zero. Consider point E on the $\dot{s} = 0$ curve in Figure 26.2, where the exchange rate does not change. If we move up in the figure, the price level is too high for financial equilibrium (see equation 26.2), which drives up the domestic interest rate (see equation 26.1), which must lead to an expected rise in the exchange rate to restore the uncovered interest parity condition (equation 26.3). This is summarized in equation (26.4), indicating that an increase in the exchange rate (starting from point E) will lead to an increase in the expected change in the exchange rate $\dot{s}$. Since it was zero at point E, it must become positive above that point, implying that the exchange rate will increase for all points above the $\dot{s} = 0$ curve. Similarly, the exchange rate will decrease for all points below this curve, as indicated by the vertical arrows in Figure 26.2.

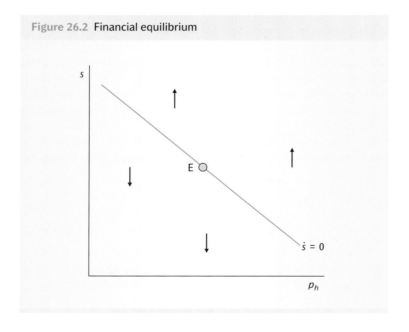

Figure 26.2 Financial equilibrium

26.3 Price stickiness and the phase diagram

As noted earlier, it is an empirical fact that goods prices are much less volatile than exchange rates for a variety of reasons; see Box 24.1. The Dornbusch model takes this fact as given; that is, it does not try to explain it, and assumes that prices are 'sticky'. This means that prices cannot adjust instantaneously (cannot 'jump'), but only gradually change in response to goods market disequilibrium. Exchange rates, in contrast, can (and will) adjust instantaneously to ensure market equilibrium. The sluggish adjustment of prices is given in equation (26.5), where λ is a parameter to measure the speed of adjustment and $\bar{s}$ is the long-run equilibrium PPP exchange rate; see equation (26.6).

(26.5) $$\dot{p}_h = \lambda(s - \bar{s})$$

(26.6) $$\bar{s} = p_h - p_f$$

By combining equations (26.5) and (26.6) we can determine the price adjustment equation, giving the speed at which domestic prices adjust to disequilibrium:

(26.7) $$\dot{p}_h = \lambda(s - p_h + p_f)$$

If the exchange rate is above its PPP value (and the domestic currency is undervalued), the price level is increasing, and vice versa if it is below its PPP value. The sluggish price adjustment is illustrated in Figure 26.3 using the two-step procedure of section 26.2. The first step determines combinations of the exchange rate s and the domestic price level p_h for which the domestic price level does not change. This gives the upward-sloping $\dot{p}_h = 0$ curve in Figure 26.3. The second step is to determine whether prices are rising or falling above and below this curve. Consider point E on the $\dot{p}_h = 0$ curve in Figure 26.3, where the price level

Figure 26.3 Sluggish price adjustment

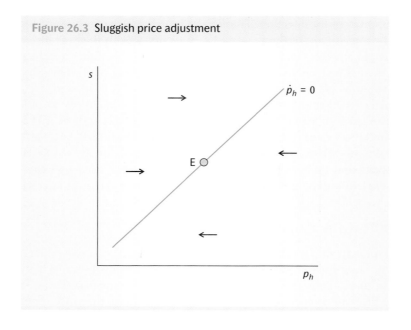

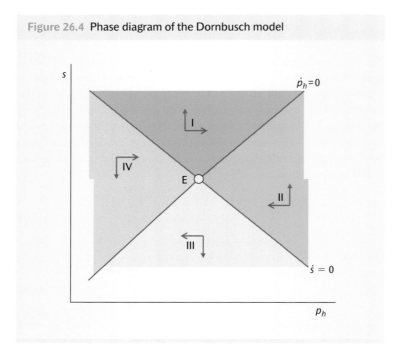

Figure 26.4 Phase diagram of the Dornbusch model

does not change. From equation (26.7) it is then clear that if we increase the exchange rate (move up in the figure), $\dot{p}_h$ will increase. Since it was zero at point E, it must become positive above point E. This implies that the price level will increase for all points above the $\dot{p}_h = 0$ curve. Similarly, the price level will decrease for all points below this curve, as indicated by the horizontal arrows in Figure 26.3.

Figure 26.4 combines the information of Figures 26.2 and 26.3 in one picture called a phase diagram. It summarizes the direction of motion for both the exchange rate and the price level. At point E, the intersection of the $\dot{s} = 0$ and $\dot{p}_h = 0$ curves, both the exchange rate and the price level do not change. Once the economy has reached this point, a full equilibrium is reached and there is no incentive to move away from this point. The intersection of the two curves subdivides the plane into four different areas, labelled I, II, III, and IV. Each of these areas is characterized by specific movements in exchange rates and prices, as indicated by the arrows in Figure 26.4. In area I, for example, both the price level and the exchange rate are increasing. Similarly, in area II the exchange rate is increasing while the price level is decreasing, etc. The next section analyses how rational expectations can be used to determine the equilibrium price and exchange rate movements. Section 26.5 then uses the equilibrium dynamics to explain the empirically observed phenomenon of exchange rate overshooting.

26.4 Equilibrium dynamics

The equilibrium dynamics for the economy are given in equations (26.4) and (26.7), for the financial equilibrium and price adjustment, respectively. They are illustrated in the phase diagram of Figure 26.4. If agents have rational expectations, they understand how the economy works; that is, they are aware of the above information and take this into account for determining their decisions and equilibrium in the economy. Figure 26.5 illustrates how this may

Figure 26.5 Dornbusch model dynamics

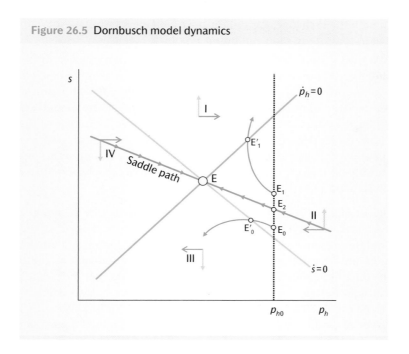

be useful for determining this equilibrium. We already know that, given the exogenous variables (such as the money stock and the foreign price level) and the parameters in this economy (such as the income elasticity of money demand and the speed of price adjustments), full equilibrium is achieved at point E, the intersection of the $\dot{s} = 0$ and $\dot{p}_h = 0$ curves. Now suppose that we are initially *not* at the equilibrium point E, but rather that the domestic price level at time 0 is too high, say equal to p_{h0}. We know that (i) prices are sticky (cannot adjust instantaneously) and (ii) exchange rates are fully flexible. This implies that the initial price level–exchange rate combination at time 0 must be somewhere along the vertical line determined by p_{h0}; see Figure 26.5.

Now that we have established that initially we must be somewhere along the vertical line in Figure 26.5, it remains to determine where exactly the equilibrium will be. The figure illustrates three possible trajectories out of an infinite number of possibilities to assist us in determining this equilibrium.

1 Suppose that the initial price level–exchange rate combination is given by point E_0 in the figure. As this point is in area II, we know that the exchange rate is increasing and the price level is decreasing. The speed at which this occurs is determined by equations (26.4) and (26.7). As we follow the trajectory in Figure 26.5, we note that at some time in the future we reach point E'_0 and cross over from area II to area III, such that henceforth both the exchange rate and the price level are decreasing. It is obvious that this trajectory will not lead us to the long-run equilibrium at point E.

2 Suppose that the initial price level–exchange rate combination is given by point E_1 in the figure. Again, this point is in area II such that the exchange rate is increasing and the price level is decreasing. As we follow the trajectory from point E_1 in Figure 26.5, we note that at some time in the future we reach point E_1 and cross over from area II to area I, such that

henceforth both the exchange rate and the price level are increasing. Again, this trajectory will not lead us to the long-run equilibrium at point E.

3 Suppose that the initial price level–exchange rate combination is given by point E_2 in the figure, a well-chosen point in between points E_0 and E_1. It is determined such that all points below E_2 will eventually cross over from area II to area III, while all points above E_2 will eventually cross over from area II to area I. Point E_2 is therefore very special as the trajectory determined by equations (26.4) and (26.7) does not cross over from area II to area I nor from area II to area III. Instead, the trajectory will lead us on a delicate path to the long-run equilibrium at point E. It is 'delicate' because if the initial exchange rate is just a little bit higher or a little bit lower, the trajectory will lead us in a completely different direction. Such a path is called a saddle path.

Agents with rational expectations are now able to determine the economic equilibrium. After all, they (i) understand the underlying economic system, (ii) know that the initial price level p_{h0} can only adjust slowly over time to the long-run equilibrium, and (iii) know that any initial exchange rate *other* than point E_2 in Figure 26.5 is *not* sustainable as it ultimately leads away from the long-run equilibrium. In short, they understand that the saddle path leading to the long-run equilibrium is eventually the only viable solution. Note that the fact that the saddle path is 'delicate' (there is only one solution leading to point E) is not a problem but actually helps the economic agents in determining the equilibrium. If there were several solutions leading to point E, the agents would have somehow to coordinate their actions in determining which one to pick. As everyone knows there is only one solution leading to the long-run equilibrium, the problem of choice does not arise. This is further discussed in Sections 26.6 and 26.7.

26.5 Exchange rate overshooting

We are now in a position to show how the model developed above can be used to explain the high variability of exchange rates caused by 'noise', 'new information', or 'exogenous shocks', as well as the empirical phenomenon of exchange rate overshooting, see Box 26.1. It should be noted from the start that, although the Dornbusch sticky-price model was the first model able to explain this type of behaviour, there are many alternative specifications using the

---

 Box 26.1   **An example of exchange rate overshooting[2]**

The term 'overshooting' is used when the short-run adjustment of an economic variable in a certain direction following an exogenous shock or policy change is larger then what is needed to restore the long-run equilibrium, necessitating a *reversal* of the direction at some time in the future. An example may clarify. Suppose that, following a policy shock, the exchange rate increases instantaneously by 40 per cent (from 1 to 1.4), while only a 20 per cent rise is necessary to restore long-run equilibrium (from 1 to 1.2). This means that after the initial *increase* of 40 per cent in the exchange rate there must be a subsequent *decrease* of 20 per cent (from 1.4 to 1.2) to reach the long-run equilibrium. The initial response is therefore 'too large' and the exchange rate 'overshoots'.[3] »

>> The currency crisis that hit a number of South-East Asian economies during 1997 provides an example of the overshooting phenomenon. In the time period preceding the crisis the South-East Asian countries maintained a fixed exchange rate relative to the US dollar. There was mounting pressure on the existing exchange rate to depreciate (it does not matter at this point why this was the case). Investors collectively started to sell their investments denominated in the currency under pressure. Initially, the authorities (particularly the central bank) tried to defy depreciation of the currency by supporting the present exchange rate, either by raising interest rates or by selling part of their foreign exchange reserves (and thus buying the local currency). As the speculative attack continued, the authorities had to give in and the currency started its (steep) decline. As illustrated for Thailand in Figure 26.6, the sharp decline following the July 1997 crisis was too large, and followed by substantial subsequent increases to restore equilibrium. These issues are further discussed in Chapter 29.

Figure 26.6 The Asian crisis in Thailand

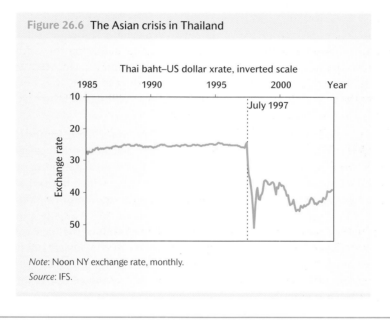

Note: Noon NY exchange rate, monthly.

Source: IFS.

same general methodology but not based on sticky prices which also give rise to exchange rate overshooting; see De Grauwe (1996) and Sarno and Taylor (2002).

The core argument is illustrated in Figure 26.7. Suppose the economy is initially in a state of rest (long-run equilibrium) at point E_0, with price level p_{h0} and exchange rate s_0. In the absence of any disturbances, exogenous shock, or policy changes, the economy will remain at point E_0 indefinitely and the price level and exchange rate do not change. At time period t_0, however, the monetary authorities unexpectedly decide to increase the money supply.[4] As is clear from equations (26.4) and (26.7), this does not affect the $\dot{p}_h = 0$ schedule associated with (long-run) purchasing power parity, but it does shift the $\dot{s} = 0$ curve up from $\dot{s}|_0 = 0$ to $\dot{s}|_1 = 0$; see Figure 26.7. Since the domestic price level is fixed in the short run and cannot adjust instantaneously, the rational economic agents know that the only path that will take the economy to the new long-run equilibrium at point E_1 is the trajectory following *saddle path*$_1$

Figure 26.7 Monetary expansion: exchange rate overshooting

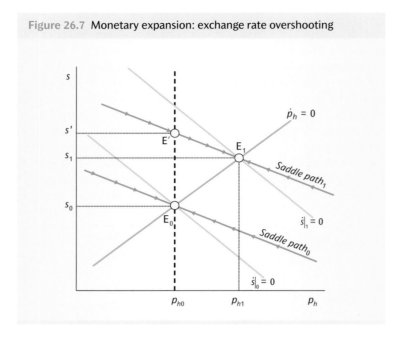

in the figure. At time period t_0 the economy therefore immediately jumps from the initial long-run equilibrium E_0 to the short-run equilibrium E' associated with the new saddle path at the price level p_{h0}. Over time, the domestic price level gradually increases, bringing about a whole sequence of short-run equilibria along the new saddle path in which the exchange rate gradually declines. This process continues until the new long-run equilibrium at point E_1 is reached.

The overshooting adjustment path is illustrated in Figure 26.8. Initially, the exchange rate is stable at s_0 until the time of the policy change t_0. As a result of the increase in the money supply, the exchange rate increases to $s_1 > s_0$ in the long run. The *impact effect* of the increase in the money supply at time t_0, however, is an immediate jump to $s' > s_1$, followed by a subsequent gradual decline to the long-run equilibrium; that is, the exchange rate 'overshoots'. Arguably, the fact that the exchange is flexible whereas the price level is not, *forces* the exchange rate to adjust by more than is necessary to restore long-run equilibrium, leading to a drastic change in the exchange rate as a result of the policy change.

Imagine, now, a world operating along the lines of the Dornbusch model, that is with sticky prices, flexible exchange rates, and agents with rational expectations, but in addition governed by uncertainty or 'news'. The latter may result from random shocks to the economic system, other components not explicitly modelled, unforeseen changes in economic policy, etc. The media (newspapers, television stations, radio programmes, the Internet, etc.) bombard us with thousands of new pieces of information every day. Some of these are important to the economic system, others are not. It usually takes some time to filter out the relevance of each new piece of information, but anything that is deemed ultimately to influence the long-run equilibrium will result in an instantaneous adjustment of the exchange rate. On the basis of rational expectations and sticky prices, even relatively small new pieces of information may give rise to substantial adjustments in the exchange rate, and possibly to overshooting. This, in a nutshell, is the explanation for the high variance of the exchange rate that we observe empirically.

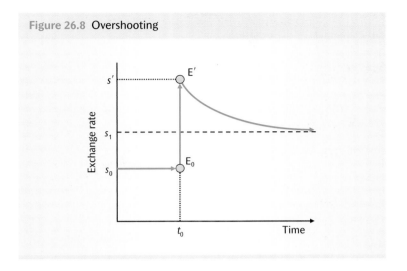

Figure 26.8 Overshooting

26.6 Expectations formation

It has become clear from the above analysis that the role of expectations formation is crucial for determining the equilibrium economic outcome. It therefore pays to delve a little deeper into the expectations formation process. Along the way it will become evident that, for expository purposes, we have cut a few corners in deriving the equilibrium in Section 26.4. This equilibrium is based on the rational expectations hypothesis introduced by Muth (1961), building on earlier work by Modigliani and Grunberg (1954). The concept is applied widely in (international) macroeconomics since the path-breaking papers by Lucas (1972, 1973), Sargent (1972, 1973), and Dornbusch (1976). Before that time, the expectations formation process was mostly based on Cagan's (1956) backward-looking adaptive expectations hypothesis; see Box 26.2.

Our core arguments are most easily explained in a discrete time framework based on the flexible price monetary model discussed in Section 24.4, including the uncovered interest rate parity condition; see Box 24.3. The model is briefly reviewed in Technical Note 26.3, which shows that the functioning of the model can be summarized in one forward-looking difference equation, namely:

$$(26.10) \qquad s_t = x_t + \Phi_t \, s^e_{t+1}, \quad 0 < \Phi < 1,$$

where s_t is the spot exchange rate, x_t is a combination of parameters, money supplies, and output levels, and $_t s^e_{t+1}$ is the value of the exchange rate at time $t + 1$ as expected by individuals forming expectations at time t. As already observed in Box 24.3, there is a nested reasoning inherent in equation (26.10) in which the exchange rate today depends on the expected exchange rate tomorrow, while the exchange rate tomorrow will depend on the expected exchange rate as of tomorrow for the day after tomorrow, etc. Essentially, the rational expectations hypothesis provides a method for dealing with this infinite-nestedness issue, as explained below and illustrated in Figure 26.9.

Box 26.2   Adaptive expectations

Before the breakthrough of rational expectations, which is widely used today in all fields of economics, the modelling of the expectations formation process was mainly based on Cagan's (1956) *adaptive expectations*. The main idea is simple as individuals use information on past forecasting errors to revise their expectations. Let $_tx^e_{t+1}$ be the value of the variable x at time $t + 1$ as expected by individuals forming expectations at time t. The adaptive expectations hypothesis is then given by:

(26.8)
$$\underbrace{_tx^e_{t+1} - {_{t-1}x^e_t}}_{\text{forecast adjustment}} = \theta(\underbrace{x_t - {_{t-1}x^e_t}}_{\text{forecast error}}), \quad 0 < \theta < 1$$

The hypothesis therefore asserts that individuals examine *ex post* in period t how accurate their prediction last period was regarding the actual value of variable x in this period (forecast error). They then revise their forecast for the variable x one period later by some fraction θ of the forecast error.

Technical Note 26.2 shows that the adaptive expectations hypothesis implies that the forecast in this period for the value of variable x in the next period is a (geometrically) weighted average of past observations, see equation (26.9).[5] This is both the main advantage and the main disadvantage of the adaptive expectations hypothesis. It is the main advantage because the *un*observable expectations term $_tx^e_{t+1}$ can be transformed into past *observations* of the variable x, which enables straightforward empirical analysis. It is the main disadvantage because any *backward*-looking expectations formation process implies that individual agents can make structural forecast errors indefinitely. In a world inhabited by rational economic agents this presents a major problem: as Bob Marley once observed, 'you can fool some people some time, but you cannot fool all the people all the time'.

(26.9)
$$_tx^e_{t+1} = \underbrace{\sum_{j=0}^{\infty} \theta(1 - \theta)^j x_{t-j}}_{\text{past observations}} + \underbrace{\lim_{n \to \infty}(1 - \theta)^{n+1} \, {_{t-n-1}x^e_{t-n}}}_{= \text{zero}}$$

Before we continue it is useful to distinguish between two different types of expectations, namely mathematical–statistical expectations and those held by individual agents.

- *Individual expectations* relate to what an economic agent today expects to hold regarding a particular value of some variable for some time in the future. It is this term denoted by $_ts^e_{t+1}$ for the exchange rate in (26.10) that is crucial for determining the economic equilibrium. In principle, agents can form their expectations regarding the future value of the exchange rate in any way they like. They could roll some dice, they could flip a coin, they could count the number of sun spots, or they could try to figure out the equilibrium value of the future exchange rate based on some economic model.

- *Mathematical–statistical expectations* relate to the expected value of some variable in the future based on an underlying mathematical–statistical model. It is denoted by the operator E_t, where the sub-index t indicates that expectations are formed given all relevant information available up to time t. Suppose we flip a fair coin in time period $t + 1$ and give the variable y_{t+1} the value 0 if the outcome is heads and 1 if the outcome is tails, then $E_ty_{t+1} = 0.5$ since the outcome heads is equally likely as the outcome tails (both occur with

Figure 26.9 Infinite nestedness, fundamentals, and bubbles

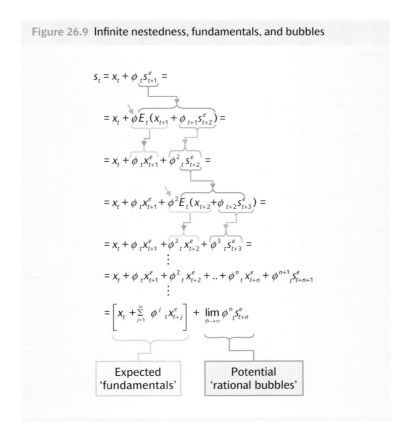

probability 0.5, indicating that $E_t y_{t+1} = 0.5 \cdot 0 + 0.5 \cdot 1 = 0.5$). Note that, in this case, the actual outcome cannot be equal to the mathematical expectation of 0.5 (it is *either* heads, in which case $y_{t+1} = 0$, *or* tails, in which case $y_{t+1} = 1$). Obviously, if we were to evaluate the expected value of this experiment two periods earlier it would still be 0.5; that is, $E_{t-2} y_{t+1} = 0.5$. In general, this need not be the case.

The rational expectations hypothesis argues that agents form expectations in a way that is consistent with the model itself; that is, the individual expectations are equal to the mathematical–statistical expectations.[6] Figure 26.9 shows how this hypothesis is applied to the flexible price monetary model summarized in equation (26.10).

1 $_t s_{t+1}^e = E_t(x_{t+1} + \Phi_{t+1} s_{t+2}^e)$ The individual expectation for the exchange rate next period is equal to the value determined by the economic model. This value is given by equation (26.10) one period ahead and depends on the underlying 'fundamentals' next period (x_{t+1}) and the value of the exchange rate expected next period by the individual agents one period ahead ($\Phi_{t+1} s_{t+2}^e$). For both of these terms expectations are formed given the available information at time t (E_t).

2 $\Phi E_t(x_{t+1}) = \Phi_t x_{t+1}^e$ The expected value for the fundamentals next period is equal to the individual expectations. If we recall that the variable x is a combination of parameters,

money supplies, and output levels (Technical Note 26.3), then this implies that the agents must find a way to forecast these values, for example based on rules imposed by the monetary authorities, or announcements concerning the future, etc.

3 $\Phi E_t(\Phi_{t+1}s^e_{t+2}) = \Phi^2{}_t s^e_{t+2}$ This uses a fundamental property of rational expectations, namely the fact that $E_t({}_{t+1}s^e_{t+2})$, which is what you expect today that you are going to expect tomorrow for the day after tomorrow, is equal to ${}_t s^e_{t+2}$, which is what you expect today for the day after tomorrow. In essence it argues that all available information is used efficiently; that is, individuals have no basis for predicting how they will change their expectations about future variables.

4 The infinite continuation of the above three arguments shows that the equilibrium solution for the exchange rate today is given by equation (26.11) below, as discussed in the next section.

26.7 Fundamentals and bubbles

As shown in the previous section and illustrated in Figure 26.9, the rational expectations solution to the flexible price monetary model is given by:

$$(26.11) \qquad s_t = \underbrace{\left[x_t + \sum_{j=1}^{\infty} \Phi^j{}_t x^e_{t+j} \right]}_{\text{fundamentals}=\tilde{s}_t} + \underbrace{\lim_{n\to\infty}\Phi^{nt} s^e_{t+n}}_{\text{potential rational bubble}}$$

We have decomposed this solution into two components, the fundamentals (which we define as $\tilde{s}_t$) and the potential rational bubble. The short cut taken in the exposition in sections 26.2–26.5 is therefore that we have focused attention exclusively on the fundamentals and ignored the possibility of bubbles (see below). This does not mean that restricting attention to fundamentals is easy or unwarranted. Indeed, it can be shown that in a long-run economic growth perspective, of which the Dornbusch model can be viewed as a simple example, it is necessary to restrict attention to the fundamentals and bubbles cannot arise, but this issue is too complex to deal with in this setting.[7]

A fundamental aspect of the rational expectations hypothesis is that it is forward looking, rather than the backward-looking adaptive expectations hypothesis, compare equations (26.11) and (26.9), respectively. This implies, as already noted above, that the economic agents must form forecasts for all relevant future economic variables, such as money supplies and outputs, in order to be able to determine today's exchange rate. Although this puts a formidable task on the shoulders of these agents, the advantage is that the expectations formation process takes place in a coherent framework and economic agents will not make structural forecast errors. They will, of course, make errors in their predictions, but there is no opportunity for the government or the central bank consistently to manipulate economic behaviour in a particular direction.

One of the disadvantages of the forward-looking character of the rational expectations hypothesis is that it creates possibilities of disturbances and coordination problems associated with 'bubbles'. The possibility arises because of the forward-looking expectations term in equation (26.11). Note that we have a very similar backward-looking expectations term in the adaptive expectations hypothesis, see equation (26.9). We have put that term equal to zero based on the argument that in retrospect the limiting expectations term is bounded from above (such that the term as a whole becomes zero). We cannot use the same argument for the forward-looking expectations term in equation (26.11), because why would we think today that the exchange rate cannot surpass some arbitrary upper bound some time into the indefinite future?

This is where the potential for rational bubbles appears, that is, 'something' that determines the current exchange rate in addition to the expected fundamentals term. From equations (26.10) and (26.11) it is clear that an arbitrary deviation from the fundamentals term that is expected to grow from period to period at the speed Φ^{-1} will provide a solution to the equilibrium condition (26.10); see Technical Note 26.4 for details. There are therefore multiple rational expectations solutions according to:

(26.12) $\qquad s_t = \tilde{s}_t + B_t, \quad$ where bubble B_t satisfies $\quad E_t(B_{t+1}) = \Phi^{-1}B_t$

So if all economic agents believe that there is a bubble B_t on top of the fundamentals $\tilde{s}_t$ which grows at the rate Φ^{-1} governing the exchange rate, then this satisfies the equilibrium condition and is thus a self-fulfilling prophecy. This, of course, poses a coordination problem, because how are the individual agents in the economy going to decide on the occurrence and size of the bubble B_t? It has been jokingly said that they perhaps count the number of sunspots to coordinate their actions, giving rise to the term 'sunspot equilibria'. Alternatively, the role of some large market players is thought to be instrumental in this respect, as discussed in Chapter 29 (financial crises). In the general foreign exchange market, however, it is now frequently argued that *chartists* play a crucial role in generating bubbles.

Chartist or 'technical' analysis involves using charts of past foreign exchange rate movements in conjunction with descriptive statistics to try to predict future exchange rate movements, which is then used as a basis for trading strategies. According to Frankel and Froot (1990: 183): 'Many so-called "chartist" forecasters, or technical analysts, are thought to use rules that are extrapolative, such as, "Buy when the 1-week moving average crosses above the 12-week moving average."' Various surveys show that the weight given to forecasting the exchange rate based on 'chartist' analysis is high for short-term forecasting horizons, while the weight given to 'fundamental' analysis increases for longer horizon forecasts; see Allen and Taylor (1990), Taylor and Allen (1992), and Lui and Mole (1998). In all cases, a substantial portion of short-run exchange rate forecasts is based on chartist analysis.

Frankel and Froot (1987, 1990) distinguish between different types of economic agents to model and explain empirical exchange rate phenomena. The 'fundamentalists' base their expectations on a Dornbusch overshooting model and the 'chartists' on extrapolation (autoregressive integrated moving average). The value of a currency is determined by portfolio managers on the basis of a weighted average of the expectations of chartists and fundamentalists, where the weight given to each varies over time.

Frankel and Froot argue that the high value of the US dollar in 1984 and 1985 as illustrated in Figure 26.10 can best be explained as a speculative bubble, based on the self-confirming market expectations driven by the increase in forecasting weight given to the chartists as a result of their previous forecasting success. They find the alternative, that the exchange rate is determined exclusively by fundamentals, unlikely (Frankel and Froot, 1990: 182): 'it is

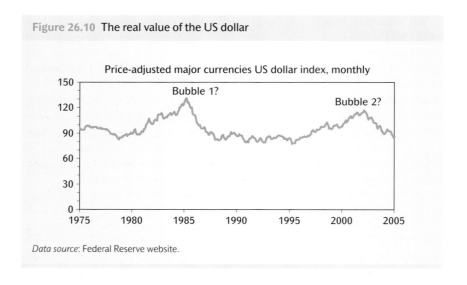

Figure 26.10 The real value of the US dollar

Data source: Federal Reserve website.

difficult to believe that there could have been an increase in the world demand for US goods (or in US productivity) sufficient to increase the equilibrium real exchange rate by more than 20 percent over a 9-month period, and that such a shift would then be reversed over the subsequent 9 months'.

In short, a speculative bubble driven by chartist behaviour is thought to be responsible for the high real value of the US dollar in 1984 and 1985. The politically driven burst in the bubble in 1985 then quickly drove the dollar down to its fundamental equilibrium value, see Section 23.4. A similar, second, bubble could be responsible for the high real value of the US dollar in 2001 and 2002, again followed by a rapid decline to restore the fundamental equilibrium. Note, however, that these are not fully rational bubbles as the three different types of economic agents (fundamentalists, chartists, and portfolio managers) do not base their forecasts on the complete information set of the model. Similar models with different types of agents are constructed, for example, by DeLong, Shleifer, Summers, and Waldmann (1990) and De Grauwe and Dewachter (1993).

26.8 Empirical evidence

The reader must have noted in this and the previous chapters that we provide ample anecdotal, historical, and heuristic information on the goodness-of-fit of the various exchange rate models based on simple graphs, statistics, and tests. So far we have not, however, thoroughly discussed and evaluated the empirical literature on econometric tests of exchange rate theories. As explained below, we will not do this here either.

Throughout this chapter we have analysed the importance of the expectations formation process for determining the exchange rate. Even in the absence of (rational) bubbles, forward-looking agents with rational expectations will take their best guess regarding the future values of all fundamental variables and expected policy responses by the monetary authorities into consideration when determining the exchange rate. This makes exchange rate models

Box 26.3   Meese and Rogoff: forecasting and random walks

Consider the following experiment. Your initial money holdings are $100. You start flipping a fair coin sequentially. Each time the outcome is heads your money holdings are increased by one dollar. Each time the outcome is tails your money holdings are reduced by one dollar. The evolution of your money holdings over time is now a simple example of a *random walk* (see also Box 28.2). The process has various obvious properties, one of which is that the expected value of your future money holdings is equal to your current money holdings. If we say that you are 'bankrupt' if your money holdings become zero, another property is, unfortunately for you, the fact that you will become bankrupt at some time in the future, for sure, no matter what your initial money holdings were.[8]

In a seminal contribution, Meese and Rogoff (1983) compare the out-of-sample forecasting accuracy of various exchange rate models with the accuracy of a random walk forecast for different, short-run time horizons. Using the root mean squared error of the forecast as a means for comparing the performance of different exchange rate models, they find that the random walk model performed as well as any of the estimated structural (monetary, Dornbusch, and portfolio) models; see Figure 26.11. Although one can always discuss the extent to which the structural models have been estimated accurately, the fact that a random walk model performed so well relative to these models did come as a shock. This is further discussed in Section 26.8.

Figure 26.11 Out-of-sample exchange rate forecasting

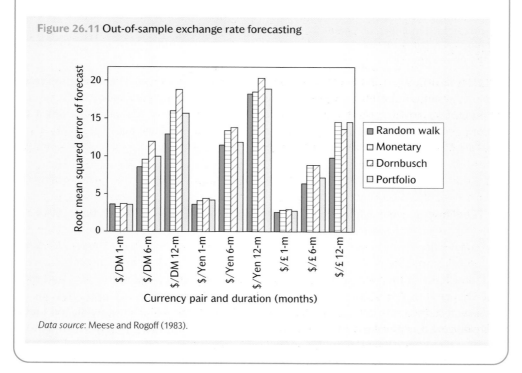

Data source: Meese and Rogoff (1983).

notoriously difficult to estimate empirically. A proper discussion of this literature, which is complex, technically advanced, and full of pitfalls and errors, requires a better understanding of econometric techniques than we take for granted in this book. We refer the reader to the overview and discussion in Sarno and Taylor (2002). At this point we want to emphasize two main results: the short-run result and the long-run result.

The *short-run result* is discussed in Box 26.3; no structural model is better in short-run fore-casting than a simple random walk model. In the presence of shocks and new information, the best forecast for tomorrow's exchange rate is today's exchange rate. In essence, this Meese and Rogoff (1983) result should not surprise us, as it is an efficiency criterion. If it was clear to everybody, based on some structural model and in the absence of interest rate differentials, that the exchange rate tomorrow is going to be higher than the exchange rate today, we could all make a profit by buying the currency today. This would immediately drive up the exchange rate today until the profit opportunity disappears, that is until the exchange rate today is equal to the expected exchange rate tomorrow.

The *long-run result* is somewhat more elusive: economic fundamentals are important for determining the long-run equilibrium exchange rate; see Koedijk and Schotman (1990). This aspect is usually emphasized in our boxes and anecdotal, historical, etc. discussions. The 'elu-siveness' relates to exactly *what* the fundamentals are (what to include and exclude). None the less, Sarno and Taylor (2002: 137) conclude:

> One finding which does, however, seem to have some validity, is that the monetary model does resurface in a number of empirical studies as a *long-run* equilibrium condition . . . . This finding . . . occurs with sufficient regularity in the empirical literature as to suggest . . . the emer-gence of a stylized fact.

It is clear that both results are important from a policy perspective. The short-run market efficiency result is important for realizing the limits and possibilities of policy interventions. The long-run (monetary) implications are important for realizing the extent to which the authorities can ultimately influence the nominal and real exchange rate. These and related issues are discussed in the Part III.C of this book.

26.9 Conclusion

The Dornbusch model analyses exchange rate adjustment in a model with sticky prices and rational expectations. Since prices are fixed in the short run and fully flexible in the long run, this framework provides a useful bridge between the fixed price analysis of Chapter 25 and the flexible price analysis of Chapter 24. At the same time, the Dornbusch model is able to shed some light on the overshooting phenomenon and the high variability of exchange rates. Basically, because prices are sticky and can adjust only gradually over time, the impact-adjustment of the exchange rate to any shocks or new information is magnified, and poten-tially adjusted by more than what is needed to restore the long-run equilibrium. In terms of historical impact in the international monetary arena, the Dornbusch model took over the baton from the Mundell–Fleming model and kept running for some twenty years before passing it on to the new open economy macro model. The latter is discussed in Chapter 31, which also provides more detail on how the economy moves from the short-run to the long-run equilibrium.

TECHNICAL NOTES

Technical Note 26.1 Derivation of the financial equilibrium

From (26.1) we can determine the domestic interest rate as a function of money supply, output, and the price level; see equation (26A.1). Equation (26A.2) first recalls the uncovered interest parity condition under perfect foresight, then substitutes equations (26A.1) and the definition of the price index (26.2), respectively.

(26A.1)
$$i_h = (1/\beta)(p + \alpha y - m)$$

(26A.2)
$$\dot{s} = i_h - i_f = (1/\beta)(p + \alpha y - m) - i_f = (1/\beta)[\gamma p_h + (1 - \gamma)(s + p_f) + \alpha y - m] - i_f$$

If we now define the auxiliary variable δ, a combination of parameters and exogenous variables, as in equation (26A.3), then (26A.2) reduces to (26.4) as used in the main text.

(26.A3)
$$\delta = (1 - \gamma)p_f + \alpha y - \beta i_f$$

Technical Note 26.2 Adaptive expectations

Equation (26.A4) is the adaptive expectations hypothesis. Rewriting leads to (26.A4′). The same equation one period earlier is given in (26.A5). A similar equation holds for all other earlier periods. Substituting first (26.A5) in (26.A4′) and subsequently the similar equation for all other earlier periods gives equation (26.A4′′) as used in Box 26.2.

(26.A4)
$$_tx^e_{t+1} - {}_{t-1}x^e_t = \theta(x_t - {}_{t-1}x^e_t), \quad 0 < \theta < 1$$

(26.A4′)
$$_tx^e_{t+1} = \theta x_t + (1 - \theta)\,_{t-1}x^e_t$$

(26.A5)
$$_{t-1}x^e_t = \theta x_{t-1} + (1 - \theta)\,_{t-2}x^e_{t-1}$$

(26.A4′′)
$$_tx^e_{t+1} = \theta x_t + (1 - \theta)[\theta x_{t-1} + (1 - \theta)\,_{t-2}x^e_{t-1}]$$
$$= \theta x_t + \theta(1 - \theta)x_{t-1} + (1 - \theta)^2\,_{t-2}x^e_{t-1}$$
$$= .. = \theta x_t + \theta(1 - \theta)x_{t-1} + \theta(1 - \theta)^2 x_{t-2} + \ldots + \theta(1 - \theta)^n x_{t-n} + (1 - \theta)^{n+1}\,_{t-n-1}x^e_{t-n}$$
$$= \sum_{j=0}^{\infty}\theta(1 - \theta)^j x_{t-j} + \lim_{n \to \infty}(1 - \theta)^{n+1}\,_{t-n-1}x^e_{t-n}$$

Technical Note 26.3 Flexible price monetary approach once more

There are two countries with monetary equilibrium given in (26.A6). Combining this with the Law of One Price (26.A7) gives (26.A8); see Chapter 24 for details.

(26.A6)
$$m - p = \alpha y - \beta i; \quad m_f - p_f = \alpha y_f - \beta i_f$$

(26.A7)
$$p = s + p_f$$

(26.A8)
$$s = (m - m_f) - \alpha(y - y_f) + \beta(i - i_f)$$

Imposing uncovered interest arbitrage in a discrete time frame gives (26.A9). Substitution in (26.A8) gives (26.A8′) and rearranging give (26.A8′′).

(26.A9)
$$_ts^e_{t+1} - s_t = (i_t - i_{f,t})$$

(26.A8′)
$$s_t = (m_t - m_{f,t}) - \alpha(y_t - y_{f,t}) + \beta(_ts^e_{t+1} - s_t)$$

(26.A8′′)
$$s_t = \frac{(m_t - m_{f,t}) - \alpha(y_t - y_{f,t})}{1 + \beta} + \frac{\beta}{1 + \beta}\,_ts^e_{t+1} = x_t + \Phi\,_ts^e_{t+1}$$

where
$$x_t = \frac{(m_t - m_{f,t}) - \alpha(y_t - y_{f,t})}{1 + \beta}; \quad \Phi = \frac{\beta}{1 + \beta} < 1$$

Technical Note 26.4 Rational bubbles in the flexible price monetary model

Equation (26.A10) recalls equilibrium condition (26.10) from the text and (26.A11) defines the fundamentals term $\tilde{s}_t$. The general rational expectations solution is then given in (26.A12) with the arbitrary bubble B_t.

(26.A10)
$$s_t = x_t + \Phi_t s^e_{t+1}$$

(26.A11)
$$\tilde{s}_t = \left[x_t + \sum_{j=1}^{\infty} \Phi^j \, _t x^e_{t+j} \right]$$

(26.A12)
$$s_t = \tilde{s}_t + B_t, \quad \text{where bubble } B_t \text{ satisfies } E_t(B_{t+1}) = \Phi^{-1} B_t$$

To verify that (26.A12) is indeed a solution to (26.A10), we first determine the expected exchange rate for the next period on the basis of (26.A12), using (26.A11):

$$_t s^e_{t+1} = E_t(s_{t+1}) = E_t(\tilde{s}_{t+1}) + E_t(B_{t+1})$$

$$= E_t \left[x_{t+1} + \sum_{j=1}^{\infty} \Phi^j \, _{t+1} x^e_{t+1+j} \right] + \Phi^{-1} B_t = \Phi^{-1} \left\{ \left[\sum_{j=1}^{\infty} \Phi^j \, _t x^e_{t+j} \right] + B_t \right\}$$

We then substitute this result in (26.A10) to get:

$$s_t = x_t + \Phi \, _t s^e_{t+1} = x_t + \left[\sum_{j=1}^{\infty} \Phi^j \, _t x^e_{t+j} \right] + B_t = \tilde{s}_t + B_t,$$

which is in accordance with the general solution (26.A12).

QUESTIONS

Question 26.1

26.1A In the Dornbusch model agents have rational expectations. Without uncertainty, this amounts to perfect foresight by agents. Can you explain why?

26.1B What causes the relative stickiness of prices?

26.1C Suppose you were to augment the Dornbusch model and introduced flexible prices. Which theory of exchange rates would we then have?

26.1D Which two important empirical observations of exchange rates are illustrated on the next page and can be explained by the Dornbusch model?

Question 26.2

26.2A Draw a phase diagram in which you indicate the exchange rate adjustment and the price adjustment equation. Indicate the long-run equilibrium point. What determines the slope of both curves?

26.2B Not all points in the phase diagram are valid combinations of the domestic price level and the exchange rate, because some points do not lead to a stable long-run equilibrium. Draw a line that indicates all valid combinations of the exchange rate and domestic price level in your diagram. What do we call this line?

26.2C In the short run, the domestic price level is fixed. Draw a line with all combinations of the exchange rate and the domestic price level in the short run after an economic shock.

26.2D Suppose now that the interest rate increases in the eurozone. Draw the consequences of this rate increase in your diagram and explain the economic intuition behind the dynamics.

Question 26.3

Suppose that you are chief economist at a bank and you are interviewed on live television about your currency views.

26.3A The journalist has heard something about overshooting, and he is curious to know whether recent labour

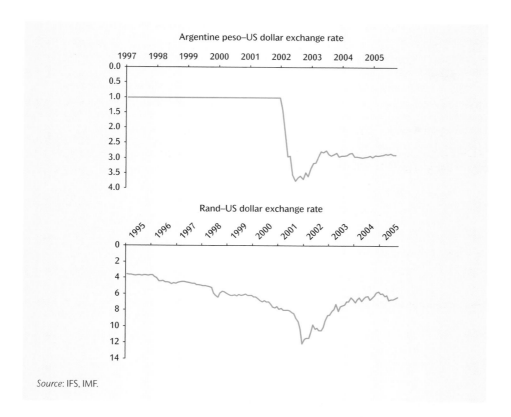

Source: IFS, IMF.

market flexibilization measures in the USA will have an exchange rate impact. Can you satisfy his curiosity and elaborate on this issue?

26.3B Delighted by your clear explanation of exchange rate economics, the journalist asks you to comment on the impact of the booming US economy on the dollar–euro rate. Explain with the help of equation (26.A3).

26.3C Despite your clear analysis, the journalist still has doubts about the current dollar–euro exchange rate. Surely, economic theory and rational behaviour can tell us something about the equilibrium exchange rate. Comment on his remarks.

26.3D If financial markets are efficient, does it make sense for you to comment on exchange rate developments for the coming year?

26.3E In light of empirical research on exchange rates, what can you tell the journalist with a reasonable degree of confidence about the dollar exchange rate?

 See the Online Resource Centre for a Study Guide containing more questions
www.oxfordtextbooks.co.uk/orc/vanmarrewijk/

NOTES

1 The qualitative implications are the same if domestic assets are simply deflated by the domestic price level only. In this case the $\dot{p}_h$ curve in Figure 26.3 is vertical, rather than downward sloping.

2 Based on Brakman et al. (2006, ch. 8).

3 The same terminology is usually also applied when the initial *decrease* is too large, although the term 'undershooting' is sometimes also used.

4 We abstain from delving into the philosophical problems associated with analysing unexpected policy changes in a perfect foresight model.

5 The limit in eq. (26.9) is equal to zero as long as the expected value term is finite (bounded from above).

6 This simultaneously implies that all agents will have the same individual expectations, as long as they all have rational expectations and have identical access to all relevant information (as we assume here). See Begg (1982) for an excellent treatment of these and related issues.

7 On economic growth models see, for example, Romer (2001) or Barro and Sala-i-Martin (2003).

8 This is not necessarily the case for random walks with 'drift'.

III.C
POLICY AND CREDIBILITY

Part III.C first provides the essence of a policy framework (objectives, targets, and instruments; Chapter 27) and applies this framework to fixed exchange rates (target zones; Chapter 28), financial crises (Chapter 29), and the process of European monetary unification (Chapter 30). This part concludes with a brief discussion of recent developments in new open economy macroeconomics (Chapter 31), which provides a bridge between international trade and international money (as discussed in Part IV).

OBJECTIVES, TARGETS, AND INSTRUMENTS

27

Objectives/key terms

- Strict inflation targeting
- Phillips curve
- Expectations-augmented Phillips curve
- Policy trade-off
- Barro–Gordon model
- Dynamic (in)consistency

- Flexible inflation targeting
- Modified Phillips curve
- Price rigidities
- Natural rate of unemployment
- Rules versus discretion
- Taylor rule

Distinguishing between objectives, instruments, and targets, we use the Phillips curve in the Barro–Gordon model to analyse policy discretion versus rules (e.g. the Taylor rule).

27.1 Introduction[1]

If you want to influence the outcome of an economic process you have to take several important steps, as summarized in Figure 27.1.

1   You have to specify what it is you want to achieve, that is specify your objectives. Although a politician may be very interested in re-election and a central bank president may wish to extend his term in office as well, we focus attention on benevolent individuals and institutions, striving to achieve some form of welfare maximization.

2   You will have to find a means for achieving your objectives. This implies, at the very least, that you have to understand how the economy functions and how you might be able to influence it by manipulating certain economic variables or parameters, which we will refer to as targets. This is not an easy job because the economic process is very complex and the result of your manipulation may be unclear, particularly if the economic agents start to take into account the actions and policies taken by you when making their decisions. None

Figure 27.1   Overview of the economic policy framework

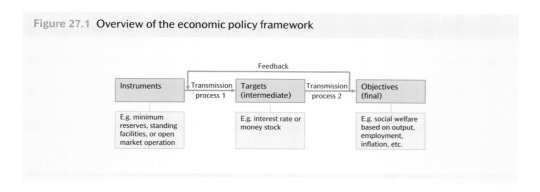

Famous economists	Robert Barro

Fig. 27.2
Robert Barro (1944 –)

The macroeconomist Robert Barro studied at Harvard and worked mainly at the University of Rochester before returning to Harvard. His initial contributions were in *dis*equilibrium macroeconomics (with Herschel Grossman), developing complete models with (Keynesian) rationing disequilibria. He soon shifted to the rational expectations revolution, elaborating on the Ricardian equivalence hypothesis: rational economic agents realize that every bond-financed debt must be met by future tax increases and adjust their savings accordingly; the method of debt financing is thus irrelevant for the economic equilibrium. He subsequently turned to dynamic inconsistency problems (with David Gordon), arguing that central banks are often tempted to violate their own inflation targets, which is taken into consideration by rational economic agents and thus raises the actual inflation rate. Consequently, as discussed in this chapter, following an externally imposed rule might be a more efficient way for the central bank to fight inflation.

the less, it is, for example, generally thought that an increase in the interest rate will reduce investments and slow down the economy, so it could potentially be used as a target variable for achieving your objectives. Similarly, if you think a rapid growth of the money supply leads to inflation and you want to fight inflation, your target variable may be the growth rate of the money supply.

3 Third, you must have means available to actually influence the target variables, such as rules that you can impose as a legislator or funds that you can invest as a government. We refer to these means as instruments. Again, there is some transmission process from the instruments to the target, indicating that the targets themselves may not be perfectly controlled by the authorities, certainly if there is complicated feedback; see Figure 27.1.

27.2 Objectives: welfare and the loss function

In the absence of personal goals, the ultimate objective of the political authorities should be the welfare of a nation's population. As an individual agent cares about thousands of different goods and services, spread across time and space, and there are millions of inhabitants in most countries, 'the' welfare function is impossible to derive from first principles. Consequently, the literature starts from a simple loss function at the macroeconomic level, to be minimized by the authorities; see Svensson (1999). If U denotes the unemployment level, π denotes the inflation rate, and an asterisk * denotes the target level for inflation or unemployment, a typical loss function L is given by:

(27.1)
$$L = b(U - U^*)^2 + (\pi - \pi^*)^2, b \geq 0$$

In this setting, both positive and negative deviations from the target levels, also referred to as the bliss points, constitute a welfare loss. As a result of the squaring, large deviations weigh

Figure 27.3 Different policy preferences; $U^* = 3, \pi^* = 0$

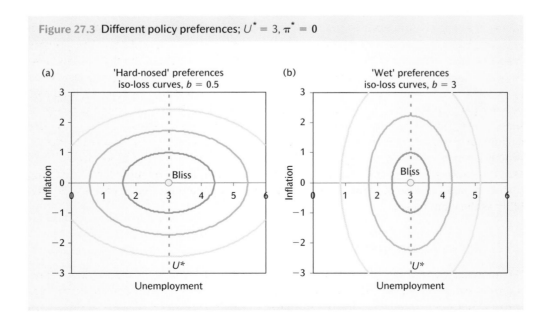

Table 27.1 Numerical inflation targets

Central bank	Inflation target (%)
Bank of Canada	1 – 3
Bank of England	2.5 (±1)
European Central Bank	0 – 2
Reserve Bank of Australia	2 – 3
Reserve Bank of New Zealand	0 – 3
Sveriges Riksbank	2 (±1)
Swiss National Bank	< 2

Source: Bofinger (2001: 130).

more heavily than small ones. For $b = 0$, the term *strict inflation targeting* is used, as the authorities then only care about inflation. For $b > 0$ the term *flexible inflation targeting* is used, as the authorities then try to balance the loss from output deviations and the loss from inflation deviations in making their decisions. The higher the welfare loss associated with unemployment deviations, that is the higher is the parameter b in equation (27.1), the more easily the authorities give in to public pressure to use monetary policy for other purposes than for fighting inflation. De Grauwe (1996) therefore uses the expression 'hard-nosed' government if b is low and 'wet' government if b is high. As illustrated in Figure 27.3 using iso-loss curves, a wet government is more willing to accept high inflation rates for a given reduction in unemployment than is a hard-nosed government.

Both inflation and employment are considered to be important in the USA, where the Federal Reserve Act (section 2A) states as objective to 'promote effectively the goals of maximum employment, stable prices, and moderate long-term interest rates'. In contrast, the current emphasis in Europe is on price stability, where Article 105(1) states: 'The primary objective of the ESCB shall be to maintain price stability.' In addition, the ESCB should also 'support the general economic policies in the Community.' Like some other central banks listed in Table 27.1, the ECB has been more explicit about its inflation target, which should be below 2 per cent per annum over the medium term; see also Chapter 30. Over the course of time, the emphasis has shifted back and forth. The international monetary system was price stability oriented in the Bretton Woods system of the 1950s and 1960s, as favored by the US Federal Reserve system. It was output stability oriented in the 1970s and 1980s, when many OECD countries were confronted with stagnation and high unemployment levels after long periods of rapid economic growth. During the 1990s, the pendulum shifted back to price stability as the main target.

27.3 From instruments to targets

The monetary authorities of a nation, say the central bank, usually have a range of instruments available for influencing economic conditions. As explained in the introduction, the instruments are used to affect the intermediate targets (interest rate or money stock), which are ultimately supposed to influence the final objective (welfare, as measured by inflation and unemployment). The instruments used today are in general more market oriented than in the decades after the second World War.[2] Bofinger (2001: 336) distinguishes between five main instruments:

– *Standing facilities for refinancing purposes*; this is essentially an overdraft facility extended by the central bank, that is a generous credit line at a given interest rate, which serves as the upper limit of the (narrow) money market rate.

– *Standing facilities for absorption purposes*; this enables banks to invest surplus central bank money at a fixed interest rate, which serves as the lower limit of the (narrow) money market rate.

– *Outright open market operations*; central-bank-initiated purchases of securities from the banks or sale of securities to the banks.

– *Securities repos* (repurchase operations); open market operations in which securities are bought or sold by the central bank for subsequent resale to or repurchase from a bank on an agreed date.

– *Minimum reserve requirements*; to be held by banks at the central bank, based on the bank's balance sheet positions and nowadays more market oriented through payment of a market interest rate.

It is useful to recall the distinction between the various types of money (monetary base, M_1, M_2 etc.); see Section 18.3 and Table 27.2. The central bank itself operates on the 'narrow' money market, where reserves are traded against claims on banks, the state, or private non-banks. The instruments mentioned above work directly on this market. Through the interaction between economic conditions and bank behaviour, the transmission process illustrated in Figure 27.1 and discussed in Chapter 18 translates the effects of the instruments on the narrow money market to the 'broad' money market, thus affecting the economic circumstances for the private non-bank sector and the state of the economy. There is thus a rather direct transmission process from the instruments to the narrow money market, and a more indirect transmission process to the broad money market, either of which could be identified as intermediate targets for policy.[3]

The demand for monetary base by the banks (B^d) is a downward-sloping function of the interest rate; see Chapter 18 and Figure 27.4. Given that demand, the central bank can, in principle, use its instruments for two targeting options on the narrow money market, namely (i) monetary base targeting, and (ii) interest rate targeting.[4] As also illustrated in Figure 27.4,

Table 27.2 The market for money

	Market participants	Assets traded
Monetary base	Central bank and commercial banks; some large companies	Central bank deposits (reserves) against claims on banks, the state, or private domestic non-banks
Money market	Commercial banks and the private non-bank sector	Commercial bank deposits against claims on non-banks

Source: adapted from Bofinger (2001: 324).

Figure 27.4 Monetary base and interest rate targeting

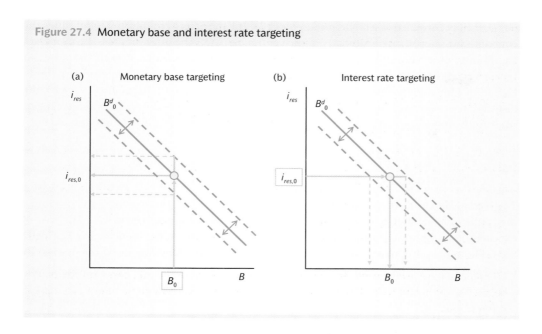

in the absence of uncertainty and shocks, that is given the stable demand function B_0^d, the two targeting options are equivalent. Associated with the monetary base target B_0 is the interest rate $i_{res,0}$. Similarly, associated with the interest rate target $i_{res,0}$ is the monetary base B_0. In practice, however, the demand function B_0^d is likely to fluctuate over time in response to uncertainty and shocks. Monetary base targeting then implies that these shocks are absorbed by fluctuations in the interest rate (panel (a) of Figure 27.4), while under interest rate targeting these shocks are absorbed by fluctuations in the monetary base (panel (b) of Figure 27.4). As explained below, most central banks have opted nowadays for interest rate targeting.

The details of the transmission process and the precise instruments used are undoubtedly important for determining the short-run equilibrium and the adjustment path of the economy to the long-run equilibrium. Suppose, for example, that a closed economy, which is initially in equilibrium, consists of an equal number of men and women. Even if we use the infamous (and unreal) method of a 'helicopter drop' to distribute a doubling of the money supply, how the helicopters are functioning is crucial for the short-run impact on the economy. If everyone receives an increase in money holdings proportional to their initial money holdings, there seems to be little reason for a change in the short-run equilibrium, other than a doubling of the price level. If, however, the extra money is equally distributed among all men in the economy and the women receive nothing, one might expect a short-run increase in the real demand for beer, and thus a more than double increase in the price of beer. Over time, as individual agents adjust their money holdings, this effect will disappear; see Laidler (1982) for a discussion. As noted in Chapters 20 and 24, eventually the quantity theory of money, adjusted for factors influencing changes in the demand for money, is crucial for understanding the long-run implications of changes in the money supply for prices and exchange rates.

Eventually, therefore, based on some type of transmission process from narrow to broad money, the monetary equilibrium determines a *combination* of money and interest rates, say

(*M, i*). If the central bank sets the money stock *M*, the monetary equilibrium determines the concomitant interest rate *i*. Similarly, if the central bank sets the interest rate *i*, the monetary equilibrium determines the money stock *M*. It is true, of course, that if there are different types of shocks and the transmission process of the two policies differs, the short-run implications of adjusting the money stock or the interest rate are different. In the end, however, the distinction between the two types of targeting policies makes little difference. If your car gets stuck in the mud, you just want to get it out and do not care if it is pushed out or pulled out.[5]

27.4 From targets to objectives: expectations and the Phillips curve

The second step in the policy framework illustrated in Figure 27.1 is to analyse the economic mechanisms that take us from (intermediate) targets to (ultimate) objectives. The role of expectations is important in this transmission process, for which the *Phillips curve* is usually used. The approach is based on *price and wage rigidities*, arising for example by the need to fix prices and wages for some period in advance to avoid excessive changes of posted prices and day-to-day negotiations regarding the wage to be paid. The economic agents therefore have to form expectations regarding the future development of the economy when posting prices and signing wage agreements.

In his original contribution Alban Phillips (1958) argued that the rate of change of nominal wages is a negative function of the unemployment rate. He provided empirical evidence to support his claim. Phillips's contribution was translated to an explanation of the inflation rate by Samuelson and Solow (1960), who showed that with mark-up pricing the rate of change of nominal wages is equal to the sum of the inflation rate and productivity increases. Their *modified Phillips curve* therefore argues that the inflation rate is a negative function of the unemployment rate, as illustrated for the USA in the 1960s in Figure 27.5.

Figure 27.5 Short-run stability of the Phillips curve, USA, 1960s

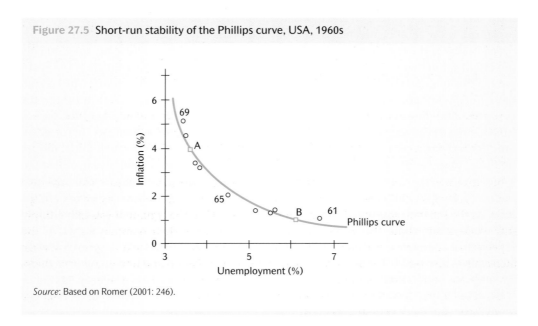

Source: Based on Romer (2001: 246).

Figure 27.6 Long-run instability of the Phillips curve, USA

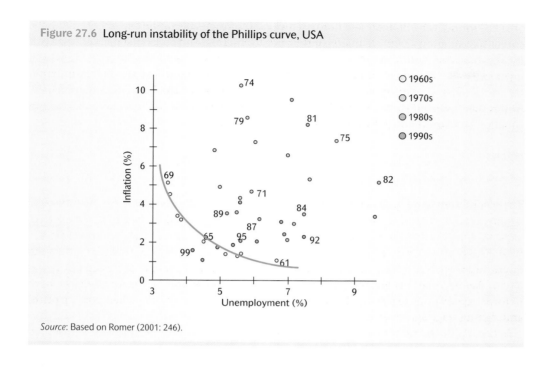

Source: Based on Romer (2001: 246).

There was immediate attention from economists, journalists, and politicians for this downward-sloping modified Phillips curve as it suggests a *policy trade-off* between inflation and unemployment, provided the underlying Phillips curve is stable. A government keen on keeping unemployment low could achieve its objective at the cost of a high inflation rate by choosing point A on the Phillips curve in Figure 27.5. Similarly, a government keen on fighting inflation could achieve its objective at the cost of a high inflation rate by choosing point B on the Phillips curve in Figure 27.5. This argument only works, of course, if the underlying Phillips curve is indeed stable. This turned out *not* to be the case for the USA, as illustrated in Figure 27.6. Fortunately, Samuelson and Solow (1960: 193) had already explicitly pointed out this possibility:

> All of our discussion has been phrased in short-run terms, dealing with what might happen in the next few years. It would be wrong, though, to think that our . . . menu that relates obtainable price and unemployment behavior will maintain its same shape in the longer run. What we do in policy ways in the next few years might cause it to shift in a definite way.

Investigating the underlying causes for the shifting short-run Phillips curve (see also Box 27.1), Phelps (1967) and Friedman (1968) developed the *expectations-augmented Phillips curve*. As the inflation rate was rising in the 1960s and 1970s, the argument was quite simply that workers care about the increase in their real wages, not their nominal wages. As the expected inflation rate was rising, the demanded nominal wage increase for a given real wage increase was also rising. The short-run trade-off between inflation and unemployment therefore depends on the expected inflation rate and the friction on the labour market. The latter is measured by the deviation between the actual rate of unemployment U and the *natural rate of unemployment* U_n; see Friedman (1968).[6]

In the sequel we will analyse a linearized version of the expectations-augmented Phillips curve, see equation (27.2). If there is no aggregate friction on the labour market, that is if $U = U_n$, the actual inflation rate π; will be equal to the expected inflation rate π^e. Otherwise, a lower unemployment rate can be obtained in the short run at the cost of a higher inflation rate. In a dynamic setting, the actual inflation rate will affect the expected inflation rate, which therefore will shift the short-run expectations-augmented Phillips curve as given in equation (27.2) and illustrated in Figure 27.7.

$$\text{(27.2)} \qquad U = U_n - a(\pi - \pi^e), \quad a > 0$$

Figure 27.7 The expectations-augmented Phillips curve

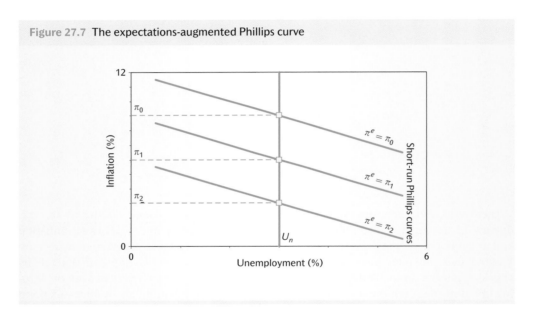

 Box 27.1   Empirical Phillips curves

The theoretical expectations-augmented Phillips curve assumes there is a short-run trade-off between unemployment and inflation, based on price and wage rigidities and the effect of a change in the real wage on the demand for and supply of labour. Monetary and fiscal policy can affect the labour market under certain conditions, for example if there is unemployment because of too high real wages. Changes in the economic agent's experience and expectations will then affect the short-run trade-off. We can also illustrate the empirical evolution over time of unemployment and inflation; see Figure 27.8 for a selection of countries. Note that, to ease comparison, the size of the scales is identical in the four panels of the graph.

The experience of the USA, UK, and Italy in the 1980s is to a large extent similar, although at a different scale. All three countries start at a high level of inflation and manage to reduce this inflation rate at the cost of rising unemployment. Once the inflation rate is lowered, which is done most quickly in the USA, people become accustomed to the lower inflation rate. Unemployment is »

⟫   then reduced in the USA and the UK during the 1990s (reaching a low point in 2000 and 2001), while Italy continues to fight inflation (in an attempt to join the EMU; see Chapter 30) and is able to reduce unemployment after 1998. Over these years the scale for Japan is quite different, with what appears to be a more stable trade-off. As the stock market collapses at the beginning of the 1990s (see Chapter 29), a period of stagnation starts, with rising unemployment levels and falling inflation rates. Eventually, the inflation rate becomes negative and prices in Japan actually start to fall.

Figure 27.8 The Phillips curve: USA, UK, Italy, and Japan

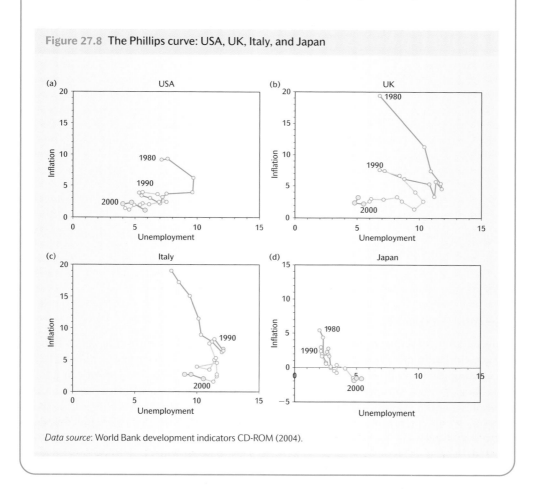

Data source: World Bank development indicators CD-ROM (2004).

27.5 The Barro–Gordon model

On the basis of the building blocks explained in Sections 27.2 and 27.4, we are now in a position to analyse and discuss some of the core issues involved in (monetary) economic policy making, for which we use a basic version of the Barro and Gordon (1983a, 1983b) model. The loss function given in equation (27.1) is combined with a linearized version of the Phillips curve, see equation (27.2), and a bliss point given by equation (27.3). We will derive

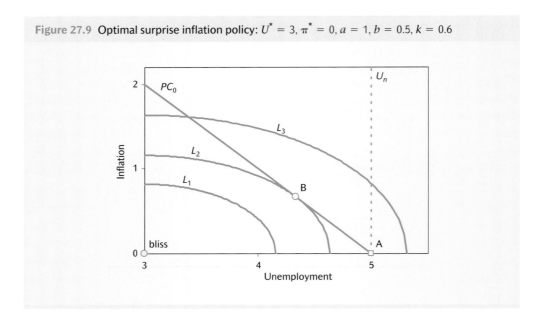

Figure 27.9 Optimal surprise inflation policy: $U^* = 3, \pi^* = 0, a = 1, b = 0.5, k = 0.6$

the optimal monetary policy under three different settings, referred to as surprise, rational expectations, and rules, respectively.

(27.3) $\pi^* = 0;\quad U^* = kU_n,\ 0 < k < 1$

I. Surprise inflation

Figure 27.9 illustrates the optimal policy response of the monetary authorities given that the expected inflation rate is zero ($\pi^e = 0$), leading to short-run Phillips curve PC_0 in Figure 27.9, intersecting the natural rate of unemployment U_n at point A. Taking this short-run Phillips curve as given, the authorities would like to select a combination of actual inflation and unemployment to minimize the loss function, as illustrated by the iso-loss curves $L_1 < L_2 < L_3$ in Figure 27.9, which is given by the tangency solution at point B in the figure. Since the actual inflation rate is clearly higher than the expected inflation rate at this point, that is the economic agents are taken by surprise by the policy chosen by the monetary authorities, we label this the 'surprise' inflation rate.[7] Obviously, this surprise inflation rate depends on the expected inflation rate; see Technical Note 27.1.

II. Rational expectations inflation

The analysis above posed an arbitrary expected inflation rate and derived the concomitant optimal policy. Uncertainty and economic shocks aside, it is unclear why the economic agents would expect the inflation rate to be different from the actual outcome. If individual economic agents are as clever as the monetary authorities and act accordingly, that is if they have rational expectations and form expectations in a way consistent with the economic model itself, this will determine the expected and actual inflation rates, as illustrated in

Figure 27.10 Rational expectations inflation: $U^* = 3$, $\pi^* = 0$, $a = 1$, $b = 2$, $k = 0.6$

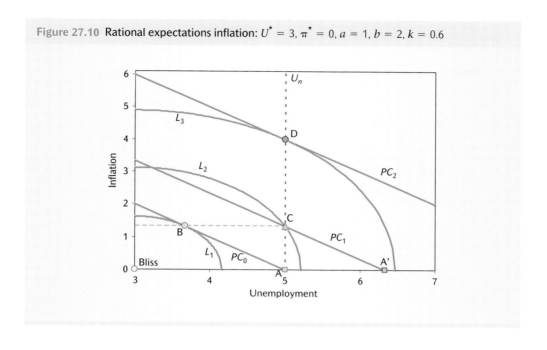

Figure 27.10. If the expected inflation rate were zero, the short-run Phillips curve would be PC_0 and intersect the natural rate of unemployment at point A. The monetary authorities would then be tempted to set the inflation rate to reach point B on curve PC_0, leading to a higher-than-expected inflation rate, making this policy inconsistent with rational expectations. If the inflation rate of point B were the expected inflation rate, it would give rise to short-run Phillips curve PC_1, intersecting the natural rate of unemployment at point C. The monetary authorities would then, similarly, be tempted to set the actual inflation rate to the north-west of C on PC_1 (not shown), again leading to a higher-than-expected inflation rate inconsistent with rational expectations. Continuing this line of reasoning, it is clear that the only inflation rate consistent with rational expectations is at point D in Figure 27.10, where the Phillips curve (PC_2) is tangent to the iso-loss curve L_3 at the natural rate of unemployment U_n; see Technical Note 27.2 for details. All other points along the natural rate of unemployment line are said to be *dynamically inconsistent*.

III. Rules

The rational expectations equilibrium derived above clearly leads to a higher welfare loss than what is potentially economically feasible in the long run. The surprise inflation rate is obviously not dynamically sustainable as it would require systematic forecast errors on the part of the economic agents. There are then, essentially, two ways in which the monetary authorities can reduce the long-run inflation rate. First, by convincing the public that they are really a 'hard-nosed' rather than a 'wet' government, that is that they really care about keeping the inflation rate in check. A change in this respect would alter the iso-loss curves in Figure 27.10 and would shift point D down accordingly. The monetary authorities will, however, face a credibility problem, as merely announcing the fact that they are a hard-nosed government

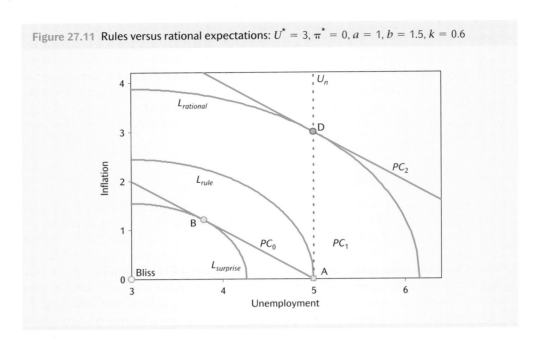

Figure 27.11 Rules versus rational expectations: $U^* = 3, \pi^* = 0, a = 1, b = 1.5, k = 0.6$

may not convince the public that they truly are. This brings us to the second option: if we impose a policy *rule* on the monetary authorities, for example by passing a law that orders the central bank to keep the inflation rate below 2 per cent per year or to keep the growth rate of the money stock below 4 per cent per year, we effectively tie the hands of the monetary authorities such that their policies become credible despite a potentially deviating underlying social loss function. This is illustrated in Figure 27.11 for a policy rule of zero inflation, leading to the long-run equilibrium at point A and welfare loss $L_{rule} < L_{rational}$; see Technical Note 27.3. In principle, therefore, prescribing (monetary) policy rules may lead to superior long-run economic outcomes as it helps to solve the dynamic inconsistency problem.

Discussion

The Barro–Gordon model above shows that under specific circumstances it may be better for the monetary authorities to follow a simple (possibly self-imposed) policy rule than to use discretionary policy to react to the economic circumstances. There are, of course, some objections to be made. Note, in particular, that the inflation bias arises because the target unemployment rate U^* is lower than the natural rate of unemployment U_n. If the target rate is the same as the natural rate of unemployment ($k = 1$), the rational outcome in this setting is zero inflation. There are, basically, two possible reasons for this: (i) the natural rate of unemployment is higher than the target rate because of allocation inefficiencies; or (ii) the natural rate of unemployment accurately reflects the preferences of private individuals. In case (i) the government should not ask the central bank to solve the inefficiencies using monetary policies, because it is not the appropriate instrument. In case (ii) the superiority of rules versus discretion arises from a deviation between private and public objective functions, and it is this deviation that should be explained.

A somewhat more balanced analysis of the choice of rules versus discretion incorporates the size and variance of stochastic shocks relative to the loss function. In this respect, Persson and Tabellini (1990) show that rules are only better if the expected costs of flexibility are higher than the expected welfare gains of reducing unemployment in case there are negative supply shocks. The Barro–Gordon model thus provides a suitable framework for thinking about the connections between credibility and expectations, as well as the trade-off between rules and discretion. In practice, many central banks rely (implicitly or explicitly) on a flexible monetary policy rule; see the next section.

27.6 The Taylor rule

Many central banks have (long-run) price stability as their primary objective, but are given discretionary power as to how to achieve this objective in response to demand and supply shocks. This holds, for example, for the European Central Bank, the Federal Reserve System, and the Bank of Japan. Although they could in principle, as explained in Section 27.3, use monetary base targeting, almost all central banks nowadays use short-term interest rate targeting, which raises the question at what level the target should be at a given point in time. This level should, of course, respond to new macroeconomic information regarding, for example, production, inflation, unemployment, and exchange rates. To assist in this decision process and to communicate its monetary policy to the public, it is useful to investigate the operating rule developed by John Taylor (1993), where the short-term interest rate is increased if the output gap is positive or the inflation rate above target, and vice versa. Clearly this policy prescription is almost directly related to the loss function posed in equation (27.1); see below.

To elaborate on Taylor's rule, which is the result of an empirical study into the monetary policies of the Federal Reserve System and not derived from a theoretical model, recall that r is the real interest rate and let x be the output gap, that is the difference between observed output and capacity output: $x = (Y-Y^\star)/Y^\star$. If the output gap is positive, actual output is above capacity output and unemployment is low. The reverse holds if the output gap is negative. The Taylor rule is given in equation (27.4), stating that the short-term real interest rate $i - \pi$ should be equal to the real interest rate r if the inflation rate is equal to the target and there is no output gap. If the inflation rate is above target, the short-term interest rate should be increased to keep inflation in check. Similarly, if the output gap is positive and the unemployment rate very low, the short-term interest rate should be increased to cool off the economy. The parameters α and β are the weights given to the deviation from the target inflation rate and the output gap, respectively. Based on the empirical work of Alesina et al. (2001), De Grauwe (2005: 186) argues that $\alpha \approx 1.5$ and $\beta \approx 0.5$ are reasonable estimates for these parameters.

(27.4)
$$i_t - \pi_t = r + \alpha(\pi_t - \pi^*) + \beta x_t$$

The Taylor rule should be thought of as a useful concept in analysis, discussions, and communication, rather than as a rule to be applied mechanically. Despite its simplicity, there are still a range of practical issues to address. First, as argued by Blinder (1998), the notion of a neutral real short-term interest rate on which the Taylor rule is based is itself a concept rather than a number. As illustrated in Chapter 21, the real interest rate has fluctuated over time

Figure 27.12 Differences in estimated output gaps: USA and Germany

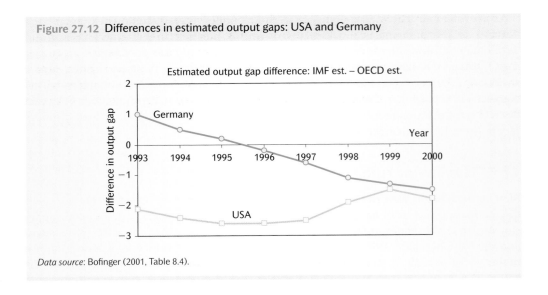

Data source: Bofinger (2001, Table 8.4).

quite substantially. Taking this into consideration, using a long-run perspective, and deducting the liquidity premium from the real intererst rate, Bofinger (2001: 272) arrives at an estimated neutral real rate of 2.8 per cent for both Europe and the USA. Second, the inflation rate used is of interest. In this respect, the concept of core inflation, derived from the consumer price index by, for example, excluding food and energy prices, is advocated by Wynne (1999). Third, and probably most importantly, it is difficult to measure the output gap, which requires an adequate estimate of the economy's growth potential. As illustrated in Figure 27.12 for Germany and the USA, even economic experts at reputable international organizations, such as the IMF and the OECD, have differing views (of up to 2.6 percentage points) regarding the estimated output gaps, and thus the growth potential of the underlying economies and the associated optimal policies. A related problem for monetary policy, further discussed in Chapter 30, is the distribution of estimated output gaps between regions within a large country, such as the USA, or between countries within a monetary union, such as EMU.

27.7 Conclusions

A government, politician, institution, or (international) organization wishing to influence the outcome of the economic process has to take several steps. First, they must specify what they want to achieve, that is specify objectives, such as welfare maximization. Second, they must understand how the economy functions, enabling them to identify certain levels of economic variables to strive for under specific circumstances, that is specify targets, such as short-term interest rate levels. Third, they must have means available to actually influence those economic variables, that is instruments at their disposal, such as minimum reserve requirements.

Monetary authorities are generally, but not exclusively, trying to achieve objectives in the best interest of the country as a whole, by fighting inflation and unemployment and by promoting (price) stability and economic growth. The expectations-augmented Phillips curve provides a simple, yet powerful view of the economic transmission process going from instruments and targets to policy objectives. Using this framework, the Barro–Gordon model shows that imposing simple policy rules may result in better long-run economic outcomes than trying to use discretionary policy to fine-tune the economy. In practice, most central banks target the short-run interest rate using a flexible interpretation of the Taylor rule, which suggests increasing the real interest rate above its neutral stance to fight inflation or temper the economy.

TECHNICAL NOTES

Technical Note 27.1 Surprise inflation in the Barro–Gordon model

Substituting the short-run Phillips curve $U = U_n - a(\pi - \pi^e)$ and the target rate of unemployment $U^* = kU_n$ in the loss function (eq. 27.1), while assuming $\pi^* = 0$, gives

(27.A1)
$$L = b[(1 - k)U_n - a(\pi - \pi^e)]^2 + \pi^2$$

To minimize the loss for a given level of expectations, the authorities determine the first-order condition by differentiating (27.A1) with respect to π and equating to zero; see (27.A2). Solving this equation gives the surprise inflation rate in (27.A3).

(27.A2)
$$2\pi - 2ab[(1 - k)U_n - a(\pi - \pi^e)] = 0$$

(27.A3)
$$\pi_{surprise} = \frac{ab(1 - k)U_n + a^2b\pi^e}{1 + a^2b}$$

Technical Note 27.2 Rational inflation in the Barro–Gordon model

Rational economic agents understand that the inflation announcements made by the authorities are not credible because the authorities will respond according to Technical Note 27.1. Accordingly, the only consistent expectation is when $\pi_{rational} = \pi_{surprise} = \pi^e$. Substituting this condition in (27.A3) and solving for the inflation rate gives (27.A4).

(27.A4)
$$\pi_{rational} = \frac{ab(1 - k)U_n + a^2b\pi_{rational}}{1 + a^2b} = ab(1 - k)U_n$$

Technical Note 27.3 Rules and the ranking of welfare loss

If the authorities are restricted by the *rule* $\pi = 0$, the expected inflation is zero and there are no surprises, so unemployment is equal to U_n and the associated welfare loss is given in (27.A5). The rational inflation rate is given in (27.A4) and the rational unemployment is U_n, so the welfare loss is given in (27.A6).

(27.A5)
$$L_{rule} = b[(1 - k)U_n]^2$$

(27.A6)
$$L_{rational} = b[(1 - k)U_n]^2 + \pi_{rational}^2 > L_{rule}$$

Similarly, the surprise inflation is given in (27.A3). Assuming $\pi^e = 0$ and solving surprise inflation and the rate of unemployment (from the Phillips curve) gives (27.A7). Substituting this in the loss function and collecting terms gives (27.A8).

(27.A7)
$$\pi_{surprise}\Big|_{\pi^e=0} = \frac{ab(1 - k)U_n}{1 + a^2b};$$

$$U_{surprise}\Big|_{\pi^e=0} = U_n - a\frac{ab(1-k)U_n}{1+a^2b}$$

(27.A8)

$$L_{surprise}\Big|_{\pi^e=0} = b\left[U_n - a\frac{ab(1-k)U_n}{1+a^2b} - kU_n\right]^2 + \left[\frac{ab(1-k)U_n}{1+a^2b}\right]^2$$

$$= b\left[(1-k)U_n - \frac{a^2b(1-k)U_n}{1+a^2b}\right]^2 + \frac{a^2b^2}{(1+a^2b)^2}[(1-k)U_n]^2$$

$$= b\left[\frac{(1-k)U_n}{1+a^2b}\right]^2 + \frac{a^2b^2}{(1+a^2b)^2}[(1-k)U_n]^2$$

$$= \frac{a^2b}{(1+a^2b)}[(1-k)U_n]^2 < b[(1-k)U_n]^2 = L_{rule}$$

Dropping the $\big|_{\pi^e=0}$ notation for convenience, we get: $L_{surprise} < L_{rule} < L_{rational}$.

QUESTIONS

Question 27.1

27.1A What is the objective of the European Central Bank (ECB)? Is the ECB hard-nosed or wet-nosed?

27.1B What instruments does the ECB have to reach its objective? Explain in detail what these instruments are and how they influence the target variable(s)?

27.1C Why do these instruments offer the ECB no perfect control over the target variable(s)?

Question 27.2

The ECB and the Fed have different policy objectives. According to the Maastricht Treaty the primary goal of the ECB is to keep price stability. The support of general economic policies is only of secondary importance. The Federal Reserve

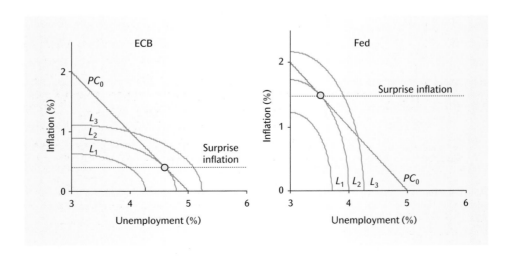

Reform Act on the other hand specifies the three objectives of the Fed: 'maximum employment, stable prices, and moderate long-term interest rates'. Unlike in the Maastricht Treaty, price stability is not given higher priority than the other goals.

In this question we will find out what consequences these different policy objectives of the ECB and Fed have in the Barro–Gordon model. For this purpose the figure above shows the Barro–Gordon model for the ECB on the left-hand side and for the Fed on the right-hand side. The figures are identical to Figure 27.9 (surprise inflation policy with an expected inflation of 0 per cent) in the main text except for the loss function. The loss function has been modified according to the policy objectives of the ECB and Fed. Assume for now that there are no policy rules.

27.2A How can you derive from the figure above which central bank is wet-nosed and which central bank is hard-nosed?

27.2B Why do the central banks fool the citizens if the expected inflation rate is larger than the realized inflation rate? Which central bank fools its citizens most? Explain.

27.2C Explain why the equilibrium indicated in the figure above is not sustainable.

27.2D Copy the figure above and indicate in both panels the sustainable equilibrium. Do you expect the inflation rate to be higher in the euro area or in the USA?

27.2E Do you stick to your conclusion of 27.2D if you know that both the ECB and the Fed have introduced a policy rule? The ECB has promised to keep inflation below 2 per cent. The FED, on the other hand, keeps inflation at such a level that 'economic agents no longer keep account of the prospective change in the general price level in their economic decisionmaking'.

Question 27.3[8]

In his 1993 paper 'Discretion versus policy rules in practice', John Taylor introduces an intuitive policy rule to determine the Federal funds rate:

Federal funds rate $= \pi + 0.5y + 0.5(\pi - 2) + 2$, where

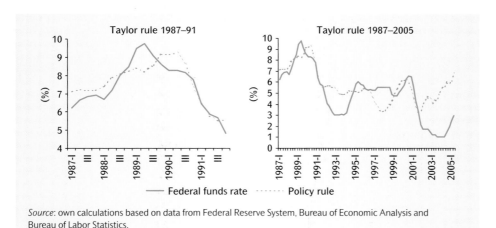

Source: own calculations based on data from Federal Reserve System, Bureau of Economic Analysis and Bureau of Labor Statistics.

π is the rate of inflation

y is the output gap or (real GDP – trend real GDP) / trend real GDP.

Taylor assumes a trend real GDP growth of 2.2 per cent during the 1987–91 period.

The left panel of the figure above shows that this policy rule fits the actual policy performance over the period analysed by Taylor (1987–91) surprisingly well. If the policy rule is extrapolated to the future (keeping the assumptions on the target inflation rate and trend real GDP constant), the results are, however, less encouraging. This is shown in the right panel of the figure.

27.3A What inflation target did the Fed have according to Taylor during the 1987–91 period?

27.3B The intuitive policy rule presented above differs from the estimation made by De Grauwe in the main text. In what respect does the policy rule above differ and why do you think Taylor has made this choice?

27.3C The policy rule above is based on quarterly data while the Fed has to determine the Federal funds rate every day. Explain whether the policy rule can still be used by policy makers in the Central Bank.

27.3D The figure in the right panel shows that at the start of the 1990s the policy rule no longer reflected the actual decisions made by the Fed. There was a good reason for the Fed to deviate from the policy rule: the spot price of oil doubled with the Iraqi invasion of Kuwait, but the futures price of oil changed very little. Why is this a good reason to deviate from the policy rule?

27.3E Also after the first Gulf War the policy rule did not reflect the actual policy of the Fed. Is the Taylor rule worthless or is there another reason for this deviation?

 See the Online Resource Centre for a Study Guide containing more questions
www.oxfordtextbooks.co.uk/orc/vanmarrewijk/

NOTES

1 This chapter builds on Bofinger (2001), chs 4–6 and 8.

2 For example, regulation Q (interest rate ceiling) was revoked in the USA in the early 1980s and quantitative restrictions, such as lending ceilings, were used by the Bank of England until 1979.

3 See Bofinger (2001, ch. 4) for details on this transmission process and a discussion of the 'money view', 'credit view', and 'banking view'.

4 Note that the targets could also be on the broad money market (money stock or interest rate), and we could also distinguish between operating targets (on the narrow money market), intermediate targets (on the broad money market), final targets (employment and inflation), ultimate objectives (welfare), etc.

5 In terms of Figure 27.3, the average long-run combination is $(B_0, i_{res, 0})$ either way.

6 The NAIRU – non-accelerating inflation rate of unemployment – is a related concept. The natural rate of unemployment is a long-run relationship based on a structural model. The NAIRU, in contrast, is a short-run relationship estimated using time series equations; see King (1998).

7 Since the authorities are tempted to set a different inflation rate than expected, we could also label it the 'temptation' inflation rate.

8 Based on John B. Taylor, 'Discretion versus policy rules in practice', *Carnegie–Rocheser Conference Series on Public Policy*, No. 39, 1993, pp. 195–214.

FIXED EXCHANGE RATES AND TARGET ZONES

Objectives/key terms

- *De jure* and *de facto* classification
- Parity rates
- European Monetary System
- Credibility
- Asymmetric shocks
- Brownian motion
- *S*-curve (honeymoon effect)

- Fear of floating and fear of pegging
- Bandwidth
- ECU
- Monetary preferences
- Target zone model
- Standard Wiener process
- Smooth-pasting conditions

We discuss some basic problems associated with fixed exchange rate regimes related to preferences and economy-wide shocks, as well as some potential benefits of these regimes related to stabilizing actual exchange rate behaviour.

28.1 Introduction

Many countries or groups of countries are involved in fixed exchange rate regimes or try to influence their exchange rate in some way; see Chapter 22. Although countries may sometimes not actually do what they say they do (as discussed in the next section), credibility problems are always of crucial importance in analysing fixed exchange rate regimes. Using the Barro–Gordon model (see Chapter 27), we discuss two credibility problems, related to a country's monetary preferences and to the exogenous business cycle shocks it faces. We continue by showing that, given complete credibility, a fixed exchange rate regime may come with the added bonus of stabilizing exchange rates inside the band. The empirical importance of this effect, however, seems to be limited.

28.2 Exchange rate regimes

There are many different types of exchange rate regimes. The IMF (2004), for example, distinguishes between eight different regimes; see Chapter 22. Its classification was based for a long time on a *de jure* system, that is based on the official exchange rate policies pursued by member countries. This led to some practical problems as countries may not actually do what they say they do. Considerable effort has therefore been devoted recently to moving to a *de facto* exchange rate classification system, based on the actual movements of exchange rates and actual monetary policies. Reinhart and Rogoff (2004), for example, use data on official and parallel exchange rates to distinguish between fourteen different types of exchange rate arrangements; see Table 28.1. The 'freely falling' category is worth mentioning, referring to cases where the 12-month inflation rate is equal to or exceeds 40 per cent per year. It accounts

Famous economists — Mark P. Taylor

Fig. 28.1 Mark P. Taylor (1958–)

After studying economics at Oxford and London Universities, while part of the time being employed as a foreign exchange dealer in the city of London, Mark Taylor worked at various institutions, including the Bank of England, the IMF, and Oxford University, and has been based at the University of Warwick since 1999. Based on his practical experience and analytical expertise, Mark Taylor evolved into one of the world's most prominent experts on all empirical matters related to international money and finance. He is a prolific researcher and has published books and articles on, for example, non-linearity in real and nominal exchange rates, the long-run behaviour of exchange rates, and the effectiveness of official foreign exchange market intervention. His versatility is also evident from his other (scientific) interests, which include horology (he is an expert on English antique clocks), beekeeping, literature and cinema (he also earned a master's degree in English literature), and languages (French, Russian, and Spanish).

Table 28.1 Reinhart–Rogoff exchange rate regimes

1 No separate legal tender

2 Preannounced peg or currency board arrangement

3 Preannounced horizontal band that is narrower than or equal to ±2%

4 *De facto* peg

5 Pre-announced crawling peg

6 Pre-announced crawling band that is narrower than or equal to ±2%

7 *De facto* crawling peg

8 *De facto* crawling band that is narrower than or equal to ±2%

9 Pre-announced crawling band that is wider than ±2%

10 *De facto* crawling band that is narrower than or equal to ±5%

11 Non-crawling band that is narrower than or equal to ±2%

12 Managed floating

13 Freely floating

14 Freely falling (includes hyperfloat)

Source: Reinhart and Rogoff (2004).

for no less than 22 and 37 per cent of the observations in Africa and the Western hemisphere (excl. Canada and the USA) in the period 1970–2001, as well as 41 per cent of the observations for the transition economies in the 1990s.

Levy-Yeyati and Sturzenegger (2004) construct a *de facto* exchange rate classification based on exchange rates and international reserves in the period 1974–2000. They find, in particular, that (i) a large number of countries have a *de facto* pegged exchange rate regime, but shy away from an explicit commitment ('fear of pegging') and (ii) a large number of *de jure* free floats are *de facto* dirty floats ('fear of floating'); see Figure 28.2. There appears to be, therefore, considerable discrepancy between deeds and words for some countries. Genberg and Swoboda (2004) argue that both the official stance and the *de facto* actions contain useful information that should be taken into account when devising exchange rate policies. This comes, in fact, very close to the more practical classification approach used by the IMF since 1999, as discussed in Chapter 22.

28.3 Fixed exchange rates

The classification problems discussed above notwithstanding, a basic fixed exchange rate regime is illustrated in Figure 28.3. The monetary authorities of a country or a group of countries determine that the exchange rate is equal to some predetermined value, the parity rate. As illustrated in the figure, the actual exchange rate is usually allowed to fluctuate within a bandwidth around this parity rate, such that it can be anywhere in between some lower limit and some upper limit. The difference between the upper limit and the lower limit is called the bandwidth. It is usually symmetrically distributed around the parity rate in level terms, say if

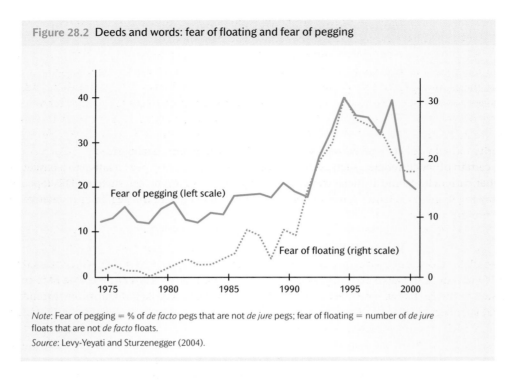

Figure 28.2 Deeds and words: fear of floating and fear of pegging

Note: Fear of pegging = % of *de facto* pegs that are not *de jure* pegs; fear of floating = number of *de jure* floats that are not *de facto* floats.
Source: Levy-Yeyati and Sturzenegger (2004).

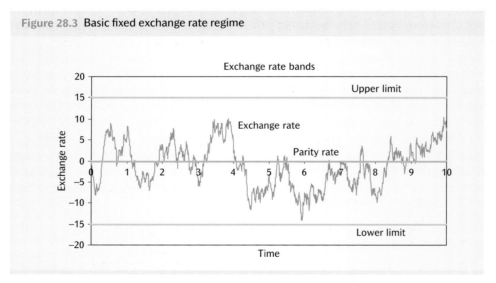

Figure 28.3 Basic fixed exchange rate regime

the exchange rate is allowed to deviate at most 2.25 per cent from the parity rate. This gives rise to an asymmetrically distributed band in logarithmic graphs, a technicality that will be ignored in the analysis below. If the exchange rate threatens to move outside the band, the monetary authorities will intervene, for example by buying or selling foreign reserves, as explained in Box 23.1. Clearly, the narrower the bandwidth, the less room there is for the exchange rate to move freely within the band, and the more frequently the monetary authorities will have to intervene in the foreign exchange market.

It is important to realize that currencies can be pegged to various international assets and the consequences this will have on actually observed exchange rate behaviour. Initially, most currencies were pegged to gold, and therefore indirectly fixed relative to each other (within the gold points; see Chapter 22). Later, the US dollar was pegged to gold and other currencies were pegged to the US dollar, effectively widening the margins within which currencies could fluctuate relative to each other over time, but still fixing the limits of fluctuation as long as the parity rates do not change. Nowadays, fixed exchange rates are characterized by pegs relative to certain other currencies, such as the US dollar or the euro, or by pegs relative to a basket of other currencies (some artificial weighted average of other currencies), such as SDRs (Special Drawing Rights). Exchange rate movements are limited relative to the peg, but not relative to non-participating currencies.

The implications of a modern peg system are illustrated using the US dollar exchange rate in France and Germany in the 1980s and early 1990s as an example; see Figure 28.4. In this period, both countries participated in the European Monetary System (EMS), which started in 1979 to reduce the large exchange rate variability of the 1970s within Europe. The EMS consisted of the Exchange Rate Mechanism (ERM) and the ECU, a basket of European currencies that later became the euro (see Chapter 30). The ERM was an adjustable peg system, in which the participating countries determined a central rate around which the exchange rate was allowed to fluctuate (plus or minus 2.25 per cent for Belgium, Denmark, France, Germany, Ireland, and the Netherlands and plus or minus 6 per cent for Italy). Using the wider band of fluctuation, Spain joined in 1989, the UK in 1990, and Portugal in 1992. There were frequent realignments (eleven in total) between March 1979 and January 1987. After that, there were no realignments until 1992; see Box 28.1. As illustrated in Figure 28.4, the French and German participation in the ERM system keeps the value of the currencies relative to each

Figure 28.4 US$ daily exchange rates: France and Germany, 1980–94

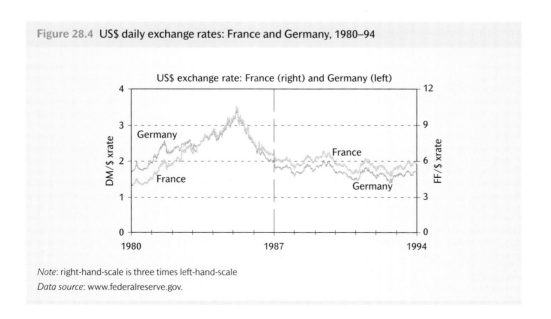

Note: right-hand-scale is three times left-hand-scale

Data source: www.federalreserve.gov.

other fixed in narrow limits, implying that their value relative to the non-participating US dollar must move up and down together. This is particularly clear in the period 1987–92, when there were no realignments. In the preceding period (1979–87) the currencies move up and down together, except for the realignments. As the curve for France is initially below and later above that for Germany, the franc was devaluated relative to the mark in this period.

28.4 Credibility of fixed exchange rate regimes I: preferences

Using the policy trilemma, we explained in Chapter 22 that a country pursuing fixed exchange rates must be willing to give up either capital mobility or policy autonomy, as it is impossible to achieve all three of these potential objectives simultaneously. In many cases, countries are confronted with new developments or circumstances that force them to give up the fixed exchange rate regime, for example if they want to lift capital controls or if they want to fight high domestic unemployment rates. This implies that market participants may not always be convinced that the announced fixed exchange rate regime will actually be enforced; that is, they may doubt its credibility. In this section and the next, we briefly discuss two credibility problems on the basis of the Barro–Gordon model introduced in Chapter 27; see equations (28.1) and (28.2).

$$(28.1) \qquad\qquad U = U_n - a(\pi - \pi^e), \quad a > 0$$

$$(28.2) \quad L = b(U - U^*)^2 + (\pi - \pi^*)^2, \quad b \geq 0, \quad \text{with } \pi^* = 0; \quad U^* = kU_n, \quad 0 < k < 1$$

Recall that equation (28.1) depicts the (linearized) expectations-augmented Phillips curve, where U is the unemployment rate, U_n is the natural rate of unemployment, π is the actual inflation rate, π^e is the expected inflation rate, and a is a parameter determining the short-run trade-off between unemployment and (surprise) inflation. Similarly, recall that equation (28.2) depicts the preferences of the monetary authorities, where L represents the welfare loss, U^* and π^* are the target rates of unemployment and inflation, and b is a parameter measuring the importance the monetary authorities attach to fighting (short-run) unemployment relative to inflation. As discussed in Chapter 27, rational economic agents take the preferences of the monetary authorities into consideration when forming their expectations. Together with the structural parameters of the model, this determines the long-run (rational expectations) rate of inflation. The fact that the preferences of the monetary authorities may differ between countries is a potential source of credibility problems in a fixed exchange rate regime.

Countries can differ, obviously, in many respects. They may have different target rates of unemployment and inflation, or different rates of natural unemployment, or different short-run trade-offs between inflation and unemployment, etc. Figure 28.5, however, illustrates the (hypothetical) rational expectations equilibrium for two countries that only differ in the weight b they attach to fighting short-run unemployment. For convenience, we label these countries Germany and Italy, where we assume that Germany has 'hard-nosed' preferences (is strong on fighting inflation) and Italy has 'wet' preferences (is more willing to fight unemployment at the cost of a higher inflation rate). Figure 28.5(a) depicts the rational expectations equilibrium for Germany (RE_{Ger}), with the short-run Phillips curve PC_{Ger} and iso-loss curve $Loss_{Ger}$. Figure 28.5(b) does the same for Italy. Clearly, the fact that the Italian

Figure 28.5 Rational expectations equilibrium for Germany and Italy

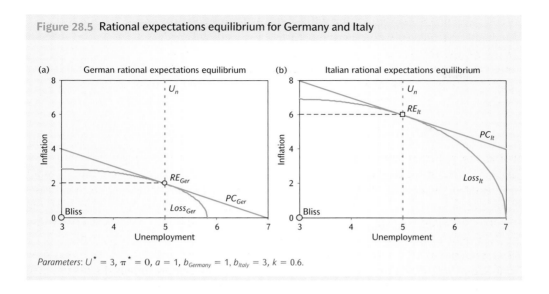

Parameters: $U^* = 3$, $\pi^* = 0$, $a = 1$, $b_{Germany} = 1$, $b_{Italy} = 3$, $k = 0.6$.

government has a 'wet' reputation, i.e. is more willing to fight unemployment at the cost of higher inflation, leads to a higher inflation rate in the long run, namely an inflation rate of 6 per cent rather than 2 per cent in the figure.

The above does not pose a problem as such. The Italian inflation rate can be structurally higher than the German inflation rate – unless the two countries enter an agreement to keep the exchange rate fixed. In the long run, the exchange rate is determined by purchasing power parity; see Chapter 20. A simple version of this is given in equation (28.3), where the exchange rate is the ratio of the price index in Germany and Italy (see Chapters 24–26 for more subtle details).

$$(28.3) \qquad\qquad S = P_{Ger}/P_{It}$$

As soon as the two countries decide to fix the exchange rate, say $S = \bar{S}$, this immediately implies that the change in the price indices in the two countries must be proportional; that is, the long-run inflation rates must be the same: $\pi_{Ger} = \pi_{It}$. Fixing the exchange rate therefore has immediate consequences for the inflation rates, and hence for the monetary policies, in the two countries. Here, a problem arises immediately. Which inflation rate will become operative after the fixed exchange rate agreement, the German rate or the Italian rate? Even if we assume that it is the German inflation rate (for example based on the argument that Germany will not enter an agreement with Italy if that is going to make it worse off), that is not going to solve the credibility problem, as illustrated in Figure 28.6. If Italy announces that it will follow the German inflation rate (point RE_{Ger} in the figure), rational economic agents know that the Italian authorities have an incentive to create surprise inflation and lower unemployment (move to point B in the figure) using a surprise devaluation of the Italian lire. The arrangement will therefore not be credible unless the preferences of the monetary authorities are the same. Before going on to the next section, which argues that even that may not be enough, we would like to point out that the European mechanism of fixed exchange rates (ERM; see section 28.3) did indeed evolve such that Germany became the leader and other countries

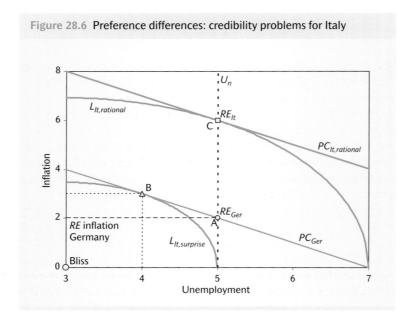

Figure 28.6 Preference differences: credibility problems for Italy

followed suit. Moreover, despite the wider bandwidth for Italy, the lire initially devaluated several times relative to the German mark, in accordance with the economic forces discussed here.

28.5 Credibility of fixed exchange rate regimes II: shocks

The previous section argued that differences in preferences of the monetary authorities between countries can cause important credibility problems when pursuing a pegged exchange rate regime. This section argues, however, that there can still be credibility problems even if the preferences of the monetary authorities are identical, namely if the participating countries are confronted with asymmetric supply and/or demand shocks. Both credibility problems seem to have played a role when the UK was forced out of the ERM system in 1992; see Box 28.1.

To understand the asymmetric shock problem, we must first realize that the rational expectations equilibrium as depicted in Figures 28.5 and 28.6 is a long-run equilibrium. During the business cycle, there can be short-run deviations from the equilibrium to which the monetary authorities respond by relaxing or tightening the money supply in order to mitigate the welfare losses caused by these fluctuations. By the nature of the equilibrium, these shocks have to be temporary and not structural, such that the average inflation rate is indeed equal to the expected inflation rate. Again using Italy and Germany as an example, Figure 28.8 illustrates the strain put on a pegged exchange rate regime if the participating countries are confronted with asymmetric shocks. This causes them to be in different parts of the business cycle, which requires different policies.

Figure 28.8 assumes that Italy and Germany have the same monetary preferences. The rational expectations equilibrium is therefore given by point RE in the figure for both countries.

Box 28.1   Black Wednesday: 16 September 1992

The European Exchange Rate Mechanism (ERM; see Section 28.3) started in 1979. After an initial period of regular realignments, the parity rates did not change from 1987 to 1992. The UK joined the ERM in October 1990 with a bandwidth of ±6 per cent around the central rate, implying a parity rate of 2.95 German marks to the pound. At this time, the British inflation rate was about three times as high as the German inflation rate and Germany had become the undisputed leader of the system. In 1989, East Germany and West Germany were reunited, causing a construction boom in Germany, which the Bundesbank tried to moderate by raising interest rates. This placed considerable pressure on the UK and Italy, which were coping with a double deficit (current account deficit and fiscal deficit) and were confronted with high unemployment rates.

Currency speculators became aware that Italy and the UK were probably no longer willing to incur the costs associated with the discipline needed to keep their currencies pegged in the ERM. Led by George Soros, the speculators launched a massive attack on the ERM system by borrowing enormous amounts in pounds and lire and selling these in German marks. If successful, the pound and lire would devalue relative to the mark. The speculators could then repay the loan in devalued currency and pocket the difference. If not, they could simply repay the loan and incur the cost of borrowing. They were therefore able to make potentially large gains at relatively small costs, with little risk.

As illustrated in Figure 28.7, the attack was successful. On 'Black Wednesday' (16 September 1992) Britain announced it would leave the ERM system. The pound devalued and the speculators made large profits. George Soros, for example, apparently earned more than $1 billion as a result of this attack. Other countries adjusted the central rates and broadened the bandwidth, as did Italy when it returned to the system. By August 1993, after an attack on the French franc, the band was widened to ±15 per cent.

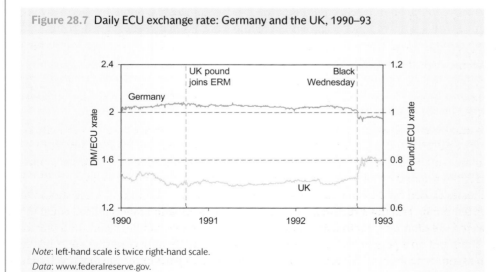

Figure 28.7 Daily ECU exchange rate: Germany and the UK, 1990–93

Note: left-hand scale is twice right-hand scale.
Data: www.federalreserve.gov.

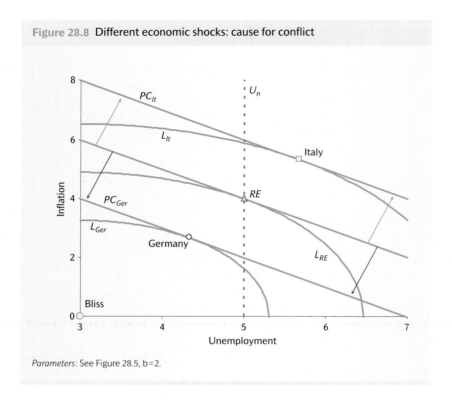

Figure 28.8 Different economic shocks: cause for conflict

Parameters: See Figure 28.5, b = 2.

We assume, however, that Italy is confronted with a negative shock which pushes the short-run Phillips curve out to PC_{It}. Given this short-run Phillips curve, the optimal response for Italy is to move to the point labelled *Italy*, incurring the welfare loss L_{It}. Similarly, Germany is confronted with a positive shock (e.g. German reunification) which pushes the short-run Phillips curve down to PC_{Ger}. Given this short-run Phillips curve, the optimal response for Germany is to move to the point labelled *Germany*, incurring the welfare loss L_{Ger}. In short, Italy wants to accommodate its negative shock with a looser monetary policy, whereas Germany wants to accommodate its positive shock with a tighter monetary policy. There is a clear conflict of interest between the participating countries caused by the asymmetric shocks.

What happens in practice depends, of course, on the specific details of the arrangement. In the ERM system, where Germany was the leader, monetary policy was largely determined in Germany. Even if the German authorities take the economic situation in the other participating countries into consideration, this creates a large bias to give in to German rather than Italian needs. In these circumstances, Italy is forced to accommodate almost all of the negative shock through rising unemployment rates, possibly reinforced by a tightening monetary policy set in Germany. In the present European system (EMU; see Chapter 30), the monetary authorities try to balance the needs of the various participating countries. Note, however, that this balancing act is difficult if the participating countries are frequently confronted with asymmetric shocks, whereas it is much easier if the countries are all confronted with the same type of shock (either positive or negative). The stress put on a pegged exchange rate regime (or a monetary union) is therefore much smaller if the shocks are highly correlated; see Chapter 30.

28.6 The basic target zone model

Having established that there are various reasons to question the credibility of a fixed exchange rate regime, it is now time to discuss how a *fully credible* regime will affect the behaviour of the exchange rate inside the band. The next section will discuss extensions of the model to incorporate limited credibility and empirical tests of actual exchange rate behaviour. The core initial contribution in this literature is Krugman (1991), a paper that inspired a range of other contributions even before it was published. It is referred to as the target zone model.[1] As explained intuitively in this section, the announcement of a fully credible target zone by the monetary authorities has a stabilizing influence on the exchange rate behaviour within the band. In principle, this could be an important bonus of fixed exchange rate regimes.

The main argument of the target zone literature is most easily explained using a simple log-linear monetary model in continuous time. This is similar to the exposition in Box 24.3, as further analysed in Section 26.6. The exchange rate s depends on the money supply m, some other fundamental variables grouped together in a term v, and a term involving the expected rate of depreciation $\Phi\,E(ds)/dt$; see equation (28.4). Note that the exchange rate reacts to two fundamental variables, namely m and v. We assume that the monetary authorities announce a fully credible target zone for the exchange rate s, implying that they only allow the exchange rate to vary within a bandwidth $2b$ around a central parity rate. We normalize the parity rate to 0, such that the exchange rate can only move freely from $-b$ to b. Moreover, we assume that the level of the money stock m only adjusts when necessary to keep the exchange rate within the target zone.

$$(28.4) \qquad\qquad s = (m + v) + \Phi\,E(ds)/dt$$

Uncertainty in the model is caused by erratic movements in the fundamentals term v, referring to all other factors that may influence the equilibrium exchange rate (such as the foreign money supply and domestic and foreign output levels). These factors are modelled implicitly, by specifying the stochastic process that governs its behaviour. We assume that this is a

---

Box 28.2 **Brownian motion (Wiener process)**

Brownian motion refers to the continuous time equivalent of a random walk process; see Box 26.3. Let t denote time and consider the stochastic process given in equation (28.5), where μ is called the drift parameter, σ is a variance parameter, and $z(t)$ is a *standard* Wiener process. This means that z is continuous, with non-overlapping increments which are independent of each other. Moreover, the increments are normally distributed with mean zero and a variance equal to the distance apart in the time increments.

$$(28.5) \qquad\qquad v(t) = \mu t + \sigma z(t)$$

Figure 28.9 illustrates some Brownian motion processes. Panel (a) shows the long-run impact of the drift parameter μ. Since the variable v fluctuates around the line μt, the variable v ultimately becomes positive if the drift parameter is positive ($\mu > 0$) and negative if the drift parameter is negative ($\mu < 0$). Panel (b) shows that the fluctuations become wilder if the standard deviation parameter σ increases. The process is frequently written in derivative form. See, for example, equation (28.6), where the drift parameter μ is equal to zero.

»

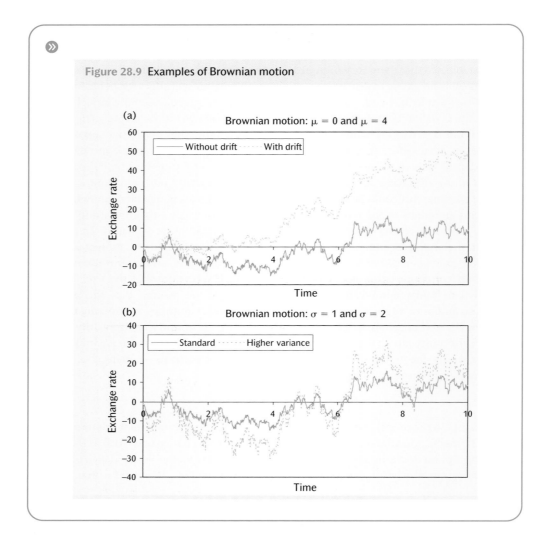

Figure 28.9 Examples of Brownian motion

(a) Brownian motion: $\mu = 0$ and $\mu = 4$

(b) Brownian motion: $\sigma = 1$ and $\sigma = 2$

Brownian motion process; see equation (28.6), where σ refers to the standard deviation and z is a standard Wiener process; see Box 28.2. There is no good economic reason for this specification other than that it allows us to illustrate the dynamic exchange rate behaviour caused by invoking a target zone in the simplest possible way.

$$(28.6) \qquad\qquad dv = \sigma dz$$

The model is completely specified by equations (28.4) and (28.6). Despite this simplicity, it has important and non-trivial implications, as illustrated in Figure 28.10. A simplistic view might argue that, since v follows a random walk and the expected value of z is zero, the exchange rate is equal to $m + v$ inside the band. Assuming that $m = 0$, this would translate to the Z-shaped curve ABCD in Figure 28.10. This cannot, however, be the real equilibrium exchange rate behaviour inside the band. To see why, consider the point labelled h_0 in the figure, which is just inside the band. If v falls a little, the exchange rate would fall along the 45-degree line to a point such as h_2. However, if v rises a little, the exchange rate cannot rise

Figure 28.10 Impossibility of a Z-shaped target zone

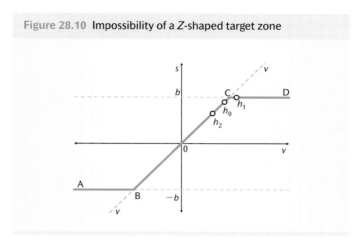

Figure 28.11 The basic target zone model: S-shaped curve (honeymoon effect)

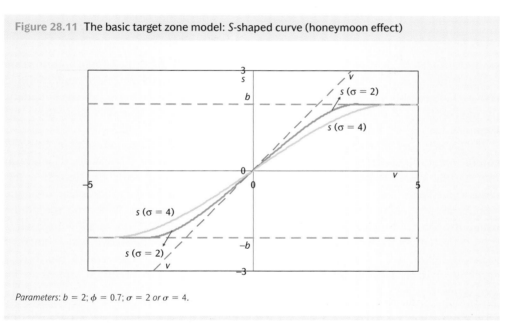

Parameters: $b = 2$; $\phi = 0.7$; $\sigma = 2$ or $\sigma = 4$.

along the 45-degree line as this would bring it outside the band. Instead, it can only rise to a point such as h_1 along the Z-shaped curve. This, in turn, implies that the expected rate of change of the exchange rate is negative. Since these expectations affect the exchange rate itself, see equation (28.4), this drags down the equilibrium exchange rate from a point such as h_0 to a point strictly below it. The equilibrium exchange rate is therefore not given by the Z-shaped curve depicted in Figure 28.10. Instead, it is given by an S-shaped curve, as shown in Figure 28.11.

We have heuristically explained why the equilibrium exchange rate inside the band must be S-shaped. There are, in principle, many S-shaped curves that could be potential equilibrium curves, two of which are illustrated in Figure 28.11 (note that these two curves are *equilibrium* curves, but for different circumstances). Actually determining the precise curve is not so easy;

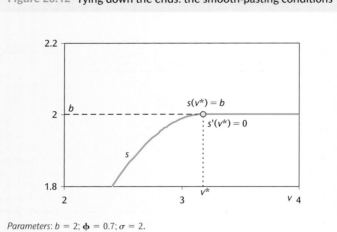

Figure 28.12 Tying down the ends: the smooth-pasting conditions

Parameters: $b = 2$; $\phi = 0.7$; $\sigma = 2$.

see Technical Note 28.1 for some of the details. The so-called smooth-pasting conditions are crucial in this respect. Following similar reasoning as illustrated in Figure 28.10 and discussed above, these conditions imply that at the point where the S-shaped curve hits the boundary, the derivative of the curve must be zero (it must touch the boundary smoothly); see Figure 28.12.

The basic model argues that announcing a fully credible target zone results in S-shaped equilibrium exchange rate behaviour inside the band. The nature of the curve depends on the specific circumstances, such as the variance associated with the fundamentals terms v; see Figure 28.11. Since the monetary authorities only have to intervene once the equilibrium exchange rate threatens to leave the bandwidth, that is beyond the points where the S-curve touches the boundaries, the announcement of the target zone itself is stabilizing. Other things equal, the other fundamentals are allowed a wider range of variation before it is necessary for the monetary authorities to intervene in the foreign exchange market. This potential bonus of a fixed exchange rate regime is known as the 'honeymoon effect'.

28.7 Target zone extensions and empirical tests

The basic target zone model has been extended into three directions, namely by allowing for (i) imperfect credibility, (ii) intramarginal interventions, and (iii) sticky prices.

- Ad (i). The argument in the previous section on the honeymoon effect is based on a fully credible target zone. Since realignments occur quite frequently in reality (see Section 28.3) or countries may discontinue the target zone (see Box 28.1), it is of course important to address the credibility issue by allowing for exogenous or endogenous risk of realignment; see e.g. Bertola and Caballero (1992) and Tristani (1994).

- Ad (ii). The basic model assumes that no intervention takes place until the exchange rate hits the boundary. Instead, it is well known that central banks intervene on the foreign

Figure 28.13 Leaning-against-the-wind intervention

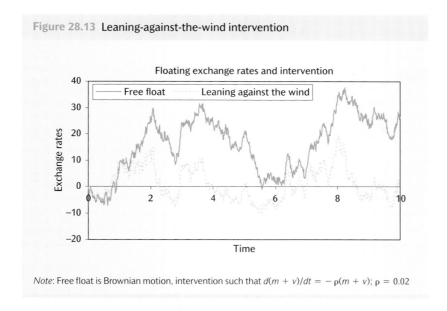

Floating exchange rates and intervention

Note: Free float is Brownian motion, intervention such that $d(m + v)/dt = -\rho(m + v)$; $\rho = 0.02$

exchange market using intramarginal intervention; see Dominguez and Kenen (1992). An example of this is 'leaning-against-the-wind' intervention in which the expected rate of change of the composite fundamentals is proportional to the deviation from parity, as illustrated in Figure 28.13 and discussed by Garber and Svensson (1995).

- Ad (iii). Since deviations from purchasing power parity can last a long time, see Chapter 20, it is useful to incorporate the empirical phenomenon of price stickiness. Miller and Weller (1991) do this by building on the Dornbusch (1976) model; see Chapter 26. Beetsma and van der Ploeg (1994) extend this approach by using a stochastic version of the Dornbusch model and allowing for (i) imperfect substitution between home and foreign goods, (ii) sluggish adjustment in wages and prices, and (iii) marginal and intramarginal interventions in the foreign exchange market.

The empirical evidence for the basic target zone model is not very strong. Pesaran and Samiei (1992) test a discrete time target zone model for France and Germany and find that their model performs better than linear exchange rate models. Using a different method for these countries, Meese and Rose (1990) find support for the model in-sample but not out-of-sample. Taking the empirical regularities of the fundamentals of the stochastic process into consideration, Koedijk, Stork, and De Vries (1992) reject the basic model for a number of EMS countries.[3] When the various extensions discussed above are taken into consideration, the empirical results improve. Various studies find support for an endogenous devaluation risk for different countries and periods; see the overview of De Arcangelis (1994). Similarly, Sutherland (1994) finds empirical support for the sticky-price target zone model. Finally, two recent, more detailed studies by Iannizotto and Taylor (1999) and Taylor and Iannizotto (2001) using daily data and incorporating weekends and holidays find statistically significant support for the basic model, although the S-curve is very weak, so there is virtually no 'honeymoon effect'.

Box 28.3   China's exchange rate peg (22 July 2005)[2]

For a period of about ten years (from 1995 to 2005) the Chinese yuan was pegged to the US dollar (about 8.28 yuan per dollar since September 1998). As documented at various places in this book, the Chinese economy prospered in this period and its exports started to rise substantially, particularly to the USA. At the same time, the current account deficit of the USA increased drastically. American public opinion attributed the rising deficit to trade with China caused by an undervalued Chinese yuan pegged to the US dollar, even though the bilateral deficit relative to China was only a part of the rising deficit (which, as we know, reflects a low American savings rate in any case).

On 22 July 2005 the Chinese authorities gave in to the rising pressure to revalue the yuan relative to the US dollar, with two twists. The first twist was that the revaluation was only 2 per cent (to about 8.10 yuan per dollar), which was certainly not enough to have any substantial influence on its trade flows relative to the USA. This is illustrated in Figure 28.14 (where we have also indicated the evolution of the Thai baht in this period for comparison purposes). The second twist was that the Chinese authorities announced that the yuan was no longer pegged to the US dollar alone, but to an undisclosed basket of other currencies. Three weeks later (on 10 August 2005), the Chinese announced which countries were in this basket, without revealing the weight attached to each currency. The most important currencies are the American dollar, the European euro, the Japanese yen, and the South Korean won. Somewhat surprisingly, the basket also contains the currencies of a number of other countries, namely Australia, Canada, Malaysia, Russia, Singapore, Thailand, and the UK. Zhou Xiaochuan, the governor of the Bank of China, argued that the selection of the countries was based on (i) China's trade pattern, (ii) the sources of its foreign direct investment, and (iii) the currency composition of its debt.

Figure 28.14 US$ exchange rates: Thailand and China, 2000–2005

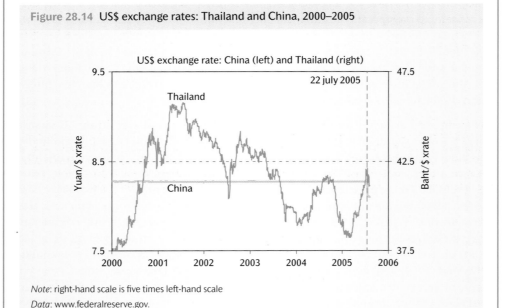

Note: right-hand scale is five times left-hand scale

Data: www.federalreserve.gov.

28.8 Conclusions

There are many different types of fixed exchange rate regimes; see Table 28.1. Differences between words (*de jure*) and deeds (*de facto*) indicate that some countries show a fear of floating and other countries show a fear of pegging. All fixed exchange rate regimes are subject to at least some credibility problems caused by the policy trilemma, which forces them to give up either on capital mobility or on policy autonomy; see Chapter 22. Using the Barro–Gordon model, we discussed two of these credibility problems, namely the need for countries engaging in fixed exchange rate regimes to have very similar monetary policy preferences, as well as the desirability to be confronted with highly correlated demand and/or supply shocks. These issues are discussed further in Chapter 30. On the positive side, the target zone literature indicates that announcing a fully credible fixed exchange rate regime has, in principle, a stabilizing influence on the actual exchange rate behaviour inside the band. This is called the honeymoon effect. Unfortunately, after allowing for several extensions of the basic target zone model, the empirical evidence indicates that the honeymoon effect is weak, at best. The next chapter analyses the potential costs involved in trying to maintain a fixed exchange rate regime that is not fully credible.

TECHNICAL NOTE

Technical Note 28.1 Solution of the basic target zone model

The structural equations (28.4) and (28.6) provide us with the expectations parameter ϕ, the bandwidth parameter b, and the variance parameter σ, which we use to define the S-curve parameter γ; see equation (28.A1). Ignoring the money stock for convenience ($m = 0$), Krugman (1991) shows, as heuristically explained in the text, that the exchange rate is given by equation (28.A2), where the parameter A still has to be determined.[4]

(28.A1)
$$\gamma = \sqrt{(2/\Phi\sigma^2)} > 0$$

(28.A2)
$$s = v + A(e^{\gamma v} - e^{-\gamma v})$$

To determine A we let $v^* > 0$ be the positive value of v where the S-curve touches the upper end of the target zone. The smooth-pasting condition gives us two pieces of information. First, the derivative of (28.A2) with respect to v must be zero; that is, $1 + \gamma A(e^{\gamma v^*} + e^{-\gamma v^*}) = 0$, as it must paste smoothly to a horizontal line at the edge of the target zone. Second, the value of the exchange rate at that point must be equal to b, the value at the edge; that is, $v^* + A(e^{\gamma v^*} - e^{-\gamma v^*}) = b$. Sarno and Taylor (2002: 183) show that these conditions imply that (28.A3) must hold. Substituting that in the second condition gives (28.A4), which is easy to solve numerically for v^*, and thus for A.

(28.A3)
$$A(v^*) = \frac{e^{-\gamma v^*} - e^{\gamma v^*}}{\gamma(e^{2\gamma v^*} - e^{-2\gamma v^*})} < 0,$$

(28.A4)
$$b = v^* + A(v^*)(e^{\gamma v^*} - e^{-\gamma v^*})$$

Question 28.1

28.1A The figures below show the development of inflation and unemployment in the USA and Argentina in the 1980s. Draw rational expectations equilibria for both countries in two diagrams. Which government has 'hard–nosed' preferences and which has 'wet' preferences?

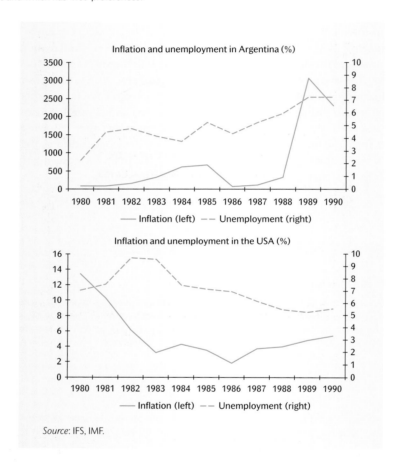

Source: IFS, IMF.

28.1B In 1991 Argentina decided to peg its exchange rate to the US dollar. What would have motivated Argentina to do so? What implications does this peg have for its long-run inflation rate?

28.1C The figures on the next page show the inflation and unemployment rates in the USA and Argentina since 1991. Was the peg successful? As a foreign exchange trader, would you trust the commitment of the Argentine government based on the figures below?

The elections are nearing and the Argentine government wants to be re-elected. A clear popularity issue is the stubbornly high unemployment rate.

28.1D Draw two loss-curves for Argentina: one assuming that the inflation–unemployment trade-off in the 1990s is in line with its preferences and another where the preferences are less 'hard-nosed'. Also depict the monetary preferences of the USA, assuming for simplicity that the natural rate of unemployment and Phillips curve are the same for both countries. Explain your graph.

28.1E What happens to the exchange rate (eventually) after the change in preferences?

28.1F What kind of relationship do you expect to exist between government elections and exchange rates?

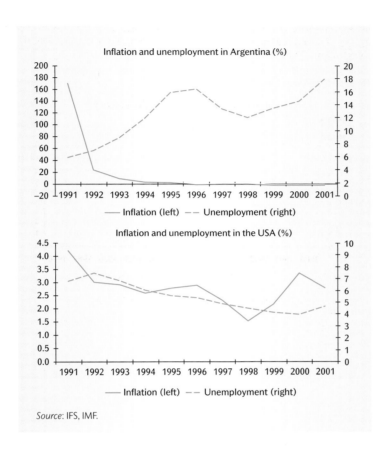

Source: IFS, IMF.

Question 28.2

In the euro area, the ECB is responsible for monetary policy. Germany, Spain and the euro area as a whole all have the same Phillips curves, policy preferences and long-run unemployment levels (5 per cent). The ECB has a long-run inflation target of 2 per cent.

28.2A Draw the equilibrium Phillips curve and loss curve for Germany, Spain and the euro area in a graph.

Spain receives a positive short-term economic shock. Germany however, experiences a negative short-term economic shock. Assume that the ECB succeeds in keeping the inflation rate at 2 per cent.

28.2B Draw in your diagram the new Phillips curves and indicate the level of unemployment and inflation for Spain and Germany after the changes.

28.2C Suppose the ECB wants to accommodate the German economic shock, because it is the biggest euro area economy. Will it tighten or loosen its monetary policy? Indicate such a change in your graph.

28.2D What is the consequence for Spain of this ECB policy?

28.2E Would a policy rule mitigate this coordination problem?

Question 28.3

28.3A What is a target zone model?

28.3B What is meant by leaning against the wind?

28.3C What is the honeymoon effect? How does this hold up empirically?

 See the Online Resource Centre for a Study Guide containing more questions
www.oxfordtextbooks.co.uk/orc/vanmarrewijk/

NOTES

1 There is no difference in principle between fixed exchange rates within a band and target zones; the idea is that the bandwidth for the latter is larger than for the former, such as for the ERM system after 1993.

2 Information source: *The Economist* (2005b).

3 That is, using a GARCH process rather than a random walk.

4 As this derivation requires some knowledge of stochastic calculus, we take it for granted here.

FINANCIAL CRISES

29

Objectives/key terms

- Exchange rates
- Characteristics of crises
- Coordination
- Banking crisis
- Twin crisis
- Currency crises
- First-generation models
- Self-fulfilling expectations

- Contagion
- Third-generation models
- Investors
- Second-generation models
- Frequency
- Central bank
- Vicious circle

We investigate the causes, characteristics, and consequences of different types of financial crises. As explained in the so-called first-, second-, and third-generation models, there is a crucial role to play for both bad fundamentals and self-fulfilling expectations leading to an exacerbating vicious circle in causing these (costly) crises.

29.1 Introduction[1]

The world economy is regularly confronted with a new financial crisis, be it a currency crisis, a banking crisis, or both simultaneously (a twin crisis); think of Mexico (1994–5), South-East Asia (1997), Brazil (1999), Turkey (2001), and Argentina (2002). As this list suggests, and we will see in this chapter, most of these crises occur in emerging market economies. The media inform us of the rapid fall in value of some currencies (see Section 29.2), and thus of the large costs that may be associated with such crises (see Section 29.7). Moreover, there is always a group of people to point at international capital mobility as the cause of the problem, in conjunction with the, perhaps ill-founded, actions of (large) investors. They have a point: in the absence of international capital mobility a currency crisis is not likely to occur. As discussed in Chapter 2, however, international capital mobility also brings many advantages, by spreading risks and channelling funds to the most productive investment opportunities. Limiting capital mobility therefore implies forfeiting these benefits, which is not the optimal response to avoiding financial crises. This chapter addresses these issues, first, by exlaining what a currency crisis is and by describing some of its characteristics; second, by analysing two models for explaining currency crises in which bad fundamentals and investors' expectations play a major role; third, by giving information on the frequency, sequencing, and costs of currency and banking crises; and finally, by providing a synthesis of the views expressed earlier in the chapter in one coherent framework (third-generation model).

29.2 What is a currency crisis?

A currency crisis occurs if investors lose confidence in an economy and its currency such that they sell their investments denominated in that currency. If this is done on a large scale in a short period of time and the speculative attack succeeds, the value of the currency can fall

Famous economists	Paul Krugman

Fig. 29.1
Paul Krugman
(1953–)

Krugman was born in a suburb of New York City and received his BA from Yale (1974) and his PhD from MIT (1977). He worked at Yale, MIT, Stanford, and MIT (again), before moving to Princeton. He is probably, and deservedly, the most influential international economist around today, well known both in the academic world and, thanks to his lucid prose, outside. As was to be expected, he described his style best himself: 'There are several different ways of doing good economics . . . But what has always appealed to me, ever since I saw Nordhaus practice it on energy, is the MIT style: small models applied to real problems, blending real-world observation and a little mathematics to cut through to the core of an issue.' He has used the MIT style splendidly to start off various new fields of study: new trade theory, geographical economics, target zone models, and financial crises. For the source of the quote, see the Collier laudatio on the Internet when Paul Krugman received his honorary doctorate in Berlin: http://www.wiwiss.fu-berlin.de/w3/w3collie/krugman/laudatio.html

Figure 29.2 Asian crisis: rapid drop in the value of some currencies

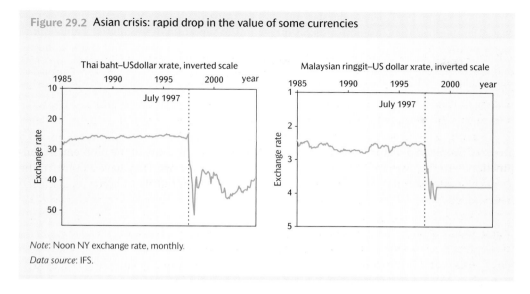

Note: Noon NY exchange rate, monthly.

Data source: IFS.

rapidly, as illustrated in Figure 29.2 for Thailand and Malaysia during the 1997 Asian crisis. This is the archetypical currency crisis. First, there is a mounting pressure on the existing exchange rate to depreciate. Investors then collectively start to sell their investments denominated in the currency under pressure. The authorities initially try to defy depreciation of the currency by supporting the present exchange rate, either by raising interest rates or by selling part of their foreign exchange reserves and buying the local currency. As the speculative attack continues, the authorities eventually have to give in and the currency starts its (steep) decline. As we will see, the speculative attack might be largely self-fulfilling, because the actions undertaken by the investors vindicate their own doubts that started the attack in the first place.

There are also less obvious aspects of a currency crisis. First, there may be *un*successful attacks, for example if the authorities respond by raising interest rates and/or selling part of their foreign exchange reserves to alleviate the doubts about their commitments. Such unsuccessful attacks should be classified as a currency crisis in view of the high economic costs associated with fighting off the attack (in terms of rising interest rates and loss of exchange reserves). Second, there is a puzzle associated with currency crises regarding the difference in outcome for economies in seemingly identical circumstances. It is not only important to understand the crises that actually occurred, but also why a crisis did not occur in very similar circumstances. As we will discuss below, the self-fulfilling nature of a currency crisis plays a large role in this respect.

We distinguish between two key players: private (portfolio) investors and the monetary authorities (the central bank). We assume that (i) the authorities want to maintain a fixed exchange rate and (ii) economic decisions have been made under the assumption that this fixed exchange rate will be maintained in the future. In these circumstances, a currency crisis can be most damaging and may ignite a full-blown financial crisis. Capital mobility is crucial for a currency crisis to occur. If investors cannot switch between currencies, or only at large (transaction) costs, a currency crisis is virtually impossible. This is one of the reasons why some economists, policy makers, and anti-globalization protesters have called for the reintroduction of restrictions on international capital mobility. Malaysia, for example, decided to re-install exchange rate controls to stabilize the exchange rate in the aftermath of the currency crisis in 1997. The Malaysian authorities, in particular former president Mohamad Mahathir, blamed the currency crisis on the whimsical and purely speculative behaviour of (foreign) investors and not on intrinsic, fundamental weaknesses of the Malaysian economy. Evidently, such controls only make sense if speculative investors rather than economic fundamentals are to blame for the currency crisis.

29.3 Characteristics of currency crises

A currency crisis typically brings about a reversal of capital flows, particularly in the case of emerging market economies. These countries have a relatively low level of domestic savings and offer a (potentially) high return on investment (high interest rates). In general, therefore, there is a large capital inflow before the crisis to take advantage of this high return to investment

Figure 29.3 Asian crisis: current account balance

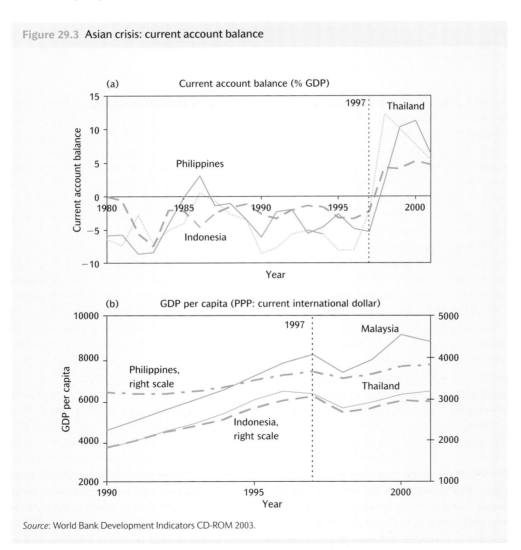

Source: World Bank Development Indicators CD-ROM 2003.

Table 29.1(a) Real income growth and capital account crises

Country	Crisis year	Real GDP growth		
		Previous year	Crisis year	Following year
Argentina	1995	5.8	−2.8	5.5
Brazil	1999	0.2	0.8	4.2
Indonesia	1998	4.5	−13.1	0.8
Korea	1998	5.0	−6.7	10.9
Mexico	1995	4.4	−6.2	5.2
Philippines	1998	5.2	−0.6	3.3
Thailand	1998	−1.4	−10.8	4.2
Turkey	1994	7.7	−4.7	8.1

Table 29.1(b) Median changes in private capital flows and current account

Year	% of GDP	
	Private capital inflows (+)	Current account deficit (−)
$t-3$	4.0	−3.0
$t-2$	4.5	−3.5
$t-1$	2.0	−3.0
crisis year = t	−2.5	2.5
$t+1$	−0.5	2.0
$t+2$	0	1.5
$t+3$	1.2	−0.5

Source: IMF (April 2002).

(on the assumption that the exchange rate remains fixed), followed by a large capital outflow if the crisis hits, as illustrated for the Asian crisis in Figure 29.3(a). A similar experience holds for the financial crises in Mexico (1994–5), Brazil (1999), Turkey (2001), and Argentina (2002).

29.4 First-generation models

Models of currency crises can be classified along two basic dimensions. The first dimension concerns the role that international investors play in bringing about the crisis. Do they merely react to a changed outlook about the exchange rate or do they themselves determine what this outlook looks like? The second dimension is the rationale for the crisis: is the currency crisis due to inherent flaws in the domestic economy that render a currency crisis inevitable or are the fundamentals of the economy sound and is the attack on the currency a purely speculative one? In the first models of currency crises, investors play a rather passive role and the currency crisis is completely due to bad fundamentals which are incompatible with the fixed exchange rate; see Krugman (1979) and Flood and Garber (1984). The basic structure of these models is outlined in equations (29.1)–(29.3):

(29.1) $$P = (V/Y)\,M$$

(29.2) $$P = S_f P^* \quad \text{with } P^* = S_f = 1$$

(29.3) $$dM = dF + dR$$

Equation (29.1) is the basic quantity theory of money; see Chapter 18. Taking the velocity of money V and the real income Y as given in the short run, the domestic price level P is a positive function of the domestic money supply M. Equation (29.2) imposes long-run purchasing power parity, see Chapter 20, where S_f denotes the fixed exchange rate and P^* is the foreign price level, both normalized to 1. To prevent a rise in the domestic price level and to maintain the fixed exchange rate, the money supply cannot increase. Equation (29.3) states that this country finances its government budget deficit F in a rather crude manner, namely by borrowing from the central bank, which increases the money supply. It represents the balance sheet of the central bank, with loans to the government F and the foreign exchange reserves R as the assets and the money supply M as the liability.

An increase in the government budget deficit dF and the resulting increase of the money supply would increase the domestic price level and thereby make it impossible to stick to the fixed exchange rate. The monetary authorities can, however, prevent the government budget deficit from increasing the money supply by selling part of the foreign exchange reserves R to the public in exchange for the domestic currency. As long as $dF = -dR$, the money supply does not increase and the country can stick to its fixed exchange rate. Since the amount of foreign exchange reserves is limited, the monetary authorities will completely run down their reserves at some point in the future. With an unchanged fiscal policy, the money supply will start to increase ($dM = dF$), such that the government can no longer stick to the fixed exchange rate and has to devalue the currency. Rational investors will not wait for this moment to happen, since the currency devaluation will imply a loss of funds expressed in foreign currency. They therefore 'attack' the currency by selling their investments well *before* reserves are depleted. The crisis occurs at some point in between the moment the government starts its money-financed expansionary fiscal policy and the moment the foreign exchange reserves are completely run down. Investors display forward-looking behaviour, understand how the economy works, and the speculative attack on the currency is inevitable and successful. The investors simply bring home the bad news a bit earlier than would have been the case if the government had had its way.

There are three points in favour of the first-generation models. First, most economists do, indeed, believe that currency crises are at least to some degree the result of bad fundamentals and that speculative attacks are not random. Kaminsky and Reinhart (1999) show, for instance, that in the eighteen months leading up to a currency crisis, countries experience a significant fall in their foreign exchange reserves R, just as the model predicts. Second, the model explains why a currency crisis can occur quite suddenly and at a time the authorities still seem able to (temporarily) stick to the fixed exchange rate. Third, the abruptness and the timing of the currency crisis implies a sudden reversal of capital flows, as illustrated above, when investors collectively decide they are no longer willing to invest in the currency.

29.5 Second-generation models

A disadvantage of the first-generation models is the rather mechanical behaviour of the agents. The government is not able to change its fiscal policies, use instruments to prevent the future devaluation, or get access to the international capital market to finance its deficit. Investors only react to the changes in the economic environment but their behaviour does not shape this environment. Their expectations only matter in determining the timing of the speculative attack, not whether or not such an attack will take place.

Since a currency crisis is like a stock market crash, see Mishkin (1992, 1999), we need a model that relates a currency crisis and the loss of confidence in the fixed exchange rate to the workings of the financial sector at large. The second-generation models of currency crises display multiple equilibria; that is, both the occurrence and the absence of a speculative attack can be an equilibrium outcome. Currency crises then not only depend on a given set of fundamentals, but also on the *behaviour* and expectations of the investors. The second-generation models are based on three core assumptions; see Krugman (1996) and Jeanne (2000: 24–5):

- *Policy makers have a reason to give up the fixed exchange rate.* They may want to devalue, for example, to boost the export sector of the economy or to reduce the debt burden of the private sector. The latter may occur if the devaluation enables a more inflationary policy, provided the domestic debt is not too heavily in foreign currency.

- *Policy makers also have a reason to stick to the fixed exchange rate.* In many cases, policy makers use the fixed exchange rate to enhance the credibility of their domestic policies. Especially in countries with a high inflation rate there is an advantage to pegging to a 'hard' currency like the US dollar or the euro in an attempt to convince the domestic private sector and foreign investors of their commitment to fighting inflation.[2]

- *The costs of maintaining the fixed exchange rate increase if a future devaluation is expected.* If investors start to doubt the sustainability of the fixed exchange rate, they want to be compensated for this perceived increased risk by demanding a higher interest rate, which increases the costs of maintaining the fixed exchange rate.

The first two assumptions above imply a trade-off for the domestic policy maker: there are costs and benefits of sticking to the fixed exchange rate. The third assumption implies that investors determine the position of the policy maker on this trade-off. If investors start to doubt the fixed exchange rate and ask for a higher interest rate, it becomes more likely that the benefits of the fixed exchange rate no longer outweigh the costs. This is summarized in equation (29.4), which gives the social loss function H the policy makers try to minimize, where S_{tar} is the desired or target exchange rate, S_{fix} is the actual fixed exchange rate, S^{exp} is the investor's expected exchange rate, and C is the credibility cost of giving up the fixed exchange rate. It incorporates the three aspects mentioned above: if $S_{tar} > S_{fix}$, the policy makers have an incentive to give up the fixed exchange rate, whereas $C > 0$ represents the welfare loss of giving up the fixed exchange rate.[3]

(29.4)
$$H = \begin{cases} [a(S_{tar} - S_{fix})^2 + b(S^{exp} - S_{fix})^2] & \text{if fixed exchange rate; } a,b > 0 \\ C & \text{if flexible exchange rate} \end{cases}$$

The first two arguments in (29.4) give the basic trade-off for the policy maker when she has to decide whether or not to try to maintain the fixed exchange rate. The third argument concerns the role of investors' expectations and their impact on social welfare. If investors expect the fixed exchange rate to hold in the future ($S^{exp} = S_{fix}$), the corresponding argument in the welfare loss function is zero and has no bearing on social welfare. If investors think the fixed exchange rate is not credible and expect the policy maker to abandon this policy at some point in the future to arrive at the target exchange rate ($S^{exp} = S_{tar}$), they will ask for a higher interest rate and thereby increase the social welfare loss. To show how this second generation model gives rise to multiple self-fulfilling equilibria, assume that the following inequalities hold:

(29.5) $$a(S_{tar} - S_{fix})^2 < C < (a + b)(S_{tar} - S_{fix})^2$$

What do these inequalities imply? Suppose the fixed exchange rate is credible, such that ($S^{exp} = S_{fix}$) and thus $b(S^{exp} - S_{fix}) = 0$. In this case, the first inequality above holds: $a(S_{tar} - S_{fix})^2 < C$, indicating that the government will not give up the fixed exchange rate and there will not be a currency crisis. If, however, investors do not find the fixed exchange rate credible and $S^{exp} = S_{tar}$, we are dealing with the second part of the inequality in (29.5): $C < (a + b)(S_{tar} - S_{fix})^2$. This time the policy makers will decide to give up the fixed exchange rate and the expectations of the investors lead to a currency crisis. Which of the two equilibria will be realized depends on the (self-fulfilling) expectations of investors about S^{exp}; see also Box 29.1.

 Box 29.1   **Coordination**

The main text deals with investors as a homogeneous group, implicitly assuming that individuals coordinate their actions and act as one. This is not an innocuous assumption because a speculative attack can only succeed if a sufficiently large number of investors decide to sell the currency in a given time period, as the following example based on Obstfeld (1996) illustrates. Suppose there are two investors and a central bank. The latter can use its foreign exchange reserves, say $R = 10$, to defend the fixed exchange rate. Each investor has funds to the amount of 6 at her disposal and must decide to either keep these funds (option *hold*) or to sell them to the central bank in exchange for reserves R (option *sell*). If a speculative attack succeeds, the central bank has to devalue the domestic currency by 50 per cent, creating a capital gain for the investors since they sold their funds (denominated in domestic currency) for foreign exchange reserves R and the foreign currency increases in value because of the devaluation. Finally, assume that each investor faces transactions costs of 1 if she decides to exchange her funds for reserves.

Table 29.2 depicts the pay-off matrix to the investors and illustrates that coordination of their decisions is needed for a currency crisis to occur. If both investors choose *hold*, there will be no transaction with the central bank, hence no speculative attack and the exchange rate will remain fixed. Given the commitment of the central bank to put up $R = 10$ of its reserves to defend the currency, it is also clear that a *single* investor cannot launch a successful speculative attack because each investor has only a total of 6 funds at her disposal. Moreover, if one of the investors chooses to *sell* while the other does not, the former will actually lose money because of the transaction costs involved in buying the reserves from the central bank. The outcome that both investors choose *hold* is an equilibrium outcome in this set-up of the game; given that the other investor chooses *hold* it is optimal to also choose *hold*. Finally, it is clear that both investors would be better off if they »

Table 29.2 Coordination of a speculative attack

Pay-off matrix (inv. 2 , inv. 1)		Investor 1	
		Sell	Hold
Investor 2	sell	(3/2, 3/2)	(−1, 0)
	hold	(0, −1)	(0, 0)

both decided to *sell*. In this case, there will be a successful speculative attack as the sources of the central bank ($R = 10$) fall short of the combined sources of the investors ($6 + 6 = 12$). Consequently, the central bank has no option but to devalue the currency by 50 per cent. This is good news for the investors who enjoy a capital gain of 10×50 per cent $= 5$, which is 5/2 for each investor and a net gain of 3/2 after subtracting the transactions costs. If the other investor chooses to *sell*, it is optimal to also choose *sell*.

The situation described above has two equilibria and a currency crisis only occurs if the individual investors can coordinate their actions, which raises the question of how they manage to do this. Two basic possibilities exist. First, the state of the economy and the perceived willingness of the central banks to defend the fixed exchange rate provide a focal point for individual investors. In this case, the economic fundamentals provide a signal to investors that they can use to coordinate their actions. Second, investors may use information as a focal point that is not necessarily related to the actual economy. Given that the currency market, like the stock market or any other speculative market, is prone to herd behaviour, any piece of information that moves the market in a certain direction might do the trick. One possibility is the (alleged) decision to sell by a large investor with a good reputation among other investors (think of George Soros or Warren Buffett), prompting the other investors to do the same.

29.6 Frequency and measurement

Eichengreen, Rose, and Wyplosz (1995) developed a widely used currency crisis indicator based on changes in the exchange rate, short-term interest rates, and official foreign exchange reserves. When a country successfully defends its fixed exchange rate by (temporarily) raising its interest rates or by drawing upon its reserves, this can also qualify as a currency crisis. Based on this indicator, Bordo et al. (2001) analyse whether currency crises have become more frequent over time. To answer this question, they define the *probability* of a crisis as the total number of crises in a period divided by the total number of country–year observations during that period, subdivided into banking crises, currency crises, and twin crises (that is banking crises combined with currency crises); see Figure 29.4. It turns out that the frequency of *currency* crises has increased (attributed by Bordo et al. to the increase in international capital mobility): in the heyday of the gold standard (1880–1913), the probability of a currency crisis was about 1 per cent compared to more than 7 per cent in the most recent period. As for banking crises or twin crises, there is no such increase.

As to the *causes* of currency crises, the bulk of the empirical research concludes that on average these crises can be attributed to economic fundamentals being at odds with the fixed

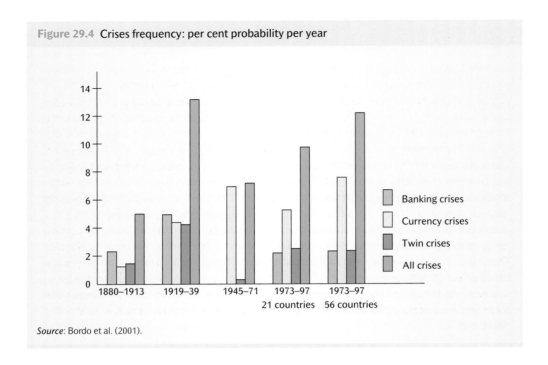

Figure 29.4 Crises frequency: per cent probability per year

Source: Bordo et al. (2001).

Table 29.3 The incidence of global contagion, 1970–98

Other countries with crises (share, %)	Probabilities (%)		
	Unconditional (A)	Conditional (B)	Difference: (B) − (A)
0–25	29.0	20.0	−9.0
25–50	29.0	33.0	4.0
50 and above	29.0	54.7	27.7

Source: Kaminsky and Reinhart (2000).

exchange rate objective. Kaminsky and Reinhart (1999) analyse sixteen macroeconomic variables or fundamentals just before and after a crisis took place, based on a sample of 76 currency crises in 20 countries in the period 1970–95. Apart from the falling reserves, countries that are hit by a currency crisis on average also have (compared to tranquil times) excessive money- and credit-growth rates, a high current account deficit (and thus a high capital inflow), an overvalued currency (in real terms), and lower output growth. After the currency crisis, these trends are often reversed within a few months. This does not imply that self-fulfilling expectations have no role to play, as indicated by various contagion studies, defined by Kaminsky and Reinhart (2000: 147) as 'a case where knowing that there is a crisis elsewhere increases the probability of a crisis at home.' Their results on contagion are summarized in Table 29.3. The *unconditional* probability (29 per cent) indicates the chance at time *t* that a

Box 29.2   Indices of intervention

As already noted in Chapter 28, there is frequently a discrepancy between what countries say they do and what they actually do. In terms of the exchange rate regime, this translates into a fear of floating and a fear of pegging. Before the Asian crisis hit, it was widely known that the South-east Asian countries had moved to a *de facto* soft dollar peg. This raises the question if, and to what extent, the countries had returned to a soft dollar peg after the crisis of 1997 subsided. Since the official announcements can be misleading, several researchers have moved to constructing an 'index of intervention' to determine the actual, rather than the announced, exchange rate policy. A good example is provided by Pontines (2006), who uses information on the volatilities of the nominal exchange rate, foreign exchange reserves, and interest rates to construct such an index. By using a Markov regime-switching approach (see Hamilton and Susmel, 1994), he is not only able to distinguish between periods of high volatility and low volatility, but also to base his index on conditional rather than unconditional variances. Figure 29.5 shows the Pontines index of intervention for Thailand and Singapore in the period 1985–2004 on a monthly basis. It indicates that Thailand maintained a clear (dollar) currency peg before the crisis, but did not return to this policy after the crisis. Singapore, on the other hand, was regularly intervening before the crisis, did little to resist the downward pressure during the crisis (unlike other countries), and returned to its narrow band policy after the crisis.

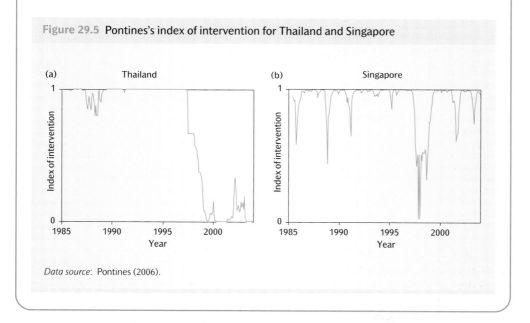

Figure 29.5 Pontines's index of intervention for Thailand and Singapore

Data source: Pontines (2006).

country is hit by a currency crisis within the next 24 months. Contagion is analysed in the next column by calculating the *conditional* probability of a currency crisis, that is the probability of a currency crisis at home when there is a currency crisis elsewhere. The conditional probability is only clearly larger than the unconditional probability if at least 50 per cent of the countries experience a currency crisis, giving some evidence of global contagion.

29.7 The costs of financial crises and sequencing

A currency crisis is a disruption on the currency market in which a speculative attack on a currency leads to a devaluation, a loss of reserves, or rising interest rates. A capital account crisis is the mirror image of a currency crisis, focusing on the sudden reversal of capital flows that accompanies the currency market disruption. These are then potential *external* channels for a financial crisis. Its domestic equivalent is a banking crisis, in which the increased fragility of a country's banking sector, potentially leading to bank runs, forces the government to intervene or banks to scale down their business. This is a potential *internal* channel for a financial crisis. It is customary to refer to a twin crisis if a banking crisis and a currency crisis occur (almost) at the same time. The estimated costs of a financial crisis, measured by the contraction of the economy, are given in Table 29.4.

As shown in Table 29.4, most currency crises and banking crises occur in emerging markets and lead to an output loss (namely 61 per cent of the currency crises and 82 per cent of the banking crises). The costs of restructuring the financial sector for the government are substantial, ranging from funds and credit injected into the banking system to the fiscal costs of closing down banks. Such costs can amount up to 20 per cent of GDP. Although these costs are already substantial for financial currency crises (about 7.1 per cent), they are substantially higher for financial banking crises (about 14.2 per cent), and even higher for financial twin crises (about 18.5 per cent).

The intrinsic weaknesses in the domestic financial sector might be *reinforced* by (quite sudden) changes in capital flows and by a currency crisis leading to a depreciation of the domestic currency. Most recent financial crises have occurred in emerging markets, where the banking sector plays a role as intermediary in the process of channelling funds to investment opportunities. Financial crises are then mainly banking crises. Mishkin (1999) argues that a banking crisis *precedes* a currency crisis, leading to the sequencing of a typical modern financial crisis as illustrated in Figure 29.6.

Table 29.4 Cost of crises in lost output (relative to trend output)

	No. of crises	Average recovery time (in years)	% of crises with output loss	Cumulative output loss per crisis*
Currency crises	158	1.6	61	7.1
Industrial	42	1.9	55	5.6
Emerging	116	1.5	64	7.6
Banking crises	54	3.1	82	14.2
Industrial	12	4.1	67	15.2
Emerging	41	2.8	86	14.0
Twin crises	32	3.2	78	18.5
Industrial	6	5.8	100	17.6
Emerging	26	2.6	73	18.8

Note: * For those crises with output loss.

Source: IMF (1998).

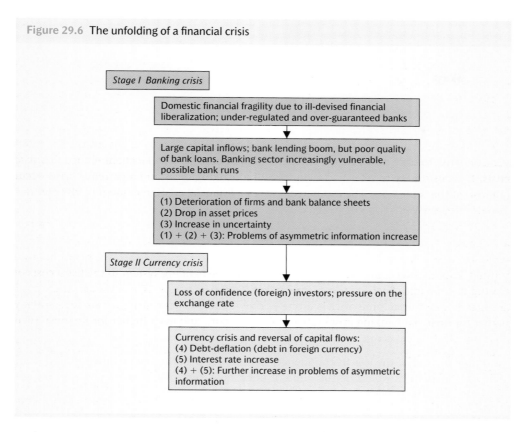

Figure 29.6 The unfolding of a financial crisis

Stage I Banking crisis

Domestic financial fragility due to ill-devised financial liberalization; under-regulated and over-guaranteed banks

Large capital inflows; bank lending boom, but poor quality of bank loans. Banking sector increasingly vulnerable, possible bank runs

(1) Deterioration of firms and bank balance sheets
(2) Drop in asset prices
(3) Increase in uncertainty
(1) + (2) + (3): Problems of asymmetric information increase

Stage II Currency crisis

Loss of confidence (foreign) investors; pressure on the exchange rate

Currency crisis and reversal of capital flows:
(4) Debt-deflation (debt in foreign currency)
(5) Interest rate increase
(4) + (5): Further increase in problems of asymmetric information

The question is, of course, if this sequence of events can be backed up with empirical evidence. Two main issues are at stake. First, is it true that banking crises typically precede the currency crises? Second, are the underlying economic conditions to blame for the crises; that is, are they the result of bad fundamentals? If self-fulfilling expectations of international investors are a necessary condition for a crisis to occur we have arrived at stage II in Figure 29.6, which then becomes the *first* stage of the financial crisis. A currency depreciation and higher interest rates (to stop the depreciation and the capital outflow) will be bad for the balance sheets of the banks and the firms, leading us to stage I in Figure 29.6, and the economy may end up with weak economic fundamentals. In a nutshell, then, Figure 29.6 is turned *upside-down* in this view.

29.8 Synthesis: third-generation model

The obvious question is: who is right: the 'fundamentalists' who blame weak domestic economic and financial conditions or the 'self-fulfillers' who blame the self-fulfilling expectations of investors? Krugman's (2000) answer is: both are correct. Figure 29.7 illustrates how aspects of both views can be reconciled in a synthesis leading to a vicious circle. The main difference between the two views above is where to start on the circle. Once the economy moves (clock-wise) around the circle, the essential differences between the two views disappear. The circular line of reasoning is as follows. Starting from a loss of confidence on the

Figure 29.7 Vicious circle of financial crises

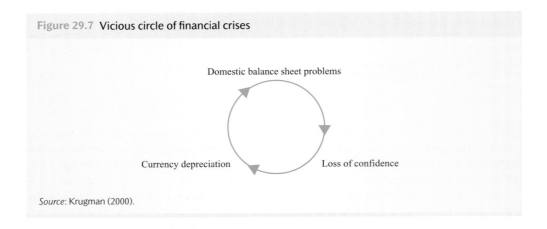

Source: Krugman (2000).

part of investors, this leads to a capital outflow → leading to a sharp real depreciation of the domestic currency required to arrive at current account surplus → leading to a worsening of firms' balance sheets (with loans or deposits denominated in foreign currency) → leading to a fall in net worth → leading to a drop in investment and output → leading to a further loss in confidence, etc.

If we take the fragility of the domestic financial sector as our starting point in this circular reasoning, instead of the loss in confidence, the starting point would be different, but from there on the analysis would be the same. It does, however, matter where you start on the vicious circle as the policy implications are quite different. If self-fulfilling expectations are to blame, international capital markets are the culprits, providing a possible rationale for restricting international capital mobility. However, if you start on the circle with the domestic balance sheet problems, you would probably call for policies that remedy the regulatory and other weaknesses in the domestic financial sector.

Finally, note that in the vicious circle approach the crucial variable is the real exchange rate. A change in the real exchange rate has two opposite effects. On the one hand, there is the standard effect that a depreciation improves competitiveness and thereby stimulates net exports, which is necessary because the capital flow calls for a current account surplus and hence for a boost in net exports. On the other hand, the depreciation increases the real value of debt denominated in foreign currency. For the group of developing countries as a whole, the current account deficit in 1998 was $68 billion, which had turned into as surplus of $67 billion in the year 2000 as a result of a substantial currency depreciation. Simultaneously, the private capital flows to developing countries dwindled. Since 2000 there has been a net debt *out*flow as banks and firms in developing countries seek to repay the now very expensive debt denominated in foreign currency; see IMF (2003) and World Bank (2003, ch. 5).

This synthesis between the 'fundamentalists' and the 'self-fulfillers' has been dubbed the *third-generation* model of currency crises. The differences with the second-generation model are twofold. First, there is a larger and more direct role for self-fulfilling expectations. In the second-generation models, self-fulfilling expectations are also possible but only in so far as these expectations influenced the trade-off for the domestic policy makers between the costs and benefits of a fixed exchange rate. In the vicious circle approach, there is a more direct impact of investors' loss of confidence on the exchange rate. Second, the interaction between the exchange rate and the domestic financial sector is only explicitly analysed in the third-generation model, which makes the vicious circle approach particularly well suited to analyse twin crises, that is the occurrence of both a banking crisis and a currency crisis. In other words, it is a useful model for analysing modern-day financial crises.

29.9 Conclusions

The number of currency crises appears to have increased over time, particularly in emerging markets, alongside the rise in capital mobility and possibly caused by the contagion phenomenon. A typical currency crisis involving a *de jure* or *de facto* fixed exchange rate can arise, for example, if the central bank is forced to use its foreign exchange reserves or raise its interest rates to fend off an attack on its currency. If such an attack is succesful, the central bank will be forced to devalue the currency or let it float, which is usually associated with a reversal of (private) funds and the current account moving from a deficit to a surplus.

The first-generation models of financial crises explain why investors will attack a currency even before the central bank runs out of reserves, based on ultimately unsustainable bad fundamentals. The second-generation models of financial crises involve a cost–benefit trade-off for policy makers for either sticking to or giving up the fixed exchange rate. The role of investors in these multiple equilibria models is more important, as the outcome chosen by policy makers crucially depends on investors' expectations, which can be based on fundamentals, but also on herd behaviour.

A currency crisis can be an external source for igniting a domestic banking crisis, in which case a twin crisis arises (a simultaneous banking crisis and currency crisis). The frequency of banking crises and twin crises does not seem to increase over time. The economic costs of all types of crises, but particularly of twin crises, is high. If a twin crisis arises, the sequencing seems to be important. Does a (bad-fundamentals-caused) banking crisis lead to a (expectations-caused) currency crisis, or vice versa? The third-generation model of financial crises is a synthesis of these two views, showing how either crisis and either underlying cause can be the starting point of a vicious circle leading to a (costly) financial crisis. As these costs are ultimately caused by trying to maintain a fixed exchange rate regime that is not fully credible, the next chapter turns to a possible solution for this credibility problem by moving to a monetary union.

QUESTIONS

Question 29.1

An important part of the Argentinian economic crisis of 2002 can be illustrated with the first-generation model of currency crises. Argentina has a long history of financial instability which is rooted in an enduring gap between the federal government's ability to raise money and the demands for spending from Argentina's politically powerful provinces. This gap was financed by borrowing from the Central Bank. In the 1980s this led to a period of hyperinflation. Inflation was only stabilized after 1991 when the Argentine peso was by law fixed to the US dollar at an exchange rate of one peso for one dollar. During the 1990s, however, government debt continued to rise. After 1997 the situation became critical when Argentina was hit by the devaluation of the Brazilian real and a considerable international revaluation of the dollar.

29.1A How, according to the first-generation model of currency crises, could Argentina keep its exchange rate fixed while government debt held by the Central Bank was rising?

29.1B Why did the situation become critical after the devaluation of the Brazilian real and the revaluation of the dollar?

29.1C In order to prevent a financial crisis, the IMF lent Argentina large sums of money in 2000. The IMF did not demand a tight fiscal policy. Why was the policy of the IMF only temporarily successful?

29.1D In 2001 the Argentina government enacted a set of measures that effectively froze all bank accounts (which first led to noisy and later to violent demonstrations). Why did the government do this?

29.1E Why do you think the government had to give up the fixed exchange rate regime at the start of 2002?

Question 29.2[4]

Box 28.1 in the main text describes the speculative attack on the British pound and the Italian lire on Black Wednesday (16 September 1991). This crisis clearly shows the importance of the second-generation crisis models.

29.2A Why can Black Wednesday not be described by the first generation models of financial crises?

29.2B In the main text the three core assumptions of second-generation models are mentioned. What are these assumptions? Explain how Britain and Italy answered these assumptions?

29.2C Describe how a full-fledged financial crisis may arise from these three assumptions.

29.2D After the exit of Britain and Italy from the European Monetary System there was mounting pressure on the French authorities to devalue the franc. Why do you think France was contaminated by the British and Italian crises?

Question 29.3

Financial crises can be disastrous for an economy. The IMF has estimated that the costs associated with a crisis can amount up to 20 per cent of GDP. Regretfully there is no standard toolkit available for governments and financial institutions to prevent a financial crisis. In some situations a certain policy may prevent a crisis while in other circumstances the same policy may instead worsen a crisis. Below a number of policies are listed that have been used in the wake of a crisis. Describe how these policies may have either a good or a bad effect on the economy. Pay special attention to the confidence of investors and the cause of a crisis (using the models from three generations).

29.3A Fiscal austerity

29.3B Capital controls

29.3C (IMF) credit line

29.3D Debt rollover and standstill

29.3E Bank holiday

 See the Online Resource Centre for a Study Guide containing more questions
www.oxfordtextbooks.co.uk/orc/vanmarrewijk/

NOTES

1 I am grateful to my co-authors Steven Brakman, Harry Garretsen, and Arjen van Witteloostuijn for allowing me to use some of our joint work (see Brakman et al., 2006) as the basis for this chapter.

2 See the Italian example in Chapter 30.

3 For a more advanced treatment of the first- and second-generation models of currency crisis, see Obstfeld and Rogoff (1996: 559–65 and 648–53).

4 This question is based on Paul Krugman's 'Currency crises'.

EUROPEAN MONETARY UNION (EMU)

30

Objectives/key terms

- Optimal currency areas
- Trade openness
- Benefits of a common currency
- Uncertainty
- Maastricht Treaty
- European System of Central Banks (ESCB)
- Convergence criteria

- Labour mobility
- Product diversification
- Transaction costs
- International currency
- European Central Bank (ECB)
- Eurosystem
- Stability and growth pact
- New euro area members

We discuss optimal currency areas, the benefits of a common currency, and the process of European monetary integration, which led to a single currency: the euro. We also review the structure of the eurosystem and the need for institutional adjustment.

30.1 Introduction

The title of this chapter is wrong. Officially, the abbreviation EMU means Economic and Monetary Union, not European Monetary Union. The latter is, however, more to the point and more commonly used, so I do the same here. If two or more countries decide to use one (virtually irrevocable) common currency, the main credibility problems analysed in Chapters 28 and 29 can be avoided. This chapter reviews the unique process of European monetary integration, which has led to the establishment of a single currency in twelve European countries on 1 January 1999. The newly established currency is called the euro, its symbol is €, and it is used in Belgium, Germany, Greece, Spain, France, Ireland, Italy, Luxembourg, The Netherlands, Austria, Portugal, and Finland. We refer to these countries as the euro area. Its total population in 2003 was 307 million people (slightly more than the USA's 291 million) and its total GNP was $8.11 trillion (about 74 per cent of the USA's $11 trillion). As such the economic power of the euro area is only surpassed by that of the USA. This chapter discusses the costs and benefits of a common currency, the historical process of European monetary integration, the role of the European Central Bank (ECB), and the associated policy coordination problems.

30.2 Optimal currency areas

The theory of optimal currency areas as pioneered by Mundell (1961), McKinnon (1962), and Kenen (1969) focuses on the differences between countries and the costs associated with introducing a common currency in responding to those differences. We can illustrate these issues in part in the framework discussed in Chapter 28, assuming that two countries that want to form a monetary union, such as Italy and Germany, are confronted with asymmetric shocks. For ease of reference, Figure 30.2 repeats Figure 28.8, where we assume that Italy is hit by a negative demand shock and Germany by a positive shock.

In response to the demand shock, the two economies will have to adjust (the extent of the adjustment depends upon whether the shock is permanent or transitory). One way to do this is by changing the relative price of Italian goods, that is by changing the real exchange rate between Italy and Germany (in logs; see Chapter 20): $s - (p_{It} - p_{Ger})$, where s is the exchange rate, p is the price index, and sub-indices refer to Italy and Germany. We immediately note one

Famous economists	Peter Kenen

Born in Ohio and educated at Columbia and Harvard, Peter Kenen first worked at Columbia for fourteen years and then moved to Princeton. He is a leading expert on the international monetary system, on which he has written numerous articles and books, as summarized in his: *The International Financial Architecture*. He closely studied the process of European monetary integration and pointed to the importance of diversification for the theory of optimum currency areas.

Fig. 30.1
Peter Kenen
(1932–)

Figure 30.2 Asymmetric shocks (Italy and Germany)

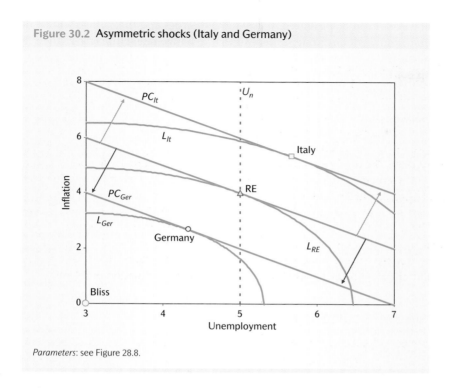

Parameters: see Figure 28.8.

problem with using a common currency: the nominal exchange rate *s* is irrevocably fixed and cannot adjust to accommodate the shocks. All the adjustment in this respect must come from price changes. Since prices are largely determined by costs and costs by wages, price flexibility is largely related to wage flexibility. Shocks can be absorbed if there is sufficient *wage flexibility*.

Wages tend to be contracted for longer time periods (one or two years) and are therefore not very flexible. Moreover, they tend to be more flexible upward than downward, implying larger adjustment problems for Italy than for Germany in our example. There is, however, an alternative adjustment channel available. Since demand and employment is increasing in Germany and decreasing in Italy, a possible solution is provided if workers migrate from Italy to Germany. As emphasized by Mundell (1961), shocks can be absorbed if there is sufficient *labour mobility*. The large cultural differences, the many languages spoken, and the other difficulties associated with migrating within Europe (e.g. different pension schemes) ensure that labour mobility within Europe is not very high.

If the shocks affecting Italy and Germany are transitory, the consequences of the shock can be mitigated through an automatic system of transfers, as operate at the regional level in most countries. Tax revenues from the increased value of production in Germany can then be transferred as unemployment benefits to Italy and mitigate the fall in demand for Italian goods. The reverse may happen some time later when Germany is affected by a negative shock. Shocks can therefore be absorbed through a system of *fiscal transfers*. At the moment, the size of such transfers within Europe is very small (the EU budget is only about 1.4 per cent of GDP), so this mechanism hardly operates in the euro area.

McKinnon (1962) points to the limited usefulness of changing the nominal exchange rate for improving a nation's competitiveness, particularly if *trade openness* is high. In that case very similar goods can be produced in different countries and their prices will be nearly the same in Italy and Germany, independent of the exchange rate. Little is lost, then, by giving up the exchange rate as an adjustment tool. Trade openness in the euro area is very high, in accordance with this criterion.

We can, of course, also wonder how frequently asymmetric shocks occur, and, if they do occur, if they are sizeable enough to be accommodated by a change in the exchange rate. Kenen (1969) points out that sectoral shocks for highly diversified countries occur regularly and are not sizeable enough to warrant a change in the exchange rate. Only for smaller countries specializing to a large extent in one or only a few products, such as Burundi which exports mainly coffee, would changing the exchange rate be a suitable method for adjusting to the shock. *Product diversification* within the euro area is very high, in accordance with this criterion.

As already analysed in Chapter 28, even if shocks are symmetric rather than asymmetric there is a need for countries to agree on the way to deal with the shock. With respect to Figure 30.2, a similar shock for Italy and Germany only leads to a similar policy prescription, and thus agreement on how to respond, if the Italian and German preferences are very similar. Regarding this *homogeneous preferences* criterion the score for the euro area is mixed. On the one hand, policies regarding inflation and unemployment have diverged strongly in the past (see Chapter 27). On the other hand, the participating countries have willingly agreed to give up their own currency and consult each other on optimal policies. Moreover, policy makers respond to the institutional environment in which they operate, and the process of monetary integration has resulted in a common institutional framework for the participating countries.

As pointed out by Baldwin and Wyplosz (2004), the final criterion is political, rather than economic. Inevitably, if some nations form a currency area there will be disagreement in the future on how to respond to symmetric or asymmetric shocks. The participating nations must then acknowledge that there may be times when the currency union transcends the national boundaries in search for a common future for the area as a whole. It is probably too early to determine if this *solidarity* criterion holds for the euro area until the euro itself has weathered some more financial storms.

Table 30.1 summarizes the extent to which the euro area can be classified as an optimal currency area according to the various criteria discussed above in the year 2006. As was to be expected, perhaps, the evidence is mixed. Labour is not very mobile within the euro area and

Table 30.1 EMU optimal currency area criteria scorecard (2006)

Optimal currency area criterion	EMU score on criterion
Wage flexibility	Low
Labour mobility	Low
Product diversification	High
Openness	High
Fiscal transfers	Low
Homogeneous preferences	Medium
Solidarity	Unclear

Source: Based on Baldwin and Wyplosz (2004, Table 13.2).

Box 30.1   The effect of a currency union on trade

The formation of a currency union affects the costs and risks associated with international transactions within the union. This raises the question to what extent the formation of a currency union affects the international trade flows of the participating countries. Glick and Rose (2002) analyse this question using a large data set involving 217 countries from 1948 to 1997. In this period there were sixteen switches into and 130 switches out of currency unions, for example in the Caribbean (related to the British pound) and in Africa (the CFA-franc zone). Since there are more exits than entries, Glick and Rose are forced to treat these switches symmetrically. They estimate a basic gravity equation (see Chapter 14) and, after controlling for many other influences affecting international trade flows (distance, GDP, language, border, regional trade agreements, colonies, etc.), come to the remarkably strong conclusion that two countries that start to use a common currency will experience almost a *doubling* of their trade flows. Similarly, two countries exiting such a currency union will experience a *halving* of their trade flows. This estimated impact is very large indeed. Others are more doubtful regarding the size and reliability of the estimates, see for example *The Economist* (2003). Indeed, early studies on the effect of the euro on the bilateral trade flows of the participating countries seem to confirm that there is a sizeable impact, although not as high as the Glick and Rose study seems to suggest, see Micco, Stein, and Ordoñez (2003).

fiscal transfers are small. International solidarity among the participating countries remains to be tested, depending on the extent to which preferences are homogeneous. Trade openness and product diversification in the euro area are, however, very high, which might make the other criteria less relevant. It is also important to realize, as indicated in the title of the table, that this 'scorecard' is a snapshot at a particular point in time. As time progresses and the euro area continues to function as a currency area, it will affect the international trade flows (see Box 30.1), the institutions, preferences, and solidarity. As such there is an 'endogeneity' issue: the currency union itself affects the criteria determining optimality of the currency union, most likely towards fulfilling the criteria. In this sense, history has ensured that the states of the USA have evolved over time toward an optimal currency area. The same might happen in Europe.

30.3 Benefits of a common currency

Whereas the main costs of a common currency are at the macroeconomic level, the main benefits are at the microeoconomic level, relating to lower costs, more transparency, and the elimination of risk. This section briefly reviews the main components.

Elimination of transaction costs

The costs associated with exchanging one currency for another disappear if the countries involved use a single currency. Since these costs are avoidable in principle, they represent a deadweight loss to society. The bank employees initially involved in these types of transactions can now produce goods and services instead, leading to a gain for society as a whole. These gains are estimated by the EC Commission (1990) to be about 0.25–0.50 per cent of GDP.

Price transparency

There is also an indirect gain of the elimination of transaction costs in terms of more price transparency. Using only one currency, consumers not only can more easily compare prices for the same goods in different countries, they can also act more easily upon this information as they do not have to incur extra costs of exchanging one currency for another to benefit from arbitrage opportunities. This increased transparency should foster competition among the providers and reduce price differences. Figure 30.3 illustrates that price dispersion for the same product does tend to be much smaller within countries than between countries. Engel and Rogers (2004) study price dispersion in the EU since 1990 and indeed conclude that there has been some reduction in price dispersion. This took place, however, in the period before the introduction of the euro, probably in response to policy pressure as a precondition of participation.

Uncertainty and welfare

The move to one currency eliminates a cause of uncertainty, namely the fluctuation in the exchange rate. We have seen on many occasions that these fluctuations can be large, persistent, and hard to predict. Eliminating this uncertainty therefore leads to a welfare gain for risk-averse individuals. There is, however, a catch in this argument, as illustrated using the standard consumer surplus concept in Figure 30.4. Suppose that the move to one currency ensures that the price for a good stabilizes at p_1, the average of the prices p_0 and p_2. Moreover, suppose that without a common currency the price is equal to p_0 with probability 1/2 and equal to p_2 the rest of the time. Evidently, with a common currency and a stable price of p_1, the consumer surplus is equal to the area A+B in Figure 30.4. In the absence of a common currency, the consumer surplus is equal to the area A if the price is p_0 and equal to the area

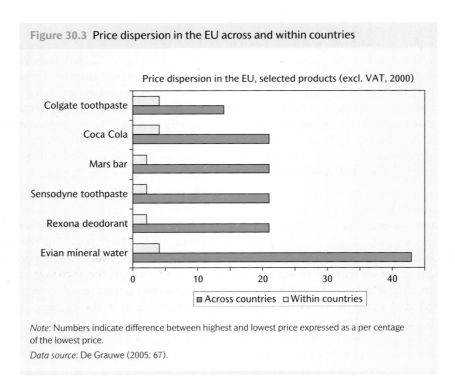

Figure 30.3 Price dispersion in the EU across and within countries

Price dispersion in the EU, selected products (excl. VAT, 2000)

Note: Numbers indicate difference between highest and lowest price expressed as a per centage of the lowest price.

Data source: De Grauwe (2005: 67).

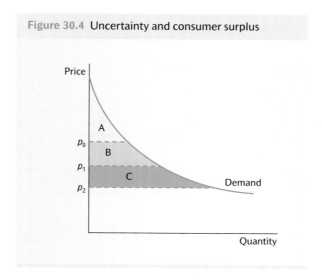

Figure 30.4 Uncertainty and consumer surplus

A+B+C if the price is p_2. Since the area C is clearly bigger than the area B, the average consumer surplus is larger if prices fluctuate than when they do not. This is caused by the fact that consumption increases to benefit from the low price and decreases to avoid the high price. In short, price fluctuations also create opportunities that may increase welfare. The net welfare effect is unclear since risk-averse consumers will compare the higher, but, risky surplus under uncertainty with the lower, but risk-free, surplus under certainty. Similar trade-off observations between opportunities and riskiness hold for firms.

Uncertainty and prices

Individuals respond to (real) price signals. We have seen in Chapter 20 that changes in the exchange rate can be persistent, leading to persistent deviations from purchasing power parity. Movements in the exchange rate and the uncertainty it creates can therefore lead to uncertainty about the correct price signals. Using the empirically observed changes in exchange rates, van Marrewijk and de Vries (1990) show that these changes have similar welfare effects as imposing tariffs and thus lead to large and persistent implicit price distortions. The movement to a common currency eliminates these distortions and leads to similar welfare gains as discussed in the theory of economic integration; see Chapter 13.

Uncertainty and growth

Individuals and firms making savings and investment decisions are particularly worried about uncertainty. Suppose the decision to export to another country involves a large sunk cost investment, for example to set up a distribution and parts supply network. Even if this is a profitable investment under the current economic conditions, fluctuations in the exchange rate may make it an unprofitable investment in the future. Since the firm is then unable to recover the large fixed, sunk costs, the uncertainty created by the movements in the exchange rate will make it think twice before committing itself to this investment. The movement to a common currency eliminates this uncertainty and allows the firm to more easily commit to the large investment. Similarly, when making savings decisions individuals are interested in their real returns, not their nominal returns. Uncertainty about the exchange rate movements creates

Box 30.2   *Monetary union and Italian interest rates*

Figure 30.5 illustrates an extreme example of the potential benefits for a country of maintaining a fixed exchange rate. Traditionally, Italy has had higher inflation rates in the second half of the twentieth century than Germany, which was keen on fighting even the threat of rapid inflation after the devastating German experience in this respect in the 1920s. Despite the fact that both countries participated in the European Monetary System (EMS) since 1979, a system of fixed, but adjustable, exchange rates, the Italians had to pay higher interest rates to investors to compensate them for the potential risk of an Italian lire devaluation (as occured, in fact, on several occasions). Only with the formation of the Economic and Monetary Union, which formally introduced one European currency on 1 January 1999, did the commitment to a fixed exchange rate become fully credible. In the period leading up to the 1 January 1999 deadline, investors became increasingly convinced of Italy's commitment, leading to a rapid reduction of the interest rate differential between Italy and Germany, as illustrated in Figure 30.5. Clearly, this saved the Italians billions of dollars (or euros) on their interest payments.

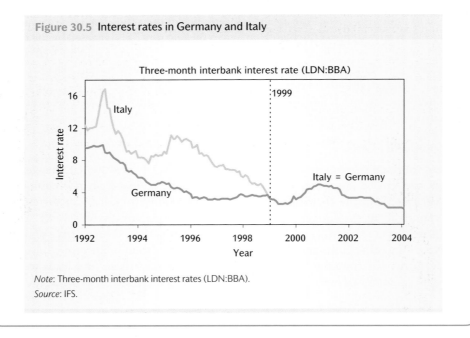

Figure 30.5 **Interest rates in Germany and Italy**

Note: Three-month interbank interest rates (LDN:BBA).
Source: IFS.

uncertainty about these real returns for which the individuals want to be compensated (risk premium). The movement to a common currency eliminates this uncertainty and reduces the risk premium, making more funds available for investment and economic growth; see Box 30.2.

International currency

A final benefit of the formation of a currency union we mention is the possibility that it may play a more prominent role as an international currency. In essence, it is based on the argument that the whole is more than the sum of the parts. Before the union, the currencies of the individual members played a role as a reserve currency in other countries. After the union, the role of the new currency is based on the combined economic clout of the member countries, making it more attractive to use as an international reserve currency worldwide. The US dollar is still the world's dominant international currency, creating seigniorage benefits for American citizens, larger profits for the central bank, and increasing the attractiveness of the USA as a location of financial activity. Since the economic power of the euro area is about 74 per cent that of the USA, its participants hope that the euro may eventually play a similar role in the international arena. As the information given in Chapter 19 on the use of international currencies in financial transactions shows, however, the role of the euro is currently still much smaller than that of the US dollar and it will certainly take a long time to substantially change this position.

30.4 The Maastricht Treaty

As outlined above, there are both advantages and disadvantages of using a common currency. The balance of the net benefits or costs may change over time, partly as a consequence of policy decisions taken along the way. Apparently, many countries in Europe eventually concluded that the benefits of a common currency are higher than the costs. Starting with the Werner Plan, a report published in 1970 by a group of experts chaired by Pierre Werner, the prime minister of Luxembourg, that proposed a monetary union, the process of monetary unification took several decades; see Figure 30.6. The movement to the EMS in 1979, a fixed exchange rate regime discussed in Chapter 28, was an important step along the way, as was the concrete time path proposed by the Delors Committee in 1989, chaired by the president of the European Commission, Jacques Delors. The most important formal steps were taken, however, in 1991 in Maastricht, a small town in the south of the Netherlands. This Maastricht Treaty created a political union, called the European Union (EU), and a series of amendments to the EEC treaty (see Chapter 13), leading to the Economic and Monetary Union. The treaty was ratified by all member states in 1993 (after a second referendum in Denmark).

Figure 30.6 The process of European monetary integration

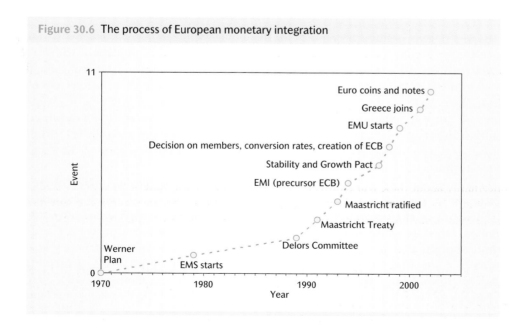

Table 30.2 **The euro conversion rates**

Currency	Value of €1 =	Currency	Value of €1 =
Belgian francs	BEF 40.3399	Italian lire	ITL 1936.27
Deutsche Mark	DEM 1.95583	Luxembourg francs	LUF 40.3399
Spanish pesetas	ESP 166.386	Dutch guilders	NLG 2.20371
French francs	FRF 6.55957	Austrian schillings	ATS 13.7603
Greek drachmas	GRD 340.750	Portuguese escudos	PTE 200.482
Irish pounds	IEP 0.787564	Finnish markkas	FIM 5.94573

Source: www.ecb.int

Table 30.3 **Convergence criteria for joining EMU**

Criterion	Details
Inflation	Not more than 1.5 per cent higher than the average of the three lowest inflation rates among EU member states
Interest rate	Not more than 2 per cent higher long-term interest rate than the average of the three low-inflation countries
EMS membership	Joined the Exchange Rate Mechanism of the EMS; no devaluation in the two years before entry into EMU
Budget deficit	Not higher than 3 per cent of GDP (government deficit)*
Public debt	Not higher than 60 per cent of GDP (government debt)*

* Some qualifications apply.

The first stage of preliminary reforms for the monetary integration process involved free movement of capital and convergence of economic policies and coordination. The second stage started with the establishment of the European Monetary Institute (EMI) in 1994, followed by the *Stability and Growth Pact* in 1997 containing the convergence criteria for being allowed to move to the third stage of the monetary union (see below). Decisions on membership and conversion rates (see Table 30.2) were made in 1998, allowing eleven countries to join the third stage: the start of EMU in 1999. Greece, which did not meet the convergence criteria initially, joined in 2001. The physical introduction of the new currency in terms of euro bank notes and euro coins was in 2002.

The convergence criteria for determining which countries were allowed to join the monetary union are summarized in Table 30.3. They stress macroeconomic conditions and are largely based on the German fear of an inflation bias. The deeply rooted German adversity to inflation, based on its devastating experience in the interbellum (see Chapter 12), and its dominant position as an international currency within Europe before the monetary union, ensured that the other countries had to prove that they adopted a sustainable German-style policy of low-inflation before they were allowed to join the monetary union. More specifically, the inflation rate and long-term interest rate should be low enough, the country should be a stable member of the Exchange Rate Mechanism of the EMS, and the government budget deficit and public debt should not be too high; see Box 30.3. The convergence criteria also apply to future candidate countries. It should be noted that many euro members (including Germany, its main initial advocate) repeatedly violate the rules of the Stability and Growth Pact, particularly regarding the maximum government budget deficit criterion (3 per cent of GDP). Reluctant to issue formal warnings and punishment for these violations, the European Council decided in March 2005 on the one hand that the Pact was still intact, but on the other hand provided exceptions that made the Pact essentially useless. Countries were given, for example, a five-year, rather than a one-year, time limit to get back under the deficit ceiling, whereas the ceiling is allowed to be breached if the government spending is supposed to 'achieve European policy goals' or 'foster international solidarity', see Feldstein (2005).

Box 30.3   Deficits and debts

It is always tempting to finance large government deficits by printing money. For that reason, one of the convergence criteria limits the size of the allowed government deficit to a maximum of 3 per cent (with some qualifications). This was based on the German golden rule that budget deficits are only acceptable if they relate to public investment (roads and other infrastructure) as these are a source of future growth, which will make it possible to pay for the investment. The idea is that such public investment amounts to about 3 per cent of GDP. So how did the convergence criteria determine that the maximum allowable government debt is 60 per cent of GDP? This number is based on some simple deficit and debt growth arithmetic.

Figure 30.7 Deficit, debt, and growth arithmetic

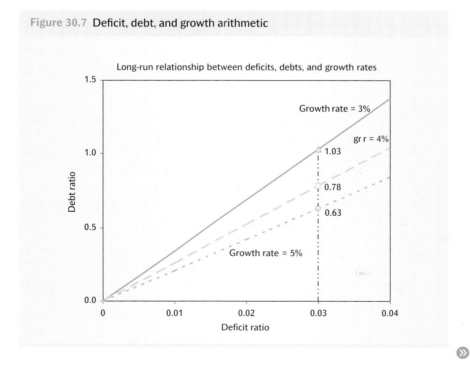

>> Let D be the government budget deficit, B the total government debt, and Y the nominal national income level. We let lower-case letters d_t and b_t denote the deficit and the debt relative to the income level. Finally, we let g_t denote the growth rate of nominal income. Since the change in this year's total debt $B_t - B_{t-1}$ is equal to this year's budget deficit D_t, dividing this equality by the nominal income level Y_t gives

(30.1) $$d_t \equiv \frac{D_t}{Y_t} = \frac{B_t - B_{t-1}}{Y_t} = \frac{B_t}{Y_t} - \frac{B_{t-1}}{Y_t} = b_t - \frac{B_{t-1}Y_{t-1}}{Y_{t-1} \ Y_t} = b_t - b_{t-1}\frac{1}{(1 + g_t)}$$

Now suppose that all the terms relative to income are constant for a long time, say d, b, and g. Equation (30.1) then shows that we must have the following relationship:

(30.2) $$d = b - b\frac{1}{(1 + g)} = \frac{bg}{1 + g}$$

This consistency requirement for the long-run convergence criteria is illustrated in Figure 30.7 for some different nominal growth rates. Basically, the larger the nominal growth rate, the lower the total government debt ratio can be. The figure also shows that a deficit of 3 per cent is about consistent with a maximum debt of 60 per cent if the nominal growth rate is about 5 per cent (= 2 per cent inflation + 3 per cent real growth?).

30.5 The Eurosystem

Usually, a single currency implies a single interest rate and a single exchange rate relative to other currencies managed by one monetary policy and a single central bank. The EMU countries are sovereign states, however, and it was not politically feasible to merge the former national central banks (NCBs) into one central bank for the euro area. The central banking system created for the euro area is therefore a bit more complicated, as illustrated in Figure 30.8. The new European Central Bank (ECB), which is located in Frankfurt, coexists with all the NCBs of the member states (Luxembourg actually had to create its NCB as it was long part of a monetary union with Belgium). The European System of Central Banks (ESCB) consists of the ECB and all the NCBs of the EU member states. Since not all EU members participate in the monetary union, the term Eurosystem refers to the ECB and the NCBs of the monetary union members.

The Eurosystem is governed by the *Executive Board*, consisting of the president, the vice president, and the four directors of the ECB, and the *Governing Council*, consisting of the executive board and the governors of the twelve NCBs. All the main decisions regarding monetary policy concerning interest rates, reserve requirements, and the like are made by the Governing Council, which meets every two weeks. Decisions in the Governing Council are taken by majority voting, with each of the members holding one vote. The Executive Board implements the decisions taken by the Governing Council through the ECB, which gives instructions to the NCBs to carry out the common monetary policy. The role of the ECB is therefore important, not only through the participation of the Executive Board in the Governing Council, but also because it sets and prepares the agenda of the meetings, which are chaired by the president of the ECB.

Up to this point (2006), the strategic role of the ECB in the Governing Council, where it holds six out of the eighteen votes, has ensured that the interests of the euro area as a whole

Figure 30.8 The European System of Central Banks in 2006

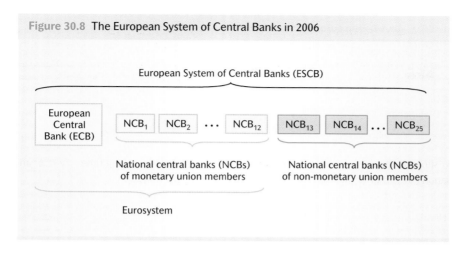

have dominated in the monetary policy deliberations and explicit voting has apparently been rare (decisions are taken implicitly unanimously). The extension of the EU in May of 2004 implies that ten more (mostly small) countries may take part in the euro area. With unchanged formal voting rules this would mean that the ECB holds only six out of a total of 28 votes. It is not hard to imagine that a coalition representing the interests of relatively small countries might then lead to monetary policy decisions not in line with the broader economic interests of the euro area. For that reason it was decided in March 2003 (still to be ratified) that the number of governors with voting rights will be limited to fifteen. The participating governors can exercise their voting right on a rotating basis (with a frequency depending on the relative size of the country).

Figure 30.9 illustrates the value of the euro since its introduction relative to the US dollar and the Japanese yen. After an initial phase in which the value of the euro declined (which led to criticism of the ECB for providing too weak a currency), the value of the euro moved back to hover around a level slightly above its introduction value (which led to criticism of the ECB for providing too strong a currency). Although the recovery can perhaps be attributed to the ECB's strong policy stance on fighting inflation (see below), it is probably wiser to acknowledge that large and persistent swings in the value of freely floating currencies is quite standard, see Chapters 19 and 20.

The objective of the Eurosystem is to deliver price stability, while taking the broader economic interests of the euro area into consideration (Article 105):

> 'The primary objective of the ESCB shall be to maintain price stability. Without prejudice to the objective of price stability, the ESCB shall support the general economic policies in the Community with a view to contributing to the objectives of the Community as laid down in Article 2. The ESCB shall act in accordance with the principle of an open market economy with free competition, favouring an efficient allocation of resources, and in compliance with the principles set out in Article 3a.'

The Eurosystem has later translated the objective of price stability to an inflation rate below 2 per cent. To ensure that the Eurosystem is not under undue political pressure, it is formally probably the most independent central bank (Article 107):

> 'When exercising the powers and carrying out the tasks and duties conferred upon them by this Treaty and the Statute of the ESCB, neither the ECB, nor a national central bank, nor any member

Figure 30.9 Value of one euro since its introduction

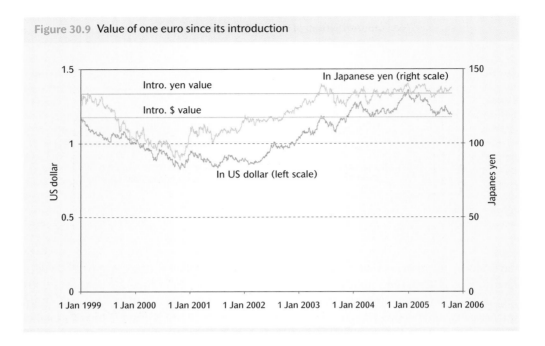

of their decision making bodies shall seek or take instructions from Community institutions or bodies, from any government of a Member State or from any other body. The Community institutions and bodies and the governments of the Member States undertake to respect this principle and not to seek to influence the members of the decision-making bodies of the ECB or of the national central banks in the performance of their tasks.'

In light of its independent status and to establish a reputation for fighting inflation early on in its existence, the ECB has become a 'hard-nosed' central bank (see Chapters 27 and 28) under the guidance of the first president (Dutchman Wim Duisenberg) and his successor (Frenchman Jean-Claude Trichet). Despite the above, the Eurosystem is, of course, held accountable for its actions as it formally operates under the control of the European Parliament. It must send an annual report to the Parliament, the Council, and the Commission. The Parliament may further request the members of the Executive Board to testify to the Economic and Monetary Affairs Committee, which the president of the ECB in practice does every quarter.

30.6 Monetary policy

The instruments of monetary policy available to the Eurosystem do not differ fundamentally from those available to other monetary authorities, as discussed in Chapter 27. The Eurosystem focuses on the European Overnight Index Average (EONIA), which is a weighted average of overnight lending transactions on the interbank market in the euro area. As illustrated in Figure 30.10, since 1 January 1999, the day the euro was introduced, the ECB has been using three key short-term interest rates to achieve its objectives.

• The interest rate on the *main refinancing operations* (MRO), which provide the bulk of liquidity to the banking system.

Figure 30.10 European Central Bank key interest rates

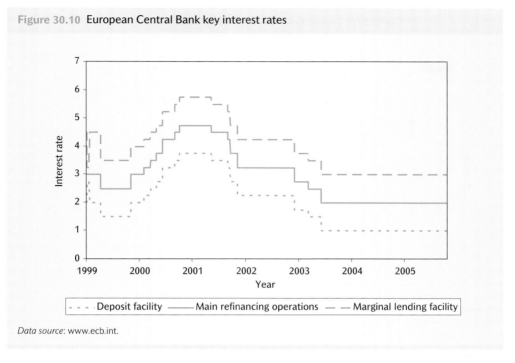

Data source: www.ecb.int.

- The rate on the *deposit facility*, which banks may use to make overnight deposits with the Eurosystem.
- The rate on the *marginal lending facility*, which offers overnight credit to banks from the Eurosystem.

We have already discussed the Taylor rule, a practical monetary policy tool used implicitly by central banks, in Chapter 27. It argues that the short-term interest rate is increased if the output gap is positive or the inflation rate above target, and vice versa:

$$(30.3) \qquad i_t - \pi_t = r + \alpha(\pi_t - \pi^*) + \beta x_t$$

Where $x = (Y - Y^*)/Y^*$ is the output gap, $i - \pi$ is the short-term real interest rate, and $\pi - \pi^*$ is the deviation from the target inflation rate. Figure 30.11 illustrates a problem for implementing this policy tool in the euro area with which monetary authorities in other countries are not or only to a lesser extent confronted. Even if we assume that the preferences of the NCBs are the same, that is they have the same values for the parameters α and β, the economic conditions with which they are confronted can be drastically different. At this stage of the business cycle, the economic interests of the Netherlands (with low inflation and low unemployment) are different from those of Spain (with high inflation and high unemployment). Similarly, Luxembourg (with high inflation and low unemployment) wants to cool down the economy, which is not in the interest of Finland (with high unemployment and low inflation).

Assuming the same preferences for the NCBs ($\alpha = 1.5$ and $\beta = 0.5$), using a long-run real interest rate r of 2 per cent, and calculating the output gap, de Grauwe (2005) constructs estimated desired interest rates for the various countries based on the Taylor rule.[1] The implied 'desired' interest rates are indeed drastically different for the various countries. As there is only one euro

Figure 30.11 Unemployment and inflation in the euro area, 2004

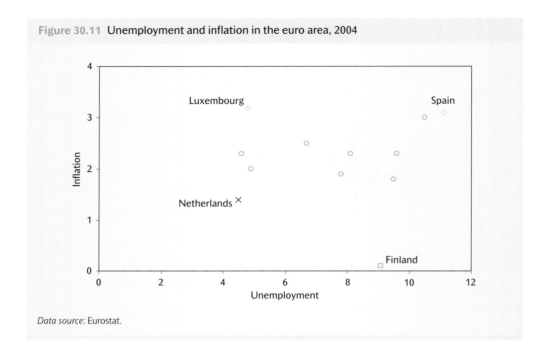

Data source: Eurostat.

interest rate, the ECB cannot possibly fulfil the wishes of all of the NCBs. Instead, the ECB must take into consideration the general interests for the euro area as a whole (its rate in Figure 30.12 is based on a weighted average), and act accordingly. The problem arises because of the sheer economic size of the euro area. In that sense, other monetary authorities of large economic entitities, such as the USA or China, are confronted with similar problems. However, the euro area difficulties are unique in the sense that it must decide on optimal policy for a collection of independent sovereign states. It is therefore crucial that its decision making process for the Governing Council (which seems to work well now as described in the previous section), is indeed properly adjusted as proposed in 2003 before new members can enter the euro area.

30.7 Extending the euro area

In 2004 no less than ten new countries entered the European Union. It is expected that at least some of them will join the euro area in the future. As already mentioned above, these coun-tries have to fulfil the same convergence criteria as the other euro area countries before they can enter the monetary union. This means, for example, that it takes at least two years after they join the Exchange Rate Mechanism of the EMS before they are allowed to join (second half of 2006 at the earliest). If all of them join the euro area, its population will increase to 381 million (plus 24 per cent) and its GDP to $9,138 billion (PPP, current $; plus 12 per cent); see Table 30.4. Further future enlargement is possible if the UK or some other countries, such as Bulgaria, Romania, and Turkey (which might join the EU and potentially the euro area) decide to participate and fulfil the criteria.

Figure 30.13 depicts the public balance and public debt criteria for some of the potential new euro area entrants. A number of countries, such as Malta, Cyprus, and Hungary, are clearly struggling to meet the entry requirements (a maximum of 60 per cent and 3 per cent

Figure 30.12 Estimated differences in desired interest rates using the Taylor rule (2003)

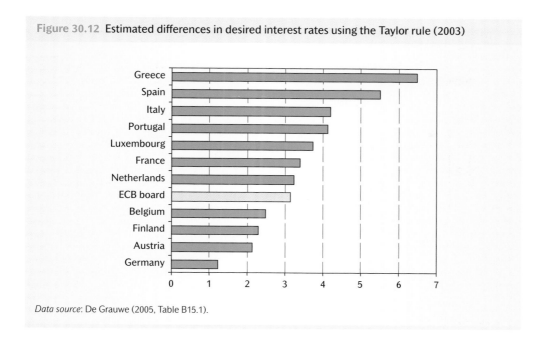

Data source: De Grauwe (2005, Table B15.1).

Table 30.4 Euro area and potential new entrant statistics, 2003

Country	Population (million)	GDP, PPP (billion, current US$)
Cyprus*	0.8	13.8
Czech Republic	10.2	166.9
Estonia	1.4	18.3
Hungary	10.1	147.7
Latvia	2.3	23.8
Lithuania	3.5	40.4
Malta	0.4	7.0
Poland	38.2	434.6
Slovak Republic	5.4	72.7
Slovenia	2.0	38.2
EMU	306.9	8,174.6
Sum	381.1	9,138.2
Bulgaria	7.8	60.5
Romania	21.7	158.2
Turkey	70.7	478.9

* GDP, PPP in 2001.
Data source: Eurostat.

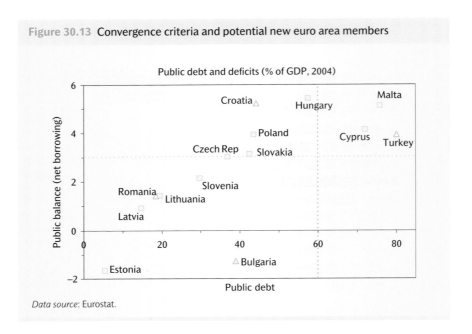

Figure 30.13 Convergence criteria and potential new euro area members

Data source: Eurostat.

of GDP). The Baltic States and Slovenia are in a better position in this respect. The inflation criterion also poses a problem for some countries, particularly for Slovakia, Hungary, and Latvia (see Figure 30.14). This may, in fact, be partially explained by the catching-up process initiated when the new entrants joined the EU, presumably resulting in more rapid productivity growth for the new entrants. Using the Harrod–Balassa–Samuelson effect discussed in Chapter 20 (see also Technical Note 30.1), the following relationship holds:

$$(30.4) \qquad \underbrace{\left(\dot{p}_{euro} - \dot{p}_{new} \right)}_{\text{inflation difference}} - \alpha \dot{s} = (1 - \alpha) \underbrace{\left(\dot{w}_{euro} - \dot{w}_{new} \right)}_{\text{productivity difference}},$$

where $\dot{s}$ is the rate of depreciation of the euro. Since a stable exchange rate is one of the convergence criteria, we can set it equal to zero for simplicity. It then follows that higher productivity growth for the new entrants, which translates into higher wage increases, also results in higher inflation rates. A succesful catching-up process thus makes it harder to fulfil the inflation criterion for joining the euro area.

30.8 Conclusions

Twelve European countries have embarked on a unique process of monetary integration by creating a new currency: the euro. Together they form a powerful economic force. We reviewed the theory of optimal currency areas, which focuses on the ability to accommodate differences between countries through wage flexibility, labour mobility, and fiscal transfers, or avoid this need through trade openness, product diversification, homogeneous preferences, and solidarity. We also reviewed the main benefits of a common currency, such as avoiding transaction costs, price transparency, reducing uncertainty, eliminating distortions, promoting growth, and the potential to become an international currency. Although

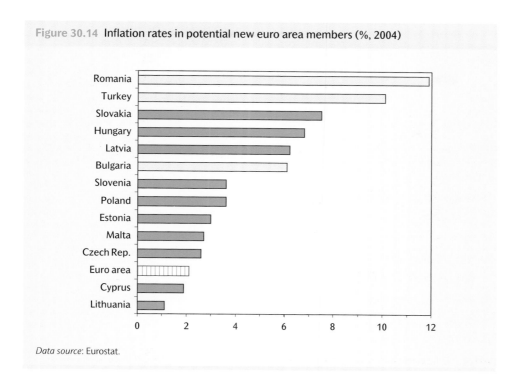

Figure 30.14 Inflation rates in potential new euro area members (%, 2004)

Data source: Eurostat.

the euro is likely to play a more prominent role in the international arena in the future, it is currently no match for the US dollar. We reviewed the history of the European integration process and discussed the institutional framework of the Eurosystem, which consists of the ECB and the twelve participating NCBs. At least ten countries may decide to join the euro area in the future, which requires a reorganization of the decision-making process to ensure that the Eurosystem protects the interests of the euro area as a whole. This is probably the most important challenge facing the euro area.

TECHNICAL NOTE

Technical Note 30.1 Harrod–Balassa–Samuelson effect

Inflation in the euro area $\dot{p}_{euro}$ is the weighted average of the price change of traded goods $\dot{p}_{euro,\,tr}$ and the price change of non-traded goods $\dot{w}_{euro}$ (which uses only Labour in a Ricardian model and is proportional to changes in the wage rate), see (30.A1). The same holds for the potential new entrants, see (30.A2).

(30.A1)
$$\dot{p}_{euro} = \alpha \dot{p}_{euro,tr} + (1 - \alpha)\dot{w}_{euro}$$

(30.A2)
$$\dot{p}_{new} = \alpha \dot{p}_{new,tr} + (1 - \alpha)\dot{w}_{new}$$

Arbitrage ensures that the price of traded goods is the same in the two countries, i.e.:

(30.A3)
$$\dot{s} = \dot{p}_{euro,\,tr} - \dot{p}_{new,\,tr}$$

where $\dot{s}$ is the rate of depreciation of the euro. There is, of course, no arbitrage possible in the non-traded-goods model. Moreover, changes in the wage rate are based on productivity improvements, as discussed in the text. Subtracting (30.A2) from (30.A1), substituting (30.A3), and rearranging gives (see the main text):

(30.A4)
$$\underbrace{\left(\dot{p}_{euro} - \dot{p}_{new}\right)}_{\text{inflation difference}} - \alpha\dot{s} = (1 - \alpha)\underbrace{\left(\dot{w}_{euro} - \dot{w}_{new}\right)}_{\text{productivity difference}}$$

QUESTIONS

Question 30.1

30.1A What are the main costs of a currency union?

30.1B Which factors can mitigate these costs?

30.1C Which two figures in Chapter 30 can tell us something about asymmetric shocks within EMU?

30.1D What is the endogeneity issue with respect to currency unions?

30.1E What are the main benefits from a currency union?

30.1F Are exchange-rate-induced price changes inherently detrimental to welfare? Explain.

Question 30.2

30.2A Why doesn't the Governing Council of the ECB adhere to the rule: one country one vote?

30.2B Why would independence be a particularly important and thorny issue for the European Central Bank?

30.2C How is the ECB kept accountable to the citizens of the EMU?

Question 30.3

30.3A What is the impact of the Balassa–Samuelson effect on the new EU member states?

30.3B What does this effect imply for the new EU member states that want to introduce the euro? How will this affect the ECB when the new EU member states are admitted today?

30.3C Can you explain the merit of each of the convergence criteria taken up in the Maastricht Treaty?

30.3D Are the convergence criteria related to the theory of optimal currency areas? Why (not)?

You are an economist at the Polish Ministry of Economic Affairs. After Poland's EU entry, the government also wants to introduce the euro. You are asked to write a report on the policy consequences of this decision.

30.3E What economic benefits would you put in your report?

30.3F Why would you stress that flexibility is important for the Polish economy?

 See the Online Resource Centre for a Study Guide containing more questions
www.oxfordtextbooks.co.uk/orc/vanmarrewijk/

NOTE

1 The main differences between conclusions based on simple unemployment rates as illustrated in Figure 30.10 and conclusions illustrated for the Taylor rule in Figure 30.11 are based on the procedure for calculating the output gap. Note also that the figures pertain to 2004 and 2003, respectively.

NEW OPEN ECONOMY MACROECONOMICS

31

We review and discuss an example of the new open economy macroeconomics literature. As this approach is based on explicit microfoundations in a general equilibrium setting with sticky prices and imperfect information, it allows welfare-based policy evaluation.

31.1 Introduction

The term *new open economy macroeconomics* refers to fairly recent developments in the international monetary literature.[1] The primary objective of this new approach is quite ambitious, as it analyses exchange rate determination and the impact of different economic policies in a dynamic general equilibrium framework. The analysis is also based on explicit microfoundations with (dynamic) optimization problems for all the economic agents involved and allows for nominal rigidities and imperfect competition. As suggested by this very brief description, incorporating all these aspects in one coherent framework is not an easy task. Not surprisingly, therefore, the analytics of the approach can be quite daunting. For that reason, we will not provide the full technical details of the model discussed below, although the most important aspects will be derived in Technical Note 31.1. Instead, we first review the core building blocks and basic structure of this type of new open economy macroeconomics models and then discuss how this approach can be used for welfare-based economic policy analysis.

Although the seminal contributions starting off the new open economy macroeconomics approach were the 'redux' article and a book written by Obstfeld and Rogoff (1995, 1996), a precursor incorporating similar aspects was provided by Svensson and van Wijnbergen (1989); see Lane (2001) for an overview of the literature. As this field is rapidly developing and many recent contributions differ regarding the details of the model, such as the specification of the utility function and whether there are nominal rigidities in the goods market or in the labour market, all of which lead to different conclusions and economic policies, Sarno and Taylor (2002: 165) argue:

> While the profession shows some convergence towards a *consensus approach* in macroeconomic modelling (where the need for microfoundations, for example, seems widely accepted), it seems very unlikely that a *consensus model* will emerge in the foreseeable future.

In the absence of such a consensus model, we restrict attention in this chapter to discussing a prominent example of the literature provided by Obstfeld and Rogoff (2000), which has the advantage that it is analytically solvable. Our explanation of the open economy macroeconomic models is based on a Dixit–Stiglitz framework as explained in Chapter 10, which is

Famous economists	Maurice Obstfeld

Fig. 31.1
Maurice Obstfeld
(1952–)

Born in New York and educated at Pennsylvania, Cambridge, and MIT, where he was one of the disciples of Rudiger Dornbusch (see Chapter 26), Maurice Obstfeld worked at Columbia and Pennsylvania before moving to Berkeley in 1989. He has had a profound influence on monetary and fiscal theory and policy in open economy macroeconomics, notably in a very fruitful collaboration with Harvard's Kenneth Rogoff (see Chapter 19). Together, they introduced, refined, and applied the 'redux' model to a range of important monetary and exchange rate problems. Maurice Obstfeld is also co-author of the best-selling textbook with Paul Krugman (see Chapter 29).

used in a nested Cobb–Douglas setting as explained in Chapter 14. Students are therefore recommended to study Chapters 10 and 14 before studying this chapter.

31.2 Exchange rates, terms of trade, and competition

Most of the discussion in this chapter will focus on two countries, the EU and the USA. We let s denote the (log) spot exchange rate of the dollar in euros. In Chapter 23 we discussed the expenditure-switching competition effect of a change in the exchange rate, through its impact on the real exchange rate q, defined as the difference between the nominal exchange rate and the price indices (p_{US} and p_{EU}) of the two countries.

(31.1) $$q \equiv s - (p_{US} - p_{EU})$$

Implicitly, that discussion ignored non-traded goods, such that the price level in a country translates more or less directly to its competitive position.

Incorporating the importance of non-traded goods in the discussion, a better indicator of competitiveness is the *terms of trade*, denoting the price of a country's exports relative to its

Figure 31.2 Correlation between exchange rate and terms of trade

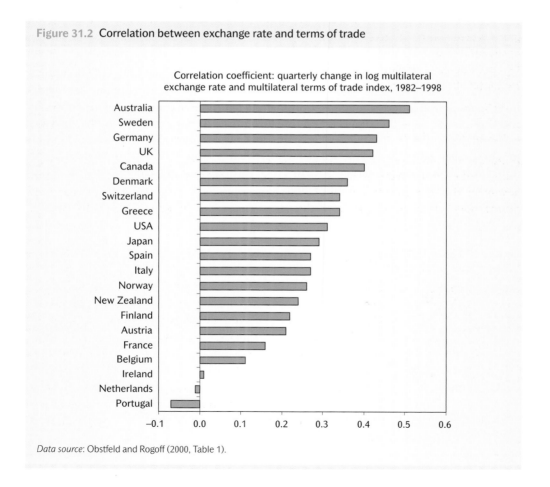

Data source: Obstfeld and Rogoff (2000, Table 1).

imports. Let $p^*_{x,EU}$ be the price of EU export goods in dollars and $p_{m,EU}$ be the price of EU import goods in euros, then the terms of trade is given by

$$(31.2) \qquad\qquad t = s + p^*_{x,EU} - p_{m,EU}$$

If t rises, the EU terms of trade is said to *improve* (although its competitive position is argued to deteriorate), because the rise in the relative price of its export goods ensures that more goods can be imported for the same level of exports, which is a welfare gain. (See Box 12.2.)

From equations (31.1) and (31.2) it is clear that changes in the nominal exchange rate s only translate in to proportional changes in the real exchange rate or the terms of trade if the respective price levels do not adjust. Similarly, changes in the nominal exchange rate s do not affect the real exchange rate or the terms of trade if the respective price levels adjust proportionally in response to these changes. We discussed this exchange rate pass-through analysis and the pricing-to-market problem in Box 24.2. As illustrated in Figure 31.2 and Table 31.1 using correlation coefficients, movements are neither completely passed through in the short run, nor is there complete pricing-to-market (as most correlations are in between zero and one). In light of this evidence, Obstfeld and Rogoff (2000) construct a model with sticky wages where changes in the exchange rate have an expenditure-switching role. We now turn to this model in more detail.

31.3 Model structure and demand

To make the model analytically tractable while at the same time providing microeconomic foundations and optimizing agents in a general equilibrium macroeconomic setting, we make many simplifying assumptions. Consider, therefore, two symmetric countries of equal size, say the EU and the USA. Consumers in both countries maximize utility, given in equation (31.3), subject to a budget constraint, given in equation (31.4). Individual i's utility function depends on three core items, namely (i) consumption (C_i, which is an index of many different varieties), (ii) real money balances (M_i/P, where P is a price index), and (iii) leisure ($-L_i$, where L_i is the individual's labour supply).

Table 31.1 Correlation between exchange rates and competitiveness, 1982–98

	Germany	Italy	Japan	UK	USA
Canada	0.87	0.85	0.74	0.88	0.51
Germany		0.65	0.67	0.74	0.88
Italy			0.73	0.79	0.87
Japan				0.76	0.73
UK					0.9

Note: correlation of monthly log changes in exchange rates and relative export competitiveness, 1982–98.

Source: Obstfeld and Rogoff (2000, Table 2).

(31.3)
$$U_i = \underbrace{\log(C_i)}_{consumption} + \underbrace{\frac{\chi}{1 - \varepsilon_m}\left(\frac{M_i}{P}\right)^{1-\varepsilon_m}}_{real\ money\ balance} - \underbrace{\frac{K}{v}L_i^v}_{leisure}$$

The parameters χ and K can shift the demand for money and leisure, while the parameters ε_m and v are price- and wage-rate-related elasticities. A pure theorist would argue, by the way, that this approach is not really based on first principles. Note that real money balances are put directly into the utility function in equation (31.3). However, money only yields utility *in*directly through the goods and services one can buy (perhaps in the future). Although there are various ways to substantiate this practice, for example in an intertemporal setting, equation (31.3) therefore constitutes a short-cut approach.

The individual has initial money holdings $M_{i,0}$, receives lump-sum transfers Tr from the goverment, earns Π_i in profits, and a wage income W_iL_i. Since total spending $M_i + PC_i$ must be equal to total income, this leads to the budget restriction:

(31.4)
$$M_i + PC_i = M_{i,0} + Tr + W_iL_i + \Pi_i$$

The individual maximizes utility by choosing the optimal level of consumption, money hold-ings, and (simultaneously) wage rate and employment. The wage-setting behaviour will be discussed in the next section. Here we just observe that $\chi(M_i/P)^{-\varepsilon_m} = 1/C_i$; see Technical Note 31.1, which indicates that the marginal utility of holding money is equated to the marginal cost of acquiring money. Moreover, we assume that individuals take the government transfer as given, but they are given in the form of money, such that $Tr = M - M_0$, where money will be a random variable below.

As illustrated in Figure 31.3, consumption goods are provided in three main types, each con-sisting of N different varieties, namely (i) locally produced non-traded goods Y_i, (ii) EU-produced traded goods $X_{EU,i}$, and (iii) US-produced traded goods $X_{US,i}$. The share of income spent on

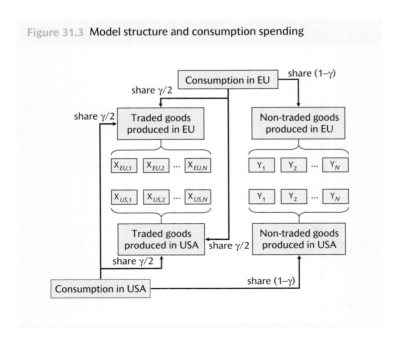

Figure 31.3 Model structure and consumption spending

non-traded goods is $1-\gamma$, while the share of income spent on domestic traded goods is $\gamma/2$, as is the share spent on foreign traded goods. If the composite index of non-traded goods is denoted by Y and of traded goods by X (where $X = X_{EU}^{1/2}\,X_{US}^{1/2}$ for composite indices X_{EU} and X_{US} denoting EU- and US-produced traded goods), the consumption index (dropping the individual index i) is given in equation (31.5). Each main consumption type is composed of a Dixit–Stiglitz-like combination of the N varieties in the group; see Chapters 10 and 14. As explained there, this leads to demand for any particular variety of goods with constant price elasticity ε_g.

$$(31.5) \qquad\qquad C = X^\gamma Y^{1-\gamma}$$

 Box 31.1   American current account imbalances

In the last 25 years the American current account deficit has reached unprecedented levels, both in absolute terms (more than \$600 billion in 2004) and in relative terms (about 5.5 per cent of GDP in 2004); see Figure 31.4. Although other countries have had larger relative current account surpluses or deficits for some time, the sheer size of the American economy implies that its deficit has important repercussions for the world economy. Consequently, this deficit has been the topic of ongoing public attention and academic research. Obstfeld and Rogoff (2005), for example, point to a range of factors underlying the large deficit, such as the low American personal savings rate (which fell to 1 per cent in 2004), the American budget deficit, and the increasing dependence on Asian central banks and oil exporters for financing the current account deficit.

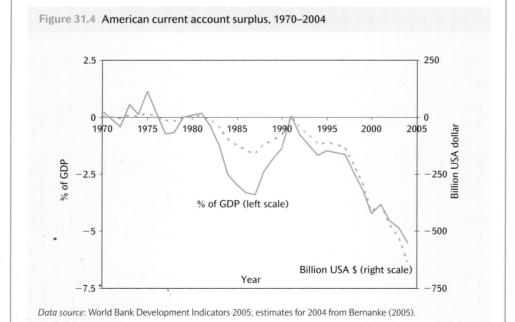

Figure 31.4 American current account surplus, 1970–2004

Data source: World Bank Development Indicators 2005; estimates for 2004 from Bernanke (2005).

>> Using a new open economy macroeconomic model similar to the one explained in this chapter, which distinguishes between three global regions, namely the USA, Europe, and Asia, Obstfeld and Rogoff analyse the consequences of three different scenarios for eliminating the USA current account deficit. The model incorporates tradable and non-traded goods, a preference for the domestically produced traded good, links between the three global regions through international trade flows, and a matrix of international asset and liability positions. The three scenarios investigate conditions under which the USA current account might improve by 5 per cent of GDP in the following settings:

- *Global rebalancing*: all current accounts go to zero; trade balances adjust to service the interest flows on the endogenously determined net stock of foreign assets.

- *Bretton Woods II*: Asia clings to its dollar peg (and raises its current account surplus), the USA current account goes to zero, and Europe's current account absorbs all changes.

- *Europe trades places*: Asia's current account is constant and Europe absorbs the entire USA current account improvement.

Table 31.2 Adjustment scenarios when USA current account goes to balance (% changes)

Log change (x100)	Scenario		
	Global rebalancing	Bretton Woods II	Europe trades places
Real exchange rate			
Europe/USA	28.6	49.5	44.6
Asia/USA	35.2	−0.5	19.4
Asia/Europe	6.7	−50.0	−25.2
Nominal exchange rate			
Europe/USA	30.0	52.0	46.8
Asia/USA	36.9	0.0	20.6
Asia/Europe	6.9	−52.0	−26.3
Terms-of-trade			
Europe/USA	14.0	21.5	22.0
Asia/USA	14.5	3.4	11.1
Asia/Europe	0.5	−18.0	−10.8

Source: Obstfeld and Rogoff (2005, Table 3).

Note: see the text for details on the scenarios.

>>

⊗ Table 31.2 summarizes some of the economic consequences of eliminating the US current account deficit. In the global rebalancing scenario, the European and Asian real exchange rate, nominal exchange rate, and terms of trade rise drastically relative to the USA, with a small appreciation of the Asian currencies relative to the euro. The euro appreciates even more in the two other scenarios, in both nominal and real terms, leading to an improvement in the terms of trade of more than 21 per cent. The changes are higher in the Bretton Woods II scenario because of the inflexibility created by the Asian peg to the dollar. Eliminating this peg in the 'Europe trades places' scenario allows for an appreciation of the Asian currencies relative to the dollar, thus mitigating the appreciation of the euro relative to the other currencies. In all cases, however, the work of Obstfeld and Rogoff suggests that a large depreciation of the dollar is necessary to balance the US current account deficit.

Information source: Obstfeld and Rogoff (2005).

31.4 Wage setting and prices

Following Blanchard and Kiyotaki (1987), firms in a country produce differentiated goods from differentiated labour inputs. The production function is based on Ethier's (1982) intermediate goods approach (see Chapter 10), where each individual supplies this interme-diate good (his or her labour) to the domestic producers of final goods at a price W_i in a Dixit–Stiglitz framework. Consequently, and analogous to the production setting, the market power of a particular type of labour is characterized by a constant price elasticty of labour demand ε_l. As usual, this implies that the wage rate charged by an individual agent is equal to a constant mark-up $\varepsilon_l/(1 - \varepsilon_l)$ over marginal costs (marginal disutility of labour). Since all individuals in the EU are confronted in equilibrium with the same circumstances and opti-mization problem, they all choose the same wage rate, W_{EU} say. Similarly, all individuals in the USA are confronted with the same circumstances and optimization problem, and choose the same wage rate W_{USA}. As shown in Technical Note 31.1, within each country wage setting is therefore determined by equation (31.6). Obstfeld and Rogoff analyse this problem in a stochastic framework with sticky wages. The wage is therefore fixed in the short run and the wage setting equation (31.6) holds in expected value terms. Clearly shocks to the system enter this problem either directly (for example K) or indirectly (through endogenous variables L, P, and C).

$$(31.6) \qquad W = \frac{\varepsilon_l}{\varepsilon_l - 1} \left[\frac{KL^{\nu-1}}{(1/PC)} \right]$$

It is now relatively straightforward to determine the price levels in the two countries. Each producer is facing a constant price elasticity of demand ε_g and therefore optimally charges a mark-up $\varepsilon_g/(1 - \varepsilon_g)$ over marginal cost, which is given by W_{EU} in the EU and by W_{USA} in the USA. Let $P_{Y,EU}$ be the price of non-traded goods in the EU, $P_{X,EU}$ the price in the EU of traded goods sold in the EU, and similarly for the USA, then:

$$(31.7) \qquad P_{X,EU} = P_{Y,EU} = \frac{\varepsilon_g}{(1 - \varepsilon_g)} W_{EU}; \quad P_{X,USA} = P_{Y,USA} = \frac{\varepsilon_g}{(1 - \varepsilon_g)} W_{USA}$$

Finally, we may wonder what the price is of exported traded goods, indicated by an asterisk (so $P^*_{X,EU}$ is the price in dollars of a traded good X produced in the EU). Even if we allow for price discrimination and pricing to market, however, firms will charge the same mark-up over marginal costs since the price elasticity of demand in the USA and the EU is the same, so the exchange rate adjusted price is the same too; see equation (31.8). This implies that the absolute Law of One Price holds. Note that, if price differentiation is possible and the elasticities of demand are different in the EU and the USA, the relative version of the Law of One Price holds; see Chapter 20.

(31.8)
$$P^*_{X,EU} = (1/S)P_{X,EU}; \quad P^*_{X,USA} = SP_{X,USA}$$

As alluded to in Section 31.2, the presence of non-traded goods implies that the real exchange rate is not constant, even though the absolute version of the Law of One Price holds for traded goods. As indicated by equation (31.5), the price index in a country is the geometric mean of the price indices of traded and non-traded goods, with the income share spent on these goods as weights. Deviations are caused by differences in the price of non-traded goods, which are based on the respective wage rates; see equation (31.7). The real exchange rate is therefore given by equation (31.1′). If the wage rates are fixed in the short run, fluctuations in the nominal exchange rate translate into larger fluctuations in the real exchange rate the larger the share of income spent on non-traded goods (the larger $1 - \gamma$). Hau (2002) finds empirical support for a related matter, namely that differences in trade openness explain a large part of the cross-country variation in the volatility of the effective real exchange rate.

(31.1′)
$$q = (1 - \gamma)(s + w_{USA} - w_{EU})$$

 Box 31.2 *Five major puzzles in international macroeconomics*

In an important contribution Obstfeld and Rogoff (2001; yes, again) identify and discuss 'six major puzzles in international macroeconomics', of which we list five, namely:

1 *Home bias in trade puzzle* International goods markets are still more segmented than frequently thought. McCallum (1995) uses a simple gravity equation (see Chapter 14) to control for distance and some other factors to argue that trade between individual Canadian provinces is *twenty* times larger than trade between a Canadian province and an American state. Although subsequent work reduced this estimate substantially, there still appears to be a large home bias effect in trade.

2 *Feldstein–Horioka puzzle* If capital flows freely across borders in search of the highest return, there is no longer a need for national savings to be equal to domestic investment. Feldstein and Horioka (1980) show, in contrast to the supposed high level of capital mobility, that national savings rates are highly correlated with domestic investment; see also Table 31.3.

3 *Home bias in equity portfolios puzzle* Equity investors in large country, such as Japan or the USA, invest more than 90 per cent in home assets. To benefit from international portfolio diversification, they should diversify much more. The problem is less pronounced for smaller countries and the share of foreign portfolios is slowly rising. »

4 *Consumption correlations* puzzle In a complete markets framework, the correlation between consumption in different countries should be high, as consumption should not depend on country-specific shocks. In contrast, these correlations are generally quite low. This observation is, of course, closely related to the Feldstein–Horioka puzzle and the home equity bias puzzle, since the obvious means of consumption smoothing (debt and equity trade) are less operative across borders.

5 *Purchasing power parity* puzzle We discussed the short-run and medium-run persistence of deviations from purchasing power parity extensively in Chapter 20.

Obstfeld and Rogoff argue that it is not the frequently used dichotomy between traded and non-traded goods (as used in this chapter) that is helpful for understanding these puzzles, but rather the more natural assumption that goods can be traded at a cost, including not only transport costs, but also tariffs, non-tariff barriers, cultural differences, and the like. We came to similar conclusions in the geographical economics approach (Chapter 14), which shares many structural details of the new open economy macroeconomics models discussed here.

Table 31.3 **Correlation between national savings and investment, 1960–99**

	1960–69	1970–79	1980–89	1990–99
Australia	0.64	0.52	0.35	0.74
Austria	−0.07	0.64	0.88	0.49
Belgium	0.86	0.59	0.46	−0.49
Canada	0.61	0.34	0.76	0.04
Denmark	−0.25	0.79	0.81	0.82
Finland	0.43	0.53	0.62	0.25
France	0.70	0.73	0.82	0.72
Germany	0.33	0.94	−0.49	0.04
Italy	0.72	−0.15	0.85	−0.38
Japan	0.80	0.92	0.23	0.93
Netherlands	−0.74	−0.95	−0.94	−0.96
Norway	0.44	−0.68	−0.68	0.79
Spain	0.66	0.83	0.64	0.47
Sweden	0.16	0.62	0.19	0.53
Switzerland	−0.70	0.95	0.85	0.84
UK	0.51	−0.67	−0.62	0.32
USA	−0.47	−0.88	0.00	−0.79
Average	0.27	0.30	0.28	0.26

Source: Ostrup (2002) based on OECD National Accounts.
Information source: Obstfeld and Rogoff (2001).

31.5 Equilibrium

Market clearing for a variety of non-traded goods implies that domestic demand equals domestic supply. Market clearing for a variety of traded goods produced in either country implies that supply of this good is equal to world demand (domestic demand plus export demand). Using some additional assumptions, Obstfeld and Rogoff (2000) derive the equilibrium equations for this model in a dynamic setting. Since the technical details of this derivation are beyond the scope of this book, we restrict attention in the sequel to discussing the main results and implications of their analysis. To this end it is useful to let z denote spending in Europe measured in terms of tradable goods. Due to the symmetric nature of the model, it turns out that z also denotes spending in the USA measured in terms of tradable goods, so we can simply refer to it as the spending level. Equations (31.9) and (31.10) give the *ex post* equilibrium conditions for spending and the exchange rate.

$$(31.9) \quad z = (\varepsilon_m/2)(m_{EU} + m_{USA}) - (\varepsilon_m/2)(w_{EU} + w_{USA}) - \log \chi - \varepsilon_m \log[\varepsilon_g/(\varepsilon_g - 1)]$$

$$(31.10) \quad s = \frac{\varepsilon_m(m_{EU} - m_{USA})}{1 - \gamma + \gamma\varepsilon_m} - \frac{(\varepsilon_m - 1)(1 - \gamma)(w_{EU} - w_{USA})}{1 - \gamma + \gamma\varepsilon_m}$$

Since the wage rates are predetermined, based on solving equation (31.6) in expected value terms, equations (31.9) and (31.10) fully describe the effects on spending and the exchange rate of unanticipated shocks. Evidently, the spending level increases if either the money supply at home or abroad increases or if the shift parameter χ decreases. In addition, an increase in the domestic money supply after the wage rates are set causes overshooting of the exchange rate (as in the Dornbusch model of Chapter 26) if $\varepsilon_m > 1$ (as it implies that $\varepsilon_m/(1 - \gamma + \gamma\varepsilon_m)$ in equation (31.10) is also larger than one).[2] A fully anticipated change in the money supply, however, results in an equiproportional increase in the wage rate at the wage-setting stage, and an equal movement in the exchange rate.

Remarkably, perhaps, it follows from equations (31.9) and (31.10) that the *ex post* spending levels and exchange rate do not depend on real shocks to the economy K; see also equation (31.3). As Obstfeld and Rogoff (2000: 141) note this happens because:

> A surprise rise in K, say, raises the attractiveness of leisure for Home residents ex post, but they are bound by their labor contracts and do not have the option of raising wages and reducing labor supply after the fact.

Productivity shocks therefore directly affect only leisure in the sticky-wage equilibrium. Other endogenous variables can still be indirectly affected by these shocks if monetary policy somehow responds to the productivity shocks. We now turn to this issue.

31.6 Monetary policy rules and exchange rate regimes

As noted in Section 31.1, a major advantage of the new open economy macroeconomics models is the ability to conduct welfare analysis of economic policies, since the approach is based on explicit utility and profit maximization problems. We briefly discuss two examples of such policies, namely efficient monetary policy rules and exchange rate regimes, using the model outlined in the previous sections for which explicit analytical solutions can be derived.

There are various 'distortions' present in the model discussed above. There is monopoly power in the goods market (which implies that goods are sold at a mark-up over marginal costs) and there is monopoly power in the labour market (which implies that wages are a mark-up over marginal disutility). Since the market power is the same for all sectors (=firms), the monopoly distortion in the goods market can be eliminated by giving firms a proportional production subsidy of $1/(\varepsilon_g - 1)$. Similarly, since the market power in the labour market is the same for all workers, the monopoly distortion can be eliminated by giving workers a proportional wage subsidy of $1/(\varepsilon_l - 1)$. In addition, there is the sticky-wage distortion (which may be based on perfectly reasonable, but not explicitly modelled, contract or menu-cost based optimization behaviour). As we have seen in Section 31.5, in the absence of an endogenous monetary policy response, the sticky-wage distortion implies that productivity shocks only affect the utility from leisure since labour is demand determined after wages are set.

31.6.1 Efficient monetary policy rules

Now suppose that the monetary authorities can observe the productivity shocks after the wage rates are set. Can they respond by setting money supplies to achieve an efficient monetary policy rule? We will focus on *constrained–efficient* monetary policy rules. They are *constrained* by maximizing an average of domestic and foreign expected utility, given the optimal price-setting behaviour of firms and wage-setting behaviour of workers. They are *efficient* in the sense that the market allocation cannot be altered, given the constraints, to make one country better off without making the other country worse off. If wages were fully flexible, workers could respond to the productivity shocks by adjusting wages and thus the labour–leisure choice. More specifically, they would respond to a positive productivity shock (a *fall* in the variable K) by supplying more labour. The question then arises if an appropriate monetary policy response can replicate the flexible wage equilibrium and if that would be a good policy. The answer is affirmative, as Obstfeld and Rogoff (2000: 146) show that 'A global monetary policy rule that gives the same real allocation as under flexible wages is efficient.' They also show that this policy rule has the form given in equation (31.11) for the EU, where E denotes the expectations operator (so Em_{EU}, for example, is the expected value of EU money supply).

$$(31.11) \qquad m_{EU} = Em_{EU} + \frac{\gamma(\varepsilon_m - 1)}{2v\varepsilon_m} \underbrace{(K_{USA} - EK_{USA})}_{USA \; surprise \; shock} - \frac{2 + \gamma(\varepsilon_m - 1)}{2v\varepsilon_m} \underbrace{(K_{EU} - EK_{EU})}_{EU \; surprise \; shock}$$

Since a similar equation holds for the USA, we can conclude that it is optimal to focus exclusively on domestic productivity shocks and not to respond to foreign productivity shocks *only* if there are either (i) no traded goods ($\gamma = 0$) or (ii) the money demand parameter is unity ($\varepsilon_m = 1$, which implies no overshooting or undershooting). Moreover, it is evident that the optimal monetary policy response is 'procyclical'. When wages are set in advance, a positive productivity shock (a fall in K) results in an expansionary domestic policy. Even though the foreign policy response will be contractionary if overshooting occurs ($\varepsilon_m > 1$), the net global monetary policy response is always positive.

31.6.2 Exchange rate regimes

The analytical structure of the model also allows for explicit welfare analysis on the impact of different exchange rate regimes. The first thing to note from the optimal policy rule in equation (31.11) is that the optimal domestic policy response is *not* the same as the optimal foreign policy response. Since the exchange rate is based on the difference between the two money supplies, see equation (31.10), productivity shocks will affect the exchange rate through the endogenous monetary response. Only if domestic and foreign productivity shocks are perfectly correlated will the exchange rate be unaffected.

The above observation makes it easy to understand the welfare implications of different exchange rate regimes in this setting. Under the *optimal floating* regime the exchange rate is allowed to adjust, such that the welfare achieved is highest. The *optimal fixed* exchange rate regime analyses monetary policy responses that ensure the exchange rate remains fixed, while optimally responding to productivity shocks given this restriction. Its achieved welfare is higher than for the third alternative, dubbed *world monetarism*, in which the exchange rate is fixed, as well as an exchange-rate-weighted average of the two national money supplies. More specifically, letting the sub-indices *opt float*, *opt fix*, and *world mon* denote optimal floating, optimal fixed, and world monetarism, Obstfeld and Rogoff (2000, pp. 147–8) show that (if σ_K^2 is the variance of the productivity shock):

$$(31.12) \qquad EU_{world\,mon} = EU_{opt\,float} - \frac{\sigma_K^2}{2\nu} < EU_{opt\,fix} = EU_{opt\,float} - \frac{\sigma_K^2}{4\nu} < EU_{opt\,float}$$

This analytic result makes it clear that the difference in expected welfare between the three regimes will be small if the variance of the productivity shock is small or if the elasticity of utility with respect to effort is large. Obviously, as repeatedly pointed out by Obstfeld and Rogoff, the ranking of the alternative policy regimes depends on the structure of the underlying analytic model. Since we did not incorporate many relevant empirical aspects into the model and made many simplifying assumptions, we should not put too much emphasis on the particular ranking derived in equation (31.12). The important point is to realize that the new open economy macroeconomic models allow us to explicitly analyse the answers to such questions under different circumstances.

31.7 Conclusions

We have discussed and analysed an example of the rapidly developing class of new open economy macroeconomic models. The main advantage of the particular model we discussed is its analytical tractability. The standard procedure of log-linear approximation around the steady state used in most new open economy models could therefore be avoided. This is an advantage indeed since shocks to the system will affect the steady state, so we are log-linearizing around a moving target. As Sarno and Taylor (2002: 154) note: 'Some researchers have argued . . . that the reliability of the log-linear approximations is low because variables wander away from the initial steady state'. This advantage, however, came at a cost. We did not point this out explicitly before, but as a result of the simplifying assumptions needed to achieve analytical tractability, the current account was shut off as a transmission mechanism for monetary and supply shocks. This makes the particular model discussed in this chapter less plausible from an empirical point of view, in which adjusting current account imbalances play a prominent role, see for example Box 31.1.[3] Apparently, we cannot have our cake and eat it too.[4]

A similar observation can be made regarding the main advantage of the new open economy macroeconomics approach in general, namely that it offers a more rigorous analytical foundation based on fully specified microfoundations. The disadvantage here is the analytical complexity of the approach and the fact that the predictions and policy conclusions are usually quite sensitive to the particular specification of the underlying microfoundations, for which it is hard to reach consensus among economists. This contrasts with the analytical simplicity and clear-cut conclusions of the more traditional approach, such as the Mundell–Fleming model (see Chapter 25). In response, I conclude with an observation already made by Sarno and Taylor (2002: 144):

> The counter-argument would be that the traditional models achieve their analytical simplicity by making a number of implicit assumptions which are simply made more specific in new open-economy models, thereby allowing economists to scrutinize them more carefully.

TECHNICAL NOTE

Technical Note 31.1 Wage setting and demand for goods and money

To maximize (31.3) subject to budget restriction (31.4) we define the Lagrangian Γ in (31.A1), where we dropped the individual index i and use the Lagrange multiplier λ.

(31.A1) $$\Gamma = \log(C) + \frac{\chi}{1 - \varepsilon_m}\left(\frac{M}{P}\right)^{1-\varepsilon_m} - \frac{K}{v}L(W)^v + \lambda[M_0 + Tr + WL(W) + \Pi - (M + PC)]$$

The equation also indicates that the labour supplied by the individual depends on the wage rate charged, that is labour supply is demand determined and $L = L(W)$. Since the elasticity of labour demand is constant (see Section 31.4):

(31.A2) $$(dL/dW)(W/L) = -\varepsilon_l \Rightarrow dL/dW = -\varepsilon_l L/W$$

The individual takes the price level, the initial money stock, the transfer, and the profits as given and chooses the optimal level of consumption, money demand, and wage rate. The first-order conditions with respect to consumption $(\partial\Gamma/\partial C = 0)$, money $(\partial\Gamma/\partial M = 0)$, and the wage rate $(\partial\Gamma/\partial W = 0)$ give rise to the following equations.

(31.A3) $$1/C = \lambda P$$

(31.A4) $$\chi\left(\frac{M}{P}\right)^{-\varepsilon_m} = \lambda P$$

(31.A5) $$K L^{v-1}\frac{dL}{dW} = \lambda\left[L + W\frac{dL}{dW}\right]$$

Combining the first two equations gives $\chi(M/P)^{-\varepsilon_m} = 1/C$, which indicates that the marginal utility of holding money is equated to the marginal cost of acquiring money. Substituting (31.A2) in (31.A5) and using (31.A3) allows us to determine the wage rate.

(31.A5') $$-\varepsilon_l K L^v/W = \lambda[L - \varepsilon_l L] \Rightarrow W = \frac{\varepsilon_l}{\varepsilon_l - 1}\frac{K L^{v-1}}{\lambda} = \frac{\varepsilon_l}{\varepsilon_l - 1}\frac{K L^{v-1}}{(1/PC)}$$

QUESTIONS

Question 31.1

The results of new open economy macroeconomics models are still highly sensitive to the specific assumptions being made. It will therefore take some time before this range of models is more widely used by policy makers than the Mundell–Fleming model. Still, the new open economy macroeconomics models have the potential to do so.

31.1A What are the main differences between new open economy macroeconomics models and the Mundell–Fleming model?

31.1B Why are these features of the new models important in the modern world economy?

Question 31.2

The model of Obstfeld and Rogoff discussed in the main text gives a policy prescription for monetary authorities when a productivity shock does not have any effect on ex post spending in an economy (characterized by sticky wages). The model suggests that monetary authorities should increase the money supply.

31.2A An improvement in productivity is modelled as a fall in K. What does a fall in K actually represent and why can it be used to model an improvement in productivity?

31.2B Why does an improvement in productivity no longer stimulate the economy when individuals have fixed their wages?

31.2C Describe how an increase in the money supply stimulates the economy.

31.2D What happens to the exchange rate, the terms of trade, and the current account when the monetary authorities raise the money supply?

31.2E Explain whether the home economy is better off when monetary authorities decide to raise the money supply after an improvement of productivity.

Question 31.3

Bayoumi, Laxton, and Presenti (2004)[5] use a new open economy macroeconomics model to estimate the economic effects of a reduction in product and labour market regulation in the euro area. They assume that market regulation will be reduced until mark-ups in the euro area become equal to those in the USA. The table below shows the estimated long-term economic effects of this deregulation policy. Explain how a reduction in mark-ups leads to the results shown in the table. Address especially how a national deregulation policy can have international repercussions.

Model estimates of more competition in Europe (percent deviations from baseline)		
	Euro area	*Rest of world*
GDP	12.4	0.8
Welfare	2.4	1.2
Labour effort	8.3	0.2
Real exchange rate	5.3	

Source: Bayoumi, Laxton, and Presenti (2004).

See the Online Resource Centre for a Study Guide containing more questions
www.oxfordtextbooks.co.uk/orc/vanmarrewijk/

NOTES

1 A disadvantage of using the term 'new' is that it will become obsolete as time progresses.

2 This contrasts with the basic redux model (Obstfeld and Rogoff, 1995), where overshooting of the exchange rate does not occur.

3 Obviously, this implies that the model used in Obstfeld and Rogoff (2005) to analyse the USA current account imbalances suffers from the log-linear approximation problems.

4 Alternatively, as Johan Cruyff, the European soccer player of the last century, so eloquently put it: 'every advantage has its disadvantage'.

5 T. Bayoumi, D. Laxton, and P. Presenti, 'Benefits and spillovers of greater competition in Europe: A macroeconomic assessment', ECB working paper series no. 341, April 2004.

PART IV
CONCLUSION

Part IV provides a summary and some concluding remarks

CONCLUDING REMARKS

32.1 Introduction

In the preface of this book we stated that the objective is to give a succinct, fairly complete, up-to-date, and thorough introduction to the forces underlying international economics. In this final chapter of *International Economics: Theory, Application, and Policy* we briefly review the most important results discussed in the previous chapters.

The world economy

Chapters 1 and 2 present basic information on the structure of the world economy, in terms of land area, population, GDP, etc. The differences between countries are large, particularly for per capita incomes. International trade flows, which are increasing faster than world production, are dominated by relatively small European and South-East Asian countries. We emphasized that a surplus on the current account translates into an outflow of capital, and vice versa. We also emphasized that international economists, in trying to explain the empirical observations, value the consistency of a general equilibrium approach, as opposed to the loose ends of a partial equilibrium approach.

32.2 International trade

After reviewing the main explanations for international trade flows, we discuss the gains from trade and the type of trade explained by each approach.

Classical technology differences

Chapter 3 analyses the classical driving forces behind international trade flows: technological differences between nations. If another country can produce a good more cheaply than we ourselves can make it (opportunity costs), it is better to import this good from abroad. To determine a country's strong (export) sectors as well as its terms of trade, only comparative costs are important, not absolute cost differences (which largely determine the welfare level and the wage rate). Comparative advantages are empirically measured using the Balassa index of normalized export shares.

Neoclassical factor abundance

Chapters 4 to 7 analyse the neoclassical incentive for international trade based on differences in relative factor abundance. The production structure uses capital and labour to produce labour-intensive food and capital-intensive manufactures under perfect competition and constant returns to scale. There is a one-to-one correlation between the prices of final goods and the rewards to the factors of production; that is, if we know the former we can derive the latter, and vice versa. If trade between nations equalizes the prices of food and manufactures, it therefore also equalizes the wage rate and the rental rate (factor price equalization). If the price of labour-intensive food rises, this raises the wage rate and reduces the rental rate. The opposite holds if the price of manufactures rises (Stolper–Samuelson). Moreover, the changes in the factor prices are larger in relative terms than the changes in the final goods prices (magnification effect). Similarly, for given prices of the final goods, an increase in the available amount of capital leads to an increase in the production of (capital-intensive) manufactures and a reduction in the production of food. The opposite holds for an increase in the available amount of labour (Rybczynski effect). When combined with neutral (identical and homothetic) preferences, the above implies that under free trade the capital-abundant country will export (capital-intensive) manufactures (Heckscher–Ohlin).

New trade: imperfect competition and increasing returns to scale

Chapters 9 and 10 discuss the new trade theories, based on imperfect competition and increasing returns to scale. Profit-maximizing firms in an imperfectly competitive market charge a mark-up of price over marginal costs, the size of which depends on the price elasticity of demand and on the degree of competition. Perceived differences in elasticity of demand lead to international trade flows, and possibly beneficial 'reciprocal dumping'. Imperfect competition leads to a deviation between the marginal rate of substitution and the marginal rate of transformation, and thus to a sub-optimal outcome. The empirically observed prevalence of intra-industry trade (two-way trade in similar products), measured using the Grubel–Lloyd index, may be explained with the Krugman model, in which each firm produces a unique variety with economies of scale under monopolistic competition.

New interactions: geography, business, and growth

Chapters 14–16 analyse more recently acquired insights derived from combining international economics with other fields of economics. The geographical economics approach blends the factor abundance model (perfect competition and constant returns to scale) and the new trade model (monopolistic competition, increasing returns to scale, and varieties of manufactures) with factor mobility (migration to regions with high real wages) to provide a simple theory of location and agglomeration. This approach explains some empirical observations and regularities, such as Zipf's Law (on the distribution of city sizes) and the gravity equation (on the size and direction of international trade flows). Similarly, the new theories on multinational firms, which are particularly active in the OECD countries and control rising shares in world production, investment, and trade flows, combine imperfect competition and returns to scale with production and strategy approaches from the business literature to endogenously determine the market structures operative in different countries of the world. In accordance with the stylized facts, multinational firms dominate if countries are more similar, while national firms dominate if countries differ in size or relative factor endowments. Chapter 16 combines economic growth theories with different approaches in international economics to explain economic dynamics and development. The neoclassical growth model focuses on investment in capital goods. It exhibits large Solow residuals and must rely on exogenous technical change to keep the economy growing. The endogenous growth models focus on entrepreneurial innovation in a world characterized by increasing returns to scale and imperfect competition. The empirically observed large swings in economic growth may be explained by a dynamic version of the geographical economics model.

32.3 Gains from trade

The gains from international trade depend on the structural details of the model in question. In the classical approach, trade is based on differences in technology between nations. If another country can produce a good (relatively) more cheaply than we ourselves can make it, it is better to import this good from abroad. In the neoclassical approach, trade is based on differences in (relative) factor abundance between nations. International trade then leads to efficiency gains by equalizing the marginal rate of substitution for all countries. In the new trade approach, international trade is based on imperfect competition and increasing returns to scale. Trade flows then lead to welfare improvements as a result of increased competition (pro-competitive gains from trade), a better use of scale economies, or an increase in the extent of the market, which raises the number of available varieties (Krugman) or the production level through positive externalities (Ethier).

Types of trade explained

International trade models are designed to explain different types of trade; that is, they are usually the result of attempts to better understand empirical observations. Classical and neoclassical trade models were developed to explain inter-industry trade, that is the exchange of different products (for example, cloth in exchange for wine). At the time of development of these models, the emphasis was on the production of homogeneous goods by firms with limited market power. Both approaches are therefore better suited to explain trade flows between *dis*similar countries than between similar countries.

Empirically, however, the largest trade flows are between similar (high-income) countries, to a considerable extent based on intra-industry trade, that is the exchange of similar products (two-way trade). New trade theories, based on increasing returns to scale and imperfect competition, were developed to explain these phenomena in a time in which product differentiation by firms with considerable market power was becoming more important. More recently still, geographical economics and the theory of multinationals were developed to better understand the location decisions of firms, the rising importance of multinationals, economic agglomeration, and the market structures of countries.

32.4 Trade policy

We distinguish between three types of trade policy: (i) standard trade policy based on the classical and neoclassical approaches of Parts I and II; (ii) new trade policy, or strategic trade policy, based on the new trade models of Part III; and (iii) applied trade policy, based on a practical mix of many different theoretical approaches. We review each of these below, with a brief digression into regional integration, to conclude with some remarks on the hidden costs of trade restrictions.

Standard trade policy

Chapter 8 analyses the impact of trade policy on the size of trade flows and the distribution of welfare effects for the classical and neoclassical models. In general, there are both winners and losers of imposing trade restrictions, which makes the demand for protection (lobbying) understandable. Among the winners are protected domestic producers and, in terms of tariff revenue, the government. The main losers are the foreign producers, the domestic consumers, who pay for the increased profits and the tariff revenue, and the country as a whole, in terms of an efficiency loss (Harberger triangles). The main difference between tariffs and quotas rests on the question who receives the tariff-equivalent government revenue. The foreign country can try to reap this benefit by establishing a 'voluntary' export restraint. Imposing a tariff always leads to a net welfare loss for a small country, which cannot influence its terms of trade. Within a neoclassical framework, a large country, which can influence its terms of trade, might benefit from a net welfare gain by imposing an 'optimal' tariff based on its monopoly power. This argument breaks down under a system of retaliation leading to tariff wars, which clarifies the necessity of multilateral trade negotiations.

New trade policy

Chapter 11 analyses the impact of trade policy based on the new trade models with imperfect competition. Tariffs and quantitative restrictions are no longer equivalent. The imposition of tariffs in general leaves the forces of foreign competition intact, albeit at a lower level. This contrasts with the imposition of quantitative restrictions, which more severely restrict the strategic possibilities of foreign firms. Quotas are therefore more restrictive than tariffs, which is one of the main reasons for the World Trade Organization to strive for 'tariffication' (the other being the clarity of the imposed trade restrictions). The so-called strategic trade policy tries to provide a competitive advantage to domestic firms by providing a credible pre-commitment. When evaluating the potential for strategic trade policy we noticed its weaknesses in a general equilibrium setting, the fragility of policy recommendations (type of strategic interactions, who moves first, strategic games, etc.), and most importantly from a practical perspective the enormous informational requirements for accurately implementing such a policy.

32.5 Applications

Regional integration

We apply the insights from both standard trade policy and new trade policy to discuss the costs and benefits of the many regional trade agreements (for example, a free trade area or a customs union). The rising popularity of economic integration known as regionalism is to be contrasted with the multilateral WTO framework of removing trade barriers. Although a regional trade agreement in general increases welfare through increased trade flows (trade-creation), the discriminatory nature of the agreement which benefits insiders may reduce welfare through a shift toward less efficient producers (trade-diversion). The European Union presents the most powerful and successful economic integration scheme to date. Many Central and East European countries want to join the EU, which requires large structural and political changes, both for the applicants and for the (rather undemocratic) political decision process of the EU.

Applied trade policy

Chapter 17 analyses applied trade policy, involving the use of accurate and current data, a model structure determined by those data, a detailed policy orientation, and the analysis of non-local changes in policy parameters from distorted base equilibria. Applied researchers have used the demand side of the economy to solve some practical problems in matching models and data, for example by incorporating demand bias, the Linder hypothesis, and the Armington assumption. For simple trade policy questions researchers use an applied partial equilibrium model, based on estimating the size of the Harberger triangles. For more complicated questions researchers use applied general equilibrium models, which take into consideration the simultaneous effects of all proposed policy measures for all sectors and countries. There are roughly three types of applied general equilibrium models: (1) constant returns and perfect competition; (2) increasing returns and imperfect competition; and (3) dynamic models. In general, the estimated costs of trade restrictions increase as we move from type (1) to type (2), and from type (2) to type (3) models. Using applied trade policy models requires the mastering of many practical tools not covered in this book. However, a rudimentary version of most theoretical analysis on which the applied policy models are based *is* covered in this book.

Hidden costs of trade restrictions

We conclude our discussion on trade policy by noting that the importance of international economic contacts through the exchange of goods, capital, foreign direct investment, knowledge, ideas, etc. can hardly be overestimated. The main reason is that imposing trade restrictions may result in goods and services *not* being introduced on the market. Using the Dupuit triangle to estimate the costs of goods that are not introduced in a simple model, we show that such costs can be substantial (and much larger than the empirically estimated costs in applied general equilibrium models). Suggestive empirical evidence in favour of this interpretation is given for example by North and South Korea, East and West Germany, and the recent developments in China.

32.6 International money

Money market

Money is used as a means of payment, a store of value, and a unit of account. There are different types of monetary aggregates (from narrow to broad: monetary base, M_1, M_2, and M_3). Money is supplied by the banking system (central bank plus commercial banks), which in the aggregate responds to price signals, notably the interest rate. The demand for money depends positively on income (transactions demand) and negatively on the interest rate (opportunity cost or the price for holding money). The interaction of these forces determines the monetary equilibrium, that is the interest rate and the money stock. The central bank can use various policies to influence this equilibrium: a tighter monetary policy implies higher interest rates and a lower money stock.

Foreign exchange market

The foreign exchange markets are the world's largest financial markets, with London, New York, and Tokyo as the main locations. The most important players are commercial banks (through intermediaries called *brokers*), firms, non-bank financial institutions, and central banks. The most traded currencies are the US dollar, the euro, the Japanese yen, and the British pound sterling. There are different types of exchange rates and instruments, such as spot rates, forward rates, swaps, and options. The difference between the banks' buying (bid) and selling (ask) exchange rate is called the spread. In view of the large traded volume, the spread is usually quite small. The exchange rate between two currencies is the price of one currency in terms of another currency. Exchange rates are characterized by high variability, changing from one day to another, and even from minute to minute. To summarize the divergent bilateral movements of a currency, we compute an effective exchange rate of that currency relative to a weighted basket of a range of other currencies. As a result of international arbitrage, the same currency sells for (virtually) the same price at different locations at the same point in time. This also holds for cross exchange rates as a result of triangular arbitrage, involving the exchange of three currencies. If the forward rate of a currency, which is the forward price of the currency, is higher than the spot rate, the currency is sold at a premium. Otherwise, it is sold at a discount.

Purchasing power parity

If there are no impediments whatsoever to international arbitrage, an identical good should sell for the same price in two different countries at the same time. This absolute version of the Law of One Price for individual goods can be used to derive a relative version of the Law of One Price (focusing on changes rather than levels) and a (relative and absolute) version relating exchange rates and price indices, referred to as purchasing power parity (PPP). The derivation is based on assumptions which, if they do not hold exactly, can cause deviations from PPP. Empirical studies do, indeed, find substantial and prolonged short-run deviations from relative PPP as measured by real effective exchange rates. In the long run, however, relative PPP holds remarkably well, certainly in view of the strict assumptions necessary for deriving PPP. The Harrod–Balassa–Samuelson effect relates to a structural bias in deviations from absolute PPP based on observed differences between countries of traded relative to non-traded goods.

Interest rate parity

The Fisher equation provides a direct relationship between interest rates and prices through the decomposition in nominal and real interest rates, where the latter is equal to the nominal interest rate minus the inflation rate. Although nominal interest rates rise with rising inflation rates to compensate for this high inflation, the real interest rate also varies considerably over time, and can be both negative and higher than the nominal interest rate. If interest rates increase for longer terms to maturity, the term structure of interest rates is said to be rising. Empirically, it can also be flat or falling. Hedged international arbitrage between two assets that are deemed perfect substitutes gives rise to the covered interest parity condition: the difference between the home and foreign interest rate is equal to the log difference between the forward and spot exchange rate. Empirically, covered interest arbitrage holds almost perfectly. If such international arbitrage between two assets is not hedged on the forward exchange market *and* investors are risk neutral, it is possible to derive the uncovered interest parity condition: the difference between the home and foreign interest rate is equal to the expected appreciation of the foreign currency. In conjunction with covered interest parity, this implies that the forward rate is equal to the expected future spot rate. Tests of uncovered interest parity are based on the additional assumption of rational expectations. These tests, which are frequently rejected empirically, are therefore based on a range of assumptions, including risk neutrality and rational expectations (together forming the simple efficient market hypothesis). Apart from the notoriously difficult econometric problems involved in the testing procedure, this may be caused by transaction costs and risk aversion leading to (time-varying) risk premia.

32.7 Exchange rates

Elasticity and abortion

The elasticities approach focuses on the relative price effects on the current account balance. According to the Marshall–Lerner condition, which states that the sum of the price elasticities of export and import demand must exceed unity, a depreciation of the domestic currency will improve the current account balance. Empirical estimates show that the Marshall–Lerner condition is fulfilled for most countries, but only after a sufficiently long period of time has elapsed to ensure that the export and import quantities can adjust to the change in relative prices. According to this J-curve effect, the initial response to a depreciation of the domestic currency is to deteriorate the current account balance, leading to an improvement only after an adjustment period of about one year. The absorption approach incorporates income effects into the analysis of the current account balance. This allows for a typology of types of disequilibria and the analysis of some simple adjustment problems. The Tinbergen rule argues that in order to achieve a certain number of economic objectives you need the same number of independent policy instruments to reach these objectives. The assignment problem argues that each instrument should be used on the target for which it has the greatest relative effect.

Monetary approach

The monetary approach to the balance of payments stresses the fact that the exchange rate is the relative price of two monies. Accordingly, a disequilibrium results if the demand for money differs from the amount supplied by the monetary authorities. In the basic monetary model with fixed exchange rates, such a disequilibrium gives rise to an adjustment process (Hume's price specie flow mechanism) which redistributes the world's money stock between the two countries until a new (stock) equilibrium is reached. In the flexible price monetary approach under flexible exchange rates, such a disequilibrium gives rise to an immediate adjustment of the exchange rate to equilibrate the demand for and supply of money. The latter approach indicates that the domestic currency depreciates one for one if the money supply increases and appreciates if the income level increases. Both of these effects are supported by empirical evidence.

Rational expectations and sticky prices

The Dornbusch model analyses exchange rate adjustment in a model with sticky prices and rational expectations. Since prices are fixed in the short run and fully flexible in the long run, this framework provides a useful bridge between the fixed price analysis and the flexible price analysis. At the same time, the Dornbusch model is able to shed some light on the overshooting phenomenon and the high variability of exchange rates. Basically, because prices are sticky and can adjust only gradually over time, the impact-adjustment of the exchange rate to any shocks or new information is magnified, and potentially adjusted by more than what is needed to restore the long-run equilibrium.

32.8 Policy framework

Policy trilemma and monetary institutions

The policy trilemma argues that of the three policy objectives (i) fixed exchange rates, (ii) capital mobility, and (iii) policy autonomy, it is possible to simultaneously achieve only two objectives at the expense of the third objective. We reviewed the main choices made in history for the four most recent international monetary systems: (a) the gold standard, (b) world wars and recession, (c) Bretton Woods, and (d) the floating rates era. During the gold standard there was broad consensus to give up policy autonomy in exchange for capital mobility and maintaining fixed exchange rates. This broke down during the world wars and recession era, as most countries pursued activist monetary policies to try to solve domestic problems at the cost of either imposing large capital controls or on giving up fixed exchange rates. In the Bretton Woods era there was again broad consensus to maintain fixed exchange rates, this time by sacrificing capital mobility (which was limited directly after the Second World War and then gradually increased). In the floating rates era, many countries have been willing to give up fixed exchange rates in return for policy autonomy and capital mobility. The International Monetary Fund is the central institution of the international monetary system, providing surveillance, technical assistance, and financial assistance in case of problems. Special Drawing Rights are artificial international reserves created by the IMF. The World Bank Group consists of five institutions focusing on poverty reduction. The Bank for International Settlements is an organization for central bank cooperation.

Objectives, targets, and instruments

A government, politician, institution, or (international) organization wishing to influence the outcome of the economic process has to take several steps. First, specify what you want to achieve; that is, specify objectives, such as welfare maximization. Second, understand how the economy functions, enabling you to identify certain levels of economic variables you should strive for under specific circumstances; that is specify targets, such as short-term interest rate levels. Third, you must have means available to actually influence those economic variables; that is, have instruments at your disposal, such as minimum reserve requirements. Monetary authorities generally try to fight inflation and unemployment and promote (price) stability and economic growth. The expectations-augmented Phillips curve provides a simple, yet powerful, view of the economic transmission process going from instruments and targets to policy objectives. Using this framework, the Barro–Gordon model shows that imposing simple policy rules may result in better long-run economic outcomes than trying to use discretionary policy to fine-tune the economy. In practice, most central banks target the short-run interest rate using a flexible interpretation of the Taylor rule, which suggests increasing the real interest rate above its neutral stance to fight inflation or temper the economy.

32.9 Economic policy

Effectiveness and capital mobility

Analysing the effectiveness of fiscal and monetary policy under various conditions, we arrived at very strong policy conclusions for small countries under conditions of perfect capital mobility: (i) fiscal policy is very effective and monetary policy entirely ineffective under fixed exchange rates, and (ii) monetary policy is very effective and fiscal policy is entirely ineffective under flexible exchange rates. Although these strong conclusions are mitigated for large countries able to influence the world interest rate and in the case of imperfect capital mobility, there is broad consensus that, in view of the generally high degree of international capital mobility, fiscal policy is more effective in the short run under fixed exchange rates and monetary policy is more effective in the short run under flexible exchange rates. Regarding international spillover effects of short-run fiscal and monetary policy there is a clear international conflict of interests. Under fixed exchange rates a small country can only boost output through a fiscal expansion, which if the country is large may reduce output abroad. Similarly, under flexible exchange rates a small country can only boost output through a monetary expansion, which if the country is large will reduce output abroad for sure. In this respect, when facing unemployment the rest of the world will always support the less effective policy expansion in Home, as it will never hurt and may benefit the foreign output level.

Fixed exchange rates and target zones

There are many different types of fixed exchange rate regimes. Differences between words and deeds indicate that some countries show a fear of floating and other countries show a fear of pegging. All fixed exchange rate regimes are subject to at least some credibility problems caused by the policy trilemma, which forces them to give up either capital mobility or policy autonomy. Using the Barro–Gordon model, we discussed two of these credibility problems, namely the need for countries engaging in fixed exchange rate regimes to have very similar monetary policy preferences, as well as the desirability to be confronted with highly correlated demand and/or supply shocks. On the positive side, the target zone literature indicates that announcing a fully credible fixed exchange rate regime has, in principle, a stabilizing influence on the actual exchange rate behaviour inside the band (the honeymoon effect). Unfortunately, empirical evidence indicates that the honeymoon effect is weak, at best.

Financial crises

The number of currency crises appears to have increased over time, particularly in emerging markets, alongside the rise in capital mobility and possibly caused by the contagion phenomenon. A typical currency crisis involving a *de jure* or *de facto* fixed exchange rate can arise, for example, if the central bank is forced to use its foreign exchange reserves or raise its interest rates to fend off an attack on its currency. If such an attack is succesful, the central bank will be forced to devalue the currency or let it float, which is usually associated with a reversal of (private) funds and the current account moving from a deficit to a surplus. The first-generation models of financial crises explain why investors will attack a currency even before the central bank runs out of reserves, based on ultimately unsustainable bad fundamentals. The second-generation models of financial crises involve a cost–benefit trade-off for policy makers for either sticking to or giving up the fixed exchange rate. The role of investors in these multiple equilibria models is more important, as the outcome chosen by policy makers crucially depends on investors' expectations, which can be based on fundamentals, but also on herd behaviour. A currency crisis can be an external source for igniting a domestic banking crisis, in which case a twin crisis arises (a simultaneous banking crisis and currency crisis). The frequency of banking crises and twin crises does not seem to increase over time. The economic costs of all types of crises, but particularly of twin crises, is high. If a twin crisis arises, the sequencing seems to be important. Does a banking crisis lead to a currency crisis, or vice versa? The third-generation model of financial crises is a synthesis of these two views, by showing how either crisis and either underlying cause can be the starting point of a vicious circle leading to a (costly) financial crisis.

EMU

Twelve European countries have embarked on a unique process of monetary integration by creating a new currency: the euro. Together they form a powerful economic force. We reviewed the theory of optimal currency areas, which focuses on the ability to accommodate differences between countries through wage flexibility, labour mobility, and fiscal transfers, or avoid this need through trade openness, product diversification, homogeneous preferences, and solidarity. We also reviewed the main benefits of a common currency, such as avoiding transaction costs, price transparency, reducing uncertainty, eliminating distortions, promoting growth, and the potential to become an international currency. Although the euro is likely to play a more prominent role in the international arena in the future, it is currently no match for the US dollar. We reviewed the history of the European integration process and discussed the institutional framework of the Eurosystem, which consists of the ECB and the twelve participating NCBs. At least ten countries may decide to join the euro area in the future, which requires a reorganization of the decision-making process to ensure that the Eurosystem protects the interests of the euro area as a whole. This is probably the most important challenge facing the euro area.

32.10 Conclusion

We have discussed and analysed the main ingredients, theories, and empirical phenomena associated with the international interaction of different countries, both from a real perspective and from a monetary perspective. After close study, the reader may remark that there is little interaction between these two fields of international economics. He or she has a point. There is little interaction between these different strands of theory. In fact, for their research most international economists specialize either in problems and theories associated with international trade or in problems and theories associated with international money. This specialization, presumably along the lines of comparative advantage, has its benefits for the academic in terms of building up more specialized knowledge and being better able to keep up with recent developments. It has its benefits for the student by allowing him/her to first study international trade (Parts II.A–C) and then international money (Parts III.A–C), or vice versa. The real–monetary (almost) dichotomy in economics in general and in international economics in particular has been frequently lamented in the past, but I do not see any signs of its imminent disappearance. This raises a final question: why do we insist on teaching *both* sub-fields to our students? The answer is given in Chapters 2 (balance of payments), 17 (applied trade policy), and 31 (new open economy macroeconomics). As a frame of reference, the balance of payments discussed in Chapter 2 is the starting point for both real and monetary analysis. As such, it provides the clearest links between the two sub-fields, indicating for example that a surplus on the current account must be accompanied by a deficit on the capital account. As discussed in Chapters 17 and 31, once confronted with practical problems and policy issues, where short-run, medium-run, and long-run economic consequences of particular instruments and suggested policies play a role in deciding what to do and why, the two sub-fields tend to move together and partially merge into one. Such complex issues as the evolution of the US current account deficit or the impact of the next WTO negotiation round can only be properly understood by building more complicated (computable) general equilibrium models, using different bits and pieces from both sub-fields and designed to answer the particular problem to be analysed. It is at this stage, where a proper mix of the different bits and pieces is required to arrive at sound economic conclusions, that a solid understanding of both sub-fields is essential.

REFERENCES

Aghion, P., and P. Howitt (1992), 'A model of growth through creative destruction', *Econometrica* 60: 323–51.

Alesina, A., O. Blanchard, J. Galí, F. Giavazzi, and H. Uhlig (2001), 'Defining a macroeconomic framework for the Euro area', *Monitoring the European Central Bank 3*, CEPR, London.

Alexander, S.S. (1951), 'Devaluation versus import restrictions as a means for improving foreign trade balances', *IMF Staff Papers*, April: 379–96.

Allen, H., and M.P. Taylor (1990), 'Charts, noise, and fundamentals in the London foreign exchange market', *Economic Journal* 100: 49–59.

Allen, W.R. (ed.) (1965), *International Trade Theory: Hume to Ohlin*, Random House, New York.

Armington, P.S. (1969), 'A theory of demand for products distinguished by place of production', *International Monetary Fund Staff Papers* 16: 159–78.

Arrow, K.J. (1962), 'The economic implications of learning by doing', *Review of Economic Studies* 29: 155–73.

Artus, J.R., and M.D. Knight (1984), 'Issues in the assessment of the exchange rates of industrial countries', *International Monetary Fund, Occasional Paper 29*, Washington, DC.

Bairoch, P. (1988), *Cities and Economic Development: From the Dawn of History to the Present*, paperback reprint, translated by C. Braider, University of Chicago Press, Chicago.

Bakker, A.F.P. (1996), *International Financial Institutions*, Longman, London.

Balassa, B. (1964), 'The purchasing power parity doctrine: a reappraisal', *Journal of Political Economy* 72: 584–96.

Balassa, B. (1965), 'Trade liberalization and "revealed" comparative advantage', *The Manchester School of Economic and Social Studies* 33: 92–123.

Balassa, B. (1966), 'Tariff reductions and trade in manufactures', *American Economic Review* 56: 466–73.

Balassa, B. (1989), ' "Revealed" comparative advantage revisited', in: B. Balassa (ed.), *Comparative Advantage, Trade Policy and Economic Development*, New York University Press, New York, pp. 63–79.

Baldwin, R., and C. Wyplosz (2004), *The Economics of European Integration*, McGraw-Hill, London.

Barrell, R., and N. Pain (1999), 'Domestic institutions, agglomeration and foreign direct investment in Europe', *European Economic Review* 43: 925–34.

Barro, R.J., and X. Sala-i-Martin (1995), *Economic Growth*, McGraw-Hill, New York.

Barro, R.J., and D.B. Gordon (1983a), 'A positive theory of monetary policy in a natural rate model', *Journal of Political Economy* 91(4): 589–610.

Barro, R.J., and D.B. Gordon (1983b), 'Rules, discretion, and reputation in a model of monetary policy', *Journal of Monetary Economics* 17(1): 101–22.

Barro, R.J., and X. Sala-i-Martin (2003), *Economic Growth*, MIT Press, Cambridge, MA.

Baumol, W.J. (1952), 'The transaction demand for cash: an inventory theoretic approach', *Quarterly Journal of Economics* 66: 545–56.

Bean, D. (1976), 'International reserve flows and money market equilibrium: the Japanese case', in: H.G. Johnson and J.A. Frenkel (eds.), *The Monetary Approach to the Balance of Payments*, Allen and Unwin, London.

Beetsma, R., and F. van der Ploeg (1994), 'Intramarginal interventions, bands, and the pattern of EMS exchange rate distributions', *International Economic Review* 35: 583–602.

Begg, D.K.H. (1982), *The Rational Expectations Revolution in Macroeconomics: Theory and Evidence*, Philip Allen, Oxford, UK.

Bekaert, G., and R.J. Hodrick (1993), 'On biases in the measurement of foreign exchange risk premiums', *Journal of International Money and Finance* 12: 115–38.

Bernanke, B. (2005), 'The global saving glut and the US current account deficit', Sandridge Lecture, Virginia Association of Economics, Richmond, Virginia, 10 March 2005, see www.federalreserve.gov

Bernhofen, D.M., and J.C. Brown (2004), 'A direct test of the theory of comparative advantage: The case of Japan', *Journal of Political Economy* 112(1): 48–67.

Bertola, G., and R.J. Caballero (1992), 'Target zones and realignments', *American Economic Review* 82: 520–36.

Bhagwati, J. (1965), 'On the equivalence of tariffs and quotas', in: R.E. Baldwin (ed.), *Trade, Growth and the Balance of Payments*, North-Holland, Amsterdam.

BIS (2002), *Triennial Central Bank Survey: Foreign Exchange and Derivatives Market Activity in 2001*, Bank for International Settlements, Basel, March.

BIS (2004), *Triennial Central Bank Survey of Foreign Exchange and Derivatives Market Activity in April 2004: Preliminary Global Results*, Bank for International Settlements.

Black, J. (1959), 'A savings and investment approach to devaluation', *The Economic Journal* 69: 267–74.

Black, S. (1973), 'International money markets and flexible exchange rates', *Princeton Studies in International Finance* 32.

Blanchard, O.J., and N. Kiyotaki (1987), Monopolistic competition and the effects of aggregate demand', *American Economic Review* 77: 647–66.

Blaug, M. (1985), *Great Economists before Keynes*, Wheatsheaf Books Ltd, Brighton, Sussex.

Blinder, A. (1998), *Central Banking in Theory and Practice*, MIT Press, Cambridge, MA.

Bloom, L. and J. Sachs (1998), 'Geography, demography, and economic growth in Africa', *Brookings Papers on Economic Activity* 2: 207–95.

Bofinger, P. (2001), *Monetary Policy: Goals, Institutions, Strategy, and Instruments*, Oxford University Press, Oxford, UK.

Bordo, M.D., M.A. Taylor, and J.G. Williamson (eds.) (2003), *Globalization in Historical Perspective*, The University of Chicago Press, Chicago.

Bordo, M.D., B. Eichengreen, D. Klingebiel, and M. Soledad Martinez-Peria (2001), 'Is the crisis problem growing more severe?', *Economic Policy*, April.

Bowen, H.P., E.E. Leamer, and L. Sveikauskas (1987), 'Multicountry, multifactor tests of the factor abundance theory', *American Economic Review* 77: 791–809.

Bowen H.P., A. Hollander, and J.-M. Viaene (1998), *Applied International Trade Analysis*, The University of Michigan Press, Ann Arbor.

Brainard, S.L. (1997), 'An empirical assessment of the proximity–concentration trade-off between multinationals, sales and trade', *American Economic Review* 87: 520–44.

Brakman, S., and C. van Marrewijk (1996), 'Trade policy under imperfect competition', *De Economist* 144: 223–58.

Brakman, S., and C. van Marrewijk (1998), *The Economics of International Transfers*, Cambridge University Press, Cambridge, UK.

Brakman, S., H. Garretsen, and C. van Marrewijk (2001), *An Introduction to Geographical Economics*, Cambridge University Press, Cambridge, UK.

Brakman, S., H. Garretsen, C. van Marrewijk, and A. van Witteloostuijn (2006), *Nations and Firms in the Global Economy: An Introduction to International Economics and Business*, Cambridge University Press, Cambridge, UK.

Brander, J.A. (1981), 'Intra-industry trade in identical commodities', *Journal of International Economics* 11: 1–14.

Brander, J.A., and P.R. Krugman (1983), 'A "reciprocal dumping" model of international trade', *Journal of International Economics* 15: 313–21.

Brander, J.A., and B.J. Spencer (1983), 'International R&D rivalry and industrial strategy', *Review of Economic Studies* 50: 707–22.

Brander, J.A., and B.J. Spencer (1985), 'Export subsidies and international market share rivalry', *Journal of International Economics* 18: 83–100.

Brown, D.K. (1992), 'The impact of a North American Free Trade Area: applied general equilibrium models', in: N. Lustig, B.P. Bosworth, and R.Z. Lawrence (eds.) *North American Free Trade: Assessing the Impact*, The Brookings Institution, Washington, DC, pp. 26–68.

Bulow, J.I., J.D. Geanakoplos, and P.D. Klemperer (1985), 'Multimarket oligopoly: strategic substitutes and complements', *Journal of Political Economy*: 488–511.

Burmeister, E., and A.R. Dobell (1970), *Mathematical Theories of Economic Growth*, Macmillan, New York.

Cagan, P. (1956), 'The monetary dynamics of hyperinflation', in M. Friedman (ed.), *Studies in the Quantity Theory of Money*, Chicago University Press, Chicago, IL.

Cassel, G. (1918), 'Abnormal deviations in international exchange rates', *Economic Journal* 28: 413–15.

Caves, R.E. (1996), *Multinational Enterprise and Economic Analysis*, Cambridge Surveys of Economic Literature, 2nd edn, Cambridge University Press, Cambridge, UK.

CBS (2004), *De Nederlandse Economie in 2003*, Centraal Bureau voor de Statistiek, Heerlen.

Chamberlin, E.H. (1993), *The Theory of Monopolistic Competition: A Re-orientation of the Theory of Value*, Harvard University Press, Cambridge, MA.

Cheung, Y.-W., and K.S. Lai (1994), 'Mean reversion in real exchange rates', *Economics Letters* 46: 251–56.

Chipman, J.S. (1965), 'A survey of the theory of international trade: Part 1, the Classical theory', *Econometrica* 33: 477–519.

Clarida, R.H., and M.P. Taylor (1997), 'The term structure of forward exchange premiums and the fore-castability of spot exchange rates: correcting the errors', *Review of Economics and Statistics* 79: 353–61.

Clinton, K. (1988), 'Transaction costs and covered interest arbitrage: theory and evidence', *Journal of Political Economy* 96: 358–70.

Coenen, G., and J.-L. Vega (1999), 'The demand for money in the euro area', *ECB working paper No. 6*, Frankfurt.

Collins, S.M. (ed.) (1998), *Imports, Exports and the American Worker*, Brookings Institution Press, Washington, DC.

Connoly, M.B., and D. Taylor (1976), 'Testing the monetary approach to devaluation in developing countries', *Journal of Political Economy*: 849–59.

Cooper, R.N. (1982), 'The gold standard: historical facts and future prospects', *Brookings Papers on Economic Activity* 1: 1–45.

Cournot, A. (1838), *Recherches sur les principes mathématiques de la théorie des riches*, translated by N. Bacon (1897), Macmillan, New York.

Davis, D.R. (1998), 'The home market, trade, and industrial structure', *American Economic Review* 88: 1264–77.

De Arcangelis, G. (1994), 'Exchange rate target zone modeling: recent theoretical and empirical contributions', *Economic Notes* 23: 74–115.

Debreu, G. (1959), *Theory of Value*, Wiley, New York.

De Grauwe, P. (1996), *International Money*, 2nd edn, Oxford University Press, Oxford, UK.

De Grauwe, P. (2005), *Economics of Monetary Union*, 6th edn, Oxford University Press, Oxford, UK.

De Grauwe, P., and F. Camerman (2002), 'How big are the big multinational companies?', *Working Paper, Belgium Senate*, Brussels.

De Grauwe, P., and H. Dewachter (1993), 'A chaotic model of the exchange rate: the role of fundamentalists and chartists', *Open Economies Review* 4: 351–79.

DeLong, J.B. (1988), 'Productivity growth, convergence, and welfare: comment', *American Economic Review* 78: 1138–54.

DeLong, J.B., A. Shleifer, L.H. Summers, and R.J. Waldmann (1990), 'Noise trader risk in financial markets', *Journal of Political Economy* 98: 703–38.

De Melo, J., and A. Panagariya (1993), *New Dimensions in Regional Integration*, Cambridge University Press, Cambridge, UK.

Diewert, W.E. (1981), 'The economic theory of index numbers: a survey', in: A. Deaton (ed.), *Essays in the Theory and Measurement of Consumer Behaviour*, Cambridge University Press, Cambridge, UK, pp. 163–208.

Dixit, A.K. (1989), 'Hysteresis, import penetration, and exchange rate pass-through', *Quartely Journal of Economics* 104: 205–28.

Dixit, A., and G. Grossman (1986), 'Targeted export promotion with several oligopolistic industries', *Journal of International Economics* 21: 233–50.

Dixit, A., and A.S. Kyle (1985), 'The use of protection or subsidies for entry promotion and deterrence', *American Economic Review* 75: 139–52.

Dixit, A., and V. Norman (1980), *Theory of International Trade*, Cambridge University Press, Cambridge, UK.

Dixit, A., and J. Stiglitz (1977), 'Monopolistic competition and optimal product diversity', *American Economic Review* 67: 297–308.

Dominguez, K.M., and P.B. Kenen (1992), 'Intramarginal intervention in the EMS and the target-zone model of exchange-rate behaviour', *European Economic Review* 36: 1523–32.

Dornbusch, R. (1976), 'Expectations and exchange rate dynamics', *Journal of Political Economy*, 84: 1161–76.

Dornbusch, R. (1980a), *Open Economy Macroeconomics*, Basic Books, New York.

Dornbusch, R. (1980b), 'Exchange rate economics: Where do we stand?', *Brookings Papers on Economic Activity* 1:143–85.

Dornbusch, R. (1987), 'Exchange rates and prices', *American Economic Review* 77: 93–106.

Dornbusch, R., S. Fischer, and P. Samuelson (1977), 'Comparative advantage, trade and payments in a Ricardian model with a continuum of goods', *American Economic Review* 67: 823–39.

Dumas, B. (1992), 'Dynamic equilibrium and the real exchange rate in spatially separated world', *Review of Financial Studies* 5: 153–80.

Dunning, J.H. (1977), 'Trade location of economic activity and MNE: a search for an eclectic approach', in: B. Ohlin, P.O. Hesselborn, and P.M. Wijkman (eds.) *The International Allocation of Economic Activity*, Macmillan, London.

Dunning, J.H. (1981), *International Production and the Multinational Enterprise*, Allen and Unwin, London.

Dupuit, J. (1844), 'On the measurement of the utility of public works', reprinted in K. Arrow and T. Scitovsky (eds.) *Readings in Welfare Economics*, Allen and Unwin, London.

Eaton, J., and G.M. Grossman (1986), 'Optimal trade and industrial policy under oligopoly', *Quarterly Journal of Economics* 2: 383–406.

ECB (2004), *Monthly Bulletin*, September, European Central Bank, Frankfurt.

EC Commission (1990), 'One market, one money', *European Economy* 35.

The Economist (1997), 'Peace in our time', 26 July (on *The Economist's* website).

The Economist (1999), 'The new trade war', 2 December (on *The Economist's* website).

The Economist (2000a), 'So that's all agreed, then', 14 December (on *The Economist's* website).

The Economist (2000b), 'Thank you, Singapore', 30 September (on *The Economist's* website).

The Economist (2001a),'A fruity peace', 19 April (on *The Economist's* website).

The Economist (2001b), 'A phoney war', 5 May (on *The Economist's* website).

The Economist (2001c), 'More tomatoes, please ', 21 June (on *The Economist's* website).

The Economist (2001d), 'Visigothenburger', 21 June (on *The Economist's* website).

The Economist (2001e), 'Picking up the pieces', 26 July (on *The Economist's* website).

The Economist (2003a), 'The euro, trade, and growth', 10 July.

The Economist (2003b), 'Sparks fly over steel', 13 November (on *The Economist*'s website).

The Economist (2004), 'Transatlantic tiff', 4 March (on *The Economist*'s website).

The Economist (2005a), 'Beet a retreat', 23 June (on *The Economist*'s website).

The Economist (2005b), 'Chinese puzzles', 13 August: 60–61.

The Economist (2005b), 'Hard truths', 20 December (on *The Economist*'s website).

Edison, H.J. (1987), 'Purchasing power parity in the long run', *Journal of Money, Credit, and Banking* 19: 376–87.

Eichengreen, B.J., (1996), *Globalizing Capital: A History of the International Monetary System*, Princeton University Press, Princeton, NJ.

Eichengreen, B.J., A.K. Rose, and Ch. Wyplosz (1995), 'Exchange rate mayhem: the antecedents and aftermath of speculative attacks', *Economic Policy*: 251–312.

Engel, C., and J. Rogers (2004), 'European product market integration after the euro', *Economic Policy*: 349–84.

Engle, R.F., and C.W.J. Granger (1987), 'Co-integration and error correction: representation, estimation, and testing', *Econometrica* 55: 251–76.

Ethier, W.E. (1982), 'National and international returns to scale in the modern theory of international trade', *American Economic Review* 72: 950–59.

Ethier, W.E. (1986), 'The multinational firm', *Quarterly Journal of Economics* 101: 805–33.

Fama, E.F. (1984), 'Forward and spot exchange rates', *Journal of Monetary Economics* 14: 319–38.

Feenstra, R.C., J.R. Markusen, and A.K. Rose (2001), 'Using the gravity equation to differentiate among alternative theories of trade', *Canadian Journal of Economics* 34: 430–47.

Feldstein, M. (2005), 'The euro and the stability pact', *NBER Working Paper No. 11249*.

Feldstein, M., and Ch. Horioka (1980), 'Domestic savings and international capital flows', *Economic Journal* 90 (June): 314–29.

Feldstein, M., and J.H. Stock (1994), 'The use of a monetary aggregate to target nominal GDP', in: N. Mankiw (ed.), *Monetary Policy*, University of Chicago Press, Chicago and London, pp. 9–40.

Fisher, I. (1911), *The Purchasing Power of Money*, 2nd edn 1926; reprinted by Augustus Kelley, New York, 1963.

Fleming, M. (1962), 'Domestic financial policies under fixed and under floating exchange rates', *IMF Staff Papers 9*.

Forslid, R., and G. Ottaviano (2003), 'An analytically solvable core–periphery model', *Journal of Economic Geography* 3: 229–40.

Francois, J.F., and H.K. Hall (1997), 'Partial equilibrium modeling', in: J.F. Francois and K.A. Reinert (eds.), *Applied Methods for Trade Policy Analysis: A Handbook*, Cambridge University Press, Cambridge, UK, pp. 122–55.

Francois, J.F., and K.A. Reinert (1997), 'Applied methods for trade policy analysis: an overview', in: J.F. Francois and K.A. Reinert (eds.), *Applied Methods for Trade Policy Analysis: A Handbook*, Cambridge University Press, Cambridge, UK, pp. 3–24.

Francois, J.F., B.J. McDonald, and H. Nordström (1997), 'Capital accumulation in applied trade models', in: J.F. Francois and K.A. Reinert (eds.), *Applied Methods for Trade Policy Analysis: A Handbook*, Cambridge University Press, Cambridge, UK, pp. 364–82.

Frankel, J.A. (1986), 'International capital mobility and crowding out in the US economy: imperfect integration of financial markets or goods markets?', in: R.W. Hafer (ed.), *How Open is the US Economy?*, Lexington Books, Lexington, MA, pp. 33–67.

Frankel, J.A., and K.A. Froot (1987), 'Using survey data to test standard propositions regarding exchange rate expectations', *American Economic Review* 77: 133–53.

Frankel, J.A., and K.A. Froot (1990), 'Chartists, fundamentalists, and trading in the foreign exchange market', *American Economic Review* 80: 181–85.

Frenkel, J.A. (1976), 'A monetary approach to the exchange rate: doctrinal aspects and empirical evidence', *Scandinavian Journal of Economics* 78: 200–24.

Frenkel, J.A. (1978), 'Purchasing power parity: doctrinal perspective and evidence from the 1920s', *Journal of International Economics* 8: 169–91.

Friedman, M. (1953), 'The case for flexible exchange rates', in: *Essays in Positive Economics*, University of Chicago Press, Chicago, pp. 157–203.

Friedman, M. (1956), 'The quantity theory of money: a restatement', in: *Studies in the Quantity Theory of Money*, University of Chicago Press, Chicago.

Friedman, M. (1968), 'The role of monetary policy', *American Economic Review* 58: 1–17.

Fujita, M., P. Kungman and A. Venables (1999), *The Spatial Economy: Cities, Regions, and International Trade*, MIT Press, Cambridge, MA.

Gandal, N., G.H. Hanson, and M.J. Slaughter (2000), 'Techonology, trade, and adjustment to immigration in Israel', *NBER Working Paper* 7962.

Garber, P.M., and L.E.O. Svensson (1995), 'The operation and collapse of fixed exchange rate regimes', in: G. Grossman and K. Rogoff (eds.), *Handbook of International Economics*, vol. III, North-Holland, Amsterdam, ch. 36.

Genberg, H. (1976), 'Aspects of the monetary approach to balance of payments theory: an empirical study of Sweden', in: H.G. Johnson and J.A. Frenkel (eds.), *The Monetary Approach to the Balance of Payments*, Allen and Unwin, London.

Genberg, H., and A.K. Swoboda (2004), 'Exchange rate regimes: does what countries say matter?', Graduate Institute of International Studies, *HEI Working Paper 07/2004*.

Glen, J.D. (1992), 'Real exchange rates in the short, medium, and long run', *Journal of International Economics* 33: 147–66.

Glick, R., and A. Rose (2002), 'Does a currency union affect trade? the time series evidence', *European Economic Review* 46: 1125–51.

Gourevitch, P., R. Bohn, and D. McKendrick (2000), 'Globalization of production: insights from the hard disk drive industry', *World Development* 28(2): 301–17.

Granger, C.W.J., and P. Newbold (1974), 'Spurious regressions in econometrics', *Journal of Econometrics* 2: 111–20.

Grossman, G.M., and E. Helpman (1991a), *Innovation and Growth in the Global Economy*, MIT Press, Cambridge, MA.

Grossman, G.M., and E. Helpman (1991b), 'Quality ladders in the theory of growth', *Review of Economic Studies* 58: 43–61.

Grubel, H.G., and P.J. Lloyd (1975), *Intra-Industry Trade: The Theory and Measurement of International Trade in Differentiated Products*, John Wiley, New York.

Grubel, H.G., and M. Walker (1989), *Service Industry Growth*, Fraser Institute, Vancouver.

Grubert, H., and J. Mutti (1991), 'Taxes, tariffs, and transfer pricing in multinational corporate decision making', *Review of Economics and Statistics* 79: 285–93.

Guittan, M. (1976), 'The balance of payments as a monetary phenomenon: empirical evidence, Spain 1955–71', in: H.G. Johnson and J.A. Frenkel (eds.), *The Monetary Approach to the Balance of Payments*, Allen and Unwin, London.

Hallwood, C.P., and R. MacDonald (2000), *International Money and Finance*, 3rd edn, Blackwell, Oxford, UK.

Hamilton, J., and R. Susmel (1994), 'Autoregressive conditional heteroscedasticity and changes in regime', *Journal of Econometrics* 64: 307–33.

Hansen, L.P., and R.J. Hodrick (1980), 'Forward exchange rates as optimal predictors of future spot rates: an econometric analysis', *Journal of Political Economy* 88: 829–53.

Harberger, A.C. (1954), 'Monopoly and resource allocation', *American Economic Review* 44: 77–87.

Harberger, A.C. (1959), 'Using the resources at hand more effectively', *American Economic Review* 49: 134–46.

Harris, R. (1985), 'Why voluntary export restraints are voluntary', *Canadian Journal of Economics* 18: 799–809.

Harrod, R. (1933), *International Economics*, James Nisbet, London.

Hau, H. (2002), 'Real exchange rate volatility and economic openness: theory and evidence', *Journal of Money, Credit, and Banking* 34: 611–30.

Head, K., J. Ries, and D. Swenson (1995), 'Agglomeration benefits and location choice: evidence from Japanese manufacturing investments in the United States', *Journal of International Economics* 38: 223–47.

Helpman, E. (1984), 'A simple theory of international trade with multinational corporations', *Journal of Political Economy* 92: 451–71.

Helpman, E. (1985), 'Multinational corporations and trade structure', *Review of Economic Studies* 52: 443–58.

Herfindanl, O.C. (1950), 'Concentration in the steel industry', unpublished PhD dissertation, Columbia University.

Hertz, N. (2001), *The Silent Take-over*, London: William Heinemann.

Hicks, J.R. (1967), *Critical Essays in Monetary Theory*, Clarendon Press, Oxford.

Hinloopen, J., and C. van Marrewijk (2001), 'On the empirical distribution of the Balassa Index', *Weltwirtschaftliches Archiv* 137: 1–35.

Horst, T. (1971), 'The theory of the multinational firm: optimal behavior under different tariff and tax rates', *Journal of Political Economy* 79: 1059–72.

Horstman, I.J., and J.R. Markusen (1986), 'Up the average cost curve: inefficient entry and the new protectionism', *Journal of International Economics* 20: 225–48.

Hume, D. (1752), *Political Discourses, volume II, essay V: of the balance of trade*: see www.econlib.org/library/LFbooks/Hume/hmMPL28.html

Hummels, D. (1999a), 'Towards a geography of trade costs', mimeo, Purdue University.

Hummels, D. (1999b), 'Have international transport costs declined?', mimeo, Purdue University.

Huriot, J.-M., and J.-F. Thisse (eds.), (2000), *Economics of Cities: Theoretical Perspectives*, Cambridge University Press, Cambridge, New York, and Melbourne.

Iannizotto, M., and M.P. Taylor (1999), 'The target zone model, non-linearity and mean reversion: is the honeymoon really over?', *Economic Journal* 109: C96–C110.

IMF (1996), *Balance of Payments Textbook*, Washington, DC.

IMF (2002), *World Economic Outlook*, Washington, DC, April.

IMF (2003), *World Economic Outlook*, Washington, DC, April.

IMF (2004), *Annual Report 2004: Making the Global Economy Work for All*, International Monetary Fund, Washington, DC.

Irwin, D. (1996), *Against the Tide: An Intellectual History of Free Trade*, Princeton University Press, Princeton, NJ.

Jeanne, O. (2000), 'Currency crises: a perspective on recent theoretical developments', *Special Papers in International Economics*, no. 20, Dept. of Economics, Princeton University, NJ.

Jones, C. (1995), 'Time series tests of endogenous growth models', *Quarterly Journal of Economics*: 495–525.

Jones, R.W. (1965), 'The structure of simple general equilibrium models', *Journal of Political Economy* 73: 557–72.

Kaldor, N. (1961), 'Capital accumulation and economic growth', in: F.A. Lutz and D.C. Hague (eds.), *The Theory of Capital*, Macmillan, London, pp. 177–222.

Kaminsky, G., and C. Reinhart (1999), 'The twin crises: the causes of banking and balance-of-payments problems', *American Economic Review* 89(3): 473–500.

Kaminsky, G., and C. Reinhart (2000), 'On crises, contagion, and confusion', *Journal of International Economics*, 51: 145–68.

Kemp, M.C., and H.Y. Wan, Jr (1972), 'The gains from free trade', *International Economic Review* 13(3): 509–22.

Kemp, M.C., and H.Y. Wan, Jr (1976), 'An elementary proposition concerning the formation of customs unions', *Journal of International Economics* 6(1): 95–7.

Kenen, P.B. (1969), 'The theory of optimum currency areas', in: R. Mundell and A. Swoboda (eds.), *Monetary Problems of the International Economy*, Chicago University Press, Chicago.

Kenen, P.B. (2000), *The International Economy*, 4th edn, Cambridge University Press, Cambridge, UK.

Kennedy, P. (1995), 'The threat of modernization', *New Perspectives Quartely*: 31–3.

Keynes, J.M. (1923), *A Tract on Monetary Reform*, in: *The Collected Writings of John Maynard Keynes*, Vol. IV; reprinted by Macmillan, London and Basingstoke, 1971.

Keynes, J.M. (1936), *The General Theory of Employment, Interest and Money*, in: *The Collected Writings of John Maynard Keynes*, Vol. IV; reprinted by Macmillan, London and Basingstoke, 1971.

Kindleberger, C.P. (1973), *The World in Depression 1929–1933*, Lane, London.

King, M. (1998), 'Monetary policy and the labour market', speech at the Employment Policy Institute's Fourth Annual Lecture (1–12–1998); see www.bankofengland.co.uk

Klein, N. (2001) *No Logo*, Flamingo, London.

Klein, M.A. (1971), 'A theory of the banking firm', *Journal of Money, Credit, and Banking* 3: 205–18.

Koedijk, K.G., and P. Schotman (1990), 'How to beat the random walk: an empirical model of real exchange rates', *Journal of International Economics* 29: 311–32.

Koedijk, K.G., P.A. Stork, and C.G. de Vries (1992), 'Differences between foreign exchange rate regimes: the view from the tails', *Journal of International Money and Finance* 11: 462–73.

Kouri, P.J.K., and M.G. Porter (1974), 'International capital flows and portfolio equilibrium', *Journal of Political Economy* 82(3): 443–67.

Krishna, K. (1989), 'Trade restrictions as facilitating practices', *Journal of International Economics* 26: 251–70.

Krugman, P.R. (1978), 'Purchasing power parity and exchange rates: another look at the evidence', *Journal of International Economics* 8: 397–407.

Krugman, P.R. (1979), 'A model of balance-of-payments crises', *Journal of Money, Credit, and Banking*, 11: 311–25.

Krugman, P.R. (1979), 'Increasing returns, monopolistic competition and international trade', *Journal of International Economics* 9: 469–79.

Krugman, P.R. (1980), 'Scale economics, product differentiation, and the pattern of trade', *American Economic Review* 70: 950–59.

Krugman, P.R. (1987), 'Pricing to market when the exchange rate changes', in: S.W. Arndt and J.D. Richardson (eds.), *Real–Financial Linkages Among Open Economies*, MIT Press, Cambridge, MA.

Krugman, P.R. (1990), *Rethinking International Trade,* MIT Press, Cambridge, MA.

Krugman, P.R. (1991), 'Is bilateralism bad?', in: E. Helpman and A. Razin (eds.), *International Trade and Trade Policy*, MIT Press, Cambridge, MA.

Krugman, P.R. (1991), 'Target zones and exchange rate dynamics', *The Quarterly Journal of Economics* 106: 669–82.

Krugman, P.R. (1993), 'Regionalism versus multilateralism: Analytical notes', in: J. De Melo and A. Panagariya (eds.), *New Dimensions in Regional Integration*, Cambridge University Press, Cambridge, UK.

Krugman, P.R. (1996), 'Are currency crises self-fulfilling?', *NBER Macroeconomics Annual 1996*: 347–407.

Krugman, P.R. (1998), 'It's baaack! Japan's slump and the return of the liquidity trap', *Brookings Papers on Economic Activity*: 137–87.

Krugman, P.R. (2000), *The Return of Depression Economics*, W.W. Norton & Co., New York.

Krugman, P.R., and M. Obstfeld (2000), *International Economics: Theory and Policy*, 5th edn, Addison-Wesley, New York, etc.

Krugman, P.R., and A.J. Venables (1995), 'Globalization and the inequality of nations', *The Quarterly Journal of Economics*, 110: 857–80.

Laidler, D. (1982), *Monetarist Perspectives*, Philip Allan, Oxford, UK.

Laird, S. (1997), 'Quantifying commercial policies', in: J.F. Francois and K.A. Reinert (eds.), *Applied Methods for Trade Policy Analysis: A Handbook*, Cambridge University Press, Cambridge, UK, pp. 27–75.

Lancaster, K.J. (1979), *Variety, Equity and Efficiency*, Columbia University Press, New York.

Lane, P.R. (2001), 'The new open economy macroeconomics: a survey', *Journal of International Economics* 54: 235–66.

Lanjouw, G.J. (1995), *International Trade Institutions*, Longman and Open University, London, New York, and Heerlen.

Lawrence, R.Z., and M.J. Slaughter (1993), 'International trade and American wages in the 1980s: giant sucking sound or small hiccup?', *Brookings Paper on Economic Activity 2: Microeconomics*: 161–226.

Leahy, M.P. (1998), 'New summary measures of the foreign exchange value of the dollar', *Federal Reserve Bulletin*, October: 811–18.

Leontief, W.W. (1956), 'Factor proportions and the structure of American trade: further theoretical and empirical analysis', *Review of Economics and Statistics* 38.

Lerner, A.P. (1944), *The Economics of Control*, Macmillan, London.

Lerner, A.P. (1952), 'Factors, prices and international trade', *Economica n. s.*: 19.

Levich, R.M. (1985), 'Empirical studies of exchange rates: price behavior, rate determination, and market efficiency', in R.W. Jones and P.B. Kenen (eds.), *Handbook of International Economics*, vol. II, North-Holland, Amsterdam, pp. 979–1040.

Levy-Yeyati, E., and F. Sturzenegger (2004), 'Classifying exchange rate regimes: deeds vs. words', *European Economic Review* 49: 1603–35.

Liesner, H.H. (1958), 'The European common market and British industry', *Economic Journal* 68: 302–16.

Linder, S. (1961), *An Essay on Trade and Transformation*, Wiley, New York.

Lipsey, R.G. (1960), 'The theory of customs unions: a general survey', *Economic Journal* 70: 496–513.

Lloyd, P.J. (1982), '3×3 theory of customs unions', *Journal of International Economics* 12: 41–63.

Lucas, R.E. Jr (1972), 'Expectations and the neutrality of money', *Journal of Economic Theory* 4: 103–24.

Lucas, R.E. Jr (1973), 'Some international evidence on output–inflation tradeoffs', *American Economic Review* 68: 326–34.

Lui, Y.H., and D. Mole (1998), 'The use of fundamental and technical analysis by foreign exchange dealers: Hong Kong evidence', *Journal of International Money and Finance* 17: 535–45.

Maddison, A. (1991), *Dynamic Force in Capitalist Development*, Oxford University Press, Oxford, UK.

Maddison, A. (2001), *The World Economy: A Millennial Perspective*, OECD, Paris and Washington, DC.

Maddison, A. (2003), *The World Economy: Historical Statistics*, OECD, Paris.

Markusen, J.R. (1981), 'Trade and the gains from trade with imperfect competition', *Journal of International Economics* 11: 531–51.

Markusen, J.R. (1984), 'Multinationals, multi-plant economics, and the gains from trade', *Journal of International Economics* 16: 205–26.

Markusen, J.R. (1995), 'Incorporating the multinational enterprise into the theory of international trade', *Journal of Economic Perspective* 9: 169–89.

Markusen, J.R. (1998), 'Multinational firms, location, and trade', *World Economy* 21(6): 733–56.

Markusen, J.R., and A.J. Venables (1998), 'Multinational firms and the new trade theory', *Journal of International Economics* 46: 183–203.

Markusen, J.R., A.J. Venables, D.E. Konan, and K.H. Zhang (1996), 'A unified treatment of horizontal direct investment, vertical direct investment, and the pattern of trade in goods and services', NBER working paper 5696, Cambridge, MA.

Marrewijk, C. van (1999), 'Capital accumulation, learning, and endogenous growth', *Oxford Economic Papers* 51: 453–75.

Marrewijk, C. van (2005), 'An overview of cross-border mergers and acquisitions for five countries,' *FM Corporate* 1: 18–19.

Marrewijk, C. van, and C.G. de Vries (1990), 'The customs union argument for a monetary union', *Journal of Banking and Finance* 14: 877–87.

Marrewijk, C. van, and J. Verbeek (1993), 'Sector-specific capital, "bang-bang" investment and the Filippov solution', *Journal of Economics* 57: 131–46.

Marrewijk, C. van, J. Stibora, A. de Vaal, and J.-M. Viaene (1997), 'Producer services, comparative advantage, and international trade patterns', *Journal of International Economics* 42: 195–220.

Marrewijk, C. van, and K.G. Berden (2007), 'On the static and dynamic costs of trade restrictions for small developing countries', forthcoming, *Journal of Development Economics*.

Marshall, A. (1923), *Money, Credit, and Commerce,* Macmillan, Basingstoke.

Martin, S. (1994), *Industrial Economics: Economic Analysis and Public Policy*, Macmillan, New York.

Martyn, H. (1701), *Considerations upon the East India Trade*: see Irwin (1996), pp. 56–9.

McCallum, J. (1995), 'National borders matter: Canada–US regional trade patterns', *American Economic Review* 85: 615–23.

McKinnon, R. (1962), 'Optimum currency areas', *American Economic Review* 53: 717–25.

Meade, J.E. (1951), *Theory of International Economic Policy: The Balance of Payments*, Oxford University Press, Oxford, UK.

Meade, J.E. (1952), *A Geometry of International Trade*, Allen and Unwin, London.

Meese, R.A., and K. Rogoff (1983), 'Empirical exchange rate models of the seventies: do they fit out of sample?', *Journal of International Economics* 14: 3–24.

Meese, R.A., and K. Rose (1990), 'Nonlinear, nonparametric, nonessential exchange rate estimation', *American Economic Review* 80: 192–96.

Melvin, M. (2000), *International Money and Finance*, 6th edn, Addison Wesley Longman, Reading.

Micco, A., E. Stein, and G. Ordoñez (2003), 'Euro's trade effect', *Economic Policy* 37: 316–56.

Midelfart-Knarvik, K.H., H.G. Overman, S.J. Redding, and A.J. Venables (2000), 'The location of European industry', *Economic Papers*, 142, European Commission, Brussels.

Mill, J.S. (1848), *Principles of Political Economy*, 2 vols, John W. Parker, London.

Miller, M.H., and P. Weller (1991), 'Exchange rate bands with price inertia', *Economic Journal* 101: 1380–99.

Mishkin, F.S. (1992), 'Anatomy of a financial crisis', *Journal of Evolutionary Economics* 2: 115–30.

Mishkin, F.S. (1999), 'Global financial instability: framework, events, and issues', *Journal of Economic Perspectives* 4(Fall): 3–20.

Modigliani, F., and E. Grunberg (1954), 'The predictability of social events', *Journal of Political Economy* 62: 465–78.

Morales, J.A. (1988), 'Inflation stabilization in Bolivia', in: M. Bruno et al. (eds.), *Inflation Stabilization: The Experience of Israel, Argentina, Brazil, Bolivia, and Mexico*, MIT Press, Cambridge, MA.

Mundell, R.A. (1961), 'A theory of optimum currency area', *American Economic Review* 51: 657–65.

Mundell, R.A. (1962), 'The appropriate use of monetary and fiscal policy for internal and external stability', *International Monetary Fund Staff Papers* 12: 70–79.

Mundell, R.A. (1963), 'Capital mobility and stabilization policy under fixed and flexible exchange rates', *Canadian Journal of Economics and Political Science* 29: 475–85.

Mundell, R.A. (1968), *International Economics*, Macmillan, New York.

Mussa, M. (1976), 'The exchange rate, the balance of payments and monetary and fiscal policy under a regime of controlled floating', *Scandinavian Journal of Economics* 78: 229–48.

Mussa, M. (1979), 'Empirical regularities in the behaviour of exchange rates and theories of the foreign exchange market', in: K. Brunner and A.H. Meltzer (eds.), *Policies for Employment, Prices, and Exchange Rates*, Carnegie-Rozhester Conference Series on Public Policy 11, pp. 9–57.

Muth, J.F. (1961), 'Rational expectations and the theory of price movements', *Econometrica* 29: 315–35.

Neary, J.P. (1978), 'Short-run capital specificity and the pure theory of international trade', *Economic Journal* 88: 477–510.

Neary, J.P. (2001), 'Of hypes and hyperbolas: introducing the new economic geography', *Journal of Economic Literature* 39(2): 536–61.

Neary, P.J. (2002), 'Globalization and market structure', Presidential Address to the European Economic Association, Venice, 22–24 August, forthcoming in the *Journal of the European Economic Association*.

Neary, P. (2003), 'Globalization and market structure', *Journal of the European Association* 1: 245–71.

Neary, P. (2004), 'Europe on the road to Doha: towards a new global trade round?', *CESifo Economic Studies* 50(2): 319–32.

NRC Handelsblad (2001a), 'Van nul naar record in grillige chipmarkt', 19 January, p.14 (in Dutch).

NRC Handelsblad (2001b), 'Minder EU-hulp suiker', 23 May (in Dutch).

NRC Handelsblad (2001c), 'Prijs van walvisspek stijgt explosief', 12 May, p. 19 (in Dutch).

NRC Handelsblad (2001d), 'Japan buigt niet in ruzie schoolboek' and 'De geschiedenis blijft Japan achtervolgen', 14 July, p. 4 (in Dutch).

NRC Handelsblad (2001e), 'Ondernemersvrouwen houden van Holland', 18 August, p. 13 (in Dutch).

NRC Handelsblad (2003), 'Hoe Amsterdam de VS verdubbelde', 20 December, p. 27.

Obstfeld, M., and K. Rogoff (1995), 'Exchange rate dynamics redux', *Journal of Political Economy* 103: 624–60.

Obstfeld M. (1996), 'Models of currency crises with self-fulfilling features', *European Economic Review*, 40(3–5): 1037–47.

Obstfeld, M., and K. Rogoff (1996), *Foundations of International Macroeconomics*, MIT Press, Cambridge, MA.

Obstfeld, M., and K. Rogoff (2000), 'New directions for stochastic open economy models', *Journal of International Economics* 50: 117–53.

Obstfeld, M., and K. Rogoff (2001), 'The six major puzzles in international macroeconomics: is there a common cause?', *NBER Macroeconomics Annual* 15: 339–90.

Obstfeld, M., and A.M. Taylor (2003), 'Globalization and capital markets', in: M.D. Bordo, A.M. Taylor, and J.G. Williamson (eds.), *Globalization in Historical Perspective*, NBER.

Obstfeld, M., and K. Rogoff (2005), 'Global current account imbalances and exchange rate adjustments', mimeo University of California, Berkeley, and Harvard University.

Officer, L.H. (1982), *Purchasing Power Parity and Exchange Rates: Theory, Evidence and Relevance*, JAI Press, Greenwich, CT.

Ohlin, B. (1933), *Interregional and International Trade*, Harvard University Press, Cambridge, MA.

O'Rourke, K.H., and J.G. Williamson (1999), *Globalization and History: The Evolution of a Nineteenth-Century Atlantic Economy*, MIT Press, Cambridge, MA.

Ostrup, F. (2002), 'International integration and economic policy', mimeo, University of Copenhagen.

Ottens, D. (2000), 'Revealed comparative advantage: an empirical analysis', unpublished master's thesis, Erasmus University, Rotterdam.

Persson, T., and G. Tabellini (1990), *Macroeconomic Policy, Credibility and Politics, Fundamentals of Pure and Applied Economics*, Harwood Academic Publishers, Chur, Switzerland.

Pesaran, M.H., and H. Samiei (1992), 'An analysis of the determination of the Deutsche Mark/French Franc exchange rate in a discrete-time target-zone model', *Economic Journal* 102: 388–401.

Phelps, E.S. (1967), 'Phillips curves, expectations of inflation, and optimal unemployment over time', *Economica* 34: 254–81.

Phillips, A.W. (1958), 'The relation between unemployment and the rate of change of money wage rates in the United Kingdom, 1861–1957', *Economica* 25: 283–99.

Pontines, V. (2006), 'On currency crises, exchange rate regimes, and contagion', unpublished PhD dissertation, University of Adelaide.

Porter, M.E. (1990), *The Competitive Advantage of Nations*, Free Press, New York.

Radelet, S., and J. Sachs (1998), 'Shipping costs, manufactured exports, and economic growth', mimeo, AEA meetings, Harvard University.

Ramsey, F.P. (1928), 'A mathematical theory of saving', *Economic Journal* 38: 543–59.

Reinhart, C., and K. Rogoff (2004), 'The modern history of exchange rate arrangements: a reinterpretation', *Quarterly Journal of Economics* 119: 1– 48.

Rivera-Batiz, L.A., and P.M. Romer (1991a), 'Economic integration and endogenous growth', *Quarterly Journal of Economics* 106: 531–55.

Rivera-Batiz, L.A., and P.M. Romer (1991b), 'International trade with endogenous technological change', *European Economic Review* 35: 971–1004.

Rogoff, K. (1992), 'Traded goods consumption smoothing and the random walk behaviour of the real exchange rate', *Monetary and Economic Studies* 10: 1–29.

Rogoff, K. (2002), 'Statement by Kenneth Rogoff on the death of Rudiger Dornbusch', International Monetary Fund News Brief 02/77, 26 July.

Rogoff, K. (2002b), 'Dornbusch's overshooting model after twenty-five years', International Monetary Fund, Working Paper 02–39.

Romer, D. (2001), *Advanced Macroeconomics*, 2nd edn, McGraw-Hill, New York.

Romer, P.M. (1986), 'Increasing returns and long run growth', *Journal of Political Economy* 94: 1002–37.

Romer, P.M. (1990), 'Endogenous technological change', *Journal of Political Economy* 98: S71–S102.

Romer, P.M. (1994a), 'The origins of endogenous growth', *Journal of Economic Perspectives* 8(1): 3–22.

Romer, P.M. (1994b), 'New goods, old theory, and the welfare costs of trade restrictions', *Journal of Development Economics* 43: 5–38.

Rybczynski, T.M. (1955), 'Factor endowments and relative commodity prices', *Economica* 22: 336–41.

Samuelson, P.A. (1948), 'International trade and the equalisation of factor prices', *Economic Journal* 58: 163–84.

Samuelson, P.A. (1949), 'International factor price equalisation once again', *Economic Journal* 59: 181–96.

Samuelson, P.A. (1964), 'Theoretical notes on trade problems', *Review of Economics and Statistics* 46: 145–54.

Samuelson, P.A. (1971), 'Ohlin was right', *Swedish Journal of Economics* 73: 365–84.

Samuelson, P.A. (1952), 'The transfer problem and transport costs: the terms when impediments are absent', *Economic Journal* 62: 278–304.

Samuelson, P.A., and R.M. Solow (1960), 'Problems of achieving and maintaining a stable price level: analytical aspects of anti-inflation policy', *American Economic Review* 50: 177–94.

Sargent, T.J. (1972), 'Rational expectations and the term structure of interest rates', *Journal of Money, Credit, and Banking* 4: 74–97.

Sargent, T.J. (1973), 'Rational expectations, the real rate of interest, and the natural rate of unemployment', *Brookings Papers on Economic Activity* 2: 429–72.

Sarno, L., and M.P. Taylor (2002), *The Economics of Exchange Rates*, Cambridge University Press, Cambridge, UK.

Schmidt, J.A. (2001), 'Background of economic transition in Central and Eastern Europe', Lecture Notes, Erasmus University, Rotterdam.

Schumpeter, J.A. (1934), *The Theory of Economic Development*, Harvard University Press, Cambridge, MA.

Schumpeter, J.A. (1954), *History of Economic Analysis*, 12th printing, 1981, Allen and Unwin, London.

Scitovsky, T. (1954), 'Two concepts of external economies', *Journal of Political Economy* 62: 143–51.

Shatz, H.J., and A.J. Venables (2000), 'The geography of international investment', in: G.L. Clark, M. Feldman, and M.S. Gertler (eds.), *The Oxford Handbook of Economic Geography*, Oxford University Press, Oxford.

Siebert, H. (1999), *The World Economy*, Routledge, London.

Smith, A. (1776), *An Inquiry into the Nature and Causes of the Wealth of Nations*, the Glasgow edition of the works and correspondence of Adam Smith, edited by R.H. Campbell and A.S. Skinner, 1981, Liberty Press.

Solow, R.M. (1956), 'A contribution to the theory of economic growth', *Quartely Journal of Economics* 70: 65–94.

Spence, A.M. (1976), 'Product selection, fixed costs and monopolistic competition', *Review of Economic Studies* 43: 217–35.

Stelder, D. (2000), 'Geographical grids in new economic geography models', paper presented at the International Conference on the Occasion of the 150th Anniversary of Johann Heinrich von Thünen's death, Rostock, 21–24 September.

Stolper, W., and P. Samuelson, (1941), 'Protection and real wages', *Review of Economic Studies* 9: 58–73.

Summers, L.H., and A. Heston (1991), 'The Penn world table (mark 5): an expanded set on international comparisons, 1950–1988', *Quartely Journal of Economics* 106: 327–68.

Sutherland, A. (1994), 'Target zone models with price inertia: solutions and testable implications', *Economic Journal* 104: 96–112.

Svensson, L.E.O. (1999), 'Inflation targeting as a monetary policy rule', *Journal of Monetary Economics* 43: 607–54.

Svensson, L.E.O., and S. van Wijnbergen (1989), 'Excess capacity, monopolistic competition, and international transmission of monetary disturbances', *Economic Journal* 99: 784–805.

Swan, T. (1955), 'Longer run problems of the balance of payments', in: *Readings in International Economics*, American Economic Association, Allen and Unwin, London.

Taylor, J.B. (1993), 'Discretion versus policy rules in practice', *Carnegie-Rochester Conference Series on Public Economics* 39: 195–214.

Taylor, M.P. (1988), 'An empirical examination of long-run purchasing power parity using cointegration techniques', *Applied Economics* 20: 1369–81.

Taylor, M.P., and P.C. McMahon (1988), 'Long-run purchasing power parity in the 1920s', *European Economic Review* 32: 179–97.

Taylor, M.P., and H. Allen (1992), 'The use of technical analysis in the foreign exchange market', *Journal of International Money and Finance* 11: 304–14.

Taylor, M.P., and L. Sarno (1998), 'The behaviour of real exchange rates during the Post-Bretton Woods period', *Journal of International Economics* 46: 281–312.

Taylor, M.P., and M. Iannizotto (2001), 'On the mean-reverting properties of target zone exchange rates: a cautionary note', *Economics Letters* 71: 117–29.

Thweatt, W.O. (1976), 'James Mill and the early development of comparative advantage', *History of Political Economy* 8: 207–34.

Tinbergen, J. (1952), *On the Theory of Economic Policy*, North-Holland, Amsterdam.

Tinbergen, J. (1962), *Shaping the World Economy*, The Twentieth Century Fund, New York.

Tirole, J. (1988), *The Theory of Industrial Organization*, MIT Press, Cambridge, MA.

Tobin, J. (1956), 'The interest elasticity of transactions demand for cash', *Review of Economics and Statistics* 38: 241–7.

Tobin, J. (1958), 'Liquidity preference as behavior towards risk', *Review of Economic Studies* 25: 65–86.

Trefler, D. (1995), 'The case of the missing trade and other mysteries', *American Economic Review* 85: 1029–46.

Tristani, O. (1994), 'Variable probability of realignment in a target zone', *Scandinavian Journal of Economics* 96: 1–14.

Twigger, R. (1999), 'Inflation: the value of the pound 1750–1998', Research Paper 99/20, House of Commons Library, UK.

UNCTAD (1999), *World Investment Report 1999*, United Nations, New York.

UNCTAD (2000), *World Investment Report 2000*, United Nations, New York.

Vanek, J. (1959), 'The natural resource content of foreign trade, 1870–1955, and the relative abundance of natural resources in the United States', *Review of Economics and Statistics* 41.

Venables, A.J. (1985), 'Trade and trade policy with imperfect competition: the case of identical products and free entry', *Journal of International Economics* 19: 1–20.

Verdoorn, P.J. (1960), 'The intra-block trade of Benelux', in: E.A.G. Robinson (ed.), *Economic Consequences of the Size of Nations*, Macmillan, London.

Viner, J. (1950), *The Customs Union Issue*, Carnegie Endowment for International Peace, New York.

Whitman, M. (1975), 'Global monetarism and the monetary approach to the balance of payments', *Brookings Papers on Economic Activity* 3: 491–536.

Wong, K.Y. (1986), 'Are international trade and factor mobility substitutes?', *Journal of International Economics* 20: 25–44.

Wood, A. (1994), *North–South Trade, Employment and Inequality: Changing Fortunes in a Skill-Driven World*, Clarendon Press, Oxford.

Wood, A. (1998), 'Globalisation and the rise in labour market inequalities', *Economic Journal* 108: 1463–1482.

World Bank (2003) *Global Development Finance*, Washington, DC.

Wynne, M.A. (1999), 'Core inflation, a review of some conceptual issues', ECB Working Paper No. 5, Frankfurt.

Young, A.A. (1928), 'Increasing returns and economic progress', *Economic Journal* 38: 527–42.

Zecher, J.R. (1976), 'Monetary equilibrium and international reserve flows in Australia', in: H.G. Johnson and J.A. Frenkel (eds.), *The Monetary Approach to the Balance of Payments*, Allen and Unwin, London.

Zipf, G.K. (1949), *Human Behavior and the Principle of Least Effort*, Addison Wesley, New York.

INDEX